THE INTERNATIONAL LIBRARY OF ESSAYS ON AVIATION POLICY
AND MANAGEMENT

THE INTERNATIONAL LIBRARY OF ESSAYS ON AVIATION POLICY AND MANAGEMENT

Edited by

LUCY BUDD AND STEPHEN ISON
De Montfort University, Leicester

Volume IV

Aviation Performance and Productivity

Routledge
Taylor & Francis Group

LONDON AND NEW YORK

First published 2020
by Routledge
2 Park Square, Milton Park, Abingdon, Oxon OX14 4RN

and by Routledge
52 Vanderbilt Avenue, New York, NY 10017

Routledge is an imprint of the Taylor & Francis Group, an informa business

British Library Cataloguing-in-Publication Data
A catalogue record for this book is available from the British Library

Library of Congress Cataloging-in-Publication Data
A catalog record has been requested for this book

ISBN: 978-0-367-28136-6 (set)
ISBN: 978-1-4724-5158-3 (volume IV)

Typeset in Times New Roman
by codeMantra

Publisher's Note
References within each chapter are as they appear in the original complete work

Contents

Part III Service delivery and service quality

Part IV Human Resources and Industrial Relations

Acknowledgments

The Publishers would like to thank the following for permission to reprint their material:

Elsevier for permission to reprint David Gillen, 'The Evolution of Airport Ownership and Governance', *Journal of Air Transport Management*, 17, 2011, 3–13.

Elsevier for permission to reprint Anming Zhang and Yimin Zhang, 'Concession Revenue and Optimal Airport Pricing', *Transportation Research Part E*, 33, 4, 1997, 287–296.

Elsevier for permission to reprint Anming Zhang and Yimin Zhang, 'Airport Charges and Capacity Expansion: Effects of Concessions and Privatization', *Journal of Urban Economics*, 53, 2003, 54–75.

Elsevier for permission to reprint Tae H. Oum, Nicole Adler and Chunyan Yu, 'Privatization, Corporatization, Ownership Forms and Their Effects on the Performance of the World's Major Airports', *Journal of Air Transport Management*, 12, 2006, 109–121.

Taylor & Francis for permission to reprint Ian Humphreys, Stephen Ison and Graham Francis, 'UK Airport Policy: Does the Government Have Any Influence?', *Public Money & Management*, 27, 5, 2010, 339–344.

Taylor & Francis for permission to reprint Robert Freestone, Peter Williams and Aaron Bowden, 'Fly Buy Cities: Some Planning Aspects of Airport Privatisation in Australia', *Urban Policy and Research*, 24, 4, 2006, 491–508.

Elsevier for permission to reprint Tae H. Oum, Jia Yan and Chunyan Yu, 'Ownership Forms Matter for Airport Efficiency: A Stochastic Frontier Investigation of Worldwide Airports', *Journal of Urban Economics*, 64, 2008, 422–435.

Elsevier for permission to reprint David Gillen and Ashish Lall, 'Developing Measures of Airport Productivity and Performance: An Application of Data Envelopment Analysis', *Transportation Research Part E*, 33, 4, 1997, 261–273.

Elsevier for permission to reprint Joseph Sarkis, 'An Analysis of the Operational Efficiency of Major Airports in the United States', *Journal of Operations Management*, 18, 2000, 335–351.

Elsevier for permission to reprint David Gillen and William G. Morrison, 'The Economics of Franchise Contracts and Airport Policy', *Journal of Air Transport Management*, 11, 2005, 43–48.

Elsevier for permission to reprint Eric Pels, Peter Nijkamp and Piet Rietveld, 'Inefficiencies and Scale Economies of European Airport Operations', *Transportation Research Part E*, 39, 2003, 341–361.

Elsevier for permission to reprint Cristina Barbot, Alvaro Costa and Elena Sochirca, 'Airlines Performance in the New Market Context: A Comparative Productivity and Efficiency Analysis', *Journal of Air Transport Management*, 14, 2008, 270–274.

Elsevier for permission to reprint Rico Merkert and David A. Hensher, 'The Impact of Strategic Management and Fleet Planning on Airline Efficiency – A Random Effects Tobit Model Based on DEA Efficiency Scores', *Transportation Research Part A*, 45, 2011, 686–695.

John Wiley & Sons for permission to reprint David R. Graham, Daniel P. Kalpan and David S. Sibley, 'Efficiency and Competition in the Airline Industry', *The Bell Journal of Economics*, 14, 1, 1983, 118–138.

Elsevier for permission to reprint Vicente Inglada, Belen Rey, Ana Rodríguez-Alvarez and Pablo Coto-Millan, 'Liberalisation and Efficiency in International Air Transport', *Transportation Research Part A,* 40, 2006, 95–105.

Sage Publications for permission to reprint Bruce K. Behn and Richard A. Riley, 'Using Nonfinancial Information to Predict Financial Performance: The Case of the U.S. Airline Industry', *Journal of Accounting, Auditing & Finance*, 14, 1, 1999, 29–56.

Emerald Publications for permission to reprint Mahour Mellat Parast and Elhan (Ellie) H. Fini, 'The Effect of Productivity and Quality on Profitability in US Airline Industry: An Empirical Investigation', *Managing Service Quality: An International Journal*, 20, 5, 2010, 458–474.

Emerald Publications for permission to reprint Fareena Sultan and Merlin C. Simpson, Jr, 'International Service Variants: Airline Passenger Expectations and Perceptions of Service Quality', *Journal of Services Marketing*, 14, 3, 2000, 188–216.

Elsevier for permission to reprint Sheng-Hshiung Tsaur, Te-Yi Chang and Chang-Hua Yen, 'The Evaluation of Airline Service Quality by Fuzzy MCDM', *Tourism Management*, 23, 2002, 107–115.

Springer for permission to reprint Michael J. Mazzeo, 'Competition and Service Quality in the U.S. Airline Industry', *Review of Industrial Organization*, 22, 2003, 275–296.

Elsevier for permission to reprint Anderson R. Correia, S. C. Wirasinghe and Alexandre G. de Barros, 'Overall Level of Service Measures for Airport Passenger Terminals', *Transportation Research Part A*, 42, 2008, 330–346.

Elsevier for permission to reprint Nicole Adler and Joseph Berechman, 'Measuring Airport Quality from the Airlines' Viewpoint: An Application of Data Envelopment Analysis', *Transport Policy*, 8, 2001, 171–181.

Elsevier for permission to reprint Fariba E. Alamdari and Peter Morrell, 'Airline Labour Cost Reduction: Post-liberalisation Experience in the USA and Europe', *Journal of Air Transport Management*, 3, 2, 1997, 53–66.

Elsevier for permission to reprint Laurie Hunter, 'Low Cost Airlines: Business Model and Employment Relations', *European Management Journal*, 24, 5, 2006, 315–321.

Elsevier for permission to reprint Geraint Harvey and Peter Turnbull, 'Employment Relations, Management Style and Flight Crew Attitudes at Low Cost Airline Subsidiaries: The Cases of British Airways/Go and bmi/bmibaby', *European Management Journal*, 24, 5, 2006, 330–337.

Sage Publications for permission to reprint Steve Taylor and Melissa Tyler, 'Emotional Labour and Sexual Difference in the Airline Industry', *Work, Employment & Society*, 14, 1, 2000, 77–95.

Disclaimer

The publishers have made every effort to contact authors/copyright holders of works reprinted in the *International Library of Essays on Aviation Policy and Management*. This has not been possible in every case, however, and we would welcome correspondence from those individuals/companies whom we have been unable to trace.

Introduction

Lucy Budd and Stephen Ison

Introduction to *the International Library of Essays on Aviation Policy and Management*

This collection comprises 6 distinct but interrelated volumes that contain previously published academic essays that collectively address important issues in international civil aviation policy and management. Despite air transport's relatively short presence in world history, it has evolved into one of the world's most significant modes of international and long-distance mobility that facilitates the routine transnational movement of billions of passengers and millions of tonnes of highly valuable freight annually. Understanding the policy and management implications of this rapidly developing transport mode has been considered by disciplines as diverse as civil engineering and the social sciences, and tens of thousands of essays, both empirical and theoretical, have been published in the field. In this collection, we limit ourselves to essays published in the English language; while we do not (and cannot) claim to be comprehensive, the aim of this collection is to present essays which showcase significant and thought-provoking essays that have sought to stimulate debate in this diverse and dynamic field of academic inquiry.

The collection comprises 6 volumes, each covering a different aspect of aviation policy and management. The collection seeks to provide useful insight into key areas of aviation that are of interest both to academics and practitioners worldwide. The choice of essays is necessarily subjective; however, every effort has been made to be as inclusive and informative as possible by drawing on a wide range of disciplinary perspectives and journal titles. Given the diversity of the empirical, theoretical and disciplinary approaches that have been applied to the study of aviation, this is no straightforward task and is inherently problematic and subjective. We appreciate that not every reader will agree with our selection and may have his or her own opinion concerning which essays should have been included or excluded. Nevertheless, it is our intention that this collection will act as a foundation from which readers can make their own further forays into the academic research base surrounding aviation.

The 6 volumes have been configured and presented as follows:

Volume 1 addresses aspects of *Aviation Law and Regulation*. This volume sets the scene for the legal and regulatory operation of international civil aviation from the earliest days to the present. It contains 4 Parts and 18 essays that cover aviation law, regulation and deregulation, competition and contestability and open skies.

Volume 2 *Aviation Planning and Operations* comprises 25 essays with Parts covering forecasting, infrastructure planning and provision, capacity, scheduling, safety and security, disruption management and resilience.

Volume 3 *Aviation Business Strategy* comprises 26 essays that cover market structure, revenue cost and pricing, mergers and acquisitions, global airline alliances and marketing and customer loyalty.

Volume 4, which focuses on *Aviation Performance and Productivity*, includes Parts relating to privatisation and commercialisation, efficiency, service delivery and service quality, human resources and industrial relations. This volume comprises 26 essays.

Volume 5 *Aviation Social and Economic Impacts* contains 26 essays divided into 5 Parts, namely airports and economic development, airports, logistics and supply chains, air transport and tourism, air transport in remote regions and environmental externalities.

Volume 6 *Aviation Design and Innovation* comprises 20 essays presented in 4 Parts – airport design and sustainability, aircraft design and manufacturing, alternative fuels and business model innovation.

Introduction to Volume 4 *Aviation Performance and Productivity*

The 26 essays in this volume are presented in 4 Parts.

Part I Privatisation and Commercialisation

Modern airports are dynamic and increasingly commercialised facilities that are designed and managed to serve the needs of a diverse group of users, including airlines, passengers and, increasingly, private shareholders. The first 4 essays in this part investigate the effects of privatisation and changes in global airport regulation on airport pricing while the final 2 examine the experience of airport privatisation in selected global markets. The first essay, by Gillen (2011), charts the evolution of airport ownership and changes in governance practices as airports transition from being public utilities to private enterprises. Arguably the most challenging and commercially contentious aspects of airport operations concern the setting of charges and the mechanisms through which expansion plans are funded.

The second essay, by Zhang and Zhang (1997), examines the optimal pricing of airports and the influence of concession revenues on pricing strategies as airports move towards being more financially self-sufficient and commercialised entities. Enhancing the proportion of revenue that is generated through non-aeronautical sources can give airports the financial flexibility to fund investment. The third essay, also by Zhang and Zhang (2003), examines the decisions relating to airport charges and capacity expansion projects made by airports. They note that the ownership structure and business approach adopted by public and private airports influences the commercial priorities and expansion decisions which are made. Commercial operators are under pressure to maximise their performance and efficiency. The fourth essay, by Oum, Adler and Yu

(2006), measures and compares the productive efficiency and profitability of airports that are Government departments, majority public owned, majority private owned and 100% privately owned. Their results suggest that private–public partnerships with minority private sector involvement and multi-level Government ownership should be avoided.

With the market for airport services increasingly liberalised, Humphreys, Ison and Francis (2010) examine the extent to which the UK Government has been able to shape airport policy. Another significant global aviation market that has experienced airport privatisation is Australia. In the final essay in this part, Freestone, Williams and Bowden (2006) examine the land use, planning and environmental impacts of Australasian airport privatisation and investigate the implications of commercial developments that are being constructed at airports that seek to generate new sources of non-aeronautical revenue for their owners.

Part II Efficiency

The essays presented in Part II continue the exploration of the impacts of airport privatisation but shift the emphasis towards cost efficiency. The essay, by Oum, Yan and Yu (2008), studies the effects of airport ownership on airport cost-efficiency through means of a stochastic frontier analysis of the world's major airports. Their findings include the fact that mixed ownership of airports should be avoided, and privatisation of one or more airports in cities with multiple airports would improve the efficiency of all airports. In recognition that many studies have examined airport efficiency purely in accounting terms, Gillen and Lall (1997) apply Data Envelopment Analysis to assess the performance of 21 US airports. This approach is also adopted by Sarkis (2000) who evaluates the performance of 44 major airports in the United States.

Issues of airport productivity and performance are of course not the exclusive concern of US airports, and the final four essays in this part examine these issues as they pertain to airports in other world regions. Gillen and Morrison (2005) explore the evolution of airport governance and policy in Canada and highlight how EU policies might promote market-based efficiency at Canadian airports. The next essay, by Pels, Nijkamp and Rietveld in 2003, focuses on the inefficiencies of European airports.

Data Envelopment Analysis has also been widely employed to measure the performance and productivity of airlines as illustrated in the essays by Barbot, Costa and Sochirca (2008) and Merkert and Hensher (2011). Research into airline efficiency and competition has a long historical pedigree, and the essay, by Graham, Kalpan and Sibley in 1983, tests the hypotheses that were central to arguments in favour of US airline deregulation. This is followed by an essay by Inglada, Rey, Rodríguez-Alvarez and Coto-Millan (2006) which compares the technical and economic efficiency of international airlines in the period 1996–2000. In addition to econometric analyses, non-financial performance information has also been used to examine airlines' financial performance as the essay, by Behn and Riley (1999), shows. The final essay in Part II, by Mahour Mellat Parast and Fini (2010), employs correlation and multivariate regression analysis to examine the effect of productivity and quality on US airline profitability.

Their research indicates that labour productivity is the most significant factor that influences airline profitability. Issues of labour and industrial relations are addressed further in Part IV of this volume.

Part III Service delivery and service quality

The five essays in this part address selected aspects of airline and airport service. The first, by Sultan and Simpson, Jr (2000), uses SERVQUAL data to determine if consumer expectations and perceptions of airline service quality differ according to nationality. Tsaur, Chang and Yen (2002) adopt a different approach and employ fuzzy set theory to evaluate airline service quality. Their research reveals that customers are most concerned by the tangible aspects of an airline's service. Issues of customer perception and experience are of course all important in highly competitive markets in which consumers can select a product from a range of potential suppliers. One factor that is known to influence customer perception of service quality is on time performance. Mazzeo (2003) utilises data from the US Bureau of Transportation Statistics to show that delays are significantly greater on routes where there is no competition. This is a significant finding and demonstrates that competition not only influences price but also key performance metrics and service characteristics.

Service characteristics are also an important consideration for airports. Correia, Wirasinghe and Barros (2008) examine levels of service (LOS) measures for passenger terminals in Brazil. As well as passengers, airlines are also consumers of an airport product and airport efficiency, and performance is known to influence an airline's choice of hub location. The final essay in this part is by Adler and Berechman (2001). Their research provides a valuable insight into how airlines measure and perceive airport quality.

Part IV Human resources and industrial relations

The final 4 essays in this volume focus on human resources and industrial relations in the aviation industry. Air travel is a safety critical commodity which is delivered through the combined efforts of hundreds of thousands of members of staff worldwide. The importance of labour productivity to aviation performance and profitability has been established earlier in this volume. Alamdari and Morrell (1997) analyse trends in airline labour costs in the United States and Europe after deregulation. Increased competition has placed pressure on staff to be more productive and has led to a reduction in wages and the erosion of favourable terms and conditions of employment. Of course, the move towards lower costs, championed in particular by the low-cost operators, has, for some carriers, led to industrial disputes and more adversarial relations between employers, unions and staff. Hunter (2006) explores different airline business models and their effect on employment relations. Although strikes by some staff can be covered through contingency planning, strikes by pilots and flight crew are typically much more disruptive as their job roles cannot be assumed by other members of airline staff for the duration of any dispute. Harvey and Turnbull (2006) examine the employment relations, management style and flight crew attitudes within two low-cost subsidiaries of UK full-service carriers.

The final essay in this Part looks at the demanding emotional labour that is required of cabin crew. Taylor and Tyler (2000) examine the world of airline cabin service delivery, in particular focusing on the often gendered nature of this work which may require female cabin crew to perform scripted routines which reinforce gender inequality in the industry.

Part I:

Privatisation and Commercialisation

1

The evolution of airport ownership and governance

David Gillen

ABSTRACT

This presentation examines the evolution of airport governance from public utility to modern business. I also briefly look at airport regulation and in this context ask the questions, do airports need to be regulated and if so, why? I consider the new thinking on two-sided platforms and examine whether this may be the new way of thinking about governance. In judging governance structures and regulation, I argue that dynamic efficiency has been underemphasized in the debate over privatization and that airline deregulation has been most important in shifting the balance of power between airlines and airports.

1. Introduction

This paper examines the evolution of airport governance and regulation over the last thirty years, and assesses the case for economic regulation and privatization. Since 1977, and the deregulation of interstate cargo aviation in the US, the aviation system has been subject to significant change, at least in the delivery and organization of air services, but it is only relatively recently that the organization and delivery of infrastructure services has progressed. What we observe now is that airports are for the most part run as modern businesses or at least in a commercial like way. There has been a transition from positioning airports solely as public utilities towards firms delivering airside services to airlines and terminal retail, and access services to passengers, plus additional ancillary services.

The modern airport is generally seen in the context of a vertical airline-airport model where the interaction moves both upstream and downstream.[1] The dramatic effects of technical change and airline liberalization are manifest in downstream markets in a number of ways; it has lowered rents placing more pressure on airports to perform in both service quality and cost efficiency. Fiscal pressure together with these changes, have led to airport governance reform and evolution. Airports are multifaceted firms and their economics are complex with multiple outputs, fixed lumpy and sunk capital, they are faced in many cases with complex regulation or political pressures. Passenger spending has become equal to or more important than aeronautical charges so airports have to marry the needed operational efficiencies of airside activity to the business and marketing of a retail terminal.

The study of airport performance and price setting under differing governance structures has only recently attracted the interest of economists and management strategists. For many years airports were owned by some level of government that treated them as a public utility and in many cases used them as a device for some broader policy initiatives. The fact that airports seemed to cover operating costs and needed government support for investment provided some evidence that airports had not, and presumably would not, use their market power. There was little interest whether airports were operating in an institutional setting which provided incentives to produce and price efficiently. There was no economic assessment of airport performance including runway pricing, runway investment and gate utilization, for example. Public ownership was assumed to yield prices close to costs, provide the range of services that users were willing to pay for, and keep costs to a minimum. Subsequent analysis dispelled these myths (Armstrong et al., 1994; Morrison and Winston, 2008).[2]

In the majority of developed countries around the world airport ownership, governance and institutional controls have undergone considerable change. Governments began to deregulate airline services and subsequently pursue new airport policies, sometimes in conjunction with aviation system reform as in the EU. The shift that occurred across many countries had several common sources. Air traffic was growing at rapid rates and airports needed to invest in capacity, there was a general rethinking of the role government should play in the economy and airports were considered a place

---

[1] This is the standard notion and places the "ownership" of passengers with the airline. I challenge this idea and argue the future may be one in which the airport owns the passenger, and the airline simply serves as the airport distribution system.

[2] While publicly owned firms did not charge prices above costs, and often allowed revenues to fall short of costs, they did not necessarily produce at minimum cost, and often did not supply what the users were willing to pay for.

4 D. Gillen / Journal of Air Transport Management 17 (2011) 3–13

where the private sector could legitimately provide the needed service and investment and, the deregulated airline sector was showing significant improvements in productivity and product innovation and many argued this could be extended to the airport sector; there was a newfound recognition of the relationship between ownership structure, governance and performance.

The paper begins with an examination of the evolution of airport governance and the various forms it has taken. Next I ask whether the governance structure matters and examine some recent work on airport cost efficiency. Following this is a brief examination of airport regulation and the differing forms it takes and in this context ask the questions; do airports need to be regulated and why, and secondly, is it reasonable to think of airports in a competitive environment? The paper finishes with an examination of the new literature on two-sided platforms and consider its usefulness in thinking about the airport business.

2. Institutions and governance

The effects of institutions on shaping the oversight, management and performance of firms are key issues in assessing competitiveness and so it is with governance and oversight in the airport sector. The institutional setting, which is generally ignored in investigating governance evolution, is important in affecting corporate governance and the strategic behaviour of firms. Institutions which establish formal rules and facilitate the development of informal rules act to constrain an economic agent's behaviour and can act to incentivize them to follow differing paths of behaviour. This occurs because institutions can affect the payoffs of various economic activities. The institutional framework can embody two types of incentives; formal (property rights under a set of laws) and informal such as reputation. Under the institutional setting we want organizational actors engaged in carrying out productive activities such as innovation, and not unproductive activities such as rent seeking.

Institutions can create increased coordination costs. For example, economies which promote competition in capital, labour and other input markets will differ from those which are more paternalistic where administrative rules are used to allocate resources. In aviation a good example of the impact of institutions on airport governance is market liberalization and in particular international bilateral agreements. Those markets which have more liberal and open skies agreements rather than restrictive bilaterals will see a change in the distribution of power between airports and airlines and in part define the competitive market for airport services.

3. Airport governance: an evolution[3]

The forces of reform have, for a number of reasons, been slow to deal with airports after air service deregulation. However, since the mid 1990s the pace of change has quickened. The move to full private ownership has been slower where there was government ownership and limited jurisdictions; Australia where they have long term leases, New Zealand and the UK notably. In many cases, governments have opted for partial rather than full privatization; Germany being a case in point. In North America where there is a long tradition of privately owned utilities and firms in the transport industries, there has been a reluctance to move away from public or local ownership of airports possibly due to a Federal tax subsidy on debt, as in the US. Canada for example chose the 'not-for-profit' governance model rather than privatization with all airport assets reverting to the

Federal government at the end of the lease and all US airports are owned by some public authority or body. In continental Europe there has been a preference for partial privatization, with the public sector retaining majority ownership in many cases.

If one differentiates between the degree and mode of the shift of airports out of public ownership, there are at least seven possible ownership/governance structures:

- Government owned/operated (US, Spain, Singapore, Finland, Sweden)
- Government owned, privately operated[4] (US (via contracts), Chile, Hamilton {Canada?})
- Major airports which have public-private partnerships in the form of BOO, BOT and management contract variants, such as in India
- Independent not-for-profit corporations(Canada)
- Fully private for-profit via IPO (Initial Public Offering) with stock widely held (originally BAA)
- Fully private for-profit via trade sale with share ownership tightly held (Australia, New Zealand).
- Partially private for-profit with private controlling interest (Denmark, Austria, Switzerland)
- Partially private for-profit with government controlling interest (Hamburg Germany, France, China, Kansai Japan

3.1. Government owned/operated airports

The general orientation of government owned and operated airports is to focus on the primary function of the airport with a limited degree of interest in other sources of commercial value. Often, government run airports have non-commercial objectives that have included the protection of national carriers or the promotion of economic activities and development. There may be periodic overinvestment with less of a long term focus on infrastructure. For such airports, investments are likely to compete with other government priorities and often there is an observed lack of consistency between aviation policy and the efficient use of airport assets. Airports can also be used for economic and development objectives; many regional airports would fit this class even in places in Europe.

3.2. Government owned, privately operated

In the US, almost all airports are government owned locally but effectively privately operated, with a high degree of contracting out.[5] US airports benefit from Federal grants and tax deductable interest bonds when investment is required, yet they typically exhibit a lack of investment in aeronautical infrastructure, albeit in many cases due to local land use restrictions, zoning laws and political pressure from vocal interest groups. US airports also exhibit some airline participation in the ownership and control of terminal buildings. The top 50 airports in the US show a significant interest in developing non-aeronautical commercial value but beyond this, there is a high degree of variability across airports (reflecting local government willingness to extend airport operations beyond the primary function).

---

[4] Some US airports have multiple contracts for services and are in effect privately managed.

[5] Stewart Airport, NY is the only example of US airports that have been privatized but its lease was sold to Port Authority of New York and New Jersey in 2009. Some analysts predicted that isolated privatization cannot succeed in the US as individual private airports must pay full market rates for their capital while their government owned competitors do not. The Midway privatization floundered with the financial crises of 2008 and remains publicly owned.

---

[3] This section draws on material in Morrison and Gillen (2008).

D. Gillen / Journal of Air Transport Management 17 (2011) 3–13   5

The US model described above, particularly of Port Authorities, has become deeply-rooted because of long term leases signed between airports and airlines giving them in many cases exclusive control of entire terminals or concourses and the right to approve or veto capital spending plans.[6] This type of arrangement made the "signatory airlines" joint ventures with the airport. For taking this risk, the incumbent airlines were able to control airport expansion and to some degree the ability of competitors to enter some markets.

As of 2010 there has been an upsurge in interest in privatization. Many airport managers are looking at alternate methods of funding capital projects, particularly terminals. A bellwether is the lease deal on Chicago's Midway Airport and if it is re-tendered. There are now 15 airports in the 'queue' or considering joining it, for just four FAA (Federal Aviation Administration) privatization slots (plus Midway), one of which is reserved for a GA airport; A significant driver of future privatization initiatives is the suggestion that the FAA Reauthorisation Bill 2010 contains an anti-privatization provision that would (1) increase the airline approval requirement for privatization from 65% to 75%, and (2) make privatized airports ineligible for federal airport improvement grants, putting them at a funding disadvantage compared with other airports.

3.3. Independent not-for-profit corporations

This structure is the regime in Canada, arising from a gradual devolution from government ownership and operation that began in the early 1990s. Canadian airport authorities operate their airports under a 60 year lease agreement (which can be extended) after which time, the land and assets, including all investments and improvements, revert to the federal government. As not-for-profit entities, Canadian airports have not been subject to direct regulation (of aeronautical charges). There has been a significant amount of infrastructure investment at Canadian airport over the last ten years however the types and levels of investment have been subject to some debate concerning the possibility of 'gold plating': over-extravagant or 'unnecessary' investment that leads to higher charges for airlines and passengers. Canadian airports exhibit varying degrees of focus on complementary non-aviation activities but all of the larger airports utilize passenger facility charges (usually bundled into airfare prices) to help finance investments.[7] An ongoing issue in Canada is the payment of 'ground rent' by airports to the Federal government, which, under the current regime, amounts on average, to 12% of gross revenues for any airport with annual revenues over $250million. Airports and airlines have argued that the form and level of rent payments led to inflated aeronautical charges. The Canadian model of airport governance has not been duplicated anywhere else in the world. It is also a model which was brought in over 15 years ago and is ready for reform. The current model limits access to equity capital, it limits transition to a true private sector business and it is less adaptable to an environment in which airline business models have changed, and there have been considerable changes in the world of aviation.

3.4. Fully private for-profit via IPO

Fully privatized airports have shown both a strong market orientation and a strong customer focus. BAA is the oldest example

of a major airport privatization implemented via the sale of all of the governments shares using an initial public offering (IPO). BAA, which include at that time, the London airports [LHR, LGW (sold in October 2009) and STN] plus four airports in Scotland (Glasgow, Edinburgh, Aberdeen and Prestwick[8]) has exhibited a strong orientation towards complementary retail business and non-complementary business on and off airport land. This is perhaps explained in part by the form of price regulation applied to these airports: a 'single till' price cap, under which revenue from all sources (aeronautical and non-aeronautical) along with costs are used at the price cap reviews held up to five years apart in deciding the level of charges or how much aeronautical prices can change. This led to low, non-market, aeronautical prices at LHR until 2003 when the price cap was set separately for the three London airports; low relative to social efficient levels. It has also led in some degree to a reduction in service quality and an 'apparent' underinvestment in some assets, mostly terminals. The UK Competition Commission (2009) report also attributed underinvestment and shoddy service quality to a lack of competition between London airports.

While these airports have shown a willingness to develop markets and make strategic investments, there is also evidence that links between airport management and the government have remained strong and that political decision-making plays a direct role in augmenting private commercial interests (for example the private demand for an additional runway at LHR and the public decision to instead support an additional runway at STN). A recent competition commission report recommended the divestment of the three London airports into separate entities and on September 17, 2008, Gatwick was purchased by Global Infrastructure Partners that also own of London City Airport, on October 20, 2009. Only the three London airports are subject to price controls, other airports are operated commercially.

3.5. Fully private for-profit via trade sale

In Australia airports still under federal ownership were first corporatized in the 1980s — which meant that the airports had a more commercial focus, were expected to achieve cost recovery as a group (though there were cross subsidies from large to smaller airports) and their accounts were publicly available. Smaller airports were either owned by federal or local governments, and in the 1980s the federal government transferred ownership of smaller airports to local governments. The main three New Zealand airports, Auckland, Wellington and Christchurch, were corporatized in the late 1980s.

Airports in Australia were privatized beginning in 1996–1997; Brisbane, Melbourne and Perth but not Sydney (which was privatized in 2002). Airports were sold to private interests via trade sales in which investment consortia bid to purchase the airports. These consortia typically have included airport management companies and/or infrastructure investment companies (along with pension funds). In Australia, airports were sold under a lease agreement of 50 years plus an automatic extension of 49 years, after which the airports revert to the federal government. Australian airports, like UK airports exhibit a strong market focus but unlike their UK counterparts Australian investors seem to have taken a more long term [investment] perspective immediately following the sale and have according to some, a more unified strategic view of how the airport should develop. This Australia-UK difference in behaviour may be due in part to how the airports were privatized, ownership by an investment firm meant less focus on short-term returns, and, the monopoly which BAA had on airport services in London and

---

[6] Examples of port authorities include New York and New Jersey, Seattle, and Boston.

[7] This is a direct consequence of the way the Airport Authorities legislation is structured and restricts access to certain types of capital.

[8] Prestwick was sold in 1991 and Southampton was purchased about the same time.

6   *D. Gillen / Journal of Air Transport Management 17 (2011) 3–13*

southern UK; also with price cap regulation a monopoly supplier can reduce quality and raise the quality adjusted price. However, the two most important differences were BAAs ability to shift investment to other airports because the regulated asset base was for a bundle of three airports (until 2003) and the single till regulation had a considerable impact. Starkie (2008) also argues the pre-2006 BAA still had all the vestiges of a nationalized industry, same culture and same management. This in combination with having a systems approach to asset regulation (bundling all three London airports) meant investment was based on planning and political decisions rather than market forces. The consequence was underinvestment at Heathrow but overinvestment in the bundle of airports, particularly at Stansted.

New Zealand followed a similar model but the airports each have a freehold on the airports assets. Government shareholdings in Auckland and Wellington were sold in the late 1990s and the airports have majority private ownership, with only Auckland being publicly listed. Christchurch remains owned by the local government. After an attempt by the Ontario Teachers Pension Fund to purchase majority ownership in Auckland Airport in 2008, the New Zealand Government placed restrictions on who could purchase shares and how many.

3.6. Partially private for-profit with government controlling interest

Athens, Rome and Hamburg are all examples of airports that are for-profit entities where private investors are limited to a minority interest; others include Belfast, Brussels, Budapest, Copenhagen, Dusseldorf and Frankfurt and airports in Argentina, Chile, Colombia and Mexico. The existence of a for-profit (commercial) objective and minority private interest has in general been viewed by the stakeholders as enough to cause a fundamental change in management attitude and an orientation towards developing commercial value. It appears that even though government remains the majority shareholder, these airports are able to make decisions and develop strategies that a government run airport would not. This includes air route development and retail development (for example, Hamburg Airport reported 20 new routes in 2007 and opened a 7000 m^2 retail plaza in 2008). It has also had a significant increase in the number of carriers serving the airport including low cost and charter carriers. In some cases such airports have pursued strategic investments with carriers and have sought to maximize the relative contribution of non-aviation revenues. The degree and intrusiveness of government intervention via regulation and oversight remains a potential issue.

3.7. Partially private for-profit with private controlling interest

Copenhagen airport is an example of an airport that has become a for-profit company with the majority share held by a single private investor (Macquarie Airports). This form of governance has, like those airports with minority private ownership, been successful in bringing a more entrepreneurial and commercial orientation to airport operations and strategy. A potential effect of this form of privatization is the possibility to raise more private capital (investors willing to pay more for controlling interest) and also the possibility of a more coherent long term investment direction. For 'hands-on' investors like Macquarie Airports, majority ownership now appears to be a minimum condition for their involvement, however there may be little *de facto* difference between minority and majority ownership.[9] The reason for this is

governments through regulation and oversight can have a significant influence and place constraints on the development of commercial value, whether there is a majority ownership.[10] Consequently in the realm of partial privatization, many factors may depend on jurisdiction-dependent government regulations, oversight, larger objectives and transparency in airport management–government relations.

4. Does the form of governance structure matter for economic efficiency?

There are numerous factors that can and do affect the performance of airports and as well there are a number of metrics one could use to describe and assess performance. Among economists the metric most often used has been productivity, measured by total factor productivity (TFP) and/or cost efficiency. However, other valid measures could be congestion, price levels for aircraft and passengers, rent per square foot of terminal space, operating profit, aviation revenue, revenue from non-aviation sources, passengers per employee and total aircraft movements, for example. The choice of which metric used will be determined by the underlying objective function of the airport of which there may be many, and some possibly conflicting.

Of interest is whether the governance structure affects airport performance where the metric is cost efficiency. A possible confounding factor in assessing the impact of governance is the liberalization of airline services in the market. Generally, changes in airport governance followed domestic airline deregulation and therefore the degree of liberalization refers to international markets. So the question is, how does the governance structure effect cost efficiency if at all, and is the country in which the airport is situated considered to be restrictive or prone to liberal bilaterals and/or open skies agreements and how does this affect efficiency?

Whether airports are operating efficiently involves three types of measures. First, are airports operating on the lowest cost function for their size, traffic composition and range of products? Second are airports operating on the correct point on the lowest function, meaning are they pricing efficiently? Third, are airports moving ahead in integrating technology whether imbedded in capital (runway or terminal), labour, governance or systems to ensure continued cost efficiency? The empirical evidence has concentrated on the first measure and only recently has research explored the second measure. The third measure has not been explored.

In a 2008 paper, Oum, Yan and Yu show, using a Bayesian stochastic frontier cost function that cost efficiency does vary with ownership form. They show that majority private and fully publicly owned airports are most cost efficient, while mixed public-private owned airports, particularly with the majority public, are less cost efficient. In developing these results there was no control for the degree of liberalization of the aviation market nor the impact of regulation, if any, on cost efficiency However, the results are telling because it appears that homogeneity of ownership leads to cost efficiency perhaps because of fewer conflicting objectives. The paper does not provide an explanation as to why the governance affects cost efficiency only that it does.

Oum et al. (2006) find similar results to Oum et al. (2008), that private majority ownership and wholly government owned or airport authorities are most cost efficient. The paper also offers some insights as to differences in behaviour such as entrepreneurship with higher non-aviation revenues associated with more

---

[9] Macquarie has a minority interest in a Rome airport and has experienced considerable difficulties.

[10] That being said, Macquarie Airports has divested all airports in which they held minority shares.

D. Gillen / Journal of Air Transport Management 17 (2011) 3–13 7

efficient airports. Vogel (2006) offers some ideas as to what the drivers are to explain why private owned airports may be more efficient. He examines the privatization and financial performance of European airports and finds that privatized airports are more cost efficient and this efficiency is driven by higher asset turnover, higher revenue productivity (return on sales), higher cash flow to revenue ratio and higher operating margins; in sum, superior operating efficiency, asset utilization and capital structure. Looking at these results as well as that of others, including Francis et al. (2002) and Vasigh and Gorjidooz (2006), it seems clear that privatized airports pursue profit while public airports are output maximizers. To meet public responsibilities, privatized airports may treat a level of output as a constraint while a public airport may find some acceptable level of profit (or cost efficiency) as a constraint. Public airports may thus not be on the lowest cost function or at the most efficient point on the cost function they are on. State airports in theory should pursue their public interest objectives and be cost effective, but it appears that agency and incentive problems may arise because of a lack of transparency and a lack of well defined property rights and incentive structures.

The difficulty with much of the empirical research is the sole focus on static productive efficiency. There is no consideration for dynamic efficiency; how well airports have been able to adjust to the wide array of changes that have taken place in the aviation industry, and their ability to deliver innovation and new products. It is also void of a reasonable treatment of capital cost. Measures of efficiency are not providing any information on the optimal size of airports nor whether there may be a range of optimal sizes. The metrics on efficiency and governance are providing information on cost performance in relation to what are effectively short run costs. Therefore, we may have state airports operating efficiently on a short run cost function but they may be the wrong scale. The implications that public-private ventures may be most inefficient is puzzling and needs greater investigation given the preference for them in Europe and India, for example. It is not clear why such joint ventures should be less cost efficient if control rests with the private partner. However, this work is silent on why cost efficiency might differ among governance structures only that it apparently does.

5. Airport regulation: experiences across jurisdictions

An airport is a multi-product firm and at its simplest it has two sides to its business: the airside market (passenger airlines and cargo companies as direct customers and fixed base operators as tenants) and the non-airside market (enplaning and deplaning passengers as direct customers and retail businesses as tenants). Each side gives rise to a multiple of products with peak and off-peak periods in both markets. However, revenues are generally bundled as airside (monies from fees and charges to airlines for runway, apron and terminal-gate use) and non-aviation (monies from retail and commercial activity including land leases).

A number of factors influence the airport's market power (ability to set airside prices). In this regard, smaller (regional) as well as larger airports can compete with road and rail transportation; for example, between Hamburg and Berlin and Madrid and Barcelona. For example, the demand for flights between London and Paris was impacted with the completion of the Chunnel connecting the UK with continental Europe; with the introduction of high speed trains the number of direct flights offered between London and Paris was reduced by approximately 50%.[11] In the case of larger airports, the number of flights an airport can attract depends on both the airport's

attractiveness as a point of departure/arrival and on its usefulness as a hub for connecting passengers. In the former case, an airport's bargaining power with airlines derives from its geographic proximity to "non-connecting" passengers and the degree to which it competes with other airports for those passengers. In the limiting case, airlines are faced with the choice of using the airport or ignoring that segment of the passenger market, allocating its equipment to an alternative market: an explicit LCC strategy. The airport may well be constrained in its pricing to the extent that non-hub airports are servicing several rival airlines. The airport has a preference to have competing sources of airside business to protect against the risk of a carrier failing or facing a bilateral monopoly. This provides a natural ceiling on airside prices particularly in countries where the domestic carriers are discount or charter airlines with low margins which are in competition with a dominant previously government owned carrier; this would be the case in Canada, Australia and New Zealand, for example. Competition Law may also constrain discrimination.

The perception that airports are monopolies has figured into the regulation of charges that airports levy.[12] This includes charges for airside activities such as landing and passenger terminal fees but also fees for non-aviation activities.[13] The form that this regulation has taken varies from country to country.[14] Essentially there are four types of price regulation: Single till price regulation takes the form of a price cap applied to all revenues deriving from the airport or all commercial activities. Price regulation is by way of a price cap using the RPI-X formula with regulatory review periods varying from three to five years.[15] With single till price regulation, carriers share in the risk portion of the airports' net commercial revenues by paying lower aeronautical charges if there are higher than expected net commercial revenues; Dual till price regulation separates aeronautical functions from non-aeronautical functions. It determines the level of aeronautical charges by considering aeronautical revenues and costs only. Consequently, the corresponding asset base includes aeronautical assets only; Rate of Return regulation benchmarks the profitability of regulated activities to the average of reference airports or businesses. It sets an allowed return on a defined asset base and may be single or dual till. Price Monitoring is currently implemented in Australia and New Zealand. The regulators use a trigger or "grim strategy" regulation where a light handed form of regulation is used until the subject firm sets prices at unacceptable levels or earns profits deemed excessive or reduces quality beyond some point and thus, triggers a long term commitment to intruding regulation.

The US is essentially a cost-of-service form of [self] regulation, which may make it a 5th form of regulation, although one could argue that those airports that still adhere to the principles of

---

[11] The drop in demand for shorter haul flights led to a reallocation of the valuable slots to longer haul flights.

[12] Some authors use 'natural' monopoly. I am not convinced the underlying cost structure of an airport exhibits both scale and scope economies which define it as a 'natural' monopoly.

[13] Airside fees would include landing, terminal, security and emergency/policing fees. Commercial fees are those negotiated for concession and lease agreements.

[14] In the debate on how to regulate airports, three features are important: the complementarity between airside and non-airside activity, the degree to which airports are congested (capacity constrained) and the level of competition in the industry (or at the airport if it is a hub). With regard to the complementarity issue, Starkie (2001) argues that the effect of increased airside movements on passenger volumes and non-airside revenues has a strong affect on airport pricing incentives. Capacity constraints influence the consequences for different price structures and just as importantly, the ability of the airport to cover its capital expenses.

[15] In the RPI-X formula where RPI is the price increase and 'X' is the limiting offset. The value of X is determined by the regulator based on a range of criteria including, for example, whether the industry is high or low productivity, the performance of the firm in the previous regulated period and whether the regulator wishes to incentivize the firm to reduce costs.

residual financing behave as if they operate under a single till form of price cap regulation.[16] The important difference in the US is that the sharing of revenues is voluntary, albeit under governance that requires break-even; the airports are required to set aeronautical fees so as to collect revenues that reflect the costs of providing the service. Thus individual prices are indirectly regulated in the sense that the aggregate of revenues cannot exceed costs. This however does not imply cost minimization.

In other parts of the world, price cap or rate of return regulation is the norm. The best examples of price cap regulation are in the UK, which regulates the BAA; France, Denmark and Ireland. With rate of return regulation (ROR) the key questions are firstly, what constitutes a 'fair' return on capital invested and secondly, what capital invested should be included in the 'allowed rate base'?[17] This form of regulation is very time intensive and generally involves lengthy regulatory hearings. ROR regulation tends to be complex, unresponsive and expensive to administer (Tretheway, 2001), however price cap regulation has become as cumbersome and resource intensive.

Price cap regulation was introduced precisely to overcome the problems associated with rate of return regulation. In particular, it was designed as a medium term 'cost recovery' mechanism, whereby at least in principle, the exogeneity of the price cap for the firm, and the fact that the price would be fixed for some years into the future, would provide incentives for firms to raise their profits by finding economies difficult for regulators to find, given the information asymmetry between regulator and those regulated. For this incentive to work, firms need to be confident of a regulatory commitment; that is, that price caps would not be re-opened to claw back savings the firm identified. Thus a key objective is to incentivize the firm to reveal its true costs by allowing the firm to keep efficiency gains within the price control period. The next period's prices are adjusted for inflation and the X-factor.[18] It was also expected initially that price cap regulation might be less resource intensive than rate of return regulation but this has not turned out to be the case; see Littlechild (2009). A criticism of price cap regulation is its short run focus and lack of incentive to invest.

Pure and hybrid price caps differ in the way in which the X in the price cap formula is set; a pure price cap sets X without reference to the costs of the airport which is regulated but may set it with reference to a broad airport benchmarked cost, while hybrid price caps set the X with reference to a firm's cost base.[19] Thus, hybrid price caps provide fewer incentives for cost reductions. For European airports none of the regulators have developed a pure price capping system. The price caps at Aeroport de Paris (ADP), Copenhagen and Dublin are based in part on the firm's costs but often adjusted for the regulators view of the scope for economies in the firm's cost base. Most important, price cap regulation does not regulate the charging structure according to arbitrary cost allocations based on historic costs.

There have been continuing debates over single versus dual till regulation. For example, there was a lengthy, detailed, and quite heated debate (i.e. disagreement) between the UK Civil Aviation Authority (CAA) (2003) and the UK Competition Commission in 2002/2003 on this issue – the CAA wanted to move to dual till; horrified airlines appealed to the UK Competition Commission which was sympathetic to their arguments and essentially a deadlock ensued which ensured no change to the price cap.

To evaluate the relative merits of dual versus single till two issues must be considered. First, do airports have, and exercise, market power in aviation and non-aviation sectors and second what represents a 'fair' distribution of the airport rents?[20] Some argue that airports can operate in a competitive environment. Schiphol, Frankfurt, Heathrow and Charles de Gaulle all compete for long haul connecting traffic. In Germany airports are close enough together they can be considered in competition to some degree as substitutes. To the extent airports are in the same market they have limited market power.

The major arguments for not including activities such as food and beverage, car and facility rental and parking concessions under a single till are that they result in perverse incentives when airports are capacity constrained and may create costs when airports have lots of capacity. When airports are capacity constrained and a single till is in place, as more revenue is made on the non-aeronautical side, it must be that aeronautical charges must be lowered to remain under the price cap. Thus in the presence of congestion, prices end up being lowered when efficiency dictates that they should be raised. If profit maximizing airports are not capacity constrained, they have every incentive to stimulate demand (and revenue) via lower prices on the aeronautical side. Thus, in the non-constrained case, single till price cap regulation is not necessary.[21] An example of where a 'single till' is chosen and not imposed is the newspaper industry which choose to sell the newspaper at less than the costs of production in order to attract the readership which attracts the advertising. In some situations, airports might, or are, doing the same thing.

What is not often considered in the debate on airport regulation is that airports can directly contribute to the degree of airline competition through pricing and capital investment decisions. Therefore policy-makers should not only consider the welfare effects of airport regulation in relation to airports and their customers, but also the associated welfare effects on airline competition that result from airport pricing and investment decisions under the various regulatory regime.[22]

At some EU airports, predominantly in Germany, we also observe revenue sharing agreements which often link the level of charges to the growth of passenger volume over a certain period. The model dictates that the airline and airport agree that airside charges will be reduced to some level if the rate of passenger growth is achieved or maintained at some agreed upon level. These so called sliding scales can be combined with price cap regulation

---

[16] Residual financing means at the end of the fiscal year, if revenues are less than costs the signatory airlines using the airport are responsible for covering the difference.

[17] Liquidity ratio, risk and conditions in the economy are also considered in setting the allowed rate of return.

[18] 'X' depends on how the regulator assesses the tradeoffs under their objectives given the cost and demand climate in which the firm operates. A high positive X-factor (i.e. RPI-X, resulting in lower real prices) might indicate that the firm revealed substantial cost savings in the past or it may indicate that the regulator sees considerable scope for further efficiency improvements during the next control period. A high negative X-factor (i.e. RPI + X, enabling a real price increase) is an indicator that the regulator might be placing more emphasis on the firm's planned investments and that the firm is facing rising incremental costs. X can be viewed as a smoothing mechanism given target revenue recovery.

[19] Hybrid price cap regulation is considered superior to cost based regulation because it is forward looking while cost plus regulation relies on historic costs.

[20] There is also the cost allocation issue with moving from single to dual till versus the efficiency gains from not regulating commercial activities.

[21] US, airports voluntarily enter into contracts with airlines to share rents if the signatory airlines agree to share the risks of costs exceeding revenues. There is no regulation requiring this type of agreement.

[22] There is one further level to this argument. Airports are in a three-level industry made up of airspace, airports and airlines. Policy at the 'top' (airspace) may cascade down to airports and airlines, just as airport decisions affect market conditions for airlines. A further reason to separate the three is that liberalisation/marketisation has gone furthest in airlines, some distance in airports, but not moved very much yet in '(not)open skies' airspace management/air traffic control. Therefore, airport governance and performance is arguably impacted by the airline market on one side and the airspace rules on the other.

D. Gillen / Journal of Air Transport Management 17 (2011) 3–13   9

as in the cases of Hamburg (Gillen and Niemeier, 2008) and Vienna.[23] At Frankfurt airport, for example, both parties agreed that with a projected passenger growth rate of 4%, average charges could be raised by 2%.[24] In the case of a higher growth rate, airlines participate with a 33% share in additional revenues. The agreement results in a sliding scale of airport charges that is related to passenger growth.

Australia and New Zealand have what has been termed 'light handed' regulation, something unique to these two countries. The major airports in both countries have been privatized since the mid 1990s. With this change in ownership and governance, formal regulation was put in place in Australia as airports were subjected to a price cap of the CPI-X form. These caps were put in place for five years, at which time there would be a review (Forsyth, 2002). It was expected that price caps would probably be continued. The caps were set by the government and they were administered by the Australian Competition and Consumer Commission (ACCC). In both cases it was a dual till system.

In 2001 The Australian Productivity Commission released a report which recommended the end of price cap regulation for all airports. In 2002 the government announced that it would be replacing regulation by monitoring for seven major capital city airports, and would not be regulating or monitoring other airports, a move from formal dual till price cap regulation to 'light handed' regulation. This regulatory form places no immediate constraints on aeronautical charges but monitors prices with a view to 'taking action' if prices are judged to be too high. After its first five years in operation, price monitoring at the major airports was reviewed in 2007 and renewed for another five years (with some adjustments). Local/municipal relations (land development) and the valuation of airport land and assets for determining aeronautical charges have been issues under this system.[25]

New Zealand did not formally regulate its airports after privatization, though it did provide for a review of airport pricing behaviour with the threat of more explicit regulation should this behaviour be unacceptable. The New Zealand approach involved a general provision set out in legislation to enable a review of pricing in industries such as airports to be initiated by the Minister at any time. In 1998, a review of pricing at Auckland, Christchurch and Wellington airports was initiated by the Minister. The Commerce Commission undertook the review, and recommended price regulation at Auckland airport (NZ Commerce New Zealand Commerce Commission, 2002).

In the Commerce Act Review undertaken in 2007, the government recommended that Auckland, Wellington and Christchurch (all international airports) be subject to much more stringent, hands-on, price monitoring and perhaps regulation, and that it be administered by the New Zealand Commerce Commission. These recommendations have not yet been introduced with legislative changes.[26]

Forsyth (2006) provides an assessment of the light handed regulatory approach. He notes that it works reasonably well with prices somewhat above what might be the case under tight regulation but well below monopoly levels. Also airports seem to be relatively cost efficient, likely on the basis that increasing profits from increased efficiency is unlikely to draw the ire of 'light handed' regulators. There are problems with investment incentives and with the 'process' of light handed regulation. It seems investments are not necessarily made on the basis of commercial objectives and economic efficiency. But this should not be surprising given the multi-product nature of airports and their continual adjustment to dynamic cost and demand functions.

6. Should airports be regulated?

The opponents of airport privatization and proponents of airport regulation argue that airports are natural monopolies and, given the opportunity, they will exploit, even abuse, this monopoly power. These claims would seem to raise two fundamental questions. First, do airports have market power, and if yes, what are the sources and is there any evidence? Second, can and will airports compete? Recent evidence from Moscow illustrates significant airport competition where two international airports, Domodedovo and Sheremetyevo, owned by rival organizations, battle for business. The result is lower fees, better service and fast-improving facilities at both airports. Domodedovo Airport, for example, recently convinced several top airlines to make it their Russian base, thanks to a major modernization that added more than 20 new restaurants, jewellery boutiques and a shop where passengers can rent DVDs to watch in booths. Sheremetyevo Airport responded by building a fast rail link to Moscow, complete with a Starbucks at the airport station.[27]

Do airports have market power? This is a complex question and many have argued that the fact that some airports seem to make high profits is evidence of such power.[28] Unfortunately the presence of economic rent may arise from market power but it may also arise from scarcity rent; an airport such as Heathrow or Chep Lak Kok or Auckland may obtain scarcity rent due to their location proximate to a desired passenger destination. The presence of rents at an airport can also result from locational rents just as stores located in a premier section of town; Oxford Street in London, 5th Avenue in New York, Bloor Street in Toronto. The rents these stores earn are not derived from market power but from location.

What are possible sources of market power for airports? One source of power would be the situation of being the sole provider of particular goods and services in the area. Airports produce a range of services for passengers, airlines and the community and derive revenues from each market segment. While they may be the sole provider of runway services they are not for other services.[29] There are a number of communities that have multiple airports; San Francisco, New York, Washington, London, Frankfurt, Paris, Los Angeles, Toronto, Vancouver to name a few. In a number of cases, large international airports are long haul connecting hubs and they

---

[23] At Frankfurt and Düsseldorf the revenue sharing agreements are the result of a Memorandum of Understanding between the airports and its users legalized as a public contract between the airport and regulator (Klenk, 2004). In case of any disagreement the charges would be fixed according to cost based regulations.

[24] These are nominal prices as the agreement is not related to the price level.

[25] Australian airports have been highly entrepreneurial. Similar to the privatized UK airports they have exhibited a strong focus on developing non-aviation revenues including non-complementary investments on airport land including factory retail outlets, shopping malls and in one case a brick factory!

[26] Under the new rules airports (Auckland, Wellington and Christchurch) would be subject to an enhanced disclosure regime, which would include information on how their charges are set based on binding input methodologies (how costs should be calculated) developed by the Commerce Commission. The Commerce Commission would monitor the way airports are setting charges against non-binding pricing principles and, if it finds stricter controls are needed; they would be able to recommend that further regulatory measures be imposed.

[27] See Daniel Michaels (2008), Moscow Points the Way With Airport Competition: While Most Nations Sport Monopolies, Rivalry Between Two Russian Gateways Ushers in Improvements for Carriers, Travelers, *Wall Street Journal*, December 1, 2008.

[28] A problem is the definition of marginal cost for calculating mark-ups. Marginal cost has little relevance given the multi-product nature of airports and the importance of fixed costs. Also a 'competitive' market structure is not realistic as the alternative to regulation.

[29] Australian Productivity Commission's 2001 report on airport price (de)regulation evaluates airport market power 'service' by 'service' (runways, check-in facilities, etc).

10   D. Gillen / Journal of Air Transport Management 17 (2011) 3–13

will compete with other long haul connecting hubs: e.g. London, Amsterdam, Paris, Frankfurt, Munich and Madrid. In other cases airports may have overlapping market catchments. This is more prevalent in areas where low cost carriers have made inroads into markets as in UK, US and many EU member states. Starkie (2008) reports that people are willing to drive up to 2 h to an airport in which there are greater services and lower fares. Therefore airports in bidding for airline services recognize that passengers can switch airports and therefore, airlines are able to be more 'footloose'.

Airports compete with one another for airline services. Airports bid for more carriers, more routes and the possibility of having an airline establish a base at their airport. If governments maintain a restrictive air services policy which does not allow entry, or if they constrain routing, frequencies or pricing, this would shift bargaining power from airlines to airports provided there are few gateway alternatives. If a carrier can move between gateways, the restrictive policy shifts power to the carriers. If there are limited gateway opportunities, airports gain relative market power. Another take on this issue is determined by the number of international carriers a country has which can serve bilateral markets. Certainly in markets such as Japan or Canada, which have large numbers of restrictive bilateral agreements and few international carriers, airports have less market power. This occurs because the airport has fewer airlines to substitute among or bid for services.[30] On the other hand, airlines in a number of countries can have a considerable influence on which airports may be designated in an air service agreement, so airports are 'beholden' to their dominant international airlines.

In a liberalized air services environment airports may gain or lose market power but it will depend on whether there is hub dominance, a limited number of gateways, and whether the liberalization removes airport designation – where the international carrier must serve a designated point. Under the new EU–US Open Skies agreement, traditional gateways will lose market power as carriers can now serve interior points in the US. However, note the existence of rents from market power is not necessarily inherent with the economics of airports but a consequence of government policy regarding international aviation. Some or all rents earned by airports may be scarcity rents arising from the aviation policy.

Domestic liberalization has had a significant impact on reducing the market power of airports. With deregulation of air services, a number of things occurred. First, airlines were able to move between markets, build networks and have airports bid for their services; rents have been reduced with competition and airlines have bargained harder with airports. A second aspect is the way in which services are now delivered. In a regulated environment, and one in which airports were viewed as public utilities, airports had a set of posted prices generally based on aircraft weight for landing charges. Airports assumed the risk of traffic loss, and airlines paid posted prices with no long term contracts. One might argue that since the airports absorbed all the risk, that any seemingly above normal returns reflected that risk. However, airline deregulation has brought about a significant change and shift in risk. Airlines are now more footloose; certainly LCCs are and the same is true for legacy carriers to some degree. Airports now have an incentive to negotiate long term contracts with carriers and engage in incentive pricing (Starkie, 2008).[31] Such contracts specify charges, conditions, service quality (turn around times, advertising, co-investments), and length of the contract. The average charge paid by larger and/or

base carriers will be less than the posted price; Starkie (2008) reports two such contracts in the UK that have this characteristic. Furthermore, airports with their lumpy capital now have an incentive to have airlines establish a base and to develop a route. Thus, competition between airports is not simply about spatial adjacency but also happens across wide geographic markets as airports bid for airline base investments.

If airports are 'natural monopolies' their cost structure should exhibit economies of scale and economies of scope. However, airports are a collection of activities which produce a range of services which could be collected into airside services and terminal services or 'other'. Airside services exhibit constant returns to scale and perhaps decreasing returns with congestion; doubling the number of runways will likely double airside throughput but it may be somewhat more or less than this depending on the configuration of runways.[32] There is also confusion when speaking about cost and airside capital. Because of lumpiness, there will be economies of utilization or economies of density.

Terminals in contrast are more puzzling. On the one hand there may be economies of scope in serving domestic and international passengers in one building. There will be economies of density initially but terminals will fill up. As they become larger there are more passengers moving over longer distances; doubling throughput more than doubles the space needed so there may well be diseconomies of scale with terminals. As terminals grow in size they become more complex, more technology is needed to move people and the mix of public to potential rental space changes.[33] Larger airports tend to have multiple terminals which may offer competing services to airlines but individual terminals may also be owned by an airline. Thus it would appear terminals offer no significant source of market power to the airport. Where land is scarce terminals may have higher charges reflecting this.

On the financial side there are two contrasting arguments. In a number of quarters there is the belief that airports are subject to high fixed costs and low marginal costs which will, in a highly competitive market, lead to setting prices below costs and incurring financial loses or setting prices at average costs and having small levels of airport traffic. The opposing argument is that airports will earn large profits because they have market power; in the first case they earn too little and in the second case too much. Starkie (2008) provides evidence from the UK that the first argument is potentially flawed. He shows that small and medium sized airports in the UK can make a 'decent' return on fixed asserts. He, at the same time, shows the return to be not that much different than what was earned in the non-financial sector in the UK. Mackenzie-Williams (2006) reports on measures of return on the capital employed for airports in various locations and these range from 9.1 to 11.3%, not particularly excessive.[34]

In most instances there is a predisposed position of regulatory intervention when an airport is privatized or there is a shift in ownership. Policy-makers should not immediately move to a regulatory tool box but rather ask the question, 'is this industry

---

[30] In cases where restrictive bilateral agreements have designated airports, such agreements provide the airport with market power.
[31] The agreement between Frankfurt Airport and Lufthansa that established landing charges based on passenger growth is a good example.

[32] Jeong (2005), for example, shows empirically that a constant returns to scale sets in at US airports at about three to five million passengers.
[33] Generalized costs, including time costs certainly rise with terminal size.
[34] Measuring profit for airports is a very difficult task for a number of reasons; in the US, for example, passenger facility charges (PFC) revenues are applied directly to construction expenditures, and so most US airport capital no longer appears on the books of US airports. Most publicly available numbers are not comparable. The most comparable number across airports would be aeronautical revenue less aeronautical costs, i.e., costs assigned as Aeronautical (this can be arbitrary). However, this number is without much meaning since almost every airport in the world is constrained so that aeronautical revenue is less than or equal to aeronautical costs; the measure of aeronautical costs usually do not assign full capital costs.

D. Gillen / Journal of Air Transport Management 17 (2011) 3–13
11

one in which a workably competitive outcome is possible, and if not, why? Can it be restructured to achieve such a competitive outcome? As Starkie (2008) points out, the unregulated airport industry has achieved solutions through long term contracts for services. Contracts which allocate risk efficiently establish service quality and protect against delay problems. Regulation, as has been shown, leads to inefficiencies such as underinvestment and loss of service quality.[35] Contracts with airlines seem rare at regulated airports. There are all sorts of unintended consequences; for example the distortion of commercial investment under the single till regime. However, those that favour regulation as a sweeping solution to a supposed problem presume that there are no costs to regulation; that there is perfect knowledge, and they impose regulation in the context of comparative statics, ignoring that the real world is full of dynamics.

Airports derive revenue from a broad array of sources. Different markets and their ability to price above cost across these markets will differ. It may, for example, be that it is the only airport serving a city (e.g. Auckland) and is therefore a single firm and a monopoly for the supply of airside services. Will it exercise monopoly power in the sense of restricting the supply of services; does it have an incentive to do this given that it would lose profits from commercial activities due to lower passenger numbers? May be, and if it does, there are regulatory measures that can be put in place; dual till regulation for example. Do airports compete? Yes, long haul connecting traffic can choose from an array of airports in Europe, for example, or North America and increasingly in Asia. Does Toronto compete with Buffalo, Vancouver with Seattle and Düsseldorf with Belgian airports? Yes, most certainly there is cross border competition. Will there always be competition? No, not necessarily, but the relevant question is, do such airports have an incentive to exercise market power? Given the high fixed cost, low marginal cost nature of airport services and the complementarity between airside movements (passenger and aircraft) there may be a tempering influence on the use (or abuse) of market power. How much market power an airport has and exercises is 'circumstantial' and must be examined on a case by case basis. The market power argument is not sufficient to reject privatization outright or to introduce heavy handed regulation in the case of full or partial privatization.

There is a large amount of theoretical and empirical work investigating airport governance, privatization and regulation. The coverage here is not exhaustive but includes the essential papers and arguments. One might contend that the justification for regulation should be made on a case by case basis. I would disagree. Restructuring airport ownership to provide for a greater role for market forces should at most involve light handed regulation. If a stronger form of regulation is deemed necessary, the case should be made for undertaking it for a particular airport; a philosophy of fit, willing and able, rather than public convenience and necessity should be the policy.

In the UK almost every airport is privatized and profitable in a competitive market. Starkie (2008) does a very good job in explaining the underlying reasons for the success of privatization of UK airports and it does not involve regulation. The success had to do with fundamental changes such as airline deregulation and the development of new airline and airport business models. It became evident that national ownership which generated excessive costs, uneconomic investments, inappropriate products and services and little innovation required a new way of doing things. Private ownership provides the right incentives for airports to adopt more

efficient production but also to be innovative. Market forces set in motion the changes that need to be made to cost and demand relationships. Putting in place a regulator creates an institution which works against the shift to private equity and competition. The impact of price controls on efficiency are non-trivial. Even in the case of RPI-X price cap regulation which was designed to reinforce the incentives for efficiency and innovation and identify how demand and costs should change, has lead to over-regulation. Regulators are presumed to know more than they do. In the effort to avoid excess profits we receive excess regulation and bureaucracy as these bodies try to identify efficient operating costs and capital expenditures. Regulation works to stifle innovation and dynamic efficiency. It preserves the conflict between airlines and airports because negotiation is always through the third party regulator. Negotiation requires customers and companies to come to agreements to reflect the needs, preferences and mutual understanding of the parties. Regulators tend to judge settlements based on outcomes rather than acceptable process. As Littlechild argues, if there are elements of monopoly the role of regulation is not to replace the market process but to reduce the market power. A good example in aviation is to push for open skies agreements to allow choice for market participants.

As with all institutional and governance changes, the key is getting enforceable property rights set with the correct incentives. There are examples of costly private sector airports, e.g. Athens, but the correct response is to understand why such an outcome occurred, not to just state that it happened. There needs to be accountability and transparency. Even in the case of a single provider, a negotiated outcome can be satisfactory to both parties provided that the process is deemed acceptable. As an example, NavCan, the sole provider of air traffic control services in Canada is generally regarded as a successful shift in governance despite being a monopoly.

6.1. A new view of the airport business – two-sided Platforms[36]

Airports have traditionally been viewed as public utilities serving the needs of airlines. More recently and in many developed countries they are seen as modern businesses pursuing their own objectives and serving the demands of carriers and passengers. Regardless of which view one takes it is a perspective of one sided markets. People went to airports to depart on an airline flight. The airport was seen as a factor of production in an airline's production function. The sources of revenue were from one side, from the airlines. Airports did not consider that passengers represented a source of revenue independently from the airlines. Indeed some airports still generate much of their total revenue from rates and charges levied on the carriers.

However, over the last decade airports have recognized with increasing frequency that non-aviation revenues are important and can be large. The important point to appreciate is that airport revenues are from two sides; from airlines and from passengers.[37] But this thinking also requires that we consider airports as platforms lying between passengers and airlines; it brings the two together. Airports add value to both sides by internalizing network effects which exist between the two demand groups; carriers are better off if there are more passengers and passengers are better off if there are more carriers, more destinations and more flights. Multi-sided markets (or platforms) serve two or more distinct customer groups who value each others participation; eBay provides markets for buyers and sellers, dating clubs bring together

---

[35] Regulators can commit for limited periods but airport investment is long lived. There will be reduced incentive to invest. Price regulated firms also can increase profits by reducing expensive services.

[36] This is a new literature with the initial stream of articles emerging in 2003.
[37] In some communities airport employees and the local community are large revenue generators.

12   *D. Gillen / Journal of Air Transport Management 17 (2011) 3–13*

people and singles bars perform the same task. Multi-sided markets must serve both sides of the market to add value. An airport cannot just serve carriers or passengers. Economists would argue that two-sided platforms (airports) internalize usage externalities that agents cannot internalize efficiently. Rochet and Tirole (2005) define two-sided markets as a situation in which the volume of transactions between end-users depends on the structure and not only on the overall level of the fees charged by the platform.

Adopting 'two-sided' thinking leads to revelations about one sided logic in two-sided markets.[38] These are particularly instructive for airports, airlines and passengers.

6.1.1. Fallacy 1: efficient price structures should reflect relative costs

ICAO (International Civil Aviation organization), IATA (International Air Transport Association) and the airlines have always taken the position that airport rates and charges should be cost based. However such pricing principles ignore the externality that exists between the customer groups on either side of the platform (airport), therefore rather than have cost based prices there should be externality based prices; relative costs are merely significant but not deterministic.

6.1.2. Fallacy 2: marginal cost pricing is efficient

The problem is two-fold here; first, non-assignable costs are allocated in some way, perhaps based on relative demand elasticities, but any assignment must consider the combination of airline and passenger demand elasticities. Second, the externality is not internalized. Subsidizing one side of the market may significantly impact utility on the other side of the market. The overall value of and to both sides' increases.

6.1.3. Fallacy 3: high price-cost margins indicate market power

In one sided markets competition generally drives prices to costs and conventional indexes of market power are price-cost margins (e.g. Lerner Index). However, two-sided market thinking suggests that competition between platforms (airports) may lead to prices above costs since the competitive structure of fees will generally not reflect costs but rather the value placed on each side of the platform by participating in the market. To draw sensible inferences about harmful market power through price-cost margins one would need to demonstrate that the *sum* of prices to airlines and passengers can be profitably raised permanently above the costs of supplying airport services to passengers and airlines.

6.1.4. Fallacy 4: a price below marginal cost indicates predation and possibly cross-subsidy

Setting prices below marginal cost may be used to generate greater surpluses by attracting those users that provide the greatest benefits to the network. For example, setting lower fees for certain types of carriers may make all carriers better off because the lower priced carriers attract more passengers to the airport.

If one side of the market receives services at below marginal cost, the view is that it must be receiving a subsidy; but this thinking ignores the fact that the service being provided to each type of user depends on whether it is provided to the other type of user. A good example is the provision of check-in kiosks at airports by airports. The airport does not charge the passenger a fee for using the kiosk because the value to the airline is higher when more passengers use the kiosks since it results in lower costs to the airlines. It is also more sensible for the airport to provide these services because the IT platform is common for all carriers and the cost of providing the service is lower for all carriers.

6.1.5. Fallacy 5: in mature markets price structures that do not reflect costs are no longer justified

One might argue that on start up a firm (an airport with a new runway) may set prices below marginal costs or even zero or the airport may provide free (or very low priced) parking; e.g. Frankfurt Hahn. But once the market is mature it may still be beneficial to keep prices low for one side and higher for the other side if the incremental value of the low priced side provides greater surplus to the higher priced side.

6.1.6. Fallacy 6: more competition may result in a more balanced price structure

Competition may or may not lead to more balanced prices. The outcome will depend on how competition interacts with each type of user. If certain airlines tend to use particular airports, greater competition may mean passengers could be subsidized by underpricing access, resulting in even more imbalance in the prices.

There are other fallacies one could list and discuss, but the main point made here is that two-sided markets require two-sided thinking. Recognizing this, airports as two-sided platforms, also requires a rethinking of the role of airlines and the ownership of the passenger. The traditional way of thinking is the airline owns the passenger and the airport serves the airlines' needs; one sided market thinking. Considering the airport as a two-sided platform places it in the centre between the airline and the passenger, the airlines serve as the airport's distribution system. The airport adds value to both passengers and airlines by bringing the two sides together.

These conclusions are drawn on the basis that in two-sided platforms the profit maximizing prices depend on the elasticities of demand by customers on both sides of the platform, the nature and magnitude of the indirect network effects between the two groups of customers and the marginal costs for both sides. The profit maximizing prices for the two sides of the market are interlinked. This fact is potentially very important for the analysis of market definition and market power as well as decisions regarding airport regulation. Starkie's insight (2001) that airports even with market power would have less incentive to use or abuse this power because of the complementarity between airside and non-airside revenues is a good example of two-sided platform thinking and well ahead of the analysis of two-sided markets.

7. Conclusions

Whether an airport is government run, a not-for-profit organization or a for-profit corporation, it is subject to market forces that define commercial value and competition along with economic costs and benefits. These costs and benefits will change depending on the set of institutions in place and the governance structure. Governance, regulation and oversight by government agencies augment or perhaps impede free-market forces by placing constraints on the actions and decisions of airports and by providing a particular set of incentives; incentives which move managers in one direction rather than another. The resulting economic impact of governance and regulatory institutions is therefore defined by the interaction of the underlying market forces with the implemented, as distinct from 'intended', constraints imposed and the behavioural responses of relevant decision-makers – airport management, airlines and passengers – to the incentives that are actually created.

The ownership and regulatory environments of airports represent compromises between conflicting objectives – efficiency has been one of the main motivations for change, but only to an extent. The varying approaches to the airport problem adopted across different countries possibly reflects different views on the best ways to pursue efficiency objectives, but it also reflects the different non efficiency objectives which governments are pursuing in their

---

[38] I borrow this expression from Wright (2004).

D. Gillen / Journal of Air Transport Management 17 (2011) 3–13

13

airport policies. Some governments are more eager to maximize revenues on privatization than others, some are more focused on promoting and protecting airline competition, some are more willing to become involved in detailed economic regulation than others and some take the view that the threat of regulation will be sufficient to discipline pricing behaviour.

Should airports be regulated? A review of airports in Australia, New Zealand, North America and Europe illustrates there are mixed feelings across jurisdictions. Continental Europe seems to have maintained a position that airports have market power, at least on the airside, and therefore must be regulated; Germany is a good example of such a view. Those predisposed to regulation should consider there is a tradeoff with the introduction of regulation at airports, the tradeoff is the economic effects of the exercise of market power and the potential (or actual) distortion that specific industry regulation can introduce. Regulators may be averse to recognizing these tradeoffs because, unlike the behaviour of prices, the welfare losses from foregone innovation may be unobservable to the regulators' constituency. Moreover, an emphasis on dynamic efficiency requires the short-term regulator to take the "long view" – fostering the competitive process rather than emulating the competitive outcome. Market economies outperform regulated economies generally because no one has enough information or foresight to understand the changing environment, so the market's seemingly messy processes of experimentation and correction yield better results than a regulator's analysis. Much of the time the regulators do not know where they are in terms of distortions. There are all sorts of unintended consequences but those that favour regulation as a sweeping solution to a supposed problem presume that there are no costs to regulation; that there is perfect knowledge, and then impose regulation in the context of comparative statics, ignoring that the real world is full of dynamics.

This being said, airline deregulation has been the single most important factor in affecting the balance of power between airports and airlines and fostering potential airport competition. It has fundamentally changed the way airlines and airports do business, largely because it has led to the introduction of new airline business models. As countries maintain strict bilaterals, or fail to put in place rights of establishment or maintain ownership limits, they create barriers to entry. In some cases such barriers convey market power to the carrier because airports cannot bid for services from other carriers. On the other hand carriers are not able to easily switch between airports. In the case of secondary airports, for example spokes in a hub-and-spoke system, the airport will have less market power regardless of the regulatory regime because it depends on the carrier to provide access to a hub. With liberalization and open skies agreements, airports can bid for airline services, and airlines are free to choose which airport best serves their needs and their business model.

Are airports two-sided platforms? This is new work that examines markets involving the bringing-together of two or more groups of distinctly different customers who value each other's participation, and these are common in the business world. Think of newspapers (wherein publishers bring together advertisers, editorial staffs and readers); or the shopping mall business (developers recruit retailers, restaurants, gasoline stations, film exhibitors, architects, highway engineers and customers); or credit card companies (merchants, banks, ATM manufacturers and customers).

The richness of this recent analysis of airports, and perhaps more broadly to transportation infrastructure, may lead to a rethinking of aviation policy and strategy. As examples, airports would be at the centre of international aviation rights negotiations, not the airlines. There would be much greater pressure to liberalize international aviation and increase the numbers of domestic carriers; actually, it would no longer matter whether an airline was domestic, nor would there be the concerns regarding cabotage or rights of establishment. These ideas are already impacting antitrust economics and enlightening the strategies of new and unfamiliar technologies. It remains to be seen if it presents a significant rethinking of airport economics.

Acknowledgements

This paper formed the basis of my Martin Kuntz Memorial Lecture. I owe an intellectual debt to Peter Forsyth, Hans-Martin Niemeier, David Starkie and Michael Tretheway for educating me over the years about airport economics, competition and regulation. This paper draws on joint work with Peter Forsyth, Hans-Martin Niemeier and others. I am grateful to the Ken Button, Cathal Guiomard, Robin Lindsey, David Starkie and Michael Tretheway for helpful comments and to Lorra Ward for her editing skills.

References

Armstrong, M., Cowan, S., Vickers, J., 1994. Regulatory Reform: Economic Analysis and British Experience. MIT Press, Cambridge, MA.

Francis, G., Humphreys, I., Fry, J., 2002. The benchmarking of airport performance. Journal of Air Management 8, 239–247.

Forsyth, P., 2006. Airport Policy in Australia and New Zealand: Privatization, Light Handed Regulation and Performance, paper to the Workshop on Comparative Political Economy and Infrastructure Performance: The Case of Airports, Madrid

Forsyth P., 2002. Privatization and Regulation of Australian and New Zealand Airports, Paper to the 4th Hamburg Aviation Conference.

Gillen, D., . Niemeier, H.-M., 2008. Comparative political economy of airport infrastructure in the European union: evolution of privatization, regulation and slot reform. In: Winston, C., de Rus, G. (Eds.), Aviation Infrastructure Performance: a Study in Comparative Political Economy. Brookings Institution, Washington DC.

Jeong, J.H., 2005. An investigation of operating costs of airports: focus on the effects of output scale, Master Thesis, University of British Columbia.

Klenk, M., 2004. New approaches to airline-airport relationships: the charges framework for Frankfurt airport. In: Forsyth, P., Gillen, D., Knorr, A., Meyer, W., Niemeier, H., Starkie, D. (Eds.), The Economic Regulation of Airports, German Aviation Research Society Series. Ashgate, Aldershot.

Littlechild, S., 2009. Regulation, over-regulation and some alternative approaches. European Review of Energy Markets 9, 153–159.

Michaels, D., 2008. Moscow points the way with airport competition: while most nations sport monopolies, rivalry between two Russian gateways ushers in improvements for carriers, travelers. Wall Street Journal December 1, 2008.

Morrison, S., Winston, C., 2008. Delayed! US aviation infrastructure policy at the crossroads. In: Winston, C., de Rus, G. (Eds.), Aviation Infrastructure Performance: a Study in Comparative Political Economy. Brookings Institution, Washington DC.

Morrison, W., Gillen, D., 2008. Airport Governance and Regulation in the 21st Century. Centre for Transportation Studies, University of British Columbia.

New Zealand Commerce Commission, 2002. Final Report. Part IV Inquiry into Airfield Services at Auckland, Wellington and Christchurch International Airports, August

Oum, T., Yan, J., Yu, C., 2008. Ownership forms matter for airport efficiency: a stochastic frontier investigation of worldwide airports. Journal of Urban Economics 64, 422–435.

Oum, T., Adler, N., Yu, C., 2006. Privatization, corporatization, ownership forms and their effects on the world's major airports. Journal of Air Transport Management 12, 109–121.

Rochet, J.-C., Tirole, J., 2005. Two–sided Markets: A Progress Report. University of Toulouse.

Starkie, D., 2008. The Airport industry in a Competitive Environment: A UK Perspective, OECD/ITF Discussion Paper No. 2008

Starkie, D., 2001. Reforming UK airport regulation. Journal of Transport Economics and Policy 35, 119–135.

Tretheway M., 2001. Airport Ownership, Management and Price Regulation, Report to the Canadian Transportation Act review Committee, Ottawa.

UK Competition Commission, 2009. BAA Airports Market Investigation: Provisional Findings Report. http://www.competition-commission.org.uk/inquiries/ref2007/airports/provisional_findings.htm.

Vasigh, B., Gorjidooz, J., 2006. Productivity analysis of public and private airports: a causal investigation. Journal of Air Transportation 11, 42–162.

Vogel, H.A., 2006. Privatisation and financial performance of European airports. Journal of Competition and Regulation in Network Industries 2, 139–162.

Williams, P.M., 2006. Benchmarking International Airport Performance: Melbourne Airport Final Report 2006, Transportation Research Laboratory. Available at: http://www.melbourneairport.com.au/downloads/pdfs/BenchmarkingReportFinal.pdf.

Wright, J., 2004. One-sided logic in two sided markets. Review of Network Economics 3, 44–64.

2

CONCESSION REVENUE AND OPTIMAL AIRPORT PRICING

ANMING ZHANG

and

YIMIN ZHANG

Abstract—In recent years airports have been under growing pressure to become financially self-sufficient and to pursue profit maximization in their non-aeronautical or concession operations. In this paper we examine the optimal pricing in a model where concession and aeronautical operations of an airport are considered together with an overall break-even constraint. We find that the optimum solution may require a subsidy from concession to aeronautical operations. However, such a cross-subsidy may or may not restore marginal-cost pricing on aeronautical operations. On the other hand, social welfare can be higher when an airport is allowed to make profits in concession operations than when marginal-cost pricing is imposed on concession operations. © 1997 Elsevier Science Ltd. All rights reserved

Keywords: airport pricing and financing, concession revenue, social welfare.

1. INTRODUCTION

In recent years, airports have been under growing pressure from governments to be more financially self-sufficient and less reliant on government support. In generating more revenue airport management needs to resolve two key questions: first, what is the 'optimum' balance between the revenue generated from aeronautical operations (referred to as 'aeronautical revenue') and the revenue from non-aeronautical or commercial activities (referred to as 'concession revenue'); and second, what pricing policies should they adopt in both operations? The purpose of this paper is to examine the two questions in a model where costs and revenues of concession operations are separated from those of aeronautical operations and where the financial break-even constraint is imposed on the overall operations.

An innovation of this approach is the explicit integration of concession operations with aeronautical operations in the examination of airport pricing policy. This is reasonable, and important, given that many airports generate a much higher proportion of their income from commercial activities than from aeronautical operations. According to recent estimates (for example, Doganis, 1992, pp. 56–58), in medium to large U.S. airports commercial operations contributed between 75–80 per cent of total airport revenues. Indeed, in 1990, more than 90 per cent of total revenue at Los Angeles airport was from commercial operations.

Below we demonstrate that, under the overall budget constraint and constant returns to scale for concession operations, the optimum solution requires a subsidy from concession to aeronautical operations. However, such a cross-subsidy may or may not restore marginal-cost pricing on aeronautical operations. On the other hand, we find that social welfare is higher when the airport is allowed to make profits in concession operations than when marginal-cost pricing is imposed on concession operations.

In practice, many airports use concession revenues to cross-subsidize aeronautical operations. The common explanation for the phenomenon is that airports appear to face a constraint on aeronautical charges either because of airline opposition to increases in aeronautical charges or because their own governments hold back or limit such increases. Our analysis suggests that the phenomenon can also emerge even without imposing the constraint on aeronautical charges, owing to the nature of airport operations. Moreover, a cross subsidy of this type can be welfare improving.

There is a large body of research in transportation economics and engineering on airports and aviation. Significant efforts have been expended in the investigation of runway costs and pricing (Levine, 1969; Carlin and Park, 1970; Walters, 1973; Morrison, 1983, 1987; Gillen et al., 1987; Oum et al., 1996) and the investigation of airport slot policy (Brander et al., 1989; Jones et al., 1993; Langner, 1995; also see BTCE, 1996, for a survey). Useful references on airport planning and management include de Neufville (1976), Wells (1986), and Doganis (1992). Doganis (1992) also contains an excellent discussion on concession revenue maximization strategies. We know of no published studies that look at airport pricing policies for both aeronautical and commercial operations in an integrated model.

The paper is organized as follows. Section 2 provides some background on the aeronautical and commercial operations of an airport which is useful in the theoretical analysis. Section 3 discusses socially optimal pricing of airport aeronautical facilities, and Section 4 examines the effects of concession revenue on optimal pricing for both aeronautical and commercial operations. Section 5 contains concluding remarks.

2. AERONAUTICAL CHARGES AND CONCESSION REVENUE

Airport income is generated from aeronautical and commercial activities. Aeronautical revenue includes aircraft landing fees, aircraft parking and hangar fees, passenger service charges and air traffic control charges (if the service is provided by the airport authority), with landing and parking charges probably being most important. Concession revenues are those generated from non-aircraft related commercial activities in the terminals and on airport land. Concession operations include running or leasing out shopping concessions of various kinds, car parking and rental, banking and catering, with terminal concessions and car parking and rental being most important.

Airport charge determination is composed of two steps. First, the airport authority sets rates for its concession operations in order to maximize concession revenue. Second, aeronautical charges are then set to make up any revenue shortfall. Higher concession revenue would mean a reduction in aeronautical charges. In the second step a decision is made on which aeronautical costs are to be allocated to users of the landing area.

This two-step practice may be considered as being advantageous to users of the landing area (airlines). There appears a 'political constraint' on aeronautical charges owing in part to bilateral air services agreements between states. For example, Article 10.3 of the Bermuda II bilateral agreement between the U.S. and the U.K. specifies that:

> "User [i.e. aeronautical] charges may reflect, but shall not exceed, the full cost to the competent charging authorities of providing appropriate airport and air navigation facilities, and may provide for a reasonable rate of return on assets, after depreciation. In this provision of facilities and services, the competent authorities shall have regard to factors such as efficiency. ... User charges shall be based on sound economic principles and on generally accepted accounting practices within the territory of the appropriate contracting Party."

In addition to political constraints, there exists airline opposition, often orchestrated through the International Air Transport Association (IATA) to increases in aeronautical charges. An example is the recent row over increased landing and parking fees at the new Hong Kong airport which is scheduled to open next year. The airport authority and IATA representatives have tried to resolve the issue for more than a year (SCMP, 1997).

The two-step rates determination has remained basically unchanged throughout the course of airport growth.* In effect, in recent years airports have tried to generate an increasing share of their revenue from their commercial activities. Indeed, maximizing concession revenue has become a goal for many airport authorities (Doganis, 1992). This is partly reflected in the manner in which the concession revenue is generated; now commercial franchises for most non-aeronautical services are awarded in an open and non-discriminatory manner. All retail licences at the new Hong Kong's airport will, for instance, be awarded by open tender. Rigorous competition in tendering for concessions is crucial in achieving the goal of maximizing commercial revenue.

---

*The manner in which the remaining revenue requirement is allocated among aeronautical users has changed since the early 1940s, however (Morrison, 1987).

One consequence of this business-like strategy for concession operations has been the growing proportion of concession revenue to total airport revenue. This can be seen clearly from Table 1 which shows the revenue structure of the Hong Kong International Airport. In 1979 the airport generated about the same amount of revenue from its aeronautical and commercial operations, while in late 1980s and 1990s concession revenue accounted for 66–70 per cent of total revenue.* Furthermore, at Hong Kong airport concession income has been rising more rapidly than its traffic; the average annual growth rates were 17.3 per cent for concession revenue as against 10.3 per cent for passenger traffic in the 1979–1995 period (HKIS, 1979–1995). This is also the case for many other airports in the world, particularly larger international airports.

However, the disproportional growth in aeronautical/concession revenues does not necessarily lead to cross subsidy between the two operations. Whether cross subsidy exists depends also on costs. A number of airports around the world have tried to split both revenue and costs between aeronautical and commercial operations.[†] Typically such analyses reveal that while aeronautical revenue fails to cover aircraft-related costs, commercial activities tend to be profitable. Examples of the cross-subsidy phenomenon are given in Table 2. In a separate study, Jones et al. (1993) further showed that, in 1990–1991, commercial activities at Heathrow, Gatwick, and Stansted airports were far more profitable to BAA than the activities financed through aeronautical charges. The operating margin from aeronautical charges was −7 per cent for the three airports as a group, while the operating margin from concession revenue was 64 per cent.

Table 1. Revenues of the Hong Kong International Airport, 1979–1995

Year[a]	Aeronautical revenues[b] (HK$M)	Commercial revenues[c] (HK$M)	Per cent of concession revenues
1979	165.2	163.2	50
1983	283.3	404.9	59
1987	242.9	575.3	70
1991	650.3	1320.0	67
1995	1074.1	2111.4	66
Annual growth	12.4%	17.3%	

[a]Fiscal year; e.g. 1979 refers to 1 April 1979–31 March 1980.
[b]Aeronautical revenue includes landing fees, aircraft parking fees, peak movement surcharges, passenger service charges, and en route navigation charges.
[c]Concession revenue includes trading concessions, airport rentals, and airport car parking.
Sources: HKIS (1979–1995).

Table 2. Profit or loss by activity area at selected U.K. BAA Plc airports 1989–1990

	Aeronautical operations[a] (£m)	Commercial operations[b] (£m)
London Heathrow	8.5	136.5
London Gatwick	−15.7	70.6
Stansted	−10.0	4.4
Glasgow	5.0	7.4
Edinburgh	2.1	4.5
Aberdeen	−0.6	2.3
Prestwick	−0.6	0.9
Total BAA	−11.3	226.6

[a]Aeronautical operations cover those activities connected with the landing, parking and take-off of aircraft including passenger charges.
[b]Commercial operations cover retailing activities such as duty- and tax-free sales, car parking, accommodation and utility charges for airport users and aircraft-related support facilities.
Source: Doganis (1992, p. 60).

---

*The 60–70 per cent range is between the number for Western European airports and the number for U.S. airports. Jones et al. (1993) showed that, in 1990–1991, approximately 40 per cent of BAA's revenue at the three South-east airports (Heathrow, Gatwick, Stansted) was obtained from aeronautical charges. The remaining 60 per cent of revenue came from other commercial activities carried on by BAA and its agents. On the other hand, Doganis (1992) reported that in medium to large U.S. airports, commercial operations had contributed between 75–80 per cent of total airport revenue. Indeed, in 1990, more than 90 per cent of total revenue at Los Angeles airport was from commercial operations.
†In effect, U.K. airports run as airport companies are required to break down their revenue and costs into aeronautical and commercial areas. See Doganis (1992) for discussion on the problems and difficulties involved in cost allocation of this kind.

3. SOCIALLY OPTIMAL AERONAUTICAL PRICING

In a congested airport, flights are delayed during peak hours. The costs of the delay are part of the social costs which should be taken into account when airport authorities consider the charges to the users of the airport. In this section, we analyze the socially optimal pricing for aeronautical operations alone. The effects of concession operations on optimal pricing will be considered in the next section.

As indicated earlier, aeronautical operations mean operations of the runway, air traffic control, aircraft parking, maintenance and services, passenger gates and terminal, and customs services for international flights. For now, we assume that airport facilities provided for passenger services are solely for passenger arrival, check-in or transfer, boarding and other related services necessary for the operations of the airlines.

Let

ρ_t $= P_t + D(Qf, K)$, the full price perceived by the passengers (De Vany, 1974) which is reflected in the carriers' demand for airport facilities.

P_t = airport charge for a flight during hour t, including both landing fees and passenger fees,

$Q_t(\rho_t)$ = demand (number of flights) for landing during hour t,

K = capacity of the airport,

$D(Q_t, K)$ = flight delay costs experienced by each aircraft during hour t,

r = the unit capacity costs of the airport,

Q $= \sum Q_t$,

$C(Q)$ = operating costs of the airport.

For simplicity, we assume that the capacity of the airport is infinitely divisible, which implies that the airport can expand capacity on a continuous basis. We define the social welfare function as the sum of consumer surplus and producer surplus. To maximize the social welfare, the airport authorities face the following problem:

$$\max_{Q_t, K} \sum \left[\int_0^{Q_t} \rho_t dQ_t - \rho_t Q_t \right] + \sum P_t Q_t - C(Q) - Kr \tag{1}$$

The first-order conditions for a maxima of the above problem lead to

$$P_t = Q_t \frac{\partial D}{\partial Q_t} + C' \tag{2}$$

$$\sum Q_t \frac{\partial D}{\partial K} + r = 0 \tag{3}$$

Equation (2) is the familiar social-marginal-cost pricing and eqn (3) gives the condition of optimal capacity. To see whether the first-best solution is financially sustainable, we can calculate the financial surplus/deficit of the airport as follows:

$$\sum P_t Q_t - C(Q) - Kr = [C'Q - C(Q)] + \sum Q_t \left(Q_t \frac{\partial D}{\partial Q_t} + K \frac{\partial D}{\partial K} \right)$$

Morrison (1983) showed that the first-best solution yields exact cost recovery when airport operating costs exhibit constant returns to scale (so the first bracketed term in the above equation vanishes) and the congestion delay cost is homogeneous of degree zero in traffic and capacity (so the second bracketed term vanishes). [Mohring and Harwitz (1962) and Mohring (1970, 1976), first proved the cost recovery theorem in the setting of highway congestion and tolls. Oum and Zhang (1990) examined the issue when capacity is lumpy.]

Doganis (1992, pp. 48–51) pointed out that there appeared to be marked economies of scale in airport operations.* Hence, $C'Q - C(Q)$ should be negative. On the other hand, the congestion delay cost estimated from steady-state queuing theory has the following form (Lave and DeSalvo, 1968; U.S. Federal Aviation Administration, 1969; Horonjeff, 1975; Morrison, 1987):

$$D(Q_t,K) = \alpha \frac{Q_t}{K(K - Q_t)} \tag{4}$$

where α is the monetary cost per unit time of delay. This functional form is not homogeneous of degree zero. In fact,

$$Q_t \frac{\partial D}{\partial Q_t} + K \frac{\partial D}{\partial K} = \frac{-\alpha Q_t}{K(K - Q_t)} < 0 \tag{5}$$

The intuition behind this inequality may be explained as follows. Consider an airport with one unit of capacity, say one runway. The probability of the runway being congested depends on the traffic volume. Now suppose that both capacity and traffic of the airport double with no consequent change of volume/capacity ratio. The probability of each runway being congested, however, is now reduced because one runway being congested implies that the other runway must also be congested *at the same time*. It follows that the expected delay is not homogeneous of degree zero in volume and capacity.

Based on (5) we conclude that,

$$\Sigma P_t Q_t - C(Q) - Kr < 0$$

which implies that the social-marginal-cost pricing would give rise to a financial deficit to the airport. Furthermore, since the magnitude of the right-hand-side of inequality (5) increases with the traffic volume, we conclude that the deficit of the airport increases when the airport becomes more congested.[†]

To make the airport financially self-supporting, a budget constraint may be imposed on the airport, which leads to the following optimization problem:

$$\max_{Q_t, K} \Sigma \left[\int_0^{Q_t} p_t dQ_t - p_t Q_t \right] + \Sigma P_t Q_t - C(Q) - Kr \tag{6}$$

$$\text{s.t. } \sum P_t Q_t - C(Q) - Kr = 0$$

The first-order conditions for a constrained maximum give the following familiar results

$$P_t - Q_t \frac{\partial D}{\partial Q_t} - C' = \frac{\lambda}{1 + \lambda \varepsilon_t} \frac{p_t}{} \tag{7}$$

$$(1 + \lambda) \left(\sum Q_t \frac{\partial D}{\partial K} + r \right) = 0 \tag{8}$$

where λ is the lagrangian multiplier and ε_t is the demand elasticity[‡] at hour t. Equation (7) shows that the markup of airport charges over the social marginal cost as a percentage of the full price perceived by the passengers is inversely related to the elasticity of demand, which is a well-known

---

*Strictly speaking, the economies of scale in airport operation may be reflections of economies of density in terminal operation. We thank David Gillen for pointing this out to us.
[†]This result may not hold in short run if capacity is indivisible and the airport is being used above long-run optimal capacity. For the analysis in case of indivisible capacity, see Oum and Zhang (1990).
[‡]ε_t is defined as $-\partial \ln Q_t / \partial \ln P_t$.

property of Ramsey pricing. It suggests that airports should charge aeronautical users on the basis of their 'ability to pay' (e.g. peak period pricing). Equation (8) indicates that the budget constraint does not change the optimality condition with respect to capacity. In other words, airport authorities which adopt Ramsey pricing should still pursue the same optimal policy of investment in capacity.

4. EFFECTS OF CONCESSION REVENUE ON OPTIMAL PRICING

As airports are under increasing pressure to be self-financing, more and more airports are moving towards commercially oriented concession operations which are not directly related to the aviation. Such operations include, for example, running or leasing out duty-free shops, car parking and rental, and airport hotels. These commercial operations provide the airport with a captive market because the main customers are the passengers, airlines, crews and airport employees. Since monopoly rents may be extracted by airports, the booming of commercially oriented airports has raised some public concern. Now we analyze this issue so as to shed light on whether concession profitability should be viewed as a cause for concern. Our analysis will take into consideration the fact that without commercial operations, aeronautical charges by the airport based on the first-best principle would not recover the costs of operating the airport.

Let

p = price of concession goods or services provided in the airport,
$x(p)$ = demand for the concession goods or services per flight,
$c(x)$ = costs of providing the concession goods or services by the airport.*

If the airport authorities are to maximize social welfare in commercial operations, marginal-cost pricing should prevail when goods or services are provided in the airport, namely, $p = c'(x)$. In the case of constant returns to scale, the marginal-cost pricing leads to financial break-even in commercial operations.

In fact, however, most airports are earning substantial profits from commercial operations, which are then used to subsidize the aeronautical operations of the airports. Below, we show that when the commercial operations and the aeronautical operations of the airports are considered together with an overall break-even constraint, some cross subsidy between commercial operations and aeronautical operations is actually socially desirable.

When the break-even constraint is imposed on the overall operations of an airport, the optimization problem facing the airport becomes;

$$\max_{Q_t, K, x} \sum \left[\int_0^{Q_t} \rho_t dQ_t - \rho_t Q_t \right] + \sum P_t Q_t - C(Q) - Kr + Q \left[\int_0^x pdx - c(x) \right] \tag{9}$$

$$\text{s.t.} \ \sum P_t Q_t - C(Q) - K_r + Q[px - c(x)] = 0$$

Note that the above formulation implicitly assumes that the demand for air travel and the demand for concession goods and services *per flight* are independent. In other words, passengers are supposed to make two separate decisions in air travel. First, they book air tickets with the airlines based on the perceived full-price which includes airline charges, 6 The costs also include user cost of capital of buildings or spaces used for the commercial operations. airport charges, and cost of congestion delay. Second, after the arrival at the airport, the passengers observe the price of goods and services in the concession areas of the airport and make purchasing decisions. This assumption may be justified by the fact that for most passengers, the purchase of an air ticket and the purchase of concession goods and services are well separated in time, except for perhaps car rental or airport hotel reservations.

---

*The costs also include user cost of capital of buildings or spaces used for the commercial operations.

Solving the first-order conditions for the constrained maxima gives

$$P_t - Q_t \frac{\partial D}{\partial Q_t} - C' + \int_0^x p \, \mathrm{d}x - c(x) = \frac{\lambda}{1+\lambda} \frac{\rho_t}{\varepsilon_t} \tag{10}$$

$$p - c' = \frac{\lambda}{1+\lambda} \frac{p}{\varepsilon_x} \tag{11}$$

$$(1+\lambda)\left(\sum Q_t \frac{\partial D}{\partial K} + r\right) = 0 \tag{12}$$

where ε_x is the elasticity of the demand for the concession goods or services.

Condition (12) indicates that the socially optimal capacity decision still holds under the budget constraint. We have the following result for pricing policy.

Proposition 1: Assuming
(i) congestion delay functional form of eqn (4),
(ii) economies of scale in aeronautical operations, and
(iii) constant returns to scale for concession operations,
then the second-best solution under the overall budget constraint requires a subsidy from concession operations to aeronautical operations.

Proof: We need to show that under the constrained maxima, the airport makes profits in concession operations. From eqns (10)–(12) and the budget constraint, we obtain

$$\frac{\lambda}{1+\lambda} = \frac{R}{\sum Q_t(\rho_t/\varepsilon_t + p/\varepsilon_x)} \tag{13}$$

where

$$R = C(Q) - C'Q - \sum Q_t\left(Q_t \frac{\partial D}{\partial Q_t} + K \frac{\partial D}{\partial K}\right) + Q\left[\int_0^x p \, \mathrm{d}x - c(x)\right] + Q[c(x) - c'x] \tag{14}$$

Under constant returns to scale in concession operations, $c(x) - c'x = 0$, which implies

$$\frac{\lambda}{1+\lambda} > 0$$

By eqn (11), the above inequality gives

$$p - c' > 0 \tag{15}$$

Hence, when aeronautical and concession operations are considered together, the constrained optimal pricing policy requires that the price of concession goods and services be set above marginal costs. Under constant returns to scale, this implies that profits are made from concession operations. *Q.E.D.*

Proposition 1 is derived under the condition of constant returns to scale for concession operations. Nevertheless, a look at the proof indicates that small deviations from this condition will not undermine the result. Also note that the conditions of eqn (4) and the economies of scale in airport costs are only sufficient conditions for Proposition 1. The result will still hold, for example, when, given eqn (4), airport costs exhibit constant returns to scale.

Since the operating costs, c, include the capital cost at fair market value,* the concession profits represent monopoly rents to the airport. Nevertheless, we show that allowing the airport to make profits is welfare improving.

---

*Basically, capital costs consist of depreciation and a fair market rate of return on the capital invested.

Proposition 2: Under the same assumptions as in Proposition 1 and the overall budget constraint, social welfare is higher when the airport is allowed to make profits in concession operations than when marginal-cost pricing is imposed on concession operations.

Proof: It is straightforward to see that combining marginal-cost pricing on concession operations and Ramsey pricing on aeronautical operations is admissible to the budget constraint in (9) but does not satisfy the first-order conditions. Therefore, marginal-cost pricing on concession goods and services is not welfare-maximizing. *Q.E.D.*

The intuitions behind the above propositions may be explained as follows. When the budget constraints are imposed separately on both aeronautical operations and concession operations, the Ramsey pricing of aeronautical operations results in airport charges being higher than the social marginal costs. The Ramsey pricing deviates from the first-best pricing by the markup on the marginal costs. When cross-subsidy is allowed, profits earned on the concession operations relax the budget constraint on aeronautical operations and thereby reduce the markup on the marginal costs. Hence, the optimal solution involves the trade-off between welfare loss due to non-marginal pricing in concession operations and welfare gain due to a reduction in the markup over marginal costs in aeronautical operations. The above analysis shows that, at the initial state of Ramsey pricing for airport charges and marginal-cost pricing for concession goods and services, the welfare gain on aeronautical operations outweighs the welfare loss on commercial operations if profits are allowed in concession operations, and a cross-subsidy is made to aeronautical operations.[*]

Using condition (12), we may rewrite eqn (14) as

$$
\begin{aligned}
R &= C(Q) - C'Q - \sum Q_t\left(Q_t\frac{\partial D}{\partial Q_t} + K\frac{\partial D}{\partial K}\right) + Q\left[\int_0^x p\,\mathrm{d}x - c(x)\right] + Q[c(x) - c'x] \\
&= C(Q) + Kr + Qc(x) - \sum Q_t\left[C' + Q_t\frac{\partial D}{\partial Q_t} + c'x - \sum_0^x p\,\mathrm{d}x + c(x)\right]
\end{aligned}
\tag{16}
$$

This suggests that R may be interpreted as the revenue required to meet the budget constraint if social-marginal-cost pricing were used. Note that the integral inside the last brackets in eqn (16) represents the consumer surplus from the consumption of goods and services offered by the airport with the concession operations. Let

$$
SMC_t = C' + Q_t\frac{\partial D}{\partial Q_t} - \left[\int_0^x p\,\mathrm{d}x - c(x)\right]
$$

Then, eqns (10), (11), and (13) reveal that

$$
Q_t(P_t - SMC_t) = R\frac{Q_t\rho_t/\varepsilon_t}{\sum(Q_t\rho_t/\varepsilon_t + Q_t p/\varepsilon_x)}
$$

$$
Q_t(p - c') = R\frac{Q_t p/\varepsilon_x}{\sum(Q_t\rho_t/\varepsilon_t + Q_t p/\varepsilon_x)}
$$

which shows that the total revenue requirement is shared between the aeronautical operations and concession operations according to the respective weighted share of revenue. The weight is the reciprocal of the demand elasticity.

Earlier, we showed that the cost-of-delay function, eqn (4), derived from queuing theory, implies that marginal-cost pricing of aeronautical operations of a congested airport would entail financial deficits. Now with the cross subsidy from concession revenue, one question that naturally arises is whether the optimal cross subsidy would restore the marginal-cost pricing on aeronautical operations. Equation (10) indicates that

---

[*]Note that the analysis does not imply that profit-maximization is socially optimal.

$$P_t > C' + Q_t \frac{\partial D}{\partial Q_t} - \left[\int_0^x p \mathrm{d}x - c(x) \right]$$

i.e. when the marginal consumer surplus derived from concession goods and services offered by the airport is taken into consideration, the optimal aeronautical charge is greater than the social marginal costs *minus* marginal consumer surplus from concession goods and services. However, if the comparison is between the optimal aeronautical charges and the social-marginal costs, we have the following result.

Proposition 3: Under the same assumptions as in Proposition 1, the optimal aeronautical charge coincides with the social-marginal-cost of the aeronautical operation, if the following condition holds:

$$\frac{\rho_t}{\varepsilon_t} = \frac{p}{\varepsilon_x} \frac{\int_0^x p \mathrm{d}x - c(x)}{p - c'}, \quad \forall t \tag{17}$$

Proof: Dividing first-order condition (11) into (10) and rearranging gives

$$P_t - Q_t \frac{\partial D}{\partial Q_t} - C' = (p - c') \frac{\rho_t/\varepsilon_t}{p/\varepsilon_x} - \left[\int_0^x p \mathrm{d}x - c(x) \right]$$

Note that social-marginal-cost pricing requires that the right-hand side of the above equation vanishes, which leads to condition (17). *Q.E.D.*

The right-hand side of condition (17) may be interpreted as the ratio of the marginal benefits to the marginal costs of the consumption of concession goods and services. Condition (17) shows that, in particular, for an airport with uniform demand throughout the day, the cross subsidy from concession profits would restore social-marginal-cost pricing in aeronautical operations if the (elasticity weighted) ratio of the full price of air travel to the price of concession goods and services equates the ratio of the marginal benefits to the marginal costs of the consumption of concession goods and services. Under this condition, the profits from concession operations would exactly cover the deficits of aeronautical operations when social- marginal-cost pricing is in place.

5. CONCLUDING REMARKS

In recent years airports have been under growing pressure to be financially self-sufficient and to pursue profit maximization in their commercial operations. However, huge commercial profits may not be acceptable to the public. In this paper we attempt to examine optimal pricing policy so as to shed light on whether concession profitability should be viewed as a cause for concern.

We find that when the commercial and aeronautical operations of airports are considered together with an overall break-even constraint, some cross-subsidy between commercial and aeronautical operations is socially desirable. When the budget constraints are imposed separately on both aeronautical operations and concession operations, the Ramsey pricing of aeronautical operations results in airport charges being higher than social marginal costs. Ramsey pricing deviates from the first-best pricing by the markup on the marginal costs. When a cross-subsidy is allowed, the profits earned on the commercial operations would relax the budget constraint on aeronautical operations and thereby reduce the markup on marginal costs. Hence, the optimal solution involves the trade-off between welfare loss due to non-marginal pricing in concession operations, and welfare gain due to reduction in the markup over marginal costs in aeronautical operations. Our analysis shows that, at the initial state of Ramsey pricing for airport charges and marginal-cost pricing for concession goods and services, the welfare gain on aeronautical operations outweighs the welfare loss on commercial operations resulting from allowing a cross-subsidy. Thus, our analysis suggests that it is important to consider commercial and aeronautical operations jointly in order to better understand airport pricing for both operations.

296   A. Zhang and Y. Zhang

Acknowledgements—The authors wish to thank David Gillen, Bill Waters and Mike Tretheway for very helpful comments and suggestions, and Sabina Cheng for her excellent research assistance. A. Zhang gratefully acknowledges financial support from the Research Grants Council of Hong Kong (RGC).

REFERENCES

Brander, J. R. G., Cook, B. A. and Rowcroft, J. E. (1989) Congestion, concentration and contestability: the case of the airline industry. *Transportation Research Record 1214*, Transportation Research Board, National Research Council, Washington, DC.

BTCE (1996) Techniques for Managing Airport Runway Congestion. Working Paper 27, Bureau of Transport and Communications Economics, Canberra, Australia.

Carlin, A. and Park, R. E. (1970) Marginal cost pricing of airport runway capacity. *American Economic Review* **60**, 310–319.

De Neufville, R. (1976) *Airport Planning: A Critical Look at the Methods and Experience.* MIT Press, Cambridge, Mass.

De Vanny, A. S. (1974) The revealed value of time in air travel. *Review of Economics and Statistics*, **56**, 77–82.

Doganis, R. (1992) *The Airport Business.* Routledge, London.

Gillen, D. W., Oum, T. H. and Tretheway, M. W. (1987) *Measurement of the Social Marginal Costs at a Congested Airport: An Application to Toronto International Airport.* Centre for Transportation Studies, The University of British Columbia, Vancouver, B. C.

HKIS (1979–1995) *Report on Civil Aviation Hong Kong, 1979–1995.* Hong Kong Information Service, Hong Kong Government Printer, Hong Kong.

Horonjeff, R. (1975) *Planning and Design of Airports.* McGraw-Hill, New York.

Jones, I., Viehoff, I. and Marks, P. (1993) The economics of airport slots. *Fiscal Studies* **14**(4), 37–57.

Langner, S. J. (1995) Contractual aspects of transacting in slots in the United States. *Journal of Air Transport Management* **2**, 151–162.

Lave, L. B. and DeSalvo, J. S. (1968) Congestion, tolls, and the economic capacity of a waterway. *Journal of Political Economy* **76**, 375–391.

Levine, M. E. (1969) Landing fees and the airport congestion problem. *Journal of Law and Economics* **12**, 79–108.

Mohring, H. (1970) The peak load problem with increasing returns and pricing constraints. *American Economic Review* **60**, 693–705.

Mohring, H. (1976) *Transportation Economics.* Ballinger, Cambridge, MA.

Mohring, H. and Harwitz, M. (1962) *Highway Benefits: An Analytical Framework.* Northwestern University Press, Evanston, IL.

Morrison, S. A. (1983) Estimation of long-run prices and investment levels for airport runways. *Research in Transportation Economics* **1**, 103–130.

Morrison, S. A. (1987) The equity and efficiency of runway pricing. *Journal of Public Economics* **34**, 45–60.

Oum, T. H. and Zhang, Y (1990) Airport-pricing: congestion tolls, lumpy investment and cost recovery. *Journal of Public Economics* **43**, 353–374.

Oum, T. H., Zhang, A. and Zhang, Y. (1996) A note on optimal airport pricing in a hub-and-spoke system. *Transportation Research B* **30**, 11–18.

SCMP (1997) No resolution on airport landing, parking fees. *The South China Morning Post*, July 18.

U.S. Federal Aviation Administration (1969) *Airport Capacity Handbook*, 2nd edn. US Government Printing Office, Washington, DC.

Walters, A. A. (1973) Investment in airports and the economist's role. In *Cost Benefit and Cost Effectiveness*, ed. J. N. Wolfe, pp. 140–154. Allen and Unwin, London.

Wells, A. T. (1986) *Airport Planning and Management.* McGraw-Hill, New York.

3

Airport charges and capacity expansion: effects of concessions and privatization

Anming Zhang and Yimin Zhang

Abstract

This paper examines the decisions on airport charges and capacity expansion made by airports with different objectives. We find that allowing an airport to have profitable concession operations may be more welfare improving than the alternative of depriving the airport of all profits from concession operations. Furthermore, the airport charge of a social welfare-maximizing airport would be lower than that of a budget-constrained public airport, which, in turn, would be lower than that of a privatized airport pursuing profit maximization. We also show that a constrained public airport would add capacity later than a social welfare-maximizing airport, whilst a privatized airport would add capacity later still. Given that constrained public airports represent the second-best situation, the capacity decisions of privatized airports would be socially suboptimal.

JEL classification: L93; L30

Keywords: Airport charges; Capacity expansion; Concessions

1. Introduction

An airport has two facets to its business: aeronautical (runway/terminal) business and non-aeronautical or concession business. Aeronautical revenues include aircraft landing fees, aircraft parking and hangar fees, passenger terminal fees and air traffic control charges (if the service is provided by the airport authority), with landing and passenger terminal charges being most important.[1] Concession revenues are those generated from non-aircraft

---

[1] For example, at Hong Kong International Airport aeronautical charges consist of three components: landing, aircraft parking, and terminal building charges (TBC). Landing fees are based on aircraft movements, while TBCs

A. Zhang, Y. Zhang / Journal of Urban Economics 53 (2003) 54–75   55

related commercial activities occurring within terminals and on airport land. Concession business includes running or leasing out shopping concessions of various kinds, car parking and rental and banking and catering, with terminal concessions and car parking and rental being the most important of these. It can also include the running of extensive office, maintenance and cargo facilities.

Many airports generate a much higher proportion of their income from concession activities than from aeronautical operations. Doganis [7, pp. 56–58] has reported that in medium to large US airports, concession operations represent between 75 and 80% of the total airport revenue. Indeed, in 1990, more than 90% of the total revenue of Los Angeles airport resulted from commercial operations. Furthermore, concession revenues have grown faster than aeronautical revenues. For example, Hong Kong International Airport generated an equal amount of revenue from its aeronautical and commercial operations in 1979, while in the late 1980s and 1990s its concession revenue accounted for 66–70% of total revenue.[2] More importantly, concession operations tend to be more profitable than aeronautical operations (Jones et al. [14], Starkie [24], and Forsyth [9]). For instance, Jones et al. [14] have shown that, in 1990–1991, approximately 60% of the revenue of BAA's three airports around London (Heathrow, Gatwick, and Stansted) resulted from concession activities.[3] The operating margin for aeronautical charges was −7% for the three airports as a group, while the operating margin for concession revenue was 64%.

The perception that airports are local monopolies and need to be regulated to prevent them from abusing their market power, has figured prominently in the regulation of airport (aeronautical) charges. The form that this price regulation has taken varies from country to country, with rate of return, price-cap and cost-based regulations being the norm. Recent studies of country-specific options and experiences of airport regulation include Forsyth [8,9], Beesley [1], Kunz and Niemeier [16], Starkie and Yarrow [25], Starkie [24], Tretheway [26], and Gillen and Morrison [12]. Tretheway [26] has pointed out that rate of return regulation tends to be complex, unresponsive and expensive to administer. Beesley [1] was critical of the approach used in the UK to regulate its airports. In particular, he argued that price-cap regulation is inappropriate in the case of Heathrow. Kunz and Niemeier [16] have argued that the cost-based regulation used in Germany is inefficient and results in the misallocation of resources. Starkie [24] further concluded that formal regulation might be unnecessary because airports are unlikely to abuse their monopoly power due to the existence of a complementarity between the demand for aeronautical services and the demand for concession services. Essentially, concession operations at a large, busy airport (e.g., Heathrow) can achieve superior locational rents for the landlord (the airport). The better the location, the greater will be the (quasi) rents. Since concession

---

are passenger based. In a "typical" case (a B747 with 418 seats, 66.8% load factor and 4-hour turnover), it has been calculated that the landing fee accounts for 68.7% of the total charge, parking 6.6% and TBC 24.7%.

[2] See Zhang and Zhang [29]. In effect at Hong Kong airport, concession income has been increasing more rapidly than its traffic. The average annual growth rate was 17.3% for concession revenue compared to 10.3% for passenger traffic during the period 1979–1995.

[3] In 1998–1999, aeronautical revenue accounted for 34% of the total revenue at BAA's regulated airports (Starkie [24]).

56   *A. Zhang, Y. Zhang / Journal of Urban Economics 53 (2003) 54–75*

activities can earn superior locational rents, increases in traffic volume at an airport will often produce significant increases in their profitability. Therefore, for a profit-maximizing airport with market power, the effect of the demand complementarity, linked to the locational rents, is to attenuate the normal, downward pressure on profits that would arise when increased air traffic volumes need to be bought at the expense of lower prices. This means that, as long as an airport combines both aeronautical and concession activities, the incentive will be to set charges lower than if runways/terminals were stand-alone facilities (Starkie [24]; see also Starkie and Yarrow [25]).

In practice, following the privatization of the British Airports Authority (BAA) in Britain in 1987, more and more countries have decided to partially or completely privatize their airports. While most of these privatized airports remain price regulated, some have been deregulated and others have been subjected to monitoring rather than regulation. It appears that some countries may move further towards a situation where there is no formal regulation, and only monitoring of some privatized airports (Forsyth [9]). In Australia, a draft report by the government's main microeconomic advisory body has recommended that explicit regulation be ended (Productivity Commission [23]). Could we expect that the profit-maximizing behavior of privatized, unregulated airports will lead to social welfare maximization, or is there a conflict between maximizing social welfare and maximizing profits? In this paper, we compare the price decisions of privatized, unregulated airports with the price decisions of public airports that maximize social welfare, using a model with general demand and cost specifications. We find that when a private airport (which is not subject to regulation) has profitable concession operations (owing, for example, to locational rents), its airport charges move closer to the social optimum than if the airport has no concession activities, or if aeronautical and concession activities are treated separately. This is the effect of concession rents discussed by Starkie [24]. However, the pricing policy of a private airport would not attain the social optimum; in effect, a private airport would charge a higher price than the socially optimal level.

Our second objective is to investigate the differences, if any, in the timing of the capacity-expansion decisions of private airports and public airports. In our model, capacity-expansion is seen as improving the quality of service by reducing or eliminating the congestion, which results from the heavy use of the existing airport. In addition to concession rents, we incorporate two other important features of the airport business. First, the demand for aeronautical services grows over time. This is because the demand for aviation services changes with general economic growth (and has over the past four decades grown at about twice the GDP growth rate). Second, airports exhibit significant indivisibilities. Particularly with large, busy airports, capacity is increased in large indivisible lumps, such as when a new runway is built. We show that given growing demand and lumpy capacity, decisions made on capacity expansion by private airports are suboptimal from a social point of view. Specifically, private airports tend to introduce capacity expansion later than comparable public airports. We also find that when a private airport has profitable concession operations, its decisions on capacity expansion are made earlier than is the case when the airport has no concession activities (or where aeronautical and concession activities are treated separately).

Since in reality public airports may deviate significantly from the maximization of social welfare, we then extend the model to include a public airport that is constrained from

A. Zhang, Y. Zhang / Journal of Urban Economics 53 (2003) 54–75   57

choosing the first-best social optimum. More specifically, we consider a public airport that is unable to charge socially optimal aeronautical fees, owing to a revenue requirement, and which needs concession profits to cover operating and capacity costs. How does this alternative behavioral assumption for the public airport affect the comparison of public vs. private pricing of aviation operations and the timing of capacity-expansion decisions? Our analysis shows that the differences in both the pricing and investment decisions of a private airport and the constrained public airport become smaller compared to the earlier case examined. Nevertheless, although the public airport would not achieve optimum solutions, it would still outperform a private airport in both pricing and the timing of capacity-expansion decisions.

There is a large body of literature on airport pricing and/or capacity investment. Useful references include Levine [18], Carlin and Park [3], Walters [28], Morrison [19,20], Gillen et al. [10,11], Oum and Zhang [21], Oum et al. [22], and Zhang and Zhang [29,30]. Oum and Zhang [21] first studied the capacity expansion of airports when capacity is lumpy and the airport is publicly owned. Zhang and Zhang [29] considered the effect of concession operations of airports in a setting where capacity is divisible, while Zhang and Zhang [30] investigated the effect of financial constraints on a publicly owned airport with lumpy capacity. The present paper contributes to the literature in that we look at decisions on airport charges and the timing of capacity expansion made by airports with different ownerships, recognizing that airport capacity is largely indivisible. We investigate the effect of concession operations on, and differences in the pricing policies and capacity decisions of airports pursuing social-welfare maximization and those pursuing profit maximization.

The paper is organized as follows. Section 2 presents the basic model. Section 3 compares the airport charges and timing of capacity-expansion decisions of private and public airports. Section 4 extends the model by considering the pricing and capacity-expansion decisions of a public airport with budget constraints. Section 5 concludes the paper.

2. Basic model

An airport supplies aviation services to airlines and passengers. These services include runway facilities for aircraft landings and take offs, terminal buildings for passenger traffic, technical services such as aircraft fueling and maintenance, and navigational services. Although the demand for aviation services is growing over time, the supply remains largely fixed for an airport during its economic life span. This is because the capacity of an airport is constrained by its runways and terminal buildings. Once put in place, the runways and terminal buildings can serve for many years and cannot be expanded quickly or in fraction. Of course, given a fixed number of runways, it is still possible to expand capacity by improving the airport's navigation and traffic control systems; these marginal expansions however are limited. In this paper, we assume that capacity can only be added in lumpy units at discrete times.

In airports with basically fixed capacity in the short run, congestion will build up as traffic increases over time. Flights are often delayed due to congestion. The costs of these delays are part of the total travel costs paid by passengers. They also constitute part of the operating costs of airlines due to increased flight times either in the air or on the ground. The delays might be anticipated and internalized by the airlines, since the airlines will over time learn where and when they need to extend or even pad the schedule.[4] In any case, these delay times, anticipated or not, increase with the level of congestion at the airport and impose costs on both passengers and airlines. Consequently, passengers view the total travel cost (the "full price") of taking a flight as the sum of the ticket price and the costs of delay.[5] Reflecting passenger demand, the airlines would then have a demand function which depends on airport charges, the costs of delay, and time.

Let $\rho = P + D(Q, K)$ be the "full price" perceived by airlines, P—airport charges for a flight, including both landing fees and passenger fees, $Q(\rho, t)$—the demand (number of flights) per period for landing which depends on the full price, ρ, and time, t, where $\partial Q/\partial t > 0$, reflecting the trend of growing demand, K—the airport's runway and terminal capacity, $D(Q, K)$—flight delay costs experienced by each aircraft (D for "delay"), which depend on total traffic level Q and airport capacity K, $C(Q)$—operating costs of the airport per period, and r—the cost of capital per period including interest and depreciation. As discussed above, we consider that the capacity, K, is fixed until the time when the airport carries out a capacity expansion.

Consider first a publicly owned airport whose objective is to maximize social welfare. Social welfare is defined here, as is common in the literature, as the sum of consumer surplus and producer surplus. Since airports usually combine aeronautical operations with concession operations, we define the social welfare function as follows:

$$\int_{\rho}^{\infty} Q(\xi, t) \, d\xi + PQ - C(Q) - Kr + Q \left[\int_{p}^{\infty} X(\xi) \, d\xi + pX - c(X) \right],$$

where, and in all subsequent expressions, Q is a function of full price and time, i.e., $Q = Q(\rho, t)$, and p—the price of concession services (or goods) provided at the airport, $X(p)$—the demand for concession services per flight, and $c(X)$—costs of providing concession services by the airport, which also include user cost of capital for buildings or spaces used for concession operations. The above formula implicitly assumes that the demand for air travel and the demand for concession services *per flight* are independent. In

---

[4] In a very interesting study, Brueckner [2] assumes non-atomistic carriers at an airport and shows that a monopoly airline fully internalizes congestion, so there is no role for congestion pricing. Under Cournot oligopoly, carriers only internalize the congestion they impose on themselves. Allocation can be improved by a toll that captures the un-internalized congestion. Airport congestion pricing has been widely discussed in policy circles as well as in the literature. Other recent academic contributions include Daniel [4,5] and Daniel and Pahwa [6].

[5] While our model includes congestion in the full price of air travel, the paper will not address the congestion externality issue per se, nor will it distinguish between public airports that internalize congestion to maximize social welfare and public airports that are unable to internalize congestion. These are important and relevant issues. As highlighted by a referee, an important motivation for airport privatization is to use profits to motivate efficient congestion pricing, while circumventing public objections to the "unfairness" of time-varying prices. We see analysis of combining inter-temporal congestion pricing with monopolistic pricing of aeronautical and concession services by public and private airports as a natural extension of the analysis presented here, although beyond the scope of the present paper. See also footnote 4.

A. Zhang, Y. Zhang / Journal of Urban Economics 53 (2003) 54–75   59

other words, it is assumed that passengers make two separate decisions, namely, to book air tickets and to purchase concession services on an airport's premises. This assumption may be justified by the fact that for most passengers, purchases of air tickets and concession services are well separated in time, except perhaps for car rentals and airport hotel reservations.

Since the demand for air travel has a growing trend, Q is a function of time t. Then the objective of the airport can be written as

$$\max_{P,p,K} \int_0^\infty \left\{ \left[\int_\rho^\infty Q(\xi,t)\,d\xi + PQ - C(Q) - Kr \right. \right.$$

$$\left. \left. + Q\left[\int_\rho^\infty X(\xi)\,d\xi + pX - c(X) \right] \right\} e^{-rt}\,dt. \right. \tag{1}$$

Here, future revenues and costs are discounted using the cost of capital as the discount rate, and the decision variables P, p, and K are all functions of time.

As the amount of traffic increases over time, the airport may expand capacity to relieve congestion. As discussed above, the capacity of the airport is fixed in the short run but can be expanded by discrete units in the long run. Without loss of generality, we may define the measurement of K in such a way that capacity can be increased one unit at a time. Letting T, T_1, T_2, etc. denote the time the capacity-expansions occur, the capacity K as a function of t can be expressed as

$$K(t) = \begin{cases} K_0, & t < T, \\ K_0 + 1, & T \leqslant t < T_1, \\ K_0 + 2, & T_1 \leqslant t < T_2. \\ \vdots \end{cases}$$

Therefore, (1) can be written alternatively as

$$\max_{P,p,T} \int_0^T \{\phi(P, p, K_0)\} e^{-rt}\,dt + \int_T^{T_1} \{\phi(P, p, K_0 + 1)\} e^{-rt}\,dt$$

$$+ \int_{T_1}^\infty \{\phi(P, p, K(t))\} e^{-rt}\,dt. \tag{2}$$

Here ϕ denotes the social-welfare function, and we are concerned only with the timing of the next expansion, T.[6]

---

[6] This is only for simplicity of exposition. As is clear in the analysis below, the optimality condition with respect to T is completely independent of the timing of subsequent capacity expansions.

For a privatized, unregulated airport, on the other hand, the objective would be to pursue profit maximization

$$\max_{P,p,K} \int_0^\infty \{PQ - C(Q) - Kr + Q[pX - c(X)]\}e^{-rt}\,\mathrm{d}t. \tag{3}$$

3. Price and capacity-expansion comparisons

Given the alternative objectives of the airports outlined above, we now analyze the resulting pricing policies and the timings of capacity expansions. In the analysis, we assume that capacity-expansion decisions are made prior to price decisions (aeronautical charges and concession fees).

3.1. Price comparison

The comparison of the pricing policies of a private airport and a public airport is carried out for a given capacity. In the case of a public airport, the Euler equation for the optimum (Kamien and Schwartz [15]) states that the following first-order conditions with respect to P and p hold for any t

$$\frac{\partial \phi}{\partial P} = 0, \qquad \frac{\partial \phi}{\partial p} = 0, \quad \forall t.$$

Differentiating the integrand of (1) with respect to P and p, we obtain

$$-Q\frac{\partial \rho}{\partial P} + Q + P\frac{\partial Q}{\partial P} - C'\frac{\partial Q}{\partial P}$$

$$+ \frac{\partial Q}{\partial P}\left[\int_p^\infty X(\xi)\,\mathrm{d}\xi + pX - c(X)\right] = 0, \quad \forall t,$$

$$Q(p - c')\frac{\mathrm{d}X}{\mathrm{d}p} = 0, \quad \forall t.$$

Since $\rho = P + D(Q, K)$,

$$-Q\frac{\partial \rho}{\partial P} + Q = -Q\frac{\partial D}{\partial Q}\frac{\partial Q}{\partial P}.$$

Hence, the first-order conditions lead to the following pricing principles:

$$P_W = C' + Q\frac{\partial D}{\partial Q} - V_W, \quad \forall t, \tag{4}$$

$$p_W = c', \qquad\qquad\qquad \forall t, \tag{5}$$

where

$$V_W = \int_{p_W}^\infty X(\xi)\,\mathrm{d}\xi + p_W X(p_W) - c\big(X(p_W)\big)$$

A. Zhang, Y. Zhang / Journal of Urban Economics 53 (2003) 54–75   61

is the consumer surplus from concession purchases plus concession profits, and the subscript W denotes that the pricing principles are derived from the welfare-maximization objective. Condition (5) simply states that for welfare maximization, concession services should be priced based on marginal costs. On the other hand, condition (4) shows that with concession operations, the airport should levy its aeronautical charges based on the social marginal cost of one flight, which is the sum of the marginal operating cost and the marginal congestion cost to other flights (the first two terms on the right-hand side of (4)), minus V_W, the social welfare generated from concession operations per flight. This implies that, for a welfare-maximizing airport, the optimal aeronautical charge is lower than social marginal costs if the airport also operates its concession business.

For a privatized, profit-maximizing airport, the first-order conditions with respect to the airport charge (P) and the concession price (p) can be derived using the same technique. We have

$$P_\pi = C' + Q\frac{\partial D}{\partial Q} + \frac{\rho}{\varepsilon} - R, \quad \forall t, \tag{6}$$

$$p_\pi = c' \Big/ \left(1 - \frac{1}{\varepsilon_X}\right), \quad \forall t, \tag{7}$$

where $\varepsilon = -(\partial Q/\partial\rho)(\rho/Q)$ is the (positive) elasticity of demand for air travel with respect to full price, ε_X is the (positive) demand elasticity for concession services, and

$$R = p_\pi X(p_\pi) - c\big(X(p_\pi)\big)$$

represents the airport's concession profits.

It is obvious that the privatized profit-maximizing airport will charge monopoly prices for its concession services. For its aeronautical services, the airport charge consists of the social marginal cost plus a markup term based on demand elasticity—a reflection of the airport's market power—and a markdown term due to the existence of concession profits. It is interesting to note that the complementarity between the demand for air travel and the demand for concession services generates an offsetting effect on the monopoly airport, such that the airport charge made tends to be closer to social marginal costs than if the airport had no concession activities, or if aeronautical and concession activities were treated separately. This is the effect of concession rents discussed by Starkie [24]. Thus, allowing the privatized airport to earn concession profits can be welfare improving.[7]

Although private airports with concession rents have good reasons to limit the extent to which they exploit their market power, would the incentive generated by a profitable concession business be strong enough to prevent airports from exploiting this market power? In other words, would their pricing policies attain the social optimum? The results of such a price comparison are contained in Proposition 1.

---

[7] To show this, first consider a private airport with concessions separate from its aeronautical operations. The airport pursues profit maximization in aeronautical operations but the concessions are based on welfare maximization (run under regulation or by a public operator). In this situation, one can show that $[\partial SW/\partial R]_{R=0} > 0$, where SW is social welfare from both aeronautical and concession operations and R is concession profits. This implies that social welfare can be improved if the airport is allowed to make profits in concessions. See Zhang and Zhang [29] for further discussion.

Proposition 1. *At any time and for a given capacity, if the social marginal cost increases with air traffic, the airport charge of a profit-maximizing airport will be higher than that of a welfare-maximizing airport.*

Proof. Consider an auxiliary function G

$$G(Q, Z) = C' + Q\frac{\partial D}{\partial Q} + Z = MC(Q) + Z,$$

where MC is the social marginal cost and Z is a parameter. From first-order conditions (4) and (6), we see that the pricing policies resulting from the two alternative airport objectives have the same functional form as G, with differences only in the value of Z. Letting $P = G$, differentiating P with respect to Z, and noting that Q also depends on P, we obtain

$$\frac{dP}{dZ} = \frac{dMC}{dQ}\frac{\partial Q}{\partial P}\frac{dP}{dZ} + 1.$$

Solving for dP/dZ gives

$$\frac{dP}{dZ} = 1\Big/\left(1 - \frac{dMC}{dQ}\frac{\partial Q}{\partial P}\right).$$

From the demand structure, $Q = Q(\rho, t)$ and $\rho = P + D(Q, K)$, Q can be viewed as an implicit function of P. Differentiating Q with respect to P

$$\frac{\partial Q}{\partial P} = \frac{\partial Q}{\partial \rho}\frac{\partial \rho}{\partial P} = \frac{\partial Q}{\partial \rho}\left[1 + \frac{\partial D}{\partial Q}\frac{\partial Q}{\partial P}\right]$$

and solving for $\partial Q/\partial P$ gives

$$\frac{\partial Q}{\partial P} = \frac{\partial Q}{\partial \rho}\Big/\left[1 - \frac{\partial D}{\partial Q}\frac{\partial Q}{\partial \rho}\right]. \tag{8}$$

This implies that $\partial Q/\partial P < 0$ and by assumption, $dMC/dQ > 0$, hence $dP/dZ > 0$.

Now, the value of Z takes the following forms, depending on the pricing policies implemented:

$$Z = \begin{cases} -V_W, & \text{for } P_W, \\ -R + \dfrac{\rho}{\varepsilon}, & \text{for } P_\pi. \end{cases}$$

Since V_W is the maximum welfare (the sum of consumer surplus and profits) attainable from concession operations while R is the maximum concession profits, it is obvious that $V_W > R$. Therefore, $Z(P_W) < Z(P_\pi)$ and it follows that $P_W < P_\pi$. $\square$

The intuition of the proposition may be explained as follows. The presence of concession operations gives the airport an incentive to reduce their airport charge, leading to a markdown term after the social marginal cost. The magnitude of the term, however, depends on the objective of the airport. For the welfare-maximizing airport, the markdown term V_W, represents the sum of consumer surplus and airport profits from concessions. For the profit-maximizing airport, the markdown term, R, represents the airport concession profits only; besides, the profit-maximizing airport also has a markup term, ρ/ε, which

A. Zhang, Y. Zhang / Journal of Urban Economics 53 (2003) 54–75   63

reflects the market power of the airport. Therefore, the airport charge of the profit-maximizing airport is higher than that of the welfare-maximizing airport.

It is interesting to compare the effects of concession operations on the differential of airport charges in terms of the Z comparisons. When there is no concessions, $V_W = R = 0$, and

$$Z(P_\pi) - Z(P_W) = \rho/\varepsilon.$$

In this case, the price differential between a public airport and a private airport is clearly due to the monopoly rents. When there are concession operations, however,

$$Z(P_\pi) - Z(P_W) = \rho/\varepsilon + (V_W - R).$$

This indicates that the price differential has an additional factor, i.e., the difference in the benefits of concessions. On one hand, the presence of concession profits would reduce ρ through a lower airport charge; on the other hand, since V_W contains both concession profits and consumer surplus from concession purchase and hence $V_W > R$, the additional factor might still make the difference between $Z(P_\pi)$ and $Z(P_W)$ larger than when there were no concessions.

This comparison can have important policy implications. When the comparison is between an airport with and without concession, we indicated earlier that concession profits would put downward pressure on airport charges of a profit-maximizing airport (also see, e.g., Starkie [24]). Our analysis here further suggests that the price differential between a private airport and a public airport might be *higher* when *both* types of airports have concession operations. In other words, the pricing policy of a private airport with concessions should be compared against a benchmark of a public airport that also operates concessions. Consequently, the effects of concession operations on airport pricing would not necessarily be in favor of privatization.

3.2. Timing of capacity expansion

Since the demand for air travel, Q, shows a growing trend, the congestion delay D, social marginal costs and airport charge P are all functions of time. These functions are also dependent on the airport capacity. For a welfare-maximizing airport, let

$$W = \int_\rho^\infty Q(\xi, t)\, d\xi + PQ - C(Q) + QV_W \tag{9}$$

represent the social-welfare level that excludes the capital costs of the airport. With P and p set by (4) and (5), respectively, W is a function of t and K. Now, problem (2) can be expressed as

$$\max_{T} \int_{0}^{T} \{W(t, K_0) - K_0 r\} e^{-rt} \, dt + \int_{T}^{T_1} \{W(t, K_0 + 1) - (K_0 + 1)r\} e^{-rt} \, dt$$

$$+ \int_{T_1}^{\infty} \{W(t, K(t)) - K(t)r\} e^{-rt} \, dt.$$

Accordingly, differentiating the objective function with respect to T leads to the following optimality condition:

$$W(T_W, K_0 + 1) - W(T_W, K_0) = r$$

or, in short notation,

$$\Delta W(T_W, K_0) = r, \tag{10}$$

where T_W denotes the optimal time for capacity expansion. This condition has a clear interpretation: the capacity should be expanded at the point where the marginal gain in social welfare per period reaches the marginal cost of capital per period.

To examine the timing of the next capacity expansion by a private airport, we let

$$\pi = PQ - C(Q) + QR \tag{11}$$

be the airport's operating profit excluding capacity costs. The optimality condition can be derived as

$$\pi(T_\pi, K_0 + 1) - \pi(T_\pi, K_0) = r$$

or

$$\Delta \pi(T_\pi, K_0) = r, \tag{12}$$

where T_π is the optimal time for the private airport to add capacity. Condition (12) states that the capacity will be added at the point where the marginal operating profits brought about by addition of the new capacity just outweigh the costs of adding this new capacity.

Before comparing the capacity-expansion decisions of these airports, we make the following trivial assumption.

Assumption 1. The delay cost function $D(Q, K)$ is differentiable with respect to K with

$$\frac{\partial D}{\partial K} < 0, \qquad \frac{\partial^2 D}{\partial Q \partial K} < 0. \tag{13}$$

This assumption is quite general, requiring only that adding capacity will reduce congestion and that the effect is more pronounced when there is more congestion.[8] For example, the following functional form estimated from steady-state queuing theory (see

---

[8] Note that we require the function $D(Q, K)$ to be differentiable only in formality. The variable K will still take only discrete values.

A. Zhang, Y. Zhang / Journal of Urban Economics 53 (2003) 54–75   65

Lave and DeSalvo [17], US Federal Aviation Administration [27], Horonjeff [13], and Morrison [20]) satisfies all our requirements

$$D(Q, K) = \alpha \frac{Q}{K(K - Q)}.$$

We then have the following result for the capacity-expansion comparison.

Proposition 2. *A profit-maximizing airport is less inclined towards capacity expansion than is a welfare-maximizing airport. Thus, the capacity-expansion decisions of private airports are suboptimal from a social point of view.*

Proof. See the proof of Proposition 4. ☐

The intuition of the above result may be explained as follows. In our model, capacity expansion improves the quality of the service by reducing the congestion, which results from heavy use of the existing airport. The socially optimal time for capacity expansion is the time when the benefits of the additional capacity, which include benefits to both passengers and the airport, just outweigh the cost of the capital investment. However, since the private airport does not care for the consumer surplus but needs to bear the cost of capital for the expansion, the benefits to the airport would be insufficient at the social optimum. The private airport will therefore add capacity only when congestion is heavy enough such that the benefits to the airport alone outweigh the cost of capital. In our model setting, therefore, the private airport tends to add capacity "too late" from a social point of view.

4. Extension: constrained public airports

In the above analysis, we compare a privatized, unregulated airport against the benchmark of a public airport that is assumed to maximize social welfare. There are several ways, however, in which public airports deviate significantly from the maximization of social welfare. One problem is that socially optimal pricing principles may lead to a financial surplus or deficit. Specifically, economies of scale or economies of density in airport operation and non-homogeneous delay functions are likely to cause a financial deficit to the airport (see Doganis [7] and Zhang and Zhang [29] for more discussion). On the other hand, with the corporatization/commercialization of airports in recent years, public airports have been under growing pressure from governments to be more financially self-sufficient and less reliant on government support. When considered together, these two observations suggest that a budget constraint could be imposed on a public airport, which would lead to the following optimization problem:

$$\max_{P, p, K} \int_0^\infty \left\{ \int_\rho^\infty Q(\xi, t) \, d\xi + PQ - C(Q) - Kr \right.$$

$$+ Q\left[\int_{p}^{\infty} X(\xi)\,d\xi + pX - c(X) \right]\Bigg\} e^{-rt}\,dt$$

such that

$$\int_{0}^{\infty} \{PQ - C(Q) - Kr + Q[pX - c(X)]\} e^{-rt}\,dt = 0.$$

In this formulation, we assume that the airport is financially self supporting in the "long run" (which extends to infinity). Implicitly, this amounts to the assumption that the deficit or surplus in the short run will be ironed out through borrowing or investing by the airport authorities in the financial market. Alternatively, the airport authorities may be given a short-run (e.g., annual) budget constraint such that the break-even condition is observed every period. Zhang and Zhang [30] discussed these two alternatives and concluded that the long-run budget constraint is socially preferable.

Furthermore, public airports may earn "profits" on their concessions. Typically, public airport authorities award concessions to private firms that maximize profits (this is the practice in Hong Kong, for example). Competition among bidders for concession operations leads to the public airport authorities capturing monopoly rents. These rents can then be used to subsidize aeronautical operations and cover capacity costs.[9] To model such a constrained public airport with cross subsidy, we make the following formal assumption.

Assumption 2. The public airport authorities capture monopoly rents through profit-maximizing concession operators. These monopoly profits are used to subsidize aeronautical operations and cover capacity costs.

Let

$$V_\pi = \int_{p_\pi}^{\infty} X(\xi)\,d\xi + p_\pi X(p_\pi) - c\big(X(p_\pi)\big)$$

be the social welfare from concessions at p_π which, given by (7), represents the profit-maximizing price that the concession operators would charge. The constrained welfare-maximizing airport then faces the following problem:

$$\max_{P,K} \int_{0}^{\infty} \left\{ \int_{\rho}^{\infty} Q(\xi,t)\,d\xi + PQ - C(Q) - Kr + QV_\pi \right\} e^{-rt}\,dt$$

such that

$$\int_{0}^{\infty} \{PQ - C(Q) - Kr + QR\} e^{-rt}\,dt = 0. \tag{14}$$

---

[9] Zhang and Zhang [29] analyzed the effects of budget constraint and concluded that allowing cross subsidy from concession operations to aeronautical operations would be socially desirable.

A. Zhang, Y. Zhang / Journal of Urban Economics 53 (2003) 54–75   67

In the following, we consider this extended model and investigate the following questions: How does this alternative behavioral assumption for the public airport affect the comparison of public vs. private pricing of aviation operations and the timing of capacity-expansion decisions? Can a private airport outperform a constrained public airport in pricing and investment decisions? Can either airport type approximate the first-best solutions?

The first-order condition with respect to P for the constrained optimum is derived as follows:

$$-Q\frac{\partial D}{\partial Q}\frac{\partial Q}{\partial P} + P\frac{\partial Q}{\partial P} - C'\frac{\partial Q}{\partial P} + \frac{\partial Q}{\partial P}V_\pi$$

$$+\lambda\left[Q + P\frac{\partial Q}{\partial P} - C'\frac{\partial Q}{\partial P} + \frac{\partial Q}{\partial P}R\right] = 0, \quad \forall t,$$

where λ is the Lagrangian multiplier. Substituting (8) into the first-order condition and simplifying, we get

$$P_B = C' + Q\frac{\partial D}{\partial Q} - \frac{V_\pi + \lambda R}{1+\lambda} + \frac{\lambda}{1+\lambda}\frac{\rho}{\varepsilon}, \quad \forall t \tag{15}$$

where the subscript B indicates that this pricing principle is applied to the budget-constrained public airport.

The multiplier λ depends on the nature of the budget constraints. It can be shown that λ will be positive if unconstrained welfare-maximization would result in a financial deficit to the airport. We are only concerned with the case where λ is positive because when λ is negative this implies that unconstrained welfare-maximization would lead to a financial surplus and so there would be no compelling reason to impose the budget constraint on the airport in the first place. Equation (15) then reveals that the (constrained) optimal aeronautical charge is based on the social marginal cost (given by the first two terms on the right-hand side of (15)), a markdown term consisting of a weighted average of concession welfare (V_π) and concession profits (R), plus a markup term. As before, the markup term is inversely related to the demand elasticity, reflecting the monopoly position of the airport.

Proposition 3. *At any time and for a given capacity, if the social marginal cost increases with air traffic, then the airport charge of a welfare-maximizing airport would be lower than that of a budget-constrained public airport, which, in turn, would be lower than that of a profit-maximizing airport. In other words,*

$$P_W < P_B < P_\pi, \quad \forall t.$$

Proof. Consider the auxiliary function G

$$G(Q, Z) = C' + Q\frac{\partial D}{\partial Q} + Z = MC(Q) + Z.$$

From first-order conditions (4), (15), and (6), we see that the pricing policies of the airports with alternative objectives all have the same functional form as G, with differences only in the value of Z. Let $P = G$. In the proof of Proposition 1, we have shown that $dP/dZ > 0$.

Now, the value of Z takes the following forms, depending on the pricing policy

$$Z = \begin{cases} -V_W, & \text{for } P_W, \\ -\dfrac{V_\pi + \lambda R}{1 + \lambda} + \dfrac{\lambda}{1 + \lambda}\dfrac{\rho}{\varepsilon}, & \text{for } P_B, \\ -R + \dfrac{\rho}{\varepsilon}, & \text{for } P_\pi. \end{cases}$$

Since V_W is the maximum welfare (the sum of consumer surplus and profits) attainable from concession operations while V_π is the welfare subject to maximum concession profits and R is the maximum concession profits, obviously, $V_W > V_\pi > R$. For the constrained public airport, due to the need for cross subsidy, the value of Z may be viewed as a weighted average of social welfare V_π and airport profits. Therefore, $Z(P_W) < Z(P_B) < Z(P_\pi)$ and it follows that $P_W < P_B < P_\pi$. □

Note that in the absence of concessions, $V_W = V_\pi = R = 0$. It can be seen that the effect of concessions on the difference between $Z(P_\pi)$ and $Z(P_B)$ is ambiguous. Therefore, the argument that concession profits would reduce airport charge of a private airport would not necessarily favor privatization because the more relevant benchmark for comparison is a public airport that also operates concessions, rather than a private airport without concessions.

Next, we analyze the timing of capacity-expansion decisions made by the airports. Similar to the case where welfare-maximization is the objective, the optimality condition for the timing of the next capacity expansion can be derived for the budget-constrained airport. Forming Lagrangian and differentiating with respect to T yields

$$\big[W(T_B, K_0 + 1) - W(T_B, K_0) \big] + \lambda \big[\pi(T_B, K_0 + 1) - \pi(T_B, K_0) \big]$$
$$= (1 + \lambda)r$$

or, in short notation,

$$\Delta B(T_B, K_0) \equiv \big[\Delta W(T_B, K_0) + \lambda \Delta \pi(T_B, K_0) \big] / (1 + \lambda) = r, \qquad (16)$$

where the function W is defined in (9) and π is defined in (11). Clearly, π is the function in the budget constraint excluding the capacity costs. Similar to W, as P is set according to the pricing principle (15), π will be a function of t and K, while λ is a constant independent of t.

Lemma 1. *At any time, the perceived benefits of the addition of an additional unit of capacity to a welfare-maximizing airport are larger than the perceived benefits to a constrained public airport, which in turn are larger than the perceived benefits to a profit-maximizing airport. In other words,*

$$\Delta W(t, K_0) > \Delta B(t, K_0) > \Delta \pi(t, K_0), \qquad \forall t.$$

Proof. See Appendix A. □

Note that the perceived benefit of adding such capacity to a public airport is the gain in social welfare excluding the cost of capital, while the perceived benefit to a private airport

A. Zhang, Y. Zhang / Journal of Urban Economics 53 (2003) 54–75   69

is the gain in operating profits. Intuitively, an expansion in capacity relieves congestion, leading to a lower congestion delay and/or an increase in the willingness to pay of consumers. Therefore, the perceived benefits to an airport depend on the marginal reduction in congestion. Since airport charges are highest (lowest) for the profit-maximizing (welfare-maximizing) airport, the congestion and thereby the perceived benefits of capacity expansion would be lowest (highest) for the profit-maximizing (welfare-maximizing) airport.

As for the optimal timing of capacity expansion, the rule is the same for all the airports, i.e., that the expansion should be made at the time when perceived benefits just outweigh the cost of capital for the expansion.

Lemma 2. *For an additional unit of capacity to a public airport or to a private airport, the perceived benefits increase over time. In other words,*

$$\frac{\partial}{\partial t} \Delta W(t, K_0) > 0, \qquad \frac{\partial}{\partial t} \Delta B(t, K_0) > 0, \qquad \frac{\partial}{\partial t} \Delta \pi(t, K_0) > 0.$$

Proof. See Appendix A. ☐

Now we are in a position to state our main results for capacity expansion.

Proposition 4. *A constrained public airport is less inclined towards capacity expansion than a welfare-maximizing airport. Furthermore, a profit-maximizing airport is even less inclined towards capacity expansion than a constrained public airport. Thus, the timing of capacity expansion decisions by privatized, unregulated airports are suboptimal from a social point of view.*

Proof. The welfare-maximizing airport will expand capacity at the time when $\Delta W = r$ is reached. By Lemma 1, however, the budget-constrained airport will find $\Delta B < r$ at this point and will therefore not expand its capacity. Further, Lemma 2 implies that the time when $\Delta B = r$ will occur later than the time when $\Delta W = r$, so that the constrained airport will expand capacity later than an unconstrained public airport. A similar argument demonstrates that the profit-maximizing airport will expand capacity even later than the constrained public airport. This proves that the timing of capacity expansion for a private airport is suboptimal from a social point of view. ☐

The intuition of the above results is quite clear. Note that the optimal timing of expansion for all airports follows the same rule, i.e., that the expansion should be made at the time when the perceived benefits of the additional capacity just outweigh the cost of capital. Lemmas 1 and 2 have established that the perceived benefits to a profit-maximizing airport are lower than those to the public airport, and that they increase over time. Therefore, it follows that expansion decisions for private airports will be made later than those for public airports.

Finally, we note that if the private airport has no profitable concession operations, benefits to the airport would be smaller than otherwise, and the timing of capacity expansion would be later still. Hence, to encourage the capacity expansion of private airports earlier, the presence of concession profits is socially desirable.

5. Conclusion

In recent years, concession operations have brought considerable revenue and profits to airports around the world. At the same time, airport privatization and deregulation have become growing trends. Our analysis in this paper suggests that allowing an airport to have profitable concession operations may be welfare improving when compared to the alternative of depriving the airport of all profits from concession operations. Specifically, for a welfare-maximizing airport, the optimal aeronautical charge is lower than social marginal costs if the airport also operates its concession business. The first-best social optimum, however, may not be financially feasible and may hence make the airport a public burden. We have considered two alternative structures that are commonly used in practice (in order to make airports financially self-supporting): a public airport with financial constraints and a privatized airport that maximizes profit.

For a constrained public airport, we have shown that the airport charge has a markup term over the social marginal cost. If the airport has profitable concession operations, however, there will also be a markdown term in the airport charge. Hence, allowing concession profits would in fact bring airport charges closer to social marginal costs. Similar results are also presented for the privatized airport pursuing profit-maximization. The concession profits would partially offset the markup over marginal costs owing to the monopoly power of the airport. Nevertheless, we have shown that the privatized airport would levy a higher airport charge than a constrained public airport, even though both would obtain the same concession profits.

Furthermore, while it is accepted that concession profits would put downward pressure on the airport charge of a privatized airport, thereby relieving some concerns over airport's market power, our analysis further suggests that the presence of concession profits could also increase the price differential between a private airport and a public airport. This implies that a more relevant benchmark for comparison against a private airport with concessions would be a public airport that operates concessions, instead of the private airport without concessions. Therefore, the argument that the presence of concession profits would reduce airport charges may not necessarily be in favor of privatization.

We have also studied the effects of the alternative airport objectives on the timing of capacity expansion. Compared with the benchmark case of a welfare-maximizing public airport, we found that a financially constrained public airport would add capacity later than the benchmark case, whilst a privatized airport pursuing profit-maximization would add capacity later still. Given that constrained public airports represent the second-best situation, our results indicate that the capacity-expansion decisions of privatized airports would be socially suboptimal.

Overall, our analysis suggests that, once the "more realistic" case of a public airport that is financially constrained is considered, the differences in both the pricing and investment decisions would now become smaller between a private airport and the (constrained) public airport, as compared to the earlier case. Nevertheless, in our model setting, the public

A. Zhang, Y. Zhang / Journal of Urban Economics 53 (2003) 54–75   71

airport would still outperform a private airport in both pricing and capacity-expansion decisions. It is worth pointing out that our model has not taken into account any potential "regulatory failures" in this latter comparison. As was indicated in the introduction, specific industrial regulation (e.g., rate of return, price-cap, or cost-based regulations) can introduce distortions. Although these distortions can be minimized by well-designed regulation, they are unlikely to be avoided entirely. If the economic effects of these distortions were significant, then a privatized airport might outperform a (constrained) public airport. The question is then how to strike the balance between the economic effects of some market power and the potential distortions of regulation. Extending our model to consider this trade-off remains an important future research.

Acknowledgments

We are grateful to an anonymous referee and the editor (Jan Brueckner) for their constructive comments, which have materially improved the paper. We also thank David Starkie, Ken Button, Robin Lindsey, Tae Oum, and participants at the 9th World Conference on Transport Research for helpful comments about an earlier version of the paper. Financial support from the Competitive Earmarked Research Grant of the Research Grant Council of Hong Kong (No. 9040384) and the Social Science and Humanities Research Council of Canada is gratefully acknowledged.

Appendix A

Proof of Lemma 1. By definition,

$$W(t, K) = \int_{\rho}^{\infty} Q(\xi, t)\, d\xi + P_W Q - C(Q) + Q V_W.$$

Differentiating W with respect to K, we obtain

$$\frac{\partial W}{\partial K} = -Q\frac{\partial \rho}{\partial K} + Q\frac{\partial P_W}{\partial K} + (P_W - C' + V_W)\frac{\partial Q}{\partial \rho}\frac{\partial \rho}{\partial K}. \tag{A.1}$$

Note that $\rho = P + D(Q, K)$,

$$-Q\frac{\partial \rho}{\partial K} + Q\frac{\partial P}{\partial K} = -Q\frac{\delta D}{\delta K},$$

where $\delta D / \delta K$ is the "full" derivative of $D(Q, K)$ with respect to K, taking into account that Q will also change as K changes:

$$\frac{\delta D}{\delta K} = \frac{\partial D}{\partial K} + \frac{\partial D}{\partial Q}\frac{\partial Q}{\partial \rho}\frac{\partial \rho}{\partial K}.$$

Substituting into (A.1), we get

$$\frac{\partial W}{\partial K} = -Q\frac{\partial D}{\partial K} + \left(P_W - C' - Q\frac{\partial D}{\partial Q} + V_W\right)\frac{\partial Q}{\partial \rho}\frac{\partial \rho}{\partial K}.$$

Use of the first-order condition (4) in the text gives us

$$\frac{\partial W}{\partial K} = -Q\frac{\partial D}{\partial K}.$$ (A.2)

Next, differentiating the operating profits $\pi = P_\pi Q - C(Q) + QR$ with respect to K yields

$$\frac{\partial \pi}{\partial K} = Q\frac{\partial P_\pi}{\partial K} + (P_\pi - C' + R)\frac{\partial Q}{\partial \rho}\frac{\partial \rho}{\partial K}.$$ (A.3)

Now,

$$
\begin{aligned}
Q\frac{\partial P_\pi}{\partial K} &= Q\left(\frac{\partial \rho}{\partial K} - \frac{\delta D}{\delta K}\right) \\
&= Q\frac{\partial \rho}{\partial K} - \left(Q\frac{\partial D}{\partial K} + Q\frac{\partial D}{\partial Q}\frac{\partial Q}{\partial \rho}\frac{\partial \rho}{\partial K}\right) \\
&= -Q\frac{\partial D}{\partial K} - \left[Q\frac{\partial D}{\partial Q} - Q\Big/\left(\frac{\partial Q}{\partial \rho}\right)\right]\frac{\partial Q}{\partial \rho}\frac{\partial \rho}{\partial K}.
\end{aligned}
$$

Substituting into (A.3) and simplifying gives

$$\frac{\partial \pi}{\partial K} = -Q\frac{\partial D}{\partial K} + \left(P_\pi - C' - Q\frac{\partial D}{\partial Q} - \frac{\rho}{\varepsilon} + R\right)\frac{\partial Q}{\partial \rho}\frac{\partial \rho}{\partial K}.$$

Using the first-order condition (6) in the text, gives

$$\frac{\partial \pi}{\partial K} = -Q\frac{\partial D}{\partial K}.$$ (A.4)

Similarly, differentiating the Lagrangian function for the objective in (14), excluding capacity costs, with respect to K yields

$$
\begin{aligned}
(1+\lambda)\frac{\partial B}{\partial K} = (1+\lambda)\Bigg\{ &-Q\frac{\partial D}{\partial K} + \left(P_B - C' - Q\frac{\partial D}{\partial Q} - \frac{\lambda}{1+\lambda}\frac{\rho}{\varepsilon}\right. \\
&+ \left.\frac{V_\pi + \lambda R}{1+\lambda}\right)\frac{\partial Q}{\partial \rho}\frac{\partial \rho}{\partial K}\Bigg\}.
\end{aligned}
$$

Using the first-order condition (15) in the text then gives

$$\frac{\partial B}{\partial K} = -Q\frac{\partial D}{\partial K}.$$ (A.5)

Although $\partial W/\partial K$, $\partial B/\partial K$, and $\partial \pi/\partial K$ all have the same functional form, they have different values. Specifically, (A.2) is evaluated with the airport charge, P_W, determined by (4), whereas (A.4) is evaluated with P_π determined by (6). Since $P_\pi > P_W$, the difference between $\partial W/\partial K$ and $\partial \pi/\partial K$ can be expressed as follows:

$$\frac{\partial W}{\partial K} - \frac{\partial \pi}{\partial K} = -Q\frac{\partial D}{\partial K}\bigg|_{P_W} + Q\frac{\partial D}{\partial K}\bigg|_{P_\pi} = \int_{P_W}^{P_\pi}\frac{\partial}{\partial P}\left(Q\frac{\partial D}{\partial K}\right)dP.$$ (A.6)

Now

$$\frac{\partial}{\partial P}\left(Q\frac{\partial D}{\partial K}\right) = \frac{\partial Q}{\partial \rho}\frac{\partial \rho}{\partial P}\frac{\partial D}{\partial K} + Q\frac{\partial^2 D}{\partial Q\partial K}\frac{\partial Q}{\partial \rho}\frac{\partial \rho}{\partial P}.$$ (A.7)

Since $\rho = P + D(Q, K)$,

$$\frac{\partial \rho}{\partial P} = 1 + \frac{\partial D}{\partial Q} \frac{\partial Q}{\partial \rho} \frac{\partial \rho}{\partial P}.$$

Solve for $\partial \rho / \partial P$,

$$\frac{\partial \rho}{\partial P} = \frac{1}{1 - (\partial D/\partial Q)(\partial Q/\partial \rho)}.$$

Hence $\partial \rho / \partial P > 0$. Combining assumption (13) in the text, we see that (A.7) and so the integrand on the right hand side of (A.6) is positive. This implies

$$\frac{\partial W}{\partial K} > \frac{\partial \pi}{\partial K}.$$

Following the same arguments, since $P_\pi > P_B > P_W$ from Proposition 1, we have

$$\frac{\partial W}{\partial K} > \frac{\partial B}{\partial K} > \frac{\partial \pi}{\partial K}.$$

Finally, by the identities

$$\Delta W = \int_K^{K+1} \frac{\partial W}{\partial K} \, \mathrm{d}K, \qquad \Delta B = \int_K^{K+1} \frac{\partial B}{\partial K} \, \mathrm{d}K, \qquad \Delta \pi = \int_K^{K+1} \frac{\partial \pi}{\partial K} \, \mathrm{d}K,$$

where integration is taken only in formality since K in fact will only take discrete values, we conclude that $\Delta W > \Delta B > \Delta \pi$. $\square$

Proof of Lemma 2. Differentiating (A.2) with respect to t, we have

$$\frac{\partial^2 W}{\partial t \partial K} = -\frac{\mathrm{d}}{\mathrm{d}t}\left(Q \frac{\partial D}{\partial K}\right) = -\left[\frac{\partial D}{\partial K} + Q \frac{\partial^2 D}{\partial Q \partial K}\right]\frac{\mathrm{d}Q}{\mathrm{d}t}.$$

Note that

$$\frac{\mathrm{d}Q}{\mathrm{d}t} = \frac{\partial Q}{\partial t} + \frac{\partial Q}{\partial \rho} \frac{\partial \rho}{\partial t}. \tag{A.8}$$

The demand has a positive trend, so $\partial Q/\partial t > 0$. Further differentiating ρ with respect to t

$$\frac{\partial \rho}{\partial t} = \frac{\partial D}{\partial Q}\left(\frac{\partial Q}{\partial t} + \frac{\partial Q}{\partial \rho} \frac{\partial \rho}{\partial t}\right)$$

and solving for $\partial \rho/\partial t$ yields

$$\frac{\partial \rho}{\partial t} = \frac{(\partial D/\partial Q)(\partial Q/\partial t)}{1 - (\partial D/\partial Q)(\partial Q/\partial \rho)}.$$

Substituting into (A.8), we obtain

$$\frac{\mathrm{d}Q}{\mathrm{d}t} = \frac{\partial Q/\partial t}{1 - (\partial D/\partial Q)(\partial Q/\partial \rho)} > 0.$$

Then by assumption (13), we have

$$\frac{\partial^2 W}{\partial t \partial K} > 0.$$

74   A. Zhang, Y. Zhang / Journal of Urban Economics 53 (2003) 54–75

With similar expressions, differentiating (A.4) and (A.5) with respect to time, we can also obtain

$$\frac{\partial^2 \pi}{\partial t\, \partial K} > 0, \qquad \frac{\partial^2 B}{\partial t\, \partial K} > 0.$$

Hence, by the identities

$$\frac{\partial}{\partial t}\Delta W = \int\limits_{K}^{K+1} \frac{\partial^2 W}{\partial t\, \partial K}\, \mathrm{d}K, \qquad \frac{\partial}{\partial t}\Delta B = \int\limits_{K}^{K+1} \frac{\partial^2 B}{\partial t\, \partial K}\, \mathrm{d}K,$$

$$\frac{\partial}{\partial t}\Delta \pi = \int\limits_{K}^{K+1} \frac{\partial^2 \pi}{\partial t\, \partial K}\, \mathrm{d}K$$

we conclude that

$$\frac{\partial \Delta W(t, K)}{\partial t > 0}, \qquad \frac{\partial \Delta B(t, K)}{\partial t > 0}, \quad \text{and} \quad \frac{\partial \Delta \pi(t, K)}{\partial t} > 0. \qquad \square$$

References

[1] M.E. Beesley, Airport regulation, in: M.E. Beesley (Ed.), Regulating Utilities: A New Era?, Institute of Economic Affairs, London, 1999.

[2] J.K. Brueckner, Airport congestion when carriers have market power, Working paper #89, Institute of Government and Public Affairs, University of Illinois at Urbana-Champaign, Champaign, IL, 2001.

[3] A. Carlin, R.E. Park, Marginal cost pricing of airport runway capacity, American Economic Review 60 (1970) 310–319.

[4] J.I. Daniel, Congestion pricing and capacity of large hub airports: A bottleneck model with stochastic queues, Econometrica 63 (1995) 327–370.

[5] J.I. Daniel, Distributional consequences of airport congestion pricing, Journal of Urban Economics 50 (2001) 230–258.

[6] J.I. Daniel, M. Pahwa, Comparison of three empirical models of airport congestion pricing, Journal of Urban Economics 47 (2000) 1–38.

[7] R. Doganis, The Airport Business, Routledge, London, 1992.

[8] P. Forsyth, Price regulation of airports: Principles with Australian applications, Transportation Research E 33 (1997) 297–309.

[9] P. Forsyth, Regulation under stress: Developments in Australian airport policy, Paper presented at the Hamburg Aviation Workshop on the State of Airport Policy—Australia, North America and Europe, Hamburg, 2002.

[10] D.W. Gillen, T.H. Oum, M.W. Tretheway, Measurement of the social marginal costs at a congested airport: An application to Toronto International Airport, Center for Transportation Studies, University of British Columbia, Vancouver, BC, 1987.

[11] D.W. Gillen, T.H. Oum, M.W. Tretheway, Airport pricing principles: An application to Canadian airports, Journal of Transportation Research Forum 29 (1989) 28–34.

[12] D.W. Gillen, W.G. Morrison, Airport regulation, airline competition and Canada's airport system, Working paper, School of Business and Economics, Wilfrid Laurier University, Waterloo, ON, 2001.

[13] R. Horonjeff, Planning and Design of Airports, McGraw–Hill, New York, 1975.

[14] I. Jones, I. Viehoff, P. Marks, The economics of airport slots, Fiscal Studies 14 (1993) 37–57.

[15] M.I. Kamien, N.L. Schwartz, Dynamic Optimization: The Calculus of Variations and Optimal Control in Economics and Management, 2nd Ed., North-Holland, Netherlands, 1991.

[16] M. Kunz, H.M. Niemeier, Regulating airports: Some lessons from the UK and Germany, Paper presented at the 4th Air Transport Research Group Conference, Amsterdam, 2000.

[17] L.B. Lave, J.S. DeSalvo, Congestion, tolls, and the economic capacity of a waterway, Journal of Political Economy 76 (1968) 375–391.

[18] M.E. Levine, Landing fees and the airport congestion problem, Journal of Law and Economics 12 (1969) 79–108.

[19] S.A. Morrison, Estimation of long-run prices and investment levels for airport runways, Research in Transportation Economics 1 (1983) 103–130.

[20] S.A. Morrison, The equity and efficiency of runway pricing, Journal of Public Economics 34 (1987) 45–60.

[21] T.H. Oum, Y. Zhang, Airport pricing: Congestion tolls, lumpy investment and cost recovery, Journal of Public Economics 43 (1990) 353–374.

[22] T.H. Oum, A. Zhang, Y. Zhang, A note on optimal airport pricing in a hub-and-spoke system, Transportation Research B 30 (1996) 11–18.

[23] Productivity Commission, Price regulation of airport services; Draft report, Productivity Commission, Australian Government, Canberra, 2001, available at http://www.pc.gov.au.

[24] D. Starkie, Reforming UK airport regulation, Journal of Transport Economics and Policy 35 (2001) 119–135.

[25] D. Starkie, G. Yarrow, The single till approach to the price regulation of airports, Civil Aviation Authority, London, 2000, available at http://www.caaerg.co.uk.

[26] M.W. Tretheway, Airport ownership, management and price regulation, Report to the Canadian Transportation Act Review Committee, Ottawa, 2001.

[27] US Federal Aviation Administration, Airport Capacity Handbook, 2nd Ed., Washington, DC, 1969.

[28] A.A. Walters, Investment in airports and the economist's role, in: J.N. Wolfe (Ed.), Cost Benefit and Cost Effectiveness, Allen and Unwin, London, 1973, pp. 140–154.

[29] A. Zhang, Y. Zhang, Concession revenue and optimal airport pricing, Transportation Research E 33 (1997) 287–296.

[30] A. Zhang, Y. Zhang, Airport charges, economic growth, and cost recovery, Transportation Research E 37 (2001) 25–33.

4

Privatization, corporatization, ownership forms and their effects on the performance of the world's major airports

Tae H. Oum, Nicole Adler, Chunyan Yu

Abstract

This paper focuses on measuring and comparing productive efficiency and profitability among airports owned and operated by government departments, 100% government-owned corporations, independent airport authorities, mixed enterprises with government majority ownership and mixed enterprises with private majority ownership. The analysis is based on a cross-sectional, time-series dataset (2001–2003) for the major Asia-Pacific, European and North American airports. There is strong evidence that airports with government majority ownership and those owned by multi-level of government are significantly less efficient than airports with a private majority ownership; there is no statistically significant evidence to suggest that airports owned and operated by US government branches, independent airport authorities in North America, or airports elsewhere operated by 100% government corporations have lower operating efficiency than airports with a private majority ownership; airports with a private majority ownership achieve significantly higher operating profit margins than other airports; whereas airports with government majority ownership or multi-level government ownership have the lowest operating profit margin; and generally, airports with a private majority ownership derive a much higher proportion of their total revenue from non-aviation services than any other category of airports while offering significantly lower aeronautical charges than airports in other ownership categories excluding US airports. The results suggest that private–public–partnership with minority private sector participation and multi-level governments' ownership should be avoided, supporting the majority private sector ownership and operation of airports.
© 2005 Elsevier Ltd. All rights reserved.

Keywords: Privatization; Ownership forms; Airports; Efficiency; Profitability

1. Introduction

Historically, airports were owned and operated by governments. Since the mid-1980s, however, significant changes have occurred in the way airports are owned, managed, and operated. With the exception of the US,[1]

corporatization, commercialization and privatization of airports have become the worldwide trend. The motives for ownership and institutional restructuring via commercialization and privatization are diverse, but normally include easier access to private sector financing and investment, and improved operational efficiency. The commercialization and privatization have taken different formats/models in different countries. For example, in 1987 the UK government sold its seven major airports including three airports in the London area (Heathrow, Gatwick and Stansted) to British Airports Authority (BAA plc), a 100%

---

[1]Contrary to the worldwide trend, airports in the US have remained mostly government owned and operated. However, the government ownership and operation of US airports are considered to be rather different from those of other countries in that there is substantial private sector involvement in management decisions concerning key airport activities and capital investment decisions. For example, because most of the major capacity expansion projects are financed through revenue bonds guaranteed by the major tenant airlines, these airlines have substantial power over airports' decisions on capacity investment, user charges, and

---

(*footnote continued*)
other key strategic decisions. Since these US airlines face a very competitive market place, they act as a pressure group, continually requiring US airports to improve operational efficiency (Bailey, 2002; Carney and Mew, 2003).

110   *T.H. Oum et al. / Journal of Air Transport Management 12 (2006) 109–121*

private sector firm. Since then, many airports around the world have been or are in the process of being privatized or commercialized, including most of the major Australian airports. Majority stakes in Copenhagen Kastrup Airport, Vienna International Airport, and Rome's Leonardo Da Vinci Airport have been sold to private owners. Many other European airports are in the process of being privatized. In New Zealand, major national airports including Auckland and Wellington International Airports are operated by 'for-profit' private sector firms with various local governments as minority owners.[2] It is interesting to note that New Zealand did not introduce any formal form of price regulation with regard to the privatized airports, whereas most of the major Australian airports were privatized utilizing price-cap regulation up until June 2002 (Productivity Commission, 2002).[3] South Africa, Argentina, Mexico, Japan and many other Asian countries are also in the process of privatizing their airports.[4] In Canada, the federal government has retained ownership of its major national airports, but these airports are managed and operated by locally based airport authorities, which are incorporated as 'not-for-profit non-share capital corporations' with long-term leases.

This paper examines how various ownership forms and institutional structures affect the performance of airports in terms of their productive efficiency, operating profits and user charges. In Section 2, we summarize the literature on privatization, ownership forms and firm performance. The general framework of our analysis for measuring the efficiency and profitability effects of airport ownership form and governance structure is presented in Section 3. The data sources, sample airport characteristics and details on variable construction are given in Section 4. Section 5 presents empirical results and a discussion of the findings. Finally, Section 6 presents a summary, conclusions and further research needs.

2. Literature on privatization, ownership and firm performance

The effects of ownership on firms' productive efficiency have been an important research topic in both the economic and management literatures. The agency theory and strategic management literature suggest that ownership influences firm performance because different owners

---

[2]There are some notable exceptions, however. For example, the City of Christchurch, through Christchurch City Holdings, owns 75% of Christchurch International Airport. The City maintains an arms length relationship with the airport, giving the airport considerable autonomy in its operation and management.

[3]Except for Sydney airport, price regulation was in place in the form of a CPI-X price-cap on declared aeronautical services. At Sydney airport, aeronautical services are subject to price surveillance, administered by the Australian Competition and Consumer Commission. The price regulation of most privately owned airports was removed in July 2002.

[4]See Hooper (2002) for the list of Asian airports that are being considered for privatization.

pursue distinctive goals and possess diverse incentives. Under government ownership, a firm is run by bureaucrats who maximize an objective function that is a weighted average of social welfare and his/her personal agenda. Under private ownership, by contrast, the firm is run for the maximization of profit (shareholder value). A common-sense view is that government-owned firms are less productively efficient than their private sector counterparts operating in similar situations. The main arguments supporting this view are: (1) the objectives given to the managers of government-owned firms are vaguely defined, and tend to change as the political situation and relative strengths of different interest groups change (Levy, 1987; De Alessi, 1983; Backx et al., 2002); (2) "the diffuseness and non-transferability of ownership, the absence of a share price, and indeed the generic difficulty residual claimants would have in expressing 'voice' (much less choosing 'exit'), all tend to magnify the agency losses" (Zeckhauser and Horn, 1989).

Neither empirical nor theoretical evidence presented in the vast management and economics literature is conclusive with respects to the above view despite its general acceptance in the popular press. De Fraja (1993) questioned the logic of the main arguments, and showed, through a principal-agent model, that government ownership "is not only not necessarily less productively efficient, but in some circumstances more productively efficient". Vickers and Yarrow (1991) suggest that private ownership has efficiency advantages in competitive conditions, but not necessarily in the presence of market power. They further suggest that even under competitive market conditions, government ownership is not inherently less efficient than private ownership, and that competition is the key to efficiency rather than ownership per se; in markets with monopoly elements, the major factor that appears to be at work is regulatory policy.

There are a number of surveys of empirical studies on efficiency that compare private- and government-owned firms. The results are far from conclusive. For example, De Alessi (1980) and Bennett and Johnson (1980) provided rather strong evidence for the view that private firms would perform better than government-owned firms, whereas Millward and Parker (1983) found that "there is no systematic evidence that public enterprise are less cost effective than private firms", Boyd (1986) agrees with this finding.

Further complicating the ownership-performance debate is the presence of a mixed ownership regime embodying elements of government and private ownership. Bos (1991) provides an excellent theoretical discussion on the behavior of mixed ownership firms. On one hand, mixed ownership may facilitate the role of the government as a "steward" in private firms that are dominated by a strategic investor or where there is a lack of market discipline. On the other hand, mixed ownership arrangements may blend the worst qualities of government and private ownership. Thus, the

T.H. Oum et al. / Journal of Air Transport Management 12 (2006) 109–121   111

resulting effects of mixed ownership on firm performance are not clear from a theoretical perspective. Empirical evidence is limited, and thus fails to provide any clarification on the issue. Boardman and Vining (1989) found that mixed ownership perform no better and often worse than government-owned firms, which may be caused by the conflict between public and private shareholders. Their finding is supported by the analytical and empirical productivity growth investigations of Ehrlich et al. (1994). On the other hand, Backx et al. (2002) found that airlines with mixed ownership tend to perform better than government-owned airlines.

The lack of consensus on the ownership-performance issue is not surprising because public vs. private firms' performance may depend on management and institutional arrangements as well as the market and competition conditions in which the firms operate. The literature in corporate governance suggests that different ownership arrangements embody distinct patterns of authority, responsibility and economic incentives that influence the quality of managerial performance (Charkham, 1996). For example, in the airport industry, major airports in Canada are owned by the federal government but operated by commercially oriented local airport authorities under long-term lease agreements. Would one expect such airports to behave in a similar manner to those owned and operated by a government agency, such as the airports operated by the Swedish Civil Aviation Administration? Similarly, under the broad umbrella of private ownership, some firms are controlled by dominant shareholders whereas others have very diffused ownership and are controlled effectively by managers. The important question here would be who actually controls the firm and thus influences its performance (Gorriz and Fumas, 1996).

Many studies have examined the performance of airports using different methodologies. For example, Hooper and Hensher (1997) examined the performance of six Australian airports over a 4-year period using the total factor productivity (TFP) method. Gillen and Lall (1997) developed two separate data envelopment analysis (DEA) models to evaluate terminal and airside operations independently from each other, and applied them to a pooled data of 21 top US airports for the 1981–1993 period. Nyshadham and Rao (2000) evaluated the efficiency of European airports using TFP and examined the relationship between the TFP index and several partial measures of airport performance. Sarkis (2000) evaluated the operational efficiency of US airports and reached the tentative conclusion that major hub airports are more efficient than spoke airports. Adler and Berechman (2001) used DEA to analyze airport quality and performance from the airlines' viewpoint. Martin and Roman (2001) and Martin-Cejas (2002) applied DEA and translog cost functions, respectively, to evaluate the performance of Spanish airports. Abbott and Wu (2002) investigated the efficiency and productivity of 12 Australian airports for the period 1990–2000 using a Malmquist TFP index and DEA.

Despite the diversity of airport ownership structures and management arrangements, the aforementioned studies with the exception of Parker (1999),[5] have largely ignored the effects of institutional factors on airports' productivity and efficiency. Advani and Borins (2001) investigated how airport service quality is affected by ownership status, privatization anticipation, competition, and a number of other factors. Using data from a questionnaire survey of 201 airports across the globe, the study found that private airports tend to provide better services. Airola and Craig (2001) appear to be the only study that explicitly examined the effects of airports' governance on efficiency performance. Based on a sample of 51 US airports, they distinguished two types of airport governance structures: city-operated airports vs. airport-authority-operated airports. Their results suggest that the authority-operated US airports out-performed city-operated US airports in terms of technical efficiency. It is noted, however, that their study uses only one output measure (number of aircraft movements) in measuring efficiency. As articulated in Oum et al. (2003), the omission of other outputs such as commercial services is likely to bias efficiency results as it underestimates productivity of the airports with proactive managers who focus on exploiting the revenue generation opportunities from non-aviation (including commercial) business.

Airport ownership/governance models can be classified into: (a) government agency or department operating an airport directly; (b) mixed private–government ownership with a private majority; (c) mixed government–private ownership with a government majority; (d) government ownership but contracted out to a management authority under a long-term lease; (e) multi-level governments form an authority to own/operate one or more airports in the region; (f) 100% government corporation ownership/operation. Since most of the previous studies have used specific continental or country-specific airport data, rather than relying on the worldwide privatization experiences and have not attempted to distinguish economic performance among the six categories of airport ownership/governance categories, this paper introduces a new analysis to the existing empirical literature. Furthermore, among the limited studies that attempted to measure the difference between privatized airports (without distinguishing the extent of privatization) and the publicly owned/operated airports, there is no consensus in their findings. Finally, almost all of the studies used a partial measure of outputs (aircraft movements and/or passengers/cargo traffic only) ignoring non-aviation service outputs (including

---

[5]Using Total Factor Productivity analysis, Parker (1999) found that BAA privatization had no noticeable impact on airport technical efficiency while Yokomi (2005) using Malmquist TFP index method found that almost all airports under BAA Plc. have improved technical efficiency after privatization.

commercial services such as concessions) that all airports produce. Given that non-aviation outputs can account for as much as 70% of total revenues an airport generates, the productivity measures ignoring the non-aviation service outputs would be seriously biased against airports that generate a high proportion of their total revenues from commercial services.

3. Model formulation

In order to test the hypotheses concerning varying degrees of privatization, other ownership forms and governance structures on the performance of airports, we propose the following framework of analysis. We will study productivity levels as a function of:

- ownership and governance form,
- management strategy variables,
- airport characteristics and business environment,
- technical (residual) efficiency.

A variable factor productivity (VFP) measure will be developed to measure the level of productivity. VFP is simply the ratio of total aggregate output over aggregate variable input. Variable inputs include labor, purchased goods and materials and purchased services including outsourcing/contracting out. VFP is used as the airport performance indicator in this research for several reasons. First, it is nearly impossible to obtain consistent capital input measures comparable across airports due to the different ownership and governance structures. Second, there is no standardized accounting or reporting system across airports worldwide. Third, airport capacity expansion and other capital projects are often subsidized to varying degrees at various levels of government, which would distort the measurement of TFP. On the other hand, data on variable input factors can be compiled with reasonable accuracy. In addition, long-term investment decisions with regard to capacity expansion are generally beyond airport managerial control, even at private airports.[6]

Ownership/governance variables: As discussed in Section 2, each airport in our sample is classified into one of the following six ownership/governance types:

(a) government agency or department operating an airport;
(b) mixed private–government ownership with private sector owning a majority share;
(c) mixed government–private ownership with government owning a majority share;
(d) government ownership but contracted out to an airport authority under a long term lease; (e) multi-level

governments form an authority to own/operate airports in the region;
(e) 100% government corporation ownership/operation.

Table 1 provides a list of airports included in the sample and their ownership and governance structure. A closer examination of the airport authorities/administrations operating outside North America indicates that they operate in a manner similar to government corporations, rather different from the airport authorities in North America. Therefore, we re-classified the airport authorities/administrations in Asia and Europe into the group of government corporation.

Management strategy variables describe an airport's management and operational strategies. Some airports focus on the traditional airport business, thus derive most of their revenue from aeronautical activities. Others have vigorously expanded into the commercial business sector. In this research, the share of non-aeronautical revenue out of total airport revenue is used as an indicator of the degree of airport business diversification.

Airport characteristics affecting productivity performance include:

- airport size (scale of output);
- average size of aircraft using the airport;
- composition of airport traffic,
- extent of capacity constraint.

Airport size is represented by an aggregate output index as constructed in the Air Transport Research Society (ATRS) (2003, 2004, 2005) global airport benchmarking reports. Airport size can vary significantly only in the very long run, through managerial design and effort. Since managers cannot alter the airport size variable significantly in the medium and short run, we regard the effect of airport size as being beyond managerial control. Average aircraft size is measured by the average number of passengers per aircraft movement and is dependent on the length of the runway(s), geographical location of the airports (intercontinental gateway airports tend to handle larger aircraft), etc. The composition of airport traffic is measured by the percentage of international traffic and the percentage of cargo traffic, both of which depend largely on the geographic location of the airport. Capacity constraints exist both with respect to runway and terminal capacity and are imposed by regulatory, environmental and investment funding concerns. They are generally beyond managerial control; however, runway and terminal capacity shortages affect productivity and quality of service to users of airport services, resulting in delays and inconvenience to airlines, passengers and shippers. Finally, service quality is another factor that may affect airport performance, a preliminary investigation by ATRS (2003) did not indicate any significant effect on the VFP, and thus was excluded from the present study.

---

[6]For example, BAA still needs approval from the British government for major capital projects, despite the fact that it is a purely private sector enterprise.

T.H. Oum et al. / Journal of Air Transport Management 12 (2006) 109–121   113

Table 1
Airport ownership and governance as of December 2003

Airport code	Airport name	Ownership/governance
ATL	Atlanta William B Hartsfield International Airport	Government department
BNA	Nashville International Airport	Authority
BOS	Boston Logan International Airport	Authority
BWI	Baltimore Washington International Airport	Government department
CLE	Cleveland–Hopkins International Airport	Government department
CLT	Charlotte Douglas International Airport	Government department
CVG	Cincinnati/Northern Kentucky International Airport	Authority
DCA	Ronald Reagan Washington National Airport	Authority
DEN	Denver-Stapleton International Airport	Government department
DFW	Dallas/Fort Worth International Airport	Authority
DTW	Detroit Metropolitan Wayne County Airport	Authority
EWR	Newark International Airport	Authority
FLL	Fort Lauderadale Hollywood International	Authority
HNL	Honolulu International Airport	Government department
IAD	Washington Dulles International Airport	Authority
IAH	Houston–Bush Intercontinental Airport	Government department
IND	Indianapolis International Airport	(Private) Authority
JFK	New York-John F. Kennedy International Airport	Authority
LAS	Las Vegas McCarran International Airport	Government department
LAX	Los Angeles International Airport	Government department
LGA	LaGuardia International Airport	Authority
MCI	Kansas City International	Government department
MCO	Orlando International Airport	Authority
MDW	Chicago Midway Airport	Government department
MEM	Memphis International Airport	Authority
MIA	Miami International Airport	Government department
MSP	Minneapolis/St. Paul International Airport	Public Corporation
ORD	Chicago O'Hare International Airport	Government department
PDX	Portland International Airport	Authority
PHL	Philadelphia International Airport	Government department
PHX	Phoenix Sky Harbor International Airport	Government department
PIT	Pittsburgh International Airport	Authority
RDU	Raleigh–Durham International Airport	Authority
SAN	San Diego International Airport	Authority
SEA	Seattle–Tacoma International Airport	Authority
SFO	San Francisco International Airport	Government department
SJC	Norman Y. Mineta San José International Airport	Government department
SLC	Salt Lake City International Airport	Government department
STL	St. Louis–Lambert International Airport	Government department
TPA	Tampa International	Authority
YEG	Edmonton International Airport	Authority
YOW	Ottawa International	Authority
YUL/YMX	Aéroports de Montréal	Authority
YVR	Vancouver International Airport	Authority
YYC	Calgary International Airport	Authority
YYZ	Toronto Lester B. Pearson International Airport	Authority
AMS	Amsterdam Schiphol International Airport	Multi-level government
BCN	Barcelona El Prat Airport	Public corporation
BRU	Brussels International Airport	Government majority
CDG	Paris Charles de Gaulle International Airport	Public corporation
CGN	Cologne/Bonn Konrad Adenauer International Airport	Multi-level government
CPH	Copenhagen Kastrup International Airport	Private majority
DUB	Dublin International Airport	Public corporation
DUS	Flughafen Dusseldorf International Airport	50–50% government private
EDI	Edinburgh Airpor	Private majority
FCO	Rome Leonardo Da Vinci/Fiumicino Airport	Private majority
FRA	Frankfurt Main International Airport	Multi-level government with minor private
GVA	Geneva Cointrin International Airport	Public corporation
HAM	Hamburg International Airport	Government majority
LGW	London Gatwick International Airport	Private majority
LHR	London Heathrow International Airport	Private majority
MAD	Madrid Barajas International Airport	Public corporation
MAN	Manchester International Airport	Multi-level government

114   T.H. Oum et al. / Journal of Air Transport Management 12 (2006) 109–121

Table 1 (*continued*)

Airport code	Airport name	Ownership/governance
MUC	Munich International Airport	Multi-level government
MXP	Milan Malpensa International Airport	Multi-level government
ORY	Paris Orly Airport	Public corporation
OSL	Oslo Airport	Public corporation
PRG	Prague International Airport	Public corporation
VIE	Vienna International Airport	Private majority
WAW	Warsaw Frederic Chopin Airport	Public corporation
ZRH	Zurich International Airport	Private majority
ADL	Adelaide International Airport	Private majority
AKL	Auckland International Airport	Private majority
BKK	Bangkok International Airport	Authority/public corporation (since September 2002)
CHC	Christchurch International Airport	Multi-level government
CNS	Cairns International Airport	Public corporation
HKG	Hong Kong Chek Lap Kok International Airport	Authority
ICN	Incheon International Airport	Public corporation
KIX	Osaka Kansai International Airport	Multi-level government with minor private
KUL	Kuala Lumpur International Airport	Government majority
MEL	Melbourne Tullamarine International Airport	Private majority
NRT	Tokyo Narita International Airport	Authority/public corporation (since April 2004)
PEK	Beijing Capital International Airport	Government majority
PEN	Penang International Airport	Government majority
PVG/SHA	Shanghai Airport Authority	Government majority
SEL	Seoul Gimpo International Airport	Public corporation
SIN	Singapore Changi International Airport	Government department
SYD	Sydney Kingsford Smith International Airport	Public corporation/private majority since July 2002

4. Sample airports and variable construction

4.1. Sources of data and construction of variables

Our sample includes up to 116 airports as listed in Table 1. These airports represent different sizes and ownership and governance structures. The data is compiled from various sources including the International Civil Aviation Organization (ICAO), Airport Council International (ACI), the US Federal Aviation Authority (FAA), International Air Transport Association (IATA), airport annual reports and direct communication with airports. Details on the data are provided in the ATRS (2003, 2004, 2005) Global Airport Benchmarking Reports.

To measure the VFP, one must first identify outputs that an airport produces and the inputs it uses in producing these outputs. The most commonly used output measures for airports are the number of passengers, the volume of air cargo, and the number of aircraft movements. Airports typically impose direct (separate) charges for their services related to aircraft movements and the handling of passengers. However, air cargo services are generally handled by airlines, third-party cargo handling companies, and others that lease space and facilities from airports. Air cargo services are not considered as a separate output in this research, as airports derive a very small percentage of their income from direct services related to air cargo. In addition to passenger traffic, cargo traffic and aircraft movements, airports also derive revenues from conces-

sions, car parking, and numerous other services. These services are not directly related to aeronautical activities in a traditional sense, but they are becoming increasingly more important for airports around the world and account for over 60% of the total revenues for many airports such as Brisbane, Tampa, Munich, etc. Thus, we consider a third output that consists of revenues from non-aeronautical services. A non-aeronautical output index is constructed by deflating the non-aeronautical revenues by purchasing power parity (PPP). For most airports, aeronautical and non-aviation inputs are not separable, thus any productivity or efficiency measure computed without including the non-aviation service output would lead to severely biased results. Inclusion of the non-aeronautical services output not only removes such bias in productivity measurement, but also allows us to examine the efficiency implications of airport business diversification strategies. An overall output index is constructed by aggregating the three output measures (passengers, aircraft movement and non-aeronautical output) using the widely accepted translog multi-lateral index procedure developed by Caves et al. (1982).

On the input side, we initially considered three variable input categories: (1) labor, measured by the number of employees (full time equivalent) who work directly for an airport operator; (2) purchased goods and materials; and (3) purchased services including outsourcing/contracting out. In practice, however, few airports provide separate expense accounts for the purchased (outsourced) services

T.H. Oum et al. / Journal of Air Transport Management 12 (2006) 109–121   115

and purchased goods and materials. Thus, we decided to combine (2) and (3) to form a so-called 'soft-cost' input. The soft-cost input includes all expenses not directly related to capital or labor input costs. As the soft-cost input is measured in monetary terms, and airports operate in countries with very different price levels, PPP is used as a deflator to derive a consistent soft-cost input index. Exclusion of the soft-cost input would bias productivity comparisons significantly in favor of the airports that outsource much of their services such as passenger terminal operations, ground handling services, fire fighting, police and security services, etc. A variable input index is constructed by aggregating labor and soft-cost input using the CCD index procedure.

VFP is defined as the ratio of the aggregate output index over the variable input index. VFP measures how productively an airport utilizes variable inputs in producing outputs for a given level of capital infrastructure and facilities.

4.2. Characteristics of some sample airports

Table 2 provides some interesting statistics for selected sample airports.[7] These statistics indicate that there are large variations among the sample airports in terms of their size, business and operating environment. For example, the annual number of airport passengers ranges from 2.3 million passengers for Penang (Malaysia) to 79 million passengers for Hartsfield–Jackson Atlanta International Airport (US) in 2003. Some airports serve mostly international traffic, such as Amsterdam, Brussels, Singapore, and Hong Kong, whereas others serve mostly domestic passengers, such as Kansas City where international traffic accounts for less than 1% of their total passenger traffic in 2003. Some airports provide services mostly to large aircraft, whereas others serve many small aircraft. For example, the average number of passengers per aircraft movement was 156 passengers at Narita and Kansai in 2003, but only 36 passengers per aircraft at Raleigh–Durham in the same year. Some airports derive most of their revenue from aeronautical activities, whereas for others, a significant portion of revenue comes from other sources including concession, car parks and rentals. For example, in 2003, aeronautical revenue accounts for 73% of New York JFK's total revenue, while it is only 32% of total revenue at Brisbane (Australia). Hub carrier's market share (in terms of frequency) varies across airports as indicated in the last column of Table 2. Oum et al. (2003) show that some of these factors are statistically significant in explaining variations in productive efficiency among the airports, yet they are beyond managerial control. Therefore, it is important to control for the effects of these variables when testing hypotheses concerning the effects of ownership and governance structure of the airports.

---

[7]Due to space limitations, not all sample airports are listed.

5. Empirical results and discussion

A series of regression analyses were conducted to examine the effects of ownership forms and other variables on airport productivity performance. Since the business environments within which these airports operate are very different across Asia, Oceania, Europe and North America, we decided to include continental dummy variables in our VFP regression models with North America as the benchmark. The private majority ownership is used as the base in all regressions. The regression results for three different sets of variables are reported in Table 3, and the results are discussed in the following sections.

5.1. The effects of regional business environments

The regression coefficients on the regional dummy variables indicate that the overall business environments in Asia and Europe appear to have negative influences on the operating efficiency of their airports, whereas the open business systems in Australia and New Zealand appear to help enhance airports' operating efficiency, as compared to the North American airports.

5.2. The effects of ownership forms

The coefficient for airports owned/operated by city/state government departments in the US is not statistically significant in any of the three models, indicating that there is no significant difference in operating efficiency performance between these US airports and those with a private majority ownership. This result provides some evidence supporting the claim by De Neufville (1999) and Dillingham (1996) that the US airports are among the most "privatized" in the world, as US airports routinely turn to airlines for financial help in facility expansion and modernization and in return offer long-term leases that often give airlines strategic control of airports through majority-in-interest (MII) arrangements. Since US carriers face a very competitive market place, they act as a pressure group continually requiring airports to improve efficiency (see Bailey, 2002; Carney and Mew, 2003). Furthermore, private companies (airlines, concessionaires and contractors) deliver most of the airports' day-to-day operations and services. In fact, the government body that owns a US airport often employs only about 10–20% of the workforce active at the airport (de Neufville, 1999).

Similarly, the coefficient for the (North American) airport authority is also not statistically significant in any of the regressions, indicating that there is no significant difference in productive efficiency between airports operated by airport authorities and those with a private majority. The airport authorities in North America appear to have sufficient freedom to operate airports in a business-like manner. Under these circumstances, ownership does not always reflect how an airport is

Table 2
Characteristics of selected airports, 2003

Airport	Passengers (000)	Passengers/movement	% International passengers	% Aeronautical revenue	% Dominant carrier
North America (50 airports)					
ATL	79,087	87	7	36	74
BOS	22,604	59	17	47	24
CLT	22,655	52	6	53	85
DFW	52,455	69	8	58	64
FLL	17,938	62	7	37	16
IND	7,360	36	1	45	19
JFK	31,735	113	48	73	22
LAX	55,307	87	26	43	30
MCI	9,573	52	7	32	34
MSP	33,200	65	4	46	79
ORD	69,509	75	13	65	47
PIT	14,267	40	3	72	82
RDU	8,344	36	2	38	16
SFO	29,165	86	23	70	56
TPA	15,311	66	3	32	22
YOW	3,263	47	24	55	58
YVR	14,322	57	49	46	41
YYZ	24,739	67	55	67	61
Mean	22,315	60	13	53	51
Europe (33 airports)					
AMS	39,960	102	100	49	52
CPH	17,714	68	91	54	50
GVA	8,049	60	99	49	46
LGW	30,058	128	86	45	45
LHR	64,261	139	88	50	41
MUC	24,193	71	65	33	64
STN	19,409	100	82	38	56
VIE	12,785	65	98	42	58
ZRH	17,025	63	95	53	51
Mean	19,417	80	75	53	52
European Airport Authorities (10 authorities)					
ADP	70,700	100	n/a	45	n/a
Aer Rianta	20,439	91	n/a	25	n/a
ANA	18,076	89	n/a	57	n/a
Berlin	12,076	56	n/a	57	n/a
Fraport AG	70,558	98	n/a	46	n/a
Mean	54,441	79		48	
Asia Pacific (33 airports)					
AKL	9,748	65	55	36	70
BNE	12,340	90	21	32	50
HKG	27,092	143	100	44	25
ICN	19,790	152	98	47	37
KIX	16,921	156	62	40	25
NRT	26,537	156	85	68	24
PEK	24,364	103	23	50	37
SIN	24,664	141	100	42	39
SYD	24,183	95	33	41	48
TPE	15,514	123	88	48	29
Mean	13,120	105	45	47	40
Asia Airport Authorities					
AAI	46,642	60	35	76	n/a
AOT	36,274	149	63	61	n/a
MAHB	34,139	65	62	76	n/a
SAA	24,756	102	33	n/a	n/a
Mean	35,453	94	48	71	

Source: Air Transport Research Society (2005).

T.H. Oum et al. / Journal of Air Transport Management 12 (2006) 109–121

Table 3
Variable factor productivity regression results–Log-linear model (Base ownership: airport with a private majority)

Model	1		2		3	
Dependent variable	VFP		VFP		VFP	
	Coeff.	t-stat	Coeff.	t-stat	Coeff.	t-stat
Intercept	0.776	—	−0.531	—	0.689	—
Output scale (index)	0.080	1.99	0.029	0.58	0.076	1.56
Runway utilization (ATM per runway)	—	—	0.101	1.71	0.045	0.80
Aircraft size (Pax/ATM)	−0.161	1.94	−0.128	1.51	−0.303	3.19
Europe	—	—	—	—	0.599	3.74
Asia-Pacific	—	—	—	—	0.628	2.83
% International	−0.010	0.51	−0.008	0.38	−0.035	1.65
Europe	—	—	—	—	−0.316	1.96
Asia-Pacific	—	—	—	—	0.139	3.52
% Non-aviation	0.574	9.04	0.565	8.92	0.504	7.70
% Cargo	0.019	0.65	0.021	0.74	0.013	0.45
Asia	−0.623	4.60	−0.612	4.52	−3.403	3.17
Europe	−0.453	3.40	0.234	0.55	−2.720	3.03
Oceania	0.410	2.72	0.432	2.86	0.508	3.58
2002	−0.066	1.35	−0.060	1.22	−0.054	1.18
2003	−0.081	1.66	−0.069	1.40	−0.067	1.45
Ownership/governance form dummy variables						
US Government Department	−0.046	0.34	−0.031	0.24	−0.056	0.44
N. America Airport Authority	0.026	0.18	0.047	0.34	0.0176	0.13
100% Public corporation	−0.047	0.54	−0.038	0.44	−0.012	0.14
Mixed Ent. (majority gov)	−0.341	2.95	−0.303	2.58	−0.225	1.98
Multi-Gov. shareholders	−0.287	2.91	−0.264	2.65	−0.331	3.51
R^2	0.6846		0.6885		0.7336	
Adjusted R^2	0.6647		0.6674		0.7107	
Log-likelihood value	−57.27		−55.71		−35.84	
Observations (n)	254		254		254	

Note: All variables including the dependent variables are in logarithmic form except for dummy variables; VFP = variable factor productivity index.

operated.[8] This result also indicates that there is no significant efficiency difference between airports operated by North American authorities and airports owned/operated by US government branches. This finding disputes those of Airola Craig (2001) who found that the authority-operated US airports out-performed city-operated airports in terms of technical efficiency. It is noted, however, that their study used only one output measure, aircraft movements, as discussed in the literature review section.

The coefficient for airports with a government majority is negative and statistically significant, indicating that airports with government majority are about one-third less efficient than the airports with a private majority. Partial privatization that gives private sector a minority interest does not appear to work well in terms of improving operating efficiency. This result is consistent with the empirical findings of Boardman and Vining (1989) in other industries, and the theoretical and empirical results of

Ehrlich et al. (1994) as discussed in the literature review section.

The dummy variable for airports with shared ownership by multiple governments has a statistically significant negative coefficient in all of the regression models in Table 3, indicating that involvement by multiple governments is likely to lead to inefficiency in airport operation. It appears that this type of airport ownership is significantly less efficient than the airports under a majority private ownership, as multiple government owners attempt to influence airport management with conflicting objectives.

The dummy variable for Government (Public) Corporation is not statistically significant. This indicates that there may not be significant differences between airports operated by a corporation under a single government ownership and those with a private majority ownership, once the differential operating environments within which these airports operate are controlled. Millward and Parker (1983) and Boyd (1986) found essentially the same results.

The most surprising result with respect to ownership is that 100% public (single government owned) airports are more efficient than the Public–Private Partnership (PPP) airports, when a government has a majority ownership and

---

[8] Results from a separate set of regressions with US airports operated by city/state department as base indicate that there is no significant difference in productive performance between the airports operated by airport authorities in North America and those operated by city/state department.

control. Given that the airports operated by 100% government-owned corporations are almost as efficient as the airports with either 100% or a majority ownership in the private sector (i.e., the benchmark airports in our regression models), it is important for governments to sell a majority stake in airports when they wish to seek private sector financing or participation in ownership and management of airports. In short, the airports with a government majority and/or with multiple government involvement tend to have significantly lower operating efficiency than those with other ownership forms.

5.3. Effects of business diversification

The % non-aviation variable is the most statistically significant variable and has a positive coefficient in all of the VFP regressions reported in Table 3. This indicates that diversifying revenue sources into commercial and other non-aeronautical business would help airports to achieve higher operating efficiency. Many airports aim to increase revenues from commercial services and other non-aeronautical activities, in order to reduce aviation user charges thus attracting more airlines. Such business diversification strategies, of course, exploit the well-known demand complementarity between aeronautical services and commercial services (Oum et al. (2004)) and appear to improve airport productive efficiency as well.

The result from a one-way ANOVA analysis (Table 4) shows that airports with a private majority ownership generally derive a higher percentage of their revenue from non-aeronautical activities than their counterparts under other ownership forms: e.g. 57% vs. 37% for airports with a government majority. If airport privatization leads to an increase in non-aviation revenue, and in turn, an airport with proportionally higher non-aviation revenue achieves greater efficiency, then this secondary effect of privatization on efficiency over and above the effect of the privatization dummy variable should be counted as the total efficiency effect of privatization. Once we take this into account, the effect of privatization on efficiency may be larger than the result presented in this section (and in Table 3).[9]

5.4. The effects of airport characteristics

All of the airports characteristic variables had the expected coefficient signs in the VFP regression. These variables are included in order to avoid bias in efficiency comparisons. The effects of these variables are as follows:

- Airport size (scale of output) has a positive coefficient in all three models, but is not always statistically sig-

Table 4
Ownership form vs. shares of non-aeronautical revenue

Groups	Count	Sum	Average	Variance
N. American Airport Authorities	78	35.87	46%	0.016
Public corporation	44	21.02	48%	0.020
Government majority	14	5.25	37%	0.014
Private-majority	32	18.20	57%	0.013
Multi-government.	16	8.72	55%	0.018
US Government Department	70	34.65	50%	0.014
Source of variation	SS	df	MS	F
Between groups	0.510	5	0.102	6.447
Within groups	3.928	248	0.016	
Total	4.439	253		

nificant. This provides some indication that the economies of output scale may have been exhausted for most of the airports included in our sample (mostly more than 3 million passengers). This is consistent with the findings of Jeong (2005).

- Runway utilization has a positive coefficient, but is not statistically significant in Model (3) and is only marginally significant in Model (2). This provides some indication that airports with congested runways tend to have higher gross VFP.
- Average aircraft size (number of passengers per air transport movement) has a statistically significant negative coefficient in the first-order term, but statistically significant positive coefficients for the cross terms with Asia and Europe regional dummy variables in Model 3. The results indicate that in North America airports handling larger aircraft tend to have lower operating efficiency as compared to a similar airport handling smaller aircraft. This may have been caused by the fact that arrivals and departures of larger aircraft tend to pose peaking and congestion problems at the terminal and landside operations thus reducing the efficient utilization of airports throughout the day. In Asia and Europe, however, airports serving larger aircraft tend to have higher efficiency than those serving smaller aircraft. This provides some indication that Asian and European airports are more concerned with runway congestion, and larger aircraft would release some runway congestion pressure, thus helping to improve overall productive efficiency.
- % International has a negative coefficient in its first-order term, but is not statistically significant. However, the cross term with the European regional dummy is statistically significant with a negative coefficient, and the cross term with the Asian regional dummy is statistically significant with a positive coefficient. The results provides some evidence that in North America and Europe, airports with a heavy reliance on international passengers are likely to have lower 'gross' VFP, whereas in Asia, airports with proportionately more international traffic tend to have a higher "gross" VFP.

---

[9]In order to test if this secondary effect of private ownership on efficiency is significant, we ran the same set of three regressions reported in Table 3 after removing % non-aviation variable. The coefficients for the ownership dummy variables in the new set regressions were not significantly different from those reported in Table 3.

T.H. Oum et al. / Journal of Air Transport Management 12 (2006) 109–121   119

- *% Cargo* has a positive coefficient, but is not statistically significant. This provides weak evidence that airports with a larger proportion of cargo traffic are expected to have higher VFP.

5.5. Ownership influences on other factors

Ownership forms are likely to influence airport pricing and profitability. A series of one-way ANOVA analysis were conducted to examine the effects of ownership form on airport profitability and airport charges.

- *Effects on profitability*: Table 5 shows that airports with a private majority achieve significantly higher profit margins (56%) than airports under other ownership forms. In particular, their average operating margins are more than double those of airports with a government majority and/or operated by multiple governments. North American airports operated by airport authorities also achieved considerably higher profit margins than other types of government-operated airports.
- *Effects on airport charges*: Table 6a and b show that airports in North America generally have lower aeronautical charges than their counterparts in other regions. Outside North America, airports with a private majority have significantly lower average aeronautical charges than other airports. The results provide some evidence that privatization has not lead to airports charging monopoly prices. Instead, privatized airports tend to enhance their profitability by diversifying their business into commercial and other non-aeronautical activities. In contrast, the airports owned/operated by multiple governments appear to rely more on aeronautical charges than the others because they are relatively inefficient.

6. Summary and conclusions

This paper investigates the effects of ownership forms and governance structure on the performance of airports around the world, focusing on productive efficiency and

Table 5
The effects of ownership on operating margin

Groups	Count	Sum	Average	Variance
N. American Airport Authorities	27	10.62	39%	0.012
Public corporation	16	5.80	36%	0.153
Government majority	5	0.98	20%	0.092
Private-majority	16	9.02	56%	0.016
Multi-government.	6	1.37	23%	0.082
US Government Department	26	8.09	31%	0.041
Source of variation	SS	df	MS	F
Between groups	0.975	5	0.195	3.771
Within groups	4.653	90	0.052	
Total	5.628	95		

Table 6

Groups	Count	Sum	Average	Variance
(a) The effects of ownership on airport charges aeronautical revenue per passenger				
N. American Airport Authorities	26	150.08	5.77	11.88
Public corporation	16	159.67	9.98	84.10
Government majority	5	42.16	8.43	15.95
Private-majority	16	106.67	6.67	13.01
Multi-government.	5	70.23	14.05	83.01
US Government Department	26	155.49	5.98	37.27
Source of variation	SS	df	MS	F
Between groups	461.196	5	92.238	2.634
Within groups	3081.453	88	35.016	
Total	3542.644	93		
(b) The effects of ownership on airport charges aeronautical revenue per work load unit[a]				
N. American Airport Authorities	26	123.55	4.75	6.93
Public corporation	16	125.67	7.85	47.13
Government majority	5	35.91	7.18	11.53
Private-majority	15	90.07	6.00	9.20
Multi-government.	5	49.56	9.91	28.30
US Government Department	26	129.43	4.98	30.05
Source of variation	SS	df	MS	F
Between groups	206.019	5	41.204	1.867
Within groups	1919.567	87	22.064	
Total	2125.586	92		

[a]A Work Load Unit (WLU) defined as one passenger or 100 kg of cargo.

operating profitability. The efficiency measure was based on a VFP index drawing from an extensive set of unbalanced panel dataset including major airports in Asia-Pacific, Europe and North America over the period of 2001–2003.

Contrary to initial expectations, we found strong evidence that airports owned and managed by a mixed enterprise with a government-owned majority is significantly less efficient than 100% publicly owned and operated airports.

Again, contrary to common belief, there is no statistical evidence indicating that the airports owned/operated by a firm with private sector majority ownership are more efficient than the airports owned/operated by the US government branches or 100% public corporations. Furthermore, no statistically significant difference in efficiency performance was found to separate airports managed by government departments/branches in the US and those managed by airport authorities such as Vancouver International Airport Authority. The data also suggests that government majority ownership and ownership by multiple governments (often federal/state/local governments) are the two most inefficient ownership forms.

Airports with a private majority, all of which are based in Europe and Oceania, achieved significantly higher profit margins (56%) than airports under other ownership forms despite the fact that they charge significantly lower aeronautical tariffs than other airports. Hence, the results provide some evidence that privatization has not lead to airports charging monopoly prices. Instead, privatized airports tend to enhance their profitability by diversifying their business into commercial and other non-aeronautical activities.

Probably the most surprising result of this analysis is that 100% public (single government owned) airports are more efficient than the PPP airports, where a government retains majority ownership and control. Given that the airports operated by 100% government-owned corporations are almost as efficient as the airports with either 100% or a majority stake in the private sector, it would appear to be important for governments to sell a majority stake in airports when they seek private sector financing or participation in ownership and management of airports. In short, the airports with a government majority and/or with multiple government involvement tend to have significantly lower operating efficiency than all other forms of ownership. Furthermore, airports with majority private ownership (including 100% private ownership) do not achieve significantly higher efficiency than the 100% government-owned airports, such as those in the US.

These results lead to the following question: why has privatization failed to improve productivity in the airport industry? The near monopoly markets for many airports (Vickers and Yarrow, 1991), the type of regulation imposed (Oum et al., 2004) and the principal-agent issues (De Fraja, 1993; Cragg and Dyck, 1999) all may have led to the problems depicted in this analysis. Consequently, institutional changes along with some or all of the following measures may help improve the airport's operational efficiency:

- In the long run, creation of a continental single aviation market would encourage greater competition amongst airport markets by providing airlines and passengers with greater choices.
- Removing bureaucratic control and duplication of administrative processes between the corporatized airport management and governmental administrative procedures.
- Giving airport managers complete authority to restructure operations and conduct business may improve efficiency e.g. the airport managers should be given the freedom to outsource terminal operations to specialized firms.

Researchers have pointed out that the empirical results of efficiency analysis may depend on the method of measurement used (Oum et al., 1999). Other methodologies, such as various forms of DEA, stochastic frontier methods, cost function methods, etc. are likely to yield different empirical results. Given that some of the findings obtained here are likely to be controversial, it is important to test different measurement methodologies before reaching a firm conclusion as to the efficiency effects of privatization, corporatization and commercialization of airports.

Acknowledgements

Financial supports via the Social Science and Humanities Research Council of Canada (SSHRC) Research Grant, and University of British Columbia's Humanities and Social Science Seed Research Grant are gratefully acknowledged.

References

Abbott, M., Wu, S., 2002. Total factor productivity and efficiency of Australian airports. The Australian Economic Review 35, 244–260.

Adler, N., Berechman, J., 2001. Measuring airport quality from the airlines' viewpoint: an application of data envelopment analysis. Transport Policy 8, 171–181.

Advani, A., Borins, S., 2001. Managing airports: a test of the new public management. International Public Management Journal 4, 91–107.

Airola, J., Craig, S., 2001. Institutional Efficiency in Airport Governance. Unpublished manuscript, Department of Economics, University of Houston, Houston, Texas.

Air Transport Research Society (ATRS), 2003. 2003 Global Airport Benchmarking Report: Global Standards for Airport Excellence, Vancouver, Canada. http://www.atrsworld.org.

Air Transport Research Society (ATRS), 2004. 2004 Global Airport Benchmarking Report: Global Standards for Airport Excellence, Vancouver, Canada. http://www.atrsworld.org.

Air Transport Research Society (ATRS), 2005. 2005 Global Airport Benchmarking Report: Global Standards for Airport Excellence, Vancouver, Canada. http://www.atrsworld.org.

Backx, M., Carney, M., Gedajlovic, E., 2002. Public, private and mixed ownership and the performance of international airlines. Journal of Air Transport Management 8, 213–220.

Bailey, E.E., 2002. Aviation policy: past and present. Southern Economic Journal 69, 12–20.

Bennett, J., Johnson, M., 1980. Tax reduction without sacrifice: Private sector production of public services. Public Finance Quarterly 8, 363–396.

Boardman, A.E., Vining, A.R., 1989. Ownership and performance in competitive environments: a comparison of the performance of private, mixed, and state owned enterprises. Journal of Law and Economics 32, 1–33.

Bos, D., 1991. Privatization: A Theoretical Treatment. Clarendon Press, Oxford.

Boyd, C.W., 1986. The comparative efficiency of state-owned enterprise. In: Negandhi, A.R., Thomas, H., Rao, K.L.K. (Eds.), Multinational Corporations and State-owned Enterprise: A New Challenge in International Business. JAI Press, Greenwich.

Carney, M., Mew, K., 2003. Airport governance reform: a strategic management perspective. Journal of Air Transport Management 9, 221–232.

Caves, D., Christensen, L.R., Diewert, W.E., 1982. Multilateral comparisons of output, input and productivity using superlative index numbers. Economic Journal 92, 73–86.

Charkham, P., 1996. Keeping Good Company: A Study of Corporate Governance in Five Countries. Oxford University Press, New York.

Cragg, M.I., Dyck, I.J.A., 1999. Management control and privatization in United Kingdom. Rand Journal of Economics 30, 475–497.

De Alessi, L., 1980. The economics of property rights: a review of the evidence. In: Zerbe, R.O. (Ed.), Research in Law and Economics. JAI Press, Greenwich.

De Alessi, L., 1983. Property rights transaction costs and X-efficiency: an essay in economic theory. American Economic Review 73, 64–81.

De Fraja, G., 1993. Productive efficiency in public and private firms. Journal of Public Economics 50, 15–30.

De Neufville, R., 1999. Airport privatization: issues for the United States. A draft paper, Massachusetts Institute of Technology, Cambridge, MA.

T.H. Oum et al. / Journal of Air Transport Management 12 (2006) 109–121 121

Dillingham, G.L., 1996. Airport privatization: issues related to the sale or lease of US commercial airports. Testimony before the subcommittee on aviation, Committee on Transportation Infrastructure, House of Representatives, GAO/T-RCED-96-82, Washington, DC.

Ehrlich, I., Gallais-Hamonno, G., Liu, Z., Lutter, R., 1994. Productivity growth and firm ownership: an analytical and empirical investigation. Journal of Political Economy 102, 1006–1038.

Gillen, D.W., Lall, A., 1997. Developing measures of airport productivity and performance: an application of data envelopment analysis. In: Proceedings of the Aviation Transport Research Group Conference, Vancouver.

Gorriz, C.G., Fumas, V.S., 1996. Ownership structure and firm performance: some empirical evidence from Spain. Managerial and Decision Economics, 575–586.

Hooper, P., 2002. Privatization of airports in Asia. Journal of Air Transport Management 8, 289–300.

Hooper, P.G., Hensher, D.A., 1997. Measuring total factor productivity of airports: an index number approach. Transportation Research E 33, 249–259.

Jeong, J., 2005. An investigation of operating costs of airports: focus on the effects of output scale. A Master of Science Thesis, University of British Columbia, Vancouver, Canada.

Levy, N., 1987. A theory of public enterprise behavior. Journal of Economic Behaviour and Organization 8, 75–96.

Martin, J.C., Roman, C., 2001. An application of DEA to measure the efficiency of Spanish airports prior to privatization. Journal of Air Transport Management 7, 149–157.

Martin-Cejas, R.R., 2002. An approximation to the productive efficiency of the Spanish airports network through a deterministic cost frontier. Journal of Air Transport Management 8, 233–238.

Millward, R., Parker, D.M., 1983. Public and private enterprise: comparative behaviour and relative efficiency. In: Millward, R.,

Parker, D.M., Rosenthal, L., Sumner, M.T., Topham, T. (Eds.), Public Sector Economics. Longman, London.

Nyshadham, E.A., Rao, V.K., 2000. Assessing efficiency of European airports: a total factor productivity approach. Public Works Management and Policy 5, 106–114.

Oum, T.H., Waters, W.G., Yu, C., 1999. Survey of productivity and efficiency measurement in rail transport. Journal of Transport Economics and Policy 33, 9–42.

Oum, T.H., Yu, C., Fu, X., 2003. A comparative analysis of productivity performance of the world's major airports: summary report of the ATRS global airport benchmarking research report—2002. Journal of Air Transport Management 9, 285–297.

Oum, T.H., Zhang, A., Zhang, Y., 2004. Alternative forms of economic regulation and their efficiency implications for airports. Journal of Transport Economics and Policy 38, 217–246.

Parker, D., 1999. The performance of BAA before and after privatization. Journal of Transport Economics and Policy 33, 133–145.

Productivity Commission, 2002. Price Regulation of Airport Services. Report No. 19, AusInfo, Canberra.

Sarkis, J., 2000. An analysis of the operational efficiency of major airports in the United States. Journal of Operations Management 18, 335–351.

Vickers, J., Yarrow, G., 1991. Economic perspectives on privatization. Journal of Economic Perspectives 5, 111–132.

Yokomi, M., 2005. Evaluation of technical efficiency at privatized airports: Case of BAA Plc. In: A paper presented at the Air Transport Research Society (ATRS) Conference, July 3–6, 2005, Rio de Janeiro, Brazil.

Zeckhauser, R.J., Horn, M., 1989. The control and performance of state-owned enterprises. In: MacAvoy, P.W., Stanbury, W.T., Yarrow, G., Zeckhauser, R.J. (Eds.), Privatization and State-owned Enterprise. Kluwer, Boston.

5

UK Airport Policy: Does the Government Have any Influence?

Ian Humphreys, Stephen Ison and Graham Francis

This article explores the UK government's influence on shaping and directing airport policy. UK air travel has increased five-fold over the past 30 years and is projected to increase by between two and three times current levels by 2030. In order to accommodate this growth the government published a new UK airports policy in 2003. The issues surrounding UK airports policy have been brought into the public eye by the takeover of BAA by the Spanish Ferrovial Group and the Office of Fair Trading's announcement that it was looking into the UK airports market (OFT, 2006).

The 2003 white paper on *The Future of Air Transport* stated that future airport development was crucial to the expansion of the UK economy, but that growth should be focused at certain airports and proceed with respect to minimizing environmental impact (Department for Transport, 2003). The white paper outlined a policy framework for the development of UK airports over the next 30 years. The recommendations included new runways at Stansted, Heathrow, Birmingham, Edinburgh and possibly Gatwick and for airports to develop terminal capacity in order to meet regional demand. This article examines the influence that the UK government actually has with respect to airport policy now that the main airports are in private hands.

Clearly, in terms of any new developments in airports there has to be a balance between the needs of the UK economy and environmental concerns in terms of air pollution, land take, noise, visual intrusion and surface access congestion. The government's policy seems to be to accommodate an increase in demand rather than managing demand. Interestingly, this is perhaps inconsistent with other transport policy the UK government is currently adopting in terms of surface transport, most notably with respect to road user charging.

UK Airport Ownership and Control

Prior to the Airports Act 1986, national or local government owned and operated the majority of UK airports and provided the finance for their development. The UK government therefore had direct influence on new infrastructure such as runway and terminal capacity. For example, the government identified the need for Terminal 4 at Heathrow in the 1970s and following the planning stage and its construction, it was opened in April 1986, directly in line with government policy.

The Airports Act 1986 privatized the British Airports Authority (now BAA) as a group of airports, which in the UK currently comprises—Aberdeen, Edinburgh, Glasgow, Gatwick, Heathrow, Southampton and Stansted. Airports owned by BAA currently handle 63% of passengers beginning or ending their journeys in the UK (OFT, 2006). The Act also required all other airports with more than £1 million turnover per annum, in two of the three previous years, to be set up as commercial companies, unable to receive subsidies and responsible for becoming commercially solvent. Airport management has become increasingly focused on commercial revenue from non-aeronautical sources of revenue, for example from retail and parking charges (Humphreys *et al.*, 2001; Graham, 2001).

Since 1986, many private companies have bought a stake in UK airports, and now the majority of UK airports are owned by private companies (see table 1).

Many of the airports have subsequently undergone ownership changes and a number of new airport groups have emerged. A further development, which was perhaps not foreseen at the time, is that a number of these airports are now under partial or total foreign ownership. Private or foreign ownership, as opposed to state ownership of airports, can raise the issue of national security. National security at airports is, however, enforced by a range of government standards and agencies that control, monitor and oversee the passage of people and goods, and this will continue to

340

Table 1. UK airport ownership.

Airport	Current owner	Part of larger group	Private interest %	Date of first privatization
Aberdeen	Ferrovial Group (Spain)	Yes	100	1987
Belfast International	Airport Concessions & Development Ltd (ACDL)	Yes	100	1994
Belfast City	Ferrovial Group (Spain)	Yes	100	2003
Biggin Hill	Regional Airports UK	Yes	100	1994
Birmingham	Local authority 49%; Macquarie 24.1; Aer Rianta 24.1%; other 2.8%	Yes/part owned by group	51	2001
Bournemouth	Manchester Airport Group	Yes	0**	1995
Bristol	Ferrovial Group and Macquarie	Yes	100	1997
Cardiff	TBI	Yes	100	1995
Coventry	CAFCO (Coventry) Ltd—joint venture between Irish-Anglo property development group Howard Holdings and Convergence-AFCO Holdings—an Anglo-American airport management and development company	No	100	2006
Doncaster Robin Hood	Peel Airports	Yes	100	2004
East Midlands Airport, Nottingham, Leicester, Derby	Manchester Airport Group	Yes	0**	1999
Edinburgh	Ferrovial Group (Spain)	Yes	100	1987
Exeter	Regional and City Airports (Exeter) Ltd (RCA)	Yes	100	N/A
Glasgow	Ferrovial Group (Spain)	Yes	100	1987
Highlands and Islands Airports	Highlands and Islands Airports Ltd	Yes/public body	0	N/A
Humberside	Manchester Airport Group	Yes	0**	1999
Kent (Manston)	Infratil (New Zealand)	Yes	100	2005
Leeds Bradford	Bridgeport Capital	No	100	2007
Liverpool	Peel Holdings Ltd	Yes	76	1990
London City	AIG Financial Products Corporation and Global Infrastructure Partners	No	100	1995
London Gatwick	Ferrovial Group (Spain)	Yes	100	1987
London Heathrow	Ferrovial Group (Spain)	Yes	100	1987
London Luton	Airport Concessions & Development Ltd (ACDL)—owned by Abertis Infraestructuras (90%), and Aena Internacional (10%) (Spain)	Yes	100*	1998
London Stansted	Ferrovial Group (Spain)	Yes	100	1987
Manchester	Local authorities: Manchester Airport Group	Yes	0	N/A
Newcastle	Part owned by Copenhagen Airport	Yes	49	2001
Norwich	80.1% Omniport/rest local authority	Yes	80.1	2004
Prestwick	Infratil (New Zealand)	Yes	100	1987
Southend	Regional Airports Ltd			
Southampton	Ferrovial Group (Spain)	Yes	100	1987
Durham Tees Valley	Local authorities and Peel Airports (which has a majority)	Yes	At least 51% private	2003

* Local authority owned, but operated on a 30-year lease.
**Airport owned by geographically remote local authority as part of Manchester Airport Group.

© 2007 THE AUTHORS
JOURNAL COMPILATION © 2007 CIPFA

341

The Nature and Form of Airport Regulation in the UK

A key aspect of the Airports Act 1986 was to introduce the economic regulation of airport charges, principally to protect the airlines from monopoly charging behaviour by the airports thus acting as a restraint on profit. The three main London airports (Heathrow, Gatwick and Stansted) and Manchester Airport were subject to price caps on their aeronautical charges imposed by the Civil Aviation Authority (CAA) (CRI/CIPFA, 2001; Francis and Humphreys, 2001).

The airport charges were, and still are, regulated under the 'single till' principle where all income (aeronautical and commercial) is considered prior to setting the aeronautical charges. This means that the revenue earned from commercial sources subsidises the aeronautical charges (Hanks, 2006). Additionally, two important facets of the Act were the requirement of all airports to produce their accounts, in a transparent manner, for inspection by the CAA, and the need for each airport to request permission from the CAA to levy charges.

With regards to BAA airports, the Act made provision for 'the national interest' by the government retaining a 'golden share'. The golden share meant that the government retained the right to intervene in BAA operations. This golden share was later ruled incompatible under EU law (Oxera, 2005). It was, however, felt that the public interest could be adequately defended through regulation by allowing the CAA to involve the Competition Commission if it considered that ownership of an airport was not in the public interest.

The Implications of the Diversity of Ownership

The ownership structure of the airport industry in the UK has a number of important implications for airport policy implementation and the development of airport capacity in line with the social, economic and environmental welfare of the UK.

With respect to airport policy, the UK government can only encourage and incentivize airport operators to invest in new capacity, when it believes capacity would best benefit the national interest. Potentially this could be encouraged by the Department for Transport via the CAA adjusting the price cap in a manner that creates incentives for airport operators to invest in new infrastructure.

The single till method of regulation is currently one which the airlines support since the commercial revenue (specifically from the airport shops and car parks) cross-subsidises the airlines' aeronautical charges. A problem that arises from this system is that the airport landing charges fail to reflect accurately airport usage, which 'makes it more difficult to manage limited capacity available' (Starkie, 1994). As a result Heathrow and Gatwick, the busiest and most congested UK airports, are two of the cheapest for the airlines in terms of aeronautical charges. One way that the UK government could improve the incentives for BAA to invest in airport capacity is if a 'dual till' regulatory system were adopted, where commercial and aeronautical revenue were regulated separately. This could provide a greater incentive for the BAA to invest in aircraft landing and handling facilities, since under the current single till regime there is little incentive to invest in these since the amount the airport can charge the airlines is restricted (CAA, 2003). It should be noted that, under single till regulation, there is an incentive to invest in expanding retail space at an airport—such a system is likely to expose the investment in airport capacity to the disciplines of the market mechanism. The dual till system has been reconsidered, but to date has not been adopted.

The final decision to invest in additional capacity at a specific airport rests with the airport operator. Prior to 1986, when the government owned and operated airports, capacity could be added directly where and when the government deemed it appropriate, subject to approval from the planning system.

Given the large capital outlay required to finance expansion of both terminal and runway capacity, it can be in the financial interests of airport owners to embark on any major developments somewhat later than earlier. This strategy would enable them to earn a higher relative return on their existing capital (Humphreys, 1999; Humphreys and Francis, 2002) and there is evidence of this happening in the UK (Learmount, 2005, p. 14). Hanks (2006), on behalf of BAA, has made it clear that, despite the incentives offered by government, the final decision to invest lies with the airport operator: 'There is no statutory or legal requirement upon the BAA to rebuild Heathrow' (Hanks, 2006, p. 7).

At Stansted, the government recommended that a second runway would be needed in 2011/2012, yet it seems the airport operator will only invest in the new runway when it is seen as financially prudent to do so. Given the apparent lack of support for an increase in charges to pay for such development from its low-cost airline tenants, the timescale for a new runway is already slipping to 2013 or even later. The timing with respect to the goals of private companies and that which favours the social and economic well being of the UK may not necessarily be congruent. However, it could be argued that the strategic long-term UK government agenda might not accord with social welfare maximization.

Averch and Johnson (1962) offer an alternative perspective and argue that private airport owners will not necessarily postpone investment—indeed, they might advance it because of the nature of regulation.

Following the privatization and commercialization of airports, a major driver for increasing terminal capacity may not in fact be solely pressure for passenger processing, but a desire for more retail space. Since the Airports Act 1986, this has become an increasingly important source of revenue for airports and, in some cases, it is the main income stream. Several airports have told us that it is in their interests to have a degree of surface access congestion since this requires passengers to arrive earlier at the airport to avoid missing their flight. Earlier arrival means that passengers spend more time at the airport which can stimulate retail spend, something that may not occur if capacity had been expanded.

An attempt by the Spanish company Ferrovial to purchase Exeter Airport was withdrawn when it was referred by the Office of Fair Trading (OFT) to the Competition Commission (Competition Commission, 2005). The takeover was referred because it was deemed that Exeter Airport would have given Ferrovial a local monopoly in the south west of England, since it also had a controlling stake in Bristol Airport, some 80 miles away. This was despite BAA having ownership of the three busiest airports in the UK (Heathrow, Gatwick and Stansted), which are responsible for over half UK airport passenger traffic and are all located in south east England (CAA 2006). In early 2006, BAA was taken over by Ferrovial and the OFT has announced looking that it is looking at referring BAA south east airports to the Competition Commission (OFT, 2006).

The government has required airports to produce master plans that detail the possible developments over the next 30 years. Given the range of runway and terminal development possible, areas around UK airports targeted for development face uncertainty and blight

until the exact runway locations are decided (see Learmount, 2005). The blight is likely to continue for a number of years as airports raise finance and bring proposals to public inquiry—a process that could take around 10 years and possibly more.

Airports may see making efficient use of their existing capacity without furthering expansion plans as more desirable than 'antagonizing their neighbours'. While this may be environmentally preferable, it may not be in the economic interests of the UK.

The system of price regulation, the Competition Commission and the planning system with its public inquiries may all be able to shape proposals and determine whether some developments should be blocked; however, this is a far cry from being able to strategically plan airport capacity provision. Even where the government has indicated that it would support the development of a new runway, a public inquiry may rule against such a proposal.

The commercial interests of private airport owners may not always be consistent with the public interest. Each case has to be evaluated on its merits. An interesting example is that of Cardiff Airport. Under local authority ownership the airport was used to attract a British Airways aircraft maintenance facility by selling land at an attractive rate. Such a decision was not in the financial interests of the airport, but for the benefit of the region by creating 870 jobs and acting as a catalyst to attracting BA supplier companies to South Wales (Humphreys 1998). Under private ownership, this development would not have been attractive since TBI (the private owners) would not entertain development unless they could see a viable financial return. As such, there can often be a dichotomy between the policy objectives of the UK government and the objectives of various airport owners.

The increasing trend towards international companies owning airports may increasingly focus an airport operator's objectives towards global financial returns, rather than a UK public service and regional economic development. So should UK national airport assets have been left to the vagaries of private markets?

Foreign Ownership
National approaches to foreign ownership of airports varies worldwide. For example, the US, Spain and France take a protectionist view. However, the UK has generally welcomed foreign ownership. The diversity of companies that own UK airports is detailed in table 1. A

Spanish group—Ferrovial—now owns BAA which has seven UK airports including the three busiest ones. Foreign private ownership of airports may pose no more of a risk than domestic private ownership. There may in fact be benefits from the influx of foreign ownership and associated investment. With foreign ownership can come a wealth of experience and expertise which could lead to improved efficiency through measures such as outsourcing, the lowering of overheads, alternative procurement methods (Teather, 2006). Surowiecki argues that preventing foreign ownership of any company and limiting the possibility of takeovers insulates managers from competition and this increases the risk of inefficiency and underperformance (Surowiecki, 2006). Overall, therefore, foreign takeovers can be good for an economy, the argument being that it can result in additional investment, new employment opportunities and the raising of managerial standards (Gapper, 2006).

Conclusion
The privatization of the UK's airports has resulted in a rich tapestry of different ownership structures that continues to evolve. The future development of UK airports is seen as crucial to the economic well-being of the UK, yet this future is primarily in the hands of private and commercialized airport operators who need to make a profit. The government had retained a 'golden share' in BAA to enable it to protect national interests, but the European Commission later deemed this incompatible with EU legislation. The interests of private airport owners may not necessarily coincide with the societal, economic and environmental interests of the UK. To ensure that airport infrastructure development is encouraged in the appropriate places and at the appropriate times, careful consideration needs to be given as to how the government can best use its regulatory, fiscal and planning levers to encourage the investment it wants. ∎

Acknowledgements
The authors wish to acknowledge the constructive comments made by the referees to earlier drafts of this article.

References
Averch, H. and Johnson, L. L. (1962), Behavior of the firm under regulatory constraint. *American Economic Review*, 52, 5, pp. 1053–1069.
CAA (2000), *The 'Single Till' and the 'Dual Till'* Approach to the Price Regulation of Airports (London).
CAA (2003), *Economic Regulation of BAA London Airports (Heathrow, Gatwick and Stansted) 2003–2008.* CAA Decision (February). See www.caa.co.uk.
CAA (2006), *UK Airport Statistics, 2005, Terminal and Transit Passengers 2005* (London).
Competition Commission (2005), CC cancels Exeter airport inquiry. News release (4 November).
CRI/CIPFA (2001), *The UK Airports Industry Airports Statistics 1999/00* (Centre for the Study of Regulated Industries, University of Bath).
Department for Transport (2003), *The Future of Air Transport*, Cm 6043 (The Stationery Office, London).
Francis, G. and Humphreys, I. (2001), Airport regulation: reflecting on the lessons of BAA. *Public Money & Management*, 21, 1, pp. 49–52.
Gapper, J. (2006), Feel the benefits of foreign. *Financial Times* (10 April).
Graham, A. (2001), *Managing Airports: An International Perspective* (Butterworth Heinemann, Oxford).
Hanks, K. (2006), How should airports be regulated? *Airport Management*, 1, 1, pp. 1–9.
Humphreys, I. (1998), Development and privatization of Cardiff airport. *Contemporary Wales*, 10, pp. 81–102.
Humphreys, I. (1999), Privatization and commercialization: changes in UK ownership patterns, *Journal of Transport Geography*, 7, pp. 121–134.
Humphreys, I., Francis, G. and Fry, J. (2001), What are the lessons from airport privatization, commercialization and regulation in the UK? *Transportation Research Record* (1744), pp. 9–16.
Humphreys, I. and Francis, G. (2002), Policy issues and planning of UK regional airports. *Journal of Transport Geography*, 10, pp. 249–258.
Learmount, D. (2005), UK runway plans face long delay. *Flight International* (3–11 July), p. 14.
Oxera (2005), *Special Rights of Public Authorities in Privatized EU Companies: The Microeconomic Impact* (Report prepared for the European Commission).
OFT (2006), OFT to look at UK airports market. Press release (25 May).
Starkie, D. (1994), Regulating airports and airlines. In Beesley, M. (Ed), *Regulating Utilities: The Way Forward* (IEA Readings 41).
Surowiecki, J. (2006), Foreign lesions: Why do we hate the idea of Americans buying the London Stock Exchange? *The Guardian* (18 March).
Teather, D. (2006), Ferrovial lands BAA with final offer of £10.3bn. *The Guardian* (7 June).

6

Fly Buy Cities: Some Planning Aspects of Airport Privatisation in Australia

ROBERT FREESTONE, PETER WILLIAMS & AARON BOWDEN

ABSTRACT *Neo-liberalism has been a dominant economic and political paradigm for several decades, legitimising the privatisation, deregulation and marketisation of many public services. The leasing of Australia's capital city airports by the Commonwealth Government to private operators exemplifies this trend. Since the late 1990s, airport companies have moved to commodify uncommitted land assets for diverse commercial developments. These trends raise important planning issues through impacts on property markets, infrastructure provision, traffic and the environment. Yet under the relevant legislation, ultimate development approval remains solely with the Commonwealth Government, with both local and state planning authorities excluded. This article presents preliminary findings on an investigation into planning aspects of non-aeronautical commercial development of major airports in Australia.*

KEY WORDS: Airports, Commonwealth Government, privatisation, neo-liberalism, urban planning

Introduction

In the prevailing neo-liberal climate, private sector involvement has grown enormously in what have been traditionally public functions and the implications of the 'privatisation bandwagon' on the form and functioning of Australian cities have been a policy concern since the early 1990s (Hayward, 1997). Institutional re-arrangements in the provision of transport services have been dramatic and arguably most profound in the aviation sector (Black, 1999). The leasing of Australia's capital city airports by the Commonwealth Government to private operators is a spectacular manifestation of the privatisation process carrying enormous implications for city functioning. In the global 'space of flows', airports are critical nodes and have latterly assumed major economic significance extending beyond core aviation functions. Airport master plans and development plans have targeted uncommitted land assets for non-aeronautical business developments such as hotels, business parks, regular and discount retail malls, and bulky goods and fast food

492　*R. Freestone* et al.

outlets. The changing urban landscape registers the evolution of airport roles from infrastructure providers to commercial entities (Gerber, 2002). More fundamentally, and on top of new facilities to accommodate increased domestic and international air traffic, such developments are transforming airports into major activity nodes with implications for urban spatial structure, transportation, commercial property markets, the environment and the efficacy of planning systems. Kasarda's (2000) concept of the 'aerotropolis' picks up on the emergence of new urban forms based around airports.

Despite the local and metropolitan context in which they sit, development approval for airports in Australia remains with the Commonwealth Government. The exclusion of local and state planning authorities from any effective determining involvement in the process raises important issues for urban planning and development. There are potential conflicts with existing planning controls and strategies. Moreover, competing development interests subject to these controls have objected to private commercial developments on airport land on public interest grounds.

This article provides a preliminary investigation of commercial development of airport land for non-aeronautical uses. It sets this in the context primarily of the broader processes of privatisation within a neo-liberal economic framework. The history of airport privatisation in Australia is reviewed. Current governance arrangements with special reference to the environmental planning framework centred on the requirement for airport master plans are described. The scale of actual and proposed non-aviation-related commercial development and reactions to this development is scoped. Concerns about these trends are categorised and discussed. Our analysis steers between the full-throttled arguments for and against privatisation that have made it such a heated political issue worldwide (Ross & Levine, 2005). It acknowledges both strengths and limitations in a planning framework ultimately configured by the Commonwealth Government's aim of maximising profits at the time of sale.

Neo-liberal Airports

Neo-liberalism aimed at privileging the role of market mechanisms has become the dominant discourse of public policy and service provision (Self, 1993). It is the "dominant ideological rationalisation for globalisation and contemporary state 'reform'" (Peck & Tickell, 2002, p. 380). Also known as 'economic rationalism' in Australia, Gleeson and Low (2000, p. 135) portray its main "political instinct" as "fundamentally hostile" to traditional planning values. But there is no singular or monolithic model. Neo-liberalism is both hegemonic and localised, assuming diverse hybrid forms in response to localised circumstances (O'Neill & Argent, 2005).

Privatisation—in the form of the transfer of assets of publicly owned enterprises by governments to private ownership—has been a dominant policy response (Bishop *et al.* 1994). Pirie (1995, p. 27) describes privatisation policy as the "most significant economic development of modern times". Key ideas that underlie the theoretical underpinnings of privatisation may be traced to the economic theories of Adam Smith, who maintained the optimum allocation of resources for the common good was best served by a free market economy based on pursuit of self-interest and guided by competition (Humphreys, 1999). In this vein, inefficiencies and losses made by state-owned industries are evidence of market failure (Pirie, 1995). Privatisation is conventionally driven by the belief that private sector ownership is more efficient than public sector ownership (Haskel & Szymanski, 1991).

The evidence for these claims is uneven, with a decidedly mixed scorecard in a range of different settings and scales. There is some evidence for a turnaround in recent years toward more active state engagement, especially on environmental grounds (Docherty *et al.*, 2004). But the 'bandwagon' rolls on, and at all political levels, privatisation is increasingly favoured "in non-ideological terms, as a means of making scarce public resources go further" (Ross & Levine, 2005, p. 368).

The neo-liberalism impulse allied to globalisation first impacted on the aviation sector in the 1980s with the privatisation of some airlines. A second wave radiating from Britain was characterised by the privatisation of infrastructure (Gerber, 2002). Traditionally airports were owned directly by the state, and administered either through a government department or by a body appointed on its behalf such as a government business enterprise. While globally the majority of airports still have some form of public ownership, the level of operational control exercised by central government has been diminished by greater commercial involvement by private sector interests. Smith (1994) asserts that airport deregulation globally has been prompted primarily by governments' desire to reduce financial burdens associated with subsidising airport capital investment given that airports have traditionally competed with other areas of public expenditure such as health, education and defence. The introduction of private financial interests in airport operations is commonly portrayed as a more efficient and cost effective way for the state to maximise revenue, whilst maintaining or improving quality of service. The level of return is increased whilst simultaneously the degree of risk is reduced as the state draws upon a specialised set of management skills. Other perceived benefits of airport privatisation include increased customer orientation, provision of opportunities for private investment, widening of share ownership, and facilitation of business expansion and diversification (Graham, 2003). The modern airport and its environs are now seen as "a model for the ideal corporate city" (Gordon, 2004, p. 251).

The capital required to develop and profitably maintain an airport is generally generated from two sources: aeronautical charges and commercial revenues (Freathy & O'Connell, 1999). Airport operators levy aeronautical charges on airlines for the utilisation of facilities, including take-off and landing payments, apron charges and baggage handling fees. Aeronautical charges may be constrained either by the charges of competing airports or through legislative intervention. While deregulation of the aviation sector has compelled airlines to operate on limited margins by minimising fares, it has also led airports to exploit their monopoly powers for commercial advantage, leading to more frequent disputes between airports and the airlines. Confronted by rising costs through heightened pressure upon existing infrastructure and expectations of corporate shareholders, airport authorities have pursued complementary means of revenue generation. Non-aeronautical revenue is increasingly important in balancing the airport bottom line (Papagiorcopulo, 1994). Freathy & O'Connell (1999) argue that this pursuit of revenue generation from non-traditional sources feeds a cyclical process of market expansion (Figure 1).

Gerber (2002, p. 30) has argued that the initial privatisation of European airports saw a simultaneous transfer to the private sector and withdrawal by the state from "active regulatory participation". That is, privatisation went hand in hand with a more liberal regulatory environment whose negative impacts have led to a selective reassertion of state intervention (Docherty *et al.*, 2004). Privatisation has meant greater tensions between the environmental and commercial strategies of airport operators. The new commercially oriented focus can attract more vehicle movements, increase congestion and landside

494   *R. Freestone* et al.

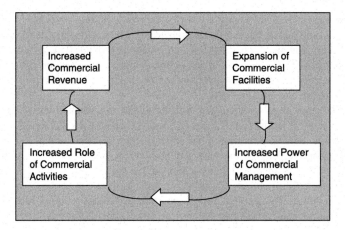

Figure 1. Airport commercial cycle. *Source:* Freathy & O'Connell (1999).

pollution, and other commercial and land use impacts (Marsh, 1991; Humphreys, 1999). With each new commercial development, there is a correlated augmentation in traffic flows and parking demands, direct economic impacts on competing retailers and other commercial operators especially within the vicinity of the airport, as well as other potential environmental and land use implications not always anticipated by local and regional planning strategies.

Privatisation of Australian Airports

In global terms, the Commonwealth Government was relatively slow to move towards the privatisation of airports, with a significant lag from the Thatcher era in Britain, but soon made up for it. The prelude was the corporatisation of airport management under the Federal Airports Corporation (Black, 1999) and by the time the Commonwealth had completed a second phase of airport lease sales in mid-1998, it had overseen what was to that time the world's largest completed airport trade sales program (ANOA, 1999).

Until the early 1940s, local communities bore the financial burden of developing and managing aerodromes. During World War II, the Commonwealth Government introduced maintenance grants for all aerodromes with regular passenger transport services. The demand for financial support increased significantly after cessation of hostilities as many airports became available for civil aviation operations. As Australian air traffic volumes grew, Commonwealth Government finance was mainly directed towards the busiest airports serving larger aircraft (Hooper *et al.*, 2000).

To temper the growing need for funding provision, in 1958 the Commonwealth Government introduced an Aerodrome Local Ownership Plan (ALOP) through which aerodromes serving a local rather than a national need were to be owned, developed, operated and maintained by local communities. The Government offered to transfer its aerodromes to local authorities free of charge, but with an agreement to pay half of the future approved maintenance and development costs for a stipulated limited time period. Despite the introduction of ALOP, over the next two decades the financial exposure of the Government grew significantly.

By the early 1980s, over 400 aerodromes were eligible for Commonwealth assistance, with the Government itself continuing to own 81 civil airports, including 12 operated by the Department of Defence. The Government subsequently set the objective of achieving full cost-recovery from the civil aviation sector, but an inquiry commissioned in 1982 calculated that only 55 per cent of costs were being recovered through aviation charges and other systemic problems within the administration of civil aviation were uncovered (Bosch *et al.*, 1984). The local ownership program was accelerated. By 1994 the Commonwealth had divested itself of the majority of Australian airports. The balance was transferred to a new body, the Federal Airports Corporation.

The Federal Airports Corporation (FAC) was a corporatised enterprise of the Commonwealth Government which commenced with 17 airports and an asset base of $1.27 billion on 1 January 1988. A further six airports were added in April 1989. The creation of the FAC occurred amidst a national program of wide-ranging micro-economic reform driven by the Hawke Labor Government. Registering the impact of neo-liberal thinking, the corporatised model afforded the administrators of airports greater commercial freedom, emulating governance, management and incentive systems employed in the private sector. The FAC had to earn a reasonable rate of return and pay dividends to the Government. It was responsible for airport operations, including terminal facilities and other commercial services, but did not include air traffic control. To protect the public interest, residual powers were reserved for the Minister for Transport to direct FAC to perform certain functions as required.

Major Australian airports recorded an impressive record of growth and profitability during the 1990s. In the five years to 1996–97, revenue per employee for all FAC airports increased by more than 54 per cent. Despite the onset of the Asian economic crisis in the middle of 1997, there was further growth across all airports in 1997–98 related mainly to increases in the number of passengers and landed tonnes. Total local passenger throughput for all FAC airports between 1987–88 and 1996–97 grew at an average annual rate of 7.8 per cent. Airports with above-average growth such as Brisbane and Perth were becoming important international gateways as Australia's popularity as a long-haul tourist destination increased. As a group, the airports serving domestic traffic grew at the slowest rate, though these were still buoyant markets over the long term (Hooper *et al.*, 2000). Aircraft movements grew at a lesser rate as larger aircraft assumed greater importance, so that landed tonnes improved in comparison with passenger numbers. Even more dramatically, the amount of landed tonnes in Sydney, Brisbane and Perth airports increased at a higher rate than passenger numbers.

When the FAC was incorporated, one of its chief aims was to keep aeronautical passenger and freight charges to a minimum, to be achieved by maximising income from other sources. Following this approach, FAC airports collectively earned a surplus before depreciation, interest and taxes of $415 million in 1996–97 (Hooper *et al.*, 2000). Some of the general aviation and smaller domestic airports did not share as fully in the growth and profits of the period, but the income-generation potential of airports was resoundingly confirmed (Table 1).

Despite or in fact because of the performance of the FAC, debate continued about the merits of comprehensively privatising major Australian airports (Mills, 1995). One event that influenced community opinion was a public inquiry into FAC charges. It had been general practice to set uniform, weight-based prices for aeronautical services for all airports, however, congestion charges were permissible at Sydney Airport as a management device.

496   *R. Freestone* et al.

Table 1. Profitability of FAC airports: 1996–97 ($000 at 1998–99 values)

Airport	Total revenue	Operating	EBDIT[a]	Assets
Sydney	251 621	81 082	170 568	1 246 927
Melbourne	128 994	42 151	85 986	487 654
Brisbane	108 102	30 017	78 083	544 640
Perth	53 763	18 459	35 305	223 487
Adelaide	28 552	11 708	16 844	4600
Darwin	8717	4767	3951	71 763
Hobart	5543	2837	2705	13 883
Canberra	8094	3614	4479	51 652
All FAC airports[b]	635 176	220 116	414 741	3 151 368

[a]EBDIT = earnings before depreciation, interest and taxes.
[b]All FAC airports = all capital city airports plus Coolangatta, Bankstown, Camden, Hoxton Park, Townsville, Alice Springs, Tennant Creek, Launceston, Essendon, Parafield, Moorabbin, Jandakot, Archerfield and Mount Isa.
Source: Adapted from FAC Annual Report 1996–97 in Hooper *et al.* (2000).

An FAC announcement in September 1992 that it intended to increase prices triggered a public inquiry by the Prices Surveillance Authority (PSA), later the Australian Competition and Consumer Commission (PSA, 1993). An important recommendation to emerge from the inquiry was that each airport should set its own fees and that cross-subsidisation between airports should cease. This brought into question whether there were any advantages from operating the airports as a system. The PSA report recommended a wide agenda for the reform of airport management, including adoption of more efficient pricing structures, improved management information systems, revaluation of FAC assets to reflect earning potential, and improved internal economic and financial appraisal of investment proposals (Hooper *et al.*, 2000).

The completion of the PSA inquiry coincided with a decisive shift in Commonwealth Government policy towards privatisation of government business enterprises. Competition in the management of airports was seen as leading to efficiency gains and sale proceeds could reduce government debt. After wide-ranging debate inside and outside parliament, the Keating Labor Government eventually resolved Caucus objections to privatisation of the airports and the stage was set for a new era in airport management and regulation.

The proposed sale of Commonwealth airport leaseholds was first unveiled in the 1994–95 Commonwealth budget. The Government subsequently announced that the leasing of airports would be conducted in two competitive rounds (SRRATC, 2000). New legislation was needed to enable assets vested in the FAC to be transferred back to the Government to enable the granting of long-term private leases. The Government introduced the draft legislation that initiated privatisation—the Airports Bill 1995—into the House of Representatives on 27 September 1995. The passage through Parliament was delayed because of a Federal election. Although the new John Howard-led Liberal–National Party Coalition Government had opposed certain aspects of the bill while in opposition, as a measure of strong bipartisan support for privatisation policy at the federal level, it moved ahead with the legislation and the *Airports Act* was assented to on 9 October 1996 (Hooper *et al.*, 2000). Although the main aim in the sale of FAC airports was the maximisation of net proceeds from the sale, several conditions and obligations had to be met by each successful airport bidder. The Government set a number of restrictions on ownership by 'airport-operator companies'. Specifically these restrictions required: (a) a 49 per cent limit on foreign ownership; (b) a 5 per cent limit on airline ownership; (c) a 15 per cent limit on cross-ownership for Sydney/Melbourne, Sydney/Brisbane and Sydney/Perth airports; and (d) a majority of the directors of an airport operator company to be Australian citizens or residents.

Finalisation of the privatisation process was a protracted procedure and preliminary preparations lasted 16 months. A public tender process was followed in two stages between 1996 and 1998. Expressions of interest were invited for the first round of sales (Phase 1)— Melbourne, Brisbane and Perth airports—in September 1996. Apart from Sydney, these three airports were regarded as the most valuable assets because of their relative size, strategic importance and commercial profit potential (ANOA, 1999). The Government announced the three winning bids in May 1997. Net proceeds of $2.22 billion had been allowed for in budget estimates, but this first round of sales alone netted $3.36 billion.

In June 1997 the Government announced that it would sell a further 15 FAC airports. Of the 15 airports in the second round of sales only Essendon Airport in Melbourne failed to attract an acceptable offer. It was subsequently withdrawn from sale and later established as a stand-alone company before being eventually sold in 2001 to Becton and logistics conglomerate Linfox. When the Phase 2 negotiations were completed, the Australian Government had received a further $740.5 million from nine different consortia (Table 2). The new owners were typically consortia of foreign airports, merchant banks, investment funds and property developers. For example, Adelaide and Parafield airports were acquired by the MSUM consortium comprising Macquarie Bank, Manchester Airport, Serco Australia, UniSuper, Local Government Superannuation Board, Legal and General Financial Services, John Laing Investment, National Australia Bank Asset Management and Hansen Yuncken Pty Ltd. Cross-ownership of some airports was permitted in the Phase 2 sales, though cross-ownership restrictions existed between Brisbane and Coolangatta; Hobart and Launceston; and Melbourne and Adelaide (ANOA, 1999).

Table 2. Australian airport leasehold sales 1996–98

Airport	Consortium	Sale ($ million 1998–99)
Adelaide, Parafield	MSUM	369.7
Archerfield	Archerfield Airport Corporation P/L	3.0
Brisbane	Australia Pacific Airports Corporation	1402.1
Canberra	Capital Airports Group	67.0
Coolangatta	Queensland Airports Group	105.2
Darwin, Alice Springs, Tennant Creek	Airport Development Group	110.3
Hobart	Hobart International Airports Corporation	36.2
Jandakot	Jandakot Airport Holdings	7.2
Launceston	Australia Pacific Airports (Launceston) P/L	17.3
Melbourne	Australia Pacific Airports Corporation	1312.9
Moorabbin	Moorabbin Airport Corporation P/L	8.1
Perth	Australia Development Group	649.8
Townsville, Mt. Isa	Australian Airports P/L	16.5

Source: Adapted from Hooper *et al.* (2000).

498   *R. Freestone* et al.

The sale of Sydney Airport proceeded outside and after the two-phase national campaign. Sydney is unlike the other airports because of its capacity constraints inhibiting ready expansion, airside or landside (Forsyth, 2002). Its sale was delayed initially by the approach of the 2000 Olympic Games and subsequently by 9/11 and the collapse of Ansett Airlines, both in the same week of 2001, as well as uncertainty about a second airport in the Sydney region. These were all cumulative risk factors making "the financial results of privatisation problematic" (Forsyth, 2003, p. 33). The airport was eventually sold in June 2002 to Macquarie Bank for $5.6 billion, more than all the other airports combined.

The Government's windfall profit was underpinned by at least three factors (Hooper *et al.*, 2000). One was the unprecedented opportunity being presented to purchase international airports. Second was the significant degree of local monopoly power enjoyed by airports. And third was successful bidders' expectation of future commercial development (Powell, 2003). In this regard, the Government had been advised that there was significant 'hidden' value potential and the marketing campaign highlighted investment opportunities presented by each airport (ANOA, 1999). Its sales team emphasised the potential for increased revenue outside the cap on aeronautical products from property development, car parking and other commercial initiatives (Hooper *et al.*, 2000). Adding to the attractiveness was the drafting of airport leases favourable to lessees with conditions effectively equating with freehold property rights (ANOA, 1999).

The Governance of Airports

Under the Australian Constitution, the legislative framework for the operation and management of major airports on Commonwealth land falls chiefly under Commonwealth law. The *Airports Act 1996* established the chief regulatory framework that would apply to airports after sales were completed. Some consideration was given to outright freehold sales of airports, especially in Phase 2. However, state and territory governments were not ready to provide the necessary legislative and policy support and the Government decided to continue with the leasehold sale approach (ANOA, 1999). Leasing of airports rather than outright sale was an absolutely crucial decision because it meant that planning approvals would remain under federal jurisdiction.

In addition to the *Airports Act*, other Commonwealth Acts and Regulations have specific implications on the planning and development of airports across Australia, including the *Environment Protection and Biodiversity Conservation Act 1999* ('the EPBC Act'). Several key stakeholders have regulatory roles, notably the Department of Transport and Regional Services (DOTARS), Department of Environment and Heritage (DEH), individual Airport Building Controllers and the relevant privatised corporate entity at each major airport known as the Airport Lessee Company (ALC).

The Airport and Regulation Branch of DOTARS is the Commonwealth Government administrative unit responsible for the development of policies intended to protect community interests in the operation of airports and air transport services. Alongside its responsibilities in respect of aircraft operations, DOTARS is also charged with the role of the continued development and implementation of the Commonwealth environment and building control regulatory regime for leased airports. The Department regards this responsibility as "aiming to balance the public interest and private sector objectives" (DOTARS, 2005). Under the provisions of the *Airports Act*, DOTARS is responsible for administration of airport leases as well as the oversight and enforcement of Airport Building Controller and Airport Environment Officer decisions.

Under the *Airports Act* an Airport Environment Strategy is required for each privatised airport subject to a long-term lease. Under the EPBC Act, assessment and approval is required for any actions likely to have a significant impact on a matter of national environmental significance, the environment of Commonwealth land (even if taken outside Commonwealth land), and the environment anywhere in the world (if the action is undertaken by the Commonwealth). When a person proposes to take an action that they believe may need approval under the EPBC Act, they must refer the proposal to the Commonwealth Minister for the Environment. DOTARS is required to refer all major development plans to the DEH under section 160 of the EPBC Act and informally may seek DEH comments on master plans submitted for approval.

Construction and building activities at leased Commonwealth airports, which do not trigger the need for a major development plan must be approved by the Airport Building Controller (ABC) appointed at each airport. Each ABC is appointed through an open tender selection process administered by DOTARS. The ABC for an airport may be a Commonwealth or State authority, a local government body, an individual or private organisation. The majority of ABCs have tended to be private organisations with multidisciplinary expertise in environmental management, surveying, engineering, planning and building. The ABC is responsible for administering the airport building control regime and ensuring that activities at leased airports meet appropriate building and engineering standards (primarily the Building Code of Australia).

The specific process for the approval of building and construction activities is set out in the *Airports (Building Control) Regulations 1996*. Activities requiring building approval by the ABC may include new buildings, terminals, hangars, shop fit-outs, demolition and civil works including runways, taxiways, roads and drains. An application for a building approval may be made either by the ALC or their representative or a sub-lessee or a person on their behalf. Pivotal to the building approval process is the consent role of an ALC. If the applicant for a building approval is a sub-lessee, they must secure consent of the ALC. If written notice of the ALC's decision has not been given to an applicant within four weeks, consent is taken to have been refused. The Regulations provide for appeals by applicants seeking a building approval to the Commonwealth Administrative Appeals Tribunal.

Major Planning and Development Assessment

Two key features of the airport planning approvals process are master plans and major development plans. Under section 75 of the *Airports Act*, when an ALC acquires or is granted an airport lease (and a final master plan for the airport is not in force at the time of acquisition) the company must provide the Federal Minister for Transport with a draft master plan within 12 months. A master plan is a long-term land use plan for the whole of an airport site and deals with broader indicative intentions, rather than individual projects in any detail. The master plan is required, under the *Airports Act*, to relate to a period of 20 years and it must be updated every five years (SRRATC, 2000). Most of the leased airports covered by the *Airports Act* have had to complete master plan reviews in the last two years.

The master plan is a strategic policy document setting out the airport's agenda for current and future airport management and development. Section 71 of the *Airports Act* lists matters that must be included in a draft master plan for an airport, including the ALC's

500   *R. Freestone* et al.

assessment of future needs of civil aviation and other users of the airport for services and facilities. Under section 79, before submitting a draft master plan to the Minister, the airport must undertake a formal 90-day public consultation process. Details of the public consultation undertaken, submissions received and details of consultation undertaken by the ALC prior to the formal public consultation period must be included in the draft master plan lodged with the Minister.

Approval of a master plan does not represent approval to build any specific major development referred to in the master plan. Major development applications must be separately approved. A separate major development plan (MDP) is required for each development that is defined as 'major' by section 89 of the *Airports Act*. This is an extensive definition, and includes development such as constructing a new runway or extending an existing one; constructing a new building wholly or principally for use as a passenger terminal where the building's gross floor area is greater than 500 m^2; constructing a new building not used wholly or principally as a passenger terminal, whose construction cost exceeds $10 million; and development of a kind that is likely to have a significant environmental or ecological impact.

The *Airports Act* prevents the Minister for Transport from approving an MDP where it is inconsistent with a master plan. Under section 69 of the *Airports Act*, an MDP must consider a number of relevant matters comparable to those addressed by the master plan. An MDP provides the detailed analysis of a specific development proposal including the identification and assessment of economic, social and environmental impacts and how these might be managed. Approval of an MDP by the Minister for Transport is based on assessment of the airport's development needs, airport carrying capacity, environmental impacts, proposed noise amelioration measures, community consultation, safety and other considerations relevant to the development at the time it is put forward for consideration. The public accountability reporting requirements are identical with the master planning process.

In several respects, the new planning requirements are a significant advance on the evaluation and approval framework provided for under the former *Federal Airports Corporation Act 1986* and the *Federal Airports Corporation Regulations 1992*. The FAC operated largely as a self-regulating government authority in respect of land use, planning and building decisions. As John Sharp, Minister for Transport and Regional Development, said in his second reading speech on the *Airports Act* on 23 May 1996, these responsibilities had to be assumed by the Commonwealth itself to ensure appropriate public interest regulation of the activities of airport lessees and other users (*House of Representatives Hansard*, 23 May 1996). The regime under the current *Airports Act*, at least for the airport operators, is more onerous, strategic and consultative with its requirements for master plans, major development plans, environmental management plans, independent building inspections and public consultation provisions. The planning regime for airport development certainly enshrines ultimate responsibility for major development with the Federal Minister for Transport.

At the same time, the provisions of the *Airports Act* set a relatively high bar in monetary terms for defining major development and bestow considerable autonomy on the part of the Airport Lessee Company. Privatisation has meant privatisation of airport building and construction approvals and ALCs appear to have considerable powers to the point of self-regulation. Master plans are generalised and hence rather flexible statements of intent, 'consultation' effectively can mean the mere provision of information, and off-site impacts are not a mandatory consideration in development decisions.

For all its internal requirements, checks and balances, the *Airports Act* also quarantines all development from local and state planning scrutiny. Section 112 explicitly excludes airport operations from any law of a State or Territory relating to land use planning. The old FAC legislation held that development not directly related to aviation should proceed only if allowed by State or Territory legislation applied as "if the land were not in a Federal airport". Under the *Airports Act*, a master plan must describe proposals in detail equivalent to that required by relevant state legislation and address the extent of any consistency with local planning schemes, but need do no more. State and Territory laws with respect to building approvals and planning have no effect on leased Commonwealth airports, except as they pertain to the registration of builders and other construction professionals, builder insurance, occupational health and safety, and fire safety (DOTARS, 2005).

Major Commercial Development

The commercial significance of airports was first seriously exploited by the FAC. One of the major manifestations was the expansion of retailing in terminals and the attempt to sell airports as leisure destinations in their own right. With privatisation since the late 1990s has come an expanded campaign of commercial development as ALCs have sought to maximise and diversify non-aeronautical revenue streams (Figure 2). The governance regime under privatisation has facilitated this process. Section 32 of the *Airports Act* prohibits an airport operator from carrying on substantial trading or financial activities other than activities relating or incidental to the operation and/or development of the airport. This provision has not prevented escalation of commercial proposals.

At May 2005 some 2837 hectares, constituting 16 per cent of total major airport lands, was dedicated under airport master plans to non-aeronautical uses (Table 3). Non-aeronautical uses represented about one-third of total proposed land use at Brisbane (36 per cent) and Perth (33 per cent) airports. Between 1996 and mid-2005, the Minister approved 19 MDPs for development at former FAC airports under the *Airports Act*. Of these 19 approvals, 12 were for non-aeronautical uses, and comprised bulky goods retailing, factory retail outlets, warehousing and distribution centres, commercial offices and car parking facilities. These figures translate to sizeable impacts, existing and proposed. The Adelaide approval relates to a \$40 million, 24 000 m^2, two-storey IKEA store at the entrance to the airport on Sir Donald Bradman Drive (*The Advertiser*, 7 May 2005). At Brisbane airport, the Brisbane Airport Corporation has developed a \$25 million, 100-outlet direct factory outlet complex (Figure 3). In Sydney there are plans for an additional 240 000 m^2 of general office, commercial and retail development. Max Moore-Wilton, when chief executive of the Sydney Airport Corporation (having previously been head of John Howard's Department of the Prime Minister and Cabinet) foresaw a whole raft of new development, from a cash-and-carry warehouse to "service stations, car-servicing facilities, motels, hotels" (*Sydney Morning Herald, Sydney Magazine*, September 2005).

Concerns about Commodification of Airport Land

Historically, airports have been one of the most contentious urban land uses in Australia and their emergence as commercial activity zones under a unique governance regime

502   *R. Freestone* et al.

Figure 2. Advertising commercial development opportunities at Sydney Airport. *Source:* Aaron Bowden.

perpetuates this status into the early 21st century. While there is widespread agreement about the importance of airports as portals for general economic growth under globalisation, considerable disquiet has been expressed on the specific issue of non-aeronautical commercial developments by diverse interests, notably state government,

Table 3. Major commercial developments at Australian airports 2001–2005

Airport	Area (ha)	Devt. area (ha)[a]	Approved major development plans
Adelaide	1569	51 (3%)	IKEA Store (2004)
Brisbane	2700	970 (36%)	Qantas Aircraft Maintenance Base (2001)
			Virgin Blue Aircraft Maintenance Facility (2003)
			Outlet Centre Development (2003)
			Parallel Runway Project (2005)
Canberra	437	12 (3%)	Terminal extension (2003)
			Runway and taxiway expansion (2003)
Essendon	305	12 (4%)	Retail and outlet centre (2003)
Gold Coast	385	40 (10%)	Extension of Common User Terminal (2001)
			Runway Extension Project (2003)
Melbourne	2369	350 (15%)	Office Accommodation (2001)
			Multi-level Car Park (2001)
			Australia Post Int'l Mail Sorting Facility (2003)
			Landside Road Office Development (2004)
Parafield	437	17 (4%)	Urban and commercial redevelopment (2003)
			Major distribution centre (2003)
Perth	2105	700 (33%)	Warehouse and Distribution Park (2003)
Sydney	905	95 (11%)	Office buildings (2001)
			Car Park and Commercial Facilities (2004)

[a]Total non-airside development approved under each respective airport master plan.
Source: Information from DOTARS and airport master plans.

Figure 3. Direct Factory Outlet at No. 1 Airport Drive Shopping Village, Brisbane Airport. *Source:* Jill Freestone.

local councils and council coalitions, local business, commercial industry groups and environmental groups. We classify and discuss concerns about non-aeronautical development under five interrelated headings:

- Constitutionality of Commonwealth protection
- Unfair competition
- Metropolitan form
- Impact on infrastructure
- Provisions of the *Airports Act*.

The constitutional argument—arguably more rhetorical than legal—questions the validity of the Commonwealth effectively transferring the privileges of its status (notably exemptions from state planning controls and local rates) to private enterprise. The Australian Mayoral Aviation Council holds this position, arguing that as airports diversify more and more away from their main function—aviation—the Commonwealth shield is less and less defensible (*Weekend Australian*, 23–24 April 2005).

The cocooning of development has led to charges of unfair competition and denials of natural justice, and calls for a 'level playing field' (Scott, 2005). There is concern that the various planning and other controls which apply to regular business operations do not apply to airport businesses, thereby bestowing an unfair competitive advantage. The Shopping Centre Council of Australia, an industry lobby group backed by powerful players like Westfield, has made submissions on master plans across Australia but with singular lack of success. Airport developers are able to produce reports that indicate no significant economic impact on existing retail hierarchies.

In relation to metropolitan form, a major concern is that airports through diversification and escalation of mixed use activity are transforming themselves into general activity centres of a kind similar to those identified by centres policies but by an entirely different process and divorced from wider planning concerns such as feasible public transport

504   R. Freestone et al.

access. Employment location policies are potentially affected. Sydney Lord Mayor Clover Moore argues that Sydney Airport is being turned incrementally by stealth into a commercial precinct half the size of Parramatta (Sandilands, 2005).

State government concerns relate to impact on infrastructure capacity, particularly congested roads. Because the *Airports Act* excises development from state planning laws, airport developers are not liable for any development contributions. The NSW Roads and Traffic Authority has estimated that the expansion of retail and commercial business at Sydney Airport in line with the master plan would generate thousands of extra vehicles requiring expenditure of $2.7 billion over 20 years, through additional lanes having to be added to motorways (*Sydney Morning Herald*, 6 January 2006). The analogy of airports as special precincts akin to the Vatican City has been made (*Independent Weekly*, Adelaide, 10 April 2005).

The provisions of the *Airports Act* itself have been questioned from 'best practice' perspectives. Master plans have been criticised as 'wish lists' with many different broad land use scenarios built in to ensure that most future development options will be consistent. A pervasive concern has been that the consultation provisions are inadequate for effective input into decision-making. 'Consultation' under the Act can effectively mean the mere provision of information and soliciting of submissions. Submissions on draft master plans are lodged with the ALC and not with DOTARS or the Minister. The legislation contains no appeal rights, moreover its deemed approval provisions mean that if a draft MDP is not determined within 90 days of submission, then it is deemed to be approved, a stark contrast to equivalent provisions under state legislation. The definition of 'major' development offers considerable discretion. Critics argue that the $10 million threshold for major development is too high, because it enables airports to segment major developments into smaller, cheaper components which can avoid the need for an MDP. Some critics see the prospect of Commonwealth land becoming safe havens for non-aeronautical land uses unwelcome and unwanted elsewhere (*Sydney Morning Herald*, 2 January 2006).

Best practice, equity, sustainability, professional critiques and industry submissions have counted for little to date. High Court challenges have been mooted by both Sydney councils and a national coalition of local governments, but none has yet eventuated. The one major legal action to date was a Federal Court case by property interests led by Westfield against the Brisbane Airports Corporation plan for a bulky goods retail outlet and other facilities. The airport won the case in February 2005. The Court held that section 32 of the Act gave the airport great discretion for commercial and other development. In April 2005 a coalition of local Sydney mayors organised a public rally at Tempe Reserve in a plea to "stop overdevelopment of Sydney Airport". The protest was only modestly attended suggesting that, amongst the general public, the prospect of greater opportunities to shop actually carried more weight than any environmental disbenefits (Figure 4). However, a storm of protest early in 2006 over Sydney Airport's plan to develop either a retail precinct with cinemas or a retail business park with offices has reportedly led to a scaling back of intentions. The NSW Government led opposition, mounting various arguments including the projected impact on road infrastructure, threats to the commercial viability of established and emerging centres nearby, inconsistency with centres policies, vulnerability to terrorism and concern at the development of land potentially needed for aviation purposes (NSW Government, 2006).

Interestingly, the major airlines have to date made little or no public comment. The overseas experience is that provided there are no immediate or long-term impacts on

Figure 4. Advertising an anti-commercial expansion rally at Sydney Airport, March 2005. *Source:* Rally flier, Coalition of Mayors Surrounding Sydney Airport.

aircraft operations, any development which might keep down the aeronautical charges levied on them is usually welcomed (Graham, 2003). This situation may change if more aggressive entrepreneurial activities were seen as compromising core airport operations. There has certainly been concern expressed that ALCs of smaller airports in the Sydney basin may be more interested in non-aeronautical opportunities than aeronautical needs, as witnessed by the closure of an entire runway at Bankstown, rising rents or non-renewal or leases for smaller aviation-related operators, and the projected closure of the Hoxton Park aerodrome in 2008 (*Sydney Morning Herald*, 4–5 March 2006).

Conclusion

The global trend towards privatisation of public transport infrastructure particularly in the field of aviation is now having major impacts on Australian airports. One impact has been the expansion of non-aeronautical business activity. A caricature of the modern British

506   *R. Freestone* et al.

airport is "a runway with a shopping mall beside it" (Graham & Guyer, 2000, p. 253) and the same trend is evident in Australia. As business operations seeking profit-making opportunities to repay large capital investments, privatised airports have sought to exploit their land assets for commercial and business development. Such development also provides a buffer against the vicissitudes of airline traffic, although despite setbacks such as 9/11 the trend seems inexorably upward. All capital city airports now boast businesses and facilities which attract both non-passenger customers and non-aviation industries.

These trends exemplify the trajectory of government policies informed by the agenda of neo-liberalism. At one level, the seeming pro-development bias of the current approvals regime illustrates Gleeson and Low's (2000, p. 138) concern at how planning is being reconstructed and redeployed as "a market dynamic in itself". As the outcome of Commonwealth Government policy-making, Troy regards airport development as one of the more 'egregious examples' of a continuing failure to consider urban issues at the national level (Troy, 2005). The approach of this article has been to show how existing planning controls under federal law provide a relatively benign environment which has facilitated a significant expansion of commercial development at Australian airports. The process has not been uncontested with growing industry, political, media and community angst across Australia.

The benign planning framework is the inevitable product of the Commonwealth seeking to maximise its return when the airports were originally privatised. This occurred in the late 1990s during an era where neo-liberal economic rationalism began to dominate and unite national and state fiscal and economic policy across the party political spectrum. The sale of airports to private consortia was ultimately just one of a series of government moves to privatise service delivery across many sectors of the economy (*vide*, Commonwealth Bank, Telstra, Qantas, AWB, etc.). When speaking in Parliament to the Airports Bill in 1996, the Minister for Transport stressed the importance of enabling airports to better serve their specific regional markets and offering them 'greater autonomy' to do so (*House of Representatives Hansard*, 23 May 1996). This required more "clarity and certainty on processes which allow government and community input". It was unlikely that the Government would have instituted a regime to compromise these aspirations, which introducing the uncertain reach of variable state and local planning laws would almost certainly have done. Guaranteeing a 'level playing field' also ensured maximum returns through the sales process. The Commonwealth presumably anticipated that it had more to gain by selling the airports with 'no strings attached' than by trying to make money through the operation of airports over the long term. Following overseas precedent, prospective operators would have also approached the privatisation process interested in the high returns on investment, entrepreneurial freedom and long-term planning security (Gerber, 2002).

In the current economic climate, the argument is not that privatisation is always bad and that non-aeronautical commercial developments in all cases are prima facie completely unacceptable. Rather, the lack of congruence across federal, state and local planning regimes is the main concern, especially whereby airport developments are legally excused from making any contributions to the upgrading of infrastructure to address wider regional impacts.

Selective and strategic reforms to the *Airports Act* might address some concerns, including insertion of concurrence provisions, prescription of minimum consultation standards, 'stop-the-clock' mechanisms to ensure due diligence, and requiring airport specific developer contributions (Bowden, 2005). These changes are unlikely. The Minister for Transport has publicly re-committed the Commonwealth Government to supporting a single regime to control airport planning and land use. A Senate Inquiry on the *Airports Act* initiated in 2002 has still yet to formally report at the time of writing (April 2006). The key outcomes foreshadowed appear to be an affirmation of present arrangements under privatisation with minor amendments to further streamline non-aviation development approvals through amendments to section 32, increasing the threshold for major development to $20 million, and actually cutting back periods for public comment on master plans and major development plans (Truss, 2005). The planning impacts of airport privatisation are likely to be an ongoing topic of public debate.

Acknowledgements

Research for this article was initiated under the UNSW Faculty of the Built Environment Research Link Program. An earlier version was presented to the 2nd State of the Australian Cities Conference in Brisbane in November–December 2005. The authors would like to thank Christine Garnaut, Anne Graham, Phil McDermott, and Pat Troy for sharing their perspectives and two anonymous referees for their critiques. Erin Cann of DOTARS and Lachlan Wilkinson of DEH responded to information requests but the findings of this article do not represent either their views or those of their departments.

References

ANOA (Australian National Audit Office) (1999) *Phase 2 of the Sales of Federal Airports* (Canberra: Commonwealth of Australia).

Bishop, M., Kay, J. & Mayer, C. (1994) Privatisation in performance, in: M. Bishop, J. Kay & C. Mayer (Eds) *Privatisation and Economic Performance* (Oxford: Oxford University Press).

Black, J. (1999) The provision of transport services, in: P. Troy (Ed.) *Serving the City: The Crisis in Australia's Urban Services*, pp. 80–105 (Sydney: Pluto Press).

Bosch, H., Hudson, H. & Linehan, D. (1984) *Independent Inquiry into Aviation Cost Recovery* (Canberra: Australian Government Publishing Service).

Bowden, A. (2005) Planning across the airport fence: a study of the impacts of non-aeronautical development of major Australian airports, BPlan Thesis, University of New South Wales.

Docherty, I., Shaw, J. & Gather, M. (2004) State intervention in contemporary transport, *Journal of Transport Geography*, 12, pp. 257–264.

DOTARS (Department of Transport and Regional Services) (2005) *Department of Transport and Regional Services* (Online). Available at www.dotars.gov.au (accessed December 2005).

Forsyth, P. (2002) Privatisation and regulation of Australian and New Zealand airports, *Journal of Air Transport Management*, 8, pp. 19–28.

Forsyth, P. (2003) Regulation under stress: developments in Australian airport policy, *Journal of Air Transport Management*, 9, pp. 25–35.

Freathy, P. & O'Connell, F. (1999) Planning for profit: the commercialisation of European airports, *Long Range Planning*, 32, pp. 587–597.

Gerber, P. (2002) Success factors for the privatisation of airports—an airline perspective, *Journal of Air Transport Management*, 8, pp. 29–36.

Gleeson, B. & Low, N. (2000) Revaluing planning: rolling back neo-liberalism in Australia, *Progress in Planning*, 53, pp. 83–164.

Gordon, A. (2004) *Naked Airport: A Cultural History of the World's Most Revolutionary Structure* (New York: H. Holt).

Graham, A. (2003) *Managing Airports: An International Perspective* (Oxford: Butterworth Heinemann).

Graham, B. & Guyer, C. (2000) The role of regional airports and air services in the United Kingdom, *Journal of Transport Geography*, 8, pp. 249–262.

Haskel, J. & Szymanski, S. (1991) Privatisation, jobs and wages, *Employment Institute Economic Report*, 6(7) (London: Economic Institute).

508   *R. Freestone* et al.

Hayward, D. (1997) The privatised city: urban infrastructure, planning and service provision in the era of privatisation, *Urban Policy and Research*, 15(1), pp. 55–58.

Hooper, P., Cain, R. & White, S. (2000) The privatisation of Australia's airports, *Transportation Research, Part E*, 36, pp. 181–204.

Humphreys, I. (1999) Privatisation and commercialisation: changes in UK airport ownership patterns, *Journal of Transport Geography*, 7, pp. 121–134.

Kasarda, J. D. (2000) Aerotropolis: airport-driven urban development, *ULI on the Future: Cities in the 21st Century*, pp. 32–41 (Washington: Urban Land Institute).

Marsh, D. (1991) Privatisation under Mrs Thatcher: a review of the literature, *Public Administration*, 69, pp. 459–480.

Mills, G. (1995) Airport users don't pay enough—and now here's privatisation, *Economic Papers*, 14(1), pp. 73–84.

NSW Government (2006) *Submission to the Preliminary Major Development Plan. Sydney Airport* (Sydney: NSW Department of Planning).

O'Neill, P. & Argent, N. (2005) Neoliberalism in Antipodean spaces and times, *Geographical Research*, 43, pp. 2–8.

Papagiorcopulo, G. (1994) The importance of non-aviation revenues to a small airport, *Commercial Airport 1994/95* (London: Stirling Publications).

Peck, J. & Tickell, A. (2002) Neoliberalizing space, *Antipode*, 34, pp. 380–404.

Pirie, M. (1995) Reasons for privatisation, in: P. Morgan (Ed.) *Privatisation and the Welfare State: Implications for Consumers and the Workforce* (Aldershot: Dartmouth).

Powell, T. (2003) *Planning, Economic Development and Canberra Airport* (Canberra: Capital Airport Group).

PSA (Prices Surveillance Authority) (1993) *Inquiry into the Aeronautical and Non-Aeronautical Charges of the Federal Airports Corporation* (Melbourne: Commonwealth of Australia).

Ross, B. H. & Levine, M. A. (2005) Privatization, in: R. Caves (Ed.) *Encyclopedia of the City*, pp. 366–368 (New York: Routledge).

Sandilands, B. (2005) Airport developments under fire, *Aircraft and Aerospace*, July pp. 25–27.

Scott, A. (2005) Building on a level playing field, Address to the Australian Mayoral Aviation Council. Shopping Centre Council of Australia.

Self, P. (1993) *Governance by the Market: The Politics of Public Choice* (London: Macmillan).

Smith, C. (1994) *Airport Industry Structure: The Trend towards Commercialisation* (London: Coopers & Lybrand).

SRRATC (Senate Rural and Regional Affairs and Transport Committee) (2000) *Report on the Inquiry into the Development of the Brisbane Airport Corporation*, Senate Committee Report tabled June 2000 (Canberra: Commonwealth of Australia).

Troy, P. (2005) Opening address to the 2nd State of the Australian Cities Conference, Griffith University, Brisbane, November–December.

Truss, W. (2005) Review confirms privatised airports regime is working. Media Release, Minister for Transport and Regional Services, 14 November.

Part II:

Efficiency

7

Ownership forms matter for airport efficiency: A stochastic frontier investigation of worldwide airports

Tae H. Oum, Jia Yan, Chunyan Yu

Abstract

We study the effects of ownership forms on airports' cost efficiency by applying stochastic frontier analysis to a panel data of the world's major airports. Our key findings are: (a) Countries considering privatization of airports should transfer majority shares to the private sector; (b) Mixed ownership of airport with a government majority should be avoided in favor of even 100% government owned public firm; (c) US airports operated by port authorities should consider to transfer ownership/management to independent airport authorities; and (d) Privatization of one or more airports in cities with multiple airports would improve the efficiency of all airports.
© 2008 Elsevier Inc. All rights reserved.

JEL classification: H11; D24; C11

Keywords: Ownership forms; Airports; *Translog* cost system; Stochastic frontier; Bayesian approach

1. Introduction

An airport links local industries and residents to new markets, products, customers, relatives and friends around the world, making it a critical component of a region's trade and commerce with other regions and countries.[1] An efficient airport provides important economic catalysts that enable the local and regional economy to thrive and improve the quality of life in the region. Governments around the world have taken measures to privatize and/or commercialize airports for various purposes including for access to private sector financing for capacity expansion and improvement of economic efficiency and productivity of airport operations. Although different ownership forms and institutional arrangements (henceforth referred

to as "ownership forms") have been adopted in different countries over the last two decades, there has been a lack of rigorous econometric evidence for the effects of various ownership forms on improving airport efficiency. This paper attempts to help fill this gap in the literature by developing an advanced form of stochastic frontier model to investigate how different ownership forms affect airport efficiency by applying it to an extensive panel data of worldwide airports.

Major airports around the world were traditionally owned and operated by national or local governments. However, starting with the privatization of the three airports in London (Heathrow, Gatwick, and Stansted) and four other major airports in the UK to British Airport Authority (BAA plc) in 1987, the role of the governments in airport ownership and management has been changing significantly over time. Many countries have introduced various forms of private sector involvement to the ownership/management of airports. For example, Rome's Leonardo Da Vinci Airport is now fully privatized, and the majority stakes of Copenhagen Kastrup International Airport, Vienna International Airport, and Brussels International Air-

---

[1] Bruckner (2003) provides some empirical evidence on the link between airline traffic and employment in US metropolitan areas.

T.H. Oum et al. / Journal of Urban Economics 64 (2008) 422–435   423

port have been sold to private and institutional shareholders. All major Australian airports have been privatized while majority stakes of Wellington International Airports in New Zealand have been privatized. In Asia, Mumbai and New Delhi airports in India have been privatized, whereas minority stakes of Beijing Capital International Airport, Shanghai Pudong Airport, Malaysia Airports Holdings Bhd, etc., have been sold to private investors. Tokyo's Narita International Airport was corporatized in 2003 and is expected to be privatized in the near future. Many airports in other Asian countries, South Africa, Argentina, and Mexico have also been and/or are in the process of being privatized partially or wholly.[2]

In contrast to this worldwide trend of privatization, however, the United States and Canada have not embraced the privatization policy. In Canada, the federal government has retained ownership of its major national airports, but commercialized these airports by transferring their management and operation to "not-for-profit" locally-based airport authorities under long term lease contracts. In the United States, airports have remained mostly municipal or regional government-owned and operated. However, the government ownership and management of the US airports are considered to be rather different from those of other countries in that there is substantial private sector involvement in management decisions concerning key airport activities and capital investment decisions. For example, because some major capacity expansion projects are financed through revenue bonds guaranteed by the major tenant airlines, these airlines have substantial power over airports' decisions on capacity investment, user charges, and other key strategic decisions. Although not strictly following the worldwide privatization trend, many airports in the United States, have in recent years begun to be organized as quasi-privatized airport authorities. These airport authorities are similar in nature to that of Canadian airport authorities, insofar as they are not-for-profit/non-shareholder entities that re-invest retained earnings into future airport development programs and are by-and-large financially self-sustaining. The US also has several airports run by local Port Authorities, whereby a Port Authority operates the local seaport(s) as well as the local airport(s).

As stated earlier, the objective of this paper is to examine how various ownership forms affect the efficiency of airport operations. To achieve this objective, we construct and estimate a stochastic cost frontier model with a flexible empirical specification. The stochastic frontier models have been very widely used as a means of measuring the deviation of a firm's (agency's) efficiency as compared to the best achievable target (frontier). Our cost frontier model is specified in a *translog* form and estimated using a Bayesian approach.

Our empirical findings suggest: (a) countries considering privatization of airports should transfer majority shares to private sector; (b) mixed ownership of airports with a government majority should be avoided in favor of even 100% government owned public corporation, despite the fact that many

countries regard P3 (Public–Private–Partnership) with government majority as a politically acceptable model to raise private funds for infrastructure capacity expansion without losing government control; (c) the US should reconsider ownership and management of airports by port authorities; these ports authorities or responsible governments should consider creating independent airport authorities to which to transfer ownership/management of airport, independently from the port management; and (d) privatization of one or more airports in cities with multiple airports would improve the efficiency of all airports.

2. Literature review and issues surrounding airport ownership

The effects of ownership on firms' productive efficiency have been an important research topic. The agency theory and strategic management literature suggest that ownership influences firm performance because different owners pursue different goals and have different incentives. Under government ownership and management, a firm is run by bureaucrats whose objective function is weighted average of social welfare and their personal agenda. Under private ownership, by contrast, the firm maximizes profit (shareholder value). A common-sense view is that government-owned firms are less efficient than their private sector counterparts operating in similar situations. The main arguments supporting this view are: (1) the objectives given to the managers of government owned firms are vaguely defined, and tend to change as the political situation and relative strengths of different interest groups change (De Alessi, 1983; Levy, 1987); and (2) the high mismatch between management's incentives and the interest of the owner (nation) increases inefficiency as documented extensively in agency theory literature (see, for example, Zeckhauser and Horn, 1989).

However, neither empirical nor theoretical evidence presented in the economics literature is conclusive with respects to relative efficiency of public vs. private firms. De Fraja (1993) questions the logic of the main arguments, and shows, via a principal-agent model, that government ownership "is not only not necessarily less productively efficient, but in some circumstances more productively efficient". Vickers and Yarrow (1991) suggest that private ownership has efficiency advantages in competitive conditions, but not necessarily in the presence of market power. They further suggest that even under competitive market conditions, government ownership is not inherently less efficient than private ownership, and that competition is the key to efficiency rather than ownership per se. Willner and Parker (2007) find that privatization may increase a firm's marginal cost.

Also, the results of empirical studies on this issue are far from conclusive. For example, Bennett and Johnson (1980) and De Alessi (1980) provide strong evidence for the view that private firms would perform better than government owned firms, whereas Boyd (1986) and Millward and Parker (1983) find no systematic evidence that public enterprise are less cost efficient than private firms.

---
[2] See Oum et al. (2004) for the ownership list of 60 major airports in Asia, Europe, North America, and Oceania.

424   T.H. Oum et al. / Journal of Urban Economics 64 (2008) 422–435

Further complicating the ownership-performance debate is the presence of mixed ownership regimes embodying elements of government and private ownership. Bos (1991) provides an excellent theoretical treatment on the behavior of mixed ownership firms. On the one hand, mixed ownership may facilitate the role of the government as a "steward" in private firms that are dominated by a strategic investor or where there is a lack of market discipline. On the other hand, mixed ownership arrangements may blend the worst qualities of government and private ownership. Thus, the resulting effects of mixed ownership on firm performance are not clear from a theoretical perspective. Empirical evidence is limited, and fails to provide any clarification on the issue. Boardman and Vining (1989) find that mixed ownership perform no better and often worse than government owned firms, which may be caused by the conflict between public and private shareholders. This finding is supported by the analytical and empirical productivity growth investigations of Ehrlich et al. (1994).

A number of studies have examined the performance of airports using different methodologies. For example, Hooper and Hensher (1997) examine the performance of six Australian airports over a 4-year period using the total factor productivity (TFP) method. Gillen and Lall (1997) develop two separate data envelopment analysis (DEA) models to evaluate terminal and airside operations separately from each other, and applied them to a pooled data of 21 top US airports for the 1989–1993 period. Nyshadham and Rao (2000) evaluate the efficiency of European airports using TFP and examine the relationship between the TFP index and several partial measures of airport performance. Sarkis (2000) evaluate the operational efficiency of US airports and reach the tentative conclusion that major hub airports are more efficient than spoke airports. Adler and Berechman (2001) use DEA to analyze airport quality and performance from the airlines' viewpoint. Martin and Roman (2001) and Martin-Cejas (2002) apply DEA and *translog* cost functions, respectively, to evaluate the performance of Spanish airports. Abbott and Wu (2002) investigate the efficiency and productivity of 12 Australian airports for the period 1990–2000 using a Malmquist TFP index and DEA. Pacheco and Fernandes (2003) examine the efficiency of 35 Brazilian domestic airports and identify the avenues for improvements, and Pels et al. (2003) investigate the technical and scale efficiency of European airports, both using the DEA method. Barros and Sampaio (2004) use DEA to evaluate the technical and allocative efficiency of Portuguese airports, and Holvad and Graham (2004) study the efficiency performance of UK airports using DEA. Martin and Roman (2006) compare the Surface Measure of Overall Performance (SMOP) and DEA in measuring the relative performance of Spanish airports. And in a later paper, Martin and Roman (2007) propose to investigate the economic efficiency of Spanish airports through airport typology. Humphreys and Francis (2002) provide a good discussion of the changing nature of the performance measurement of airports in response to changing organizational contexts.

In addition to the efficiency and productivity performance, there have been studies on administrative and strategic aspects of airport ownership and governance structures. For example,

Bacot and Christine (2006) conduct a survey of airport managers of primary US airports to examine the administrative setting of airport authorities/airport operators in the US within local governments. Lyon and Francis (2006) explore the challenges facing airports managers in New Zealand where airports are run as commercial entities under a variety of ownership structures. Halpern and Pagliari (2007) investigate the relationship between governance structures and the market orientation of airports with the focus on Europe's peripheral areas.

Despite the diversity of airport ownership and institutional arrangements, the aforementioned studies, with the exception of Parker (1999),[3] have largely ignored the effects of institutional factors on airports' productive efficiency. Airola and Craig (2001) and Craig et al. (2005) appear to be the only studies that explicitly examine the effects of US airports' institutional arrangement on efficiency. Based on a sample of 51 US airports, they distinguish two types of airport governance structures: city operated airports versus airport authority operated airports. Their results suggest that the authority-operated US airports out-perform city-operated US airports in terms of technical efficiency. It is noted, however, that their study uses only one output measure (number of aircraft movements) in measuring efficiency. As articulated in Oum et al. (2003), the omission of other outputs such as commercial services is likely to bias efficiency results as it underestimates productivity of the airports with proactive managers who focus on exploiting the revenue generation opportunities from non-aviation business. Given that non-aeronautical outputs can account for as much as 70% of total revenue an airport generates, the productivity measures ignoring the non-aeronautical services (including concession) would be seriously biased against the airports generating a high proportion of their total revenues from commercial services.

Furthermore, an important issue that has not received due attention in the ownership-performance debate for airports is whether the effects of ownership forms on airport efficiency would depend on the competitive condition in which an airport operates. Many airports are considered to possess considerable market power as the only airport serving a region or a metropolitan area,[4] whereas some major metropolitan areas are served by multiple airports,[5] such as London, Paris, Los Angeles, New York–New Jersey, Washington DC, etc., that may potentially compete against each other. The extent to which the market structure influences the effects of ownership forms on airport efficiency has important implications for ownership restructuring. What would be the most effective ownership form for improving airport efficiency in the presence of multiple airports? Would a non-profit airport authority be more efficient than a government corporation? The answers to such questions would be critical for policy makers in deciding the forms/formats for

---

[3] Using Total Factor Productivity analysis, Parker (1999) found that BAA privatization had no noticeable impact on airport technical efficiency while Yokomi (2005) using Malmquist TFP index method found that almost all airports under BAA Plc. have improved technical efficiency after privatization.

[4] Note that the market power for these airports applies to the origin-destination traffic only.

[5] In many cases, these airports are owned and operated by the same operator.

T.H. Oum et al. / Journal of Urban Economics 64 (2008) 422–435   425

airport ownership restructuring. Unfortunately, there does not appear to be any clear consensus among the theoretical arguments in this regard as discussed earlier in this section. Therefore, this issue is more of an empirical question. There are, however, some studies on airline competition and network structure that may have implications for airport efficiency performance. Examples include: Flores-Fillol (2007), Grammig et al. (2005), Daniel and Thomas Harback (2005), Bhadra and Texter (2004), and Cohen and Morrison Paul (2003).

The above discussion leads us to conclude that there is a need for a rigorous econometric study for measuring the effects of ownership and institutional arrangements on the efficiency of airports using a comprehensive cost model which is formulated consistently with micro-economic theory.

3. The econometric model

The empirical model to quantify the effects of ownership forms on airport efficiency is under the stochastic frontier framework first developed by Aigner et al. (1977) and Meeusen and van den Broeck (1977). The stochastic frontier method postulates that some firms fail to achieve the cost (production) frontier. That is, inefficiencies exist, and these inefficiencies cannot be fully explained by measurable variables. Thus, a one-sided error term, in addition to the traditional symmetric noise term, is incorporated in the model to capture inefficiency that cannot be explicitly explained.

In the short run, if the airport management tries to minimize production cost (C) given outputs (Q), variable input prices (W), and fixed capital inputs (K), the outcome can be summarized by a short run variable cost function, $C_i^*(Q_{it}, W_{it}, K_{it}, t)$, where i indexes airports and t indexes time. In reality, airports may deviate from the cost minimization objective for various reasons including airport ownership forms, and such deviations indicate the existence of inefficiency. For airport i, the deviation of its actual cost from the frontier, Δ_i, is regarded as a random draw from a distribution conditional on its ownership form (Z_i). The density function of the distribution, $f(\Delta_i|Z_i)$, is restricted to the positive range because it measures cost inefficiency. The conditionality of the deviation on ownership forms captures the effects of ownership on cost efficiency, and the random part of the deviation captures the effects of all unobserved factors. By modeling the deviation from the frontier as random, our model is an example of the random effects stochastic frontier model described in Kumbhakar and Lovell (2000).

Formally, the observed actual production cost (after taking log) of airport i at time t is expressed as

$$\ln C_{it} = \ln C_i^*(Q_{it}, W_{it}, K_{it}, t) + \Delta_i + \varepsilon_{it}^c \tag{1}$$

where ε_{it}^c represents the noises associated with the cost observation. Our model includes three outputs in vector Q_{it} (number of passengers q_{1it}; number of aircraft movements q_{2it}; and non-aeronautical output q_{3it}), two variable input prices in vector W_{it} (labor price w_{1it}; and non-labor variable input price w_{2it}), and two fixed capital inputs in vector K_{it} (number of runways k_{1it}; and terminal size k_{2it}).

3.1. Specification of the cost frontier

To estimate the empirical model, the log variable cost frontier is approximated by the following *translog* functional form:

$$\ln C_i^*(Q_{it}, W_{it}, K_{it}, t)$$
$$\approx \ln \tilde{C}_i(Q_{it}, W_{it}, K_{it}, t)$$
$$= \alpha_{it} + \sum_{j=1}^{3} \beta_j \ln q_{jit} + \sum_{j=1}^{2} \lambda_j \ln k_{jit} + \sum_{j=1}^{2} \delta_j \ln w_{jit}$$
$$+ \frac{1}{2} \sum_{j=1}^{3} \sum_{n=1}^{3} \phi_{jn} \ln q_{jit} \ln q_{nit} + \sum_{j=1}^{3} \sum_{n=1}^{2} \gamma_{jn} \ln q_{jit} \ln w_{nit}$$
$$+ \sum_{j=1}^{3} \sum_{n=1}^{2} \rho_{jn} \ln q_{jit} \ln k_{nit}$$
$$+ \frac{1}{2} \sum_{j=1}^{2} \sum_{n=1}^{2} \tau_{jn} \ln w_{jit} \ln w_{nit} + \sum_{j=1}^{2} \sum_{n=1}^{2} \zeta_{jn} \ln k_{jit} \ln w_{nit}$$
$$+ \frac{1}{2} \sum_{j=1}^{2} \sum_{n=1}^{2} \psi_{jn} \ln k_{jit} \ln k_{nit}. \tag{2}$$

The intercept α_{it} varies across airports in order to capture the difference in cost frontier (individual heterogeneity across airports in adopted technologies) caused by the factors beyond managerial control; and varies over time in order to reflect technical change. Cost frontiers may be different from airport to airport because of differences in operating environments (such as weather conditions), general labor skills, culture factors, etc., which are not included in our model explicitly. Therefore we specify α_{it} as:

$$\alpha_{it} = \tilde{\alpha} + [\Pi_i, D_{it}]\Theta + \nu_i, \ \nu_i \sim N\left(0, \sigma_\nu^2\right) \tag{3}$$

where Π_i is the vector of airport i's characteristics; D_{it} is the year dummy variables; the random term ν_i captures the difference in cost frontiers that cannot be explained by factors in Π_i.

3.2. Specification of the random deviation

The random deviation from the frontier is parameterized as:

$$\Delta_i = \exp(Z_i \Gamma_i), \tag{4a}$$
$$\Gamma_i \sim N(\bar{\Gamma}, \Omega) \tag{4b}$$

where Ω is a diagonal matrix; Z_i is the dummy variable vector indicating ownership forms; $Z_i = j$ indicates that the ownership form of airport i is j.

With this model specification, the observed cost is $C_{it} = C_i^*(Q_{it}, W_{it}, K_{it}, t) \exp(\Delta_i)$, where $\exp(\Delta_i)$ captures the deviation from the efficiency frontier, and is defined as cost inefficiency. When an airport is on the frontier, $\exp(\Delta_i)$ equals to one. For ease of interpretation and following the common practice, we use the following indicator as the measure of the mean efficiency level of all airports under ownership form j

$$h(j) = \frac{1}{\exp(E(\Delta_i|Z_i = j))}. \tag{5}$$

This efficiency level can be interpreted as the percentage of achieving the frontier, and is the parameter of our interest for identifying the effects of ownership forms on cost efficiency.[6]

3.3. Variable input share equation

To improve the efficiency of estimation, it is customary to estimate the stochastic cost frontier equation jointly with input share equations. In order to avoid the singularity problem, we chose to add the labor share equation only,[7]

$$
S_{it}^* \equiv \frac{\partial \ln C_i^*(Q_{it}, W_{it}, K_{it}, t)}{\partial \ln w_{1it}} \approx \frac{\partial \ln \tilde{C}_i(Q_{it}, W_{it}, K_{it}, t)}{\partial \ln w_{1it}}
$$

$$
= \delta_1 + \sum_{j=1}^{3} \gamma_{j1} \ln q_{jit} + \sum_{j=1}^{2} \tau_{j1} \ln w_{jit} + \sum_{j=1}^{2} \zeta_{j1} \ln k_{jit}. \quad (6)
$$

In order to reflect the panel data structure, we add the following noise term into the labor share equation, and the noise term is divided into two components:

$$
\mu_{it} = \xi_i + \varepsilon_{it}^s, \quad \text{with } \xi_i \sim N\left(0, \sigma_\xi^2\right) \quad (7)
$$

where ξ_i is the random individual effects of airport i. The labor share equation is estimated jointly with the frontier cost function in (2) via the seemingly unrelated regression (SUR) specification.

4. Estimation procedure

The Markov Chain Monte Carlo (MCMC) simulation under the Bayesian framework is used to make inference about the unknown parameters Ξ. Examples of Bayesian analysis on stochastic frontier models include Atkinson and Dorfman (2005a, 2005b), Fernandez et al. (1997), Huang (2004), Kleit and Terrell (2001), Koop et al. (1995, 1997), Kumbhakar and Tsionas (2005), Lewis and Anderson (1999), McCauland (2008), O'Donnell and Coelli (2005), and Tsionas (2002). The Bayesian inference can be facilitated by the data augmentation proposed by Tanner and Wong (1987). In particular, rather than working directly on the posterior of $p(\Xi|Data)$, we work on the posterior of $p(\Xi, \{v_i, \xi_i, \Gamma_i\}|Data)$ by taking the unobserved individual airport level parameters as missing data to be augmented. $\{v_i, \xi_i, \Gamma_i\}$ is used to denote the collection of the individual level parameters for all airports. The data augmented posterior is

$$
p\left(\Xi, \{v_i, \xi_i, \Gamma_i\}|Data\right)
$$

$$
\propto p(\Xi) \cdot \prod_{i=1}^{N} \left\{ \phi(\Gamma_i; \bar{\Gamma}, \Omega) \cdot \phi\left(v_i; \sigma_v^2\right) \cdot \phi\left(\xi_i; \sigma_\xi^2\right) \right.
$$

$$
\left. \times \prod_{t=1}^{T_i} BVN(y_{it}, S_{it}; \Xi) \right\} \quad (8)
$$

where $p(\Xi)$ is the prior of the parameters; $\phi(\cdot)$ represents the univariate normal density function, and $BVN(\cdot, \cdot)$ represents the bivariate normal density function; T_i is the number of observations on airport i.

Since the functional form of the data augmented posterior is complicated, it is impossible to derive its analytical properties. Therefore, we use the Monte Carlo simulation to take random draws from the posterior and the empirical properties of the draws will be used to approximate the theoretical ones. The MCMC simulation is a special way to implement Monte Carlo simulation, and it takes random draws by simulating a Markov process in the space of $(\Xi, \{v_i, \xi_i, \Gamma_i\})$ that converges to $p(\Xi, \{v_i, \xi_i, \Gamma_i\}|Data)$. A good introduction to the MCMC simulation can be found in Gelman et al. (2004). Appendix A of this paper outlines the algorithm for implementing the MCMC simulation, and more details of the algorithm can be found in Oum et al. (2007).

The Bayesian estimation approach adopted in this paper has many advantages. First, since the data likelihood without data augmentation involves multiple integrations over the random parameter space, evaluating such a likelihood function in Maximum Likelihood Estimation is not a trivial problem. Relying on random sampling rather than optimization, the MCMC based on the data augmented posterior provides exact finite sample results rather than relying on asymptotic approximation as well as saving computational costs very significantly. Second, the MCMC approach provides exact finite sample estimates for the individual-level inefficiency measures. Finally, the MCMC approach allows us to formally take parameter uncertainty into account in computing predictive moments and quantiles of any functions of interest, because each parameter is assigned a probability distribution and can easily be integrated out. For example, we can compute $\text{Prob}(h(j) > h(j')|Data)$, the probability that mean efficiency level of ownership form j is larger than that of ownership form j'. Both interpretations and analyses for such functions under the Bayesian approach are transparent and straightforward.

As usual in estimating *translog* cost system, certain regularity conditions on parameters must be imposed in estimation in order to get a well-defined variable cost frontier in terms of economic theory. We impose the following conditions explicitly in estimation. First, the coefficients associated with the interactions among outputs (ϕ's), the interactions among capital inputs (ψ's), and the interactions among variable inputs' prices (τ's), are symmetric. Second, the variable cost frontier in (2) is homogeneous of degree 1 with respect to variable input prices. Lastly, the variable cost frontier is concave in variable input prices. The monotonicity of the variable cost frontier (non-decreasing in outputs and variable input prices) is verified after estimation. Please see Appendix B for the details of these conditions as well as how we incorporate them in estimation.

5. Sample and variables

Our sample consists of an unbalanced panel of 109 airports around the world, representing different sizes, ownership and institutional arrangements. The data is compiled from vari-

---

[6] As was done in Oum and Yu (1998, 2004), researchers may be also interested in identifying efficiency levels of individual firms (agents), measured by $h_i = \frac{1}{\exp(\Delta_i)}$.

[7] Our empirical results are invariant to the choice of either labor cost share equation or other variable input cost share equation.

T.H. Oum et al. / Journal of Urban Economics 64 (2008) 422–435   427

ous sources including Airport Council International (ACI), the US Federal Aviation Authority (FAA), International Air Transport Association (IATA), and airport annual reports. Some data were obtained directly from the airports. Details on the data are provided in various issues of the ATRS Global Airport Benchmarking Report (for example, Air Transport Research Society, 2007).

To estimate airport cost frontiers, one must first identify outputs that an airport produces and the inputs it uses in producing these outputs. The most commonly used output measures for airports are the number of passengers, the volume of air cargo, and the number of aircraft movements (ATM). Airports typically impose direct (separate) charges for their services related to aircraft movements and the handling of passengers. However, air cargo services are generally handled by airlines, third party cargo handling companies, and others that lease space and facilities from airports. Air cargo services are not considered as a separate output in this research, as airports derive a very small percentage of their income directly from air cargo services. In addition to passenger traffic, cargo traffic and aircraft movements, airports also derive revenues from concessions, car parking, and numerous other services. These services are not directly related to aeronautical activities in a traditional sense, but they are becoming increasingly more important for airports around the world and account for over 60% of the total revenues for many airports. Thus, we consider a third output that consists of revenues from non-aeronautical services. Since non-aeronautical services include numerous items and activities, it is very difficult, if not impossible, to construct an "exact" price index that is consistent across airports in different countries and over time. The Purchasing Power Parity (PPP) appears to be the only viable option that is consistent multi-laterally (across airports in different countries and over time) as a proxy for price index for non-aeronautical outputs, as it adjusts for changes in market exchange rates and changes in real (overall) price levels of different countries over time. A non-aeronautical output index is constructed by deflating the non-aeronautical revenues by the PPP. Inclusion of the non-aeronautical services output also allows us to examine the efficiency implications of airport's business diversification strategies.

On the input side, we initially considered three variable input categories: (1) labor, measured by the number of (full time equivalent) employees who work directly for an airport operator; (2) purchased goods and materials; and (3) purchased services including outsourcing/contracting out. In practice, however, few airports provide separate expense accounts for the purchased (outsourced) services and purchased goods and materials. Thus, we decided to combine (2) and (3) to form a so-called "non-labor variable input". This non-labor variable input includes all expenses not directly related to capital or labor input costs. The price of labor input is measured by the average compensation per employee (including benefits). Similar to the non-aeronautical output, the non-labor variable input includes numerous items, thus the Purchasing Power Parity (PPP) is also used as a proxy for the non-labor input price. In addition to the variable inputs, two fixed capital inputs are considered: number

of runways and total size of passenger terminal area measured in square meters.

Airport efficiency performance are undoubtedly affected by variations in the regulatory and institutional environments in which airports operate, as well as airport characteristics, and operating and market conditions. Some of these factors are beyond the managerial controls of airport operators, thus should be considered as factors affecting the heterogeneity of cost frontier across individual airports. We compile the following variables to control for the observed heterogeneity in cost frontier: percentage of international passengers in total passenger traffic, percentage of cargo traffic in total airport traffic,[8] and regional dummy variables.

To examine the effects of ownership forms on airport efficiency, we classify the airports into the following categories that are reflected by ownership dummy variables:

(a) Majority private ownership including 100% private ownership: i.e., private-government mixed ownership with a private majority (private majority);
(b) Government-private mixed ownership with a government majority (government majority);
(c) Government ownership but contracted out to an independent and autonomous management authority via a long term lease (Authority);
(d) 100% government corporation ownership/management/ operation (public corp.);
(e) Government ownership and a branch of government operates airport including US city owned airports (government branch); and
(f) Shared ownership by multiple governments including multi-level governments (multi-level government).
(g) Quasi-Public Port Authorities (in the US) that operate both seaports and airports (US port authority).

Table 1 presents some summary statistics of the sample. These summary statistics indicate that there are large variations among the sample airports in terms of their size and business and operating environment. For example, the annual number of airport passengers ranges from 900,000 passengers to 83 million passengers in 2004. Some airports serve only international traffic, whereas others serve mostly domestic passengers. Some airports derive most of their revenue from aeronautical activities, whereas for others, a significant portion of revenues comes from other sources including concession and rentals. Labor cost shares range from 9 to 73%, and average annual employee compensation ranges from US $5030 to US $101,618 in 2004. It would be interesting to see how such variations would affect the observed performance of the airports.

---

[8] Measured in terms of Work Load Unit (WLU), a commonly used output measure in the aviation industry that combines passenger and cargo traffic volume. One WLU is defined as one passenger or 100 kg of cargo.

Table 1
Summary statistics[a]

	2001	2002	2003	2004
Output measures				
Number of passengers (million)	20 (15)	18 (15)	18 (15)	19 (16)
Number of aircraft movements (000's)	283 (177)	261 (177)	258 (177)	262 (185)
Non-aeronautical revenue (000's PPP deflated $)	119 (152)	112 (150)	125 (163)	138 (191)
Variable inputs				
Number of employee (000's)	1.0 (1.8)	1.1 (2.3)	1.1 (2.6)	1.1 (2.6)
Non-labor variable cost (000's US $)	91 (115)	87 (103)	96 (115)	100 (121)
Fixed inputs				
Number of runways	2.87 (1.15)	2.82 (1.16)	2.90 (1.24)	2.89 (1.28)
Terminal size (000's squared meter)	170 (162)	170 (161)	184 (171)	187 (179)
Variable inputs' prices				
Wage rate (000's US $)	54 (28)	54 (25)	60 (25)	63 (28)
Non-labor variable input price (000's US $)	0.95 (0.15)	0.92 (0.17)	0.97 (0.16)	0.99 (0.19)
Variable input's share				
Labor cost share	0.38 (0.14)	0.39 (0.14)	0.38 (0.14)	0.38 (0.14)
Airport characteristics				
Percentage of international passengers	0.29 (0.34)	0.31 (0.35)	0.30 (0.35)	0.32 (0.35)
Percentage of cargo	0.15 (0.14)	0.16 (0.14)	0.16 (0.15)	0.16 (0.15)
Geographic distribution of airports in percentage				
Asian airports (%)	9	7	8	10
Australian–New Zealand airports (%)	4	7	7	9
European airports (%)	17	22	19	21
North American airports (%)	70	64	66	60
Airport ownership in percentage				
City/state (%)	32	28	29	27
Public corporation (%)	12	15	14	12
Majority government (%)	3	3	1	5
US airport authority (%)	28	28	28	25
US port authority (%)	8	7	7	7
Majority private (%)	9	11	13	16
Shared government (%)	8	8	8	8
Number of observation	89	99	96	104

[a] The numbers in parentheses are the standard errors.

6. Estimation results and interpretation

The details of the empirical estimation can be found in Appendices B and C. Under Bayesian approach, estimation results are represented by the posterior distribution of parameters. For each of the parameters of interest, we report the median and the 90% interval (5%-ile and 95%-ile) of its posterior distribution.

6.1. Results of the base model

Table 2 presents the estimation results of the cost frontier. The first section of Table 2 reports the results of the intercept differentials of the cost frontier across airports and over the years. The variation in the intercept across airports is interpreted as individual heterogeneity in technology, and reflects the effects of the factors beyond airports' managerial control. The cost frontiers of Asian and European airports are significantly higher than those of North American airports. The results of the year dummies indicate upward shifts of the cost frontier in the post-2001 period, indicating the negative effects of

September 11 on airport costs. Finally, the results of σ_v^2 indicate the existence of a substantial heterogeneity in technology caused by variables other than the observable ones (percentage of international passengers, percentage of cargo, and regional dummies).

Since it is difficult to interpret directly the results of the second order terms in a *translog* function, at the bottom of Table 2 we report the cost elasticities with respect to the three outputs, own price elasticities of the two variable inputs, and the predicted variable input share. The positive cost elasticities and predicted variable input share imply that the monotonicity conditions in outputs and variable input prices are satisfied. Since we impose the concavity condition (concave in variable input prices) in estimation, own price elasticities of the variable inputs have the expected signs.

Finally, the estimation results of the variances and covariance of noise terms indicate that: (a) there are significant variations in costs and labor shares across different airports that are not accounted for by the variables included in our model, justifying the need for a stochastic frontier model; (b) the cost equa-

T.H. Oum et al. / Journal of Urban Economics 64 (2008) 422–435   429

Table 2
Estimation results of the cost frontier (the Base Model)[a]

Parameters	Posterior median [5%-ile, 95%-ile]
Individual and time varying intercept[b]	
$\bar{\alpha}$ constant	−0.5990 [−0.7654, −0.4486]
θ_1 (% cargo × constant)	−0.1409 [−0.5300, 0.2527]
θ_2 (% international passengers × constant)	0.2038 [−0.1014, 0.5103]
θ_3 (Australia/New Zealand dummy × constant)	−0.4423 [0.6959, −0.1843]
θ_4 (Europe dummy × constant)	0.6518 [0.3501, 0.9652]
θ_5 (Asia dummy × constant)	0.8512 [0.5203, 1.1824]
θ_6 (Year 2002)	0.0721 [0.0423, 0.1018]
θ_7 (Year 2003)	0.0854 [0.0536, 0.1168]
θ_8 (Year 2004)	0.0663 [0.0329, 0.0991]
σ_v^2 (unobserved heterogeneity)	0.1007 [0.0837, 0.1216]
Coefficients of outputs	
β_1 (passenger)	0.2018 [0.0076, 0.3932]
β_2 (aircraft movements)	0.2025 [0.0202, 0.3861]
β_3 (non-aeronautical output)	0.3417 [0.2429, 0.4408]
Coefficients of capital inputs	
λ_1 (runway)	0.0022 [−0.1247, 0.1288]
λ_2 (terminal size)	0.0692 [0.0069, 0.1316]
Coefficients of variable inputs' prices	
δ_1 (wage rate)	0.3532 [0.3201, 0.3851]
Coefficients of interactions among outputs	
ϕ_{11} (passenger with passenger)	0.4608 [−0.1229, 1.0432]
ϕ_{22} (aircraft movements with aircraft movement)	0.0056 [−0.5579, 0.5639]
ϕ_{33} (non-aeronautical with non-aeronautical)	0.0810 [−0.0766, 0.2393]
ϕ_{12} (passenger with aircraft movement)	−0.4072 [−0.9122, 0.1009]
ϕ_{13} (passenger with non-aeronautical)	−0.3117 [−0.5747, −0.0488]
ϕ_{23} (aircraft movement with non-aeronautical)	0.3331 [0.1152, 0.5536]
Coefficients of interactions between capital inputs	
ψ_{11} (runway with runway)	0.0511 [−0.3262, 0.4293]
ψ_{22} (terminal with terminal)	0.0751 [−0.0257, 0.1752]
ψ_{12} (runway with terminal)	−0.2521 [−0.4078, −0.0966]
Coefficients of interaction between inputs' prices	
τ_{11} (wage rate with wage rate)	−0.0040 [−0.0160, −0.0003]
Coefficients of interactions between outputs and variable inputs' prices	
γ_{11} (passenger with wage rate)	−0.0810 [−0.1479, −0.0134]
γ_{21} (aircraft movement with wage rate)	0.0570 [−0.0109, 0.1252]
γ_{31} (non-aeronautical with wage rate)	−0.0055 [−0.0396, 0.0287]
Coefficients of interactions between outputs and capital inputs	
ρ_{11} (passenger with runway)	0.2286 [−0.1475, 0.6080]
ρ_{12} (passenger with terminal)	−0.0347 [−0.2136, 0.1440]
ρ_{21} (aircraft movement with runway)	0.2167 [−0.1945, 0.6278]
ρ_{22} (aircraft movement with terminal)	0.0724 [−0.1107, 0.2541]
ρ_{31} (non-aeronautical with runway)	−0.1448 [−0.3470, 0.0575]
ρ_{32} (non-aeronautical with terminal)	0.0296 [−0.0598, 0.1197]
Coefficients of interactions between capital inputs and variable inputs' prices	
ζ_{11} (runway with wage rate)	0.0910 [0.0410, 0.1412]
ζ_{21} (terminal with wage rate)	−0.0006 [−0.0264, 0.0254]
Noise variances	
σ_ξ^2	0.0356 [0.0333, 0.0385]
σ_{cs}	−0.0012 [−0.0021, −0.0004]
σ_{ec}^2	0.0144 [0.0125, 0.0168]
σ_{es}^2	0.0049 [0.0043, 0.0057]
Elasticities and variable input shares[c]	
Cost elasticity with respect to aircraft movements	0.1135 [0.0270, 0.2919]
Cost elasticity with respect to passengers	0.3366 [0.1596, 0.5145]
Cost elasticity with respect to non-aeronautical revenue	0.2905 [0.1971, 0.3844]
Own price elasticity of labor inputs	−0.6552 [−0.6977, −0.6219]
Own price elasticity of non-labor variable inputs	−0.3672 [−0.4002, −0.3365]
Labor input share[d]	0.3590 [0.3303, 0.3873]
# of observations	776

[a] In estimation, variable cost, outputs, fixed inputs, and variable input prices are all normalized at their sample means.
[b] The intercept of the cost frontier is specified as $\alpha_{it} = \bar{\alpha} + [\Pi_i, D_{it}]\Theta + v_i$, $v_i \sim N(0, \sigma_v^2)$, where Π_i is the vector of airport's characteristics and D_{it} is the vector of time dummies.
[c] The elasticities and variable input share are evaluated at the sample means of variables.
[d] Non-labor variable input share equals one minus labor input share.

Table 3
Estimation results—efficiency parameters[a]

Parameters	Base Model	Model 2
$\bar{\Gamma}_1$ (majority private)	−4.6287	−4.7205
	[−7.6041, −2.6674]	[−7.3802, −2.8804]
$\bar{\Gamma}_2$ (public corporation)	−3.5040	−3.5839
	[−6.8685, −2.1401]	[−7.0752, −2.1797]
$\bar{\Gamma}_3$ (airport authority)	−4.3957	−3.9756
	[−7.9183, −2.3585]	[−6.4890, −2.4356]
$\bar{\Gamma}_4$ (corporation × multi-airport)[b,c]		0.2374
		[−5.9733, 2.0763]
$\bar{\Gamma}_5$ (majority government)	−2.6637	−3.2477
	[−6.3502, −1.0384]	[−6.3296, −1.3452]
$\bar{\Gamma}_6$ (US city/state)	−2.1684	−2.5027
	[−5.9045, −1.2560]	[−4.0673, −1.5163]
$\bar{\Gamma}_7$ (shared government)	−1.6043	−1.8957
	[−3.4218, −0.6897]	[−3.8801, −1.1185]
$\bar{\Gamma}_8$ (US port authority)	−0.8398	−1.5871
	[−1.7294, −0.1831]	[−2.9813, −0.6590]
$\bar{\Gamma}_9$ (government × multi-airport)[c,d]		1.1179
		[0.2606, 2.2434]
$\sigma_{\bar{\Gamma}}^2$ (variance of Γ_i)[e]	0.5938	0.4274
	[0.3006, 1.2761]	[0.2306, 0.9104]

[a] We report the median and the 90% highest density region [5%-ile, 95%-ile] of the posterior distribution of each parameter. Changing the specification of inefficiency term has negligible effects on estimation results of cost frontier parameters. To save space, we do not report the results of cost frontier across different inefficiency specifications.

[b] Corporation dummy equals to one if the ownership of an airport is majority private, public corporation, or airport authority.

[c] Multi-airport is a dummy indicating whether an airport is in a multiple airport market.

[d] Government dummy equals to one if the ownership of an airport is US city/state, majority government, US port authority, or shared government.

[e] Our model specifies $\Gamma_i \sim N(\bar{\Gamma}, \sigma_{\bar{\Gamma}}^2 \mathbf{I})$, with $\mathbf{I}$ denoting the identity matrix.

tion and the labor input share equation are negatively correlated; suggesting that it is beneficial to estimate the cost equation and the variable input share equation jointly.

6.2. Effects of ownership forms on cost efficiency

Table 3 summarizes and compares the effects of the seven different ownership forms on airport efficiency. Two alternative specifications of the inefficiency term (the random deviation from the frontier) are estimated with the identical specification of the cost frontier. It is noted that results of the cost frontier parameters between the two alternative models are rather stable, not unduly influenced by alternative specifications of the inefficiency term. Below we discuss and summarize the results from the two alternative models: the Base Model and Model 2.

6.2.1. The Base Model results

The Base Model is specified by Eqs. (4a) and (4b). Under this model specification, the random deviation of airport i with ownership j is determined by $\Delta_i = \exp(\Gamma_i)$, $\Gamma_i \sim (\bar{\Gamma}_j, \sigma_{\bar{\Gamma}}^2)$. The smaller the deviation is relative to its own cost frontier, the more efficient the ownership form is. The posterior distributions of $\bar{\Gamma}_j$, presented in column 2 of Table 3, reflect the extent of deviations from the cost frontier under different ownership forms. For example, airports under majority private ownership

are more efficient than those under US port authority because the posterior density of $\bar{\Gamma}_1$ lies in the left of the posterior density of $\bar{\Gamma}_8$.

The results from the Base Model can be summarized as follows:

- Airports with the ownership forms of majority private, public corporation, and airport authority are more efficient than those with various forms of government ownership and management (majority government, shared government, and US port authority). This suggests that ownership forms in which management can exercise a larger degree of autonomy and face less political influence are helpful to improve the efficiency of airports;
- Among airports with the four government ownership/management forms, those operated by US port authorities[9] are the least efficient;
- The results of the variance of inefficiency parameters ($\sigma_{\bar{\Gamma}}^2$) reported in the last row of Table 3 imply that besides ownership forms and other variables included in our cost model, unobserved variables also affect airport efficiency.

6.2.2. Model 2—An alternative model to incorporate the effects of multiple airports

Some metropolitan areas are served by multiple airports, such as New York/New Jersey, Los Angeles, San Francisco Bay area, Chicago, Washington DC, London, Paris, Rome, etc. These airports may potentially compete against each other. Would the presence of multiple airports influence the effects of ownership forms on airport efficiency? To answer this question, we estimate an alternative model (Model 2) that includes a "Multi-Airport" dummy variable, and another set of ownership form variables. The "Multi-Airport" dummy is given the value of ONE if an airport is in a multiple airport market, and zero otherwise. To construct the second set of ownership form variables, we re-group the airports in multi-airport markets into two ownership groups: (1) "Corporation" that includes *Majority Private, Public Corporation*, and *Airport Authority*: These airports enjoy significant managerial autonomy and are reasonably free from political interference; and (2) "Government" that includes *Majority Government, US city/state, Shared Government*, and *US Port Authority*. We also include two interaction terms in Model 2: Multi-Airport * Corporation and Multi-Airport * Government.

The results from Model 2, presented in column 3 of Table 3, indicate that the presence of multiple airports has no effect on the efficiency of airports under the 'Corporation' ownership forms, whereas the presence of multiple airports has a significant negative effect on the efficiency of airports under the 'Government Group' ownership forms. At first glance, these results appear to be somehow counter-intuitive since a "common-sense" view would be that airports in a multi-airport market faces stronger competition than airports in sin-

---

[9] Airports operated by US port authorities include the three airports in New York/New Jersey area, Boston airport, Seattle airport, Portland airport, and Oakland airport.

T.H. Oum et al. / Journal of Urban Economics 64 (2008) 422–435   431

Table 4
Efficiency levels conditional on ownership forms (results of Model 2)[a]

	Single-airport market	Multiple-airport market
$h(1)$: majority private	0.9888	0.9751
	[0.9309, 0.9992]	[0.7501, 1.00]
$h(2)$: public corporation	0.9651	0.9478
	[0.8670, 0.9989]	[0.6957, 1.00]
$h(3)$: airport authority	0.9766	0.9334
	[0.8977, 0.9979]	[0.6217, 1.00]
$h(4)$: majority government	0.9525	0.8549
	[0.7184, 0.9977]	[0.3347, 0.9347]
$h(5)$: US city/state	0.9015	0.7220
(government branch)	[0.7672, 0.9770]	[0.4959, 0.9125]
$h(6)$: shared government	0.8282	0.5743
	[0.6089, 0.9735]	[0.1693, 0.9016]
$h(7)$: US port authority	0.7732	0.4543
	[0.5230, 0.9344]	[0.1772, 0.7232]

[a] Under our model specification, $h_i \equiv \exp(-\Delta_i)$ captures the deviation from the efficiency frontier, and is defined as cost inefficiency. The mean efficiency level under ownership form j is measured by $h(j) = \exp(-\bar{\Delta}^j)$, where $\bar{\Delta}^j = E(\Delta_i | Z_i = j)$; Z_i is the vector of ownership dummies and $Z_i = j$ means that the ownership form of airport i is j ($j = 1, \ldots, 8$). The efficiency results here are based on the results of Model 2 in Table 3.

gle airport markets. However, in reality, it is quite common that airports in a metropolitan area with multiple airports are owned and operated by a single airport operator. Such examples include the three airports in New York/New Jersey area, the two airports in Chicago, the two airports in Washington DC, etc. Even in some cases with different airport operators, airports in the multi-airports areas are often complementary, such as one mainly for domestic passengers and the other one mainly for international passengers. Consequently, the Multi-Airport market variable does not seem to indicate the presence of competition. One possible explanation for the results of Model 2 is that these airports are located in large metropolitan areas, and as such, they are likely to face larger bureaucracy and more political influence from powerful city/state governments, and consequently, become less efficient.

The basic findings on the effects of ownership forms on airport efficiency from the Base Model still hold after controlling the multiple-airport market effects. One implication of the results from Model 2 is that since government-controlled ownership forms in multiple airport cities (Government ∗ Multi-Airport) are less efficient than other airports in similar situation, privatization, corporatization or creation of independent authority for managing an airport in multiple airport city would help improve the efficiency of the airport.

6.3. Comparison of ownership effects in single airport vs. multiple-airport cities

Table 4 presents the median along with the 5%-ile and 95%-ile of the posterior distributions of efficiency levels[10] for different ownership forms in both single-airport and multiple-airport

---

[10] Recall from Section 3 that the mean efficiency level of all airports under ownership form j is measured by $h(j)$ in Eq. (5).

Table 5
Hypothesis tests for comparing efficiency between ownership forms[a]

	Single-airport market	Multiple-airport market
$\Pr(h(j) > h(j'))$:	0.93	0.93
(US city/state > US port authority)		
$\Pr(h(j) > h(j'))$:	0.89	0.93
(airport authority > US city/state)		
$\Pr(h(j) > h(j'))$:	0.99	1.00
(airport authority > US port authority)		
$\Pr(h(j) > h(j'))$:	0.75	0.86
(majority private > majority government)		

[a] The hypothesis tests report the posterior probability measures on whether the mean airport efficiency under ownership form j is greater than the one under ownership j'. These posterior probabilities are calculated based on estimation results of Model 2 in Table 3.

markets. The posterior medians of the efficiency levels for majority private, public corporation, and airport authority are all above 90% of the frontier in both markets.

The efficiency levels of airports with 'Government' ownership forms are affected by market structure: their posterior distributions shift to the left indicating lower efficiency in multiple-airport markets. The airports operated under shared ownership of multi-level governments and the airports operated by the US port authorities are the least efficient groups in terms of cost efficiency: the posterior medians of their efficiency levels are only about 80% of the frontier in single-airport markets, and about 50% of the frontier in multiple-airport markets.

The findings on the effects of ownership forms on airport efficiency are of course subject to statistical uncertainty. In order to address such uncertainty, we compare the efficiencies between different ownership forms in terms of posterior probability using the results of Model 2 in Table 3. The results of the comparisons are presented in Table 5, and can be summarized as follows:

- There is a 93% probability that airports owned and operated by the US cities/states are more efficient than those owned and operated by the US port authorities in both single-airport and multiple-airport markets; whereas there is an almost 100% probability that airports owned and operated by independent airport authorities are more efficient than those owned and operated by the US port authorities in all markets.

- There is an 89% probability and a 93% probability that airports owned and operated by independent airport authorities are more efficient than the US city/state owned and operated airports in single-airport markets and multiple-airport markets, respectively.

- There is a 75% probability that airports owned and operated by operators with private majority than those owned and operated by mixed enterprises with government majority in single-airport markets; and the probability increases to 86% in multiple-airport markets.

432   T.H. Oum et al. / Journal of Urban Economics 64 (2008) 422–435

6.4. Robustness of the results to underlying assumptions

Our data include the year of 2001, and the event of 9/11 is treated as a random shock that led to the increased costs in the years of 2002–2004. However, it is also possible that the rising costs at some airports after 9/11 are a result of decreased efficiency. In order to test the 9/11 effects on our results, we re-estimated the models after removing the year 2001 data. The conclusions from the Base Model and Model 2 did not change.

To further ensure the robustness of our results, we also examined the issue of endogeneity between ownership forms and airports' efficiency. This issue arises if governments are more likely to be pressured to privatize or commercialize inefficient airports. After careful considerations, we conclude that the endogeneity issue does not pose any serious problem in our analysis because of the following reasons.

First, as discussed in the introduction, the choice for airport ownership and institutional arrangements is related more to the economy, law, and political systems of a country and/or a region rather than to the efficiency level of individual airports. For example, in reforming airport ownership forms over the last two decades, many governments in Europe, Asia, Australia and New Zealand have fully or partially privatized the major airports in their countries, whereas Canada has chosen to transfer the management and operation of major Canadian airports to independent airport authorities under long-term lease contracts, but retain the ownership of these airports. Some US airports are operated by port authorities mainly because they are located close to major seaports with long history and operated by powerful port authorities. The regional dummy variables are included partly to capture the systematic differences in the choices of airport ownership forms across the regions. If consistent data were available, we would include country-specific indicators of economy, law, and political systems to better control such effects.

Second, the motives for governments to privatize/commercialize airports are diverse, not just for improving operational efficiency. Lack of funding has often been the one of main factors that forces governments to seek creative means to finance the necessary infrastructure improvement and/or expansion. For example, the $2.3 billion Thatcher government received from privatizing the seven major UK airports in 1987 was not negligible, it was as important a motive as improving the efficiency of these airports. Similarly, the expected $2 billion–$3 billion cash windfall is a big reason behind Chicago Mayor Richard Daley's push to privatize Midway Airport.

7. Conclusion

In this paper, we estimated a stochastic frontier cost model in *translog* form via a Bayesian approach in order to measure the effects of ownership and institutional forms on the efficiency of airports. Our key empirical findings are: (a) airports owned and/or controlled by majority private firms, autonomous public corporations or independent authorities are more efficient than those owned and/or controlled by government branch (city/state), multiple level governments, or US ports authori-

ties; (b) there is an almost 100% probability that airports controlled/operated by independent airport authorities are more efficient than those controlled/operated by US port authorities, and there is 93% probability that US city/state run airports are more efficient than those operated by US port authorities; (c) there is about 80% probability that airports owned/operated by a majority private firm achieve higher efficiency than those owned/operated by the mixed enterprise with government majority ownership; and (d) airports owned/operated by a Government controlled agencies (US ports authorities, shared government ownership, US city or state government, mixed enterprises with government majority ownership) have significantly lower efficiency in multiple airport markets than in single airport markets. These findings imply the following:

- Countries considering to privatize airports should transfer 100% or a majority ownership to private sector; and should avoid the mixed ownership with government majority in favor of even 100% government owned public firm;
- US should reconsider ownership and management of airports by port authorities;
- although average efficiency of the airports owned and operated by cities/states are lower than those operated by independent airport authorities, the difference is not statistically significant. As such, this issue needs careful further examinations.

Acknowledgments

We are grateful for comments from Jayendu Patel, Kenneth Small, and Clifford Winston; from seminar participants at the University of British Columbia, Washington State University, the American Economic Association 2007 conference, and the INFORMS 2007 conference; and from the referees and a co-editor of this journal. We are also grateful for the research assistance of Yunfei Zhao. This research is financially supported by the Social Science and Humanities Research Council (SSHRC) of Canada, UBC-P3 Research Program, and the Hong Kong Polytechnic University.

Appendix A. Outline of the bayesian approach

Our econometric model can be expressed in the following hierarchical form

$$\ln C_{it} = a_i + X_{it}B + \exp(Z_i\Gamma_i) + \varepsilon_{it}^c, \tag{A.1a}$$

$$S_{it} = X_{it}B + \xi_i + \varepsilon_{it}^s, \tag{A.1b}$$

$$\alpha_i = \bar{\alpha} + [\Pi_i, D_{it}]\Theta + v_i, \tag{A.1c}$$

$$\Gamma_i \sim N(\bar{\Gamma}, \sigma_\Gamma^2 \mathbf{I_M}), \tag{A.1d}$$

$$\xi_i \sim N(0, \sigma_\xi^2), \tag{A.1e}$$

$$v_i \sim N(0, \sigma_v^2), \tag{A.1f}$$

$$(\varepsilon_{i1}^c, \varepsilon_{i1}^s, \varepsilon_{i2}^c, \varepsilon_{i2}^s, \dots, \varepsilon_{iT_i}^c, \varepsilon_{iT_i}^s)' \sim N(\mathbf{0_{T_i}}, \Sigma \otimes \mathbf{I_{T_i}}). \tag{A.1g}$$

Since the labor share equation only provides information to estimate a subset of B, the entries in X_{it} corresponding to the

T.H. Oum et al. / Journal of Urban Economics 64 (2008) 422–435   433

parameters outside this subset are set as zeros. In (A.1d), the subscript of M denotes the size of Z_i. The inference to the unknown parameters is done by sampling from the augmented posterior $p(\varXi, \{v_i, \xi_i, \varGamma_i\}|Data)$. The empirical moments of the marginal draws of $\varXi$ are the estimation results of the parameters; the sample mean of the draws of v_i is used to measure the unobserved individual effects; since $h_i = \exp(-\exp(Z_i \varGamma_i))$, the draws of $\varGamma_i$ is used to measure individual efficiency level.

The random sampling is done by the Gibbs sampling, in which the full parameter space $(\varXi, \{v_i, \xi_i, \varGamma_i\})$ is divided into several components, and the iterations of the Gibbs sampler cycle through the components, drawing each component conditional on the value of all the others. Under certain regularities, the draws from the iteration process converge to the augmented posterior.

The priors on parameters used in estimation are all non-informative and changing the priors has no substantial effects on the posteriors. In order to check the convergence of the random draws, we run the Gibbs sampler from different starting values for the parameters, and plot the time-series of the draws for each of the runs in order to check the convergence. In general, the Gibbs draws converge after about 20,000 draws. To overcome high autocorrelation among the draws, we generate very long chains—300,000 Gibbs draws, and drop the first 100,000 and use the remaining 200,000 to summarize the posterior means and standard deviations. Tests for Robustness are done by increasing the post-convergence draws to 400,000, and there is very little change in the results.

We specify two airport-specific random terms in our model specification: (v_i) controls the variation in cost frontier from unobserved sources (the factors which are not included in $\varPi_i$), $(\varDelta_i)$ measures the deviation from the frontier. Greene (2005) refers such specification as true random effects stochastic frontier model. From the estimation results of Model 2 in Table 3, we plot the posterior means of $p(h_i|Data)$ and $p(v_i|Data)$ to confirm that these two random effects can be separated in estimation. We also find that airport efficiency could be substantially underestimated if the unobserved frontier variation was ignored ($v_i = 0$).

The details of the Gibbs sampler and results of the sensitivity analysis can be found in Oum et al. (2007).

Appendix B. Regularity constraints on the cost frontier

The following constraints on cost frontier are imposed explicitly in estimation.

1. Symmetric constraints: $\phi_{12} = \phi_{21}$, $\phi_{13} = \phi_{31}$, $\phi_{23} = \phi_{32}$, $\tau_{12} = \tau_{21}$, $\psi_{12} = \psi_{21}$;

2. Homogeneity constraints: The variable cost frontier is homogeneous of degree 1 with respect to variable input prices, so we have

$$\delta_1 + \delta_2 = 1, \qquad \gamma_{11} + \gamma_{12} = 0, \qquad \gamma_{21} + \gamma_{22} = 0,$$

$$\gamma_{31} + \gamma_{32} = 0, \qquad \frac{1}{2}\tau_{11} + \tau_{12} + \frac{1}{2}\tau_{22} = 0, \qquad \tau_{11} + \tau_{12} = 0,$$

$$\tau_{12} + \tau_{22} = 0, \qquad \zeta_{11} + \zeta_{12} = 0, \qquad \zeta_{21} + \zeta_{22} = 0;$$

3. Concavity constraint: The variable cost frontier is concave with respect to variable input prices. To impose this constraint in estimation, we first derive the Hessian matrix of the variable cost frontier with respect to variable input prices as

$$\nabla^2_W C_{it}(Q_{it}, W_{it}, X_{it}, t)$$
$$= \begin{pmatrix} \frac{C_{it}}{w_{1it}^2}(\tau_{11} + S_{1it}^2 - S_{1it}) & \frac{C_{it}}{w_{1it}w_{2it}}(S_{1it}S_{2it} + \tau_{12}) \\ \frac{C_{it}}{w_{1it}w_{2it}}(S_{1it}S_{2it} + \tau_{12}) & \frac{C_{it}}{w_{2it}^2}(\tau_{22} + S_{2it}^2 - S_{2it}) \end{pmatrix} \quad \text{(B.1)}$$

where S represents the observed variable input share. As shown by Diewert and Wales (1987), the Hessian matrix is negative semidefinite if and only if $\tau \equiv \left(\begin{smallmatrix} \tau_{11} & \tau_{12} \\ \tau_{12} & \tau_{22} \end{smallmatrix}\right)$ is negative semidefinite. Combining this with homogeneity constraints, the concavity constraint can be implemented by restricting $\tau_{11} \leqslant 0$.

In estimation, we incorporate the linear constraints associated with symmetry and homogeneity into the cost frontier. We then assign a normal prior truncated above 0, to τ_{11} to incorporate the concavity constraint. An alternative approach of imposing regularity constraints in estimating flexible functional forms with Bayesian approach can be found in Terrell (1996).

Since the monotonicity properties of the cost frontier (nondecreasing in outputs and variable input prices) could be violated even the concavity constraint is imposed, as suggested by Barnett and Pasupathy (2003), we calculate the cost elasticities with respect to the three outputs, own price elasticities of the two variable inputs, and the predicted variable input share in order to verify the monotonicity properties. As reported in Table 2, they have the expected signs, implying that the monotonicity conditions in outputs and variable input prices are satisfied.

References

Abbott, M., Wu, S., 2002. Total factor productivity and efficiency of Australian airports. Australian Economic Review 35, 244–260.

Adler, N., Berechman, J., 2001. Measuring airport quality from the airlines' viewpoint: An application of data envelopment analysis. Transport Policy 8, 171–181.

Aigner, D., Lovell, K., Schmidt, P., 1977. Formulation and estimation of stochastic frontier function models. Journal of Econometrics 6, 21–37.

Airola, J., Craig, S., 2001. Institutional efficiency in airport governance. Unpublished manuscript, Department of Economics, University of Houston, Houston, Texas.

Air Transport Research Society, 2007. Global airport benchmarking report: Global standards for airport excellence. Vancouver, Canada, Various Issues. http://www.atrsworld.org.

Atkinson, S.E., Dorfman, J.H., 2005a. Multiple comparison with the best: Bayesian precision measures of efficiency rankings. Journal of Productivity Analysis 23, 359–392.

Atkinson, S.E., Dorfman, J.H., 2005b. Feasible estimation of firm-specific allocative inefficiency through Bayesian numerical methods. Working Paper, University of George, Athens, GA.

Bacot, H., Christine, J., 2006. What's so 'special' about airport authorities? Assessing the administrative structure of US airports. Public Administration Review 66 (2), 241–251.

Barnett, W., Pasupathy, M., 2003. Regularity of the generalized quadratic production model: A counterexample. Econometric Reviews 22, 135–154.

Barros, C.P., Sampaio, A., 2004. Technical and allocative efficiency in airports. International Journal of Transport Economics 31 (3), 355–377.

Bennett, J., Johnson, M., 1980. Tax reduction without sacrifice: Private sector production of public services. Public Finance Quarterly 8, 363–396.

Bhadra, D., Texter, P., 2004. Airline networks: An econometric framework to analyze domestic US air travel. Journal of Transportation Statistics 7 (1). Paper #6.

Boardman, A.E., Vining, A.R., 1989. Ownership and performance in competitive environments: A comparison of the performance of private, mixed, and state owned enterprises. Journal of Law and Economics 32, 1–33.

Bos, D., 1991. Privatization: A Theoretical Treatment. Clarendon Press, Oxford.

Boyd, C.W., 1986. The Comparative efficiency of state-owned enterprise. In: Negandhi, A.R., Thomas, H., Rao, K.L.K. (Eds.), Multinational Corporations and State-owned Enterprise: A New Challenge in International Business. JAI Press, Greenwich, CT.

Bruckner, J.K., 2003. Airline traffic and urban economic development. Urban Studies 40 (8), 1455–1469.

Cohen, J.P., Morrison Paul, C.J., 2003. Airport infrastructure spillovers in a network system. Journal of Urban Economics 54 (3), 459–473.

Craig, S., Airola, J., Tipu, M., 2005. The effects of institutional form on airport governance efficiency. Unpublished manuscript, Department of Economics, University of Houston, Houston, Texas.

Daniel, J.I., Thomas Harback, K., 2005. Do airlines that dominate traffic at hub airports experience less delay? Working Paper #05-09, Department of Economics, University of Delaware.

De Alessi, L., 1980. The Economics of property rights: A review of the evidence. In: Zerbe, R.O. (Ed.), Research in Law and Economics. JAI Press, Greenwich, CT.

De Alessi, L., 1983. Property rights transaction costs and x-efficiency: An essay in economic theory. American Economic Review 73, 64–81.

De Fraja, G., 1993. Productive efficiency in public and private firms. Journal of Public Economics 50, 15–30.

Diewert, W.E., Wales, T.J., 1987. Flexible functional forms and global curvature conditions. Econometrica 55, 43–68.

Ehrlich, I., Gallais-Hamonno, G., Liu, Z., Lutter, R., 1994. Productivity growth and firm ownership: An analytical and empirical investigation. Journal of Political Economy 102, 1006–1038.

Fernandez, C., Osiewalski, J., Steel, M.F.J., 1997. On the use of panel data in stochastic frontier models. Journal of Econometrics 79, 169–193.

Flores-Fillol, R., 2007. Airline competition and network structure. UFAE and IAE Working Papers #683.07, Edi.ci B, Universitat Autònoma de Barcelona, Spain.

Gelman, A., Carlin, J.B., Stern, H.S., Rubin, D.B., 2004. Bayesian Data Analysis, second ed. Chapman & Hall/CRC.

Gillen, D.W., Lall, A., 1997. Developing measures of airport productivity and performance: An application of data envelopment analysis, in: Proceedings of the Aviation Transport Research Group Conference, Vancouver, Canada.

Grammig, J., Hujer, R., Scheidler, M., 2005. Discrete choice modelling in airline network management. Journal of Applied Econometrics 20 (4), 467–486.

Greene, W., 2005. Reconsidering heterogeneity in panel data estimators of the stochastic frontier model. Journal of Econometrics 126, 269–303.

Halpern, N., Pagliari, R., 2007. Governance structures and the market orientation of airports in Europe's peripheral areas. Journal of Air Transport Management 13, 376–382.

Holvad, T., Graham, A., 2004. Efficiency measurement for UK airports: An application of data envelopment analysis. Empirical Economics Letters 3 (1), 29–39.

Hooper, P.G., Hensher, D.A., 1997. Measuring total factor productivity of airports: An index number approach. Transportation Research E 33, 249–259.

Huang, H.C., 2004. Estimation of technical inefficiencies with heterogeneous technologies. Journal of Productivity Analysis 21, 277–296.

Humphreys, I., Francis, G., 2002. Performance measurement: A review of airports. International Journal of Transport Management 1, 79–85.

Kleit, A.N., Terrell, D., 2001. Measuring potential efficiency gains from deregulation of electricity generation: A Bayesian approach. Review of Economics and Statistics 83, 523–530.

Koop, G., Steel, M.F.J., Osiewalski, J., 1995. Posterior analysis of stochastic frontier models using Gibbs sampling. Computational Statistics 10, 353–373.

Koop, G., Osiewalski, J., Steel, M.F.J., 1997. Bayesian efficiency analysis through individual effects: Hospital cost frontiers. Journal of Econometrics 76, 77–105.

Kumbhakar, S.C., Lovell, C.A.K., 2000. Stochastic Frontier Analysis. Cambridge University Press.

Kumbhakar, S.C., Tsionas, E.G., 2005. Measuring technical and allocative inefficiency in the translog cost system: A Bayesian approach. Journal of Econometrics 126, 355–384.

Levy, N., 1987. A theory of public enterprise behavior. Journal of Economic Behaviour and Organization 8, 75–96.

Lewis, D., Anderson, R., 1999. Residential real estate brokerage efficiency and the implications of franchising: A Bayesian approach. Real Estate Economics 27, 543–560.

Lyon, D., Francis, G., 2006. Managing New Zealand's airports in the face of commercial challenges. Journal of Air Transport Management 12, 220–226.

Martin, J.C., Roman, C., 2001. An application of DEA to measure the efficiency of Spanish airports prior to privatization. Journal of Air Transport Management 7, 149–157.

Martin, J.C., Roman, C., 2006. A benchmarking analysis of Spanish commercial airports: A comparison between SMOP and DEA ranking methods. Networks and Spatial Economics 6 (2), 111–134.

Martin, J.C., Roman, C., 2007. Political opportunists and Mavericks? A typology of Spanish airports. International Journal of Transport Economics 34 (2), 245–269.

Martin-Cejas, R.R., 2002. An approximation to the productive efficiency of the Spanish airports network through a deterministic cost frontier. Journal of Air Transport Management 8, 233–238.

McCauland, W., 2008. On Bayesian analysis and computation for functions with monotonicity and curvature restrictions. Journal of Econometrics 142, 484–507.

Meeusen, W., van den Broeck, J., 1977. Efficiency estimation from Cobb–Douglas production function with composed error. International Economic Review 8, 435–444.

Millward, R., Parker, D.M., 1983. Public and private enterprise: Comparative behaviour and relative efficiency. In: Millward, R., Parker, D.M., Rosenthal, L., Sumner, M.T., Topham, T. (Eds.), Public Sector Economics. Longman, London.

Nyshadham, E.A., Rao, V.K., 2000. Assessing efficiency of European airports: a total factor productivity approach. Public Works Management & Policy 5, 106–114.

O'Donnell, C.J., Coelli, T.J., 2005. A Bayesian approach to imposing curvature on distance functions. Journal of Econometrics 126, 493–523.

Oum, T.H., Yan, J., Yu, C., 2007. Technical notes for "Ownership Forms Matter for Airport Efficiency: A Stochastic Frontier Investigation of Worldwide Airports". Unpublished manuscript, School of Economic Sciences, Washington State University.

Oum, T.H., Yu, C., 1998. Winning Airlines: Productivity and Cost Competitiveness of the World's Major Airlines. Kluwer Academic Press, New York/London.

Oum, T.H., Yu, C., 2004. Measuring airports' operating efficiency: A summary of the 2003 ATRS global airport benchmarking report. Transportation Research E 40, 515–532.

Oum, T.H., Yu, C., Fu, X., 2003. A comparative analysis of productivity performance of the world's major airports: Summary report of the ATRS global airport benchmarking research report—2002. Journal of Air Transport Management 9, 285–297.

Oum, T.H., Zhang, A., Zhang, Y., 2004. Alternative forms of economic regulation and their efficiency implications for airports. Journal of Transport Economics and Policy 38, 217–246.

Pacheco, R.R., Fernandes, E., 2003. Managerial efficiency of Brazilian airports. Transportation Research A 37 (8), 667–680.

Parker, D., 1999. The performance of BAA before and after privatization. Journal of Transport Economics and Policy 33, 133–145.

Pels, E., Nijkamp, P., Rietveld, P., 2003. Inefficiencies and scale economies of European airport operations. Transportation Research E 39 (5), 341–361.

Sarkis, J., 2000. An analysis of the operational efficiency of major airports in the United States. Journal of Operations Management 18, 335–351.

Tanner, M.A., Wong, W.H., 1987. The calculation of posterior distribution by data augmentation. Journal of the American Statistical Association 82, 528–549.

Terrell, D., 1996. Incorporating regularity conditions in flexible functional forms. Journal of Applied Econometrics 11, 179–194.

Tsionas, E.G., 2002. Stochastic frontier models with random coefficients. Journal of Applied Econometrics 17, 127–147.

Vickers, J., Yarrow, G., 1991. Economic perspectives on privatization. Journal of Economic Perspectives 5, 111–132.

Willner, J., Parker, D., 2007. The performance of public and private enterprise under conditions of active and passive ownership and competition and monopoly. Journal of Economics 90, 221–253.

Yokomi, M., 2005. Evaluation of technical efficiency at privatized airports: Case of BAA Plc. A paper presented at the Air Transport Research Society (ATRS) Conference, July 3–6, 2005, Rio de Janeiro, Brazil.

Zeckhauser, R.J., Horn, M., 1989. The control and performance of state-owned enterprises. In: MacAvoy, P.W., Stanbury, W.T., Yarrow, G., Zeckhauser, R.J. (Eds.), Privatization and State-owned Enterprise. Kluwer, Boston, MA, pp. 7–57.

8

DEVELOPING MEASURES OF AIRPORT PRODUCTIVITY AND PERFORMANCE: AN APPLICATION OF DATA ENVELOPMENT ANALYSIS

DAVID GILLEN

and

ASHISH LALL

Abstract—Many studies have investigated the financial results and economic productivity of airlines but few have investigated the productivity or performance of airports, and how changes in the industry may have affected them. Most airports measure performance strictly in accounting terms by looking at only total costs and revenues and the resulting surpluses or deficits. Few utilize any type of productivity measure or performance indicator. This paper applies Data Envelopment Analysis to assess the performance of airports. It is used to construct performance indices on the basis of the multiple outputs which airports produce and the multiple inputs which they utilize. In particular we develop productivity measures for terminals and airside operations. The performance measures are then used in a second stage Tobit regression in which environmental, structural and managerial variables are included. The regression results provide a 'net' performance index and also identify which variables the managers have some control over and what the relative importance of each variable is in affecting performance. The data set contains a panel of 21 U.S. airports over a five-year period. © 1997 Elsevier Science Ltd. All rights reserved

Keywords: DEA, airport, performance, productivity.

1. INTRODUCTION

Over the last two decades a great deal of effort and resources have been expended in developing measures of performance for carriers in the different modes of transportation. This has been stimulated by both deregulation and privatization initiatives. Measures of productivity performance, efficiency and effectiveness are now available for railways, airlines, trucking, and public transit firms. The measures range from relatively simple quantities, such as output per employee, to more sophisticated measures such as TFP (Total Factor Productivity)—a standard which takes account of all inputs in the production process. These measures have been used to assess alternative management actions and strategies in developing, for example, more effective means of satisfying the objectives of the owners or operators. They have also been used to measure technical progress and to rank carriers by their productivity gains. In other cases, measures of cost and service effectiveness have been developed in order to evaluate financing for capital projects and changes in public policy such as deregulation.

The motivation for this paper stems from the evolving trends of 'redefining the way in which government operates' and the growing tendency to shift major capital investments and operations in transportation away from direct government control. This can mean anything from privatizing or commercializing infrastructure to creating incentives for managers so that they pursue particular financial targets and perform in a way that maximizes the objectives of the owners. World-wide this has taken such forms as airport and roadway privatization as well as commercialization through joint public/private ownership or the contracting out of various services. In many cases these enterprises are break-even or not- for-profit. Under such circumstances standard financial measures of performance such as the rate of return on capital or profits are not meaningful. It is also difficult to define a measure of output or service as well.

A major impetus behind the desire to privatize or at least commercialize airports, roadways and ports throughout the world is the lack of investment capital available from governments to meet the needs of these infrastructure to invest in new facilities, terminals and equipment. Furthermore, management is under increasing pressure to wean them from government support by becoming more efficient. Airports, in particular, are recognized as mature 'firms' that should be able to stand-alone and operate without government support or interference.

Continued deregulation of carriers has provided an additional stimulus to improve airport performance. Despite airport charges being only 5–7 per cent of total operating costs, airlines operate in highly competitive markets and cannot easily pass rate increases on to customers.* They have continued to place pressure on airports to increase their efficiency. A set of performance measures would allow an airport to demonstrate any improvements. We also develop a linkage between the performance measure and management strategies arguing that it is not sufficient to simply describe performance but also to be able to assess it and understand how managers can affect their performance. The focus in this paper is upon air transportation infrastructure but we believe the approach has broad application.

In this paper we suggest that a method which can be used to assess the performance of the management of transportation infrastructure is Data Envelopment Analysis (DEA). Section 2 provides a brief overview of airport operations and issues to consider in developing performance measures. In Section 3 we examine performance measures and compare these to DEA. Section 4 contains the description of the data and measures of airport performance. The empirical results from the Tobit estimation are reported and discussed in Section 5 while the conclusions are contained in Section 6.

2. AIRPORT OPERATIONS AND ORGANIZATION

While all business enterprises, whether in the public or private sector, need to continuously monitor their performance, it is especially important in the airport industry due to the specific characteristics of airports. Doganis (1992) points out that in a competitive environment, market forces will ensure that optimal performance is equated with profitability. However, the conditions under which airports operate are far from competitive. Regulatory, geographical, economic, social and political constraints all hinder direct competition between airports. At the same time, the extent to which airports can attract other airports' traffic with different prices or service levels is also limited. In other words, the demand for airport services is likely to be relatively inelastic.

The competitive environment of the aviation industry in North America and elsewhere means greater market mobility for carriers and freedom to establish linkages and alliances. Carriers enter and exit markets and change frequency of service and gauge of aircraft. They form partnerships, alliances and take equity positions in other national and global carriers. All of these factors have an impact upon airport demands and utilization. With all of the turmoil brought about by consolidation and restructuring of the air carrier industry and the desire to have an efficient aviation system (air carriers and airports) it seems reasonable that the impact of the domestic policy decisions or policies on efficient use of resources should be investigated.[†]

Airports are subject to peak demands. To have perfectly satisfied customers (the airlines and their passengers) airports would need to supply sufficient runway and terminal capacity to avoid

---

*These figures are for North America. The costs in Europe and Asia are somewhat higher due to higher fees for navigation and airport rates and charges.

† Even as 'mere' landlords, however, the business of airport planning and management is extremely challenging. As Doganis (1992) points out: "Airport authorities must invest substantial capital sums in large and immovable assets that have no alternative use, to satisfy a demand over which they have little control except indirectly. It is the airlines and not the airports who decide where and how the demand for air travel or air freight will be met. Airports merely provide a facility for bring together airlines and their potential customers. Thus, matching the provision of airport capacity with the demand while achieving and maintaining airport profitability and an adequate level of customer satisfaction is a difficult task. It is made particularly difficult because investments to expand airport capacity are lumpy, increasing effective capacity by much more than is needed in the short term, and because they must be planned long in advance."

delays at even the busiest periods, allowing the airlines to maximize fleet utilization and improve load factors by providing service when their customers most desire. Airports, conversely, would like the airlines to spread their flight over the entire day so as to minimize runway and terminal requirements. The advent of hubbing has exacerbated this dichotomy with its concentration of arrivals and departures in narrow time bands. Even at those airports that are not used as hubs by any airline, aircraft movements are not evenly distributed. Among the other factors listed by Ashford *et al.* (1984) that affect an airport's peaking characteristics is the domestic/international traffic mix as well as the long haul/short haul mix.

Doganis (1992) gives an interesting illustration of the pressures being brought to bear on runway capacity. Between 1971 and 1982, a period in which the average annual increase in the number of passengers was 5.2 per cent, all of the growth was accommodated by higher load factors (33%) and increased aircraft size (67%) with the number of departures remaining unchanged. Between 1982 and 1986, however, when the annual average growth rate rose to 8.8%, the increase in demand was met almost entirely (97%) by increasing the number of departures.

While airports should be asked to adhere to private financial standards, they must also be judged in the context of their overall goals. These can be "diverse, often not clearly articulated, and frequently specified (or influenced) less by professional managers than by public policy and political considerations within various sponsoring governments" (Doganis and Graham, 1987). In the case of airports, it has been argued, federal support has resulted in facilities that are not so much what is needed as what the government is willing to pay for (Wells, 1992). Bhargava *et al.* (1993) found little in the way of "goal/objectives as a criterion" in much of the work he reviewed, finding instead the assumption that "financial measures appropriately capture the objectives of the firm". Given the unique position of airports, profit measures are an inadequate, if not totally misleading means of assessing management performance.

Airports face many of the same problems of any public utility in which capital is lumpy and marginal operating costs low. For a manufacturing firm at a constant level of production, a slowdown in sales would be reflected as an increase in inventory and not a decrease in efficiency. If the slowdown were to be anticipated and production reduced, the amount of inputs consumed would likewise be reduced leaving the output/input ratio (i.e. productivity) unchanged (ignoring possible economies of scale). With most airports, however, the factors of production (inputs) usually do not change year to year and there can be no inventory of production. Efficiency, therefore, will suffer any time there is a slowdown in the economy or by the airlines utilizing the airport, regardless of airport management ability or efforts.*

Since such exogenous factors do exist, how does one account internally for a change in output? If output is down, does this mean anything under the airport's control has become less productive? This exogenous slowdown needs to be accounted for in order to provide an accurate measure of managerial performance. In essence we want to determine how much variation in airport performance can be attributed to managerial decision-making and initiatives and what are the important decisions or strategies within that portion of airport performance an airport manager can affect.

3. DATA ENVELOPMENT ANALYSIS

Development of a strategic performance measure requires that the multiple outputs and objectives be accommodated. It should also be possible to translate the performance indicator into effective management strategies. Methods of measuring efficiency can be broadly classified into non-parametric and parametric. Non-parametric methods include indexes of partial and total factor productivity, and data envelopment analysis. The latter is essentially a linear programming based method. Parametric methods involve the estimation of neoclassical and stochastic cost and or production functions.

The data requirements for the various methods differ, as do their ability to inform managerial decisions. The use of partial productivity measures is pervasive and though these measures are easy to understand and compute, they can be quite misleading, because they do not reflect differ-

---

*A graphic example, though atypical in magnitude, is Anchorage International which has seen its concession revenue shrink from $19.5 million in 1990 to $5.4 million in 1993 due to the cessation of layovers of aircraft flying between the U.S. and Japan. Another example is Dayton International, where passenger traffic has been cut in half between the time of the US Air merger with Piedmont Aviation on August 5, 1989 and the final closure of their Dayton hub in January of 1992.

ences in factor prices nor do they take account of differences in the other factors used in production. Partial productivity measures are also unable to handle multiple outputs.

One solution to some of these problems is to construct an index of total factor productivity (TFP). This measure does not suffer from the shortcomings of partial productivity measure, but taken alone it is not very informative for ranking management strategies. Extracting more information from measures of total factor productivity typically requires reliance on estimating parametric neo-classical cost or production functions.* The data requirements are more onerous than partial measures. In addition to data on physical inputs and outputs, this measure also requires information on prices, which is used to aggregate inputs and outputs.

Data Envelopment Analysis (DEA) is another alternative and has found favor in applications where the outputs are not easily or clearly defined; for example in measuring productivity in schools, hospitals or government institutions (Bedard, 1985). It is also useful in determining the efficiency of firms that consume or produce inputs or outputs, which lack natural prices (Button and Weyman-Jones, 1993a; 1993b). DEA is a (linear) programming based technique and the basic model only requires information on inputs and outputs. Indeed, this is also a major drawback of DEA, as it does not incorporate any information of factor prices or costs of production.[†] DEA can incorporate multiple outputs and inputs; in fact, inputs and outputs can be defined in a very general manner without getting into problems of aggregation.[‡] If more of a measure is desirable it can be modeled as output and if less of something is better, it can be interpreted as input. This is an attractive feature as in many service industries such as banking, it is difficult to determine whether something is an input or an output. DEA can also make use of proxy outputs including output combinations that would not be used with other efficiency measures.[§]

DEA provides a scalar measure of relative efficiency by comparing the efficiency achieved by a decision-making unit (DMU) with the efficiency obtained by similar DMUs. The method allows us to obtain a well-defined relation between outputs and inputs. In the case of a single output this relation corresponds to a production function in which the output is maximal for the indicated inputs. In the more general case of multiple outputs this relation can be defined as an efficient production possibility surface or frontier. As this production possibility surface or frontier is derived from empirical observations, it measures the relative efficiency of DMUs that can be obtained with the existing technology or management strategy. Technological or managerial change can be evaluated by considering each set of values for different time periods for the same DMU as separate entities (each set of values as a different DMU). If there is a significant change in technology or management strategies this will be reflected in a change in the production possibility surface.[¶]

4. DATA, METHOD AND DEA RESULTS

The data used in the DEA calculations represent a cross section of airports in the US which have differing ownership, financing and operational characteristics. A brief discussion of some of the variables is useful. Airport financing falls into two categories; residual or compensatory. At a residual financed airport, carriers have the responsibility for meeting any shortfall that occurs after all revenues have been collected from various sources. At a compensatory financed airport, the airport has full responsibility and the carriers simply pay a negotiated fee. The residual airport would be closer to a privatized airport while the compensatory would be akin to a public airport. Airport managers can affect the efficiency of their airport by allowing the runways and facilities to

---

*These have their own problems. For example, though in theory all flexible functional forms can approximate an unknown production technology, in practice, results may differ quite substantially. Thus choice of functional form becomes an important issue. In addition, flexibility has a price, that is, violation of theoretical consistency requirements for cost minimization. Stochastic or frontier cost and production functions suffer from the same shortcomings though unlike neoclassical functions, they are able to distinguish technical progress (movement in the frontier) from technical inefficiency (distance from the frontier).

[†]For this reason DEA cannot be used to analyze or comment on cost efficiency. Firms may be technically efficient but cost inefficient. Furthermore it may be possible that firms ranked technically inefficient by DEA may be able to produce their outputs at a lower cost than those ranked as technically efficient.

[‡]All productivity measures have the shortcoming that they do not directly include user-borne costs. Using proxies can include these.

[§]For example, gross-ton-miles and car-miles or gross-ton-miles and revenues as alternative measures of outputs in the rail industry.

[¶]For a detailed explanation of DEA see Charnes et al. (1994). For a good illustration see Førsund and Hernaes (1994).

be used in different manners. The access to gates, for example, can affect the number of movements and passengers handled; both measures of output. Noise management, a key issue at major
US airports, can be handled in a number of different ways. Each noise management strategy can
have a different affect on the number of aircraft using the airport, runways and gates, in a given period
of time. A noise budget allows a carrier to emit an aggregate amount of noise. If it uses noisy
aircraft it can have fewer flights while use of newer quieter aircraft allows more flights.

Our data set is composed of information from 21 of the top 30 airports in the United States for
the period 1989–1993 (Cooper and Gillen, 1994). We have 114 observations organized in a panel.*
The first part of our analysis involves deriving a scalar measure of relative efficiency for 114
DMUs. To do this, we define airports as producing two separate classes of services, these being
terminal services and movements. Terminal services are modeled as having two outputs—number
of passengers and pounds of cargo and six inputs—number of runways, number of gates, terminal
area, number of employees, number of baggage collection belts and number of public parking
spots. Movements have two outputs—air carrier movements and commuter movements and four
inputs—airport area, number of runways, runway area and number of employees.† Movements are
assumed to be produced under constant returns to scale (Gillen, 1994) whereas returns to scale are
variable in the production of terminal services.

The models used here to obtain a scalar measure of relative efficiency are the output-oriented
models.‡ For our purposes, orientation is not of crucial importance and our decision is based on
convenience.§ The output-oriented model fits in more naturally with the second stage of our analysis, which estimates a Tobit model. Movements are modeled under the assumption of constant
returns to scale. The model is as follows for a given DMU:¶

$$\min_{\mu,v} g_0 = v'X_0$$

$$s.t.$$

$$\mu'Y_0 = 1 \tag{1}$$

$$-\mu'Y_0 + v'X_0 \geq 0$$

$$\mu'' \geq 0$$

$$v' \geq 0$$

where X_0 is a vector of inputs, Y_0 is a vector of outputs and, μ and v are weights to be determined
by solving the programming problem. Terminal services are modeled using the following variable
returns to scale model:‖

$$\min_{\mu,v,v_0} f_0 = v'X_0 + v_0$$

$$s.t.$$

$$\mu'Y_0 = 1 \tag{2}$$

$$-\mu'Y_0 + v'X_0 + v_0 t \geq 0$$

$$\mu' \geq 0$$

$$v' \geq 0 \, free$$

where v_0 is the measure of returns to scale or the constant term in the hyperplane and t is a unit
vector. The measure of efficiency we report in Table 1 represents two types of inefficiency, that

---

*Data for Dayton Airport are only available for the period 1989–1992.
†We do not have disaggregated data on employees involved in the provision of terminal services and those involved in
  producing movements. In addition, we do not have data on fuel and other inputs such as materials.
‡In the 'output oriented' model the two sources of inefficiency are that which can be eliminated by a proportional aug-
  mentation of all outputs and residual inefficiency or output slack. In the 'input oriented' model there are two sources of
  inefficiency, one that can be eliminated by a proportional reduction in input use and a residual or excess input.
§Note that if a unit is inefficient according to the input-oriented model, it will also be so according to the output-oriented
  model.
¶See eqn (4) in Charnes et al. (1978).
‖See page 34 in Charnes et al. (1994).

AVIATION PERFORMANCE AND PRODUCTIVITY

D. Gillen and A. Lall

which can be removed by a proportional augmentation of all outputs and residual inefficiency. A value of 1 implies that the DMU is efficient *and efficiency score increases with increase in relative inefficiency*. Tables 2 and 3 show changes in efficiency between the years 1989 and 1993.

An examination of Table 1 reveals the following outcomes for the different airports. In the majority of cases the index is falling implying an increase in efficiency (or reduction in inefficiency). This can reflect in part the emergence from the recession in the late 1980s. However there are some interesting differences. Anchorage for example shows in increase in inefficiency for terminals but a

Table 1. Efficiency measures from DEA calculation

Airport	DMU	Terminals	Movements	Airport	DMU	Terminals	Movements
Anchorage	ANC-89	1.0000	2.5554	Memphis	MEM-92	1.0533	1.1728
	ANC-90	1.0947	2.5421		MEM-93	1.0000	1.2105
	ANC-91	1.0333	1.9672	Milwaukee	MKE-89	2.1333	2.3538
	ANC-92	1.1331	1.6731		MKE-90	2.0326	1.9366
	ANC-93	1.1319	1.9505		MKE-91	2.7135	1.8979
Atlanta	ALT-89	1.0658	1.1327		MKE-92	2.5597	1.8847
	ALT-90	1.0000	1.0000		MKE-93	2.5059	1.8513
	ALT-91	1.2093	1.2793	Minneapolis	MSP-89	1.3675	1.8736
	ALT-92	1.1126	1.2635	—St Paul	MSP-90	1.3011	1.7099
	ALT-93	1.0000	1.1856		MSP-91	1.2958	1.8051
Boston	BOS-89	1.1583	1.7050		MSP-92	1.1760	1.6196
	BOS-90	1.1721	1.5258		MSP-93	1.1395	1.3588
	BOS-91	1.2093	1.3533	Ontario	ONT-89	1.0000	2.6907
	BOS-92	1.2014	1.1593		ONT-90	1.0000	2.7001
	BOS-93	1.1311	1.0000		ONT-91	1.0000	2.6846
Baltimore/	BWI-89	1.6761	1.9109		ONT-92	1.0000	2.7248
Washington	BWI-90	1.6331	1.8677		ONT-93	1.0000	2.3619
	BWI-91	1.6900	1.9422	Phoenix	PHX-89	1.0000	1.0752
	BWI-92	1.7923	2.1235		PHX-90	1.0000	1.0357
	BWI-93	1.9216	1.9613		PHX-91	1.0000	1.0027
Charlotte/	CLT-89	1.2254	1.0000		PHX-92	1.0411	1.0000
Douglas	CLT-90	1.2980	1.0176		PHX-93	1.0000	1.0274
	CLT-91	1.2657	1.0273	Portland	PDX-89	1.8053	1.2376
	CLT-92	1.1127	1.0402		PDX-90	1.8614	1.1867
	CLT-93	1.1447	1.0000		PDX-91	1.8185	1.1678
Chicago	MDW-89	1.0000	1.0000		PDX-92	1.7312	1.0861
	MDW-90	1.0000	1.0000		PDX-93	1.5044	1.0085
	MDW-91	1.0000	1.1251	St Louis	STL-89	1.1029	1.8893
	MDW-92	1.5640	2.4514		STL-90	1.0860	1.7998
	MDW-93	1.0000	2.7807		STL-91	1.1371	1.8077
Cincinnati/	CVG-89	1.4838	1.1329		STL-92	1.0572	1.7895
Northern Kentucky	CVG-90	1.5269	1.0000		STL-93	1.1073	1.8025
	CVG-91	1.4059	1.0000	Salt Lake City	SLC-89	1.4605	2.0072
	CVG-92	1.2417	1.0216		SLC-90	1.3358	2.1787
	CVG-93	1.4439	1.0000		SLC-91	1.3085	2.1127
Cleveland Int'l	CLE-89	1.9690	1.8371		SLC-92	1.2312	2.0320
	CLE-90	1.8451	1.6372		SLC-93	1.0912	2.0392
	CLE-91	1.9278	1.7012	San Diego	SAN-89	1.0000	1.0000
	CLE-92	1.5158	1.4295		SAN-90	1.0000	1.0000
	CLE-93	1.4377	1.6833		SAN-91	1.0111	1.0098
Dayton	DAY-89	1.0000	1.9072		SAN-92	1.0099	1.0000
	DAY-90	1.0000	1.9623		SAN-93	1.0000	1.0000
	DAY-91	1.1825	1.7849	San Francisco	SFO-89	1.0505	2.1147
	DAY-92	1.3434	2.4312		SFO-90	1.0800	2.1741
Fort Lauderdale	FLL-89	1.7584	1.0000		SFO-91	1.0381	2.1026
	FLL-90	1.6486	1.8308		SFO-92	1.0205	2.2579
	FLL-91	1.7950	1.9414		SFO-93	1.0000	2.4530
	FLL-92	1.7562	2.2228	San Jose	SJC-89	1.0000	2.4739
	FLL-93	1.6305	1.8133		SJC-90	1.0000	1.8111
Kansas City	MCI-89	1.6473	1.5304		SJC-91	1.4144	1.6095
	MCI-90	1.9107	2.1834		SJC-92	1.5807	1.5900
	MCI-91	2.2568	2.6458		SJC-93	1.5957	1.6722
	MCI-92	2.2317	2.3277	Seattle—Tacoma	SEA-89	1.1407	1.0729
	MCI-93	2.8372	2.2539		SEA-90	1.0677	1.0000
Memphis	MEM-89	1.0000	1.5758		SEA-91	1.0000	1.0209
	MEM-90	1.0385	1.7755		SEA-92	1.0000	1.0126
	MEM-91	1.1009	1.6779		SEA-93	1.0000	1.0632

reduction in inefficiency for movements. This reflects the reduction in passengers due to long haul jets being able to bypass this technical stop as well as the growth of hubbing out of the west coast gateways such as San Francisco and Seattle.

Figures 1 and 2 illustrate the Terminal and Airside efficiency measures contained in Table 1. They provide a better display of both differences between terminal and airside efficiency in an airport and also relative efficiency across airports. The differences are quite striking.

Table 2. Terminal-efficiency in 1993 compared to 1989

Worse	Better	Same
Anchorage	Atlanta[a]	Chicago[b]
Baltimore/Washington	Boston	Phoenix[b]
Dayton	Charlotte/Douglas	San Francisco[b]
Fort Lauderdale	Cincinnati/Northern Kentucky	Seattle—Tacoma[b]
Kansas City	Cleveland International	
Milwaukee	Memphis[a]	
Portland	Minneapolis—St Paul	
San Jose	Ontario[a]	
	St Louis	
	Salt Lake City	
	San Diego[a]	

[a]Indicates efficiency of 1 in 1993.
[b]Indicates efficiency of 1 in 1989 and 1993.
Data for Dayton are for 1989 and 1992.

Table 3. Movement-efficiency in 1993 compared to 1989

Worse	Better	Same
Atlanta	Anchorage	Charlotte/Douglas[b]
Baltimore/Washington	Boston[a]	
Chicago	Cincinnati/Northern Kentucky[a]	
Dayton	Cleveland International	
Kansas City	Fort Lauderdale	
Milwaukee	Memphis	
Ontario	Minneapolis—St Paul	
St Louis	Phoenix	
Salt Lake City	Portland	
San Francisco	San Diego[a]	
	San Jose	
	Seattle—Tacoma	

[a]Indicates efficiency of 1 in 1993.
[b]Indicates efficiency of 1 in 1989 and 1993.
Data for Dayton are for 1989 and 1992.

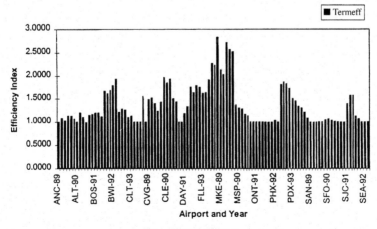

Fig. 1. Thermal efficiency.

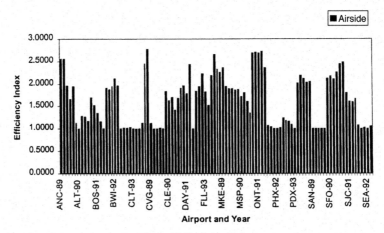

Fig. 2. Airside efficiency index

Boston's Logan Airport, for example, has terminal inefficiency rising and movements ineffi-ciency falling. However, the relative values of efficiency are very different. Terminal efficiency is quite high while airside efficiency was relatively poor but improved markedly over five years. As is true of Salt Lake City but in most of cases the inefficiencies are moving in the same direction. The hub airports exhibit some loose similarities. It appears that as hubbing rises terminal efficiency improves but movement efficiency decreases most likely due to the feed from small commuter aircraft. San Francisco exhibits this pattern of performance but the level of inefficiency on the movement side is quite startling. San Jose illustrates the impact of American developing their hub there with terminal efficiency rising and movement efficiency gradually falling.

Summary tables of the changes in terminal and movements efficiency between 1989–1993 are shown in Tables 2 and 3. Terminals doing worse are those in which airlines have moved elsewhere or the economy has not picked up. Terminals doing better reflect new and expanding hub opera-tions, and traffic growth from economic growth above the average (e.g. San Diego). Those doing the same are well-established hub airports.

Table 3 exhibits a clear bifurcation in the results for changes in movement efficiency. Both hub and non-hub airports showed degradation in efficiency. Those airports doing better were those which tended to have more homogenous traffic and fewer wide-bodied aircraft.

5. TOBIT RESULTS

At this point we have addressed only the first of our questions. We have a measure of relative airport efficiency and we can rank airports by year and to each other by airside as well as terminal efficiency. This is one of the significant benefits of the DEA measure in that it is useful for both inter-temporal as well as cross-sectional comparisons. However, it is also our purpose to explain the variation in performance measures both over time and across airports. We develop a set of variables for each airport which we roughly classify as structural (e.g. number of runways, land area and numbers of gates), environmental variables (e.g. annual service volume or ASV) and managerial variables (e.g. use of gates, financing regime, noise strategies, proportion of GA traffic, existence of hubs at airport). We are interested in two issues. What proportion of the variation in efficiency that can be explained by the managerial variables and which managerial variables are most important in affecting this proportion of efficiency?

To obtain the true or net efficiency index we undertake a second stage of analysis. In this we utilize the efficiency index generated from the DEA methodology and use it as the dependent variable in order to identify the variables which affect efficiency. The DEA efficiency measure has a lower bound of 1 or, as we have done here, if one take natural logs of the efficiency measure, a lower bound of zero. Thus we use the censored regression or Tobit model (Tobin, 1958). The standard Tobit model can be represented as follows for observation i:

Developing measures of airport productivity and performance: an application of data envelopment analysis   269

$$y_i^* = \beta' x_i + \varepsilon_i$$
$$y_i = 0 \ \text{if} \ y_i^* \le 0 \qquad (3)$$
$$y_i = y_i^* \ \text{if} \ y_i^* > 0.$$

The estimated coefficients of the Tobit model do not provide the marginal effects. The marginal effect for variable j is derived as follows:*

$$\frac{\partial E[y_i]}{\partial x_j} = \beta_j \Phi_i. \qquad (4)$$

In addition, conditional marginal effects are also reported. The conditional marginal effect for variable j is derived as:

$$\frac{\partial E[y_i \mid y_i > 0]}{\partial x_j} = \beta_j \left[1 - \left(\frac{\beta' x_i}{\sigma} \right) \cdot \frac{\phi_i}{\Phi_i} - \left(\frac{\phi_i}{\Phi_i} \right)^2 \right]. \qquad (5)$$

In the above two equations, ϕ_i and Φ_i are the respective probability and cumulative density functions of a standard normal variable evaluated at $\beta' x_i / \sigma$. Since a unique marginal (and marginal conditional) effect can be calculated for each observation, we report the mean of the marginal effects. The results of the estimation are reported in Tables 4 and 5, for movements and terminals respectively.

Table 4 reports the Tobit regression results for movement (airside) efficiency and Table 5 does the same for Terminal efficiency explanations. The marginal and conditional marginal effects are reported in the last two columns respectively of the tables. The two measures are quite similar but the conditional marginal effect is always less. In the movements efficiency regression we are trying to determine which managerial and non-managerial variables have the most impact on the

Table 4. Tobit regression on efficiency related to movements

Variable	Regression coefficient	t statistic	Marginal effect	Conditional marginal effect
Number of airline hubs	-0.2725	-4.40	-0.2315	-0.2158
Square feet of airside capacity	0.0001	6.05	0.0001	0.0001
Number of runways	0.0386	0.99	0.0328	0.0305
Total number of gates	-0.0091	-3.03	-0.0077	-0.0072
Proportion of GA movements	2.8554	8.30	2.4258	2.2609
Year 1989 dummy	-0.0491	-0.81	-0.0417	-0.0389
Year 1990 dummy	-0.0431	-0.72	-0.0366	-0.0341
Year 1991 dummy	-0.0045	-0.08	-0.0038	-0.0035
Year 1992 dummy	-0.0118	-0.20	-0.0100	-0.0093
Residual financing	-0.3394	-3.84	-0.2883	-0.2687
Rotational runways	0.3864	3.33	0.3282	0.3059
Preferential flight path	-0.2351	-2.90	-0.1997	-0.1861
Preferential runway use	0.2761	2.57	0.2345	0.2186
Limit on operations	0.0717	0.31	0.0609	0.0568
Limit on stage II aircraft	0.6970	3.82	0.5921	0.5519
Limit on operating hours	-1.1286	-4.01	-0.9588	-0.8936
Noise budget	2.0797	5.50	1.7667	1.6467
Atlanta dummy	1.9590	4.63	1.6643	1.5512
San Francisco dummy	0.5089	3.11	0.4323	0.4029
Minnesota and St Paul dummy	2.1189	5.94	1.8000	1.6777
Seattle—Tacoma dummy	-0.5997	-0.97	-0.5094	-0.4748
Phoenix dummy	-0.1389	-0.57	-0.1180	-0.1100

Dependent variable log of efficiency index of movements.
Log of the likelihood function 12.390.
Estimate of sigma 0.1833.
Asymptotic t-ratio for estimate of sigma 12.986.

*See p. 963 in Greene (1997) or p. 799 in Judge et al. (1988). Note that this is also a good approximation for the marginal effects of dummy variables.

Table 5. Tobit regression on efficiency related to terminals

Variable	Regression coefficient	t statistic	Marginal effect	Conditional marginal effect
Number of airline hubs	0.2811	4.013	0.2016	0.1686
Total number of gates	−0.0086	−2.103	−0.0062	−0.0052
Square feet of terminal	0.0000	3.148	0.0000	0.0000
Baggage belts per gate	3.1222	3.671	2.2387	1.8729
Proportion of gates common use	−0.8853	−3.848	−0.6348	−0.5311
Proportion of gates exclusive use	−0.4193	−2.634	−0.3006	−0.2515
Compensatory financing	−0.0908	−1.106	−0.0651	−0.0545
Year 1989 dummy	−0.0568	−0.675	−0.0407	−0.0341
Year 1990 dummy	−0.0362	−0.437	−0.0259	−0.0217
Year 1991 dummy	0.0662	0.821	0.0474	0.0397
Year 1992 dummy	0.1019	1.288	0.0731	0.0612
Atlanta dummy	−0.9668	−4.106	−0.6933	−0.5800
San Francisco dummy	−1.6732	−5.148	−1.1998	−1.0037
Minnesota and St Paul dummy	−1.3211	−6.517	−0.9473	−0.7925
Seattle—Tacoma dummy	−2.0175	−7.238	−1.4466	−1.2102
Phoenix dummy	−1.4534	−5.177	−1.0422	−0.8719
Proportion international passengers	−5.2258	−3.079	−3.7471	−3.1349

Dependent variable log of efficiency index of terminals.
Log of the likelihood function −14.717.
Estimate of sigma 0.2412.
Asymptotic t-ratio for estimate of sigma 12.048.

efficiency with which airside can yield aircraft movements. Since the efficiency index has a lower limit of 1, a higher number implies more *inefficiency*. Once you take natural logs the lower limit is zero. So a *positive coefficient implies inefficiency* is going up.

There are four sets of variables; dummy variables for the time period, dummy variables for hub airports, noise strategy variables and management operational and investment variables. The time dummies are not significant so there is no apparent trend in the data or anomalies in one year or another. The hub dummies show clearly that primary hubs increase the efficient use of the airside. However, there are differences among hubs. At Minneapolis—St Paul, the hub for Northwest Airlines and Atlanta, the hub for Delta Airlines we see quite similar (positive) effects on efficiency but San Francisco a second hub for United shows a smaller impact. San Francisco is also a gateway and tends to have a greater proportion of wide body aircraft traffic. The former hubs have a large number of feeder flights hence increasing the level of efficiency.

The noise strategy variables are all significant save for limiting operations. Using a preferential flight path or limiting the hours of operation reduces inefficiency while all the remaining noise management strategies tend to increase inefficiency. It appears counterintuitive that limiting the hours an airport is open could reduce inefficiency. However, two explanations are offered. First, if limits on hours and primary hubs are correlated this could explain the result. Airlines will not bring complexes into the airport in the middle of the night to hub since there would be little demand. The second explanation is that given limitations on night use the airport utilizes its' resources very efficiently while those without such constraints do not feel compelled to operate with such efficiency.

The management variables contain a broad cross section of strategies and investments. Increasing the number of boarding gates can increase airside efficiency while increasing the number of runways has no impact and increasing the area of airside capacity has the opposite effect, reducing efficiency. Given scarce resources, the airport manager can obtain more cost efficiencies from investing in terminal gates than expanding the size of the airport or increasing the number of runways. Airports with a larger number of hub airlines have greater cost efficiencies. Some airport managers feel hubs can place an airport in jeopardy but the evidence implies there may be a cost to such a position. The one variable that stands out as significantly affecting airport efficiency is the proportion of general aviation traffic. An increase in this type of traffic has a sizable impact on increasing inefficiency. Such evidence provides support for the introduction of peak pricing for small GA aircraft at major airports.

The way the airport arranges its finances has some impact on efficiency. Airports that have residual financing have a higher level of efficiency (note this is the opposite of terminal efficiency as discussed below). Under residual financing the airlines are at risk for revenue shortfalls. They will bring pressure to bear on the airport to ensure greater efficiency on the airside. Unlike terminals here are no alternative revenue sources so one would expect a greater emphasis on efficient resource use. This would also tend to increase revenue from landing fees.

Looking at the marginal effects the best thing airport management can do to improve efficiency is create pressures of productive and dynamic efficiency through corportization or privatization. This interpretation comes from the 'residual financing' variable. An almost equally effective strategy is to attract a hub airline. Adding gates has a positive but small impact on airside efficiency. The preferred noise management strategy appears to be limiting operating hours and the use preferential flight paths. The limitation on operations is clearly counter-intuitive and one would need to explore this result further.

In Table 5 we report the results for the explanation of terminal efficiency. As in the previous case the variables can be divided into three sets as the noise variables have been excluded. In the time dummies only the 1992 dummy appears significant. It is positive, implying that in 1992 the level of efficiency fell relative to previous years. The hub dummies are all significant and of the same sign. Terminals at airports that are hubs operate at a higher level of efficiency than non-hubs. Unlike airside efficiency there appears not to be any real differences among the hubs. The proportion of international passengers has a profound impact on efficiency. However, unlike with movement efficiency, as the number of carriers hubbing at an airport rises the level of inefficiency of terminals rises. Without co-ordination of the banks airlines will sacrifice some flights as carriers compete for the same times for establishing times for banks to arrive and depart straining gates and baggage systems.

There were a number of strategic variables examined for terminal efficiency. First, the way in which gates are managed has an impact on efficiency. The greater the proportion of common and exclusive use gates the greater the reduction in inefficiency. Common use gates means the airport controls gate use and will ensure they are used most efficiently. Similarly when a gate has been given to a carrier for exclusive use it is in the carriers best interest to use the resource efficiently. As the proportion of preferential use gates rises we get the opposite result; efficiency falls. A carrier that has preferential treatment may try to use gates as a barrier to entry and not necessarily use them efficiently.

Investing in gates has a positive impact on efficiency while increasing the size of the terminal does not. Bigger terminals are not the solution to improving efficiency but allowing greater access to aircraft and passengers with greater numbers of gates will. A surprising result is that increasing the number of baggage belts per gate raises inefficiency. One would have expected the opposite result. It may be that hub airports which process larger numbers of passengers but tend to use baggage belts less are driving this result.

Unlike airside, terminals have greater levels of efficiency if they are financed on a compensatory basis. This means the airport owner accepts responsibility for any revenue shortfall. In terminals there are a number of alternatives for revenue generation and airports will have an incentive to develop these and run the terminal efficiently. Airlines see the terminal as a check-in and departure facility. This focus would not necessarily lead to greater terminal efficiency.

Having greater proportions of international passengers is one strategy that has a marked impact on improving terminal efficiency. Adding gates is also effective but how one manages those gates is important. Increasing the proportion of gates for common use raises efficiency as does reserving some for exclusive use. With common use the airport can improve efficiency by allocating it across airlines while with exclusive use gates the airline has an incentive to use the gates most efficiently. If gates are placed in 'preferential use' airlines have an incentive to protect their strategic position by not giving them up for competitors use. The increase in baggage belts per gate is a surprising result. It may reflect the importance of hubs that has more through traffic and hence less need for baggage belts.

6. SUMMARY

Public infrastructure such as airports, air traffic control, air navigation systems, roadways and ports represent sizable capital investments that yield a service that is difficult to define. In addition, in most all cases there is no market measure of performance since the services are not transacted in a 'traditional' economic market setting. As we privatize, commercialize or defederalize these various assets it seems important that we are able to judge whether the new managers are doing a good job. Because there are obligations to serve placed upon the new owners when the transfer or sale takes place, the use of pure profit or rate of return measures to judge performance may not be appropriate.

The economics of airports has changed in the last decade. As airlines have developed hubs, airports can now compete for the long haul connecting passenger. Inter-airport competition was an anomaly in the past. Airports are now perceived as multi-product firms producing airside services, terminal space services, terminal passenger handling services, land development services and cargo handling services. Many airports have adopted new retail plans and genrate more revenue from this source than for airside fees. When airports lower prices and profits increase, one has elasticity proof that airport retail is not a natural monopoly. Every airport that has been privatised has lowered landing fees and retail prices and increased revenues dramatically. There appear to be significant X-inefficiencies in government airports and the question is, why?

There has been extensive literature discussing the measurement of performance for both private and public enterprise. Unfortunately, 'conventional indicators (partial and total factor productivity, average cost, and financial ratios) of performance are restricted to measuring the achievement of allocative objectives but they fall quite short of the true concept of efficiency' (Pestieau, 1989). In order to develop a strategic performance measure it requires that the multiple outputs and multi-dimensional objectives be accommodated. What's more, it is desirable to be able to translate the performance indicator into effective management strategies. Our idea is to not only measure performance but also to be able to assess what the manager can affect of this performance variation and what are the most effective strategies.

We selected the use of DEA to create our performance measures. This methodology has been used in applications where the outputs are not easily or clearly defined; for example in measuring productivity in schools, universities and government institutions. It is also useful in determining the efficiency of firms that consume or produce inputs or outputs, which lack natural prices. DEA can incorporate multiple outputs and inputs and inputs or outputs can be defined in a general manner and avoid problems of aggregation. If more of a measure is desirable it can be modeled as output and if less of something is better, it can be interpreted as input. This is an attractive feature as in many service industries such as banking, it is difficult to determine whether something is an input or an output.

Our approach in the assessment of airport performance has been to separate airside and terminals in exploring management strategies to improve efficiency. These two components of the airport, although conditionally related, have different production technologies and certainly different strategies available to them. On the airside having hub airlines and expanding gate capacity improves efficiency. Reducing the number of GA movements has a dramatic impact on improving efficiency as well. In fact it is the single most important factor affecting airside efficiency. Market discipline is also an important factor. If the airport absorbs the risk of revenue shortfalls, there is less incentive for the efficient use of the available capacity.

Terminal efficiency is improved by expanding the number of gates and managing them in a way to ensure their effective utilization. Placing them in common or exclusive use but not preferential use can best accomplish this. We would not argue these results are the final word in adopting certain management or regulatory strategies. The numbers need to be confirmed. What we do argue is that measuring for management of the modern airport is imperative.

This research represents a start. The next steps are to integrate cargo information to take account of this output and to represent more outputs. It also seems important that we better integrate the airside and terminal operations. They are clearly contingent on one another as there are externalities. Estimating a conditional efficiency measure would seem the next logical step.

Acknowledgements—An earlier version of this paper was presented at the ATRG Conference, Vancouver, Canada, June 1997. We thank Bill Waters for his constructive comments on an earlier draft.

REFERENCES

Ashford, N., Martin Stanton, H. P. and Moore, C. (1984) *Airport Operations*. John Wiley & Sons, New York.
Bedard, J. C. (1985) Use of data envelopment analysis in accounting applications: evaluation and illustration by prospective hospital reimbursement. Ph.D. dissertation, University of Wisconsin—Madison, UMI, Ann Arbor, MI.

Developing measures of airport productivity and performance: an application of data envelopment analysis 273

Bhargava, Dubelaar, C. and Ramaswani, S. (1993) *Reconciling diverse measures of performance: a conceptual framework and a test of methodology*, Working paper, Faculty of Business, University of Alberta.

Button, K. and Weyman-Jones, T. (1993a) X-inefficiency and regulatory shift in the UK. *Journal of Evolutionary Economics* **3**, 1–15.

Button, K. and Weyman-Jones, T. (1993b) X-inefficiency and technical inefficiency. *Public Choice*, 1–22.

Charnes, A. *et al.* (1994) *Data Envelopment Analysis: Theory, Methodology and Applications*. Kluwer Academic Publishers, Boston.

Charnes, A., Cooper, W. W. and Rhodes, E. (1978) Measuring the efficiency of decision making units. *European Journal of Operation Research* **2**(6), 429–444.

Cooper, D. and Gillen, D. (1994) Measuring airport efficiency and effectiveness in the california aviation system. Research Report no. UCB-ITS-WP-94, Air Transportation research Center, Institute of Transportation Studies, University of California, Berkeley.

Doganis, R. (1992) *The Airport Business*. Routledge, London.

Doganis, R. and Graham, A. (1987) Airport management: the role of performance indicators. Transport Studies Group Research Report No. 13.

Førsund, Finn R., and Erik Hernaes (1994) A comparative analysis of ferry transport in Norway. In *Data Envelopment Analysis: Theory, Methodology and Applications*, eds A. Charnes *et al.* Kluwer Academic Publishers, Boston.

Gillen, D. Measuring management performance for deregulated commercialized and privatized public infrastructure. Paper presented to the Center for Law & Economic Analysis Conference, Sept., Toronto.

Greene, W. H. (1997) *Econometric Analysis*, 3rd edn. Prentice Hall, New Jersey.

Judge, G. G., et. al. (1988) *Introduction to the Theory and Practice of Econometrics*, 2nd edn. John Wiley and Sons Inc., New York.

Pestieau, P. (1989) Measuring the performance of public enterprises: a must in times of privatization. *Annals of Public and Co-operative Economics* **60**(3), 293–305.

Tobin, J. (1958) Estimating the relationship for limited dependent variables. *Econometrica* **26**, 24–36.

Wells, A. T. (1992) *Airport Planning & Management*. Tab Books, Blue Ridge Summit, PA.

9

Technical Note

An analysis of the operational efficiency of major airports in the United States

Joseph Sarkis

Abstract

Recently, considerable attention has been focused on the performance of various airlines and air carriers in terms of efficiency. Although it is obvious that air carriers use airports, few studies have focused on airport operational efficiency. This empirical study evaluates the operational efficiencies of 44 major U.S. airports using data envelopment analysis and some of its recent developments. Various airport characteristics are evaluated to determine their relationship to an airport's efficiency. Efficiency measures are based on four resource input measures including airport operational costs, number of airport employees, gates and runways, and five output measures including operational revenue, passenger flow, commercial and general aviation movement, and total cargo transportation. The results of this study have operational as well as public policy implications. © 2000 Elsevier Science B.V. All rights reserved.

Keywords: Data envelopment analysis; Productivity; Logistics; Service operations

1. Introduction

The operational performance of various air carriers is the subject of numerous studies. Yet, airports, major service providers to air carriers, have not been evaluated from the perspective of their management or operational efficiency. Instead, as noted by Wiley (1986) and Inamete (1993), much of the literature on airports focuses on technical subjects, such as planning, design, construction, and legal and environmental issues.

The analysis and evaluation of airport operational efficiency have implications for a number of airport customers. Air carriers want to schedule and locate at airports that are more efficient. Municipalities want airports to be as efficient, and, thus, as competitive as possible to attract business and passengers, and to show local governments that they provide good service. The federal government, in funding airport improvement projects, could use airport efficiency evaluation to help determine the effectiveness of these programs and whether various airport improvement projects that focus on reengineering or capital improvements impact relative airport efficiency. Benchmarking their own airports against comparable airports is one way for airport operations managers to ensure competitiveness. Factors beyond operations decisions that may impact airport operational efficiency are investigated here.

These, and other important managerial and operations issues focusing on the productivity and effi-

336   *J. Sarkis / Journal of Operations Management 18 (2000) 335–351*

ciency measurement of U.S. airports, set the stage for this study. The primary objective of this paper is to determine those characteristics that impact the operations of major U.S. airports and to obtain results that will aid operations managers and communities in improving their airports by benchmarking their airports against similar airports. Data are gathered directly from the airports and also from the Airports Council International (ACI) and are input to a series of models that evaluate the relative efficiency of sets of airports. The modeling techniques, which are based on a set of mathematical programming formulations defined as data envelopment analysis (DEA), are briefly described in Section 3, with additional detail presented in Appendix A.

As well as showing the applicability of the various DEA models, results are investigated to determine characteristics that may impact airport operational efficiency (e.g., whether an airport is a hub to a major air carrier, is in a snowbelt [regions with more than 10 in. of snow per year], and part of a multiple airport system [MAS]). This paper incorporates many versions of DEA for efficiency analysis; a brief comparison and analysis of these techniques and their results are also included, followed by a summary and discussion of the results and future research potential.

2. Background

Airports are critical, dominant forces in a community's economic development (e.g., Dallas–Fort Worth and Atlanta). Inamete (1993) states that since 1970, airports have redrawn the economic map of the U.S. Locating airports in communities to further their economic development has been exacerbated by the deregulation of the airline industry, which has allowed airlines to expand services and pressured airports to provide additional services to the airlines' customers.

Inamete (1993) states that airport operational efficiencies may be improved through internal and external measures. Government policies are strong external measures, while communication and close management of operational, technical, and managerial functions are clear internal measures. The relationship between the key elements of airport management and policy milieu also impacts airport operations.

Improvements and evaluations of airport operational efficiencies have not been well researched by the literature, perhaps due to the relatively recent introduction of operational improvement paradigms such as total quality management and business process reengineering. External forces for operational improvement include efforts by regulatory organizations such as the Federal Aviation Administration (FAA), which itself has experienced government reengineering.

We review literature focusing on related efficiency studies, as well as issues and external characteristics that may impact airport operational efficiency. Airport operations managers may benchmark their airports' performances against those of comparable airports on input and output measures used in these studies and consider these factors to interpret their findings more accurately.

2.1. Analysis of airport operations

Few studies have focused on the productivity and efficiency of major U.S. airports. Productivity can be defined as a general measure of a ratio of output(s) to input(s). The focus on productivity measurement in this industry typically has been on organizations that use the services of airports and on general transportation infrastructure (e.g., Schefczyk, 1993; Truitt and Haynes, 1994; Windle and Dresner, 1995). Efficiency, which is defined in more detail in the discussion on DEA models in Appendix A, considers the relative productivity of a set of units (in this case, airports). An efficient unit is said to lie on the efficient frontier of a set of units.

The deregulation of the airline industry has put pressure on airports to be more competitive and productive because airlines choose airports that are more cost effective. Ashford (1994, p. 59) makes a cogent argument for the improved management of airports in a deregulated airline environment: "Facilities which are efficient, inexpensive, cost effective and offering a high level of service to airlines and passengers can expect higher passenger flows and consequently increased revenues and increased profitability. In a deregulated climate, such a facility

J. Sarkis / Journal of Operations Management 18 (2000) 335–351   337

could expect to attract air carrier operation in an environment where the airline is free to move its base of operations.'' Simply put, an air carrier's willingness to remain at an airport may be deter- mined by that airport's efficiency. Airport opera- tions, and the role of airport operations managers, have critical strategic implications for an airport's long run viability.

Table 1
Listing of airports and characteristic categorizations

Airport abbreviation	Location	Airport name	Major carrier hub	Airport system category	Snowbelt (> 10 in.) snow annually
ATL	Atlanta, GA	Hartsfield Intl.	Yes	SAS	No
BUF	Buffalo, NY	Greater Buffalo Intl.	No	SAS	Yes
BWI	Maryland	Baltimore/Washington Intl.	Yes	MAS	Yes
CLE	Cleveland, OH	Cleveland–Hopkins Intl.	Yes	MAS	Yes
CLT	North Carolina	Charlotte/Douglas Intl.	Yes	SAS	No
DAL	Dallas, TX	Love Field	Yes	MAS	No
DAY	Dayton, OH	Dayton Intl.	Yes[a]	SAS	Yes
DEN	Denver, CO	Denver Intl.	Yes	SAS	Yes
DFW	Irving, TX	Dallas–Fort Worth Intl.	Yes	MAS	No
FLL	Florida	Fort Lauderdale Exec.	No	MAS	No
GEG	Spokane, WA	Spokane	No	SAS	Yes
GRR	Grand Rapids, MI	Kent County Intl.	No	SAS	Yes
HNL	Hawaii	Honolulu	No	SAS	No
HOU	Houston, TX	Houston Intercontinental	Yes	MAS	No
IAD	Maryland	Dulles Intl.	Yes	MAS	Yes
IAH	Houston, TX	William P. Hobby	Yes	MAS	No
IND	Indiana	Indianapolis Intl.	No	SAS	Yes
JAX	Florida	Jacksonville Intl.	No	SAS	No
JFK	New York, NY	John F. Kennedy	Yes	MAS	Yes
LAS	Las Vegas, NV	McCarran Intl.	Yes	SAS	No
LAX	Los Angeles, CA	Los Angeles Intl.	Yes	MAS	No
LGA	New York, NY	La Guardia	No	MAS	Yes
MCI	Kansas City, MO	Kansas City	No	SAS	Yes
MCO	Orlando, FL	Orlando Intl.	Yes	SAS	No
MEM	Memphis, TN	Memphis Shelby County	Yes	SAS	No
MIA	Miami, FL	Miami Intl.	Yes	MAS	No
MKE	Milwaukee, WI	General Mitchell	No	SAS	Yes
MSP	Minnesota	Minneapolis–St. Paul	Yes	SAS	Yes
MSY	Louisiana	New Orleans Intl.	No	SAS	No
OAK	California	Oakland Intl.	Yes	MAS	No
ONT	Los Angeles, CA	Ontario Intl.	Yes	MAS	No
PDX	Portland, OR	Portland Intl.	No	SAS	No
PHX	Phoenix, AZ	Sky Harbor Intl.	Yes	SAS	No
PIT	Pittsburgh, PA	Pittsburgh Intl.	Yes	SAS	Yes
RNO	Reno, NV	Reno/Tahoe Intl.	No	SAS	Yes
SDF	Louisville, KY	Louisville Intl.	Yes	SAS	Yes
SEA	Seattle, WA	Seattle–Tacoma Intl.	Yes	SAS	No
SFO	California	San Francisco Intl.	No	MAS	No
SJC	California	San Jose Municipal	Yes[b]	MAS	No
SLC	Utah	Salt Lake City Intl.	Yes	SAS	Yes
SMF	California	Sacramento Metro	No	SAS	No
SNA	Los Angeles, CA	John Wayne	No	MAS	No
STL	St. Louis, MO	Lambert	Yes	SAS	Yes
TPA	Tampa, FL	Tampa Intl.	No	SAS	No

[a] Before 1992.
[b] Before 1993.

338   *J. Sarkis / Journal of Operations Management 18 (2000) 335–351*

Airports seek funding from the FAA's airport improvement program (AIP), a program critical for airport operations because its spending represents a substantial portion (20–25%) of the national airport system's capital costs (see DeLuca et al., 1995). Similar to most other governmental programs, it is undergoing evaluation and reengineering. The areas of change of the FAA airports reengineering project include national planning, master agreement development, resource reallocation, performance measurements, information technology development, and outreach programs. Three of these areas focus on the performance measures of airports related to any AIP funding and operations. The first, national planning, includes the development and publication of a report that measures actual and temporal improvements in airport system performance. In the second, the reallocation of FAA resources will depend heavily on performance measures after AIP completion at an airport and on airport resource utilization. The third major area of change, performance measures, addresses an important need for the national planning process because (1) it is the basis for determining national airport system performance, and (2) it guides the creation of a prioritized inventory of airport improvement projects. Six performance measurement areas have been defined for airport development systems: infrastructure, environment, accessibility, capacity, and investment (FAA, 1997, p. 26). The FAA adds that the priority system will be adjusted depending on the measurement of system performance as determined by performance measures (FAA, 1996, 1997) such as efficiency evaluations.

In addition to the consideration of airport efficiency, the results of this study are used to evaluate some characteristics of airports and their relationships to the efficiency measures, which will help the FAA and communities to compare airports. It will also show airport management that certain external characteristics may result in varying performances and that to benchmark their performances meaningfully, they need to consider these characteristics.

2.2. Airline hub location and relation to airport operational efficiency

Most of the major air carriers (except Southwest Airlines) have a transportation system based on the hub and spoke network model. The location of a hub at an airport greatly increases many airport output measures, including revenue and passenger flow. Thus, we expect that the operational efficiency of hub airports will be greater because either they are major air carrier hubs or air carriers chose these airports as hubs because they are more efficient. This study will not discern the causation, but will focus on the relationship between operational efficiency and whether an airport has an air carrier hub. The limited empirical and theoretical research on hub airport characteristics has focused on "fortress hub" and hub duopoloy/monopoly relationships with airport fare prices (see Borenstein, 1989; Windle and Dresner, 1993). The effects on airport operations of whether an airport is a hub have not been considered by any research.

A hub airport is defined as one that is officially a hub for a major airline in the U.S. (except Southwest Airlines). The major private airlines and carriers include: Alaska Airlines, American Airlines, America West, Continental Airlines, Delta Airlines, Federal Express, Northwest Airlines, Southwest Airlines, Trans World Airlines, United Parcel Services, United Airlines, and US Airways. For Southwest Airlines, airports where over 25% of passenger traffic is from the Southwest are considered hubs. The air carriers themselves (American Airlines, United Parcel Services, Federal Express) and *Air Transport World*, a major trade journal, provide data sources. The categorization of airports as hub/nonhub is shown in Table 1. Only those airports that responded to this study are included in Table 1. We thus have our first proposition.

Proposition 1. *Airports that are hubs for major air carriers are more efficient than those that are not hubs.*

2.3. Multiple airport systems

Hansen and Weidner (1995) have studied the characteristics of a variety of MAS and the potential and need for additional MAS. The relative efficiency scores from the DEA execution in our data also may be used to evaluate the differences between MAS airports and those of single airport systems (SAS).

J. Sarkis / Journal of Operations Management 18 (2000) 335–351 339

According to Hansen and Weidner (p. 9), an MAS is two or more airports with scheduled passenger enplanements, and which satisfy both of the following criteria.

· Each airport is included in the same community by the FAA or within 50 km (30 miles) of the primary airport of an FAA designated 'large hub' community, or each airport is in the same Metropolitan Statistical Area or Consolidated MSA.

· The Herfindahl concentration index [1] (HCI) for the airports is less than 0.95.

MAS airports, typically, have more passenger enplanements due to their locations in densely populated areas, which may increase their efficiency scores. In addition, airports within MAS compete with each other, further emphasizing the need for efficiency. Hansen and Weidner imply that competition in MAS provides a foundation for privatization of airports. SAS airports also may be efficient because they represent the major passenger enplanement traffic in a geographical region and have relatively higher outputs, which the DEA models utilize. Categorization of MAS/SAS airports is identified in Table 1. MAS airports are identified according to Hansen and Weidner (1995).

Proposition 2. *Airports in Multiple Airport Systems are more efficient than those in Single Airport Systems.*

2.4. Geographical considerations and relationship to airport operational efficiency

While providing the data, some respondents expressed concern about the fact that geographic location, especially snowbelt vs. nonsnowbelt, may strongly influence relative airport productivity and efficiency. A brief analysis of these categories is presented. Airport categorizations of snowbelt or nonsnowbelt locations are shown in Table 1. We now state our third proposition.

---

[1] The HCI is a measure of the degree to which passenger activity is concentrated at a single airport within the region. It is calculated as the sum of the squared traffic shares of each airport in an MAS. For an SAS the HCI is equal to 1.

Proposition 3. *Airports that are not in snowbelts are more efficient than those in snowbelts.*

3. Methodology

Airport operational efficiency is calculated using various DEA models, which are detailed in Appendix A. The following models and their efficiency scores are calculated for each airport in this study.

· Simple Efficiency (Charnes et al., 1978 [CCR]; Banker et al., 1984 [BCC]) refers to efficiency scores (technical and scale efficiencies) calculated by the basic CCR and BCC models for each airport.

· Simple Cross-Efficiency (SXEF) (Doyle and Green, 1994) is the efficiency score calculated for an airport s by multiplying the optimal weights of an airport k from the CCR model by the original ratio of inputs and outputs of the airport s. The cross-efficiency scores are then averaged for each airport to get a mean SXEF.

· Aggressive Cross-Efficiency (AXEF) (Doyle and Green, 1994) is the efficiency score calculated for an airport s by multiplying the optimal weights of an airport k from Doyle and Green's *scaled* aggressive formulation by the original ratio of inputs and outputs of the airport s. The cross-efficiency scores are then averaged for each airport to get a mean AXEF value.

· Ranked Efficiency (RCCR) (Andersen and Petersen, 1993) is the efficiency score calculated by the reduced CCR model for each airport.

· Radii of Classification Rankings (GTR) (Rousseau and Semple, 1995) is the efficiency score calculated by the Rousseau and Semple generalized Tchebycheff radius of classification formulation.

Over the past two decades, DEA has become a popular methodology for evaluating the relative efficiencies of decision-making units within a relatively homogenous set (see Emrouznejad and Thanassoulis, 1996a,b,1997; Seiford, 1996 for comprehensive bibliographies). This study represents, to date, one of the more comprehensive applications of the DEA methodology and its variants. Using a variety of DEA-based models allows for additional insights and determines the consistency of the results. Appendix A describes the major limitations of the models and

340   *J. Sarkis / Journal of Operations Management 18 (2000) 335–351*

how the results of these models supplement one another.

4. Data and data acquisition

The Data for DEA models include both input and output factors from which relative technical, scale, and cross-efficiency measures are determined (each of these types of efficiencies is defined below). Input data, composed of resources that are common to all airports, include financial costs (measured in operating costs), labor (measured in the number of full-time equivalent employees directly employed by the airport), and the number of gates and runways. These are standard resources that are available to all airports and airport operations managers to help generate the necessary outputs. Output data are comprised of operating revenue generated, number of aircraft movements, general aviation movements, passenger movements, and amount of cargo shipped. General aviation includes all aircraft not flown by scheduled airlines or the military. Movements for aircraft and general aviation represent a landing and take-off of an airplane or helicopter at an airport. A passenger movement can be either: (a) passengers arriving or departing via commercial airplane or helicopter; or (b) passengers stopping temporarily at a designated airport and departing on an aircraft with the same flight number and counted only once. General aviation refers to private consumer aircraft that use the airport. All data are self-reported by the airports.

The data set is acquired from two major sources, the ACI (ACI, 1995) and two mail surveys sent to selected airports. Only the top 80 U.S. airports based on the FAA's 1993 passenger revenue enplanement number found in Table 4.11 of the *FAA Statistical Handbook of Aviation* (FAA, 1994) are included, although they are not necessarily the largest in cargo movements. Output data are taken from the ACI annual database of airport activities, which ACI gathers from self-reported data from member airports. The surveys are used to acquire information on the major inputs (and operating revenue). There are 43 usable responses for 1990, and 44 for the years 1991 through 1994, constituting a 55% response rate.

Table 1 lists airports that responded to this survey, as well as three characteristics used to deter-mine if statistically different efficiency scores occur within these classifications. The characteristics include whether an airport is a hub for a major airline, is part of an MAS, and is in a snowbelt location. Table 2 is composed of descriptive statistics that include means and standard deviations (SD) for each of the input and output factors in each of the 5 years in our study. There are no statistically significant differences between early and late respondents, which implies that nonresponse bias may be negligible (this procedure is suggested by Armstrong and Overton, 1977 to help evaluate nonresponse bias). Closer evaluation of the mean statistics (see Table 3; 1990 is not included due to the lack of a complete data set for that year) from the ACI database of those airports that did not respond reveals some bias in our data set. In terms of aircraft movements, total passengers, and cargo moved, the nonresponding airports are smaller, while the general aviation numbers are comparable.

The discussion of assumptions and definitions concerning airport operating cost and revenue data is warranted. Airport cost data specifically focus on operating costs, not other expenses such as depreciation. Operating revenues are derived from a number of sources including concessions, parking fees, landing fees, user charges, and commercial development revenue. While one airport reports that due to nonprofit and federal regulations, it has equal revenues and costs, the vast majority of revenues and costs are not equal.

A good rule-of-thumb in applying DEA is to include a minimum set of data points in the evaluation set (i.e., the number of inputs multiplied by the number of outputs, Boussofiane et al., 1991) to discriminate better between efficient and inefficient units. In our example with a total of four input and five output factors, a good minimum set is 20 data points; we have 44 data points. Even if the problem of too few data points were encountered, the ranking and cross-efficiency models, as described in Appendix A, could be used as good discriminators.

Before the data are executed to determine their efficiency scores, the original absolute values are mean normalized by dividing each value of a respective airport for a given factor by the mean value of all the airports for that respective input or output factor. Mean normalization lessens the impact of

Table 2
Descriptive statistics for 44 airport samples

Year	1990[a]		1991		1992		1993		1994	
	Mean	SD	Mean	SD	Mean	SD	Mean	SD	Mean	SD
Inputs										
Operating cost (millions of dollars)	50.523	60.811	55.113	63.750	59.176	65.497	65.018	75.867	67.216	72.170
Employees	399.872	357.472	411.243	370.191	425.568	389.261	426.657	379.436	441.302	394.737
Gates	65.256	67.972	57.886	38.306	58.022	38.323	58.682	38.403	59.341	40.219
Runways	3.023	1.123	2.977	1.089	2.977	1.089	2.977	1.089	3.023	1.045
Outputs										
Operating revenues (millions of dollars)	72.680	78.190	78.906	82.845	85.870	89.822	90.766	92.030	93.288	89.581
Aircraft movements	245,402.6	166,641.6	238,460.8	150.627	246,667.9	159,533.5	251,169.8	162,053.7	264,496.7	166,138.7
General aviation	75,689.5	74,132.6	73,597.55	78,232.78	74,340.48	75,989.19	75,270.73	69,647.47	75,093.41	74,413.42
Total passengers	14,343,567	12,367,961	13,889,568	11,551,961	14,695,819	12,332,889	15,146,487	12,563,788	16,622,186	13,429,564
Total freight	249,253.4	311,970.5	272,401.5	329,390.1	304,262.5	371,260.5	335,452.8	402,849.9	37,1321	447,925.2

[a] 1990 has only 43 airports in sample.

Table 3
Averages for 36 nonresponding airports

Year[a]	1991	1992	1993	1994
Aircraft movements	159,913	167,364	168,827	175,636
General aviation	75,676	74,772	73,131	72,249
Total passengers	8,375,119	8,953,951	8,951,126	9,575,120
Total freight	127,148	143,594	149,277	172,738

[a]1990 data were incomplete and not included.

large differences in data magnitudes (scaling difficulties) that may not be adequately handled by many commercial software linear programming packages. This ratio scale adjustment does not influence the final DEA efficiency score and is empirically tested on this and other data sets.

5. Study results

In this section, we conduct an overall airport industry data evaluation that includes average technical and scale efficiency analysis, as well as a brief evaluation of the airport rankings. In addition, we consider the impact on efficiency of airport characterizations (i.e., whether an airport is a hub, in an MAS region, or in a snowbelt).

5.1. Overall airport analysis

The results of the CCR and BCC efficiency scores are shown in Table 4. At least 22 different airports are considered to be technically- or scale-efficient in at least 1 of the 5 years under consideration; 14 airports are efficient for all 5 years. Sengupta (1995) states that industrial competitiveness or efficiency can be evaluated through analysis of average efficiencies. The average efficiencies from the CCR model show an upward trend from 1990 to 1992, then a drop, then another increase during 1993 and 1994. The average efficiency scores from the BCC model showed a continuous increase over each year, except for the drop in 1993 and rebound in 1994. The differences in average CCR and BCC efficiency scores point to some varying returns to scale in the data set. That is, relationships among the input and output values depend on the magnitude of the data set.

Even though there was a slight drop in average airport efficiencies during 1993, airports seemed to rebound in their technical and scale efficiencies during 1994. While 1993 may have been a poor performing year in terms of average efficiencies for all airports, it was also the year in which the largest percentage of respondents performed most efficiently (34% for CCR and 48% for BCC). This result may also imply that certain airports were targeted for less air carrier business during a period of airline downsizing that occurred during the recessionary (for the air carriers) years of 1993 and 1994. One such example is San Jose Municipal Airport, which in 1993 was no longer a hub for any of the major air carriers due to airport gate and landing charges, according to a deputy director of aviation finance and administration. Difficult economic and financial pressures on air carriers made these charges prohibitive and thus, air carriers decided to close hub operations at San Jose.

The slight upward trends in both percentage of efficient airports and average efficiency scores mean that airport operations are becoming more competitive. Yet, with less than half of the airports in this sample still not obtaining an efficiency score equal to 1, there is ample room to increase efficiency compared to that of other airports. On the other hand, an average technical efficiency of over 0.50 (a range of 0.74–0.78), may mean that most airport organizational resources and capacities are well utilized or are reaching their limitations. It is difficult to interpret overall airport industry efficiency by comparison with other industries because it is not clear which industries are comparable. For example, in a study of the 100 largest U.S. banks, Thompson et al. (1991) found 88% to 97% mean technical efficiency scores, which may mean that airports are less competitive or less efficient (or both) than the U.S. banking industry. As more data become available and more industries are evaluated using DEA, comparative analyses across industries may provide insights into competitiveness and overall efficiency.

Using the SXEF, AXEF, GTR, and RCCR ranking models, it seems that the most consistently efficient airports are Fort Lauderdale Executive and Oakland International (appearing in the top ten rankings in each year and among various ranking models), while the least efficient airports include Jack-

J. Sarkis / Journal of Operations Management 18 (2000) 335–351 343

Table 4
DEA model results of BCC and CCR models for major U.S. airports
See Table 1 for explanation of abbreviations.
CCR *xx* is the Charnes, Cooper and Rhodes DEA model efficiency score for year 19*xx*. BCC *xx* is the Banker, Charnes and Cooper model efficiency score for year 19*xx*.

Airport	CCR90	CCR91	CCR92	CCR93	CCR94	BCC90	BCC91	BCC92	BCC93	BCC94
ATL	**1.000**	**1.000**	**1.000**	**1.000**	**1.000**	**1.000**	**1.000**	**1.000**	**1.000**	**1.000**
BUF	0.602	0.464	0.553	0.438	0.564	0.766	0.764	0.752	0.759	0.809
BWI	0.514	0.490	0.518	0.432	0.529	0.569	0.531	0.522	0.438	0.552
CLE	0.474	0.401	0.432	0.386	0.426	0.506	0.440	0.460	0.433	0.505
CLT	**1.000**	**1.000**	**1.000**	**1.000**	**1.000**	**1.000**	**1.000**	**1.000**	**1.000**	**1.000**
DAL	0.478	0.506	0.543	0.553	0.554	0.574	0.609	0.608	0.612	0.641
DAY	0.864	0.704	0.621	0.686	0.731	0.957	0.716	0.648	0.687	0.735
DEN	0.743	0.855	0.880	0.794	0.718	0.751	0.997	**1.000**	**1.000**	0.876
DFW	0.908	**1.000**	**1.000**	0.951	0.938	**1.000**	**1.000**	**1.000**	**1.000**	**1.000**
FLL	**1.000**	**1.000**	**1.000**	**1.000**	**1.000**	**1.000**	**1.000**	**1.000**	**1.000**	**1.000**
GEG	0.521	0.524	0.546	0.610	0.696	0.790	0.826	0.771	0.776	0.846
GRR	0.693	0.791	0.813	0.729	0.675	**1.000**	**1.000**	**1.000**	**1.000**	0.864
HNL	**1.000**	**1.000**	**1.000**	**1.000**	**1.000**	**1.000**	**1.000**	**1.000**	**1.000**	**1.000**
HOU	0.460	0.720	0.604	0.725	0.719	0.490	0.724	0.620	0.762	0.789
IAD	0.469	0.519	0.533	0.495	0.584	0.486	0.519	0.539	0.496	0.598
IAH	0.898	0.613	0.994	0.546	0.575	**1.000**	0.616	**1.000**	0.557	0.577
IND	0.611	0.632	0.632	0.582	0.676	0.626	0.722	0.711	0.639	0.691
JAX	0.339	0.335	0.380	0.304	0.441	0.559	0.551	0.531	0.518	0.630
JFK	**1.000**	**1.000**	**1.000**	**1.000**	**1.000**	**1.000**	**1.000**	**1.000**	**1.000**	**1.000**
LAS	0.916	0.887	0.915	0.856	0.945	0.926	0.997	0.943	**1.000**	**1.000**
LAX	**1.000**	**1.000**	**1.000**	**1.000**	**1.000**	**1.000**	**1.000**	**1.000**	**1.000**	**1.000**
LGA	**1.000**	**1.000**	**1.000**	**1.000**	**1.000**	**1.000**	**1.000**	**1.000**	**1.000**	**1.000**
MCI	0.452	0.483	0.493	0.486	0.384	0.549	0.529	0.528	0.527	0.392
MCO	0.719	0.836	0.899	0.844	0.941	0.763	0.843	0.906	0.845	0.951
MEM	0.612	**1.000**	**1.000**	**1.000**	**1.000**	0.616	**1.000**	**1.000**	**1.000**	**1.000**
MIA	**1.000**	**1.000**	**1.000**	**1.000**	**1.000**	**1.000**	**1.000**	**1.000**	**1.000**	**1.000**
MKE	0.360	0.544	0.546	0.494	0.511	0.388	0.614	0.619	0.606	0.638
MSP	0.778	0.924	0.972	0.934	0.913	0.790	0.939	0.989	**1.000**	**1.000**
MSY	0.447	0.470	0.473	0.438	0.489	0.636	0.536	0.549	0.516	0.528
OAK	**1.000**	**1.000**	**1.000**	**1.000**	**1.000**	**1.000**	**1.000**	**1.000**	**1.000**	**1.000**
ONT	0.597	0.584	0.528	0.487	0.558	0.701	0.665	0.608	0.579	0.609
PDX	0.615	0.593	0.591	0.598	0.731	0.615	0.604	0.599	0.628	0.771
PHX	**1.000**	**1.000**	**1.000**	**1.000**	**1.000**	**1.000**	**1.000**	**1.000**	**1.000**	**1.000**
PIT	0.576	0.847	0.981	**1.000**	0.734	0.579	**1.000**	**1.000**	**1.000**	**1.000**
RNO	0.478	0.547	0.585	0.559	0.617	0.668	0.725	0.717	0.718	0.733
SDF	**1.000**	**1.000**	**1.000**	**1.000**	**1.000**	**1.000**	**1.000**	**1.000**	**1.000**	**1.000**
SEA	**1.000**	**1.000**	**1.000**	**1.000**	**1.000**	**1.000**	**1.000**	**1.000**	**1.000**	**1.000**
SFO	0.942	0.988	0.996	0.971	**1.000**	0.998	**1.000**	**1.000**	**1.000**	**1.000**
SJC	0.515	0.539	0.511	0.472	0.604	0.520	0.554	0.533	0.534	0.612
SLC	0.753	0.749	0.796	0.860	0.877	0.754	0.755	0.800	0.885	0.925
SMF	0.692	0.708	0.686	0.636	0.758	0.814	0.909	0.843	0.840	0.886
SNA	**1.000**	**1.000**	**1.000**	**1.000**	**1.000**	**1.000**	**1.000**	**1.000**	**1.000**	**1.000**
STL	0.632	0.630	0.647	0.572	0.610	0.772	0.734	0.706	0.795	0.857
TPA		0.605	0.632	0.638	0.753		0.620	0.641	0.644	0.786
Average efficiency	0.736	0.761	0.780	0.752	0.778	0.794	0.819	0.821	0.813	0.836
Percent efficient	30%	34%	34%	34%	34%	37%	41%	45%	48%	43%

sonville International, Kansas City, Milwaukee's General Mitchell, and New Orleans International (appearing in the bottom ten rankings in each year and among the various ranking techniques). Because the efficiencies (or inefficiencies) and rankings may be due to circumstances beyond the control of airport operations management, we evaluate three possible underlying characteristics (circumstances) that may cause variation in the results.

5.2. Characteristics affecting airport operational efficiency

To determine whether differences exist in various airport characteristics (i.e., hub or nonhub, MAS or SAS, snowbelt or nonsnowbelt) for each type of efficiency score measurement (i.e., CCR, BCC, SXEF, AXEF, RCCR, GTR), a nonparametric analysis (Mann–Whitney U-test) is used. These tests are executed on a PC version of SPSS. The Mann–Whitney test is recommended for nonparametric analysis of DEA results by Brockett and Golany (1996) and Grosskopf and Valdmanis (1987); it is used here because the efficiency score results do not fit within a standard normal distribution. The final results for each DEA method and year are shown in Tables 5–7.

Table 5 presents the results for the statistical differences on efficiency scores between hub and nonhub airports. For the most part, Proposition 1 is supported. Significant differences exist using AXEF, CCR, and SXEF efficiency scores, especially between the years 1991 and 1994; differences become more significant for later dates in our study. The hub airports are more efficient for each year that there is a significant difference, implying that major carriers may be locating at more efficient hubs or starting to consolidate operations at their major hubs in more recent years. Two airports, Dayton International and San Jose Municipal (see Table 1), lost their major air carrier hub status during this period, while their rankings and efficiency evaluations are consistently in the bottom half of the results. This observation may support the contention that deregulation has allowed air carriers to seek out efficient airports. These changes in hub sets also support the stronger differentiation in efficiencies between hub and nonhub airports in more recent years. Although the GTR

Table 5
Nonparametric statistical analysis of hub and nonhub airports
AXEF.*xx* is the Aggressive Cross-Efficiency DEA model efficiency score for year 19.*xx*. **BCC**.*xx* is the Banker, Charnes and Cooper DEA model efficiency score for year 19.*xx*. **CCR**.*xx* is the Charnes, Cooper and Rhodes DEA model efficiency score for year 19.*xx*. **GTR**.*xx* is the Rousseau and Semple Radii of Classification model efficiency score for year 19.*xx*. **RCCR**.*xx* is the Andersen and Petersen Reduced CCR DEA model efficiency score for year 19.*xx*. **SXEF**.*xx* is the Simple Cross-Efficiency DEA model efficiency score for year 19.*xx*.

Model	Mann–Whitney U	Z	Asymptotic significance (two-tailed)
AXEF90	156.000	−1.508	0.132
AXEF91	145.000	−2.037	**0.042****
AXEF92	142.000	−2.196	**0.028****
AXEF93	146.000	−2.168	**0.030****
AXEF94	159.000	−1.860	**0.030****
BCC90	202.500	−0.348	0.728
BCC91	200.000	−0.737	0.461
BCC92	187.000	−1.179	0.239
BCC93	173.000	−1.619	0.106
BCC94	167.000	−1.742	0.106
CCR90	162.500	−1.363	0.173
CCR91	159.000	−1.734	**0.083***
CCR92	167.000	−1.632	0.103
CCR93	159.000	−1.898	**0.058***
CCR94	179.000	−1.414	**0.058***
GTR90	199.000	−0.427	0.669
GTR91	199.000	−0.735	0.462
GTR92	192.000	−1.003	0.316
GTR93	169.000	−1.623	0.105
GTR94	153.000	−2.002	0.105
RCCR90	175.500	−1.018	0.309
RCCR91	174.000	−1.338	0.181
RCCR92	181.000	−1.265	0.206
RCCR93	173.000	−1.528	0.126
RCCR94	184.000	−1.268	0.126
SXEF90	159.500	−1.420	0.156
SXEF91	147.000	−1.989	**0.047****
SXEF92	139.000	−2.268	**0.023****
SXEF93	150.000	−2.073	**0.038****
SXEF94	159.000	−1.860	**0.038****

** Indicates significance at 10% level.
* Indicates significance at 5% level.

results are on the verge of showing a statistically significant difference, no such differences exist in hub/nonhub efficiencies for each of the DEA efficiency metrics. However, there are strong overall indications that hub airports are more efficient, which somewhat support Proposition 1.

J. Sarkis / Journal of Operations Management 18 (2000) 335–351 345

Table 6
Nonparametric statistical analysis of multiple airport and single airport systems
+: **AXEF**xx is the Aggressive Cross-Efficiency DEA model efficiency score for year 19xx. **BCC**xx is the Banker, Charnes and Cooper DEA model efficiency score for year 19xx. **CCR** xx is the Charnes, Cooper and Rhodes DEA model efficiency score for year 19xx. **GTR** xx is the Rousseau and Semple Radii of Classification model efficiency score for year 19xx. **RCCR** xx is the Andersen and Petersen Reduced CCR DEA model efficiency score for year 19xx. **SXEF**xx is the Simple Cross-Efficiency DEA model efficiency score for year 19xx.

	Mann–Whitney U	Z	Asymptotic significance (two-tailed)
AXEF90	188.000	−0.820	0.412
AXEF91	202.000	−0.663	0.507
AXEF92	202.000	−0.663	0.507
AXEF93	203.000	−0.639	0.523
AXEF94	187.000	−1.024	0.306
BCC90	201.500	−0.497	0.619
BCC91	229.500	0.000	1.000
BCC92	222.000	−0.190	0.849
BCC93	212.000	−0.447	0.655
BCC94	222.000	−0.189	0.850
CCR90	189.500	−0.793	0.428
CCR91	204.000	−0.627	0.531
CCR92	207.000	−0.553	0.580
CCR93	223.000	−0.160	0.873
CCR94	214.000	−0.381	0.703
GTR90	195.000	−0.646	0.518
GTR91	221.000	−0.205	0.838
GTR92	211.000	−0.446	0.656
GTR93	223.000	−0.157	0.876
GTR94	203.000	−0.639	0.523
RCCR90	183.500	−0.932	0.352
RCCR91	200.000	−0.711	0.477
RCCR92	203.000	−0.639	0.523
RCCR93	211.000	−0.446	0.656
RCCR94	208.000	−0.518	0.604
SXEF90	181.000	−0.994	0.320
SXEF91	205.000	−0.591	0.555
SXEF92	206.000	−0.556	0.571
SXEF93	206.000	−0.566	0.571
SXEF94	187.000	−1.024	0.306

** Indicates significance at 10% level.
* Indicates significance at 5% level.

Because no statistically significant differences exist between MAS and SAS airports, Proposition 2 is not supported by our study (see Table 6). Although MAS puts pressures on airports to be more efficient because consumers and carriers have more airport service choices in a relatively close geographical region, SAS may be more efficient because all consumers and carriers choose a single airport in a geographical area. Thus, MAS/SAS characteristics may not strongly affect airport operational efficiency.

Table 7
Nonparametric statistical analysis of snowbelt and nonsnowbelt airports
+: **AXEF**xx is the Aggressive Cross-Efficiency DEA model efficiency score for year 19xx. **BCC**xx is the Banker, Charnes and Cooper DEA model efficiency score for year 19xx. **CCR** xx is the Charnes, Cooper and Rhodes DEA model efficiency score for year 19xx. **GTR** xx is the Rousseau and Semple Radii of Classification model efficiency score for year 19xx. **RCCR** xx is the Andersen and Petersen Reduced CCR DEA model efficiency score for year 19xx. **SXEF**xx is the Simple Cross-Efficiency DEA model efficiency score for year 19xx.

	Mann–Whitney U	Z	Asymptotic significance (two-tailed)
AXEF90	129.000	−2.421	**0.015****
AXEF91	136.000	−2.405	**0.016****
AXEF92	133.000	−2.476	**0.013****
AXEF93	133.000	−2.476	**0.013****
AXEF94	136.000	−2.405	**0.016****
BCC90	158.00	−1.758	**0.078***
BCC91	181.500	−1.375	0.169
BCC92	183.000	−1.356	0.175
BCC93	193.000	−1.117	0.264
BCC94	171.000	−1.643	**−0.100***
CCR90	152.500	−1.872	**0.061***
CCR91	155.000	−1.995	**0.046****
CCR92	159.000	−1.898	**0.058***
CCR93	171.000	−1.608	0.108
CCR94	141.000	−2.333	**0.20****
GTR90	174.000	−1.321	0.187
GTR91	182.000	−1.315	0.189
GTR92	182.000	−1.315	0.189
GTR93	192.000	−1.078	0.281
GTR94	165.000	−1.718	**0.086***
RCCR90	155.500	−1.773	**0.076***
RCCR91	157.000	−1.907	**0.056***
RCCR92	164.000	−1.742	**0.081***
RCCR93	171.000	−1.576	0.115
RCCR94	147.000	−2.144	**0.032****
SXEF90	124.500	−2.531	**0.011****
SXEF91	135.000	−2.429	**0.015****
SXEF92	135.000	−2.429	**0.015****
SXEF93	141.000	−2.286	**0.022****
SXEF94	135.000	−2.429	**0.015****

** Indicates significance at 10% level.
* Indicates significance at 5% level.

Of the three characteristics that may affect airport operational efficiency, the one that seems to be the best discriminator is the natural environment, which strongly supports Proposition 3. Whether an airport is located in a snowbelt seems to have the strongest influence on its operational efficiency. Table 7 shows that for almost every efficiency measure there is at least 1 year that has a statistically significant difference (at the 0.05 and 0.10 levels of significance) in efficiency scores. Thus, for most airport operations managers, poor weather conditions may lead to less airport operational efficiency.

One of the advantages of studying the impact of airport characteristics on operational efficiency is the ability to regroup DEA evaluation sets. In future studies, it may be more prudent to evaluate (or control for) relative airport efficiency within sets and groupings based on weather conditions and whether airports serve as hubs for major air carriers. These initial results present some circumstances beyond the control of most airport operations managers that account for differences in airport efficiency (i.e, airports that are in snowbelts or do not contain major air carrier hubs are more likely to be inefficient).

6. Discussion of models and study limitations

As we have mentioned, one of the limitations of DEA is its sensitivity to data and parameter selection. If we had selected other parameters (inputs and outputs) or fewer parameters for evaluation, we may have obtained different outcomes. Even though this study provides a random sample of the full population, some extensions to overall industry competitiveness and efficiency may need to be evaluated further, especially because there is a bias toward larger airports in our data set. The three characteristics and their impacts on efficiency scores may in turn be influenced by differing sample sizes, but not to the extent of their impacts on overall average efficiency scores. Issues related to the influence of sample sizes on results need to be studied by DEA theorists and researchers.

One assumption made for the data set may cause an outlier to occur, which is evident in the RCCR and GTR results. We assume that the Fort Lauderdale Executive Airport (FLL), which does not have traditional terminals and gates, has only six gates (the same as the number of fixed-based operations located at the airport), a significantly smaller number of gates than the average of approximately 60 gates. The GTR analysis shows that FLL would need to have a reduced improvement (smaller value for outputs, larger value for inputs) of at least 789% in all its factors in 1994 (a larger percentage in other years) for it to become inefficient. The actual number of gates at FLL needs to increase to at least 46 before it can possibly become inefficient. In actuality, this value (if it is the only factor that is varied) may have to be much larger because it is assumed that all factors need to increase or decrease in value by this amount for a change in classification. Thus, we can say with some certainty that FLL, based on its large classification score, is a robust efficient solution for all years. The cross-efficiency scores, which tend to force nonzero weightings across input and output factors, also support the robustness of FLL's efficiency. Because the assumption of only six gates at FLL may also affect the efficiency of units that it dominated, FLL is removed from the data set and the CCR efficiency scores are determined again. The revised results do not make any inefficient units efficient, even though some inefficient units do increase slightly in efficiency, which is to be expected.

Six DEA-based models were used to evaluate airport operational efficiency. By using CCR and BCC in tandem, we can tell if varying returns to scale occur within the data set (some differences exist in average efficiency scores). Because both techniques truncate the efficiency score at 1, and they may not serve as good discriminators for airport ranking. Another disadvantage is that extreme weighting of the factors occurs, which may cause unrealistic efficiency evaluations. SXEF and AXEF cross-efficiency approaches are included to address this issue. However, SXEF and AXEF average out the weightings of the models, which may not be the true measure of importance levels associated with each of the factors. The RCCR and GTR techniques are better overall discriminators because they do not truncate the efficient scores. The results provide more continuous (rather than truncated at 1 or 0 values) airport efficiency scores, as well as evaluating robustness. However, RCCR and GTR also allow extreme weighting to occur.

J. Sarkis / Journal of Operations Management 18 (2000) 335–351 347

As we have stated, the efficiency models presented in this paper allow for complete flexibility of weights on the inputs and outputs. That is, there are no restrictions on the values of the coefficient weights (u and v) in the DEA formulations. Information that prioritizes the data inputs and outputs, which may be elicited from airport operations managers, may lead to more realistic evaluations of airport efficiency. In the conclusion, we define research issues not covered in this study for evaluating airport operations efficiency.

7. Summary and conclusion

Evaluating airport operational efficiency is important for a number of reasons: communities rely on airports for economic well-being, deregulation allows air carriers to choose among competing airports, and federal funding for airport improvements is based on performance measures. Data are acquired from the airports and the ACI database. Various DEA models provide diverse and complementary insights into evaluating overall efficiencies and factors that may influence airport efficiency. Results, which are based on external empirical data and an empirical evaluation of airport characteristics, show that overall mean efficiencies of major U.S. airports have been increasing (with a slight drop in 1993) over the last few years. This tends to confirm the notion of increasing competitiveness and improving resource utilization by airports. Some external factors and characteristics may influence an airport manager's control over operations. Whether an airport is a hub for a major air carrier and whether it is located in a snowbelt seem to relate strongly to an airport's efficiency. Whether an airport is a part of an MAS or an SAS does not have a significant relationship with its efficiency.

The tools and data used in this study have a number of limitations, one of which is the bias toward larger airports. Although this bias is not necessarily bad from a DEA perspective, which seeks to consider airports with more homogeneous characteristics, our generalization of results to smaller airports (from among the largest 80) must be evaluated. In addition, data variations in input and output parameters and the size of the data sample may provide

varying results. The data variables selected are not exhaustive. For example, additional data detailing costs and where these costs are budgeted could be used. Evaluation of airport efficiencies using other, additional modeling assumptions might provide further insights into this area.

This paper makes a number of major contributions. It provides some initial analysis on airport service operations, an area where there has been limited research, and identifies characteristics that may explain differences in airport operational efficiency. Results indicate that operations managers should evaluate and benchmark their performances with airports having similar characteristics. Federal agencies may find this study useful in determining how well their funding aids airports in maintaining and improving their operational efficiencies (e.g., through the AIP). This paper also contributes methodologically in its comprehensive use of various DEA techniques that provide complementary information for industry analysis.

There are several areas worthy of future consideration. International surveys can be used to determine how various categories of ownership (private, centralized government, decentralized government) and national economic, social, and political characteristics may impact airport operational efficiency. Even though almost all airports in the U.S. are publicly owned and operated, a significant portion of their operations are run by private commercial organizations. Airport operations privatization and its effect on airport efficiency is a potentially interesting area of research that would require a determination of total expenditures and revenues of airport operations by private and public sources (ratios of public to private employees may also be used as proxy measures). It would be difficult to determine the roles and significance of airlines, concessionaires, and other management groups in airport operations. Because debt financing is expected to be of increasing importance in airport management, using debt financing in productivity models may enhance future analysis.

Inamete (1993) lists a number of factors that can affect performance including: changes in public ownership structure through privatization; contracting out various functions of airports to private organizations; combining government and private airport

348 *J. Sarkis / Journal of Operations Management 18 (2000) 335–351*

ownership; increasing autonomy for government-owned airport organizations; creating government holding corporations; commercializing the activities of airport organizations; and creating competitive dynamics by having two or more public airport organizations. Many of these policy initiatives, which will have profound implications for operations managers, have not yet been introduced but may be implemented in the near future. A longitudinal study extending the results presented here could provide insights into whether these initiatives actually provide more efficiency in airport operations and how operations managers might react to them. Another extension of this work would be field and case studies of airports that provide internal operational reasons for the differences in airport operational efficiency.

Overall, there seems to be ample opportunity to examine a number of dimensions of airport operations using a variety of research tools.

Acknowledgements

We wish to thank Maria Hinayon of the Airports Council International for her assistance in acquiring data for this study.

Appendix A. Data envelopment analysis models

Here, we provide a review of basic DEA and some cross-efficiency and ranking extensions to the DEA models that are used to evaluate the airport data.

A.1. Basic DEA models

Productivity models have traditionally been used to measure the efficiency of systems. Typically, DEA productivity models for a given decision-making unit use ratios based on the amount of outputs per given set of inputs; here a decision-making unit is an airport. DEA allows for the simultaneous analysis of multiple inputs to multiple outputs, a multi-factor productivity approach. Using the notation of

Doyle and Green (1994), the general efficiency measure used by DEA is best summarized by Eq. (A1).

$$E_{ks} = \frac{\sum\limits_{y} O_{sy} v_{ky}}{\sum\limits_{x} I_{sx} u_{kx}} \tag{A1}$$

where E_{ks} is the efficiency or productivity measure of airport s, using the weights of test airport k; O_{sy} is the value of output y for airport s; I_{sx} is the value for input x of airport s; v_{ky} is the weight assigned to airport k for output y; and u_{kx} is the weight assigned to airport k for input x.

In the basic DEA ratio model developed by Charnes et al. (1978) (CCR), the objective is to maximize the efficiency value of a test airport k from among a reference set of airports s, by selecting the optimal weights associated with the input and output measures. The maximum efficiencies are constrained to 1. The formulation is represented in expression (A2).

$$\text{maximize} \quad E_{kk} = \frac{\sum\limits_{y} O_{ky} v_{ky}}{\sum\limits_{x} I_{kx} u_{kx}}$$

subject to: $\quad E_{ks} \leq 1 \quad \forall \quad \text{Airports} \quad s \tag{A2}$

$u_{ks}, v_{ky} \geq 0$

This nonlinear programming formulation (A2) is equivalent to formulation (A3) (see Charnes et al., 1978 for a complete transformation explanation):

$$\text{maximize} \quad E_{kk} = \sum\limits_{y} O_{ky} v_{ky}$$

subject to: $\quad E_{ks} \leq 1 \quad \forall \quad \text{Airports} \quad s$

$$\sum\limits_{x} I_{kx} u_{kx} = 1 \tag{A3}$$

$u_{kx}, v_{ky} \geq 0$

The transformation is completed by constraining the efficiency ratio denominator from (A2) to a value of 1, represented by the constraint $\sum_{x} I_{kx} u_{kx} = 1$.

The result of formulation (A3) is an optimal simple or technical efficiency value (E_{kk}^*) that is at most equal to 1. If $E_{kk}^* = 1$, then no other airport is more efficient than airport k for its selected weights. That is, $E_{kk}^* = 1$ has airport k on the optimal frontier and is not dominated by any other airport. If $E_{kk}^* < 1$,

J. Sarkis / Journal of Operations Management 18 (2000) 335–351

349

then airport k does not lie on the optimal frontier and there is at least one other airport that is more efficient for the optimal set of weights determined by (A3). Formulation (A3) is executed s times, once for each airport. The first method in the analysis uses the CCR model to calculate the simple efficiency.

The dual of the CCR formulation (also defined as the envelopment side) is represented by model (A4):

minimize θ,

subject to:

$$\sum_s \lambda_s I_{sx} - \theta I_{sx} \le 0 \quad \forall \quad \text{Inputs } I$$

$$\sum_s \lambda_s O_{sy} - O_{ky} \ge 0 \quad \forall \quad \text{Outputs } O \qquad (A4)$$

$$\lambda_s \ge 0 \quad \forall \quad \text{Airports } s$$

The CCR model has an assumption of constant returns to scale for the inputs and outputs. To take into consideration variable returns to scale, a model introduced by Banker et al. (1984) (BCC) is utilized. The BCC model aids in determining the scale efficiency of a set of units (which is a technically efficient unit for the variable returns to scale model). This new model has an additional convexity constraint defined by limiting the summation of the multiplier weights (λ) equal to 1, or:

$$\sum_s \lambda_s = 1 \qquad (A5)$$

The use of the CCR and BCC models together helps determine the overall technical and scale efficiencies of the airport respondents and whether the data exhibits varying returns to scale.

A.2. Cross-efficiency and ranking models

One of the difficulties with simple efficiency scores is a resulting set of false positives. A false positive airport score weighs heavily on a single input or output, thus making that airport more efficient than any other airport (Sexton et al., 1986 define these units as mavericks). A procedure for discriminating between true efficient airports and false positive airports is to analyze the cross-efficiencies. Sexton et al. (1986) introduced the concept of cross-efficiencies and the cross-efficiency matrix (CEM). The CEM provides information on

the efficiency of a specific airport with the optimal weighting schemes determined for other airports. The table in this section summarizes a generalized CEM. The kth row and the sth column represent the efficiency measure of airport s by the optimal weights for airport k(E_{ks}). Each of the columns of the CEM is then averaged to get a mean cross-efficiency measure (defined as the SXEF measure when the optimal weights used for the CEM are from the basic CCR model) for each airport (e_s). A false positive airport score may be associated with an efficient airport that has a relatively small cross-efficiency value or a value that is less than that of an initially inefficient airport.

A pitfall in determining a cross-efficiency score is that the weights, derived from the CCR model, used to calculate the optimal simple efficiencies (and eventually used in cross-efficiency measures) may not be unique. To overcome this difficulty, a formulation (A6) developed by Doyle and Green (1994), one that will help generate a less ambiguous set of optimal weights, may be used for cross-efficiency calculation and development of a CEM.

$$\text{minimize} \quad \sum_y \left(\nu_{ky} \sum_{s=k} O_{sy} \right),$$

$$\text{subject to:} \quad \sum_x \left(u_{kx} \sum_{s=k} I_{sx} \right) = 1,$$

$$\sum_y O_{ky} \nu_{ky} - E_{kk}^* \sum_x I_{kx} u_{kx} = 0 \qquad (A6)$$

$$E_{ks} \le 1 \quad \forall \quad \text{Airports } s \ne k$$

$$u_{kx}, \nu_{ky} \ge 0$$

The Doyle and Green formulation as presented in (A6) has a primary goal of obtaining a maximum simple efficiency score for airport k (the test unit) and a secondary goal of determining a set of weights that minimize the other airports' aggregate output, as defined by the objective function. The test unit k is defined as an average unit whose efficiency is minimized. This model has been defined as an aggressive formulation (AXEF). To make the Doyle and Green formulation benevolent, where the secondary goal is to maximize the other airport's aggregate output, requires changing the "minimum" to "maximum" in (A6). The data required in (A6) includes the optimal efficiency scores (E_{kk}^*) from the CCR model, as shown by the second constraint set. This procedure for cross-efficiency calculation requires a two-phased approach to determine the optimal weights.

A simple alteration to the Doyle and Green formulation (A6) provides for more accurate results when executed using commercial linear programming software. The variation takes an average unit expressed in the objective function of (A6) and scales it by dividing the value by the $n - 1$ units that form the average units, where n is the total number of airports in the model. This scaling allows for a similar scale of optimal weights (v^* and u^*) as the basic CCR model. We find in initial tests of formulation (A6) that as the set of units under evaluation gets larger, the optimal weights get smaller to offset the average unit size. As the optimal weights become smaller, truncation and roundoff errors tend to occur with the commercial LP solution package. The scaling of the optimal weights does not impact the efficiency score of the units under consideration. The new objective function we introduce for formulation (A6) is:

$$\text{minimize} \quad \sum_y \frac{\left[v_{ky} \sum_{s \neq k} O_{sy} \right]}{n - 1} \qquad (A7)$$

where n is the total number of airports.

The mean cross-efficiency scores calculated using this formulation can be used to rank the airport alternatives. The false positives or mavericks are defined through a maverick index score, which may be calculated with expression (A8).

$$MI_k = \frac{E_{kk}^*}{e_k} \qquad (A8)$$

where MI_k is the maverick index score for test unit k, E_{kk}^* is the optimal value from the CCR formulation for test unit k, and e_k is the cross-efficiency score (either SXEF or AXEF) for test unit k. We call test unit k a false positive if it is initially technically efficient using the CCR formulation, and its maverick index score is greater than a sum of the mean of the maverick indices and a factor (which will be some fraction of the standard deviation of the sample). This result is represented by expression (A9).

$$MI_{k \in E} > \overline{MI} + \rho\sigma \qquad (A9)$$

where $MI_{k \in E}$ is the test unit k which is initially technically efficient, $\overline{MI} = (\sum_{j=1}^m MI_j) / m$ and is the

mean of the maverick indices (over the full set of airports m), $\sigma =$ the standard deviation of the full set of airports, and $\rho =$ a false positivity factor (in this study, we arbitrarily set $\rho = 1$).

Another DEA-ranking approach is a variation of the CCR model proposed by Andersen and Petersen (1993). In their model, they simply eliminate the test unit from the constraint set. The new formulation is represented by (A10).

$$\text{maximize} \quad E_{kk} = \sum_y O_{ky} v_{ky}$$

$$\text{subject to:} \quad E_{ks} \leq 1 \quad \forall \quad \text{Airports } s \neq k$$

$$\sum_x I_{kx} u_{kx} = 1 \qquad (A10)$$

$$u_{kx}, \quad v_{ky} \geq 0$$

Expression (A10), which we call the reduced CCR (RCCR) formulation, allows for technically efficient scores to be greater than 1. This result allows for a more discriminating set of scores for technically efficient units and thus can be used for ranking purposes.

Another DEA-based model that can help rank individual units (including efficient units) is one proposed by Rousseau and Semple (1995), which focuses on preservation of a unit's classification (e.g., changes required to input and output values to maintain a unit's classification as efficient or inefficient). This approach is based on determining a unit's sensitivity to changes in the data values. The formulation used here to evaluate the data set is the generalized Tchebycheff radius of classification preservation (GTR) model (A11).

$$\text{minimize} \quad \alpha^+ - \alpha^-$$

subject to:

$$\sum_{s = k} \lambda_s I_{kk} - \alpha^+ I_{kx} + \alpha^- I_{kx} - I_{kx} \leq 0 \quad \forall \quad \text{Inputs } I$$

$$\sum_{s = k} \lambda_s O_{sy} + \alpha^+ O_{ky}$$

$$\quad - \alpha^- O_{ky} - O_{ky} \geq 0 \quad \forall \quad \text{Outputs } O$$

$$\sum_{s = k} \lambda_s = 1 \qquad (A11)$$

$$\lambda_s, \alpha^+, \alpha^- \geq 0$$

where α^+ is the distance of an efficient unit from the Pareto frontier and α^- is the distance of an inefficient unit from the Pareto frontier.

J. Sarkis / Journal of Operations Management 18 (2000) 335–351 351

Unlike the other DEA models discussed above, the optimal value for this formulation can be either negative (inefficient unit) or positive (efficient unit). The magnitude of the objective value is also significant because it defines the robustness of the unit's score. Magnitudes of objective values can serve as good measures to discriminate among units with similar classifications, and thus to rank the various units either efficient or inefficient. Whereas the RCCR model is based on the CCR formulation, the GTR model is underpinned by the BCC formulation. We may also use the results of the GTR formulation to evaluate the sensitivity of the data used in this study.

References

ACI, 1995. ACI monthly airport traffic statistics collection, Airports Council International, Geneva, Switzerland.

Andersen, P., Petersen, N.C., 1993. A procedure for ranking efficient units in data envelopment analysis. Management Science 39, 1261–1264.

Armstrong, J.S., Overton, T.S., 1977. Estimating nonresponse bias in mail surveys. Journal of Marketing Research 14, 396–402.

Ashford, N., 1994. Airport management in a changing economic climate. Transportation Planning and Technology 18, 57–63.

Banker, R.D., Charnes, A., Cooper, W.W., 1984. Some models for estimating technical and scale inefficiencies in data envelopment analysis. Management Science 30, 1078–1092.

Borenstein, S., 1989. Hubs and high fares: dominance and market power in the U.S. airline industry. Rand Journal of Economics 20, 344–365.

Boussofiane, A., Dyson, R.G., Thanassoulis, E., 1991. Applied data envelopment analysis. European Journal of Operational Research 52, 1–15.

Brockett, P.L., Golany, B., 1996. Using rank statistics for determining programmatic efficiency differences in data envelopment analysis. Management Science 42, 466–472.

Charnes, A., Cooper, W.W., Rhodes, E., 1978. Measuring the efficiency of decision making units. European Journal of Operational Research 2, 429–444.

DeLuca, J.M., Dewitt, C.E., Lewis, S.P., 1995. Airport finance challenges for the next decade. Airport Magazine, May/June, http://www.airportnet.org/depts/publications/airmags/am5695/fin.htm.

Doyle, J., Green, R., 1994. Efficiency and cross-efficiency in DEA: derivations, meanings and uses. Journal of the Operational Research Society 45, 567–578.

Emrouznejad, A., Thanassoulis, E., 1996a. An extensive bibliography of data envelopment analysis (DEA), Vol. 1, Working papers, Working paper 244, Business School, University of Warwick, Coventry CV4 7AL, England.

Emrouznejad, A., Thanassoulis, E., 1996b. An extensive bibliography of data envelopment analysis (DEA), Vol. 2, Journal papers, Working paper 245, Business School, University of Warwick, Coventry CV4 7AL, England.

Emrouznejad, A., Thanassoulis, E., 1997. An extensive bibliography of data envelopment analysis (DEA), Vol. 3, Supplement 1, Working paper 258, Business School, University of Warwick, Coventry CV4 7AL, England.

FAA, 1994. FAA statistical handbook of aviation. Department of Transportation, Washington, DChttp://www.bts.gov/ntda/shafaa/.

FAA, 1996. FAA airports reengineering. Washington, DC, http://www.faa.gov/arp/.

FAA, 1997. Airport planning and development process: analysis and documentation report. Federal Aviation Administration, Washington, DC.

Grosskopf, S., Valdmanis, A., 1987. Measuring hospital performance: a non-parametric approach. Journal of Health Economics 6, 89–107.

Hansen, M., Weidner, T., 1995. Multiple airport systems in the United States: current status and future prospects. Transportation Research Record 1506, Transportation Research Board, National Research Council, Washington, DC, pp. 8–17.

Inamete, U.B., 1993. Key elements in managing airports: the policy environment and increasing efficiency. International Journal of Public Sector Management 6, 12–23.

Rousseau, J.J., Semple, J.H., 1995. Radii of classification preservation in data envelopment analysis: a case study of 'program follow-through'. Journal of the Operational Research Society 46, 943–957.

Schefczyk, M., 1993. Operational performance of airlines: an extension of traditional measurement paradigms. Strategic Management Journal 14, 301–317.

Seiford, L.M., 1996. Data envelopment analysis: the evolution of the state of the art (1978–1995). Journal of Productivity Analysis 7, 99–137.

Sengupta, J.K., 1995. Dynamics of Data Envelopment Analysis. Kluwer Academic Publishers, Dordrecht, The Netherlands.

Sexton, T.R., Silkman, R.H., Hogan, A.J., 1986. Data envelopment analysis: critique and extensions. In: Silkman, R.H. (Ed.), Measuring Efficiency: An Assessment of Data Envelopment Analysis Jossey-Bass, San Francisco, pp. 73–104.

Thompson, R.G., Dharmapala, P.S., Humphrey, D.B., Thrall, R.M., 1991. DEA/AR efficiency of large U.S. commercial banks, Working paper No. 91, Jesse H. Jones Graduate School of Administration, Rice University, Houston, TX.

Truitt, L.J., Haynes, R., 1994. Evaluating service quality and productivity in the regional airline industry. Transportation Journal 33, 21–32.

Wiley, J.R., 1986. Airport Administration and Management. Eno Foundation for Transportation, Westport, CT.

Windle, R., Dresner, M., 1993. Competition at 'duopoly' airline hubs in the U.S. Transportation Journal 33, 22–30.

Windle, R., Dresner, M., 1995. A note on productivity comparisons between air carriers. Logistics and Transportation Review 31, 125–134.

10

The economics of franchise contracts and airport policy

David Gillen, William G. Morrison

Abstract

In this paper, we apply insights from the economics of franchise contracts to the governance of airports and the evolution of airport policy in Canada. Some aspects of the devolution of airports in Canada could be consistent with a 'public franchise' approach to airport policy. An examination of Canada's National Airport Policy and subsequent policy decisions, however, suggests that the government may have made the right decision for the wrong reasons. Applying the franchise perspective to European airport policy, recent decisions by the European Union regarding exclusive agreements between publicly owned airports and low-cost carriers suggest a departure from the incentive-compatibility requirements of franchise contracts that would promote market-based efficiency.

1. Introduction

What happens when a government picks the right policy for the wrong reasons? At first pass, one might have reason to believe that the right policy, irrespective of the motivation will yield the right results. In this paper, we argue that this is by no means certain because the motivation for policy decisions affects the way that a policy is implemented and the evolution of future policy decisions. The context of our discussion is Canada's National Airport Policy (NAP), which administered the devolution of airports from direct federal operation and control to local airport authorities (LAAs). We view this episode in Canadian airport policy through the lens provided by the economics of franchise contracts. The franchise model suggests a governance system that emphasizes the economic efficiency properties of in-centive compatible contracts. While the NAP case recounts some unique aspects of Canadian airport policy, the implications of viewing airports as a franchise system for policy purposes are far more general. Consequently, our analysis provides a new perspective on recent EU decisions regarding the interaction between publicly owned regional airports and low-cost carriers.

2. A recent history of Canadian Airport Policy

We document the evolution of the Canadian airport system in more detail elsewhere (Gillen and Morrison, 2004; Gillen, Henrikkson and Morrison, 2001). It is useful, however, to summarize the recent evolution of policy in Canada as a means to discuss potential contradictions in interpreting the intent, and economic implications of policy decisions.

Historically, in Canada, planning and managing airports was one of the most important responsibilities of the Federal Ministry of Transport (later renamed Transport Canada). However, in 1986, the Airport Authorities Group (AAG) was created with the explicit task of introducing commercialization and financial self-sufficiency in the airport system. When the AAG took over, the system contained 200 airports with an estimated replacement value of some $8 billion in 1985. The AAG then had a capital budget of $200 M, an operating budget of about $400 M, and about 4500 employees.

44   *D. Gillen, W.G. Morrison / Journal of Air Transport Management 11 (2005) 43–48*

Rather than a simple change in internal governance, the creation of the AAG signalled a distinct policy shift with respect to airports with the contemporaneous creation of a new policy directive *Future Framework for the Management of Airports in Canada* (1989) (Transport Canada, 1988). This directive proposed to transfer a subset of airports to LAAs and to transfer the remaining designated airports to local municipalities, for a nominal fee. Thus, the government set in motion, a process culminated in the devolution of airports from Federal control—a strategy that evolved and was eventually synthesized as the NAP in 1994.

This devolution of airports can be identified with five elements of the evolving environment. First, the increased growth of passenger traffic meant new investment in capacity would have to be made and the federal government did not have sufficient resources to provide this capital. Second, there was pressure for governments to downsize and transfer activities that could be provided outside the government to alternative agencies or privatize it. This reflected the broad movement of less government in the US and UK as well as elsewhere. Third, the environmental review process lengthened the airport planning process. It also provided local constituents with a federal political power point. Fourth, the general movement of deregulation particularly among transportation enterprises, airlines, trucking, rail and bus, had led to measurable welfare gains and the next step was to deregulate infrastructure. Finally, devolution can be seen as a response to the growing worldwide interest in alternative airport governance mechanisms. Some within the AAG recognized that market-based incentives and demand management had a very low likelihood of being introduced under continued federal ownership and management.

The NAP changed the role of the federal government from one of owner, operator and regulator to one of owner, landlord and regulator. However, this was to be true for only the top 26 airports in the country, measured by aggregate enplaned and deplaned passengers.[1] These larger airports became part of the *National Airport System* (NAS). Smaller facilities designated as regional or local airports were to be sold to local communities for a nominal fee; generally $1. In cases where communities had no interest in owning the airport, other groups (such as not-for-profit enterprises) as well as for-profit enterprises (e.g. Sault St. Marie) were encouraged to take over the airport.

With pending devolution came the need to devise new ways for airports to meet their capital requirements. The

federal government assumed that the 26 airports in the NAS would have the fiscal capacity to attract capital necessary for infrastructure investment and that they would have strong enough markets to generate revenues from airside and groundside activities. Fiscal capacity refers to the ability of an airport to achieve a particular level of revenue and/or capital access (bonds) because of the markets it serves and traffic level it attracts. Those airports within the NAS had access to private capital markets (bonds), as well as Airport Improvement Fees (AIFs) in addition to revenues from both airside and groundside activities.[2]

Under the NAP, smaller regional and municipal airports were to be provided with assistance from internal capital market funds under the Airports Capital Assistance Program (ACAP). These funds were designated for safety-related airside investment projects—the funds were project specific—and the monies were derived from the lease payments from the NAS airports. Local operators were required to contribute to a maximum of 15% of project costs. The problems with this capital market were the amounts were highly variable, the access rules were not clearly defined and the allocation of funds across projects was not clearly defined. One justification for this internal capital market was the role the regional/local airports played in the country's aviation network. In a hub-and-spoke system, hub airports derive benefit from spoke airports and the more spokes the greater the value of the network. Private markets would tend to under invest in spoke airports unless there was some means of internalizing this network externality. As we move towards more direct flights in the domestic market, this justification becomes less tenable.

Under the NAP, the federal government continued to set safety and security standards for all airports in Canada, presumably following International Civil Aviation Organization (ICAO) guidelines. For the larger NAS airports, these standards were in some cases, written directly into the transfer agreements during the devolution process. Irrespectively, these standards became part of the airport certification process at all NAS airports.

2.1. A change in direction

The evolution of airport policy in Canada changed towards the end of the 20th century. In Canada, Canadian Airlines International failed and was subsumed into Air Canada, creating concerns about the sustainability of domestic airline competition. These structural changes in conjunction with other economic and political events placed the airports at greater risk in

---

[1] The government noted the top 26 airports handle 94% of passenger traffic in Canada. Actually, the top 8 airports handle 86% and the 18 remaining airports account for only 8%. Clearly, such diversity creates problems in having one set of policies for capital access and emergency services.

[2] AIFs are sometimes referred to as passenger facility charges (PFCs).

D. Gillen, W.G. Morrison / Journal of Air Transport Management 11 (2005) 43–48

several ways including fewer flights, lower traffic levels and higher costs as well as the shift in market power.

In response to the changes occurring in the airline industry, the government proposed modifications to the National Transportation Act, the Competition Act, the Competition Tribunal Act, and the Air Canada Public Participation Act. A new bill, Bill C-26 took aim at curtailing the [anticipated] market power of Air Canada and to protect consumers and the economy from potential abuses of changes to service quality and service reductions or stoppages.

Bill C-26 represented the first in a series of policy initiatives that signalled the reintroduction of an activist interventionalist government. Changes to the Competition Act were not just aimed at a particular industry but at a particular firm, an unprecedented change in any country. The National Transportation Act was amended to introduce a consumer complaints commissioner as well as new powers for the National Transportation Agency (NTA) to review and possibly alter fares. The NTA could also review route and service abandonment and possibly force a continuance. In all cases, these changes represented a move away from deregulation where market solutions had been encouraged.

In the spring of 2001, the Canadian Transportation Act Review Committee (CTARC) was struck to offer advice/solutions to the pressures evolving in the Canadian market for transportation services.[3] These included investment requirements in infrastructure, integrating transportation policy with environmental concerns (e.g. Kyoto Agreement) and ensuring the institutional environment did not hinder the ability of firms and industries to integrate with the new global economy. The NTA had mandated a review of the Act within 4 years and the airline and railway industries were under continuing pressure as the growth and evolution of markets was making the present institutional structures near obsolete. Interestingly, the airport sector, viewed by many as evolving along the lines envisaged by the policy of the 1990s, was placed on the agenda. A key concern of the government was the failure of the current airport authorities to have accountability and transparency in their policies and strategies. In the end, the review committee provided over 100 recommendations covering rail, air and airport policy; however, the results of this process were delayed by the events of September 11th.

Canada's federal government reacted quickly in response to the events of 9–11 and announced new initiatives to enhance security at Canada's airports. This included a plan to purchase new explosive detection equipment with a price tag of around $58 million the creation of a new Federal body: the Canadian Air

Transport Security Authority (CATSA), which was formally constituted (under Bill C-49) in March 2002.

The negative shock provided by 9–11 to the industry was amplified by the knee-jerk reaction from policymakers in the federal government with the creation of a security tax as a fixed fee on all routes to and from Canadian airports. As a result of the tax, Canada's troubled airline (Air Canada) and its low-cost competitor West Jet were faced with significant losses in revenues, particularly on shorter-haul domestic routes where both business and leisure demand are price elastic.[4] In some cases, it was simply a profits tax as carriers absorbed the tax by lowering net fares.

Beyond the undesirable effects of the security tax, the whole idea of creating a new federal government institution to implement a uniform set of security changes across the country was another policy that went against the devolution set out by the NAP. While the Federal government (through Transport Canada) had a justifiable mandate to assess and set security standards, there were no justifiable grounds for the government centralizing the *implementation* of these changes. Giving airports the flexibility to manage their own security improvements could have allowed for airports to price and manage these improvements in a way that minimized any undesirable effects on passenger volumes.

In 2003, the results of the process that began with the Transportation Act Review finally gave rise to new proposed legislation for airports. Bill C-27: the Airports Act, emerged from the committee recommendations. Bill C-27 contained over 215 clauses…more provisions than the entire Competition Act! The bill represented a significant reintroduction of government oversight and intervention and a move away from a market orientation to effect efficiency and service quality. If implemented, it would increase the organizational and administrative costs to airports, all in the name of transparency and apparent accountability. The emphasis was on fairness and the public role of aviation, in effect a supply side view of airport services that appeared to revert back to the 'old days'.[5]

3. Airport networks and the economics of franchise contracts

The economic analysis of franchising has spurned a relatively large literature, some of which is based upon

---

[3]The Committee was interested in both railway and aviation issues.

[4]Gillen, Morrison and Stewart (2002) report a median estimate of price elasticity for short-to-medium haul domestic travel of −1.5 for both business and leisure travel.

[5]Examples of the government increasing its grip on airports and creating a Federal oversight include the control over slots (Paragraph 28), limited access to data (paragraph 23), control over fee setting (Paragraphs 144–147), establishing performance measures and Federal control over ownership and directors (paragraphs 50, 53, 54, 57 and 136).

46 *D. Gillen, W.G. Morrison / Journal of Air Transport Management 11 (2005) 43–48*

viewing the interaction between franchisors and franchisees through the lens of the principal-agent model.[6] The franchisor as principal, wishes to develop a national brand for a good or service, the demand for which in part depends upon the franchisor's success in developing and maintaining national standards. The franchisor also wishes to harness the ability of potential franchisees that can provide capital and possess local market expertise. The franchisees as agents recognize the benefits from trading their expertise and labour in return for participating in the franchise, but the contractual relationship creates both a vertical and a horizontal shirking problem. In the vertical relationship between the franchisor and a single franchisee, the franchisor knows the effort required from the franchisee to maximize the profits of the overall business, but often cannot observe effort directly. This creates an incentive for franchisees to under-provide effort if their shirking cannot be detected.

The horizontal shirking problem can be thought of both as a prisoner's dilemma problem or as 'market for lemons' problem: each franchisee has an incentive to free-ride on the effort put forth by other franchisees as they all contribute to a public good—the reputation of the national brand. Also, suppose that consumers attribute some average effort or quality level to the product based on the distribution of effort levels provided by franchisees. As in the standard 'lemons' model of asymmetric information, the existence of franchisees providing low effort undermines the consumers' willingness-to-pay for the product.

The analytics of the problem thus focus our attention on the extent to which the franchisor as principal can design a governance structure that mitigates the shirking problems and maximizes the principal's objective function. A corner solution to the incentive compatibility problems in franchise contracts is to make each franchisee a full residual claimant to their efforts in return for a fixed fee as compensation to the franchisor. However, this solution is unlikely to be implemented because (a) franchisees are unlikely to have the wealth necessary to pay a sufficiently large fee and (b) such an arrangement would severe the interests of the franchisor who would then have no incentive to promote the overall franchise.

In practice, what we observe in private franchise contracts are a combination of three instruments: fixed fees, revenue sharing and resources spent on monitoring the efforts of individual franchisees.[7] In particular, revenue sharing helps to motivate 'good' incentives on both the part of the franchisees and the franchisor.

---

[6]A seminal article in this literature is Mathewson and Winter (1985).

[7]Including in some cases conditons placed on suppliers and/or minimum input quality (e.g. McDonalds contracts for it smeat from specific suppliers for the franchisees in a particular geographic area.

4. Was the National Airport Policy an attempt to create a public franchise system?

Now let us return to the NAP in Canada and evaluate its implementation in relation to the public franchise model. There are three key elements of the implementation of the NAP that differentiate the network structure that one might have expected if the intent had been to create a public franchise. First, LAAs were legislated to be non-profit organizations. The government thus created institutions with for-profit motives that were nevertheless prohibited from making profit. From our model then, how does the addition of a zero profit constraint affect the incentives and behaviour of airports? Clearly, prohibiting a monopoly or a firm with significant market power from earning positive profits does not change the fact that it is a monopoly, so what happens to the monopoly rents? Our model would suggest that the airport will attempt to reinvest its profits in retail investments rather than increase its throughput effort level or infrastructure investments. Increases in retail investments increase retail spending per customer and retail profits which again must be reinvested to satisfy the zero-profit constraint. This 'gold-plating' issue is often discussed in relation to the market power of airports, but seldom is it linked to the governance structure of the airport system.

The second differentiating factor in the implementation of the NAP was the absence of revenue sharing in the contracts between the federal government and LAAs. The devolution of airports was a gradual process over 12 or so years and in each case an independent process of contract bargaining took place, with different lump-sum transfers and lease agreements signed. Again, within our model, assuming that the government opts (for whatever reason) to generate revenues solely through fixed fees, and assuming asymmetries in the market conditions facing individual airports, then the government needs to assess the optimal fixed fee for each airport. However, the informational demands and uncertainty that accompany this problem suggest that either the government will have to adjust these fixed fees on a regular basis (as market demand increases or contracts for example) or will have to create more complex formulas that attempt to effect automatic adjustments in the fee schedules. Why then did the government opt for fixed fees over revenue-sharing? One might guess that the decision was prompted by the inability of the government to provide infrastructure funds for these newly created organizations, while requiring them to make infrastructure investments. Many of the lease agreements for newly devolved airports set out initial lease payments that would eventually rise steeply after some initial start-up period. For some airports the end of this 'grace' period is approaching (Edmonton airport's rents increase

D. Gillen, W.G. Morrison / Journal of Air Transport Management 11 (2005) 43–48   47

dramatically in 2006 for example), and there has been some public concern about the ability of airports to withstand the increases in rents when they occur.

Another possible contributory factor in explaining the apparent government preference for fixed fees is connected to the decision to create non-profit enterprises. Finally, the ownership structure of the airport system under the NAP was that the government retained ownership of airport assets and lands. This has naturally created a distortion in the capital market for airport authorities. The alternative would have been to privatize the airports with the government retaining a non-controlling share of profits. This would have been more consistent with the public franchise model in terms of providing two-way incentive compatibility, and would also have provided more access (or less distorted access) to capital markets for airports. One might also expect that capital markets and shareholders would help to discipline any 'gold-plating' incentive on the part of airports.

In summary, examination of Canada's NAP in relation to our analytical framework suggests that if the government had really intended to create a public franchise network, then the airport system would have been privatized with the government as a non-controlling shareholder. Further, the privatization process would have set out revenue sharing conditions with each airport. This governance structure would have provided much needed flexibility in the financing of the system and would have mitigated the perceived need for a reversion to intervention and centralist legislation.

5. The franchise model and European regional airport policy

In 2001, the Walloon regional authorities and Brussels South Charleroi Airport (BSCA), the airport management company in which the Walloon region has a 100% stake, awarded Ryanair a 50% reduction in landing fees and set a fee of EUR 1 per passenger for ground-handling assistance (10% of the airport's basic rate). Ryanair also received from BSCA substantial start-up benefits such as a contribution to accommodation costs, subsistence, and the recruitment and training of pilots and cabin crew. In addition, BSCA paid EUR 4 per passenger by way of contributing to Ryanair's advertising costs and to reductions in ticket prices. In return, Ryanair had committed to base between two and four planes at the airport, and to have at least three flights per plane leaving Charleroi every day. Ryanair serviced 12 destinations from Charleroi, generating traffic of two million passengers a year (Barrett, 2004). It estimates that its operation in Charleroi had led to the creation of 200 direct jobs, and calculates that each passenger saves about EUR 100 on average by opting

for Ryanair rather than for one of the competing airlines using Zaventem airport in Brussels.

Ryanair established service at Charleroi since 1997, and has been attacked by rivals on the grounds of unfair competition. For example, Virgin Express, which also offers low-cost airfares, estimates that the direct and indirect aid given by Charleroi airport provides Ryanair with a benefit worth €30 per passenger. The matter was brought to the attention of the European Commission.[8]

In February 2004, the EU Commission disallowed the airport arrangements between Charleroi Airport and Ryanair on the grounds of lack of transparency, infringement of the private market investor principle, discriminatory exclusivity to Ryanair and the length of the agreement between the airport and Ryanair. The commission also ruled in February that approximately €4million out of €15million of incentives paid to date to Ryanair by Charleroi, the airport south of Brussels that is owned by the Walloon government, amounted to illegal state aid.

In its ruling, the Commission did state that airports may enter into similar contracts with airlines as had been the case with Charleroi and Ryanair provided such contracts were for a limited duration, were transparent, available to all carriers, were used to develop *new* routes and were proportional to the expected route revenue.

The Commission is saying there can be no exclusive contracts. However, with any investment the value of the returns must exceed the value of the initial investment otherwise less or no investment will take place. In route development airlines incur sunk costs and airlines do not wish to abandon routes once they begin since there is a significant downside to route abandonment. Therefore, any contract developed between airports and airlines must be consistent with the business model of the airline, in this case low-cost carriers. These carriers develop small markets and therefore need exclusive contracts. In the absence of such contracts, less investment in small markets will take place with a potential resultant loss in economic welfare.

One interpretation of the EU decision and statement of guidelines for future airline–airport relationships is that it appears to maintain the dated perspective that an airport is a cost centre for an airline. From this perspective, the decision fails to recognize that even publicly held airports are more efficient when they operate like private businesses. Such businesses will seek to form strategic partnerships whenever mutual benefits result. The only remaining question then is whether net social benefits are positive. An airport operating as a business has an incentive to ensure its services are consistent with the business model of the airlines it serves. Similarly, these airlines have an incentive to

---

[8]The Commission also received official complaints concerning Ryanair's activities at Strasbourg and Pau in France.

48   *D. Gillen, W.G. Morrison / Journal of Air Transport Management 11 (2005) 43–48*

maximize the passenger throughput and service access of the airport. If the French government held a 'per-passenger' revenue-sharing contract with Charleroi airport, the resulting revenues would by definition offset the value of concessions offered to Ryanair. More than anything, the EU decision thus reflects the inadequacies of the current airport governance system in France.

6. Conclusion

International experience in evolving airport policy has been to shift to privatization, in whole or in part accompanied by some form and intensity of regulation; for example, Germany and the UK have a relatively heavy-handed form of regulation compared with Australia and New Zealand. Proponents of privatization base their argument in part on a belief that airports will not have an incentive to exercise their market power where it exists. In other cases, airports are viewed as being in competition; for example, Germany has numerous airports in close proximity to one another. Opponents of privatization argue that first airports do possess and will exercise market power and that under privatization, there will be an underinvestment in the aviation network due to vertical externalities.

The economics of franchise contracts suggests that these apparently opposing views can be reconciled by an airport system which is owned by a single entity, public or private, but where airports are franchised to local private market entrepreneurs. The problems to overcome are ensuring that there is sufficient investment in both system and airport capacity to maximize the value of the system as a whole while providing incentives for airports to provide a level of effort (through services or investments) that does not free ride on the other airports in the system.

Our analysis suggests that a revenue-sharing contract between each airport (with a separation between airside and non-aviation revenues) and the franchisor could be used to eliminate horizontal free-riding externalities and could be implemented as a 'payment-per-passenger' contract.[9] It would also achieve the objective of moving away from fixed lease payments that place all the risk on the airports (and airlines) and result in exacerbating the cyclical exposure of the industry.

Share contracts of the type just described between airports and airlines have the potential to generate net revenue gains for governments. These revenues can then be redistributed amongst stakeholders if so desired, without introducing distortions in competitive airline

markets. That is, one may set the objective of promoting equal treatment of competitors, but this should be accomplished without losing socially efficient incentive-compatibility. The current EU ruling against Ryan Air does not appear to be successful in this regard.

In this paper, we have applied insights from the economics of franchise contracts to the governance of airports as a franchise system and related this to airport policy in Canada and Europe. The next step is to develop a formal analytical model of this sort of airport governance system which will provide more concrete analytical results. Indeed, there are several complicating but interesting extensions one could add in to the analysis, such as the role of airlines as both airport customers of and investors in airports. Similarly, one could examine the interplay between raising airport revenues through passenger chargers and private debt.

Nevertheless, we would argue that the franchise perspective developed in this paper has significant potential in providing an analytical structure that not only provides an economic rationale for appropriate airport policy decisions, but also addresses important issues relating to the *consistent* implementation of these policies. It is after all better to make the right decision for the right reason.

Acknowledgements

We benefitted from comments received from participants at the HWWA-GARS Workshop on Congestion and Competition, held at the Hamburg Institute of International Economics, Hamburg in 2004. Any errors remain our responsibility alone.

References

Barrett, S., 2004. Airports and Communities in a derugulated market. Presentation to Seventh Hamburg Aviation Conference.

Gillen, D., Morrison, W.G., 2004. Airport pricing, financing and policy. In: Gillen, D., Forsyth, P., Knorr, A., Mayer, O., Martin, H.-M., Starkie, D. (Eds.), The Economic Regulation of Airports: Recent Developments in Australasia, North America and Europe. Ashgate, Aldershot.

Gillen, D., Henrikkson, L., Morrison, W.G., 2001. Airport financing, costing and performance. The Canada Transportation Act Review Board, Government of Canada, Ottawa.

Gillen, D., Morrison, W.G., Stewart, C., 2002. Air travel demand elasticities: concepts, issues and measurement. Department of Finance, Government of Canada, Ottawa.

Mathewson, F., Winter, R., 1985. The economics of franchise contracts. Journal of Law and Economics 28, 503–526.

Starkie, D., 2002. Airport regulation and competition. Journal of Air Transport Management 8, 63–72.

Starkie, D., Yarrow, G., 2000. The single till approach to the price regulation of airports. Civil Aviation Authority, London.

Transport Canada, 1988. A new policy concerning a future management framework for airports in Canada. Government of Canada, Ottawa.

---

[9]The separation of airside and groundside revenue streams is required to avoid the distortions and social inefficiencies created by a 'single till' approach (Starkie, 2002; Starkie and Yarrow, 2000).

11

Inefficiencies and scale economies of European airport operations

Eric Pels, Peter Nijkamp, Piet Rietveld

Abstract

In this paper we argue that European airports, on average, are inefficient. Airline inefficiency (low load factors) appears to contribute significantly to airport inefficiency in terms of air passenger movements. We find that the average airport in Europe operates under constant returns to scale in "producing" air transport movements and under increasing returns to scale in producing passenger movements. These operating characteristics are statistically tested in a stochastic frontier model. Using data envelopment analysis, in which the number of runways is used as a fixed factor, technical and scale efficiency coefficients have been assessed. There appears to be no region-specific effect in that an airport in a certain country or region is on average more (in)efficient.
© 2003 Elsevier Ltd. All rights reserved.

Keywords: Airports; Efficiency; Data envelopment analysis; Stochastic frontier

---

1. Introduction

Aviation has grown rapidly in recent years, and will most likely continue to grow, while many airports face capacity shortages. Reynolds-Feighan and Button (1999) examine the capacity of the EU's airports. Athens, Linate (Milan), Barcelona, Madrid, London Heathrow, Paris Charles de Gaulle, Paris Orly, New York, Nice and Tenerife are mentioned as the 10 "most penalized" destination airports (based on delay per movement). Athens, Madrid, Palma de Mallorca, Nice, Dusseldorf, Geneva, Lyon, Marseille, Barcelona and Brussels are mentioned as the 10 most penalized departure airports. Many airports are planning or building additional capacity (e.g. a fifth runway at Amsterdam Schiphol, terminal five at Heathrow, Frankfurt is investigating the construction of a new runway). Additional runway capacity at Heathrow is not planned at the moment. Clearly, in the London case, there are multiple airports (most of them operated by the British Airport Authority), of which e.g. Stansted might be used to relieve Heathrow (see e.g. Tolofari et al. (1990) a detailed study). Whether the principal airline(s) operating from these airports think this is a good idea is another question. It now appears that British Airways will center its activities at Heathrow, while some low cost carriers are located at Stansted and Gatwick. These airports can therefore not be seen as reliever airports.

Many airports are also privatized (e.g. British airports operated by the British Airport Authority), or are expected to be privatized (e.g. the privatization of Amsterdam Airport Schiphol was planned, but postponed in the light of the parliamentary elections in May 2002 and the economic downturn later that year). Both regulators and investors in private airports need information on the cost structure and efficiency of airports. For example, a regulator needs information on the development over time of an airport's efficiency to determine price caps (when the airport is regulated by means of a price cap). Investors may be more willing to invest in a relatively efficient airport, since it may have higher expected profits. Given the relatively large investments and the impacts of aviation outside of the airport, also operators of public airports need to be aware of the cost structure and efficiency to be able to operate efficiently. Is it, for example, beneficial to open a new airport (or reconstruct an older airport) further away from the city to act as a reliever airport and thus reduce the noise impact around the city? Maybe private airports are more efficient, so that (partial) privatization may be advisable.

In this light, it is important to know whether (existing) airports are able to operate efficiently from an economic perspective using the current capacity, and whether or not scale economies are prevailing. In relation to that, we aim to examine whether smaller airports are equally efficient compared to larger airports. If not and/or if increasing economies to scale are prevailing, moving only part of the airport (e.g. intercontinental flights) to a new airport (or subsidiary thereof) would be unwise from an economic perspective. Then one would end up with two smaller, relatively inefficient airports. An airport can be labeled as inefficient for different reasons, the first of which are "indivisibilities", a well-known problem in public goods provision. An expansion of the runway system may in a lot of cases automatically create an over-capacity. It may be necessary to construct a new runway, but due to technical (and safety) requirements, it is usually not possible to fit its capacity to the expected (additional) demand. To a lesser extent, the same holds true for airport terminals. Second are governmental regulations (e.g. limits to the hours of airport operation, noise contours) and constraints imposed by physical circumstances (e.g. fog and wind) under which airports must operate. Next to the (purely technical) inefficiencies described above, X-inefficiency also is important. [1] Finally, airline inefficiency, resulting in low load factors, may cause airport inefficiency. The idea here is that an airport may have an "optimal" design; runway and terminal capacity are related (e.g. runway capacity is used to control the terminal usage). When the number of passengers per aircraft movement (i.e. the average load factor) decreases,

---

[1] Note that "regulators" do not necessarily have an incentive to reach a social optimum. Hence, regulations can also be a cause of X-inefficiency.

E. Pels et al. / Transportation Research Part E 39 (2003) 341–361   343

terminal efficiency also decreases in this line of reasoning. When airline inefficiency indeed causes airport inefficiency, this may be caused by airport prices (for aircraft movements) that are too low. [2]

European airports are controlled by a wide variety of agents (local governments to private enterprises) offering services that may include anything from (local) air traffic control (approach and landing) to catering services (restaurants at airports). In this paper we focus on the efficiency and economies of scale in the "production" of passenger and aircraft movements. In addition to these production-oriented economies, demand-related economies are also important: a large airport has the potential to offer higher frequencies and better and more connections in a hub and spoke network. These demand related aspects will not be discussed in this paper, although they should be kept in mind while interpreting our results. Even if economies of scale in airport operations were to be small or absent, there may nevertheless be economies on the demand side, thus implying that customers would benefit, so that consequently airports are in a better position to charge users for their services.

The determination of the economic efficiency of an airport entails the estimation of a (cost or production) frontier; an airport is (technically) efficient only if it operates on the frontier. [3] The elasticity of scale is evaluated at the frontier (even when the airport is not efficient, i.e. does not operate at the frontier). A frontier can be estimated by using parametric (e.g. stochastic frontier analysis) or non-parametric methods (e.g. data envelopment analysis (DEA)); see e.g. Gillen and Lall (1997) for a DEA analysis of North-American airports. Using the parametric method, one estimates a stochastic cost or production frontier. The estimation of a "standard" cost or production function fits a curve through the middle of a data cloud. Firms (airports) are on average efficient, but both positive and negative random fluctuations (with zero expected value) around the optimal production do exist. If not all firms reach the theoretical efficient frontier in practice, calibration of the "traditional" cost function will not yield the efficient frontier. To overcome this problem, a stochastic inefficiency term can be added to the traditional cost function to form a stochastic frontier. If a firm does not reach the optimal frontier (i.e. the stochastic inefficiency term is statistically different from 0), it is technically inefficient, a result that may be due to misinformation, so that wrong decisions are taken, or due to circumstances or occurrences beyond the control of the management, such as regulation or weather. According to Diewert (1992), statistical estimation of the parameters that characterize technology is more accurate using cost functions (than using production functions). However, in that case input prices are required, but there are no clear market prices for inputs. [4] A production frontier may therefore still be more useful.

DEA uses a sequence of linear programming problems to create a piecewise linear frontier, and implicitly assumes that outputs can be fully explained from the inputs. Any deviation from the

---

[2] The idea is simple. Higher landing fees means lower profit margins when the load factor does not change. Increasing the load factor may also lead to a higher profit margin (per flight). In practice, this point may be far more complicated, because airlines can decide to increase the ticket price to recover the landing fee. Pricing of airport capacity is, however, not an issue in this paper.

[3] Note that although a technically efficient firm generates the maximum output from a given input set, it is not guaranteed the firm uses a cost-minimizing input set or is scale efficient.

[4] See Button (1999) for a general survey of aviation data.

344   *E. Pels et al. / Transportation Research Part E 39 (2003) 341–361*

efficient frontier is labeled as inefficient; random (unexplained) deviations are not possible. Stochastic production frontier analysis, conversely, determines inefficiency as the distance to the stochastic frontier; stochastic deviations from the optimal frontier are allowed.

In this paper, we use both methods as "complements" rather than as "competitors", as explained below (in Section 3). The parametric method allows for statistical testing of the presence of a deviation from the efficient frontier and returns to scale. Because DEA is non-parametric, no statistical tests are available.

The outline of this paper is as follows. In Section 2 stochastic production frontier analysis and DEA is concisely discussed. In Section 3 the data and models to be estimated are presented. In Section 4 the estimation results are presented, while Section 5 concludes.

2. Frontier analysis

As discussed in the previous section we use two methods for determining a production frontier, viz. stochastic frontier analysis and DEA. Each is discussed briefly here. There exists a large body of literature on both topics, see e.g. Coelli (1996a,b) and the references therein. Although both methods are similar in that they determine a frontier and inefficiency based upon that frontier, there is a significant difference. The DEA approach provides a "measurement" of inefficiency (the "Farrell approach" (Button and Weyman-Jones, 1994)). As we will explain below, the stochastic frontier approach estimates inefficiency, but it can also be used as an "explanation" for inefficiency (the "Leibenstein approach").

2.1. The stochastic production frontier

We have noted in the introduction that a deviation from the optimal production frontier may have a variety of causes. Using a stochastic production frontier, the production process is characterized (approximated) by a flexible functional form, while inefficiency (the deviation from the frontier) is modeled explicitly.

Consider the following stochastic production frontier:

$$
\begin{aligned}
y_{j,t} &= f(x_{j,t}, \exp(R)) \times \exp(E_{j,t}) \\
E_{j,t} &= V_{j,t} - U_{j,t}(z_{j,t})
\end{aligned}
\tag{1}
$$

where $y_{j,t}$ is the output of airport j in period t, $x_{j,t}$ is a vector of inputs of airport j in period t, and R represents the state of technology. This is discussed in greater detail in Section 3.2. $f()$ is a transformation function which represents the deterministic part of the production frontier. $V_{j,t} \sim N(0, \sigma_V^2)$ and IID is a standard error term. $U_{j,t}$ represents the non-negative (stochastic) deviation from the production frontier; for $U_{j,t} > 0$ airport j does not reach the (efficient) frontier due to technical inefficiency. $U_{j,t} \sim N(m_{j,t}, \sigma_U^2)$, truncated at 0, and $m_{j,t} = z_{j,t}\delta$. $U_{j,t}$ and $V_{j,t}$ are independent. $z_{j,t}$ is a vector of airport attributes that are not considered as inputs, but can explain inefficiency (e.g. variables representing the degree of regulation).

E. Pels et al. / Transportation Research Part E 39 (2003) 341–361 345

If Eq. (1) is estimated in log–log form, then the technical efficiency is

$$TE_j = \frac{E(y_{j,t}|\widehat{U}_{j,t}, x_{j,t}, z_{j,t})}{E(y_{j,t}|U_{j,t} = 0, x_{j,t}, z_{j,t})} = \exp(-\widehat{U}_{j,t}) \tag{2}$$

where $\widehat{U}_{j,t}$ is the predicted value of $U_{j,t}$. Again, based on a log–log form, and assuming fixed proportions, returns to scale can be determined as (see also Fuss et al., 1978):

$$RTS = \sum_j \frac{\partial y_{j,t}}{\partial x_{j,t}} \tag{3}$$

After this brief introduction to stochastic frontier analysis we continue with DEA in the next subsection. The econometric models corresponding to Eq. (1) are presented in Section 3.

2.2. Data envelopment analysis

In DEA one uses a series of linear programming problems to determine a (production) frontier. The efficiency of each airport [5] is evaluated against this frontier. Hence the efficiency of an airport is evaluated relative to the performance of other airports. Both input and output-oriented models can be used, depending on which variable is the target variable. For example, if the objective is to produce as much output as possible using the given input, one should use an output-oriented model. If the objective is to produce a given output using a minimum of inputs, an input-oriented model is more suitable. Although airports are the decision making units in this analysis, they may have complete control over the outputs; in the end, the airlines are the agents selling aircraft seats and transporting passengers. Seen from that perspective, an input-oriented program seems to be more appropriate for the problem analysed in this paper. [6, 7] Note that both models estimate the same frontier, but the efficiency measures of the inefficient decision making units may be different (since the models generate the same frontier, the efficient decision making units will be the same in both models).

The efficiency measure proposed by Charnes et al. (1978) maximizes weighted outputs over weighted inputs, subject to the condition that for every airport this efficiency measure is smaller than or equal to 1. Assume that we have L airports with m outputs and n inputs, then for an airport denoted by a subscript 0, the measure of efficiency is [8]

---

[5] Charnes et al. (1978), and a significant proportion of the literature that followed that paper, use the term "decision making unit" for the firm or agent analysed to emphasize that their interest lies in the decisions made by non-profit organizations rather than (in theory) profit maximizing firms.

[6] In the remainder of this paper, all models are input-oriented. For output-oriented specifications see e.g. Banker et al. (1984) and Coelli (1996b).

[7] One could of course also ask how much output could be generated with a given input set, including environmental capacity. This could be useful for airports like Amsterdam Airport Schiphol, where environmental restrictions are becoming increasingly important, but requires an exact definition of the input "environment", which is unavailable. Ultimately, the orientation of the model depends on the status and policy of the airport operator. These are, of course, not the same for all airports, but, in general, the input-oriented model probably suits the "average airport" best.

[8] This maximization problem is repeated for each of the L airports.

$$\max_{u,v} \quad \frac{\sum_{i=1}^{m} u_i y_{i,0}}{\sum_{j=1}^{n} v_j x_{j,0}}$$

$$\text{s.t.} \quad 1 \geqslant \frac{\sum_{i=1}^{m} u_i y_{i,l}}{\sum_{j=1}^{n} v_j x_{j,l}}; \quad l = 1, \dots, L, \tag{4}$$

$$u_i, v_j \geqslant 0$$

The maximization problem in (4) can have an infinite number of solutions. Assume that u^* and v^* are solutions to the above problem. Then it can be shown that for any θ, θu^* and θv^* are also solutions to the (same) problem (Coelli, 1996b). Since θ cannot be identified, there is an infinite number of solutions. Charnes et al. (1978) show that the above fractional programming program has the following linear programming equivalent, which avoids this problem:

$$\max_{u,v} \quad \sum_{i=1}^{m} \mu_i y_{i,0}$$

$$\text{s.t.} \quad 0 \geqslant \sum_{i=1}^{m} \mu_i y_{i,l} - \sum_{j=1}^{n} v_j x_{j,l}; \quad l = 1, \dots, L, \tag{5}$$

$$\sum_{j=1}^{n} v_j x_{j,0} = 1$$

$$\mu_i, v_j \geqslant 0$$

The dual to this linear programming problem is

$$\min_{h,\lambda} \quad h_0$$

$$\text{s.t.} \quad \sum_{l=1}^{L} \lambda_l y_{i,l} \geqslant y_{i,0}; \quad i = 1, \dots, m,$$

$$h_0 x_{j,0} - \sum_{l=1}^{L} \lambda_l x_{j,l} \geqslant 0; \quad j = 1, \dots, n, \tag{6}$$

$$h_0, \lambda_l \geqslant 0$$

which has fewer constraints and is therefore usually preferred in the literature. [9]

Banker et al. (1984) show that the efficiency coefficient h_0 in (6) is the product of a technical and scale efficiency measure. Hence, if not all decision making units are operating at the optimal scale level, the technical efficiencies determined using the model in (6) are confounded by scale inefficiencies. [10] To overcome this problem, Banker et al. (1984) add the convexity restriction [11]

---

[9] The linear programming problem in (5) has $L + 1$ restrictions; the linear programming problem in (6) has $m + n$ restrictions.

[10] In effect, the model in (6) assumes that all decision making units are operating at their optimal scale, even when they, in fact, may not do so.

[11] This restriction implies convexity of the production set and input requirement set. This in turn implies a quasi-concave production function (frontier) (see e.g. Varian (1992) for details).

E. Pels et al. / Transportation Research Part E 39 (2003) 341–361   347

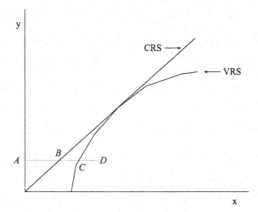

Fig. 1. Production frontiers.

$$\sum_{l=1}^{L} \lambda_l = 1 \tag{7}$$

to the program in (6). Call the efficiency coefficient determined by this program h_0^{VRS}. The difference between the two approaches is plotted in Fig. 1 for the case with one input and one output.

In this graph the efficiency of a decision making unit operating at D as determined by program (6) is $h_0 = AB/AD$. Adding the convexity constraint (7) to (6) yields an efficiency of $h_0^{\text{VRS}} = AC/AD$. Note that this efficiency coefficient is always larger than or equal to the unconstrained efficiency coefficient, as the frontier fits the data more tightly. The scale efficiency is $h_0^{\text{scale}} = h_0/h_0^{\text{VRS}} = AB/AC$; if $h_0^{\text{scale}} = 1$, the decision making unit is scale efficient. If $h_0^{\text{scale}} < 1$, the scale efficiency estimate only indicates whether or not variable returns to scale are prevailing. The direction of these returns is not determined. Whether increasing or decreasing returns to scale are prevailing can be determined by running another program, in which the constraint in (7) is changed to $1 \geqslant \sum_{l=1}^{L} \lambda_l$ and added to (6); call the efficiency coefficient from this program h_0^c. Note that the linear program used to determine h_0^c cannot envelop the data more closely than the program used to determine h_0^{VRS}, as the latter program is the most constrained ($\sum_{l=1}^{L} \lambda_l = 1$) and the former program is the least constrained ($1 \geqslant \sum_{l=1}^{L} \lambda_l$) of the two (Banker et al., 1996). Then if $h_0^{\text{scale}} < 1$ and $h_0^c = h_0^{\text{VRS}}$, decreasing returns to scale prevail. If $h_0^{\text{scale}} < 1$ and $h_0^c < h_0^{\text{VRS}}$, increasing returns to scale prevail. [12]

---

[12] There is another approach used to estimate returns to scale. Using the linear program in (6) to determine h_0 (i.e. without restriction 7), $\sum_{l=1}^{L} \lambda_l^*$ estimates returns to scale, where the asterisk * means an optimal solution. If this sum is smaller than 1 (in all alternate optima), increasing returns to scale are prevailing. If this sum is larger than 1 (in all alternate optima), decreasing returns are prevailing and if it is equal to 1 (in any alternate optimum), constant returns are prevailing; see Banker et al. (1996) for details. Banker et al. (1996) show that these two alternative approaches are equivalent.

348   *E. Pels et al. / Transportation Research Part E 39 (2003) 341–361*

3. Specification of the model

After the theoretical exposition in the previous section, we will now describe the parametric and DEA models to be estimated. We first present a general model of airport activities, before continuing with the econometric models to be estimated in Section 4.

3.1. A general model of airport activities

"An airport's primary function is to provide an interface between aircraft and the passengers or freight, including mail, being transported by air" (Doganis, 1992). From this perspective, an analysis of airport outputs requires data on air passenger movements (APM) and air transport movements (ATM), with the corresponding necessary inputs. The necessary inputs for these two outputs are quite different and that it is not uncommon to model these outputs separately, see e.g. Gillen and Lall (1997). The airport can also be regarded as an interface between airlines and passengers rather than aircraft and passengers, although the difference is ambiguous. One could even go as far as to say that the airport is an interface between a large number of agents, including rail companies, taxi companies etc. Due to data restrictions, we focus on the efficiency of passenger and airline operations. The airlines' primary objective is to sell aircraft seats. ATM is essential, but is not a goal in itself. Seen from that objective, ATM can also be considered as an input from the airport's perspective. Note that as APM changes, ATM does not necessarily follow; the airlines can adjust the load factors, seating arrangements or size of their aircraft; ATM can be, but is not necessarily endogenous.

From this line of reasoning, ATM can be considered as an intermediate good that is "produced" and then "consumed" in the production of APM. The various relationships between ATM, APM, runway efficiency and terminal efficiency are depicted in Fig. 2. If ATM is low, given the runway capacity or given the inputs, runway inefficiency will be high; this is estimated using the stochastic production frontier. ATM is considered to be an input for APM. Given the terminal capacity and given the airlines' load factors, a high value of ATM (corresponding to low runway inefficiency) corresponds to a high value of APM (low terminal inefficiency); a positive relationship between ATM and APM is expected in the stochastic production frontier. If terminal

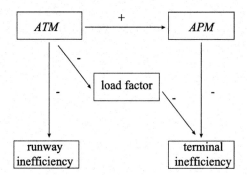

Fig. 2. Relations between dependent variables and efficiency.

E. Pels et al. / Transportation Research Part E 39 (2003) 341–361   349

inefficiency however, is relatively high, this could be explained by the average load factors. If load factors are low, airports "need" a proportionally large number of flights (high ATM) to move a given number of passengers. This means that, ceteris paribus, the airport is relatively inefficient. [13] This inefficiency is, however, beyond the control of the airport authorities. A similar line of reasoning holds when airlines decide to use smaller aircraft. When a relatively large amount of aircraft movements is needed to yield the same number of passengers. Load factors may be included in the analysis, but we do not have sufficient data on the aircraft size (mix).

The production frontiers (and inefficiency model) will be estimated using pooled cross-section—time series data for 33 European airports between 1995 and 1997. Data on ATM (annual number of domestic and international movements) and APM (the annual number of domestic and international passengers, including transit and non-scheduled passengers) was obtained from the British Airport Authority. The primary source for the data on inputs is IATA's Airport Capacity/Demand Profiles (1998). This publication contains detailed information on a large number of international airports. The list of European airports used in the analysis is given in Appendix A; when the Airport Capacity/Demand Profiles contained enough information for an airport, it was included in the analysis. In addition, individual airports were contacted in order to obtain (additional) information.

After this brief introduction, the parametric and the DEA model will be specified in the next two subsections. As explained above, the parametric model allows for statistical testing and can be used to explain inefficiencies. But the model used (the translog) is a second-order approximation of an unknown function (frontier). Although the approximating function may be precise at the point of approximation, the precision at more extreme data points is not clear. [14] The parametric approach will therefore be used to test for the presence of returns to scale and inefficiencies (deviations from the optimal frontier). DEA will be used for an analysis of inefficiencies and returns to scale of individual airports; because DEA fits a piecewise linear curve, it does not have the problem described above.

3.2. The parametric model

Based on the discussion in the previous section, we model the efficiency of an airport as follows. First, a stochastic production frontier for ATM is estimated. A stochastic production frontier for

---

[13] Assume that an increase in ATM results in an increase in APM (i.e. ATM is a significant explanatory variable in the production function explaining APM). If the frequency elasticity of demand is smaller than 1, an increase in ATM will likely result in a less than proportional increase in APM, if at all. A downward adjustment of airline load factors is likely and has a positive effect on terminal inefficiency.

[14] The translog function is a flexible functional form that can achieve arbitrary scale elasticities at any data point. Once the parameters of the function are estimated, the elasticities are determined for every point along the curve. It may be that the curve satisfies curvature conditions imposed by economic theory only for a specific range (Caves and Christensen, 1980). For example, Caves et al. (1984) find that the neoclassical curvature conditions on their (estimated translog) cost function are satisfied around the sample mean and violated at extreme sample points (as a result of "dominant" second order effects). Wales (1977) has shown that such problems do not necessarily undermine the validity of the elasticities evaluated at the sample mean. Caves et al. (1984) test the robustness of the specification by fixing all the second order coefficients at 0; although that specification is rejected on statistical grounds, the coefficients of the first order effects are "remarkably similar" to the unrestricted estimates.

APM is then estimated, in which the predicted value of ATM is an explanatory variable. The model

$$\ln(\text{ATM}_{j,t}) = \alpha_0 + \sum_i \alpha_i \ln(x_{j,t}^{i,\text{ATM}}) + \frac{1}{2} \sum_h \sum_i \alpha_{h,i} \ln(x_{j,t}^{h,\text{ATM}}) \ln(x_{j,t}^{i,\text{ATM}}) + \gamma_1 R_j + \frac{1}{2} \gamma_2 R_j^2$$
$$+ \sum_i \eta_i \ln(x_{j,t}^{i,\text{ATM}}) R_j \tag{8}$$

where $x_{j,t}^{i,\text{ATM}}$ is the ith input used by airport j in the production of $\text{ATM}_{j,t}$; the "x-variables" used are the airport's surface area (ha), the number of aircraft parking positions at the terminal and the number of remote aircraft parking positions. R_j is the number of runways. Each airport uses a number of runways which is fixed, at least in the short run. One could include the total runway capacity rather than the number of runways. In a long run analysis, that would probably be the preferable modelling strategy. In a short run analysis like this, however, one would have to adjust the capacity for utilization because a runway is a long run investment that may be built with growth figures for the next decade(s) in mind. A newly delivered runway may therefore have a capacity that (far) exceeds realized demand. [15] Therefore, the number of runways will be used as a fixed factor, representing a stage of technology rather than as a traditional input. The number of runway crossings (as a proxy for crossing flight paths or ATMs) was also included in the analysis because crossing flight paths may lead to a lower output per runway due to e.g. waiting times. This variable was, however, insignificant. The inefficiency model is

$$U_{j,t}^{\text{ATM}} = \sum_j \delta_j z_j^{\text{ATM}} \tag{9}$$

The "z-variables" explaining inefficiency include a dummy variable, which has the value 1 if the airport in question is a slot coordinated airport, and a dummy variable, which takes the value 1 if there is a time restriction.

The model explaining APM is

$$\ln(\text{APM}_{j,t}) = \beta_0 + \sum_i \beta_i \ln(x_{j,t}^{i,\text{APM}}) + \frac{1}{2} \sum_h \sum_i \beta_{h,i} \ln(x_{j,t}^{h,\text{APM}}) \ln(x_{j,t}^{i,\text{APM}}) \tag{10}$$

and

$$U_{j,t}^{\text{APM}} = \sum_j \delta_j z_j^{\text{APM}} \tag{11}$$

where $x_{j,t}^{i,\text{APM}}$ is the ith input used by airport j in the production of $\text{APM}_{j,t}$; these inputs are $\text{ATM}_{j,t}^* = E(\text{ATM}_{j,t} | U_j, x_{j,t}^{\text{ATM}}, z_j)$, the number of check-in desks and the number of baggage claim units. Other possible inputs are terminal size (m^2) and number of aircraft parking positions at the

---

[15] Oum and Zhang (1991) discuss the utilization of quasi-fixed inputs in the context of cost function estimation. They point out that parameter estimations for quasi-fixed inputs may be biased when the quasi-fixed inputs are not adjusted for utilization. In this paper, we use production functions rather than cost functions. Whether Oum and Zhang's conclusions carry over to the case of production functions is not the issue in this paper. Moreover, we do not have sufficient data to adjust runway capacity for utilization, and even if we would have the necessary data, we might run into specification problems.

E. Pels et al. / Transportation Research Part E 39 (2003) 341–361 351

terminal (as an approximation of number of gates), but specifications in which these variables are also used are rejected because of insignificance of parameters of both of these variables and the variables finally used (probably due to multicollinearity, these variables are highly correlated with the variables actually used), and unexpected parameter signs. Note that including terminal size may introduce a bias because part of the terminal space may be dedicated to commercial activities (that may be more important at some airports than others), while commercial outputs are not included in this analysis. Although we assume that ATM "causes" APM, it is not straightforward that ATM is fully exogenous. Moreover, the airport has no (direct) control over the number of ATM; it merely provides the capacity. Therefore, the predicted value of ATM (i.e. the frontier value) is used as an explanatory variable rather than as the actual value. The variables explaining inefficiency are a time dummy as described above and secondly, the airlines' load factor. The average load factor is calculated as the weighted average of the aggregate load factors between the city in which the airport is located and a number of important destinations (Amsterdam, London, Frankfurt, Paris, Zürich and Singapore). For certain airports (in London, Milan and Paris) no specific load factors could be computed; e.g. London Gatwick, Heathrow and Stansted have the same load factor because only data on routes originating in *London* is available.

All data (except for the dummies) are standardized around the mean. In both models a constant and two dummy variables (for 1996 and 1997) are included. The constant estimates the difference between the (unknown) output evaluated at the mean input levels and the mean output in 1995. [16] The difference in the next two years is the constant plus the dummy variable for that year

Data on labor, both the number of people working *at* the airport and working *for* the airport, is only available for a limited number of airports. For example, the number of people employed *by* the operator of FRA (Flughafen Frankfurt Main AG) in 1997 is 12,500 (ACI, 1999). According to the ACI airport database, FRA is the only airport operated by Flughafen Frankfurt Main AG. The British Airport Authority (BAA) had 8393 employees and operates, among others, Heathrow, Gatwick and Stansted (BAA, 1999). The numbers of passengers at these airports in 1997 were 58 million for Heathrow and 40 million for Frankfurt. We may assume that such numerical differences reflect differences in the way workers have been classified in the various airports. Since it is not clear how many employees are actually involved in the handling of aircraft, passengers and luggage, and because data on labor is simply unavailable for a large number of airports, this variable is not used in the analysis.

3.3. The DEA model

The DEA models for estimating the frontier are described in detail in Section 2.2, and the data are identical to those in the previous subsection. Two remarks are in order, however. Firstly, the number of runways is used as a fixed factor to keep consistency with the stochastic frontier model. The DEA program then is (see e.g. Banker and Morey (1986))

---

[16] Note that these were equal if $f(\cdot\cdot)$ would be homogeneous of degree 1 and linear.

$$\min_{h,\lambda} \quad h_0$$

$$\text{s.t.} \quad \sum_{l=1}^{L} \lambda_l y_{i,l} \geq y_{i,0}; \quad i = 1, \ldots, m,$$

$$h_0 x_{j,0} - \sum_{l=1}^{L} \lambda_l x_{j,l} \geq 0; \quad j = 1, \ldots, n-1, \qquad (12)$$

$$x_{j,0} - \sum_{l=1}^{L} \lambda_l x_{j,l} \geq 0; \quad j = n,$$

$$\sum_{l=1}^{L} \lambda_l = 1, \quad h_0, \lambda_l \geq 0$$

where the number of runways is the nth input. This input cannot be adjusted by the management to "fit" the output, but it is used in the determination of the frontier. If the first $n - 1$ inputs can be reduced, by keeping the last input (number of runways) fixed, we find that the airport in question is not efficient. Of course a convex combination of all airports does not necessarily have a meaningful interpretation in our case (an airport cannot have 1.5 runways), but it should be noted that: (i) runways at different airports may be different lengths and (ii) runways are considered as categorical variables in the sense that for one (unit) input (i.e. one runway), there is a range of possible outputs (see the previous subsection). This means that a portion of the frontier will run parallel to the axis (see Section 2.2), and that the presence of input (runway) slacks is not necessarily an indication of an inappropriate input mix. If the slack is smaller than 1, runway capacity is not fully used, but it cannot be reduced. If it is larger than 1, there could be an inappropriate input mix in the sense that the same output could be obtained with one less runway. Secondly, the DEA model does not suffer from multicollinearity, so that, in principle, "all" available inputs can be used. However, to maintain consistency between both models, the same input set is used in both models. The only difference is that in the DEA model with APM as the output, the actual— rather than the predicted-value of ATM is used because the DEA model has no endogeneity problem and measures efficiency rather than it predicts outcomes.

4. Estimation results

In this section the estimation results from both models are discussed.

4.1. Estimation results from the stochastic frontier model

Estimation results for the ATM model are given in Table 1. The number of parking positions (both at the terminal and remote) and the airport area are significant. The first order effects (parking positions and remote parking positions) are clearly significant. The parameter of the number of runways is, however, not significantly different from 0. The second order effect for the number of runways (i.e. the squared number of runways) is negative, indicating that a number of runways larger than the average number (2) does not lead to an increase in ATM, ceteris paribus.

E. Pels et al. / Transportation Research Part E 39 (2003) 341–361   353

Table 1
Estimation results, ATM

Parameter	Estimate	(s.e.)
$\alpha_{constant}$	0.713	(0.083)*
α_{96}	0.670	(0.032)*
α_{97}	0.154	(0.061)*
α_{area}	0.403	(0.059)*
$\alpha_{\#runways}$	0.002	(0.115)
$\alpha_{positions}$	0.268	(0.211)
α_{remote}	0.280	(0.055)*
α^2_{area}	−2.207	(0.458)
$\alpha^2_{\#runways}$	−0.456	(0.077)*
$\alpha^2_{positions}$	−0.606	(0.130)*
α^2_{remote}	−0.308	(0.137)*
$\alpha_{area \times \#runways}$	0.591	(0.068)*
$\alpha_{area \times positions}$	1.208	(0.043)*
$\alpha_{area \times remote}$	−0.090	(0.012)*
$\alpha_{\#runways \times pos.}$	−0.218	(0.157)
$\alpha_{\#runways \times rem.}$	−0.286	(0.128)*
$\alpha_{positions \times remote}$	0.343	(0.152)*
$\delta_{slot\ coordination}$	−0.278	(0.726)
$\delta_{time\ restriction}$	−2.363	(1.447)
$\sigma^2_U + \sigma^2_V$	0.734	(0.106)*
$\gamma = \sigma^2_U / (\sigma^2_U + \sigma^2_V)$	0.999	(0.6E−05)*
Log-L	−10.689	
$LR^{one-sided\ error}$	73.761	
Observations	102	

From the estimates of the inefficiency model, it appears that the slot coordinated airports are less inefficient and also airports with limited hours of operation are less inefficient. [17] This could be explained as follows. Assume that all inputs are multiplied with the fraction of time the airport is open. For example, when an airport is open for 18 h a day, all inputs would be multiplied by 18/24. In such a situation one could expect that the time constrained airports would be more efficient since during night time the unconstrained airports are likely to have little traffic. This approach of adjusting the input levels to the hours of operation has not been applied in this analysis; instead, the (possible) influence of time constraints on efficiency is modeled explicitly in the inefficiency model using a dummy variable. Another explanation could be the following. The production function and inefficiency model together determine the output. Airports with a relatively high output (which, given the input set, can result in a low inefficiency) cause higher environmental pressures compared to airports with a relatively low output. Because of the environmental pressures, a political decision to impose time constraints may result. This could explain the finding that airports with limited hours of operation are less inefficient. Two remarks are in order though.

---

[17] Both parameters are insignificant, although this is probably due to multicollinearity. Estimations with either of these variables does not lead to significant changes of the estimated frontier or the sign of the variable in question. The variables are then significant, but the log-likelihood is lower of course.

First, environmental pressures are not the only reason to impose time constraints. For example, when the output is simply too low at certain hours, the airport can be closed because of economic reasons. Second, in the line of reasoning above we have reversed causality; the value of the time restrictions dummy is dependent on the output. This calls for a different (two-stage) estimation method, but first, further theoretical analysis is necessary to determine the exact relations between the variables concerned.

Estimation results for the APM-model are presented in Table 2. While the (first order) parameters for ATM* and the number of check-in desks are significant, the parameter for the number of baggage claims is not significant. The second order coefficient for the number of baggage claims is, however, significant. Note that the interaction terms are not significant, indicating that the inputs are not complementary. The load factors have the expected sign; as load factors increase, inefficiency decreases. Airline inefficiency (reflected by low load factors) is apparently carried over to airports; *given* ATM*, a larger passenger flow could have been possible. Again, time-restricted airports are less inefficient.

The role of the inefficiency term in the total disturbance becomes clear from the values of γ reported in Tables 1 and 2. In both models, γ is close to 1 (i.e. the variance of the inefficiency term is large compared to the variance of the disturbance term), indicating the significance of the inefficiency effect. This also becomes clear from the likelihood ratio test of the one-sided error; the hypothesis $H_0 : \gamma = \delta_0 = \cdots = \delta_n = 0$ is rejected in both cases. Hence, there is a distinct inefficiency effect. In the following subsection, through the use of DEA, these inefficiency effects are analysed for individual airports.

Table 2
Estimation results, APM

Parameter	Estimate	(s.e.)
β_{constant}	0.213	$(0.061)^*$
β_{96}	0.016	(0.041)
β_{97}	0.050	(0.051)
β_{ATM^*}	0.848	$(0.096)^*$
$\beta_{\text{check-in desks}}$	0.490	$(0.160)^*$
$\beta_{\text{baggage claims}}$	−0.129	(0.191)
$\beta^2_{\text{ATM}^*}$	−0.586	$(0.162)^*$
$\beta^2_{\text{check-ins}}$	−0.851	(0.772)
$\beta^2_{\text{baggage claims}}$	−0.905	$(0.268)^*$
$\beta_{\text{ATM}^* \times \text{check-ins}}$	0.353	(0.477)
$\beta_{\text{ATM}^* \times \text{baggage claims}}$	0.209	(0.469)
$\beta_{\text{check-ins} \times \text{baggage claims}}$	0.436	(0.561)
δ_{constant}	0.815	(0.562)
$\delta_{\text{time restriction}}$	−0.592	$(0.222)^*$
$\delta_{\text{load factors}}$	−1.454	$(0.119)^*$
σ^2	0.377	$(0.064)^*$
γ	0.999	$(0.5\text{E}{-}07)^*$
Log-L	−32.252	
$LR^{\text{one-sided error}}$	36.81	
Observations	102	

E. Pels et al. / Transportation Research Part E 39 (2003) 341–361   355

Using the production frontier estimates and Eq. (3), returns to scale can be calculated. For the average airport (i.e. with average inputs), the elasticities (standard errors) are 0.951 (0.065) for the ATM model and 1.209 (0.029) for the APM-model; the "average" airport (approximately 12.5 million passengers and 150,000 ATM) is operating under constant returns to scale when generating ATM and under increasing returns to scale when moving passengers. Doganis (1992) suggests that "early" studies of British airports show that the long run average cost (per passenger) falls sharply until a passenger level of about 3 million is reached, suggesting there are hardly any scale economies at higher passenger levels. The methodology underlying this result is not discussed by Doganis, the results are thus difficult to compare. Based on the estimates from the APM model, there is a strong negative relation between the airport size (measured in APM) and the scale elasticity as predicted by the model; the correlation coefficient is −0.83. This indicates there is some support for the common conjecture that smaller airports operate under (strong) increasing returns to scale. The corresponding correlation coefficient in the ATM model is 0.11. As mentioned above, the translog production frontier is a second order approximation of an unknown frontier at a certain point (the average). The estimated elasticities may only be plausible in a certain range of data (around the average); see Footnote14. In fact, it appears that the airports MXP and OTP have negative estimated scale elasticities. [18] Deleting these observations and calculating the correlation coefficient between the scale elasticity and the airport size measured in ATM for 1997, only (which is the most efficient year) yields −0.09. [19] If we ignore MXP and OTP, there is a very weak or insignificant relation between the elasticity of size and airport size.

The finding that airports are operating under constant returns to scale "producing" ATM and under increasing returns to scale generating APM is not uncommon; see e.g. Gillen and Lall (1997). Although, the general picture is that the scale elasticity decreases with size (expressed in APM), a detailed analysis of efficiency (for individual airports) is made using DEA.

4.2. Estimation results from the DEA model

The efficiency coefficients for the ATM model are reported in Table 3. To save space, only the estimates for 1997 are given. In the second column the technical efficiency from the variable returns to scale model (i.e. the linear program composed by Eqs. (6) and (7)) is given. For most airports efficiency increases over time (as ATM increases over time). The third column gives the scale efficiency and the last column contains the returns to scale characterization; *drs* means decreasing returns to scale and *irs* means increasing returns to scale. If an airport operates under decreasing returns to scale, the scale efficiency decreases over time (as the output increases), and if an airport operates under increasing returns to scale, the scale efficiency increases over time. If the scale efficiency is 1, there is no need for the airport to increase or decrease the scale of its operations. Note that if the scale efficiency is 1, the airports in question were operating under increasing returns in the previous years (because the output and technical efficiency increased over time). If 1998 were to be added to the dataset, the (absolute) values of the efficiency coefficients

---

[18] In the APM model all elasticity estimates are positive.
[19] The figure for 1997 for the APM model is −0.84.

Table 3
DEA efficiency results, ATM[a]

Airport	Technical	Scale	rs
AMS	0.804	0.767	drs
BLL	1	0.515	irs
BRU	0.755	0.760	drs
CDG	1	1	–
CPH	1	1	–
DUB	0.442	0.830	irs
FAO	1	0.294	irs
FCO	0.880	0.850	drs
FRA	1	0.909	drs
GOT	1	0.493	irs
GVA	0.993	0.669	irs
HAJ	0.819	0.689	irs
HAM	0.650	0.864	irs
LGW	1	1	–
LHR	1	1	–
LIN	1	1	–
LIS	0.760	0.612	irs
LYS	0.368	0.768	irs
MAN	0.794	0.821	irs
MRS	0.699	0.702	irs
MUC	1	0.942	drs
MXP	0.955	0.316	irs
NUE	1	0.506	irs
OTP	0.734	0.199	irs
ORY	0.601	0.921	drs
PRG	0.541	0.673	irs
STN	0.614	0.595	irs
STO	0.999	0.821	drs
STU	1	1	–
SXF	0.504	0.275	irs
TRN	1	0.272	irs
TXL	0.516	0.883	irs
VIE	0.518	0.998	irs
ZRH	1	0.983	drs

[a] rs = returns to scale, irs = increasing returns to scale, drs = decreasing returns to scale.

would change (decrease if the output increases), and airports that were operating under constant returns to scale in 1997 will now operate under increasing returns to scale in that year, because the efficiency is evaluated relative to the most efficient decision making units.

The average technical efficiency in the ATM model (0.82) appears to be quite high; almost half of the airports are technically efficient, and GVA, MXP and STO are (very) close to the efficient frontier. Yet there are a number of airports (DUB, LYS, PRG, SXF, TXL and VIE) that have a rather low efficiency coefficient. There seem to be no region-specific effects in that airports in a one country are on average more efficient than airports in other countries. The correlation coefficient between the technical efficiency (Table 3) and the airport size measured in ATM is 0.19; there only

E. Pels et al. / Transportation Research Part E 39 (2003) 341–361   357

Table 4
DEA efficiency results, APM

Airport	Technical	Scale	rs
AMS	0.788	1	–
BLL	0.971	0.461	irs
BRU	1	1	–
CDG	0.695	0.991	irs
CPH	1	1	–
DUB	0.932	0.963	irs
FAO	1	0.996	irs
FCO	1	0.995	drs
FRA	0.809	0.998	drs
GOT	0.972	0.593	irs
GVA	0.448	0.951	irs
HAJ	0.674	0.928	irs
HAM	0.643	1	–
LGW	0.954	1	–
LHR	1	1	–
LIN	1	1	–
LIS	0.707	0.886	irs
LYS	0.513	0.970	irs
MAN	0.774	0.990	drs
MRS	1	0.970	irs
MUC	0.757	0.994	drs
MXP	0.842	0.771	irs
NUE	0.917	0.494	irs
OTP	0.949	0.401	irs
ORY	0.927	1	–
PRG	0.672	0.785	irs
STN	0.711	0.748	irs
STO	0.896	0.988	irs
STU	0.923	0.836	irs
SXF	1	0.507	irs
TRN	0.750	0.601	irs
TXL	0.687	1	–
VIE	0.798	0.911	irs
ZRH	0.986	0.988	drs

seems to be a weak "size" effect, if any. The same conclusions hold true for the APM model (Table 4, the correlation coefficient is 0.17). The average technical efficiency in the APM model is 0.82. Although there are fewer technically efficient airports, there are also less airports with relatively low technical efficiency coefficients. [20]

In Tables 3 and 4 we can see that a number of airports are operating under decreasing returns to scale. FCO, FRA, MUC and ZRH operate under (slight) decreasing returns to scale in both models. AMS, BRU, ORY and STO are operating under (slight) decreasing returns to scale in the ATM model and constant or increasing returns to scale in the APM model, while the opposite

---

[20] Only GVA and LYS have a coefficient below 0.5.

holds true for MAN. The correlation coefficient between the scale efficiency (Table 4) and the airport size measured in APM is 0.53. It should be kept in mind that scale efficiency says nothing about the orientation of the returns to scale; both increasing and decreasing returns are reported in Table 4. From Table 4 it can be seen that a number of relatively smaller airports, BLL, GOT, MXP, NUE, OTP, PRG, STN, SXF, and TRN are operating under increasing to scale and have a relatively low scale efficiency. Similarly, a number of relatively large airports, AMS, CDG, FCO, FRA, LGW, LHR, LIN, MAN, MUC, ORY, and ZRH are operating under (near) constant returns to scale or decreasing returns to scale. Hence, although the correlation between the scale efficiency and airport size (measured in APM) is apparently not very high, the finding in the previous subsection that scale elasticity decreases with airport size also becomes apparent from Table 4.

The correlation between the scale efficiency in the ATM model and the airport size (measured in ATM) is 0.18; so there is no apparent relation between scale efficiency and airport size. Whereas some of the larger airports are operating at (near) constant returns to scale (CDG, CPH, LGW, LHR and LIN) or (slight) decreasing returns (AMS, BRU, FCO, FRA, MUC and ORY), some of the smaller airports are operating at increasing returns to scale and have a relatively low scale efficiency (BLL, FAO, GOT, LIS, MXP, NUE, OTP, STN, SXF and TRN). There is a negative relation between the returns to scale characterization of an airport and the size of the airport (measured in ATM). In the previous section we found that this relation was negative, but very weak; judging by the correlation coefficient of −0.09, there is hardly any relation. The 10 smaller airports just mentioned are operating under strong increasing returns to scale, while larger airports are operating under near constant (increasing or decreasing) returns to scale.

The from the DEA is that on average airports operate under constant returns to scale and that the smallest airports (BLL, FAO, MXP, NUE, OTP, SXF and TRN), which are responsible for 4.6% of the total traffic in 1997, almost surely operate under increasing returns to scale. The conclusion of Section 4.1, that the average airport (i.e. an airport operating at mean input levels) is operating at constant returns to scale, is thus maintained here.

5. Conclusion

In this paper we have estimated production frontiers for European airports, using both stochastic frontier analysis and DEA. From the stochastic frontier analysis, it appears that there is a significant inefficiency effect. In the ATM model, airports with a time restriction and/or slot co-ordination appear to be less inefficient. One could think that within the limited time frame inputs are used more efficiently, but time is not considered as an argument in the production function. With or without the limited time frame, airports need the same expected peak capacity and hence can be expected to be more inefficient when there is a time restriction. During that period the airports are closed and the capacity is not used. More research into this aspect is necessary. Inefficiency in the APM model is explained by a time restriction dummy and airline load factors; apparently, airline inefficiency is carried over to airports. This link between efficiency of airlines and airports has not yet been demonstrated in the (empirical) literature, as far as we know. In the DEA model distinction is made between technical and scale efficiency. Overall it seems that many European airports can improve their efficiency. Privately operated airports such as LGW, LHR

E. Pels et al. / Transportation Research Part E 39 (2003) 341–361   359

and corporatized airports like CPH (of which 49% of the shares were in private hands during the period under consideration) seem to be more efficient on average, and can act as a "peer" for many (public) airports (that may be privatized in the future). VIE (of which 47% was in private hands in 1997) is, however, inefficient.

Based on the estimates of the stochastic frontier model, we conclude that the average airport is operating under constant returns to scale when handling ATM and increasing returns to scale when moving passengers; the scale elasticity is decreasing in the number of passengers (i.e. on average, smaller airports are operating under strong returns to scale and larger airports are operating under weak returns to scale). This relation is rather strong in the APM model, but is rather weak in the ATM model. Using DEA, similar conclusions are drawn, the only difference being that the relation between airport size measured in ATM and returns to scale seems to be much stronger than in the case of the stochastic frontier model. The conclusion of the analysis in this paper is that the average airport is operating under constant returns to scale in the ATM model and increasing returns to scale in the APM model, where the returns in the latter model are decreasing in APM. These conclusions are in line with the results found in the literature (see e.g. Gillen and Lall, 1997). These results also suggest that larger airports may not be natural monopolies. Some large airports even operate under decreasing returns to scale. Starkie (2001) discusses airport regulation, and suggests airport regulation under the assumption that airports are natural monopolies may lead to inefficiently low prices. This is not to say that airports do not have market power, but for many large airports, scale economies may not be the source of monopoly power.

One should, however, realize that the model in this paper concerns the physical capacity of the airport. Data on the environmental capacity (determined by regulation) and schedule delays, which can or even should be included in the analysis, is not available. For example, in the case of Amsterdam Airport Schiphol (and other airports), the physical capacity exceeds "environmental capacity", and a new runway is under construction to increase environmental capacity, although this may not be optimal from a purely economic point of view. The physical capacity of the existing runway has not (yet) been reached.

From the analysis in this paper it appears that, although the average airport is operating under constant returns to scale in the ATM model and increasing returns to scale in the APM model, a number of airports is operating under decreasing returns to scale. From a cost perspective these airports should decrease their scale of operations. Therefore, given the present configurations of these airports, a hub strategy which asks for an increase in both outputs, is not necessarily optimal. If such a strategy would be followed, a reconfiguration of the airport would also be necessary, and such a strategy would also entail high costs.

It should be noted, that the estimations of the scale and efficiency parameters (from a short run production function) are conditional on the available data. The number of runways was treated as a fixed factor. Including the number of runways as a flexible input may change the conclusion (because then the parameter for the number of runways would also be included in the evaluation of scale economies; in this specification it is not significant, but it is also treated differently than the flexible inputs). In this paper the distinction between fixed and flexible factors thus becomes clear in the way the variables are included in the frontier functions. In practice one can wonder whether the variables used are truly flexible; other factors may also not be very flexible in the short run. In this sense one could also speak of "capacity utilization" rather than efficiency, since the latter implies that airport management should be able to reduce inefficiency by changing the input mix. To "truly" incorporate variable factors in an analysis of airport efficiency and returns to scale, a cost function may be more appropriate. However, then one faces the problem that some airports may have significantly lower costs than others because of outsourcing of various activities; a problem similar to the problem mentioned above concerning the numbers of employees. Such data issues need to be resolved, for both cost and production function estimation, since the analysis of the airport is an important field of research now that more and more airports are corporatized or privatized.

Acknowledgements

The authors thank three anonymous referees for valuable comments on an earlier draft of this paper.

Appendix A. Airports used in the analysis

Airport	City	Airport	City
AMS	Amsterdam	LYS	Lyon
BLL	Billund	MAN	Manchester
BRU	Brussels	MRS	Marseille
CDG	Paris–Charles de Gaulle	MUC	Münich
CPH	Copenhagen	MXP	Milan–Malpensa
DUB	Dublin	NUE	Nüremberg
FAO	Faro	OTP	Bucharest–Otopeni
FCO	Rome	ORY	Paris–Orly
FRA	Frankfurt	PRG	Prague
GOT	Göthenborg	STN	London–Stansted
GVA	Geneva	STO	Stockholm
HAJ	Hannover	STU	Stuttgart
HAM	Hamburg	SXF	Berlin–Schönefeld
LGW	London–Gatwick	TRN	Turin
LHR	London–Heathrow	TXL	Berlin–Tegel
LIN	Milan–Linate	VIE	Vienna
LIS	Lisbon	ZRH	Zürich

References

Airport Council International (ACI), 1999. Airport Database.
Banker, R., Morey, R.C., 1986. The use of categorical variables in data envelopment analysis. Management Science 32 (12), 1613–1627.

Banker, R., Charnes, A., Cooper, W.W., 1984. Some models for estimating technical and scale inefficiencies in data envelopment analysis. Management Science 30 (9), 1078–1092.

Banker, R., Chang, H., Cooper, W.W., 1996. Equivalence and implementation of alternative methods for determining returns to scale in data envelopment analysis. European Journal of Operational Research 89, 473–481.

Button, K.J., 1999. The usefulness of current international air transportation statistics. Journal of Transportation and Statistics 2 (1), 71–88.

Button, K.J., Weyman-Jones, T.G., 1994. X-efficiency and technical efficiency. Public Choice 80, 83–104.

Caves, D.W., Christensen, L.R., 1980. Global properties of flexible functional forms. American Economic Review 70, 422–432.

Caves, D.W., Christensen, L.R., Tretheway, M., 1984. Economies of density versus economies of scale: why trunk and local service airline costs differ. Rand Journal of Economics 15 (4), 471–489.

Charnes, A., Cooper, W.W., Rhodes, E., 1978. Measuring the efficiency of decision making units. European Journal of Operational Research 2, 429–444.

Coelli, T., 1996. A guide to FRONTIER version 4.1: a computer program for stochastic frontier production and cost function estimation. CEPA Working Paper 96/07. Centre for Efficiency and Productivity Analysis, University of New England, Armidale.

Coelli, T., 1996. A guide to DEAP version 2.1: a data envelopment analysis (computer) program. CEPA Working Paper 96/08. Centre for Efficiency and Productivity Analysis, University of New England, Armidale.

Diewert, W.E., 1992. The measurement of productivity. Bulletin of Economic Research 44 (3), 163–198.

Doganis, R., 1992. The Airport Business. Routledge, London.

Fuss, M., McFadden, D., Mundlak, Y., 1978. A survey of functional forms in the economic analysis of production. In: McFadden, M., Fuss, D. (Eds.), Production Economics: A Dual Approach to Theory and Applications. North-Holland, pp. 219–268.

Gillen, D., Lall, A., 1997. Developing measures of airport productivity and performance: an application of data envelopment analysis. Transportation Research 33E (4), 261–274.

IATA, 1998. Airport Capacity/Demand Profiles.

Oum, T.H., Zhang, Y., 1991. Utilization of quasi-fixed inputs and estimation of cost functions. Journal of Transport Economics and Policy 25 (2), 121–134.

Reynolds-Feighan, A.J., Button, K.J., 1999. An assessment of the capacity and congestion levels at European airports. Journal of Air Transport Management 5, 113–134.

Starkie, D., 2001. Reforming UK airport regulation. Journal of Transport Economics and Policy 35 (1), 119–135.

Tolofari, S., Ashford, N., Caves, R.E., 1990. The cost of air service fragmentation. Loughborough University of Technology, Department of Transport Technology, TT9010.

Varian, H.R., 1992. Microeconomic Analysis. W.W. Norton and Company, New York.

Wales, T.J., 1977. On the flexibility of flexible functional forms: an empirical approach. Journal of Econometrics 5, 183–193.

12

Airlines performance in the new market context: A comparative productivity and efficiency analysis

Cristina Barbot, Álvaro Costa, Elena Sochirca

ARTICLE INFO

Keywords:
Efficiency
Productivity
Airlines

ABSTRACT

This paper analyses airlines' efficiency and productivity using two different methodologies: data envelopment analysis and total factor productivity, and we additionally investigate which factors account for differences in efficiency. Our main findings show that low-cost carriers are in general more efficient than full-service carriers, efficiency and the dispersion of both data envelopment analysis and total factor productivity indexes amongst airlines differ according to geographical areas, which may be a result of different legislation and de-regulation processes, and so of specific competitive conditions, labour is the only input that definitively influences productivity, and larger airlines are more efficient, suggesting the existence of economies of scale.

1. Introduction

The air transport market has undergone considerable change. De-regulation in Europe, North America and Australia, have led to a significantly increased competition, and along with de-regulation, many European airlines that were formerly state-owned have been either fully or partially privatised. Also, adjustments following the events of September 11 have affected the environment in which air services are provided. Finally, the large-scale market entry of low-cost carriers (LCCs) has increased competition and affected the fares charged by incumbent airlines. As a consequence of these and other developments, it is probable that the relative efficiency of the world's airlines has changed.

This paper performs analysis on the comparative efficiency of airlines in this new market context looking at a large sample of airlines and using two different methods of measuring performance efficiency. The sample is of 49 carriers with 2005 data. Additionally, possible factors that may account for higher productivity are examined. Data envelopment analysis (DEA) and total factor productivity (TFP) methods are used for analysis. Further, we use regression analysis to find out which factors account for productivity differences.

DEA efficiency studies of airlines are numerous. Some of the recent studies include Scheraga (2004), who, using data for 38 airlines from around the world for 1995 and 2000 found that relative efficiency had changed little. Fethi et al. (2001) looked at 17 European carriers for 1991 and 1995 and found that by 1995 it

was too soon to find any improved efficiency. Oum and Yu (1995) analysed 23 airlines over the period from 1986 to 1993 and found that those that most improved their efficiency were European airlines, in particular, having had low indexes in 1986. Fare et al. (2007) studied the effects of deregulation on the productivity of 13 US airlines. Except for Sheraga, other studies used data prior to 1995 before LCCs were important and too soon in most cases to examine the medium-term effects of deregulation and liberalisation. Our analysis captures the effects of the new market environment introduced by these new conditions.

2. The airlines

Forty-nine airlines from different parts of the world are grouped by the regional classification of International Air Transport Association (IATA). These are—Europe and Russia (21 airlines), North America and Canada (11), China and North Asia (8), Asia Pacific (7), Africa and Middle East (2). The aim was to include each region's largest airlines as well as a representative sample of LCCs. Of the airlines, 10 are European, North American, and Asia Pacific LCCs. Data for 2005 are used and sources include airlines' annual reports, direct information from airlines' websites, the International Air Transport Association (various years) yearly publication (*World Air Transport Statistics*), the Association of European Airlines (2007) and *Yearbook* 2006.

Tables 1 and 2 show some of the main features of the airlines. Passenger revenues range from 49% for Eva Airways to 98% for Norwegian Airlines. As most LCCs do not carry cargo, they have the highest shares of passenger revenues. Other revenues come

C. Barbot et al. / Journal of Air Transport Management 14 (2008) 270–274   271

Table 1
Input and output mix

	Mean	St. dev.	Highest	Lowest
Revenue shares				
Passenger (%)	80	17	95	49
Cargo (%)	8	9	45	0
Other (%)	10	7	27	1%
Inputs cost shares				
Labour (%)	23	8	33	8
Capital (%)	11	4	18	2
Fuel (%)	25	9	57	11
Others (%)	41	10	59	13
Input use				
Labour per min ASKs	0.37	2.10	1.09	0.08
Block hours (day average)	9.90	0.21	15.3	4.7
Fuel (min gallons per billion ASKs)	7.8	8.6	13.4	3.4
Size (min ASKs)	66155	68017	283364	3067

Table 2
Per cent of inputs and outputs by airline type

Shares of output revenues	Passenger	Cargo	Other	Salaries	Capital	Fuel	Other
Full service airlines							
Average	78.1	10.3	10.9	22.2	11.3	25.3	41.5
Standard Deviation	10.6	8.5	7.2	7.8	4.0	8.4	8.5
Low-cost airlines							
Average	93.5	0.2	6.3	23.2	11.0	27.2	38.6
St. dev	4.4	0.6	4.5	10.4	4.5	12.3	14.0

mainly from selling maintenance and engineering services, catering, leasing of own aircraft, sale of fuel and sale of goods but these are a small share, and account only for 27% for Japan Airlines, the carrier with the largest share. The airlines vary considerably in size, with an average doing 66,155 million available seat kilometres (ASKs), The largest company is American Airlines doing 283,364 million while the smallest one, Cyprus Airways, registers 3067 million.

The input and output mix used in DEA is generally uniform for the airlines examined, with the only major difference being a lack of cargo carriage amongst the LCCs. The share of "other inputs" in operating costs is relatively high across the board, with a mean of 41% and a highest value of 59%, for Malev. "Other inputs" differ amongst airlines and their shares in operating revenues depends much on the company's decision between outsourcing and internalising the production of some of these services. Labour costs shares range from 8% for Eva Airways to 33% for SAS. This reflects greater international differences amongst salaries than effective labour use. As an example, Asian airlines have lower shares of salaries in costs but higher levels of employment per ASK. For example, PIA's ratio of employees per million ASKs is of 0.93, while Ryanair ratio is of 0.08. Block hours range from a maximum of 15.3 for American Airlines to a low of 4.7 for SAS.

3. Efficiency and productivity analysis

3.1. Data envelopment analysis

The DEA performance analysis applies the input-oriented Banker–Charnes–Cooper model (Banker et al., 1984), using variable returns to scale, with each airline considered as a

separate decision-making unit (DMU). The model is

$$\min_{\theta, s_i^-, s_r^+} \left(\theta - \varepsilon \left(\sum_{i=1}^{m} s_i^- + \sum_{r=1}^{s} s_r^+ \right) \right) \quad (1)$$

$$\sum_{j=1}^{n} x_{ij} \lambda_j + s_i^- = \theta x_{i0}, \quad i = 1, \ldots, m$$

$$\sum_{j=1}^{n} y_{rj} \lambda_j - s_r^+ = y_{r0}, \quad r = 1, \ldots, s$$

$$\sum_{j=1}^{n} \lambda_j = 1, \quad j = 1, \ldots, n$$

$$\lambda_0 = 0$$

$$\lambda_j \geqslant 0, \ s_r^+ \geqslant 0, \ s_i^- \geqslant 0, \quad \forall i, j, r$$

where x_{ij} is the ith input of DMU j; where; y_{rj} is the rth input of DMU j; θ is the efficiency score of the considered DMU; $\sum_{j=1}^{n} \lambda_j = 1$ is the convexity constraint in the Banker–Charnes–Cooper model: s_i^- is an input slack parameter; s_r^+ is an output slack parameter; $\lambda_0 = 0$ is a constraint for applying the super-efficiency measure.

To distinguish between airlines' efficiency and effectiveness, as well as different efficiency sub-analyses are performed using slightly differentiated data sets, i.e. for efficiency, effectiveness and three airlines groups; all carriers, FSCs, and LCCs.

The DEA data set includes as inputs—labour (number of core business workers), fleet (number of operated aircraft) and fuel (in gallons consumed) and as outputs—ASKs, RPKs and revenue tonne kilometres (RTKs).

The DEA results are presented in Table 3. Overall, we see that LCCs perform better than full service airlines. The two exceptions are Air Tran and West Jet; both have very low efficiency and effectiveness scores. Their weaker performance or could be due to not being able to get the most of their inputs, or by the influence of factors not considered here. Among the full service airlines, the lowest performance scores are for Aeroflot. In general, it is not possible to draw a simple conclusion, as to any correspondence between efficiency and effectiveness patterns. However, a number of airlines display best performance results (values of unity) in both efficiency and effectiveness cases (about 45% of these are LCCs). Geographic area of operations also seems to account for certain parallels. The majority of European and American carriers have higher effectiveness than Asia Pacific and China/North Asia airlines, which on their turn generally appear more efficient than effective. Similarly, the difference in performance between LCCs and FSCs is greater for European operators than for American ones. LCCs do not appear sensitive to either of these effects but are highly efficient across the board with no significant variations in their efficiency or effectiveness scores.

3.2. Total factor productivity analysis

We use three outputs and four inputs to look at TFP. Outputs are passenger service (measured in RPKs), cargo service (measured in RTKs) and ancillary output. This last measure includes items related to operations other than passengers and cargo and they were computed following Oum and Yu (1995). Hence, revenues are residuals of passengers and cargo services and quantities are calculated dividing residual revenues by the purchasing power parity (PPP) index obtained from Penn World Table. PPP was converted in euros and normalised to Germany's PPP.

Table 3
DEA results on operational efficiency and effectiveness

Classification	Unit name	Efficiency	Effectiveness
Full-service carriers			
Europe and Russia	Iberia	0.7391	0.7254
	Alitalia	0.5773	0.5272
	KLM	0.5011	0.5494
	SAS	0.3423	0.4752
	Austrian	0.4979	0.6094
	British Airways	0.8387	1.0000
	Lufthansa	0.6449	0.7529
	AirFrance	0.5821	0.7281
	Turkish Airlines	0.6922	0.7424
	TAP	0.8120	0.7471
	Cyprus Airways	1.0000	1.0027
	Aeroflot	0.3348	0.3921
	Malev	0.5566	0.5510
	Finnair	0.6709	0.9412
	CSA	0.4186	0.4246
	Iceland Air	0.8897	0.8657
	LOT	0.4713	0.4593
US and Canada	Delta	1.0000	1.0000
	Northwest	0.6088	0.8410
	American Airlines	1.0000	1.0000
	United Airlines	0.9567	1.0000
	Midwest Airlines	0.5446	0.5097
	Air Canada	1.0000	1.0000
	Continental	0.5970	0.7497
China and North Asia	China Southern Airlines	0.6744	0.6710
	All Nippon Airways	0.8471	0.7193
	Japan Airlines	1.0000	1.0000
	Korean Air	0.7235	0.6615
	Malaysian Airlines	0.6828	0.6330
	Singapore Airlines	1.0000	1.0000
	PIA	0.7483	0.6900
	Cathay Pacific	1.0000	1.0000
Asia Pacific	Eva Airways	0.9083	1.0000
	Thai Airways	0.9993	0.9346
	Jet Airways	0.4827	0.4543
	Qantas	0.8685	0.9948
	Air New Zealand	0.7931	0.8430
Middle East and Africa	Emirates	1.0000	1.0000
	Kenya Airways	0.7738	0.7593
Low-cost carriers			
Europe and Russia	EasyJet	0.9030	0.9438
	Norwegian	1.0000	1.0000
	Ryanair	1.0000	1.0000
	Virgin express	1.0000	1.0000
Asia Pacific	Virgin blue	0.8587	0.8440
	Air Asia	0.8817	0.8600
US and Canada	Southwest	0.9403	0.9109
	AirTran	0.3286	0.3087
	JetBlue	1.0000	1.0000
	West Jet	0.5750	0.5634
	Mean	0.7605	0.7837
	Standard deviation	0.2124	0.2081

Table 4
TFP results

Airlines	Output index	Input index	TFP index
Ryanair	0.51	0.20	253
Air Asia	0.08	0.04	210
Eva Airways	0.65	0.35	186
Japan Airlines	2.72	1.49	182
Korean Air	1.24	0.75	164
Cathay Pacific	1.19	0.75	160
Jetblue	0.30	0.20	151
Virgin Blue	0.24	0.16	150
Virgin Express	0.04	0.03	141
Emirates	0.99	0.71	139
EasyJet	0.43	0.31	135
Quantas	1.70	1.26	133
Southwest	1.27	0.96	133
Continental	2.12	1.61	131
All Nippon Airways	1.35	1.05	128
Westjet	0.23	0.19	125
British Airways	2.06	1.67	123
Norwegian	0.04	0.03	123
American Airlines	3.41	2.80	122
Northwest	1.98	1.70	117
Lufthansa	3.33	2.86	116
United Airlines	2.88	2.51	115
Iberia	0.89	0.78	115
KLM	1.21	1.09	112
Air New Zealand	0.32	0.29	110
Cyprus Airways	0.05	0.04	108
Singapore Airlines	1.52	1.41	108
Delta	2.59	2.47	105
Thai Airways	0.96	0.92	104
Air Canada	1.00	1.00	100
Air France	2.05	2.12	97
Finnair	0.27	0.28	0.96
Alitalia	0.72	0.77	93
Malaysian Airlines	0.70	0.77	91
Midwest Airlines	0.08	0.09	90
Turkish Airlines	0.37	0.42	90
Austrian	0.35	0.41	86
Kenya Airways	0.09	0.11	84
TAP	0.24	0.29	84
China Southern	1.09	1.39	78
SAS	0.76	1.00	76
Malev	0.10	0.14	72
Air Tran	0.17	0.25	69
Aeroflot	0.38	0.63	61
PIA	0.24	0.46	51
Jet Airways	0.17	0.36	47
CSA	0.09	0.21	44

As inputs, we used labour (the number of employees), capital (the airline's fleet), fuel, (gallons), and "other operating inputs". Other operating inputs are computed by dividing residual operating costs (salaries and benefits, capital cost, measured by aircraft depreciation and aircraft leasing costs, and fuel cost) by the same PPP index used for outputs. This was done because

"other operating inputs" represent a mix of goods and services that are similar to residual outputs, and differ from the ones adopted by Oum and Yu (1995) that are based on land and property.

Output and input were aggregated into a single measure following the methodology of Caves et al. (1982). TFP was normalised to Air Canada, which was selected as the base company because it has a unitary score in the DEA analysis thus, offering a reasonable basis of comparison of the TFP and DEA results. Output, input and TFP indexes are presented in Table 4. Results should be read taking into consideration Oum and Yu's (1995) observation regarding TFP's limitations. With the exception of Air Tran, low-cost airlines exhibit higher productivity as anticipated. In fact, and as stated by Hansson et al. (2003) being "low cost" means adopting a business model focused on simple, streamlined processes and products. Simplicity and business speed rely on minimal inputs that enable high productivity levels.

Regional differences among companies' productivity levels might be expected. Legislation and de-regulation processes are specific to each region giving potentially different level of

C. Barbot et al. / Journal of Air Transport Management 14 (2008) 270–274   273

Table 5
Regression analysis results

Dependent variable	N	Constant	H	EMP	LCC	F	SZ
Full data set							
TFP	47	149.8**	−0.23	−112.2***	38.9	−1338.6	0.103*
	–	0.00	0.90	0.00	0.02	0.27	0.10
TFP	47	139.5***	–	−113.6***	40.6	–	1.68***
	–	0.00	–	0.00	0.01	–	0.01
Full-service carriers							
TFP	37	139.1***	0.5	−115.9***	–	−482.4	0.11*
	–	0.00	0.79	0.00	–	0.74	0.10
TFP	37	141.9***	–	−118.4***	–	–	0.11*
	–	0.00	–	0.00	–	–	0.07

* Significant at 10%.
** Significant at 5%.
*** Significant at 1%

competitive pressure on carriers with resultant implications for productivity and X-efficiency. The North American group of airlines exhibits greater homogeneity in TFP scores, with a standard deviation of 22.5, probably reflecting more intensive competitive conditions and similar legal frameworks. European carriers reveal a high standard deviation (43.5) and confirm the findings of Scheraga (2004) on the large dispersion in efficiency amongst European airlines. The dispersion is also large (45.2) in China and North Asia. The Asia Pacific group is also heterogeneous (49.4), with efficient companies, like Cathay Pacific and Qantas competing with poorly performing airlines, like Pakistan International Airlines and Jet Airways. India and Pakistan companies register very low levels of productivity and the same is true of small and medium-sized European airlines, such as SAS, CSA, Aeroflot and Malev. The group of China and North Asia exhibits the highest average TFP score (148), considerably above the other groups.

When comparing DEA and TFP, due to a higher degree of data correspondence between effectiveness measurements, the analysis focuses on this measure. Our results indicate that the performance dynamics of the methodologies are very similar. Where there are disparities, variations may be due to dissimilarities in the inputs/outputs used. In particular, the TFP measure uses one more input and one more output than the DEA. In the case when the input or output not omitted in DEA has a large weight in one airline's costs or revenues, the two methodologies may yield different results. Despite these problems, both DEA and TFP analysis are consistent in showing that LCCs are in the vast majority of cases more efficient than traditional carriers.

3.3. Regression analysis

To investigate which inputs explain better productivity differences, TFP scores are regressed against indexes reflecting the use of labour, fleet and fuel—namely EMP (employees per million ASK), H (block hours per day) and F (fuel consumption per million ASKs). Variable SZ (airlines' size, in billions ASKs) was included to check for the existence of economies of scale. As the analysis of TFP's results clearly shows that low-cost airlines have higher productivity scores, a dummy variable was added taking a unitary value for LCCs and zero otherwise. Two specifications are examined; one with all independent variables and the second omitting non-significant variables.

The first equation is

$$TFP = b_0 + b_1 H + b_2 EMP + b_3 LCC + b_4 F + b_5 SZ \qquad (2)$$

It is expected that H will have a positive sign—the more the fleet is used, the higher the productivity of capital, and of the airline. EMP should have a negative sign, as a higher use of labour per ASK would lower productivity. Fuel consumption per ASK should not differ much across airlines, depending mainly on the types of aircrafts used, and so it is expected that this variable is not significant. A positive and significant coefficient of SZ indicates the existence of economies of scale. The LCC dummy variable is anticipated to have a positive sign.

Table 5 summarises the results of the regression analysis. Of the three inputs, only EMP is significant. Employment per ASK has the expected sign and its coefficient shows that a reduction of 112 employees per million ASKs leads producing a one point increase in an airline's TFP index. It was expected that higher aircraft use should contribute to higher productivity indexes but this does not materialize. The LCC dummy is significant and has the expected positive sign and there is some weak indication of the existence of economies of scale. In the modified specification without the insignificant variables there is little change. The adjusted R^2 remains near 0.6, and F-statistic is high, but the LCC dummy increases in significance as does SZ.

As the influence of the variable LCC is strong, other variables' influence may be dampened within the full data set. Therefore, the second regression was performed using only observations for traditional carriers

$$TFP = b_0 + b_1 H + b_2 EMP + b_3 F + b_4 SZ \qquad (3)$$

Using all variables, the results, however, do not change much. All input variables keep similar levels of significance, and the value of the adjusted R^2 and F do not change. Size becomes less significant in this second equation, implying that LCCs also account for some of the overall scale effects. This confirms that there are reasons for concentration in the LCC segment of the industry (Alamdari and Mason, 2006); economies of scale making it easier for such concentration to occur. To gain some insights into the factors leading to these economies of scale, SZ was regressed with all other variables reflecting inputs' use: H, EMP and F. Only EMP proved to be significant at any reasonable level suggesting that scale economies are caused mainly by relative savings in labour as airlines expand their operations; an effect also reported by Association of European Airlines (2004) for 2000–2003.

4. Conclusions

Examining our results from a large sample of airlines using two alternative methodologies: DEA and TFP shows that LCCs are, in general, more efficient than FSCs because of the business model they follow, and not because of their size and input mix. Further, DEA analysis suggests that both efficiency and effectiveness are not always correlated; while some airlines emerge efficient and effective, this is not always the case. TFP analysis shows that in airlines from regions that have more homogeneous regulatory structures, like North America, are more uniform in their productivity. The general results are robust regardless of whether programming or statistical analysis is applied.

References

Alamdari, F., Mason, K., 2006. EU network carriers, low cost carriers and consumer behaviour: a Delphi study of future trends. In: 10th Air Transport Research Society Conference, Nagoya.

Association of European Airlines, 2004. Yearbook 2003. AEA, Brussels.

Association of European Airlines, 2007. Yearbook 2003. AEA, Brussels.

Banker, R., Charnes, A., Cooper, W., 1984. Some models for estimating technical and scale inefficiencies in data envelopment analysis. Management Science 30, 1078–1092.

Caves, D., Christense, L., Diewert, E., 1982. Multilateral comparisons of output, input, and productivity using superlative index numbers. Economic Journal 92, 73–86.

Fare, R., Grosskopf, S., Sickles, R., 2007. Productivity of US airlines after deregulation. Journal of Transport Economics and Policy 41, 93–112.

Fethi, M., Jackson, P., Weyman-Jones, T., 2001. European Airlines: a stochastic DEA study of efficiency with market liberalization. In: Paper Presented at the Seventh European Workshop on Efficiency and Productivity Analysis, University of Oviedo.

Hansson, T., Ringbeck, J., Franke, M., 2003. Flight for survival: a new business model for the airline industry. Strategy+Business 31, 78–85.

International Air Transport Association, (various years), World Air Transport Statistics, IATA, Geneva.

Oum, T., Yu, C., 1995. A productivity comparison of the world's major airlines. Journal of Air Transport Management 2, 181–195.

Scheraga, C., 2004. Operational efficiency vs. financial mobility in the global airline industry: a data envelopment analysis and Tobit analysis. Transportation Research A 38, 383–404.

13

The impact of strategic management and fleet planning on airline efficiency – A random effects Tobit model based on DEA efficiency scores

Rico Merkert, David A. Hensher

ABSTRACT

As a result of the liberalisation of airline markets; the strong growth of low cost carriers; the high volatility in fuel prices; and the recent global financial crisis, the cost pressure that airlines face is very substantial. In order to survive in these very competitive environments, information on what factors impact on costs and efficiency of airlines is crucial in guiding strategic change. To evaluate key determinants of 58 passenger airlines' efficiency, this paper applies a two-stage Data Envelopment Analysis (DEA) approach, with partially boot-strapped random effects Tobit regressions in the second stage. Our results suggest that the effects of route optimisation, in the sense of average stage length of the fleet, are limited to airline technical efficiency. We show that airline size and key fleet mix characteristics, such as aircraft size and number of different aircraft families in the fleet, are more relevant to successful cost management of airlines since they have significant impacts on all three types of airline efficiency: technical, allocative and, ultimately, cost efficiency. Our results also show that despite the fuel saving benefits of younger aircraft, the age of an airline's fleet has no significant impact on its technical efficiency, but does have a positive impact on its allocative and cost efficiency.

Keywords:
Data Envelopment Analysis
Airlines
Efficiency
Strategic management
Fleet planning

1. Introduction

While cost management has been traditionally a crucial part of airline management, in the recent past it has become a substantial part of an airline's survival strategy. Although the financial situation of most international airlines has improved since the recent global financial crisis, it is far too early to conclude that more airlines will not get into financial difficulties or will be forced into some kind of merger or acquisition activity. As competition and economic pressures increase in many airline markets worldwide, yields for premium products in particular, decline, which adds to the current cost pressure. In addition, the substantial growth of the low cost carriers (LCC) and the high volatility in fuel and foreign exchange markets, complement the picture of an era where costs and efficiency are placed much higher in the agenda's of airline management than they have ever been before.

The question is then, what survival and cost management strategies should airlines choose in order to remain in the market or to grow and perform well under current market conditions? One strategy has been to adopt the LCC model, by either setting up own subsidiary low cost operations (such as Jetstar Airways affiliated with Qantas) or through following the general trend of de-frill, which most aviation markets have experienced in the recent past. Another observed strategy is that of increasing market power through alliances, as well as growth through mergers and acquisitions (M&A – e.g. see Lufthansa/BMI/Austrian/Swiss and Iberia/BA in Europe or United/Continental in the US). Given the often observed cubic cost function

(Vasigh et al., 2008), it is worth questioning to what extent growth makes sense, as there might be diseconomies of scale also present. In other words, as in other industries (e.g. see Merkert et al., 2010), airlines can also become too big to operate cost efficiently.

Perhaps even more importantly, the previous literature suggests that operational factors have, at least at the micro level, significant impacts on costs and the efficiency of aircraft operations. Among others, Doganis (2009, p. 104) shows that aircraft size and stage length have a substantial impact on aircraft costs, in the sense that bigger aircraft and longer sectors result in lower average unit cost of the aircraft in question. In addition, we aim to highlight the potential impact of the fleet mix on the cost efficiency of airlines. As the LCC carriers have specifically shown as a reason for moving to greater homogeneity in assets, the unit costs of airline operations increase when there are a large number of different aircraft types/families (e.g. A320 versus A380) and different aircraft manufacturers (e.g. Boeing, Airbus or Embraer) in the fleet (e.g. see Gillen, 2006). This is mainly a consequence of increased maintenance cost, administration and safety cost, spare part cost and staff costs (as one needs different pilots, engineers and crew for different types of aircraft), but also of reduced purchasing power. Often the number of aircraft manufacturers in an airline fleet is driven by political rather than operational or economically rational decisions.

The aim of this paper is to analyse the impact on airline efficiency of fleet planning and strategic management decisions. The paper is structured as follows: Section 2 presents the background and previous research that has dealt with similar issues. Section 3 details the methodology and Section 4 presents the data. The results are presented and discussed in Section 5, whilst Section 6 offers some conclusions.

2. Background and previous studies on airline efficiency

The key aim of this paper is to investigate the impact of strategic management (i.e. growth and business model) and fleet planning decisions on the efficiency of international airlines. There are a large number of studies measuring the productivity and efficiency of airlines using a range of econometric methods such as traditional partial productivity or unit cost measurement (e.g. see Oum and You, 1998), total factor productivity (TFP) methods (e.g. see Siregar and Norsworthy, 2001; Barbot et al., 2008), stochastic frontier approaches (SFA – e.g. see Assaf, 2009), and Data Envelopment Analysis (DEA) methods (e.g. see Fethi et al., 2001; Bhadra, 2009). The benefit of SFA and DEA is that they compute, for multiple inputs and outputs, single efficiency measures that can then be used to benchmark airlines against each other.

To discuss DEA in more detail, it is useful to first introduce the different concepts of efficiency. Technical efficiency is the most common efficiency measure. It is similar to physical productivity, as it refers to the optimal use of resources in the production process (maximal output from a given set of inputs), and hence considers physical indicators. However, if information on input prices is available, and if cost minimisation is assumed for all firms (in our case airlines), then a DEA model is appropriate to additionally calculate the *allocative efficiency* (AE) and the total (operating) *cost efficiency* (CE) of the relevant firms. Whilst technical efficiency is concerned about the quantity of inputs only, allocative efficiency refers to the optimal mix of these inputs (assuming cost minimisation). The concept of cost efficiency is the combination of technical and allocative efficiency and refers to choosing inputs at a given level of service so that the cost of production is minimised.

A key advantage of DEA compared to parametric methods such as SFA is that it does not require any assumption on the functional form of cost or production frontiers, and it also does not have to assume that firms always aim to minimise cost. DEA (if used for technical efficiency analysis) also does not require any information on prices, which is most helpful in data sensitive industries such as aviation. A disadvantage of DEA is that it does not cater for stochastic errors as SFA does. Recent papers that have applied a DEA approach to airlines, usually with truncated regression models in the second stage, include Barros and Peypoch (2009), who found for their sample of 27 European airlines (for 2000–2005) that demographics in the home country of the relevant airlines and membership in an alliance network, impact on airline efficiency. By applying a similar approach to 2005 data of 49 international airlines, Barbot et al. (2008) also find economies of scale, and show in addition that low cost carriers are usually more technically efficient than full service operators. Hong and Zhang (2010) find, for their sample of 29 airlines (1998–2002), that carriers with a high share of cargo in the overall operation are more efficient than those with a low cargo share (note that only mixed airlines and no specialised freight-only operators were included in that analysis). Finally, Ouellette et al. (2010) apply the DEA approach to show the impact of deregulation on the Canadian air carrier industry, and find that deregulation explains large parts of the measured inefficiency of their sample.

What these papers have in common is that they have examined technical efficiency only. This is limiting their findings in two ways. Firstly, most of the previous studies use both physical and cost data as input factors to determine technical efficiency. Methodologically, one could, however, argue that technical efficiency is about measuring the output to inputs ratio (e.g. see Banker et al., 1984) and therefore it should primarily consist of physical measures. This also has the advantage that one has not to make assumptions on the distribution of individual staff or material costs. Secondly, we find cost efficiency much more interesting and relevant to decision-making in airline management. As the three relevant efficiency measures are linked to one another, with cost efficiency being a combination of technical and allocative efficiency (CE = TE·AE), only an analysis of the values of all three types of efficiency will provide the full picture of the efficiency of the entities in question. Whilst the positive impacts of airline size and the chosen business approach (LCC versus full-service carrier) on technical efficiency are well discussed in the existing literature, the impacts on allocative and cost efficiency are less clear. Moreover, none of the previous papers recognise the potentially substantial impacts of fleet mix and stage length on technical, allocative and cost efficiency.

688   *R. Merkert, D.A. Hensher/Transportation Research Part A 45 (2011) 686–695*

3. Method and model specification

This paper builds on Merkert et al. (2010) by applying a two-stage DEA total efficiency approach to determine impact factors on airline efficiency. The first stage is concerned with a number of bootstrapped and non-bootstrapped DEA approaches to measure the efficiency of the relevant airlines (for details on bootstrapping in DEA, see Simar and Wilson, 2008 and Thanassoulis et al., 2008). This is followed by a number of second-stage random effects Tobit regression models which seek to evaluate the impact that strategic management and fleet planning have on technical, allocative and cost efficiency.

DEA (Charnes et al., 1978) is a linear programming technique for evaluating the relative performance of individual organisations or decision-making units (in our case airlines) based on observed data. The relative performance of an airline is hence defined as the ratio of the weighted sum of its outputs to the weighted sum of its inputs. The weights are not predetermined, but rather allocated by the model, avoiding bias resulting from subjectively assigned weights (such as Analytic Hierarchy Process). Generally, a DEA production frontier can be operationalised non-parametrically either with an input or output orientation, under the alternative assumptions of constant returns to scale (CRS) or variable returns to scale (VRS).

This paper uses an input oriented function because it assumes that airlines have a higher influence on the inputs than other features of performance identification (since output volumes are substantially influenced by macro-economic factors and often predetermined by long-term slot contract interests). By applying an input oriented CRS model, an efficiency score for firm i in a sample of I firms is estimated through the following optimisation system (Coelli et al., 2005):

$$
\begin{aligned}
& \min_{\theta \lambda} \theta, \\
& \text{s.t.} - qi + Q\lambda \geqslant 0 \\
& \qquad \theta xi - X\lambda \geqslant 0 \\
& \qquad \lambda \geqslant 0,
\end{aligned}
\tag{1}
$$

where λ represents the weights for the inputs and outputs which is an $I \times 1$ vector of constants, X and Q are input and output matrices, and θ measures the distance between the observations x_i and q_i and the frontier (where the frontier represents efficient operation). In other words, the distance (θ) represents the efficiency score. A value of $\theta = 1$ indicates that a firm is efficient, and thus located on the determined frontier.

A key limitation of the CRS model is its assumption that all observed firms operate at the optimal scale (Banker et al., 1984). In the aviation sector, imperfect competition, budgetary restrictions and regulatory constraints on entries and mergers may often result in firms operating at an inefficient scale. Hence, in this paper, in addition to the CRS efficiency scores (TE^{CRS}), the variable returns to scale efficiency scores (TE^{VRS}) are estimated. For the evaluation of the latter, it is necessary to assume an additional convexity constraint ($I1'\lambda = 1$), which ensures that inefficient firms are only benchmarked against firms of a similar size. For technical efficiency, we calculate both CRS and VRS scores to see whether they are different, which would indicate scale inefficiency. Since we believe that the VRS scores reflect reality much better than the CRS scores, for allocative and cost efficiency we then focus on VRS scores, and the second-stage regressions are based on VRS scores only. By applying an input oriented VRS DEA model, we estimate allocative and cost efficiency through the following optimisation system (Coelli et al., 2005):

$$
\begin{aligned}
& \min_{\lambda, x_i^*} w_i' x_i^*, \\
& \text{s.t.} - qi + Q\lambda \geqslant 0 \\
& \qquad \xi^* - X\lambda \geqslant 0 \\
& \qquad I1'\lambda = 1 \\
& \qquad \lambda \geqslant 0,
\end{aligned}
\tag{2}
$$

where w_i' represents a $N \times 1$ vector of input prices and x_i^* is the cost-minimising vector of input quantities for the ith firm. Whilst the former needs to be pre-assigned, the latter is estimated by the linear programming procedure. All other notions are as defined for technical efficiency. Cost efficiency is then calculated as:

$$
\text{CE} = \frac{w_i' x_i^*}{w_i' x_i},
\tag{3}
$$

and allocative efficiency is derived from:

$$
\text{AE} = \frac{\text{CE}}{\text{TE}}.
\tag{4}
$$

In the second stage of the analysis we follow previous studies (e.g. Barros and Peypoch, 2009; Merkert et al., 2010) by applying a two-stage model which regresses the first-stage DEA efficiency scores (dependent variable) against explanatory variables in the second stage (with the efficiency scores bounded at both ends of the 0–1 distribution). However, according to Simar and Wilson (2007, 2008), a two-stage approach results in inconsistent and biased parameter estimates (e.g. as a result of the dependence of the DEA efficiency scores on each other) unless the DEA efficiency scores are corrected by a bootstrapping procedure. In this paper we apply the smoothing homogenous bootstrap approach (for a detailed discussion see Simar

R. Merkert, D.A. Hensher/Transportation Research Part A 45 (2011) 686–695   689

and Wilson, 1998, 2000) that provides a means of incorporating stochastic elements in the DEA by performing repeated sampling, not from the empirical distribution per se but from its smoothed version. This avoids the serial correlation problem of conventional two-stage DEA studies, and allows us to estimate a robust regression model in the second-stage analysis in order to determine the impacts of strategic and fleet planning decisions on the overall efficiency of airlines. Our bias-corrected scores are derived from 2000 bootstrapped iterations. We note that there is a lively debate in the literature on the value of different bootstrapping methods (e.g. Tsionas and Papadakisa, 2010), with uncorrected efficiency scores (e.g. Barbot et al., 2008) and double bootstrapping methods (e.g. Barros and Peypoch, 2009) still frequently used in second-stage Tobit regressions. In addition to the bootstrapped technical efficiency scores, we also use the conventional non-biased corrected efficiency scores in the second-stage regression models. Since we also want to control for both cross-firm and time errors in our censored panel data set, we use the following random effects Tobit regression model:

$$y_{it} = \alpha + \beta_1 AIRLINE\_SIZE_{it} + \beta_2 AIRCRAFT\_SIZE_{it} + \beta_3 STAGE\_LENGTH_{it} + \beta_4 FLEET\_AGE_{it} + \beta_5 AIRCRAFT\_FAMILIES_{it}$$
$$+ v_{it} + u_i \tag{5}$$

where y_{it} is the VRS efficiency score of the individual airlines i in the relevant year t, $AIRLINE\_SIZE_{it}$ represents available tonne kilometres of that airline (as a proxy of its size), $AIRCRAFT\_SIZE_{it}$ indicates the average number of seats of the aircraft in service under the relevant airline in the relevant year, $STAGE\_LENGTH_{it}$ presents the average stage length that has been flown by the aircraft of the airline, $FLEET\_AGE_{it}$ reflects the age of its fleet, and $AIRCRAFT\_FAMILIES_{it}$ represents the number of different aircraft families[1] (e.g. A380 or B777) that the relevant airline fleet consisted of at that point in time. Our analysis clusters the relevant aircraft; therefore, at the aircraft family level (e.g. aircraft that the same pilot can fly) rather than the specific aircraft type level. The essential assumptions of the random effects model are that the unique effect v_{it} is uncorrelated across periods, that the random effect u_i is the same in every period, and that all effects are uncorrelated across individuals (see Greene, 2002, R16-100).

4. Data

This paper analyses 58 of the largest passenger airlines over the two fiscal years of 2007/2008 and 2008/2009.[2] In order to ensure comparability of the analysed airlines, we have only selected those that operated and reported for the full 12 months in each of the two relevant years. It is worth noting that the sample was not significantly affected by M&A activities in the two analysed years. Only two of the analysed airlines have been involved in M&A transactions, namely Air Berlin and Air India. However, as some large M&A airline transactions have happened before 2005 and then again from late 2009, particularly in the US and in Europe, some airlines experienced either costs/benefits of a recent M&A activity (e.g. Lufthansa/SN Brussels) or prepared for an upcoming merger during our analysed period (e.g. Delta/Northwest). Since this can be said for many airlines, we decided to leave these airlines in the sample. In terms of the DEA models, we have used the same two input factors and two output factors in each of the models. In line with previous studies, we see the major trade-off in airline management (as in other industries) between capital and labour. Because both need to be operationalised, we use, as shown in Table 1, available tonne kilometres (ATK) as a proxy for capital (again in line with the existing literature) and full-time equivalent (FTE) staff as the measure of labour. As both are physical measures, they are useful for evaluating technical efficiency. In order to evaluate the allocative and cost efficiency of each airline in the sample, we also include the price of a unit of capital, proxied by ATK_Price (determined by dividing the sum of all operating costs,[3] other than staff cost, by ATK), and average staff cost as the price for one unit of labour.

The two outputs used in all three DEA models are revenue passenger kilometres (RPK) and revenue tonne kilometres (RTK). These are commonly used to reflect the output of both passenger and cargo (including mail) flight operations. At this point it is worth mentioning that this paper focuses on operational efficiency, and hence ancillary revenues (e.g. from selling travel insurances, hotel accommodation, etc.) are not captured in the DEA models.

In terms of the second-stage explanatory variables, we pool the data over the two analysed years, which means that we have 116 observations for the 58 airlines of our sample. The size of each airline is thereby expressed in terms of its capacity, in other words as available seat kilometres (ASK). With airlines such as Emirates adding substantial capacity to their fleet, and mergers being seen as a measure to perform better, it is interesting to analyse whether big is indeed beautiful in the context of airline efficiency. Whilst the average stage length (shown in km) was chosen to evaluate the impact of route/network optimisation on airline efficiency, aircraft size (measured in average seats per aircraft across the operated fleet) was selected to test whether the earlier discussed productivity measures of individual aircraft would have an impact on overall airline efficiency. As shown in Table 1, there are substantial differences across airlines, which is not only a result of different aircraft types and families in the fleets, but also attributable to different seat and cabin configurations that airlines chose (number of seats in different classes, leg room, etc.). It is worth noting, that because of the focus on passenger airlines

---

[1] This means, for example, that the A318, A319, A320 and A321 aircraft types are part of the A320 family (with the A380 being the biggest aircraft family) whilst at Boeing the aircraft types from B737-200 to B737-900 are, for example, all members of the B737 family (including ER (extra range) types).

[2] We used the Airline Business 2007/08 (Flightglobal, 2007) ranking of the top 200 passenger airlines (based on RPK), and aimed to get both physical and cost data of the top 50 of these airlines. As we could not get hold of the annual reports of a small number of airlines (mainly from the Middle East), we decided to replace them with and add some of the top 50–100 airlines of which we had the required data readily available.

[3] In our analysis, operating costs include rent/leasing charges and depreciation but exclude both taxes and interest expenses.

690   R. Merkert, D.A. Hensher / Transportation Research Part A 45 (2011) 686–695

Table 1
Descriptive statistics for first- and second-stage analysis. *Source:* Own analysis.

	N	Mean	Std. dev.	Min	Max
First-stage DEA models					
Output 2007/2008					
RPK (000s)	58	53,069,326	48,286,405	1,302,807	222,763,439
RTK (000s)	58	6,540,683	5,946,058	1,20,163	23,321,412
Input 2007/2008					
LABOUR (FTE)	58	18,840	15,879	1079	71,818
ATK (000s)	58	10,266,018	9,281,515	220,155	38,978,784
FTE_Price (USD/FTE)	58	51,555.3	26,508.6	1890	115,836
ATK_Price (USD/ATK)	58	0.5164	0.1638	0.2552	0.9861
Output 2008/2009					
RPK (000s)	58	54,266,600	47,344,773	1,371,653	211,993,968
RTK (000s)	58	6,616,855	5,834,049	126,361	22,176,043
Input 2008/2009					
LABOUR (FTE)	58	19,191	15,869	1132	70,926
ATK (000s)	58	10,508,685	9,109,562	232,285	37,416,956
FTE_Price (USD/FTE)	58	53,134.9	27,417.2	1998	123,352
ATK_Price (USD/ATK)	58	0.5874	0.2010	0.3002	1.4342
Second-stage explanatory variables					
AIRLINE_SIZE (m ASK)	116	69,345	58,999	2008	273,371
STAGE_LENGTH (km)	116	1977	1167	633	7281
AIRCRAFT_SIZE (seats)	116	195.6	53.5	101.1	340.2
FLEET_AGE (years)	116	8.49	3.35	2.8	19.26
AIRCRAFT_FAMILIES (#)	116	4.59	2.06	1	11
AIRCRAFT_MANUFACTURERS(#)	116	2.33	1.10	1	7

and limited data availability/consistency, our analysis does not include specialised freight aircraft. However, as Hong and Zhang (2010) point out, in many regions 50 or even up to 60% of airfreight is carried in the belly compartment of passenger aircraft. As a result, air cargo and passenger operations overlap in some airlines substantially, which again is one of the reasons why we use ATK and not ASK as the input proxy for capital in the first stage of our analysis.

The other important variables in terms of fleet optimisation are the number of different families of aircraft (e.g. A320 versus A380), number of different manufacturers (e.g. Airbus or Embraer) in the fleet, and the age of the fleet. Having a more homogenous fleet enables airlines reportedly to keep crew, training, maintenance, purchasing, safety and other costs low, and it also increases the airlines' market power when negotiating with aircraft manufacturers and suppliers. This explains in large part, we believe, why particularly low cost carriers such as Ryanair and Southwest have only one type of aircraft (in this case the Boeing 737) in service. However, there are other airlines such as China Eastern and Air India that have a large range of different families of aircraft (more than 10) in their fleet. It is hence interesting to see whether the fleet mix has an impact of an airline's overall efficiency. Regarding the fleet age, one would assume that this variable is correlated with fuel efficiency, and hence airlines with very young fleets should be more efficient compared to their peers.

The input and output data for the DEA models, as well as the stage length data, were mainly sourced from ICAO/ATI (2011) databases. However, since the ICAO data was often incomplete (particularly in terms of staff data) and inconsistent (particularly in terms of traffic data), we complemented and verified our database with data from IATA (2008, 2009) and data from a review of a large number of annual reports of the sampled airlines. The unit of analysis is the airline company itself rather than their parent companies. The data on the fleet mix (average aircraft size and age, average number of families and manufacturers of aircraft in fleet) were obtained from Flightglobal (2010). Since parked, ordered and retired aircraft were excluded, we collected such data for some 8500 individual aircraft in service in the fleets of the 58 airlines for each of the two relevant fiscal years.

Since we had to complement the ICAO data (which is provided in US$) with data from the airline annual accounts, a number of the two input price figures were obtained in local currency units. To make the data comparable, we converted all data into US$ by using the average exchange rate in the relevant year (OANDA, 2010). Ideally we would have liked to use the purchasing power parity (PPP) method (European Communities and OECD, 2006), but for a number of countries that host airlines of our sample, no PPP data exists.

5. Results

The first-stage DEA results, presented in Table 2, can be presented in a number of different ways. Initially we have estimated the DEA scores separately for 2007/2008 and 2008/2009. Obtaining the DEA estimates for two separate years improves the robustness of the results, particularly given the recent volatility in the aviation market. From the separate scores, we then calculate the averages over the 2 years, and compare that with the scores of two years of data pooled in the DEA models. Not surprisingly, the average DEA scores of the two separate models come out higher (although once the results are bootstrapped, that difference becomes marginal) than the pooled DEA scores, which is a result of comparing

R. Merkert, D.A. Hensher / Transportation Research Part A 45 (2011) 686–695   691

Table 2
First-stage DEA results. Source: Own analysis.

Year	N	Computed with FEAR 1.15				Computed with DEAP 2.1		
		TE^{VRS}	TE_{Corr}^{VRS}	TE^{CRS}	TE_{Corr}^{TRS}	TE^{VRS}	AE	CE
Overall results								
2007/2008	58	0.8413	0.7856	0.7873	0.7502	0.8413	0.6803	0.5900
2008/2009	58	0.8242	0.7643	0.7708	0.7306	0.8242	0.6637	0.5639
Av. 07–08/08–09	58	0.8328	0.7750	0.7790	0.7404	0.8327	0.6720	0.5769
Pooled 07–09	116	0.8259	0.7730	0.7774	0.7402	0.8259	0.6567	0.5583
Av. 07–08/08–09 Results by region								
Africa/middle east	7	0.7715	0.7306	0.7275	0.7006	0.7714	0.6960	0.5557
Asia/Pacific	19	0.8149	0.7701	0.7894	0.7569	0.8149	0.5964	0.5008
Europe	18	0.8522	0.7834	0.8053	0.7551	0.8522	0.7087	0.6149
N_America	11	0.8939	0.8129	0.7615	0.7201	0.8939	0.8135	0.7438
S_America	3	0.7479	0.7188	0.7407	0.7146	0.7478	0.3545	0.2692

like with like, and also because of the smaller sample sizes for each of the separate years rather than for the pooled data. The results suggest that the airlines' average technical, allocative and cost efficiency has deteriorated over the analysed 2 years. This decrease in efficiency can be explained by the fact that airlines faced a much more difficult business environment in 2008/2009 compared to the situation in 2007/2008. The year 2008 saw the beginning of the recent global financial crisis, with high and very volatile fuel prices and a number of airline financial failures (note that none of the airlines in our sample went into administration).

The first columns of efficiency scores show the average technical efficiency scores of the airlines (under both assumptions VRS and CRS) and reveal that on average all of them are associated with a degree of scale inefficiency (because the VRS and CRS scores differ). As mentioned above, according to the recent literature (e.g. Simar and Wilson, 2008) for robust second-stage regression results, the first-stage DEA should be bootstrapped/bias-corrected. As expected, in our DEA models (VRS and CRS) the average bias-corrected technical efficiency scores (TE_{Corr}) are smaller than the average uncorrected scores (TE). This indicates that a traditional DEA, without the bootstrapping procedure, tends to overestimate technical efficiency for the analysed sample. The standard deviation of the bias-corrected values is also smaller than that of the uncorrected values. Thus, the bootstrapping procedure appears to be beneficial for obtaining the more realistic efficiency scores. While these technical efficiency scores are estimated with the software package FEAR 1.15 (Wilson, 2010), all allocative and cost efficiency (plus a control technical efficiency) DEA estimations are undertaken with the software DEAP 2.1 (Coelli et al., 2005). The benefit of DEAP 2.1 is that it allows, in contrast to FEAR 1.15, estimation of the three types of efficiency. DEAP 2.1, however, is not able to apply any bootstrapping procedures, and hence both software packages were used.

As mentioned above, the overall efficiency of the airlines has decreased over the analysed two years. Our results suggest that the relatively poor cost efficiency was a result of allocative inefficiency rather than of the technical inefficiency of the airlines in both years, and also across the analysed geographic regions. This indicates that some airlines use not only more inputs, particularly in Africa and South America, but also an inefficient mix of inputs, particularly in Africa (the latter became apparent after an analysis of the individual results).

Although our sample includes airlines from each continent, for some regions, particularly South America and the Middle East, we were able to collect financial data for only a limited number of operators (because many operators in these regions are publicly owned and do not publish annual reports/accounts). However, from the physical data (e.g. staff numbers) of other Middle East carriers such as Etihad, Qatar and Saudi Arabian, we know that these airlines have a very similar technical efficiency to Emirates. Emirates is not only relatively technically efficient, but also allocative and cost efficient, but it is not the most efficient airline in our sample; in terms of TE_{Corr}^{VRS}, that is United Airlines, and in terms of CE, it is a number of airlines ($CE = 1$) including Cathay Pacific Airways and Singapore Airlines. The average scores of North American airlines were much better than expected, which could be explained by recent substantial staff cuts in these airlines, and the fact that 2008 saw a very large number of aircraft taken out of service in this region (particularly those that were least fuel efficient). The relatively poor efficiency scores of the South American carriers is primarily a result of the relatively low efficiency scores of the two Brazilian airlines. That has to do with their very low system load factor (less than 60%) and the general trend for South American and African airlines in high labour intensity of flight operations in these regions.

Although the first-stage efficiency scores are worth presenting on their own, we find it even more interesting to reveal some of the key determinants of the differences in efficiency across airlines. We estimated a series of second-stage random effects Tobit regressions to investigate the determinants of technical, allocative and cost efficiency (the first-stage VRS DEA scores of the separate DEA models for each year being the dependent variable). Although we use two statistical packages in the first-stage DEA models, our analysis still relies on non-bootstrapped allocative and cost efficiency scores in the second-stage regressions, instead of their bootstrapped values. However, as discussed earlier, the debate on the value of bootstrapping methods is ongoing. In this analysis, the random effects Tobit regression models were run for bootstrapped (TE_{Corr}^{VRS}) and original (TE_{Corr}^{VRS}) technical efficiency scores. As shown in Table 3, the results are similar in terms of the significance of the reported impacts, and in terms of their magnitude, and suggest that for the given sample, bootstrapping is not as important as

692   R. Merkert, D.A. Hensher/Transportation Research Part A 45 (2011) 686–695

Table 3
Second-stage random effects Tobit regression results based in DEA scores. *Source*: Own analysis.

	TE_{Corr}^{VRS}	TE^{VRS}	AE^{VRS}	CE^{VRS}
Constant	0.75822***	0.79093***	0.32303***	0.26225***
AIRLINE_SIZE (m ASK)	0.57223D-06***	0.95770D-06***	0.15838D-05***	0.20017D-05***
AIRCRAFT_SIZE (seats)	0.00019*	0.00024	0.00113***	0.00085**
STAGE_LENGTH (km)	−0.11768D-04**	−0.10262D-04	0.19051D-04	0.16135D-04
AIRCRAFT_FAMILIES (#)	−0.01170***	−0.01776***	−0.04619***	−0.04731***
FLEET_AGE (years)	0.00202	0.00368	0.02276***	0.02292***
Sigma (v)	0.08806***	0.10360***	0.20799***	0.20766***
Sigma (u)	0.00881	0.01036	0.02080	0.02077

*** Significance at 1% level.
** Significance at 5% level.
* Significance at 10% level.

perhaps for other industries. Consequently, the regression coefficients of the non-bootstrapped allocative and cost efficiency scores are likely to show statistically significant effects of the explanatory variables.

The second-stage regressions were performed using Limdep 9.0 (NLOGIT 4.3), and the results are summarised in Table 3. The coefficients are the marginal effects on technical, allocative and cost efficiency. As indicated in Eq. (5), the variable AIR-CRAFT_MANUFACTURERS had to be dropped because of its strong correlation with the variable AIRCRAFT_FAMILIES. Otherwise, multi-collinearity did not appear to be an issue, based on the partial correlation coefficients between the explanatory variables.

As Table 3 shows, the second-stage regression models produced interesting and statistically significant results.[4] In terms of robustness, we have greatest confidence in the coefficients based on technical efficiency. This is because the technical efficiency scores are likely to be most reliable, as they are not associated with any potential foreign exchange or different international accounting principle distortions (physical inputs only).

While the average stage length operated by the analysed airlines has a relatively small but significant negative impact on technical efficiency, there appears to be no significant impact of that specific element of route optimisation on allocative and cost efficiency. This is interesting, as it highlights a trade off in terms of operating cost. On the one hand, longer sectors result in lower unit costs because of increased fuel efficiency. Longer sectors suggests, on the other hand, that the carriers need to factor in costs associated with cabin crew accommodation, maintenance and other essential facilities at the destinations (which is something that LCC airlines such as easyJet try to avoid). Hence, in total, the presence of longer sectors has no significant impact on overall efficiency. This finding could, however, be confounded by the nature of the sample with respect to the actual length of sectors operated (e.g. for specialist long-haul carriers, the number and extent of refuelling stops could have an influence), and the specific nature of the extent and location of hub-and-spoke networks.

The size of the airline (if measured in ASK) has a relatively small but very significant positive impact on technical, allocative and cost efficiency. Whilst this suggests that, on average, big is beautiful, an analysis of the individual efficiency scores revealed that this scale economy advantage has limits (at around 100bn ASK). Similarly, our results suggest that the average size of the aircraft in an airline's fleet has a significant positive effect on all three types of efficiency, particularly on allocative and cost efficiency. Aircraft regulations, for example, on staff (1 crew member per 50 seats is required) add to aircraft costs; at the macro-airline level, we find that airlines with the larger aircraft in their fleet (measured in available seats per aircraft) are on average the most efficient.

The results regarding the average fleet age of the airlines suggest, contrary to our predictions, that fleet age has no significant impact on technical efficiency, and a small but very significant positive impact on allocative and cost efficiency. This means that airlines with an older fleet are, on average, relatively more efficient than those with a younger fleet. Younger aircraft tend to be, in general, much more fuel efficient; the airlines with the youngest fleet in our sample (Ryanair with some 3 years) are indeed relatively efficient. But then there are also airlines with much older fleets (such as Cathay with about 10 years or Lufthansa with around 13 years), that are similarly, or even more efficient. In addition, some airlines with young fleets have very low allocative and cost efficiency scores (such as Jetblue with a fleet of 3.56 years of age or Virgin Blue with 4.5 years). Although this alone explains our findings sufficiently, one should also note that in 2008 a large number of aircraft were taken out of service (particularly those that were least fuel efficient) in North America, and that happened in airlines that had, on average, a relatively old fleet. As a result these airlines, with a relatively old fleet, became more allocative and cost efficient and have contributed to the trend displayed in our regression results.

The most substantive findings of our analysis are related to the fleet mix variables. The results suggest that the average number of different aircraft families in the fleet of an airline has, as expected, a negative and statistically very significant impact on technical, allocative and cost efficiency. We also tested to replace the AIRCRAFT_FAMILIES with the AIRCRAFT_MAN-UFACTURERS variable in our regression models (because of multi-collinearity we could not have both variables in the same

---

[4] Besides the presented variables, we also included a dummy to control for the business model (9 LCCs in sample) of the airlines, but the results came out insignificant. What this shows is that for LCC operations in particular (which could have been an important dimension of heterogeneity and hence distortion), it is not significantly impacting on our airlines' efficiency. Hence, we present our results at aggregate level and not clustered into different business models.

R. Merkert, D.A. Hensher / Transportation Research Part A 45 (2011) 686–695 693

model), and found a similarly significant impact of the number of manufacturers (in airline fleets) on all three types of efficiency. This clearly shows that homogenous fleets are best in terms of technical, allocative and cost efficiency.

6. Conclusions

This paper set out to examine the impact of strategic management and fleet mix decisions on technical, allocative and cost efficiency. While the previous literature has shown (although the methodology is not fully convincing) that the growth of airlines has an impact on technical efficiency, our results suggest a similar positive impact on allocative, and ultimately, cost efficiency. The analysis of the individual efficiency scores shows, however, that this impact is limited, and for an airline size of around 100bn ASK diseconomies of scale make further growth less attractive. In terms of fleet mix, the results of the second-stage random effects Tobit regressions show, as expected, that airlines that have, on average, large aircraft and only a few (if possible one) aircraft families and manufacturers in their fleet, are associated with relatively high technical, allocative and cost efficiency. This finding supports some of the qualitative arguments in the previous literature on the likely consequences of heterogeneity in aircraft fleets. The findings for the influence of the age of airline fleets suggest that a younger fleet does not necessarily result in higher efficiency. While there is individual airline evidence on efficiency gains, a result of very young and homogenous fleets (e.g. Ryanair), the overall results show that airlines with relatively old fleets can be very efficient, particularly allocative and cost efficient.

The impact of aircraft size on airline efficiency shows, additionally, that the known impact of aircraft size on aircraft unit cost (micro level lens) has a notable effect on the overall efficiency of airlines (macro level lens). This, to some extent, varies with the average stage length flown by the aircraft of our analysed airlines. While it is well known that longer sectors tend to reduce the average unit cost of aircraft, the results show at the macro level that the average sector length of the fleet of an airline has a negative impact on technical efficiency, but it has no statistically significant effect on allocative and cost efficiency of the airlines. Virgin Atlantic, for example, has flown the longest sectors in our sample and has a technical efficiency that is substantially lower than the sample average. This means that it is less productive than its peers, using too much labour and capital in the production process. However, its allocative efficiency is much higher than the sample average, and hence its cost efficiency (which is usually most important to airlines) is in line with the sample average. Hence, stage length in relation to total cost appears not to be an important factor. However, we acknowledge that more research is required in this area, as these effects may change when other input (such as ASK) and output (such as revenues) factors are considered in the DEA analysis. The same conclusion can be made with regard to our findings on the fleet age of airlines. While a few airlines with very young fleets are very efficient, on average the airlines with older aircraft are more allocative and cost efficient than those with younger fleets.

Methodologically, our findings suggest that bootstrapping of the first-stage efficiency scores improves the second-stage random effects Tobit regression results only marginally. Hence we argue that our regression results based on non-bias-corrected allocative and cost efficiency are as informative and valuable as the regression results of the bias-corrected technical efficiency scores. In terms of limitations, our approach does not capture all potential strategic management decisions. An airline might, for example, consider, in addition to stage length, its hub-and-spoke strategy and how traffic and capacity are matched on all routes, in order to optimise its network. Non-aeronautical revenues are becoming increasingly important in airline management, and hence should be included in efficiency analysis. Moreover, we are aware that any cross-country benchmarking is associated with a degree of distortions (for example, as a result of different purchasing powers of local currencies used to present costs). Further research is therefore required in that respect.

To conclude, with a focus on operational efficiency, this paper has shown econometrically that not only the size of airlines but also fleet mix decisions such as the size of aircrafts and number of families of aircraft in the fleets, have an impact on technical, allocative and, ultimately, cost efficiency. Although stage length has an impact on an aircraft's unit cost, its impact at the airline level is limited to technical efficiency. Conversely, the age of fleets has no significant impact on technical efficiency but delivers, on average, a small positive effect on allocative and cost efficiency. The analysis of the individual efficiency scores shows examples in which very young fleets result in relatively high efficiency; however, further research is required on this issue. What our results clearly show is that airline management that aims to reduce cost should focus less on stage length and fleet age and more on the other variables, particularly on the optimisation of the airlines' fleet mix.

Acknowledgements

The authors gratefully acknowledge the valuable comments of two anonymous referees. We are also grateful for the advice of Rigas Doganis, Andy Foster and Andrew Melvin on the methodology and data used in this paper. The financial support from the Royal Economic Society, through its Small Academic Expenses Scheme, is also greatly appreciated and enabled the first author to spend three months at ITLS (The University of Sydney) in 2010. Any remaining errors are the responsibility of the authors.

Appendix A

See Table 4.

Table 4
Sample of 58 airlines. *Source:* Sample based on Flightglobal (2007) ranking of the top passenger airlines (measured in RPK).

Region/state	Airline	Region/state	Airline
Africa/middle east		*Asia/Pacific*	
Egypt	Egypt Air	Australia	Qantas Airways
Ethiopia	Ethiopian Airlines	Australia	Virgin Blue
Israel	El Al Israel Airlines	China	Air China
Kenya	Kenya Airways	China	China Eastern
Mauritius	Air Mauritius	China	China Southern
South Africa	South African Airlines	China	Hainan Airlines
UAE	Emirates	Hong Kong	Cathay Pacific Airways
		India	Air India
Europe		India	Jet Airways
Austria	Austrian Airlines	Japan	All Nippon Air.
Croatia	Croatia Airlines	Japan	Japan Airlines
Czech Republic	Czech Airlines	Malaysia	Malaysian Airlines
Finland	Finnair	New Zealand	Air New Zealand
France	Air France	Philippines	Philippine Airlines
Germany	Air Berlin	Rep. of Korea	Asiana Airlines
Germany	Lufthansa	Rep. of Korea	Korean Air
Ireland	Aer Lingus	Singapore	Singapore Airlines
Ireland	Ryanair	Thailand	Thai Airways
Portugal	Tap Air Portugal	Vietnam	Vietnam Airlines
Russia	Aeroflot Russian Airlines		
Spain	Iberia	*North America*	
Switzerland	Swiss	Canada	Air Canada
Turkey	Thy Turkish Airlines	USA	Airtran Airways
UK	British Airways	USA	Alaska Airlines
UK	easyJet Airlines	USA	American
UK	Monarch Airlines	USA	Continental
UK	Virgin Atlantic	USA	Delta
		USA	Jetblue Airways
South America		USA	Northwest
Brazil	GOL Linhas Aéreas Inteligentes	USA	Southwest
Brazil	Tam Linhas Aereas	USA	United
Chile	LAN Airlines	USA	US Airways

References

Assaf, A., 2009. Are US airlines really in crisis? Tourism Management 30 (6), 916–921.
Barbot, C., Costa, A., Sochirca, E., 2008. Airlines performance in the new market context: a comparative productivity and efficiency analysis. Journal of Air Transport Management 14, 270–274.
Banker, R.D., Charnes, A., Cooper, W.W., 1984. Some models for estimating technical and scale inefficiencies in data envelopment analysis. Management Science 30, 1078–1092.
Barros, C.P., Peypoch, N., 2009. An evaluation of European Airlines' operational performance. International Journal of Production Economics 122, 525–533.
Bhadra, D., 2009. Race to the bottom or swimming upstream: performance analysis of US airlines. Journal of Air Transport Management 15, 227–235.
Charnes, A., Cooper, W.W., Rhodes, E.L., 1978. Measuring the efficiency of decision making units. European Journal of Operational Research 2, 429–444.
Coelli, T.J., Rao, P.D.S., O'Donnell, C.J., Battese, G.E., 2005. An Introduction to Efficiency and Productivity Analysis, second ed. Springer, New York.
Doganis, R., 2009. Flying off course – airline economics and marketing, fourth ed. Routledge, London.
European Communities and OECD, 2006. EUROSTAT – OECD Methodological manual on purchasing power parities, 2005 ed. Luxembourg.
Fethi, M.D., Jackson, P.M., Weyman-Jones, T.G., 2001. European Airlines: a Stochastic DEA study of efficiency with market liberalisation. Paper presented at the Seventh European Workshop on Efficiency and Productivity Analysis (7EWEPA), University of Oviedo, Oviedo, Spain.
Flightglobal, 2007. Airline Business – Airline Industry Guide 07/08, Flightglobal/Reed Business Information, Rugby.
Flightglobal, 2010. acas3 fleet database, Flightglobal/Reed Business Information, Rugby.
Gillen, D., 2006. Airline business models and networks: regulation, competition and evolution in aviation markets. Review of Network Economics 5, 366–385.
Greene, W.H., 2002. LIMDEP Version 8.0 Reference Guide. Econometric Software, Inc., New York.
Hong, S., Zhang, A., 2010. An efficiency study of airlines and aircargo/passenger divisions: a DEA approach. World Review of Intermodal Transportation Research 3, 137–149.
IATA, 2008. World Air Transport Statistics, WATS, 52rd ed. Montreal/Geneva.
IATA, 2009. World Air Transport Statistics, WATS 53rd ed., Montreal/Geneva.
ICAO/ATI, 2011. Statistics for 2007–2009 sourced from ICAO's Statistical Air Transport Reporting Forms. <www.ICAOData.com> (accessed March 2011).
Merkert, R., Smith, A.S.J., Nash, C.A., 2010. Benchmarking of train operating firms – a transaction cost efficiency analysis. Journal of Transportation Planning and Technology 33, 35–53.
OANDA, 2010. Historical Exchange Rates, OANDA Corporation. <www.oanda.com> (acessed August 2010).
Ouellette, P., Petit, P., Tessier Parent, L.P., Vigeant, S., 2010. Introducing regulation in the measurement of efficiency, with an application to the Canadian air carriers industry. European Journal of Operational Research 200, 216–226.
Oum, T.H., You, C., 1998. Cost competitiveness of major airlines: an international comparison. Transport Research Part A 32, 407–422.
Simar, L., Wilson, P.W., 1998. Sensitivity analysis of efficiency scores: how to bootstrap in nonparametric frontier models. Management Science 44, 49–61.
Simar, L., Wilson, P.W., 2000. A general methodology for bootstrapping in non-parametric Frontier models. Journal of Applied Statistics 27, 779–802.
Simar, L., Wilson, P.W., 2007. Estimation and inference in two-stage, semi-parametric models of production processes. Journal of Econometrics 136, 31–64.
Simar, L., Wilson, P.W., 2008. Statistical inference in nonparametric frontier models: recent developments and perspectives. In: Fried, H.O., Lovell, C.A.K., Schmidt, S.S. (Eds.), The Measurement of Productive Efficiency and Productivity Change. Oxford University Press, New York, pp. 421–522.

Siregar, D.D., Norsworthy, J.R., 2001. Pre- and post-deregulation financial performance and efficiency in US Airlines. Change Management and the New Industrial Revolution, 200. IEMC '01 Proceedings, pp. 421–429.

Tsionas, E.G., Papadakisa, E.N., 2010. A Bayesian approach to statistical inference in stochastic DEA. Omega 38, 309–314.

Thanassoulis, E., Portela, M.C.S., Despić, O., 2008. Data envelopment analysis: the mathematical programming approach to efficiency analysis. In: Fried, H.O., Lovell, C.A.K., Schmidt, S.S. (Eds.), The Measurement of Productive Efficiency and Productivity Change. Oxford University Press, New York, pp. 251–420.

Vasigh, B., Tacker, T., Fleming, K., 2008. Introduction to Air Transport Economics: From Theory to Applications. Ashgate, Aldershot.

Wilson, P.W., 2010. Package 'FEAR' – Frontier Efficiency Analysis with R. Clemson, Department of Economics, Clemson University.

14

Efficiency and competition in the airline industry

David R. Graham

Daniel P. Kaplan

and

David S. Sibley

After reviewing some recent developments in the airline industry, this article tests two hypotheses that were central to the argument for deregulation: (1) that CAB regulation caused airlines to employ excess capacity relative to the capacity that would be provided under unregulated competition; and (2) that potential competition would keep fares at cost even in highly concentrated markets. An econometric analysis of these hypotheses based on postderegulation data suggests that the excess capacity hypothesis is essentially confirmed. In contrast, the pattern of fares in late 1980 and early 1981 does not support the potential competition hypothesis that fares are independent of market concentration.

1. Introduction

■ The deregulation of the airline industry provides an invaluable opportunity to compare the performance of an industry with and without economic regulation, as well as an important test of economists' predictions of the consequences of deregulation.[1] After reviewing some of the recent developments in the airline industry, this article tests two hypotheses that were central to the arguments for deregulation. First, Civil Aeronautics Board (CAB) fare regulation was thought to promote service competition and thus cause the airlines to employ excess capacity, so that market-determined fares were predicted to yield more efficient capacity utilization. Second, because capital is highly mobile in the airline industry, potential competition was predicted to keep fares at competitive levels, even in highly concentrated markets. The article also describes the added efficiencies afforded by the realignment of airline routes, and the role of the new "low cost" airlines in the long-term development of the industry.

The industry has not yet adapted fully to the new competitive environment. Nevertheless, some basic developments signal the direction in which the industry is evolving. The analysis presented here suggests several provisional conclusions:

We would like to acknowledge the helpful comments of two anonymous referees and the Editorial Board of this Journal. Steve Cooperman, Steve Davis, John Panzar, Jack Schmidt, and most notably, Tadas Osmolskis provided valuable assistance. The views expressed do not necessarily represent those of the Department of Labor, the Civil Aeronautics Board, or Bell Laboratories.

[1] See, for example, Jordan (1970), Keeler (1972), Levine (1965), MacAvoy and Snow (1977), Pulsifer *et al.* (1975), and the Report of the Kennedy Hearings on airline regulation (U.S. Senate, Committee on the Judiciary (1975)).

(1) Rising load factors as well as changes in the patterns of load factors across markets since the late 1960s suggest that more efficient levels of capacity are provided today. Together with the adoption of peak-load pricing and improvements in the system of airline routes, this indicates that the industry is operating more efficiently now than under regulation.
(2) Fares appear to be closely related to the cost of service. Market characteristics, such as distance and the time sensitivity of passengers, explain most of the variation in fares across markets.
(3) There appears to be some price-setting power exercised by airlines in relatively concentrated markets. But if the Herfindahl index is .5 or higher, further increases in concentration have little effect on fares.
(4) New, low cost airlines have a substantial negative effect on fares in the markets they serve. Their increasing role is contributing to the evolution of a more efficient industry.

2. Events since deregulation

■ The transition from regulation has been gradual and has involved both legislative and regulatory initiatives. Hence, it is impossible to pinpoint an exact end of regulation. The CAB took a major step in liberalizing fare regulation when it approved the first "Super Saver" fares in the spring of 1977. In the fall of 1978, carriers were allowed to set fares as much as 10% above or 50% below a CAB standard fare. In May 1980 this "zone of reasonableness" was expanded to give carriers unlimited downward flexibility and expanded upward flexibility.[2]

The Board was able to take pricing initiatives under longstanding authority; however, it was not until the Airline Deregulation Act was passed in October, 1978, that the Board got clear authority to liberalize route awards. Three months after the Act was passed, the Board essentially gave carriers the ability to serve any routes they wished. The airlines have taken advantage of these new freedoms to dramatically change their route networks and pricing strategies.

□ **Routes.** The CAB's authority over routes gave it control over entry into the industry as well as into markets. The Board not only restricted entry by new firms, but also restricted the number of existing carriers competing in a given market. (Usually only 2 or 3 airlines were authorized to serve any given route.) Moreover, only the trunks, the largest airlines, were permitted to serve major long-haul markets, while other airlines were restricted to serving regional markets. These route policies caused a degree of regional and market specialization to develop. Consequently, many travelers had to change airlines enroute, even though passengers prefer online connections.[3] Online connections afford greater assurance that bags will not be lost or connections missed, and they allow passengers to avoid long walks between terminals at large airports. An analysis of travel patterns in a sample of more than 4,000 markets shows that the fraction of trips that require passengers to change planes has remained about the same since 1978, but the proportion of passengers that must change airlines in route has decreased by 38%.[4]

Along with this shift towards single carrier service have come changes in traffic patterns. Table 1 depicts the changes in the number of flights between cities of four size

[2] Initially, ceilings were lifted altogether for markets of less than 200 miles. They were set at 50% above the standard fare in markets of 201 to 400 miles and at 30% above the standard fare in longer haul markets. In September 1980, the ceilings were changed to equal the standard fare plus 30% plus $15 in all markets.

[3] Carlton, Landes, and Posner (1980) estimated that an online connection is worth more to the traveler than an interline connection.

[4] For a discussion of connecting patterns and more detailed empirical support, see Graham and Kaplan (1982).

TABLE 1   Changes in Weekly Departures between Airport Categories:
             Week of June 1, 1978 vs. June 1, 1981

City Category	Number of Cities	Percentage Changes in Weekly Flights			
		City Category			
		Large Hubs	Medium Hubs	Small Hubs	Nonhubs
Large Hubs	23	9.3			
Medium Hubs	36	10.5	0.0		
Small Hubs	66	18.3	−7.1	−23.2	
Nonhubs	517	12.3	10.5	−21.1	−12.6

Source: *Official Airline Guide*, Oak Brook, Ill.: Official Airline Guides, Inc.

categories.[5] Large and medium hubs had more flights in 1981 than in 1978. Total flights declined at smaller communities (small hubs and nonhubs), but these communities had more flights to big cities (large and medium hubs). The decrease in total service at nonhubs is entirely explained by reduced service to other small communities, and the increase in direct service to larger airports has improved the convenience of service to many of these communities.[6]

These changes in the route networks have been accompanied by corresponding changes in the competitive structure of the industry. The share of domestic traffic served by the trunks fell from 87% to 80% between the second quarters of 1978 and 1981. On the other hand, local service airlines grew markedly as they entered longer haul markets, thereby offering an increasing amount of online service to their passengers. Also, newly certificated airlines have begun service in many heavily traveled markets. As Table 2 shows, between May 1978 and May 1981 the Herfindahl index of concentration did not increase in any category of market and fell in most categories. (To be sure, there is enough variation across markets so that the differences in the average Herfindahls for May 1978 and May 1981 are not statistically significant.) To an important degree, declining concentration is due to entry by additional airlines into markets. Specifically, 69% of the 100 most heavily traveled markets were entered by one or more airlines.[7]

□   **Fares.** Under regulation the Board generally set fares based on distance. But even among markets of a given distance, the cost of air service differed widely. For example, the volume of travel in a market affects costs. Moreover, the Board deliberately set fares below cost in the short-haul markets and above cost in the long-haul markets.

With increased fare flexibility, the fare structure has changed dramatically. For a sample of markets, Table 3 compares the average fares paid in 1980 with the Board's fare

---

[5] The Federal Aviation Administration classifies communities on the basis of their relative sizes. Large hubs have at least 1% of domestic passenger enplanements; medium hubs, .25 to .99%; small hubs, .05 to .24%; and nonhubs have less than .05%.

[6] Small communities in which commuter carriers have replaced larger airlines have, on average, experienced increases in the number of flights. Since the Deregulation Act was passed in October, 1978, trunk and local airlines have dropped service at 72 cities; those cities have experienced a 30% increase in flights. Though these communities no longer have the opportunity for online service for long-haul trips, commuters and larger airlines are developing interline agreements that offer commuter passengers some of the advantages of online service. For a further discussion of the Board's regulation of service to small communities as well as changes since deregulation, see Graham and Kaplan (1982).

[7] There was entry into 54% of the second 100 markets, and 35% of the smaller markets. These markets are ranked by origin-destination traffic volume.

TABLE 2 Herfindahl Indexes of Market Concentration* (May 1978 vs. May 1981)

Market Distance (in miles)	Top 100 Markets			Second 100 Markets			Sample of Smaller Markets		
	Number of Markets	1978 Herfindahl	1981 Herfindahl	Number of Markets	1978 Herfindahl	1981 Herfindahl	Number of Markets	1978 Herfindahl	1981 Herfindahl
Less Than 500	36	.40 (.13)	.36 (.13)	40	.54 (.17)	.44 (.17)	79	.75 (.29)	.66 (.27)
501 to 1000	26	.50 (.10)	.41 (.11)	31	.55 (.15)	.46 (.14)	25	.66 (.24)	.59 (.21)
1001 to 1500	17	.52 (.12)	.43 (.12)	12	.58 (.21)	.48 (.18)	11	.79 (.24)	.65 (.20)
1500+	17	.44 (.13)	.42 (.13)	15	.53 (.09)	.53 (.12)	6	.78 (.16)	.62 (.15)
Average of All Distances:	96	.46 (.13)	.40 (.13)	98	.55 (.16)	.46 (.16)	121	.74 (.27)	.64 (.25)

* Standard deviations in parentheses.
Source: Herfindahl indexes are based on each airlines' share of nonstop flights in a market as reported in the *Official Airline Guide*.

122 / THE BELL JOURNAL OF ECONOMICS

TABLE 3   Average Fares as a Percentage of DPFI Fare Formula Year Ending June 1981*

| | Market Size Category | | | | | |
| | Top 100 Markets | | Second 100 Markets | | Sample of Smaller Markets | |
Market Distance	Number of Markets	Fares	Number of Markets	Fares	Number of Markets	Fares
0–500 mi.	36	89 (20)	40	97 (24)	79	113 (22)
501–1000 mi.	26	98 (16)	31	96 (14)	25	101 (12)
1001–1500 mi.	17	82 (11)	12	89 (12)	11	97 (17)
1500+ mi.	17	66 (11)	15	84 (11)	6	91 (5)
Average of all Distances:	96	86 (20)	98	94 (19)	121	108 (21)

* Weighted average of all coach fares. Weights are based on the number of passengers. The average *DPFI* formula fare is the average of the three different formula fare levels effective during the period, weighted by the number of origin and destination passengers carried during the effective period of each fare level. Standard deviations are in parentheses.

Sources: Fare data are obtained from CAB, *Origin-Destination Survey of Airline Passenger Traffic*, Domestic Fares. Data are not published, but are retained in a CAB computerized data bank.

formula adjusted for inflation.[8] Of course, even when the industry was regulated, average fares in a market differed from the fares prescribed in the Board's distance-based formula (commonly referred to as the *DPFI* formula).[9] Average fares were sometimes less than *DPFI* coach fares because of the availability of discounts. Before the Super Saver fares, however, discounts did not generally exceed 25% and were offered to relatively few passengers. At the same time, local service carriers could charge 30% above the fare formula so that fares were generally higher than the formula fare in markets where local service carriers were the dominant ones.

In 1980, as expected, fares in small, short-haul markets were above the *DPFI* formula. Average fares were below the formula in the top 200 markets, and in smaller markets above 1,000 miles. Fares tended to decline as a percentage of the *DPFI* coach fares as distance and market density increased, with the top markets between 501 and 1,000 miles as the sole exception. Average fares varied widely around the *DPFI* coach fare, which suggests that airlines are exercising their fare flexibility to a considerable degree.

---

[8] Market fare data are not available prior to 1979; therefore, it is not possible to compare directly fares paid before and after deregulation.

Keeler (1981, p. 74) shows that in 1980, 58 of the largest 90 interstate markets had available unrestricted fares that were 15% or more below the standard CAB fare.

[9] The formula was developed in the *Domestic Passenger Fare Investigation*, U.S. Civil Aeronautics Board (1974). The *DPFI*, which was completed in 1974, made significant changes in the CAB's regulatory policies. In the *DPFI* the Board decreased the price of long-haul travel relative to short-haul travel, adopted a 55% load factor and seating density standards, and limited the degree to which airlines could use discount fares. The *DPFI* reduced, to some extent, airlines' incentives to engage in nonprice competition. Nevertheless, since the *DPFI* was based on industry average costs, it established fares that were substantially different from the cost of service in most markets. Because the Board based its fare policies on the *DPFI*, that formula provides a useful baseline for considering the average fare levels in the deregulated environment.

☐ **Load factor and equipment size.** There are economies of scale and economies of utilization in providing air service on a given route: airlines can reduce costs by operating larger aircraft at higher load factors. Passengers' demand for convenient service, however, generally requires carriers to operate more frequent flights, using smaller aircraft at lower load factors, than simple cost minimization dictates. This is especially true in short-haul markets, where surface transportation is quite competitive with air travel. Deregulation has given carriers the operating flexibility to choose the combination of fares, aircraft size, and load factor to maximize profits in each market.

Aircraft size and load factor will tend to be higher in markets where travelers place relatively little value on convenience; passengers in vacation markets, for example, are generally not very time sensitive.[10] In addition, heavily traveled routes should have larger aircraft and higher load factors because there are probably diminishing returns in terms of passenger's willingness to pay for increased convenience. As traffic increases, carriers will substitute larger aircraft and operate them at higher load factors rather than increase the number of flights proportionately. (Moreover, in large markets it is likely that a given level of convenience can be achieved with a higher load factor, because the law of large numbers will tend to smooth out the random fluctuations in demand.) Finally, longer haul markets will tend to have larger aircraft and higher load factors. The economies of larger aircraft are greatest in longer markets. Load factors will tend to rise because the cost of available capacity increases with distance, whereas there is no reason to expect that the typical traveler's willingness to pay for convenience will increase.

Table 4 relates load factor and equipment size to distance and density. Average aircraft size increases with market size. Also, for each density interval, average aircraft size increases with market distance. The relationship between load factor and distance and density is less clear. Nevertheless, a statistical analysis in the next section indicates that load factors do indeed increase with market distance and density.

Table 5 presents the load factor and equipment size for 32 long-haul markets which are classified according to whether they are tourist markets. Since travelers in tourist markets are by definition less time-sensitive, we would expect the demands for low cost service—large aircraft operated at higher load factors—to be greatest in these markets. Indeed, this table suggests that tourist markets have lower operating costs than do non-tourist markets.[11] Table 5 indicates that these cost savings contribute to lower fares in tourist markets. Such fare differentials were not permitted under regulation, and the fact that they have evolved under deregulation suggests that markets have become more efficient. In general, the pattern of fares, load factors, and aircraft sizes across markets are roughly consistent with market efficiency. The price and quality of service appear to vary by distance, density, and passenger time sensitivity in the way predicted by Douglas and Miller (1974).

3. Excess capacity hypothesis

■ The excess capacity hypothesis posits that regulated fares were too high in most markets, so that service competition led the airline industry to supply more than the economically efficient number of flights and seats. Moreover, the hypothesis implies that excess capacity would be more pronounced in some markets than others, because the structure of regulated fares did not match the structure of costs. Under this hypothesis, the pattern of load factors and equipment sizes under regulation should have differed from those just described in Tables 4 and 5. In this section, we develop tests of the excess

---

[10] For a discussion of these issues, see Douglas and Miller (1974). They examine the surplus maximizing solution to this choice problem. Our discussion is based on their analysis.

[11] We define tourist markets as those involving service to Florida, Hawaii, and Reno and Las Vegas, Nevada.

TABLE 4   Average Load Factor and Equipment Size (Available Seats per Flight), Year Ending June 30, 1981*

	Market Size Category								
	Top 100 Markets			Second 100 Markets			Sample of Smaller Markets		
Market Distance	Number of Markets	Load Factor	Average Equipment	Number of Markets	Load Factor	Average Equipment	Number of Markets	Load Factor	Average Equipment
0–500	36	59	130	40	57	126	79	55	108
		(5)	(20)		(5)	(28)		(11)	(20)
501–1000	26	57	146	31	58	133	25	56	125
		(3)	(21)		(4)	(17)		(6)	(24)
1001–1500	17	58	164	12	59	141	11	58	137
		(3)	(22)		(3)	(14)		(4)	(12)
1500+	17	63	269	15	54	214	6	56	216
		(7)	(61)		(5)	(62)		(2)	(62)
All Distance:	96	59	162	98	57	140	121	56	122
		(5)	(59)		(5)	(40)		(9)	(37)

* Standard deviations in parentheses.
Source: *Service Segment Data* (ER-586).

TABLE 5   Fares, Load Factors and Aircraft Size: Long-Haul Tourist Markets
              vs. Nontourist Markets, Year Ending June 1981

	Top 200 Markets		
	Number of Markets	Mean	Standard Deviation
Fares as Percent of *DPFI:*			
Nontourist Markets	27	75	12
Tourist Markets	5	56	5
Average Load Factor:			
Nontourist Markets	27	58	5
Tourist Markets	5	70	5
Average Seats per Aircraft:			
Nontourist Markets	27	240	59
Tourist Markets	5	308	58

Source: Fare data are obtained from CAB, *Origin-Destination Survey* of Airline Passenger Traffic, Domestic. Load factor and seating capacity data are obtained from CAB,
Service Segment Data, (ER-586).

capacity hypothesis based on the pattern of load factors observed before and after deregulation.

Under CAB fare regulation, the airlines chose the profit-maximizing level of convenience, given the fare. Consequently, the load factors in any given market depended
upon CAB policies as well as on the market characteristics described above.[12] *Ceteris
paribus,* load factors are expected to have been lower in markets where fares were set
high relative to costs. The CAB deliberately set fares higher than cost in the long-haul
markets and did not consider density or the value of convenience. Hence, in moving to
a competitive pricing regime, load factors should have risen most in long-haul markets
and in relatively dense markets.

The number of airlines serving the market could also be expected to affect load
factors under regulation. A monopolist would add flights only up to the point where the
added revenues from increased travel stimulated by the increase in convenience covered
the cost of the flight. But if several carriers were allowed in the market, each would also
perceive that added flights would draw traffic away from its competitors' flights. The
perceived payoff to adding flights increases as the number of airlines increases, so that
a greater expansion of capacity and lower load factors will result.

Under deregulation, increased emphasis on price competition and decreased emphasis on service competition should reduce the relationship between market structure
and load factor from the one that existed when the industry was regulated.

To test the excess capacity hypothesis, we compare the relationships between load
factor, distance, concentration and traffic volume observed in 1980 and 1976 with the
relationship reported by Douglas and Miller (1974) for 1969. The year 1976 provides a

---

[12] Douglas and Miller (1974), Panzar (1975), and Schmalensee (1977) have examined the comparative
static behavior of airlines under regulation. Panzar and Schmalensee provide explicit models of monopolistic
competition for predicting airline behavior. Airlines are assumed to choose the profit-maximizing capacity, given
the market fare. The models predict that with limited entry, profits will not be driven to zero by nonprice
competition. Whereas the earlier studies examine the case in which each airline's demand is assumed to be
proportional to its share of flights in the market, Schmalensee considers three general demand assumptions. He
shows that when the regulated fare is increased, there is a corresponding decrease in load factor. Profits may
rise, fall, or remain unchanged depending upon the exact form of the demand function. He also shows that
entry will reduce load factors and profits.

transitional observation because it comes after the *DPFI*, but before fare regulation was liberalized.

Using a sample of 324 markets, we estimated the same type of equation used by Douglas and Miller.[13] The main difference between our approach and that of Douglas and Miller is that instead of measuring concentration by the number of carriers, we use the Herfindahl index, based on carriers' shares of departures. This allows us to account for the fact that carriers' market shares may differ widely from each other. We estimate load factor equations for 1976 and 1980 by using ordinary least squares (OLS) and two stage least squares (2SLS). Use of 2SLS is suggested because the preceding discussion of density and service quality implies possible correlation between the density variable and the error term. High load factors reduce service quality and thereby reduce traffic.[14] Our results are presented in Table 6. The Herfindahl index was treated as exogenous in each case.

Equations (1) and (2) present the OLS and 2SLS coefficient estimates for 1980. They both show that load factor increases with distance, density, and concentration. The coefficients are all highly significant. The 1976 relationship is similar. In 1969, however, the distance coefficient is negative. Fitted values of load factor are plotted against distance in Figure 1.

Douglas and Miller interpreted the downward sloping load factor curve in 1969 as strong evidence that airlines were supplying excess capacity in potentially profitable long-haul markets. The estimated relationships in 1976 and 1980, in contrast, indicate that load factor rose with distance in these years and was higher than the 1969 load factor overall at each distance. This latter finding is particularly notable because 1980, like 1969, was a recession year in which demand for long-haul travel was hard hit.[15] These findings indicate that the CAB had imposed the wrong structure of fares in the late 1960s. They also suggest that the fare structure created in the *DPFI* helped mitigate the excess service competition caused by the mismatch between fares and costs in long-haul markets.

Load factors increase with market density in each of the three sample years. As noted above, the excess capacity hypothesis implies that if there were economies of scale at the

---

[13] Our sample of markets came from the top 200 markets ranked in terms of origin and destination traffic, in the year ending June 1978, and a random sample of 129 smaller markets. Fifteen of the top markets had insufficient data.

[14] In the 2SLS equation, we estimated the number of passengers by using data on population, income, and distance. Population and income data come from "Survey of Buying Power," *Sales and Marketing Magazine* (July 23, 1979). We used coach load factor from the Board's Service Segment Data (ER-586); Herfindahl indexes were derived from the November *Official Airline Guide*, in the various years. Generally, load factors during the periods under consideration were probably not high enough to have substantially affected traffic. In that case, OLS gives a reliable parameter estimate.

When both the Herfindahl index and the number of passengers were treated as endogenous, each of their coefficients doubled. (This is true in 1976 as well as in 1981.) We believe this reflects a high degree of collinearity between the systematic portion of Herfindahl and passengers, such that the two coefficients are not truly partial effects. While the correlation between passengers and Herfindahl is .56 in 1980, the correlation between the fitted values is .79. Although the relative magnitudes between 1976 and 1980 are consistent with the pattern reported in the text, they are far different from the 1969 estimates. Since we believe these results are not comparable with the 1969 results, we have reported the 2SLS estimates only for the case in which the number of passengers, and not the Herfindahl index, is endogenous. We performed specification tests similar to those described in footnote 26 below to test the exogeneity of the Herfindahl index in the 1980 equation; we found that we could not reject the hypothesis that the index was exogenous.

[15] It should be noted that in 1976 the economy was expanding rapidly after the recession of 1974 and 1975. In addition, there was considerable technological change between 1969 and 1976 involving the introduction of wide-bodied aircraft. On balance, this would be expected to cause load factors to fall in long-haul markets because the wide bodies were specifically designed for long-haul routes, and they offered many more seats per flight with reduced costs per seat. On the other hand, the rapid increases in fuel prices in 1973–1974 and again in 1979–1980 would have led to an increase in equilibrium load factors regardless of changes in regulatory policies.

TABLE 6   Equations Explaining Average Load Factors*

	Constant	ln *Distance*	ln *(Passengers Per Day)*	ln *(Herfindahl)*	$\bar{R}^2$
1980–1981 **(324 Observations):**					
(1) OLS	.130 (3.87)	.026 (5.09)	.045 (8.14)	.061 (4.37)	.33
(2) 2SLS	.056 (1.21)	.018 (2.81)	.068 (6.25)	.103 (4.66)	
1976 **(324 Observations):**					
(3) OLS	.123 (3.21)	.029 (5.88)	.047 (7.83)	.127 (8.20)	.29
(4) 2SLS	.042 (.77)	.025 (4.53)	.067 (5.87)	.162 (6.93)	
Douglas-Miller 1969 Estimates **(347 Observations):**				ln (number of carriers)	
		−.019 (−1.8)	.073 (7.0)	−.146 (−5.5)	.14
(5) OLS	.357				

* Herfindahl indexes are based on each airline's share of nonstop flights in a market as reported in the *Official Airline Guide.* Equation (5) is taken from Douglas-Miller (1974, p. 53). The *t*-statistics are in parentheses.

market level, load factors should have risen most in denser markets, *ceteris paribus,* as the result of deregulation. In our equations this would be reflected by a larger coefficient for the density variable in 1980. In fact, in the ordinary least squares regressions, the passenger volume coefficient for 1969 is larger than for either 1976 or 1980. In 1969, however, wide-bodied aircraft were not widely available, so that any economies of scale in serving high volume markets would have been much smaller than in subsequent years; therefore, the inducement for providing excess capacity in large markets was smaller in

FIGURE 1

LOAD FACTORS AND DISTANCE*

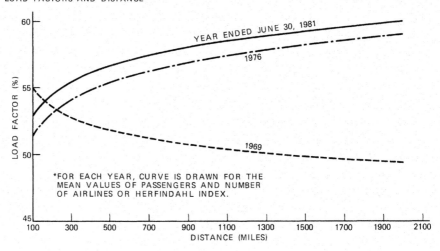

*FOR EACH YEAR, CURVE IS DRAWN FOR THE MEAN VALUES OF PASSENGERS AND NUMBER OF AIRLINES OR HERFINDAHL INDEX.

1969. (Wide bodies accounted for about 35% of trunk airline capacity in 1976 and 1980.) Comparing 1976 with 1980, we find that the density coefficients are virtually identical. The implications of the excess capacity hypothesis for the effects of density appear not to be observed in this sample of markets.

In 1980, under deregulation, market concentration had a smaller effect on load factor than it had (before deregulation) in either 1976 or 1969. This is true whether the OLS or the 2SLS estimates are used. To illustrate, suppose the number of equally sized firms in a market increases from two to three. Our OLS estimate of the Herfindahl coefficient for 1980 predicts a drop in load factor of 2.1 points. The 1976 OLS estimate is 7 points, and the Douglas and Miller coefficient on the number of firms predicts a 7.3 point drop in load factor. Using the 2SLS estimates (available only for 1980 and 1976), we find that the estimated 1980 effect is a 3.4 point drop as compared with a 5.5 point decrease in the 1976 equation. These results support the hypothesis that carriers engaged in service competition under regulation and that this has been substantially replaced by price competition since deregulation. Figure 1 shows that the 1980 load factor curve lies everywhere above the 1976 and the 1969 curves.

Although the higher load factors in 1980 imply that average convenience has deteriorated, because flights are less accessible when load factors are higher, there is evidence that the quality of service has not deteriorated for time-sensitive passengers—those who value high-convenience service most. Carriers have increasingly moved to peak-load pricing systems; this shifts some travelers to offpeak flights, thereby increasing time-sensitive passengers' access to peak flights. Other airlines achieve the same effects with reservation systems that set aside a number of seats on each flight for full-fare passengers, thereby providing these time-sensitive passengers with low load-factor, high-access service. Remaining seats are sold at a discount to passengers who usually must satisfy advance purchase or minimum stay requirements, which are often chosen to take account of the carrier's system load. The net effect of both pricing systems is to provide high quality service to those who value it most. Therefore, the quality of service for time-sensitive passengers has not fallen so much as the rise in average load factors would seem to suggest; conceivably, it has not fallen at all.

4. The potential competition hypothesis: testing for market power

■ To estimate the effect of market concentration on fares, we begin by developing a model of the equilibrium average fare in an airline market. This model explains the equilibrium fare by using the variables discussed above (distance, concentration, traffic volume, and travelers' valuations of time) as well as an airline-specific variable related to airlines' cost structures. Our test of the potential competition hypothesis is based on the extent to which firms in highly concentrated markets set fares above the levels prevailing in less concentrated, but otherwise similar markets.

□ The model. As we have already observed, the cost of air service depends on a market's distance and traffic volume, as well as on the level of convenience demanded. A number of other variables affect the costs of serving a market. First, the opportunity cost of serving a market depends on whether the market involves one of the four airports at which the FAA constrains access: Chicago O'Hare, Washington National, and New York's Kennedy and LaGuardia airports. To serve one market that includes a slot-constrained airport is necessarily to forego serving another profitable market that also involves that airport.[16]

---

[16] Service to New York City includes service to Newark International Airport, which is not slot-constrained. The CAB O&D Survey, however, does not distinguish among service to the New York City airports and thus, neither do we. Service to Washington National is restricted to cities that are less than 650 miles away and to

Dummy variables are included to account for this effect. Also, costs are affected by a host of airline-specific factors. There is a fairly clear difference in costs between newly certificated carriers and the trunk and local airlines with the new carriers' costs being lower. This will reduce average fares in markets where the new carriers are present.

Thus, we can write the long-run marginal cost of providing a particular level of service convenience as follows:

$$LRMC = C(D, Q, LF, NYC, CHI, WAS, NEWCERT), \tag{6}$$

where

D = distance
Q = number of passengers
LF = load factor
$NEWCERT$ = presence of newly certificated carrier
NYC = New York City dummy
CHI = Chicago dummy
WAS = Washington dummy.

Quantity demanded depends on price and service quality, which in our simple model depend upon load factor and flight frequency. Demand for service quality derives from a desire to minimize the difference between a passenger's desired and actual arrival time; it is related to his time sensitivity. Time sensitivity cannot be measured directly, but two proxies are readily available. First, wage rates reflect consumers' marginal valuations of time. Therefore, per capita incomes of the cities served by a market provide a proxy for the time sensitivities of passengers traveling between those cities. Second, we have already noted that passengers in tourist markets are less time-sensitive. Thus, a tourist-market variable provides another proxy for the demand for service convenience. These variables will affect the equilibrium level of service quality and, hence, the equilibrium fare. The reduced form expression for service quality is

Service Quality $\equiv S = S(TOURIST, INC,$ other exogenous variables)
$TOURIST$ = 1 for markets involving service to Florida, Hawaii, Las Vegas, Reno and 0 otherwise;
INC = product of per capita income in the two cities at the ends of the markets.

The ability of carriers to mark fares up above $LRMC$ is a function of the price elasticities of demand faced by incumbent firms. Demand elasticities are smaller if there are entry barriers and the market is highly concentrated. If there are no entry barriers, and entry can be accomplished quickly and cheaply, firm demand is highly elastic regardless of market concentration. The presence of entry barriers means that the elasticity of firm demand will fall as market concentration increases.

Since surface transportation is less attractive as distance increases, fare markups over $LRMC$ presumably can increase with distance, at least up to a point. In very long distance markets, however, passengers have many routing and connecting possibilities open to them. Thus, the theoretical net effect of distance on markup is unclear. Finally, firms' price elasticities of demand should be higher in tourist markets than in nontourist markets, because tourists are often willing to use alternate modes of transportation or even to

---

certain grandfathered cities. Nevertheless, many long-haul markets receive substantial amounts of either one-stop or connecting service from National Airport in addition to nonstop service to other airports in the metropolitan area. We, therefore, do not distinguish between cities that are served nonstop from National and those that are not.

change destination if air fares rise. For nontourist travelers, the options are often limited to telecommunications or the mail.

Summarizing this discussion, the equilibrium market price can be written as[17]

$$P = LRMC \times MARKUP,$$

where *MARKUP* depends on barriers to entry, concentration, the competitiveness of ground transportation, and whether a market is a tourist market. Thus *MARKUP* can be written as a function $M(H, D, Tourist)$ where $\partial M/\partial H > 0$ if there exist any entry barriers.

Substituting the reduced form expression for *S* into the function for *LRMC*, we have the following price equation:

$$P = LRMC \times M(H, D, Tourist)$$

$$= P(D, Q, H, NYC, CHI, WAS, TOURIST, INC, NEWCERT). \qquad (7)$$

We wish to estimate the magnitude of $\partial P/\partial H$ and to test whether it is significantly greater than zero. On the right-hand side of (2), *Q* and *H* may be considered endogenous variables. Therefore, we provide two-stage least squares estimates as well as ordinary least squares estimates of the price equation.

☐ **Data and measurement of variables.** Our model is most applicable to large markets where there typically is a substantial amount of local traffic. It does not explicitly treat the phenomenon of networking, i.e., the joint production of air service in a number of markets. Hence, we limit our estimates of the model to a sample of 194 of the most heavily traveled markets.[18]

We measure price by average yield (coach fare per revenue passenger mile) for local coach passengers (including discount and normal economy). Yields are obtained from the CAB's *Passenger Origin and Destination Survey* and cover nonstop, one-stop, and multistop traffic. The other variables reflect only nonstop service. This should not cause significant measurement error, because the markets in our sample are large and passengers in these markets generally use nonstop service. Density is measured by the total number of passengers transported in the market as reported in the CAB's Service Segment Data. Distance is the nonstop distance reported in the *Origin and Destination Survey.* The Herfindahl index is based on departure shares and is derived from the *Official Airline Guide.*[19] Income is obtained from a survey of buying power published in July, 1979.[20]

The model is estimated using data for the fourth quarter of 1980 and the second

---

[17] The fare equation arrived at below can be thought of as arising from a Cournot equilibrium in which firms choose price, number of flights, load factor, and capacity. Let *b* equal the constant marginal operating cost and *B* the marginal capacity cost, which we assume constant in our sample of 194 large markets. Then in Cournot equilibrium price is given by

$$P = \frac{\eta}{\eta - 1}\left(b + \frac{B}{LF}\right),$$

where LF = load factor and η is the firm-specific price elasticity of demand. Substitute the reduced form load factor equation into this expression, define $\eta/(\eta - 1)$ as the *MARKUP*, and the resulting expression motivates our estimating equation.

[18] See, however, Sibley, Jollie *et al.* (1982) for a discussion of networking and entry barriers. Our results are consistent with those obtained for a much larger sample of markets. See Graham and Kaplan (1982).

[19] In regressions not reported here, we also estimated the fare equation by using Herfindahl indexes based on true *O&D* traffic in each market and on online feed traffic in each market. The results were similar to those reported here.

[20] "Survey of Buying Power," *Sales and Marketing Management Magazine* (July 23, 1979). The population data also came from this publication. The income variable used is disposable income divided by the number of households in each metropolitan area. In estimating the equations, we divided the computed income variable by 10^9.

quarter of 1981.[21] Table 7 presents the sample means and standard deviations of the variables for the two quarters.

□ **Findings.** The fare equation was estimated in the semilog form, with interaction or polynomial terms included for distance, density, and the Herfindahl index. This function is fairly flexible, and results in an estimating equation in which terms involving H are multiplicatively separable from other variables, as suggested by equation (7). Ordinary-least squares estimates are reported in Table 8; Table 9 reports the estimates using two-stage least squares.[22] The results of the OLS and 2SLS estimates are quite similar.

As we shall discuss below, the presence of newly certificated carriers apparently has a substantial impact on fares in the markets they serve. Therefore, to determine the robustness of our estimates, we also estimated the model for a subsample of markets where these airlines do not operate. These regressions also appear in Tables 8 and 9.

TABLE 7   **Sample Means and Standard Deviations**

	1980—Fourth Quarter		1981—Second Quarter	
	Mean	S.D.	Mean	S.D.
Yield	.170	.070	.177	.072
Herfindahl	.467	.160	.465	.160
Distance*	868	669	868	669
Density*	170379	167270	186139	183122
Tourist	.160		.160	
Newly Certificated Carrier	.201		.247	

* For purposes of scaling the estimated coefficients, distance is entered in the regressions in units of 1,000s of miles and density is entered in millions of passengers.

---

[21] A high degree of fare flexibility was not introduced until May, 1980. The PATCO strike and subsequent firing of air traffic controllers in the summer of 1981 probably distorted traffic and fare data. Hence, our two sample periods, which lie between these major events, are as representative of an unregulated environment as any data presently available.

[22] Our 2SLS estimates are based on the following four-equation model, which can be derived from the Cournot model described in footnote 17 above:

$$Fare = F(D, Q, S, TOURIST, INC, NYC, CHI, WAS, NEWCERT, H) + u_1 \qquad \text{(i)}$$
$$Q = Q(D, FARE, S, POP, INC) + u_2 \qquad \text{(ii)}$$
$$H = H(D, Q, S, LHUB, SHUB, BAL, FLL) + u_3 \qquad \text{(iii)}$$
$$S = S(FARE, Q, H, D, INC, TOURIST) + u_4. \qquad \text{(iv)}$$

The variables that have not yet been defined are:

POP = the product population in city A and city B;
$LHUB$ = 1 if the endpoints of a market are both large hubs, and 0 otherwise;
$SHUB$ = 1 if either of the endpoints of a market is a small hub, and 0 otherwise;
BAL = 1 if a market serves Baltimore, and 0 otherwise;
FLL = 1 if a market served Fort Lauderdale, and 0 otherwise.

Since we are primarily interested in fares, we have in effect substituted for S in equations (i)–(iii) and have not estimated equation (iv).

The specification of the H equation derives from assuming that concentration depends on the carriers' route networks, of which the market in question is part. For this purpose, it is important to know whether a market involves a large hub, a small hub, or a satellite airport. The $LHUB$ and $SHUB$ variables are intended to reflect the fact that concentration will tend to be lower in markets which have many airlines serving at the end points, and concentration should tend to be higher when few airlines operate at the endpoints. Baltimore and Fort Lauderdale are satellite airports operating near major hubs. Typically their markets were more concentrated than those of other similar airports, and hence dummies were included to account for the differences.

TABLE 8 OLS Fare Equations for Semilog Specification, Dependent Variable = ln (Average Yield)*

	C	D	D²	D³	QD	Q	H	H²	NYC	CHI	WAS	TOURIST	INC	NEWCERT	R̄²
All Markets							*Fourth Quarter 1980*								
(194 Observations):															
(8)	−1.405	−2.02	1.08	−.206	.035	−.155	.961	−.718	.131	.120	.076	−.090	.608	−.141	.84
	(−10.33)	(−11.18)	(6.69)	(−5.10)	(.38)	(−1.54)	(3.20)	(−2.98)	(4.52)	(3.64)	(1.60)	(−2.78)	(2.19)	(−4.03)	
Markets without Newly Certificated Airlines															
(155 Observations):															
(9)	−1.419	−2.15	1.19	−.233	−.061	−.040	1.189	−.874	.076	.061	.025	−.092	.626		.88
	(−9.25)	(−12.23)	(7.69)	(−6.02)	(−.32)	(−.21)	(3.94)	(−3.75)	(2.75)	(1.95)	(.54)	(−2.76)	(2.20)		
All Markets							*Second Quarter 1981*								
(194 Observations):															
(10)	−1.197	−1.76	.844	−.154	.119	−.155	.288	−.133	.112	.133	.058	−.104	.513	−.220	.83
	(−9.03)	(−9.56)	(5.16)	(−3.77)	(1.38)	(−1.70)	(.97)	(−.56)	(3.81)	(3.98)	(1.19)	(−3.15)	(1.81)	(−6.78)	
Markets without Newly Certificated Airlines															
(146 Observations):															
(11)	−1.161	−1.92	.964	−.182	.092	−.325	.630	−.393	.073	.074	−.010	−.137	.478		.83
	(−7.68)	(−10.58)	(5.95)	(−4.50)	(.45)	(−1.39)	(2.09)	(−1.68)	(2.39)	(2.31)	(−.20)	(−3.87)	(1.62)		

* The *t*-statistics are in parentheses.

TABLE 9 2SLS Fare Equations for Semilog Specification, Dependent Variable = ln (Average Yield)*

	C	D	D^2	D^3	$\hat{Q}D$	$\hat{Q}$	H / H^2	NYC	CHI	WAS	$TOURIST$	INC	$NEWCERT$
Fourth Quarter 1980													
All Markets (194 Observations):													
(12)	-1.538	-2.02	1.11	-.213	-.160	.516	1.311	.109	.126	.089	-.090	.353	-.185
	(-9.54)	(-9.72)	(6.00)	(-4.59)	(-1.16)	(1.89)	(3.59)	(3.19)	(3.42)	(1.65)	(-2.46)	(1.07)	(-4.31)
							H^2 -.886						
							(-3.18)						
(13)	-1.072	-1.97	1.08	-.209	-.195	-.406	-.462	.104	.112	.083	-.109	.322	-.217
	(-2.80)	(-8.54)	(5.28)	(-4.07)	(-1.22)	(-1.20)	(-.36)	(2.52)	(2.48)	(1.44)	(-2.77)	(.91)	(-3.64)
							H^2 .734						
							(.60)						
Markets without Newly Certificated Airlines (155 Observations):													
(14)	-1.631	-2.11	1.19	-.234	-.306	.686	1.536	.061	.062	.021	-.098	.546	
	(-8.30)	(-10.89)	(7.30)	(-5.78)	(-.98)	(1.56)	(4.14)	(2.02)	(1.89)	(.45)	(-2.79)	(1.83)	
							H^2 -1.038						
							(-3.96)						
Second Quarter 1981													
All Markets (194 Observations):													
(15)	-1.340	-1.82	.895	-.165	.065	.293	.770	.094	.140	.068	-.091	.339	-.259
	(-8.58)	(-8.95)	(5.00)	(-3.68)	(.56)	(1.26)	(2.03)	(2.89)	(3.88)	(1.29)	(-2.54)	(1.07)	(-6.69)
							$\hat{H}^2$ -.427						
							(-1.49)						
(16)	-.874	-1.71	.820	-.150	.046	.173	-1.268	.087	.126	.061	-.110	.343	-.274
	(-2.15)	(-6.55)	(3.60)	(-2.64)	(.29)	(.47)	(-.90)	(1.84)	(2.60)	(.92)	(-2.48)	(.87)	(-5.01)
							$\hat{H}^2$ 1.648						
							(1.24)						
Markets without Newly Certificated Airlines (146 Observations):													
(17)	-1.501	-2.03	1.06	-.200	-.104	.968	1.261	.076	.077	.034	-.129	.354	
	(-6.01)	(-8.41)	(5.31)	(-4.08)	(-.23)	(1.34)	(2.59)	(2.03)	(1.96)	(.53)	(-2.96)	(.97)	
							H^2 -.703						
							(-2.12)						

* $\hat{Q}$ and $\hat{H}$ were fitted using OLS reduced form equations and the fitted values were used to calculate $\hat{Q}D$ and $\hat{H}^2$. These fitted values were then used to obtain OLS estimates of the fare equation. The fare equations' residuals and coefficient standard errors were adjusted as specified in Maddala (1977, p. 239). The numbers in the parentheses are the adjusted t-statistics.

The estimated parameters generally conform with our expectations, and typically are statistically significant. The OLS equations have $\bar{R}^2$'s ranging from .83 to .88, indicating that the equations explain a large share of the variation in the average fare per mile. The coefficients of distance are all highly significant. The average fare per mile declines over a broad range up to about 1,000 miles, and then remains relatively flat until about 2,000 miles, where it declines again.[23] Density, however, has a small and insignificant effect on fares. In 1981 it is positive in the 2SLS equations, though it is negative in the OLS specifications. Although we expected market density to influence fares, this regression finding is consistent with the results in Table 3, which showed that, except for markets of 1,500 miles or more, there were not substantial differences between fares in the top 100 and the second 100 markets.

As expected, fares are related to the passengers' value of time. The coefficient of *TOURIST* is consistently negative and significant, and indicates that fares in tourist markets are approximately 10% lower than fares in other markets. The coefficient *INC* is positive, as predicted, though it is significant only in the OLS estimates for 1980 (equations (8) and (9)).

Fares in markets served by the slot-constrained airports tend to be higher; except for Washington, the coefficients are significantly positive. For the sample that excludes markets served by newly certificated carriers, the coefficients of the slot dummies all decline. This reflects the fact that a substantial proportion of the top 200 markets involving these airports is served by newly certificated airlines.

The coefficients of *NEWCERT* show that average fares in markets served by newly certificated carriers were 19% lower in 1980 (equation (12)) and 26% lower in 1981 (equation (15)).[24] The estimated effect of *NEWCERT* was four percentage points less in the comparable OLS equations. The sharp jump in the coefficient of *NEWCERT* between 1980 and 1981 probably reflects the fact that the newly certificated airlines' share of traffic grew between the two periods, as well as the fact that the larger established airlines increasingly cut fares to meet the competition from these new, lower cost airlines.

We estimated the fare equation by assuming first that the Herfindahl index and the error term were uncorrelated and then that they were correlated. When H (and H^2) are treated as exogenous but density is endogenous, the coefficient of H is positive, that of H^2 is negative, and both tend to be significant (equations (12), (14), (15), and (17)). The results are roughly similar for the OLS equations (equations (8)–(11)), except that the OLS regression for the second quarter of 1981 yields insignificant coefficients for H and H^2 (equation (10)). This overall uniformity in the effect of H holds for both the full sample and the subsample with *NEWCERT* markets excluded.

When H and H^2 are considered endogenous variables, the point estimates often switch signs, and the estimates become insignificant (equations (13) and (16)).[25] We conducted specification tests to determine whether H (and H^2) are correlated with the error term in the fare equation. The test results suggest that H is not significantly correlated with the error term of the fare equation, and thus the specification treating them as exogenous is appropriate.[26]

---

[23] The B-727-200, the most widely used aircraft in the industry, is well suited for markets of about 1,500 miles, but begins to operate at a cost penalty in longer haul markets. Larger, wide-bodied aircraft are best suited for use in dense, longer haul markets. Thus, the predicted relation between average fare and distance is consistent with the existing fleet mix.

[24] Since we do not have data on the fares of Midway in 1980 and People Express in 1981, the true effect of the *NEWCERTS* is undoubtedly greater.

[25] An *F*-test of the joint significance of these variables indicates that the total effect of the Herfindahl index is not statistically different from zero in equations (13) and (16).

[26] Two different tests of the endogeneity of H and H^2 were tried. The first was proposed by Revankar (1978), the second by Hausman (1978). Nakamura and Nakamura (1981) have shown that Hausman's test is equivalent to Wu's proposed T_2 test. See Wu (1973, 1974).

The fact that the Herfindahl index may be treated as exogenous may be due in part to the fact that regulation determined the broad outlines of carriers' route networks and that changes under deregulation have not removed the CAB's stamp on the networks. Alternatively, this finding may reflect the fact that airlines choose routes on the basis of how they fit entire networks of routes so that concentration in the city pair market is mainly determined by the networking characteristics of the market itself. This suggests that the network, rather than the city-pair concentration, be thought of as endogenous. For these reasons, we shall rely on the fare equations in which the Herfindahl index is treated as exogenous.

Our results show that the effect of concentration on fares is not uniform. As Figure 2 shows, the relation between fares and H is increasing and concave in the relevant region of H. This suggests that the effects of increased concentration are small for markets with medium to high levels of concentration. When the Herfindahl index reaches .5 or so, the percentage increase in fares that results from a .1 rise in H is very small.

Overall, the model yields a pattern of results that is quite plausible and robust. With the exception of market density, which has no consistent or statistically significant effect, the estimated effects of the variables agree with our expectations. Several interesting issues are touched upon by these results. First, we find that markets serving the slot-constrained

FIGURE 2

FARES AND MARKET CONCENTRATION*

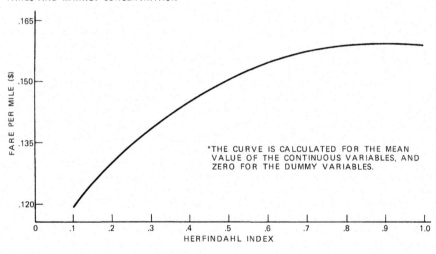

*THE CURVE IS CALCULATED FOR THE MEAN VALUE OF THE CONTINUOUS VARIABLES, AND ZERO FOR THE DUMMY VARIABLES.

Let

$$H = \pi_{11}X_1 + \pi_{12}X_2 + v_1$$

$$H^2 = \pi_{21}X_1 + \pi_{22}X_2 + v_2$$

be the reduced form equations for Herfindahl and Herfindahl squared. X_1 is the vector of X's that appear in the fare structural equation. In Revankar's test, the variables $T_1 = \pi_{12}X_2$ and $T_2 = \pi_{22}X_2$ (where the π are reduced form estimates) are entered into the fare equation and their joint significance is tested. The $F(2, 180)$ for this test was 2.64 in 1980 and 1.51 in 1981; thus we cannot reject the hypothesis that H and H^2 are exogenous. In Hausman's test the fitted values $\hat{H}$ and $\hat{H}^2$ are entered into the fare equation, along with H and H^2. The $F(2, 180)$ for the joint significance of three variables is 4.90 in 1980 and 2.57 in 1981; thus we reject the hypothesis of exogeneity in 1980 but not in 1981. We conclude that the weight of the evidence argues that H should be treated as an exogenous variable.

We found it impossible to explain more than about 25% of the variation in the Herfindahl index. A study of the determinants of market concentration in the airlines would be a useful topic for future research.

airports in New York and Chicago have higher fares. Second, our estimates suggest that airlines tailor operations and fares in a market to reflect travelers' valuations of time. Third, market concentration appears to have a positive impact on fares in the relatively unconcentrated markets, but not much incremental effect for markets with a Herfindahl index above .5 or so. Finally, the newly certificated airlines are producing lower fares in the markets they serve.

5. The new entrants

■ Since the passage of the Airline Deregulation Act, a dozen new carriers have begun scheduled interstate service and even more have applied for certification. Some are former intrastate carriers, others are former charter carriers, and seven are new enterprises. The operations of these carriers are significantly different from those of the formerly regulated carriers, and their rapid growth suggests that they will have far reaching effects on the industry.

The new entrants tend to offer fewer amenities and higher seating densities than the formerly regulated carriers. The most striking difference between the new entrants and the incumbents, however, is their cost structure. The new entrants generally pay lower wages and have much less restrictive work rules. For example, pilots at Southwest, a former intrastate carrier, average more than 50% more flying hours per month than pilots of the formerly regulated carriers. Moreover, the new entrants are less likely to have labor contracts that prohibit cross utilization of employees as, for example, using baggage handlers to load in-flight meals.

For the year ending June, 1981, Southwest's costs of operating a B-737 in a 200-mile segment are estimated to have been much less than the cost of two formerly regulated carriers who operated the same equipment, United and Piedmont. (See Table 10.) A major part of the difference between Piedmont's and United's cost of operating a B-737 stemmed from a union contract which required United to use a three-man cockpit crew. Piedmont and Southwest were able to use two-man crews; in the Fall of 1981 United renegotiated its labor contract so it too now uses a two-man crew.

In 1981 the new entrants accounted for 6.9% of the domestic traffic (as measured in revenue-passenger-miles), and they were the most rapidly growing segment of the

TABLE 10   Comparison of Airline Costs of Operating
               B-737-200 over a 200-Mile Market*

Cost Category	Southwest	Piedmont	United
Operating and Aircraft Service			
Expense	1,345	1,720	2,144
Passenger Expense	273	713	659
Reservations, Sales and			
Advertising Overhead	135	403	508
Other	107	108	302
Fully Allocated Costs	1,860	2,944	3,613

* Estimates were derived from the CAB, "Domestic Fare Structure Costing Program, Version 6, Update." Data are for 12 months ending June 30, 1981. For all three airlines, we valued the aircraft at the used aircraft price as of January 1, 1981, and assumed that the average capital cost was 14%. United's stock of B-737-200s is relatively old; hence, their maintenance cost was high. We, therefore, assumed that United's maintenance costs were equal to their (lower) expense on a B-727-200, a larger, and typically more costly aircraft to maintain. This expense was comparable to Piedmont's maintenance expense for the B-737-200.

industry. In response to the competition posed by these carriers, the established airlines, as evidenced by United's agreement with its pilots, are taking steps to pare their costs.

6. Concluding remarks

■ Our analysis, which is based on the two quarters of available data, shows that in several important respects the airline industry appears to be evolving in the ways economists predicted it would. Load factors have risen. Market characteristics, such as distance and the demand for convenient service, explain a large share of the variation in fares across markets in ways which are broadly consistent with market efficiency criteria. Competition from newly formed airlines has had a substantial effect on fares. On the other hand, fares seem to be positively related to concentration, thereby indicating that potential competition is not strong enough at present to eliminate all attempts to raise price in concentrated markets.

It is tempting to ask whether the evidence reported in this article is consistent with the assertion that airline markets are perfectly contestable, as suggested in recent work by Bailey and Panzar (1981) and Baumol, Panzar, and Willig (1982).

This issue can be viewed from two perspectives. First, do airline markets display characteristics which are favorable to contestability? Second, is behavior in airline markets consistent with that implied by contestability?

Two factors have been proposed as features favoring contestability: the absence of sunk costs and an expectation by prospective entrants that incumbents' prices will not change in response to entry. It is frequently argued that sunk costs of entry are low in airline markets because capital is extremely mobile. Although capital may be highly mobile, other sunk costs may exist. In many cases, passengers exhibit a preference for incumbent carriers' flights because incumbents' schedules and service reliability are better known than the entrants' until the latter have been in the market for a while. In addition, price rigidity by incumbent firms is not characteristic of the deregulated airline industry. It is commonplace for incumbent carriers to announce publicly that they will match the fares of any entrants.

The literature on contestability does not provide an explicit way of empirically determining whether a market is contestable. Hence, it is not entirely clear whether our empirical results are consistent with what one would expect to observe in a contestable market. In the simplest, single homogeneous product case, Baumol, Panzar, and Willig (1982, ch. 2) show that in a perfectly contestable market the only effect that concentration has on price is that a monopoly market may have a higher price than one served by two or more firms. (Increasing the number of firms beyond two has no additional effect on price.) But even this effect is absent when one corrects for market size, as we do in our regressions. Thus, our finding that the Herfindahl index has a positive and significant effect on fares is inconsistent with this simplest version of the contestability hypothesis.[27]

References

BAILEY, E.E. AND PANZAR, J. "The Contestability of Airline Markets During the Transition to Deregulation." *Law and Contemporary Problems*, Vol. 44 (Winter 1981), pp. 125–145.

BAUMOL, W., PANZAR, J., AND WILLIG, R. *Contestable Markets and the Theory Industry Structure*. San Diego: Harcourt, Brace, Jovanovich, 1982.

[27] It should be pointed out, however, that a major tenet of the contestability model is that market structure is determined endogenously, along with price and quantity. Equations (13) and (16) incorporate this endogeneity of market structure. They present 2SLS estimates of the H and H^2 coefficients. If markets are dense enough that economies of equipment size are exhausted, however, as they probably are in our sample of 194 large markets, concentration is not necessarily correlated with the error term of the fare equations. If it is not, then the 2SLS estimates in equations (13) and (16) may be adversely affected by our inability to predict H and H^2 well in the first stage.

138 / THE BELL JOURNAL OF ECONOMICS

CARLTON, D., LANDES, W., AND POSNER, R. "Benefits and Costs of Airline Mergers: A Case Study." *Bell Journal of Economics*, Vol. 11 (Spring 1980), pp. 65–83.

CAVES, R.E. *Air Transport and Its Regulators*. Cambridge: Harvard University Press, 1962.

DEMSETZ, H. "Industry Structure, Market Rivalry and Public Policy." *Journal of Law and Economics*, Vol. 16 (April 1973), pp. 1–10.

DORMAN, G. "Air Service to Small Communities after Airline Deregulation." *NERA Topics*. New York: National Economic Research Associates, Inc., 1982.

DOUGLAS, G. AND MILLER, J. *Economic Regulation of Domestic Air Transport*. Washington, D.C.: Brookings Institution, 1974.

FRANK, R.R. "Is the Current Air Fare Structure Discriminatory?" Washington, D.C.: U.S. Civil Aeronautics Board Memorandum, 1980.

GRAHAM, D.R. AND KAPLAN, D.P. "Competition and the Airlines: An Evaluation of Deregulation." Staff Report of Office of Economic Analysis. Washington, D.C.: U.S. Civil Aeronautics Board, 1982.

HAUSMAN, J.A. "Specification Tests in Econometrics." *Econometrica*, Vol. 46 (November 1978), pp. 1251–1271.

JORDAN, W. *Airline Regulation in America*. Baltimore: John Hopkins Press, 1970.

KEELER, T. "Airline Regulation and Market Performance." *Bell Journal of Economics and Management Science*, Vol. 3 (Autumn 1972), pp. 399–424.

LEVINE, M. "Is Regulation Necessary? California Air Transportation and National Regulatory Policy." *Yale Law Journal*, Vol. 74 (July 1965), pp. 1416–1447.

MACAVOY, P. AND SNOW, J., EDS. *Regulation of Passenger Fares and Competition among the Airlines*. Washington, D.C.: American Enterprise Institute, 1977.

MADDALA, G.S. *Econometrics*. New York: McGraw-Hill, 1977.

NAKAMURA, A. AND NAKAMURA, M. "On the Relationships among Several Specification Error Tests Presented by Durbin, Wu, and Hausman." *Econometrica*, Vol. 49 (November 1981), pp. 1583–1588.

PANZAR, J. "Regulation, Service Quality, and Market Performance: A Model of Airline Rivalry." Ph.D. dissertation, Stanford University, 1975.

———. "Regulation, Deregulation, and Economic Efficiency: The Case of the CAB." *American Economic Review*, Vol. 70 (May 1980), pp. 311–315.

PELTZMAN, S. "The Gains and Losses from Industrial Concentration." *Journal of Law and Economics*, Vol. 20 (October 1977), pp. 229–263.

PULSIFER, R. *et al.* "Report of the CAB Special Staff on Regulatory Reform." Washington, D.C.: U.S. Civil Aeronautics Board, 1975.

REVANKAR, N.S. "Asymptotic Relative Efficiency Analysis of Certain Tests of Independence in Structural Systems." *International Economic Review*, Vol. 19 (February 1978), pp. 165–179.

——— AND HARTLEY, M.J. "An Independence Test and Conditional Unbiased Predictions in the Context of Simultaneous Equation Systems." *International Economic Review*, Vol. 14 (October 1973), pp. 625–631.

SCHERER, F.M. *Industrial Market Structure and Economic Performance*, 2nd ed. Chicago: Rand McNally, 1980.

SCHMALENSEE, R. "Comparative Static Properties of Regulated Airline Oligopolies." *Bell Journal of Economics*, Vol. 8 (Autumn 1977), pp. 565–576.

SIBLEY, D.S. AND JOLLIE, S.B. "Antitrust Policy for the Aviation Industry, Report of the Civil Aeronautics Board." Washington, D.C.: U.S. Civil Aeronautics Board, 1982.

U.S. CIVIL AERONAUTICS BOARD. *Domestic Passenger Fare Investigation*. CAB Reports, Special Volume. Washington, D.C.: U.S. Government Printing Office, 1974.

U.S. SENATE, COMMITTEE ON THE JUDICIARY. "CAB Practices and Procedures." Report of the Subcommittee on Administrative Practice and Procedure. Washington, D.C.: U.S. Government Printing Office, 1975.

WU, D.-M. "Alternative Tests of Independence between Stochastic Regressors and Disturbances." *Econometrica*, Vol. 41 (July 1973), pp. 733–750.

———. "Alternative Tests of Independence between Stochastic Regressors and Disturbances: Finite Sample Results." *Econometrica*, Vol. 42 (May 1974), pp. 529–546.

15

Liberalisation and efficiency in international air transport

Vicente Inglada, Belen Rey, Ana Rodríguez-Alvarez, Pablo Coto-Millan

Abstract

This paper sets out to compare the economic and technical efficiency of international air transport companies, within the new liberalisation framework that characterises the period of 1996–2000. For this purpose, two stochastic frontiers are estimated, one for cost function, the other for production function. From these estimations we obtain indexes for, respectively, economic and technical efficiency. Our evidence suggests that the benefits of increasing competition in terms of efficiency, is being large for the Asian companies.
© 2005 Elsevier Ltd. All rights reserved.

Keywords: Efficiency; Deregulation; Air transport; Stochastic frontier

1. Introduction

International air transport has gone through profound changes since the end of the 1970s. Air transport in the United States became totally liberalised in 1978, while Europe embarked on the same road 10 years later, the full process being completed in 1997.[1] Where the Asian countries are

---

[1] A detailed review of the liberalisation process in Europe is to be found in Rey (2000).

96   *V. Inglada et al. / Transportation Research Part A 40 (2006) 95–105*

concerned, today's domestic markets continue to be very fragmented, these countries still being bound by very restrictive bilateral agreements (Oum and Lee, 2002). However, the threat posed by the creation of international alliances between American and European companies is pushing these countries towards air transport liberalisation. In Chin (1997), we observe that one of the first measures was the entry onto the market of "second-level" companies,[2] thereby increasing competition within the domestic markets, to the detriment of the traditional national companies, which had been operating as large monopolies.

As for company ownership, the 1980s and 1990s witnessed the privatisation of numerous international companies, among which we find British Airways, Singapore Airlines, Japan Airlines (JAL) and Iberia.

These changes were introduced in order to stimulate competitiveness in domestic and international markets and improve the results of air companies, many of which have been fundamentally restructured in a deep way so as to survive in more competitive contexts. The international alliances and code-share agreements[3] that have been arrived at constitute good examples of this.

Such a transformation of the industry calls for an analysis of the consequences on air transport companies efficiency, and this is what our article sets out to do. Previous studies of the subject, such as Forsyth et al. (1986), Encaoua (1991), Oum and Yu (1995) and Inglada et al. (1999), compared periods of regulation and liberalisation, reaching the conclusion that liberalisation led to gains in efficiency for air companies.

This article is structured into three sections: firstly there is an exposition of the methodology used, secondly, there is a description of data and variables and, lastly, we present the results of the estimation with our conclusions.

2. Methodology

The most common way of estimating both economic and technical efficiency is by using efficiency frontier methodology. This approach basically consists in adjusting data to a particular technological frontier and estimating the efficiency measures, comparing the values observed with the optimums defined by the frontier. In this kind of estimation one needs to assume a special frontier type and choose a procedure for the estimation.

As Bauer (1990) points out the are two competing paradigms on how to construct frontiers. One uses mathematical programming techniques, the other employs econometric techniques. The chief advantage of the mathematical programming or Data Envelopment Analysis (DEA) approach is that no explicit functional form need be imposed on the data. However, the calculated frontier may be warped if the data are contaminated by statistical noise (such as luck and weather). Frontier estimation employing DEA methodology has often been applied in the transport field, see for instance Alam et al. (1998), Gillen and Lall (1997) or Adler and Golany (2001) for air transport.

---

[2] To name some of them: Silk Air, Eva Airways, Japan Asia Airways, All Nippon Airways, Asiana, Saempati and Dragon Air.

[3] There are many examples, but one of the most recent is the code-share agreement between the air companies of Vietnam and American Airlines in July 2001.

V. Inglada et al. / Transportation Research Part A 40 (2006) 95–105   97

On the other hand, the econometric approach (with stochastic frontier analysis) can handle statistical noise, but it imposes an explicit, and possibly overly restrictive, functional form for technology (flexible functional forms allow for a more sophisticated technology).[4] This technique was originally developed within a cross-sectional context, in which the objective is to compare the efficiencies of producers. More recently alternative techniques have been extended for use in a panel data context (see Schmidt and Sickles, 1984 in a stochastic frontier context or Charnes et al., 1985 for DEA). Unless panel data are available, an explicit distribution for the inefficiency term must be imposed as well. If panel data is disposable the researcher can relax many of the more restrictive assumption about the inefficiency disturbances. In particular with panel data, researchers no longer have to assume that the level of inefficiency is independent of the regressors and no longer have to impose a particular distribution for the inefficiency terms, making these restrictions testable propositions. We have used these advantages in this paper where we present an empirical exercise with panel data.

2.1. Economic efficiency

The frontier cost function represents the minimum cost of producing a particular output level, given the technology and the prices of the production inputs used.

Our study involves the estimation of a stochastic parametric cost function using the corresponding econometric model. These types of cost functions have been widely employed in the transport field, with appropriate modifications, by Nash and Preston (1996) for rail transport, and by Oum and Zhang (1991) for air transport.

To calculate economic efficiency, a cost function is estimated via the application of the methodology developed by Schmidt and Sickles (1984) using a panel data. With panel data techniques, each producer is observed over a certain time period. The cost function can be defined as:

$$c_{at} = \alpha + c(w_{at}, y_{at}; \beta) + v_{at} + u_a \tag{1}$$

where c is the observed cost; α is the constant; w is the input price vector; y is the output; β is a technological parameter vector, $a = 1, \ldots, A$ are indices of the different producers and $t = 1, \ldots, T$ are years.

The residue v_{at} is a random disturbance with the usual properties: independently and identically distributed (iid) with zero mean and constant variance, and registers the effects of statistical noise. On the other hand, u_a records the degree of economic efficiency of the ath company. Thus, $u_a \geq 0$ for all a, and it is distributed identically with mean μ and variance σ_u^2, and independent of v_{at}, that is to say, $u_a \approx D(\mu, \sigma_u^2)$. The fact that the inefficiency term has no time specification signifies that economic efficiency only varies between companies and not over time.

Given that $E(u_a) = \mu$ we can define:

$$u_a^* = u_a - \mu \quad \alpha^* = \alpha + \mu;$$

---

[4] In the specific case under study, the functional form selected was flexible functional form: the translogarithmic. This is a quadratic function corresponding to a second order Taylor-series progression.

98   *V. Inglada et al. / Transportation Research Part A 40 (2006) 95–105*

so that the u_a^* is iid with mean 0. Then in Eq. (2)

$$C_{at} = \alpha^* + c(w_{at}; y_{at}; \beta) + v_{at} + u_a^* \tag{2}$$

the error terms v_{at} and u_a^* have zero mean, and most of the results of the panel data literature can be apply directly. Thus, we can apply the fixed effects model or the random effects model depending on whether or not one is willing to assume that technical inefficiency is uncorrelated with the regressors (output and input prices vector, in this case). If we can assume that there is not this correlation we can estimate consistently the random effects model using generalised least squares (GLS). However, it may be incorrect to assume that inefficiency is independent of the regressors. In this case, we can estimate by means the so-called *within* estimator which treats the u_a term as fixed, that is to say, it estimates a separate intercept for every firm.[5] Then, the model (2) becomes

$$C_{at} = \alpha_a + c(w_{at}; y_{at}; \beta) + v_{at} \tag{3}$$

where $\alpha_a = \alpha + \mu_a = \alpha^* + \mu_a^*$.

This can be done by suppressing the constant term and adding a dummy variable for each of the N firms or, equivalently, by keeping the constant term and adding $(N-1)$ dummies.[6]

The chief advantage of the within estimator is that its consistency does not hinge on uncorrelatedness of the regressors and the individual effects. Is also does not depend on the distribution of the effects, since in treating them as fixed it simply proceeds conditionally from whatever their realisations may be.

Once the individual intercepts have been estimated we simply define

$$\hat{\alpha} = \min(\hat{\alpha}_a) \quad \text{and} \quad \hat{u}_a = \hat{\alpha}_a - \hat{\alpha}$$

Finally, once u_a has been estimated, and if we assume a model with the cost in logarithmic terms we have that:

$$\text{Ln} \, EE_a = C_{at}^* - C_{at} = -\hat{u}_a \Rightarrow EE_a = \exp(-\hat{u}_a) \tag{4}$$

where EE is the economic efficiency index; C is the observed cost (in logarithm) and C^* is the cost function (in logarithm) which represents the minimum cost given the actual output and the input prices vector.

2.2. Technical efficiency

Koopmans (1951) provided a formal definition of technical efficiency: a producer is technically efficient if an increase in any output requires a reduction in at least one other output or an increase in at least one input, and if a reduction in any input requires an increase in at least one other input or a reduction in at least one output. Thus, a technically inefficient producer could produce the

---

[5] To contrast the null hypothesis that effects and regressors are uncorrelated it is possible to apply the Hausman specification test which is based on the differences between the various estimators.

[6] Another equivalent procedure is to apply OLS after expressing all data in terms of deviations from the firm means. In the latter case, the N intercepts are recovered as the means of the residuals by firm. Moreover, it is possible to have a consistency problem with the estimated intercepts (α_a) because the theory requires that $T \to \infty$.

V. Inglada et al. / Transportation Research Part A 40 (2006) 95–105   99

same outputs with less of at least one input, or could use the same inputs to produce more of at least one output.

In this sense, there are two approaches for analysing technical efficiency. The first, known as input-orientated technical efficiency, analyses the ability of a firm to use the minimum quantity of inputs to produce a given set of outputs.

The second approach, output-orientated technical efficiency, centres on the possibility of increasing the output without changing the number of inputs. In this study, to estimate the degree of technical inefficiency of air companies, a parametric production function was used, making it possible to obtain indicators of technical efficiency for different companies. To do this, we use the panel data methodology originally proposed by Schmidt and Sickles (1984).

The model runs as follows: with a panel of T periods of observations of A companies, technology can be represented by the following production function

$$y_{at} = b + f(x_{iat}; \beta) + \varepsilon_{at} - \partial_a \tag{5}$$

where y is the output; x is the input vector $(i = 1, \ldots, n)$; b is the constant; β is a technological parameter vector; $a = 1, \ldots, A$ are indices of the different producers and $t = 1, \ldots, T$ are years.

The ε_{at} error term represents statistical noise and is assumed to be iid with zero mean and constant variance. The ∂_a term represents technical inefficiency and, correspondingly $\partial_a \geqslant 0$ for all a. We assume the ∂_a to be iid with mean d and variance σ_∂^2 and independent of the ε_{at}. That is to say, $\partial_a \approx D(d, \sigma_\partial^2)$.

We can rewrite the model as follow. First, given that $E(\partial_a) = d$ we can define:

$$\partial_a^* = \partial_a - d \quad b^* = b - d$$

so that the ∂_a^* is iid with mean 0. Then in Eq. (6)

$$y_{at} = b^* + f(x_{iat}; \beta) + \varepsilon_{at} - \partial_a^* \tag{6}$$

the error terms ε_{at} and ∂_a^* have zero mean and we can estimate as we have explained in the previous section. Then, applying the fixed effects model, we have:

$$y_{at} = b_a + f(x_{iat}; \beta) + \varepsilon_{at} \tag{7}$$

where $b_a = b - \partial_a := b^* - \partial_a^*$.

To obtain technical efficiency indexes we define

$$\widehat{b_a} = \max(\widehat{b}_a) \quad \text{and} \quad \widehat{\partial}_a = \widehat{b} - \widehat{b}_a$$

and finally, if the output is in logarithm terms we have that:

$$\operatorname{Ln} TE_a = Y_{at} - Y_{at}^* = -\widehat{\partial}_a \Rightarrow TE_a = \exp(-\widehat{\partial}_a) \tag{8}$$

where TE is the output oriented technical efficiency index; Y_{at} is the observed output (in logarithm) and Y_{at}^* is the maximum output (in logarithm) given the actual inputs.

2.3. Empirical specification

In order to determine the economic and technical efficiency of various air companies, it is necessary to estimate a cost and a production frontier function.

100   *V. Inglada et al. / Transportation Research Part A 40 (2006) 95–105*

Following Eq. (3) the translog total cost function used would adopt the following expression:

$$C_{at} = \alpha_a + \alpha_y \ln y_{at} + \alpha_{yy} \frac{1}{2} \ln y_{at}^2 + \sum_{i=1}^{n} \beta_i \ln w_{iat} + \frac{1}{2} \sum_{i=1}^{n} \sum_{j=1}^{n} \beta_{ij} \ln w_{iat} \ln w_{jat}$$

$$+ \sum_{i=1}^{n} \rho_{yi} \ln y_{at} \ln x_{iat} + \sum_{t=1}^{T} \alpha_T T + v_{at} \tag{9}$$

Similarly, following Eq. (7) the production function would take on this form:

$$y_{at} = b_a + \sum_{i=1}^{n} \beta_1 \ln x_{iat} + \frac{1}{2} \sum_{i=1}^{n} \sum_{j=1}^{n} \beta_{ij} \ln x_{iat} \ln x_{jat} + \sum_{t=1}^{T} \alpha_T T + \varepsilon_{at} \tag{10}$$

where $i,j = 1,\ldots,n$ is the number of inputs; $a = 1,\ldots,A$ is the number of air companies; $t = 1,\ldots,T$ are years; α_a and b_a are the individual effects; α_T are the coefficient of the variable time dummy T; and v_{at} and ε_{at} are the error terms with the characteristics explained above.

3. The data

A panel of 20 international air companies over the period 1996–2000 was selected, seven of which are European (Lufthansa, KLM, SAS, Finnair, Spannair, Iberia, British Airways), six North American (American Airlines, United, Delta, Northwest, USAir, Continental), one Canadian (Canadian), two Mexican (Aeroméxico and Mexicana), and four from Asia, Japan Airlines (JAL), Korean Air, Cathay Pacific (Hong Kong) and Singapur Airlines (SIA). They are all large-scale companies carrying out international flights. There are annual observations for them all. ICAO statistics form the basic reference (Digest of Statistics from the International Civil Aviation Organisation). These are completed with the data published by the IATA (International Air Transport Association),[7] World Air Transport Statistics. Using both sources of information we constructed our own data base, with the purpose of estimating a production function and a cost function for the air transport industry, in line with the methodology described in the previous section. The production function would run like this:

$$Y = F(L, K, E) \tag{11}$$

where Y, is production, arrived at using the number of km-tons available (as a joint indicator comprising km-passengers and km-tons available), L, represents the total number of workers in the air industry, K, represents the capital, arrived at using the capacity of the planes available (expressed as tons available per plane) and E is a proxy for the energy used, calculated using the number of kilometres covered.

The cost function would run like this:

$$C = f(Y, W_L, W_K, W_E, W_S) \tag{12}$$

---

[7] Published financial data supplied by countries in their national currencies is transformed into US dollars by the ICAO. To cut out the effects of inflation, all the statistics are deflated using the GNP deflator measured in constant 1991 currency.

V. Inglada et al. / Transportation Research Part A 40 (2006) 95–105   101

where each of the variables represents the following: C is the operating costs or operational total; Y is the output, being available ton-km, which includes both passengers and cargo; W_L is the labour factor price, obtained as the cost of cabin staff divided by the number of cabin workers; W_E is the energy price, obtained by the energycost divided by the number of kilometres flown; W_K is the capital price, arrived at by the capital cost divided by available capacity (capital costs include insurance, hiring of equipment, maintenance, depreciation and amortisation); W_S is the price of materials and other services, arrived at as the cost of all the other components not previously included, divided by the number of departures executed by the aircraft.

In addition, we tested the inclusion of other variables to record additional output characteristics, such as load factor and average distance covered in a flight stage (total kilometres flown/number of departures). Nevertheless, none of these variables proved to be significant.

4. Results of the estimation

The results of the estimations are shown in Tables 1–4.[8] With regard to the cost function (Table 1), both the total cost and the regressors are in logarithms and have been normalised (divided by the geometric mean). In this way, the first order coefficients can be interpreted as cost elasticity. The heteroscedasticity was corrected using White's method (1980). All the coefficients display the expected signs, and are significant.

This function was estimated with the fixed effects panel data model. The Hausman test (1978) was performed to verify if it was possible to maintain the null hypothesis of an absence of correlation between individual effects and explanatory variables. From the result obtained (see Table 1), it was confirmed that it is not possible to sustain that hypothesis and, consequently, the appropriate course of action is to use the fixed effects model.

So 20 dummy variables (α_a) were used, one per company, with the purpose of capturing specific individual effects for each of them. As we have explained in Section 2.1, in efficiency studies these effects are interpreted as economic efficiency indices for each company (EE).

The economic efficiency index, constructed from Eq. (4), ranges from 0 to 1. The results are shown in Table 2, and reveal that the Asian companies are economically the most efficient, with Cathay Pacific and SIA out in the lead, followed by Korean Air and JAL. The American companies exhibit indices for economic efficiency that are very low by comparison. The same situation is to be observed in the European companies, while the German Company LUFHTANSA and SAS from Scandinavia display the lowest index values.

In Table 3, meanwhile, we show the estimation of the stochastic production function. The estimated first order coefficients (which have been also normalised) are also significant and have the expected sign. Using this estimated frontier, it is possible to obtain the indices for technical efficiency (TE), calculated in accordance with Eq. (8). The values obtained from the TE (see Table 4)

---

[8] The estimation was carried out with the statistical program TSP43.

Table 1
Estimation of the cost function

Variable	Coefficients	t-Statistic
$L(Y)$	0.6789	6.5151[**]
$L(W_L)$	0.1057	2.1112[**]
$L(W_E)$	0.2312	3.8480[**]
$L(W_K)$	0.2905	5.4448[**]
$L(W_S)$	0.3725	5.7286[**]
$L(Y)L(Y)$	−0.1850	−2.9415[**]
$L(W_L)L(W_L)$	−0.0506	−0.8998
$L(W_L)L(W_K)$	0.1501	2.0327[**]
$L(W_L)L(W_E)$	0.0067	0.1184
$L(W_L)L(W_S)$	−0.1061	−1.4642
$L(W_E)L(W_E)$	0.0906	0.6215
$L(W_E)L(W_K)$	−0.1028	−1.9301[*]
$L(W_E)L(W_S)$	0.0054	0.0469
$L(W_K)L(W_K)$	0.1078	−1.0039
$L(W_K)L(W_S)$	0.0605	0.8773
$L(W_S)L(W_S)$	0.0402	0.3426
$L(Y)L(W_L)$	0.0814	2.6877[**]
$L(Y)L(W_E)$	−0.0231	−0.6551
$L(Y)L(W_K)$	−0.0793	−3.0743[**]
$L(Y)L(W_S)$	0.0209	0.4846
D_{T97}	0.0177	1.3333
D_{T98}	0.0339	1.5569
D_{T99}	0.0368	1.6106
D_{T00}	0.0012	0.0467
R-squared	DW	SE regression
0.99	1.71	0.05

Hausman test, Chi squared (20) = 56.77.
[*] Significant at 10%.
[**] Significant at 5%.

generally prove to be higher than the EE indexes but also situate the Asian companies in first place.

Our evidence suggest that the benefits of increasing competition in terms of efficiency is large for Asian airline industry. From the end of the 1980s, the national company monopoly was broken and entry was granted to "second-level" companies, whose interests left a powerful mark on air transport policy in Asia. Hooper (1996) describes how various competing companies sprang up in a number of Asian countries and the effect this had on international traffic in Korea, the Philippines, China, India and Japan.

As a consequence, the Asian air market is powerful and growing very rapidly. But, apart from the introduction of competition, some Asian companies possess characteristics that make them more efficient when compared to their American and European counterparts. To take the examples of SIA and Cathay Pacific, both companies have a prestigious reputation, for their passenger customer service, efficient collection and delivery of baggage, the cleanliness of their aircraft, and so on.

V. Inglada et al. / Transportation Research Part A 40 (2006) 95–105   103

Table 2
Indixes of economic efficiency

Company	Indixes of economic efficiency (EE)
Lufthansa (Germany)	0.2801
KLM (Holland)	0.5392
SAS (Scandinavia)	0.2142
Finnair (Finland)	0.3690
Spannair (Spain)	0.4172
Iberia (Spain)	0.3487
British airways (UK)	0.4250
American (USA)	0.2333
United (USA)	0.2345
Delta (USA)	0.2205
Northwest (USA)	0.2871
USAir (USA)	0.2040
Continental (USA)	0.2913
JAL (Japan)	0.6143
Canadian (Canada)	0.5696
Aeromexico (Mexico)	0.3502
Mexicana (Mexico)	0.3367
Korean AIR (Korean Republic)	0.7334
Cathay Pacific (China)	1
SIA (Singapore)	0.9763

Table 3
Production function estimators

Variable	Coefficients	t-Statistic
$L(L)$	0.1417	1.9677[**]
$L(K)$	0.4690	7.6228[**]
$L(E)$	0.4180	4.3762[**]
$L(L)L(L)$	1.3253	3.1259[**]
$L(K)L(K)$	0.2263	2.0861[**]
$L(E)L(E)$	0.2734	1.1041
$L(L)L(K)$	−0.6449	−4.2967[**]
$L(L)L(E)$	−0.6524	−2.0121[**]
$L(K)L(E)$	0.3632	3.4078[**]
D_{T97}	0.0077	0.7565
D_{T98}	0.0221	1.5089
D_{T99}	0.0247	1.5755
D_{T00}	0.0187	0.8442
Average	0.432	
R-square	DW	SE regression
0.99	1.43	0.03

Hausman test, Chi squared (9) = 17.09.
[**] Significant at 5%.

Table 4
Indixes of technical efficiency

Companies	Indixes of technical efficiency (TE)
Lufthansa (Germany)	0.5407
KLM (Holland)	0.7359
SAS (Scandinavia)	0.3476
Finnair (Finland)	0.4689
Spannair (Spain)	0.5403
Iberia (Spain)	0.4186
British Airways (UK)	0.6571
American (USA)	0.5419
United (USA)	0.5922
Delta (USA)	0.5431
Northwest (USA)	0.5531
USAir (USA)	0.3827
Continental (USA)	0.4656
JAL (Japan)	0.8344
Canadian (Canada)	0.6194
Aeromexico (Mexico)	0.5073
Mexicana (Mexico)	0.4880
Korean Air (Korean Republic)	0.8906
Cathay Pacific (China)	1
SIA (Singapore)	0.9286

With respects to inputs, labour market is much more flexible than European and American and their aircraft incorporate planes of the latest generation.

Lastly, but of strategic importance, we must mention their "Computer Reservation System" (CRS). In Asia, Abacus is a system that was established by the six regional airlines, including Cathay Pacific and SIA. It is in operation in Singapore and Hong Kong. Likewise, Abacus has reached an agreement with the Japanese company All Nippon, which will allow it to control the Asian market.

The European CRS, Amadeus, by comparison, despite having come into operation before the Asian system, shows many deficiencies in performance. The Asian companies, in consequence, are right up front, exploiting the evident advantages that allow them to control the market.

5. Conclusions

In this article, we have compared the technical and economic efficiency of 20 international air companies for 1996–2000. The companies are based in countries whose exposure to the liberalisation process varies. In the USA, for instance, the market has been completely liberalised since 1978, while the European market reached completion in 1997, yet the most recent experience of opening up to competition is that of the Asian countries, whose clearest liberalisation agreements were struck at the end of the 1990s.

Four air companies from these countries, Cathay Pacific (Hong Kong), SIA (Singapore), Korean Air (Korean Republic) and JAL (Japan), actually obtain the highest values for economic and technical efficiency, leaving the American and European countries far behind.

Therefore there are benefits of increasing competition for Asian airline industry. Additionally, we can point the well established reputation for quality enjoyed by some of their companies, their flexible labour market and the Abacus Computer Reservation System's far greater efficiency when compared to the European equivalent, Amadeus.

References

Adler, N., Golany, B., 2001. Evaluation of deregulated airline networks using data envelopment analysis combined with principal component analysis with an application to Western Europe. European Journal of Operational Research 132 (2), 260–273.

Alam, I., Semenick, M., Sickles, R.C., 1998. The relationship between stock market returns and technical efficiency innovations: evidence from the US Airline Industry. The Journal of Productivity Analysis 9 (1), 35–51.

Bauer, P.W., 1990. Recent developments in the econometric estimation of frontiers. Journal of Econometrics 46, 39–56.

Charnes, A., Cooper, W.W., Golany, B., Seiford, L.M., Stutz, J., 1985. Foundations of data envelopment analysis for Pareto–Koopmans efficient empirical production functions. Journal of Econometrics 30 (12), 91–127.

Chin, T.H.A., 1997. Implications of liberalisation on airport development and strategy in the Asia Pacific. Journal of Air Transport Management 3 (3), 125–131.

Encaoua, D., 1991. Liberalising European airlines: cost and factor productivity evidence. International Journal of Industrial Organisation 9, 109–124.

Forsyth, P.J., Hill, R.D., Trengrove, C.D., 1986. Measuring airline efficiency. Fiscal Studies 7, 61–81.

Gillen, D., Lall, A., 1997. Developing measures of air transport productivity and performance: an application of data envelopment analysis. Transportation Research 33, 261–273.

Hausman, J., 1978. Specification test in econometrics. Econometrica 46, 1251–1272.

Hooper, P., 1996. Airline markets in Asia: the domestic/international regulatory interface. In: Dick, H. (Ed.), Towards "Open Skies"; Airline Deregulation in Asia-Pacific. Institute of Transport Studies, University of Sydney, London.

Inglada, V., Coto-Millán, P., Rodriguez-Alvarez, A., 1999. Economic and technical efficiency in the World Air industry. International Journal of Transport Economics XXVI (2), 219–236.

Koopmans, T.C., 1951. An analysis of production as an efficient combination of activities. In: Koopmans, T.C. (Ed.), Activity Analysis of Production and Allocation, Cowles Commission for Research in Economics, Monograph no. 13, John Wiley and Sons, Inc., New York.

Nash, C., Preston, J., 1996. El Transporte por Ferrocarril en Europa y el Futuro en RENFE. In: La regulación de los transportes en España. Biblioteca Civitas, Economía y Empresa, pp. 263–312.

Oum, T.H., Zhang, Y., 1991. Utilisation of quasi-fixed inputs and estimation of cost functions. Journal of Transport Economics and Policy 25, 121–138.

Oum, T.H., Yu, C., 1995. A productivity comparison of the world's major airlines. Journal of Air Transport Management 2, 181–195.

Oum, T.H., Lee, Y.H., 2002. The Northeast Asian air transport network: is there a possibility of creating open skies in the region? Journal of Air Transport Management 8, 325–337.

Rey, M.B., 2000. Efectos de la liberalización del transporte aéreo sobre el mercado español de vuelos regulares (1989–1997). Ph.D. Thesis. Universidad Complutense de Madrid, España.

Schmidt, P., Sickles, R.C., 1984. Production frontiers and panel data. Journal of Business and Economic Statistics 2, 367–374.

White, H., 1980. A heteroscedasticity-consistent covariance matrix and a direct test for heteroscedasticity. Econometrica 48, 721–746.

16

Using Nonfinancial Information to Predict Financial Performance: The Case of the U.S. Airline Industry

BRUCE K. BEHN
RICHARD A. RILEY, JR.

To enhance traditional financial reporting, academics and policymakers have suggested that financial statement users be provided with nonfinancial performance information that may enhance users' ability to evaluate and predict financial performance. This study tests this proposition by examining whether timely nonfinancial performance information is a useful predictor of financial performance in the airline industry. From analysts' written pronouncements and financial press articles we identify a number of fundamental metrics, including customer satisfaction, purportedly used by analysts and investors to assess airline performance. We empirically examine these metrics and find that on-time performance, mishandled baggage, ticket oversales, and in-flight service are significantly associated with our proxy for customer satisfaction. Using an instrumental variable for customer satisfaction, we find that customer satisfaction, load factor, market share, and available ton miles are contemporaneously associated with operating income and revenues and that customer satisfaction and available ton miles are contemporaneously associated with expenses. Finally, using one and two months of nonfinancial data, we find that nonfinancial performance information appears to be useful in predicting quarterly revenues, expenses, and operating income.

1. Introduction

The purpose of this research is to evaluate the association between nonfinancial information and financial performance in the U.S. domestic airline industry and to examine whether this nonfinancial information can be useful in predicting future financial performance. Both academics and policymakers, including Birchard

We would like to thank Susan Ayers, Joe Carcello, Kathleen Hethcox, Al Nagy, Terry Neal, Jan Williams, Jeff Wong, the University of Oregon seminar participants at the 1997 American Accounting Association national meeting, and Holly Johnston (the reviewer) for their helpful comments on earlier versions of this paper. We gratefully acknowledge the financial support of the University of Tennessee.

(1994), the AICPA (1994) Jenkins Committee, and Wallman (1995, 1996), have expressed concern that corporate financial reporting and disclosure are not keeping pace with a dynamic and constantly changing business world. To enhance traditional financial reporting, one consistent suggestion from this group has been to provide financial statement users with nonfinancial performance information that may enhance users' ability to evaluate and predict financial performance. As Birchard (1994) argues, there is a missing link between companies' progress in operating activities and companies' financial results, and this link will come from research that demonstrates that nonfinancial performance variables are indicative of bottom line results. This study contributes to this debate by providing empirical evidence that timely nonfinancial performance information is contemporaneously associated with, and can be useful in predicting, financial performance in the U.S. airline industry.

Using analysts' written pronouncements and financial press articles we identify a number of fundamental metrics purportedly used by analysts and investors to assess airline performance. From this search, it appears that fundamental operating metrics such as load factors, market share, and available ton miles differentiate airline performance. While these measures appear to be important indicators of future earnings, customer satisfaction measures such as on-time arrival, mishandled baggage, ticket oversales (i.e., involuntarily "bumped" passengers), in-flight service levels and customer complaints also differentiate future financial performance.[1]

We develop hypotheses for these metrics based on analysts' and financial press suppositions. The customer satisfaction hypothesis is tested using an instrumental variables approach, and we find that on-time performance is negatively associated with customer complaints (our proxy for customer satisfaction). In contrast, mishandled baggage, ticket oversales, and crowded flights are positively associated with customer complaints. Further, we find that load factor and market share are positively associated with contemporaneous operating income, while customer complaints (our instrumental variable for customer satisfaction) and available ton miles are negatively associated with contemporaneous operating income. With respect to revenues, customer complaints are negatively associated with revenue and load factor, and market share and available ton miles are positively associated with revenue. In addition, customer complaints and available ton miles are positively associated with operating expenses. The explanatory power of these models (i.e., adjusted R^2) ranges from 0.41 to 0.71 and the results are robust to a variety of alternative measures of financial performance.

We also develop and empirically test whether monthly nonfinancial information can be used to predict quarterly financial performance. Using nonfinancial

---

1. For example, in a recent *Wall Street Journal* article (Carey [1996]), John Edwardson, United Airline's (UAL) president and chief operating officer, stated the UAL is spending $386 million to replace aircraft seats, refurbish cabin interiors, upgrade passenger entertainment systems and improve food and in-flight service to bolster UAL's lackluster standing with customers. Further, UAL plans to link executive compensation to airline on-time performance.

information provided in months 1 and 2 of a particular quarter, we develop a model to predict quarterly revenues, expenses, and operating income. The explanatory power of these models (i.e., adjusted R^2) ranges from 0.35 to 0.71 and associations similar to those already noted are observed for the one- and two-month prediction periods. Based on these findings, it appears that fundamental nonfinancial performance metrics are indicators of future financial performance in the airline industry. Because many of the nonfinancial performance variables incorporated in this research are disclosed monthly, whereas financial statement data are systematically released quarterly, these results may be of particular interest to policymakers and others interested in the timely release of relevant performance metrics.

This research is organized in the following manner. The accounting and financial reporting issues surrounding nonfinancial metrics are presented in Section 2. In Section 3, pertinent prior research is discussed. Section 4 includes an overview of the airline industry. Model and variable development are discussed in Section 5. The data sources and sample selection procedures are outlined in Section 6. The results are presented in Section 7. Finally, contributions, limitations and extensions are considered in Section 8.

2. Nonfinancial Performance Variables and the Accounting Profession

The AICPA Jenkins Committee was charged with identifying information that companies should provide to investors and creditors. In 1994, the committee published *Improving Business Reporting—A Customer Focus: Meeting the Needs of Investors and Creditors*. One of the recommendations of the Jenkins Committee for meeting users' needs is that financial reporting should focus more on the factors that create value, including nonfinancial measures indicating how key business processes are performing.

In addition, SEC Commissioner Wallman (1995, 1996) notes that the SEC has relied on the assistance of the accounting profession for the past 60 years to satisfy the commission's statutory responsibility to craft accounting standards for public companies. The commissioner's commentary encourages the accounting profession to consider financial reporting issues more pervasive than those addressed by the Jenkins Committee.[2] As part of a preliminary proposal to enhance financial reporting, Wallman (1996) suggests a five-layer corporate reporting system that de-emphasizes recognition and focuses on providing relevant information. Pertinent to our research, "layer 3" would include information that is "highly relevant, ... consistently measurable with a high degree of reliability" but does not meet the definition of an asset, liability or component of equity. For the airline industry, performance indicators that might be included in layer 3 are measures such as load

---

2. For example, the commissioner suggests that the accounting profession consider how to address disclosure for "virtual" companies and intellectual assets.

factor and on-time arrival.[3] These measures are readily determinable and, because of systematic collection methods, are reliable and potentially auditable.

The preceding arguments and proposals are consistent with FASB *Statement of Financial Accounting Concepts Number 1*: financial reporting should provide information that is useful (i.e., relevant) to present and potential investors and creditors and other users in making rational investment, credit and similar decisions. Although there are many advocates of changing financial reporting, such views are not universal. For example, Francis and Schipper (1998) state that the common (and unacceptable) goal of the AICPA Jenkins Committee initiatives is to improve financial reporting by altering some or all of the elements of the current financial reporting model and/or by altering the fundamental nature of the assurance function. The authors conclude that, overall, their tests yield no systematic evidence that financial statements have lost relevance over the 43-year sample period (1951–1993). We contribute to this debate by examining whether nonfinancial operating metrics are contemporaneously associated with and useful predictors of short-term financial performance.

3. Prior Research

While a large body of financial accounting literature examines the association between firm market values (i.e., stock prices) and accounting variables, these relationships have been tested with little regard for their underlying economic structure (Bernard and Noel [1991]). Therefore, to better understand how company fundamentals map into financial performance, Bernard and Noel (1991), Stober (1993), and others have investigated the ability of financial statement metrics to predict future earnings. These particular authors find that inventory and receivable information are leading indicators of future financial performance. While this research explores the relationship between accounting financial statement metrics and financial performance, it does not investigate the association between nonfinancial metrics and traditional financial performance measures.

Amir and Lev (1996), however, extend research related to nonfinancial performance metrics by examining the value-relevance of nonfinancial performance variables in the high-technology wireless communications industry. The authors note that in times of rapid change, financial information of firms, especially in fast-changing technology-based industries, may be of limited value to investors. For example, telecommunications, biotechnology, software producers, and other growth companies create value through production and investment activities; yet, key financial variables such as earnings and book value are negative or excessively depressed and appear unrelated to market values. Based on these observations, Amir and Lev (1996) examine the value-relevance of financial information and nonfinancial information using quarterly data for 14 companies over 10 years. Their

---

3. Amir and Lev (1996) argue that nonfinancial information will typically be industry-specific.

analyses document the value relevance of rights acquired by potential subscribers and penetration of markets and their findings suggest that, on a stand-alone basis, traditional financial statement information is largely irrelevant for the wireless communications industry. The authors conclude that the results indicate the importance, in both practice and research, of expanding the domain of fundamental variables examined to include nonfinancial information.

Two studies address the relation between nonfinancial measures and financial performance in the airline industry. Schefczyk (1993) uses data envelopment analysis (DEA) to evaluate airline operating efficiency (i.e., the ratio of outputs to inputs). The author hypothesizes that available ton kilometers may reflect aircraft capacity more accurately than flight equipment depreciation and amortization. Further, Schefczyk (1993) argues that load factor (alone) may be an incomplete nonfinancial performance measure because nonflight inputs and outputs are ignored and inputs besides airline capacity are disregarded (e.g., operating costs). Available flight tons per kilometer (representing flight assets), flight operating costs, and nonflight assets are used as inputs and revenue per passenger kilometer and nonpassenger service revenues are used as outputs to estimate efficiency. The findings indicate that estimated efficiency, load factor, and the percentage of passenger revenues are positively associated with return on equity.

Dresner and Xu (1995) examine the effect of three customer service variables on customer satisfaction and in turn on profitability for U.S. airlines, testing links in the customer service, customer satisfaction, and corporate performance chain. The study examines the effects of on-time performance, mishandled baggage, and ticket oversales on customer satisfaction (proxied by customer complaints) and the effect of these customer service variables and estimated customer satisfaction on corporate profitability. The findings suggest that increasing customer service raises customer satisfaction and improves corporate performance.

Our work complements and extends that of Schefczyk (1993) and Dresner and Xu (1995). By incorporating fundamental operating measures in addition to customer satisfaction metrics in a comprehensive model, we test whether this nonfinancial airline information is contemporaneously associated with financial performance and whether this information can also be used to predict short-term revenues, expenses, and operating income. In addition to incorporating a richer set of variables, we argue that these nonfinancial measures may have different relative effects on airlines' revenues and expenses. Given the potential for differing effects on revenues and expenses, analyzing only the association between nonfinancial information and operating earnings may dampen the informational content of these airline nonfinancial metrics.

4. The Airline Industry

In any industry-specific analysis, knowledge of industry economics and aspects of value relevance, including the impact of nonfinancial performance variables, must be developed.[4] Since the Airline Deregulation Act became law in 1978, industry performance has been turbulent.[5] The industry recovered from an economic slump in 1984 as the deregulation process was completed. In the latter part of the 1980s, as a result of economic recovery and relatively low fuel prices, the largest three carriers, American, Delta, and United, were profitable, and new capacity was continually added within the industry. As the 1980s came to an end, however, airlines suffered from declining revenues and spiraling costs. In addition, in 1990, Iraq invaded Kuwait, further escalating operating costs (i.e., fuel costs). An overall economic recession in the United States in 1989–90 resulted in decreased consumer travel budgets, and the threat of terrorism depressed passenger levels even further.

In 1991, airline traffic declined for the first time in its then 67-year history. Now defunct airlines such as Eastern bore the burden of industry decline; however, most airlines added debt to their financial structure as a result of accepting aircraft ordered during prosperous times and funding deficits. In response, airlines retreated into profitable markets, cut operating costs, restructured operations, and prepared for an immediate future of low fares and fierce competition. By 1996, airline traffic had begun to rise, capacity had leveled off, and load factor (the percentage of seats sold) had improved. Ott and Neidl (1995) argue that the turbulent financial past is a prologue for the future. Competition, especially from "no-frills" airlines such as Southwest, will continue to be problematic, and the industry will continue to be cyclical (*Value Line*, March 22, 1996).[6]

O'Connor (1995) describes airline service as an undifferentiated product. In such highly competitive environments, price is usually the only factor differentiating homogeneous goods and services. However, it appears that U.S. airlines do not consider their products as commodities and have gone to great lengths to differentiate themselves and their services in the market place. U.S. airlines exhort the benefits of hub systems (Delta); nonstop flights (United); inexpensive flights (Southwest); and differences in frequent flyer programs, destinations, and anticipated service levels. As an example, Continental promotes the fact that they have been consistently ranked first or second in on-time performance.[7]

Amir and Lev (1996) chose to analyze wireless communications companies because the industry is emerging and dynamic and, thus, the role of traditional (historical) financial information is unclear. Similarly, in the competitive airline industry, the role of nonfinancial information is also unclear. Airlines tend to have significant fixed costs related to the acquisition and operation of aircraft; therefore, the information content of historical financial statements may be limited. Nonfi-

---

4. The basis for this discussion is O'Connor (1995) and Ott and Neidl (1995), though other sources cited in the reference section were also consulted.

5. The primary effects of airline deregulation were to eliminate controls over entry and exit for both specific airline routes and the airline industry and to eliminate controls over airline ticket prices.

6. "No-frills" airlines provide minimum service levels (e.g., no preassigned seating and limited in-flight services) and charge lower airfares (by comparison to full service airlines).

7. See Continental's full-page *Wall Street Journal* advertisement on Wednesday, May 22, 1996, p. A17.

nancial information may fill this void by providing important signals about financial performance in the airline industry.

5. Model and Variable Development

Similar to Lev and Thiagarajan (1993), we review analysts' written pronouncements from *Value Line* and *Standard & Poors* and relevant financial press articles from the *Wall Street Journal* and the *Wall Street Journal Transcripts* to identify a set of nonfinancial performance variables.[8] We then incorporate these nonfinancial metrics in linear regression models to examine the contemporaneous relationship with quarterly financial performance and the ability of these nonfinancial metrics to predict quarterly financial performance. Based on this search we find that load factor, market share, capacity, and customer satisfaction are fundamental drivers of financial performance. These variables are discussed in the following and descriptions and predicted signs are summarized in Table 1.

5.1 Customer Satisfaction Model

While metrics such as load factor, market share, and capacity are readily available from public sources, information about customer satisfaction is difficult for analysis and investors to obtain because firms do not disclose the results of internal customer satisfaction surveys. Even if airlines disclosed such information, it is unlikely that the information would be standardized across companies. Based on anecdotal evidence, it appears that analysts and investors use customer service proxies such as mishandled baggage, customer complaints, on-time arrivals, ticket oversales, and in-flight service to assess customer satisfaction. To model this relationship, similar to Dresner and Xu (1995), we create an instrumental variable (CMPLNTFT) for customer satisfaction, and use this customer satisfaction proxy in our models. Specifically, the following ordinary least-squares regression is used to develop the customer satisfaction proxy used in the contemporaneous and prediction models discussed in the next sections:

---

8. The following excerpt from *Value Line* (March 22, 1996) illustrates how analysts use nonfinancial performance measures to draw inferences about airlines' current performance and future earnings.

> Airline traffic is continuing to rise, although at a relatively slow pace. . . . The good news is that capacity has been leveling off. . . . Last year (1995), the available seat miles actually declined slightly (less than 1%). . . . The result has been that the load factor (the percentage of seats sold) has risen. Last year's industry load factor rose 1.6 percentage points, to 65% and this year there has been a further increase. That is generally good news for the industry.

According to this excerpt, available seat miles and load factor are proposed as leading indicators of financial performance. Because it is difficult to develop a theoretical analysis that derives the effect(s) of nonfinancial performance variables on financial performance, we use analysts' and investors' interpretations as the basis for including nonfinancial performance variables in our empirical models.

TABLE 1

Variable Definitions and Predicted Signs

Panel A. Fundamental operating variables[a]

	OPINC (operating income)	OPREV (operating revenue)	OPEXP (operating expense)	Variable Definitions
				Percentage change in the quarterly operating income from the same quarter in the prior year
				Percentage change in quarterly operating revenue from the same quarter in the prior year
				Percentage change in quarterly operating expense from the same quarter in the prior year
CMPLNTFT		−	?	Estimated percentage change in quarterly complaints from eq. (1)
LOADFCTR		+	+	Percentage change in the quarterly revenue load factor from the same quarter of the prior year; load factor equals revenue ton miles divided by available ton miles
MKTSHR		+	+	Percentage change in the quarterly market share from the same quarter in the prior year based on the largest 10 airlines listed in the mishandled baggage report
AVLMILES		?	+	Percentage change in the available ton miles from the same quarter in the prior year

Panel B. Customer service variables[b]

		Variable Definitions
	CMPLNT (complaints)	
ONTIME	−	Percentage change in the quarterly rate of complaints per 100,000 passengers from the same quarter of the prior year
		Percentage change in quarterly rate of on-time flights from the same quarter of the prior year
MISBAGS	+	Percentage change in the quarterly rate of mishandled baggage per 1,000 passengers from the same quarter of the prior year
OVERSALE	+	Percentage change in the quarterly rate of passengers involuntarily denied boarding ("bumped") per 10,000 passengers from the same quarter of the prior year
INFLIGHT	+	Percentage change in the quarterly revenue load factor from the same quarter of the prior year

[a] Source: Department of Transportation, *Air Carrier Statistics Monthly*, except market share, which was computed from the *Air Travel Consumer Report*.
[b] Source: Department of Transportation, *Air Travel Consumer Report* (monthly).

$$\text{CMPLNT} = \alpha_0 + \alpha_1\text{ONTIME} + \alpha_2\text{MISBAGS} + \alpha_3\text{OVERSALE}$$

$$+ \alpha_4\text{INFLIGHT} + \sum_{\text{year}=1}^{8} \alpha_{\text{year}+4}\text{YR89} - \text{YR96} + \qquad (1)$$

$$\sum_{n=1}^{6} \alpha_{n+12}\text{AIRLINE} + \varepsilon.$$

Here CMPLNT refers to the percentage change in the quarterly number of complaints per 100,000 passengers from the same quarter (denoted q) in the prior year (i.e., [complaints$_q$ − complaints$_{q-4}$]/complaints$_{q-4}$). We use percentage changes with respect to the same quarter in the previous year to alleviate the effects of seasonality in the airline industry and nonstationarity in financial statement data.[9] Further, we include airline and year dummy variables in all equations to control for firm and time variation.[10] All the remaining variables are discussed in the following and defined in Table 1.

5.2 Independent Variables: Customer Satisfaction

ONTIME: ONTIME is measured as the percentage change in on-time arrivals (i.e., [on-time arrivals$_q$ − on-time arrivals$_{q-4}$]/on-time arrivals$_{q-4}$), where flights are considered on-time when they land within 15 minutes of the scheduled time shown in the carriers' computerized reservations system (CRS). On-time performance measures are periodically published in the *Wall Street Journal* and mentioned in articles related to the airline industry. For example, the financial press often notes that monthly (on-time) statistics reported to the Department of Transportation (DOT) have become powerful marketing tools.

In fact, the *Wall Street Journal* alludes to assertions by some airlines that on-time numbers being reported to the DOT were being manipulated by other airlines to improve their on-time rankings.[11] Further, Continental pays each worker $65 for finishing second or third in on-time rankings and $100 for each month the airline finishes with a first-place ranking. According to the *Wall Street Journal* (McCartney [1995]), bonus checks for on-time performance equal half of the $6 million of expenses incurred monthly to book delayed or stranded passengers on other carriers. On-time performance is predicted to have a positive effect on customer sat-

---

9. Airlines experience seasonality. For example, November (Thanksgiving), December (Christmas holidays), and the summer months (vacations) are usually peak airline traffic months. In addition, it has been shown that financial statement data, especially income statement figures, are nonstationary and should be first-differenced before being included in an ordinary least-squares regression.

10. The panel data set includes a limited number of firms and several quarterly periods. Ordinary least-squares (OLS) coefficients generated from panel data regressions results in heterogeneity bias (i.e., model misspecification) because the OLS error term consists of unobservable firm (state) and time effects. As a result, OLS estimates are biased and the variance-covariance matrix is inconsistent. The firm and period dummy variables account for the unobservable firm and time period effects. We use annual time period dummy variables, as opposed to quarterly dummy variables, to conserve degrees of freedom.

11. Incorrectly reported nonfinancial performance variables bias against our finding significance.

isfaction and thus a negative association with the dependent variable customer complaints.

MISBAGS: MISBAGS represents lost, damaged, delayed, or pilfered bags and is measured as the percentage change in the rate of mishandled baggage per 1,000 passengers (i.e., [mishandled baggage$_q$ − mishandled baggage$_{q-4}$]/mishandled baggage$_{q-4}$). The importance of the mishandled baggage statistic is noted in the following *Wall Street Journal* (McCartney [1995]) excerpt: "Under him (Chief Executive Bethune, Continental Airlines), the Houston-based carrier has consistently ranked first or second in measures such as on-time performance, baggage handling and customer complaints . . . and has posted four consecutive quarters of record profits." In addition, airlines often mention mishandled baggage rankings in advertisements. Mishandled baggage is predicted to have a negative effect on customer satisfaction and thus a positive association with the dependent variable customer complaints.

OVERSALE: OVERSALE is measured as the percentage change in the number of passengers who hold confirmed reservations and are involuntarily denied boarding (i.e., bumped) per 10,000 passengers arrivals (i.e., [involuntarily bumped$_q$ − involuntarily bumped$_{q-4}$]/involuntarily bumped$_{q-4}$). Oversales are reported to assist consumers with information on the quality of services provided and are discussed in financial press articles. Ticket oversales are predicted to have a negative effect on customer satisfaction and thus a positive association with the dependent variable customer complaints.

INFLIGHT: INFLIGHT (which is identical to LOADFCTR) is measured as the percentage change in the ratio of revenue ton miles to total available ton miles and reflects the percentage of airline capacity used to generate revenues (i.e., [load factor$_q$ − load factor$_{q-4}$]/load factor$_{q-4}$). This variable is hypothesized to affect customer service because the higher the percentage of sold seats, the less in-flight service (i.e., individual attention) passengers receive and the more crowded the flights.[12] In-flight service is predicted to have a negative effect on customer satisfaction and thus a positive association with the dependent variable customer complaints.

5.3 Contemporaneous Model

Using this instrumental variable CMPLNTFT as a proxy for customer satisfaction, along with the other identified fundamental drivers of financial performance, we develop the following model that examines the contemporaneous relationship between this nonfinancial information and traditional quarterly financial performance:

---

12. LOADFCTR is hypothesized to have both indirect effects through customer satisfaction and direct effects on financial performance. Therefore, this variable appears in the customer satisfaction and the fundamental driver models.

$$\text{Dependent variables} = \beta_0 + \beta_1 CMPLNTFT + \beta_2 LOADFCTR$$
$$+ \beta_3 MKTSHR + \beta_4 AVLMILES + \qquad (2)$$
$$\sum_{year=1}^{8} \beta_{year+4} YR89 - 96 + \sum_{n=1}^{6} \beta_{n+12} AIRLINE + \varepsilon.$$

Three different dependent variables are used: operating income (OPINC),[13] operating revenues (OPREV), and operating expenses (OPEXP). Each of these variables is measured as the percentage change in its value in the current quarter from the same quarter in the prior year (e.g., [operating income$_q$ − operating income$_{q-4}$]/ operating income$_{q-4}$). As discussed previously, we include airline and year dummy variables in all equations to control for firm and time specific variation.

5.4 Independent Variables: Contemporaneous Model

CMPLNTFT: CMPLNTFT is measured as the predicted (fitted) values from regressing CMPLNT on the customer satisfaction metrics in eq. (1). Marketing research has demonstrated that the longevity of customers' relationships favorably influences company profitability (e.g., Zeithaml, Berry, and Parasuraman [1996]). Reichheld and Sasser (1990) contend that customer defections have a stronger impact on companies' net income than market share and other factors usually associated with competitive advantage. Therefore, customer satisfaction is expected to be positively associated with operating revenues and operating income because satisfied customers are expected to continue flying with the same airline.

Customer satisfaction's influence on expenses is difficult to predict. For example, airlines may spend millions of dollars to replace aircraft seats; refurbish cabin interiors; upgrade passenger entertainment systems; and improve on-time punctuality, food, and in-flight service to bolster customer service, which would indicate a positive relationship. In contrast, the factors associated with increased customer satisfaction may actually reduce operating expenses. For example, less replacement costs are incurred if fewer bags are lost or fewer costs may be incurred (e.g., overtime) if more aircraft arrive on time. Therefore, we do not make a pre-

---

13. When raw percentage changes in operating income are used as the dependent variable, the model is econometrically unstable. This situation is primarily because the scalar (net income$_{q-4}$) has significant variability: the smallest decrease in operating income is −8,823 percent and the largest increase is 2,066 percent. To stabilize the model we bound ("winsorize") the percentage changes by ± 100 percent. Approximately 10.4 percent of the observations were affected by this technique. These results are presented. Results similar to those presented later in Table 4 are obtained when the "raw" percentages are incorporated in the model and three outlier observations are excluded. However, the removal of these three observations did not result in an econometrically stable model; therefore, the more formal winsorizing procedure was applied to the data. Similar results are also found when changes in operating income, operating revenue, and operating expenses are scaled by available ton miles. In these regressions, the coefficients are additive across the operating revenue, expense, and income models (i.e., revenue minus expense model coefficients are approximately equal to the operating income model coefficients).

diction regarding the association between customer satisfaction and operating expenses.

LOADFCTR (same as INFLIGHT): Analysts and the financial press often refer to load factor as a key variable in the airline industry because it appears to be a fairly good indicator, at least in the short term, of how management is handling pricing and marketing in relation to performing their capacity management function. For example, *Value Line* reports load factor for each airline for the past 10 years as well as projections for the current and subsequent year as a single line-item statistic. Increases in load factor are predicted to have a positive direct effect on operating earnings, operating revenues, and operating expenses. As the percentage of aircraft seats sold rises, revenues should increase proportionately. Expenses, on the other hand, are more difficult to evaluate. Some expenses may not vary significantly over an individual route (e.g., aircraft costs, fuel), but others may be impacted (e.g., food, baggage handling); overall, we predict that operating expenses will increase as load factor increases.

MKTSHR: MKTSHR is measured as the change in market share percentage (i.e., [market share$_q$ − market share$_{q-4}$] / market share$_{q-4}$), where market share is defined as the number of passengers who flew during the period with the sample airline as a percent of passengers that flew with the 10 largest airlines. Prior research on the relation between market share and profitability is mixed (see Fraering and Minor [1994] for a summary). Further, since deregulation, the airline industry is notorious for its fierce competition. The following excerpt from *USA Today* (Jones [1995]) exemplifies this competition and the impact of market share on performance: "Continental and United have been able to steal (Southwest's) passengers and (Southwest's) fourth quarter earnings sank 47% from the previous year." Based on review of analysts' reports and financial press articles, we predict a positive association between revenue and market share as well as a positive association between operating expenses and market share. However, the relationship to profitability will be determined by the stronger effect (i.e., market share's relative impact on revenues versus expenses). Consistent with the preceding anecdote, we predict that as market share increases, operating income will also increase.

AVLMILES: Airlines' capacity to service passengers is proxied by the change in available ton miles (i.e., [available ton miles$_q$ − available ton miles$_{q-4}$] /available ton miles$_{q-4}$). Available ton miles is explicitly discussed in analysts' reports related to the airline industry and mentioned in *Wall Street Journal* articles. On a quarterly basis, airlines have the potential to alter their capacity. Management can decide to move out of unprofitable routes, adjust fleet composition, and change route structures. While the intent of these actions would, of course, be to enhance long-term value, whether these decisions will be profitable in the short term is questionable. While airlines are making positive operating revenue, factors that are associated with increases in capacity could have negative association with operating income. For example, if an airline leases a new plane for a new route to Denver, the costs of starting up this new route (e.g., advertising costs, gate rentals, discounts to passengers, etc.) could be increasing at a faster rate then operating income earned for this new route. Therefore, we cannot predict, at least on a quarterly basis, how changes in operating capacity will affect operating income. While we predict that increases in capacity will be positively associated with increases in operating revenues and expenses, we do not make a prediction for operating income.

5.5 Predictive Model

Another important motivation for examining the relationships between financial and nonfinancial measures of performance is understanding the role of nonfinancial performance measures as leading indicators of financial performance. In this role, we initiate the examination of these relationships by specifying models that include lead relationships and empirically test the ability of nonfinancial measures to predict future quarterly financial performance. Specifically, since most of the nonfinancial data is available on a monthly basis, we use data from the first month and first two months of a quarter to predict quarterly financial performance.

As discussed in Section 6.1, the *Air Carrier Traffic Statistics Monthly* and *Air Travel Consumer Report* are issued monthly. Further, the nonfinancial data provided in these reports are available approximately 4–5 weeks (28–35 days) after month-end.[14] In contrast, the release of the quarterly financial results occurs approximately 45 days after quarter-end.[15] Given this timing, approximately two months of nonfinancial performance data are available to predict the financial results of any given quarter. The release of the nonfinancial performance data for the third (and final) month of the quarter approximately coincides with the release of the quarterly financial results.

We use eq. (2) and the dependent variable definitions noted earlier and in Table 1 to examine the predictive ability of nonfinancial performance metrics with the following changes to the independent variable definitions. For the first analysis using the first month of the quarter, all independent variables are calculated as the percentage change in the independent variable for month 1 of the quarter from the same month in the prior year (e.g., [load factor$_{m1 \ of \ q}$ $-$ load factor$_{m1 \ of \ q-4}$]/load factor$_{m1 \ of \ q-4}$).[16] For the second analysis, we add variables representing the information contained in the second month of the nonfinancial performance variables (e.g., [load factor$_{m2 \ of \ q}$ $-$ load factor$_{m2 \ of \ q-4}$]/load factor$_{m2 \ of \ q-4}$). Because the

---

14. Based on discussions with Department of Transportation Officials, the *Air Travel Consumer Report* is issued approximately 4–5 weeks after month-end and the data is not made public prior to the release of the report. The *Air Carrier Traffic Statistics Monthly* is issued approximately 60 days after month-end. However, the data are made available to the public on request after submission to the DOT. In some cases, individual airlines may be observed releasing nonfinancial performance information a few weeks after month-end; however, such releases are not observed consistently or by all airlines.

15. SEC filing requirements allow companies to issue their year-end financial statements 90 days after year-end. To examine the financial statement report timing, the report date of quarterly earnings variable (Compustat quarterly industrial file) is examined. For the period of study, all financial statements, including year-end, were released within 45 days after quarter-end.

16. The instrument variable CMPLNTFT is also estimated using monthly data.

monthly changes in independent variables are highly correlated, we perform the following procedure to isolate the incremental explanatory power of the second month. We regress the percentage change in month 2 on the month 1 value (including year and time dummy variables) and calculate the residual for each observation. We then incorporate the residuals from each of these individual regressions along with the month 1 values in the month 2 model.[17]

6. Data Sources and Sample Selection

6.1 Data Sources

Nonfinancial performance data were obtained from two sources. Since 1987, the U.S. Department of Transportation, Office of Consumer Affairs, has published the *Air Travel Consumer Report* (monthly), which provides airline operating statistics for major airlines related to on-time performance, mishandled baggage, ticket oversales and customer complaints.[18] Similarly, in 1973, the Department of Transportation began issuing the *Air Carrier Traffic Statistics Monthly*. This report provides operating statistics such as revenue passenger miles, revenue load factor, passenger enplanements, etc.[19] Both of these reports, which are compiled by an independent third party, provide timely information that enables comparability among industry members.[20] All financial data were obtained from the Compustat tapes, *CD Disclosure*, 10-Ks, or annual reports.

6.2 Sample Selection

To evaluate the contemporaneous association and the predictive ability of nonfinancial performance variables, the 10 largest airlines that consistently appeared in the *Air Travel Consumer Report* between 1988 and 1996 were identified. Compustat tapes, 10-Ks, and/or annual reports were examined to identify public airlines filing with the Securities and Exchange Commission. As a result of this screening procedure, three of the ten largest airlines, Continental, Northwest, and TWA, were

---

17. The overall explanatory power of the models (adjusted R^2 and F statistics) are identical whether the raw values or the residuals from the month 2 variable regressions are included in the model. However, this technique has the effect of removing the significant correlations while incorporating the additional information provided by the month 2 data.

18. The current set of service quality measures and format used in the DOT's *Air Travel Consumer Report* dates back to 1987 but similar data have been reported, in different formats, for many more years.

19. Both sources provide monthly and some quarterly data. Where necessary, quarterly variables were calculated using monthly figures. The quarterly calculation typically involved weighting monthly measures based on the number of monthly passengers. Similarly, with regard to the predictive models, two-month calculations typically involved weighting monthly measures based on the number of monthly passengers.

20. The data are gathered by the DOT on Form 41. Form 41 data are generally comparable across carriers and time periods because they are filed according to the DOT's Uniform System of Accounts. Also, the DOT has an auditing process for these data.

TABLE 2

Descriptive Statistics and Correlation Table

Panel A. Descriptive statistics

Variable	Mean	Std. Dev.	Min.	Median	Max.
ONTIME	−0.99	7.23	−23.64	−1.40	26.02
MISBAGS	−0.45	21.04	−55.72	−0.45	63.65
OVERSALE	19.08	89.32	−81.25	0.78	866.70
INFLIGHT/LOADFCTR	1.57	5.53	−9.44	0.99	29.59
CMPLNTFT	−4.55	24.97	−64.02	−4.58	77.06
MKTSHR	4.48	10.87	−20.53	3.85	54.16
AVLMILES	8.32	9.77	−16.88	7.69	48.63

Panel B. Correlation matrix

	ONTIME	MISBAGS	OVERSALE	INFLIGHT/ LOADFCTR	CMPLNTFT	MKTSHR	AVLMILES
ONTIME	1						
MISBAGS	−0.52	1					
	(0.01)						
OVERSALE	−0.20	0.08	1				
	(0.01)	(0.22)					
INFLIGHT/	−0.18	0.03	0.08	1			
LOADFCTR	(0.01)	(0.63)	(0.22)				
CMPLNTFT	−0.53	0.44	0.49	0.23	1		
	(0.01)	(0.01)	(0.01)	(0.02)			
MKTSHR	−0.08	−0.03	0.01	0.48	−0.04	1	
	(0.22)	(0.64)	(0.92)	(0.01)	(0.41)		
AVLMILES	0.05	0.09	−0.02	−0.14	−0.07	0.56	1
	(0.49)	(0.17)	(0.77)	(0.04)	(0.09)	(0.01)	

Numbers below the diagonal represent Spearman rank correlations. Numbers in parentheses represent *p*-values, two-tailed tests.

deleted due to various data limitations.[21] The remaining seven airlines include Alaska, American, America West, Delta, Southwest, United, and USAir.[22] The final sample totals 213 quarterly observations—approximately 30 quarterly observations per airline. Descriptive statistics and the correlation matrix are presented in Table 2.

---

21. Northwest was taken private in 1989. It remained a private company until 1994. TWA was taken private in late 1988. It remained a private company until 1995. Continental airlines did not file with the Securities and Exchange Commission for various quarters in 1991 and 1992.

22. According to the *Air Travel Consumer Report*, the 10 largest airlines account for more than 90 percent of domestic operating revenues. The seven remaining airlines average 85 percent of the total passengers included in the top 10 airlines. Therefore, data for this study represent approximately 76.5 percent of domestic operating revenue (i.e., 90% * 85% = 76.5%).

TABLE 3

Customer Satisfaction Model Regression of Customer Service Variables on Complaints[a]

Variable[b]	Full Model		ONTIME Removed		MISBAGS Removed	
	Coefficient	t Stat.	Coefficient	t Stat.	Coefficient	t Stat.
Constant	−34.14	−3.69***	−31.66	−3.40***	−33.38	−3.52***
ONTIME	−1.14	−2.51***			−1.90	−4.72***
MISBAGS	0.47	3.35***	0.65	5.26***		
OVERSALE	0.11	3.55***	0.12	3.94***	0.10	3.37***
INFLIGHT	0.69	1.40*	0.80	1.59*	0.62	1.23
Y1996	47.21	4.86***	48.31	4.92***	46.27	4.65***
Y1995	36.17	3.64***	36.35	3.61***	34.91	3.43***
Y1994	47.35	4.75***	44.48	4.44***	45.16	4.44***
Y1993	16.61	1.69*	12.91	1.31	19.51	1.94**
Y1992	42.54	4.22***	37.24	3.73***	42.41	4.11***
Y1991	54.24	5.20***	49.01	4.74***	49.32	4.66***
Y1990	29.46	2.80***	22.14	2.16**	32.28	3.01***
Alaska	−11.60	−1.26	−10.75	−1.15	−11.07	−1.17
American	−9.04	−0.97	−7.41	−0.79	−10.81	−1.14
America West	−1.29	−0.14	2.14	0.23	−4.54	−0.48
Delta	−5.71	−0.63	−3.42	−0.37	−8.24	−0.88
Southwest	−16.45	−1.80*	−15.99	−1.73*	−16.33	−1.74*
United	−14.56	−1.60	−14.21	−1.55	−14.38	−1.55
Adjusted R^2	0.28		0.26		0.24	
Model F statistic	6.05***		5.88***		5.46***	

*** Significant at the 0.01 level.
** Significant at the 0.05 level.
* Significant at the 0.10 level.
The coefficients for ONTIME, MISBAGS, OVERSALE and INFLIGHT are one-tailed tests. The coefficients for all other variables are two-tailed tests.
[a] The sample consists of 213 quarterly observations from 1989 to 1996.
[b] All variables are defined in Table 1.

7. Findings and Sensitivity Testing

7.1 Customer Satisfaction Model

Results from estimating customer satisfaction are presented in Table 3 under the full-model caption. As predicted, changes in on-time arrival have a significant negative effect on changes in customer complaints (positive effect on customer satisfaction) suggesting that as the percentage of on-time arrivals increases, complaints decline. In contrast, changes in mishandled baggage, load factor, and ticket oversales are positively correlated with changes in customer complaints. This finding suggests that increases in mishandled baggage, deteriorating in-flight service, and being involuntary "bumped" increases customer complaints. The adjusted R^2

and F statistic for the model are 0.28 and 6.05, respectively, suggesting that the model appears to reasonably explain changes in customer satisfaction as proxied by complaints.

While the model appears to reasonably proxy for customer satisfaction, as described in Table 2 ONTIME and MISBAGS are highly correlated at −0.52. To determine whether this colinearity could be influencing these findings, we reran the customer satisfaction equation dropping one of these variables at a time. The results of these two regressions are shown in Table 3 under the ONTIME and MISBAGS removed captions. When ONTIME or MISBAGS is removed from the model very little changes. The significance levels and coefficient values for most of the variables remain approximately the same. When ONTIME is removed the coefficient value and t statistic on MISBAGS change from 0.47 and 3.35 to 0.65 and 5.26, respectively. When MISBAGS is removed the coefficient value and t statistic on ONTIME change from −1.14 and −2.51 to −1.90 and −4.72, respectively. Therefore, it does not appear that multicollinearity is influencing the results.

7.2 Contemporaneous Model

Results from estimating eq. (2) for the contemporaneous association between nonfinancial information and financial performance as proxied by operating income, operating revenues and operating expenses are presented in Table 4. With regard to eq. (2) and consistent with our predictions, the fitted values for complaint changes (CMPLNTFT) is significant and negatively associated with percentage changes in operating income (OPINC). Thus, as complaints increase, financial performance as proxied by operating income decreases. Available miles is also significant and negatively associated with changes in operating income.[23] Thus, at least in the short term, it appears that as management increases capacity, profitability decreases.[24] In contrast, changes in load factor and market share are pos-

---

23. As previously mentioned, on a quarterly basis, airlines have the potential to alter their capacity. Management can decide to move out of unprofitable routes, adjust fleet composition, and change route structures. While the intent of these actions would, of course, be to enhance long-term value, whether these decisions will be profitable in the short term is questionable. We attempt to proxy for these capacity actions by incorporating the variable AVLMILES. Although we could not obtain the requisite data on a quarterly basis we gathered annual information for number of aircraft, route changes, and airports used. We regressed these variables (and other control variables) on AVLMILES (see the Appendix). The results suggest that available ton miles (AVLMILES) appears to be reasonable proxy for capacity.

24. In the long term, rational decision makers would not choose to increase AVLMILES unless they expected the resulting percentage increase in operating revenues to exceed or equal the resulting increase in expenses. Therefore the regression coefficient sign on AVLMILES would be contrary to expectations. This situation could be due to multicollinearity because some of the correlations noted in Table 2 were relatively large. Therefore, we perform the following additional analyses. First, we examined the VIF scores for all our independent variables. The highest VIF score was 3.74, which suggests that multicollinarity is not affecting the results (VIF > 10 are normally a sign of significant multicollinearity). Next, we removed the variable LOADFCTR from the regression models and reran the regression models (LOADFCTR and MKTSHR are correlated at 0.47—see Table 2). The statistical significance remained almost identical to those specified in Tables 4–6. Next, we removed the variable

TABLE 4

Contemporaneous Model Regressions of Fundamental Operating Metrics On Financial Performance[a]

Variable[b]	Operating Income		Operating Revenue		Operating Expense	
	Coefficient	t Stat.	Coefficient	t Stat.	Coefficient	t Stat.
Constant	−30.78	−1.72*	8.42	4.61***	12.68	6.51***
CMPLNTFT	−1.13	−5.19***	−0.03	−1.47*	0.08	3.19***
LOADFCTR	1.90	1.70**	0.35	3.09***	0.13	1.07
MKTSHR	1.50	2.09**	0.21	2.80***	0.05	0.64
AVLMILES	−2.08	−3.16***	0.46	6.87***	0.67	9.36***
Y1996	84.12	4.30***	−1.39	−0.70	−9.74	−4.59***
Y1995	79.31	4.49***	−7.01	−3.90***	−14.09	−7.34***
Y1994	77.54	4.31***	−9.64	−5.27***	−16.06	−8.22***
Y1993	82.85	5.21***	−2.66	−1.64*	−11.19	−6.48***
Y1992	23.87	1.37	−6.22	−3.50***	−11.08	−5.85***
Y1991	14.46	0.84	−7.09	−4.03***	−9.98	−5.31***
Y1990	−8.54	−0.50	−2.31	−1.32	−1.41	−0.75
Alaska	−8.87	−0.56	−2.49	−1.55	−1.62	−0.94
American	0.84	0.06	1.98	1.30	1.08	0.67
America West	15.00	0.99	2.49	1.61	0.96	0.58
Delta	6.99	0.46	−0.87	−0.57	−1.15	−0.71
Southwest	−5.48	−0.32	4.28	2.48***	5.85	3.17***
United	−7.29	−0.49	0.05	0.03	0.65	0.40
Adjusted R^2	40.5%		65.5%		70.9%	
Model F statistic	9.47***		24.66***		31.4***	

*** Significant at the 0.01 level.
** Significant at the 0.05 level.
* Significant at the 0.10 level.
For all the equations, the coefficients for LOADFCTR and MKTSHR are one-tailed tests. For the operating income and revenue equations, the coefficients for CMPLNTFT are one-tailed tests. For the operating revenue and expense equations, the coefficients for AVLMILES are one-tailed tests. The coefficients for all other variables are two-tailed tests.

[a] The sample consists of 213 quarterly observations from 1989 to 1996.
[b] All variables are defined in Table 1.

itively associated with financial performance as proxied by changes in operating income. This result suggests that airlines that are successful at selling their available seats and attracting customers from other airlines exhibit increased operating income.

AVLMILES from the regression models outlined in Table 4 and reestimated the models. While most of the findings remain unchanged the significance level on MKTSHR changed from 0.04 to 0.12. The sign on all coefficients remained the same as those in Tables 4–6. Finally, to ensure percentage changes in available ton miles is not proxying for size, we add the natural logarithm of assets to the model and the results are qualitatively identical to those presented in Tables 4–6. Based on these tests, it appears that multicollinearity is not influencing the results of our regressions.

Results consistent with expectations were noted when financial performance was proxied by percentage changes in operating revenues (OPREV). Fitted complaints has a significant negative (p-value $= 0.07$) impact on same quarter revenue changes.[25] Thus, when complaints rise due to poor customer service, revenues tend to deteriorate. Load factor is positively associated with revenue changes. As predicted, available miles and market share changes have a positive association with revenue changes. Thus it appears that as airlines expand their fixed capacity by adding more flights and increase the percentage of seats filled on the plane, revenues tend to rise. MKTSHR is also significant, suggesting that after taking into account capacity changes, increases in market power are also associated with increases in revenues.

With regard to percentage changes in expense (OPEXP), available mile changes is a significant positive predictor. In contrast to expectation, load factor and market share have no statistical association with operating expenses. Intuitively, the load factor result appears to be because expenses fixed at the airline and flight levels constitute a significant portion of total operating expense in the airline industry; thus, a higher percentage of seats sold may have a negligible effect on operating expenses. Fitted complaints, our proxy for customer satisfaction, also appears to be positively associated with expenses (i.e., as customer satisfaction decreases, expenses increase). An interpretation of this result is that customer dissatisfaction may not only impact future revenues but also impact current profits by increasing expenses.

Finally, as previously discussed in the airline industry section, during the early 1990s airlines retreated into profitable markets, cut operating costs, restructured operations, and prepared for an immediate future of low fares and fierce competition and by 1996 capacity had leveled off. Our results on the dummy variables are consistent with this anecdotal evidence. From 1990 to 1996 the year dummy coefficients for the operating income equation increased from -8.87 to 84.12. However, the coefficients have remained somewhat stable over the last four years. Finally, the explanatory power of models (i.e., adjusted R^2) ranges from 0.40 to 0.71. The models' F statistics are all significant at the 0.01 level.

---

25. One may question whether the impact of complaints on revenues would occur in the same quarter or for some lagged period(s). Our choice to examine same quarter changes in complaints and financial performance is because business passengers (versus recreational passengers) are the major source of airline revenue. Business passengers are airlines' important customers for two reasons: (1) business passengers tend to purchase tickets more often and (2) business passengers tend to pay higher ticket prices. Anecdotally, the *Wall Street Journal* (Petzinger [1995]) notes that "on American, a full-fare coach traveler (business passenger) pays $1,074 for a New York-Miami round trip, while the rock-bottom restricted fare is $169 (vacation passenger)." Assuming business passengers fly a second time in the same quarter that they have a complaint and assuming that complaints impact business travelers' choice of airline, testing the association of current quarter changes in complaints and current quarter changes in financial performance appears reasonable. To the extent that passengers do not make their next ticket purchase in the same quarter, the model is misspecified.

7.3 Predictive Models

Results from using eq. (2) for predicting quarterly results, where financial performance is proxied by operating income, operating revenues, and operating expenses, are presented in Tables 5 and 6. The explanatory power of predictive models (i.e., adjusted R^2) ranges from 0.35 to 0.71. The models' F statistics are all significant at the 0.01 level. It appears that these models explain quarterly financial results reasonably well. Based on these findings, there is evidence to suggest that these nonfinancial metrics can be useful in predicting quarterly financial performance.

In Table 5, all independent variables are calculated as the percentage change in the independent variable for month-one of the quarter from the same month in the prior year (e.g., [load factor$_{m1 \text{ of } q}$ − load factor$_{m1 \text{ of } q-4}$]/load factor$_{m1 \text{ of } q-4}$). Even though only one month of nonfinancial data is used to predict financial performance for the quarter, the results are remarkably similar to those presented in Table 4. First, the fitted values for complaint changes (CMPLNTFT) and changes in available ton miles are significant negative predictors of operating income (OPINC). Thus, as complaints increase, financial performance as proxied by operating income decreases. Similarly, as available ton miles increase, operating income decreases. In addition, percentage changes in market share are positively associated with financial performance, as proxied by changes in operating income. In contrast to the contemporaneous results, however, load factor does not appear to be significantly associated with percentage changes in operating income (p-value = 0.11).

Fitted complaints has a significant negative impact on percentage changes in revenues (OPREV). Thus, when complaints rise due to poor customer service, revenues tend to deteriorate. Load factor and market share changes are positively associated with revenue changes. As predicted, but in contrast to the operating income finding, available mile changes has a positive association with revenues. Thus it appears that as airlines expand their capacity by adding more flights, revenues tend to rise.

With regard to the prediction of operating expense changes (OPEXP), customer complaints and available mile changes are significant positive predictors in the one-month model. In addition, market share changes are associated with increases in expenses. In contrast to expectation, load factor has no statistical association with operating expenses. Intuitively, this appears to be because expenses fixed at the airline and flight levels constitute a significant portion of total operating expense in the airline industry; thus, a higher percentage of seats sold may have a negligible effect on operating expenses. An interpretation of the fitted complaints (customer satisfaction proxy) result is that customer dissatisfaction not only may impact future revenues but also impact current profits by increasing expenses.

In Table 6, we add variables representing the information contained in the second month of the nonfinancial performance data (e.g., [load factor$_{m2 \text{ of } q}$ − load factor$_{m2 \text{ of } q-4}$]/load factor$_{m2 \text{ of } q-4}$). For each independent variable, we regress month

TABLE 5

One-Month Predictive Model Regressions Using Fundamental Operating Metrics to Predict Quarterly Financial Performance[a]

Variable[b]	Operating Income		Operating Revenue		Operating Expense	
	Coefficient	t Stat.	Coefficient	t Stat.	Coefficient	t Stat.
Constant	−25.43	−1.36	8.61	4.74***	12.26	6.20***
CMPLNTFT—One	−1.12	−4.51***	−0.04	−1.84**	0.07	2.56***
LOADFCTR—One	1.30	1.23	0.19	1.82**	0.07	0.58
MKTSHR—One	1.36	1.98**	0.28	4.26***	0.15	2.07**
AVLMILES—One	−1.79	−2.88***	0.46	7.63***	0.63	9.59***
Y1996	55.87	2.91***	−1.24	−0.66	−6.34	−3.12***
Y1995	84.86	4.14***	−5.80	−2.91***	−13.35	−6.16***
Y1994	92.77	4.29***	−7.81	−3.71***	−15.91	−6.96***
Y1993	80.72	4.74***	−1.49	−0.90	−9.96	−5.53***
Y1992	23.37	1.22	−5.03	−2.69***	−9.81	−4.83***
Y1991	27.94	1.39	−6.06	−3.10***	−10.29	−4.85***
Y1990	−0.65	−0.03	−0.83	−0.44	−0.45	−0.22
Alaska	−30.39	−1.69*	−3.28	−1.88*	−0.40	−0.21
American	−3.78	−0.24	1.16	0.76	0.82	0.50
America West	13.66	0.86	1.49	0.96	0.66	0.40
Delta	9.82	0.62	−1.84	−1.19	−2.42	−1.45
Southwest	14.36	0.80	3.05	1.75*	2.65	1.40
United	−12.67	−0.79	−1.33	−0.85	−0.62	−0.04
Adjusted R^2	35.1%		65.4%		70.2%	
F statistic	7.74***		24.6***		30.4***	

*** Significant at the 0.01 level.
** Significant at the 0.05 level.
* Significant at the 0.10 level.
For all the equations, the coefficients for LOADFCTR and MKTSHR are one-tailed tests. For the operating income and revenue equations, the coefficients for CMPLNTFT are one-tailed tests. For the operating revenue and expense equations, the coefficients for AVLMILES are one-tailed tests. The coefficients for all other variables are two-tailed tests.
[a] The sample consists of 213 quarterly observations from 1989 to 1996.
[b] All variables are defined in Table 1.

2 values on month 1 values (and year and time dummy variables) and incorporate the residuals from these regressions along with the month-1 values examined in Table 5. With the exception of load factor, the statistical association between the month 1 nonfinancial performance variables and operating income is consistent with the results presented in Table 5. Month 1 fitted complaints, market share and available ton miles are significant explanatory variables for operating income. The p-value on load factor declined from 0.11 to 0.21. In addition, the month 2 data for fitted complaints, load factor and market share are all significantly associated with quarterly operating income. Only the month 2 residual for available ton miles has no statistical association. These results suggest that, consistent with expecta-

TABLE 6

Two-Month Predictive Model Regressions Using Fundamental Operating Metrics to Predict Quarterly Financial Performance[a]

Variable[b]	Operating Income		Operating Revenue		Operating Expense	
	Coefficient	t Stat.	Coefficient	t Stat.	Coefficient	t Stat.
Constant	−20.46	−1.10	10.55	5.61***	12.93	6.52***
CMPLNTFT—One	−1.13	−4.62***	−0.04	−1.73**	0.06	2.18**
Two	−0.68	−1.82**	−0.04	−1.12	0.02	0.40
LOADFCTR—One	0.88	0.83	0.22	2.08**	0.14	1.23
Two	1.50	1.50*	0.21	2.10**	0.09	0.85
MKTSHR—One	1.83	2.50***	0.29	3.99***	0.11	1.41*
Two	1.16	1.64**	0.06	0.89	−0.10	−1.35*
AVLMILES—One	−2.15	−3.29***	0.41	6.25***	0.63	9.07***
Two	0.68	0.53	0.31	2.42***	0.39	2.83***
Y1996	60.64	3.14***	−2.39	−1.23	−7.81	−3.81***
Y1995	90.05	4.43***	−5.63	−2.75***	−14.17	−6.56***
Y1994	95.77	4.48***	−8.35	−3.88***	−16.03	−7.05***
Y1993	81.19	4.74***	−2.71	−1.57	−11.14	−6.12***
Y1992	30.99	1.64*	−5.08	−2.67***	−10.34	−5.15***
Y1991	23.25	1.14	−6.54	−3.19***	−9.75	−4.50***
Y1990	5.87	0.30	−0.59	−0.30	−0.77	−0.37
Alaska	−48.65	−2.67***	−5.18	−2.82***	−0.18	−0.09
American	−4.21	−0.28	0.24	0.16	0.43	0.27
America West	8.82	0.57	0.22	0.14	0.54	0.32
Delta	3.00	0.19	−3.22	−2.04**	−2.49	−1.50
Southwest	4.61	0.026	2.06	1.15	3.39	1.79*
United	−18.26	−1.15	−2.49	−1.56	−0.26	−0.15
Adjusted R^2	38.7%		64.8%		71.2%	
F statistic	7.37***		19.6***		25.9***	

*** Significant at the 0.01 level.
** Significant at the 0.05 level.
* Significant at the 0.10 level.
For all the equations, the coefficients for LOADFCTR, MKTSHR are one-tailed tests. For the operating income and revenue equations, the coefficients for CMPLNTFT are one-tailed tests. For the operating revenue and expense equations, the coefficients for AVLMILES are one-tailed tests. The coefficients for all other variables are two-tailed tests.
[a] The sample consists of 213 quarterly observations from 1989 to 1996.
[b] All variables are defined in Table 1.

tions, the second month of data reinforces and improves predictions that incorporate only one month of data.

With regard to revenues, the association between the month 1 variables and percentage changes in operating income is virtually identical to the results presented in Table 5, where percentage changes in month 1 fitted complaints, load factor, market share, and available ton miles are significantly associated with revenue changes. With regard to the month 2 information added to the model, only month

2 percentage changes in load factor and available ton miles are statistically associated with percentage changes in revenue.

The results for the regression of percentage changes in operating expenses on two months of nonfinancial performance measures appear in the last two columns of Table 6. The month 1 values for percentage changes in fitted complaints, market share, and available ton miles continue to be positively associated with percentage changes in operating expense. Consistent with Tables 4 and 5, month 1 load factor changes demonstrate no statistical association with operating expense changes. With regard to the month 2 information added to the model, the residuals from the market share regression have a mild association with percentage changes in operating expense and month 2 available ton miles residuals are significantly associated with operating expense changes. Overall, the predictive results presented in Table 5 and 6 are consistent with the contemporaneous associations observed in Table 4, and one can conclude that even one month of nonfinancial performance information can be used as a basis for prediction of quarterly financial performance in the airline industry. Further and consistent with expectation, the second month of data also enhance the explanatory power (i.e., adjusted R^2) of the models.

7.4 Sensitivity Testing

Although the results from the prior analyses are generally consistent with expectations, we perform several additional tests to ensure the results are robust to alternative measures of financial performance. First, we substitute profitability ratio changes, used by Dresner and Xu (1995) (i.e., the ratio of operating revenues to operating expenses [revenues/expenses]) for changes in operating income (OPINC) as the dependent variable in the contemporaneous model. Second, we substitute changes in the natural log of operating earnings (natural log of operating revenues less natural log of operating expenses) for operating income changes (OPINC) as the dependent variable. Finally, we substitute changes in the natural log of revenues and changes in the natural log of expenses for percentage changes in revenues and expenses (i.e., OPREV and OPEXP). The results from all these tests are virtually unchanged from those presented in Table 4. Fitted complaint (CMPLNTFT) and available ton mile (AVLMILES) changes continue to be negatively significant, while load factor (LOADFCTR) and market share (MKTSHR) changes are significant and positively associated with profitability ratio changes. As a result of these sensitivity tests, it appears that the results in this paper are fairly robust to alternative specifications.

8. Conclusions, Limitations, and Future Research

In this research we have examined the association between nonfinancial performance variables and financial performance in the U.S. airline industry and examined whether this nonfinancial information can be used to predict quarterly financial performance. From analysts' written pronouncements and financial press articles we identify a number of fundamental metrics purportedly used by analysts and investors to assess airline performance. Using an instrumental variables approach, we find that on-time performance, mishandled baggage, ticket oversales, and in-flight service are significantly associated with customer satisfaction. Using this proxy for customer satisfaction in our contemporaneous model, we find that customer satisfaction, load factor, market share, and available ton miles are associated with operating income and revenues and that customer satisfaction and available ton miles are associated with expenses. In addition, using one and two months of nonfinancial data, we find that nonfinancial performance information appears to be useful in predicting quarterly revenues, expenses, and operating income. Based on these findings, it appears that timely nonfinancial performance metrics are associated with, and can be useful in predicting, financial performance for the U.S. airline industry.

This research is important because both academics and policymakers, including Birchard (1994), the AICPA (1994) Jenkins Committee, and Wallman (1995, 1996), have expressed concern that corporate financial reporting and disclosure are not keeping pace with a dynamic and constantly changing business world. To enhance traditional financial reporting, one consistent suggestion from this group has been to provide financial statement users with nonfinancial performance information that may enhance users' ability to evaluate and predict financial performance. This study contributes to this debate by providing empirical evidence that timely nonfinancial performance information is a useful predictor of financial performance in the airline industry. However, this study has its limitations.

One of the main limitations of this research is that nonfinancial performance variable hypotheses are developed from analysts' written pronouncements and anecdotal assertions from financial press articles. Therefore, neither a solid theoretical nor an analytical modeling foundation exists for our predictions. Although the results are intuitive, the explicit means by which nonfinancial performance variables track into revenues, expenses, and operating earnings eludes us. Thus, one extension may be for researchers to theoretically model the association between nonfinancial and financial performance. Another extension may be to determine if this information is valued by using the capital market's reaction to the variables incorporated in this study. This may be especially important because in the airline industry, many of the nonfinancial performance variables incorporated in this research are disclosed monthly, whereas financial statement data is systematically released quarterly.

Another limitation is that the research is completed at the industry level. Both sample size and generalizability of the results are adversely impacted. However, Amir and Lev (1996) argue that the specificity of analyses and insights gained from industry studies are often more explicit than general cross-sectional studies. Another concern is that the listing of nonfinancial performance variables incorporated in this study may not be complete. One may argue that variables related to geographic coverage, hub concentration, haul length, and frequent flier membership are important nonfinancial performance variables. One could also argue that by examining quarterly associations we are not addressing the fundamental drivers of long-term value. For example, do long-term investments in computerized reservation systems increase market share and therefore enhance long-term company value? While these limitations exist, however, we initiate the analysis of short-term financial performance and nonfinancial performance information, leaving the exploration of their association with longer-term financial performance for subsequent research.

While this paper concentrated on the relationships among nonfinancial variables and quarterly financial performance in the airline industry, research that provides a better understanding of the internal linkages among these variables could be very promising. Using a framework such as Kaplan and Norton's (1992) Balanced Scorecard or similar tools to better understand the cause and effect relationships between operational data, long-term investments, and long-term financial performance could be very beneficial. In addition, enhancing our understanding of the relationship between customer satisfaction and financial performance could be a fruitful avenue of research to pursue.

APPENDIX: FURTHER ANALYSIS OF AVLMILES AS A PROXY FOR CAPACITY

AVLMILES (the percentage change in available ton miles from the same quarter in the prior year) was designed to capture strategic uses of capacity. Short-term strategic uses of capacity include (1) adjustments in fleet composition, (2) movement in and out of unprofitable routes, and (3) changes in airports serviced by the airline. While we could not obtain the requisite data to include these proxies in our quarterly regressions, we gathered the following information on an annual basis and performed the following regression:

Dependent Measure: Percent Change in Available Ton Miles

Variable[a]	Coefficient	t Stat.
Constant	0.09	2.29**
ACRFTC	0.20	2.31***
ROUTEC	0.01	2.89***
AIRPORTC	1.12	5.55***
Y1996	0.02	0.50
Y1995	0.07	1.76*
Y1994	0.06	1.63
Y1993	0.02	0.54
Y1992	0.03	0.78
Y1991	0.04	1.16
Y1990	0.06	1.78*
Alaska	−0.07	−2.02**
American	−0.04	--1.09

USING NONFINANCIAL INFORMATION   55

Variable[a]	Coefficient	t Stat.
America West	−0.10	−2.62***
Delta	−0.10	−2.69***
Southwest	−0.11	−2.88***
United	−0.05	−1.46
Adjusted R^2	68.4%	
Model F statistic	8.42***	

*** Significant at the 0.01 level.
** Significant at the 0.05 level.
* Significant at the 0.10 level.
[a] The sample consists of 56 annual observations from 1989 to 1996.

ACRFTC = Percentage change in the number of aircraft (year$_t$ − year$_{t-1}$/year$_{t-1}$); source: annual report or 10-K.

ROUTEC = Number of route changes for a given year, where a route change is defined as at least a 20 percent change in arrivals at the 26 largest airports where such change is sustained for at least two quarters. Source: *Air Travel Consumer Reports.*

AIRPORTC = Percentage change in the number of airports used during the year (year$_t$ − year$_{t-1}$/year$_{t-1}$); Source: *Air Travel Consumer Report.*

The results of the preceding analysis suggest that aircraft increases, changes in route structure and airport increases are positively associated with increases in capacity (available ton miles). The model's R^2 is 0.68 and the F statistic is significant at the 0.001 level. Based on this analysis it appears that available ton miles (AVLMILES) appears to be a reasonable proxy for capacity metrics.

REFERENCES

AICPA. 1994. *Improving Business Reporting: A Customer Focus.* New York: American Institute of Certified Public Accountants.

Amir, E., and B. Lev. 1996. "Value-Relevance of Non-Financial Information: The Wireless Communications Industry." *Journal of Accounting and Economics* 22 (August–December): 3–30.

Bernard, V., and J. Noel 1991. "Do Inventory Disclosures Predict Sales and Earnings?" *Journal of Accounting, Auditing & Finance* 6 (Spring): 145–181.

Birchard, B. 1994. "The Call for Full Disclosure." *CFO Magazine* 10 (December): 31–42.

Carey, S. 1996. "UAL Net Soars 40% on Ticket Prices and Traffic as Revenue Climbs 8.7%." *Wall Street Journal* 228 (October 23): B11.

Dresner, M., and K. Xu. 1995. "Customer Service, Customer Satisfaction and Corporate Performance in the Service Sector." *Journal of Business Logistics* 16:23–40.

Financial Accounting Standards Board (FASB). 1978. *Objectives of Financial Reporting by Business Enterprises.* Statement of Financial Accounting Concepts No. 1, Norwalk, CT: FASB.

Fraering, J. M., and M. S. Minor. 1994. "The Industry-Specific Basis of the Market Share-Profitability Relationship." *Journal of Consumer Marketing* 11:27–37.

Francis, J., and K. Schipper. 1998. "Have Financial Statements Lost Their Relevance?" Working Paper, University of Chicago.

Jones, D. 1995. "Low-Cost Carrier Still Challenges Industry." *USA Today* 13 (July 10): 5B.

Kaplan, R. S., and D. P. Norton. 1992. "The Balanced Scorecard: Measures that Drive Performance." *Harvard Business Review* 70 (January–February): 71–79.

Lev, B., and S. R. Thiagarajan. 1993. "Fundamental Information Analysis." *Journal of Accounting Research* 31 (Autumn): 190–215.

McCartney, S. 1995. "Back on Course: Piloted by Bethune, Continental Air Lifts Its Workers Morale." *Wall Street Journal* 225 (May 15): A1.

O'Connor, W. E. 1995. *An Introduction to Airline Economics.* Westport, Conn.: Praeger.

Ott, J., and R. E. Neidl. 1995. *Airline Odyssey: The Airline Industry's Turbulent Flight into the Future.* New York: McGraw Hill.

Petzinger, T., Jr. 1995 "Hard Landing: Four Lessons Our Airlines Need to Learn." *Wall Street Journal* 226 (November 6): B1.

Reichheld, F., and W. E. Sasser, Jr. 1990. "Zero Defections: Quality Comes to Services." *Harvard Business Review* 68 (September–October): 105–111.

Schefczyk, M. 1993. "Operational Performance of Airlines: An Extension of Traditional Measurement Paradigms." *Strategic Management Journal* 14:301–317.

Stober, T. L. 1993. "The Incremental Information Content of Receivable in Predicting Sales, Earnings, and Profit Margins." *Journal of Accounting, Auditing & Finance* 8 (Fall): 447–473.

Wallman, S. M. H. 1995. "The Future of Accounting and Disclosure in an Evolving World: The Need for Dramatic Change." *Accounting Horizons* 9 (September): 81–91.

Wallman, S. M. H. 1996. "The Future of Accounting and Financial Reporting Part II: The Colorized Approach." *Accounting Horizons* 10 (June): 138–148.

Zeithaml, V. A., L. L. Berry, and A. Parasuraman. 1996. "The Behavioral Consequences of Service Quality." *Journal of Marketing* 60 (April): 31–46.

17

The effect of productivity and quality on profitability in US airline industry
An empirical investigation

Mahour Mellat Parast

Elham (Ellie) H. Fini

Abstract

Purpose – This study aims to investigate the effect of productivity and quality on profitability in the US airline industry.

Design/methodology/approach – Airlines operations and performance data were used to determine the effect of productivity and quality on profitability. Correlation and multivariate regression analysis have been used for data analysis.

Findings – The results show that labor productivity is the most significant predictor of profitability. On-time performance has no relationship with profitability. The findings suggest that labor productivity, gas price, average annual maintenance cost and employee salary are significant predictors of profitability. The relationship between labor productivity and employee salary with profitability is positive, while gas price and average annual maintenance cost have a negative relationship with profitability.

Research limitations/implications – The research could be more detailed by taking into account measures of airline safety. Additional measures for service quality could be considered.

Practical implications – Operational performance (labor productivity) is the main source of profitability in the US airline industry followed by customer satisfaction and service quality.

Originality/value – The study captures the performance of the airline industry based on longitudinal data from 1989 to 2008. Previous studies have used either quarterly or monthly observations. Second, the study examines the significance of productivity and quality on profitability. Previous studies have provided little insight regarding the effect of productivity and quality on profitability.

Keywords Productivity rate, Quality, Profit, Airlines, United States of America

Paper type Research paper

1. Introduction

In the pursuit of better operational performance and profitability, organizations are looking for strategies to improve their operational performance and boost their profitability. As competition intensifies due to changes in the industry structure and the emergence of new technologies, organizations are determined to reduce their operational cost while enhance their profitability. This holds true for the airline industry as well.

The airline industry is experiencing some tough times. Previous studies has indicated that there are inherent problems in the airline industry due to cyclical and seasonal demand, high labor/capital, fuel intensity, government intervention, and organized labor (Taneja, 1988; Williams, 2002; Taneja, 2003; Raghavan and Rhoades, 2008). In addition to the structural changes in the industry, the unpredictable and stochastic nature of demand (i.e. customers) in the airline industry contributes to the complexity of the management of day-to-day operations (Listes and Dekker, 2005). Accordingly, it is important to determine internal factors that contribute to the performance of the airlines. This helps airlines to more effectively allocate their resources and emphasize practices that contribute to the overall organizational performance.

This paper seeks two objectives: First, it investigates the effect of productivity and quality on profitability. Second, it determines the operational factors that affect profitability in the US airline industry. To do so, operational and performance data of airlines during 1989-2008 was used to examine the effect of quality and productivity on profitability.

2. Literature review

The US airline industry was completely deregulated after the Airline Deregulation Act of 1979. The new environment enabled the airline industry to initiate and develop business practices that could not be easily implemented during the regulated era. The effect of deregulation on improving airline industry is a debatable issue. In fact, productivity of the airline industry was improving before the deregulation due to the technological advancement, even at a higher rate than the entire US economy (Murphy, 1969). While there is the presumption that organizations functioning in regulated environments cannot achieve sustainable competitive advantage, empirical findings suggest that in the regulated airline industry firms enhanced their profitability through two sets of practices:

(1) effective utilization of their strategic resources; and

(2) pursuing an efficiency-oriented strategy.

In the US airline industry (during the regulated area) it has been found that the profitability of an air carrier was ultimately determined by organizational leaders (Ramaswamy et al., 1994). Therefore, in the regulated area of the US airline industry managers' operational and business strategies were significant determinants of profitability.

It has been argued that the deregulation of the US airline industry has resulted in improving productivity, efficient management practices and higher quality services to customers (Adrangi et al., 1997). After deregulation, the competition in the airline industry shifted from emphasis on frequency of flights, geographical coverage and in-flight service to focus on operational excellence (Treacy and Wiersema, 1995). Operational excellence was considered as an effective business strategy business strategy before the deregulation as well (Ramaswamy et al., 1994). This suggests that the airline industry had acknowledged the role of operational excellence and efficiency-driven strategy on profitability.

While the effect of deregulation on the US airline industry has been widely discussed (e.g. Trapani and Olson, 1982; Moore, 1986; Bailey and Williams, 1988;

MSQ
20,5

Adrangi *et al.*, 1997), little attention has been devoted to the effect operational performance on airline profitability. This study aims to bridge the gap in the literature by investigating the effect of operational factors on airline profitability. More specifically, this study addresses the effect of productivity and quality on profitability in the US airline industry.

460

2.1 The relationship between operational performance and profitability in services
The effect of operational performance on profitability has been extensively discussed in both manufacturing and service organizations. From quality management perspective, several studies show that certain practices such as employee training, employee involvement, and process improvement enhance profitability (e.g. Douglas and Judge, 2001; Kaynak, 2003; Yeung *et al.*, 2006). Empirical findings suggest a direct link between quality and profitability in both manufacturing and service organizations (Buzzell *et al.*, 1987). In case of the service organizations several studies have addressed the role of service quality, customer satisfaction, and business performance (Zhao *et al.*, 2004; Voss *et al.*, 2005). Smith and Reece (1999) found a link between productivity and financial performance in the distribution sector. It has been suggested that understanding the relationship between service quality and profitability requires simultaneous investigation of the link between productivity and profitability (Zeithaml *et al.*, 1996).

Few studies have addressed the effect of operational performance on profitability in the airline industry. Schefczyk (1993) studied the effect of total factor productivity on financial performance in the international airline industry. The findings suggested that productivity is related to return on equity. According to Schefczyk (1993), using productivity alone will be misleading in addressing profitability since in the context of the airline industry, productivity may not take into account the operational aspects (such as on-time departure, in flight service, baggage handling, etc.) that are important to the customer. Lapré and Scudder (2004) showed that performance improvement in the airlines can be achieved depending upon their proximity of operations to their asset frontiers[1]. Their findings suggest that airlines operating closer to their asset frontiers cannot improve both quality and cost simultaneously. Alternatively, those airlines that are operating away from their assent frontiers can achieve simultaneous improvement in both quality and cost. In another study, Tsikriktsis (2007) empirically investigated the relationship between operational performance and profitability. Utilizing the concept of "focused factory" the findings suggested that airline profitability is contingent upon the organization's operation model. Focused airlines show a negative link between late arrivals (i.e. new entrants) and profitability while full-service airlines do not show such a link. In addition, capacity utilization is a stronger driver of profitability for the full-service airlines compared to the focused airlines. In terms of performance, focused airlines outperform full service airlines[2].

This study differs from the previous studies in several aspects. First, this study captures the performance of the airline industry based on the longitudinal data from 1989 to 2008. Previous studies have used either quarterly or monthly observations. Second, this study examines the significance of productivity and quality on profitability. Previous studies have provided little insight regarding the effect of productivity and quality on profitability. Finally, in this paper different measures for quality and productivity have been utilized.

3. Theoretical background

Several theoretical frameworks can be used to address the link between quality, productivity, and performance in services. The "service profit chain" argues that certain human resource management practices can enhance customer satisfaction resulting in improvement of productivity and quality of service which in return increase financial performance (Heskett *et al.*, 1997; Loveman, 1998). This perspective is in line with the resource-based view of the firm, which argues that resources and capabilities of an organization can be a source of competitive advantage (Barney, 1991, 1995; Wright *et al.*, 1994).

Previous studies have addressed the effect of productivity in improving performance (Roth and Jackson, 1995; Anderson *et al.*, 1997). Within the airline industry there are a few studies that show the link between productivity and performance (Murphy, 1969; Schefczyk, 1993; Tsikriktsis, 2007). While the above studies have utilized different forms and/or definitions for productivity, the general findings suggest that productivity is related to performance in the airline industry. With reference to the "service profit chain" one can argue that human resource practices in the airline industry are directly linked to profitability. One of the measures that can capture both human resource practices and productivity is labor productivity. Therefore, it is hypothesized that:

> *H1.* Labor productivity is directly linked to the profitability in the US airline industry.

In service organizations, quality is directly linked to profitability (Roth and Jackson, 1995). Empirical evidence suggests that there is a link between service quality and profitability (Nelson *et al.*, 1992; Anderson *et al.*, 1994; Rust *et al.*, 1995; Loveman, 1998; Voss *et al.*, 2005). Within services it has been shown that both customer satisfaction and productivity enhance profitability (Anderson *et al.*, 1997). In addition, in the context of the airline industry it is expected that conformance quality (i.e. on-time performance) would be related to profitability since it results in cost reduction and eliminates reworks/rescheduling (e.g. rebooking due to missing the original and/or the connecting flights). Suzuki (2000) found that airlines market share increases with improvement in on-time performance. Therefore, it is hypothesized that:

> *H2.* Quality (on-time performance) is directly related to profitability in US airline industry.

Finally, to explain the similarities and/or differences among airlines (e.g. Delta vs Airtran) we utilize the institutional theory. According to the institutional theory, to be more adaptive and flexible to environmental uncertainty and complexity firms tend to imitate the structure, processes, norms, rules, and practices of a dominant institution. The outcome of such adaptive processes will lead to organizational isomorphism -"the resemblance of a focal organization to other organizations in its environment (Deephouse, 1996). From this perspective, firms, which share common norms and practices will become similar over time. Therefore, we can argue that within the US airline industry airlines develop similar organizational processes and routines over time through observing and benchmarking industry best practices[3]. In addition, in relatively homogenous industries (such as the airline industry) the average could be a good indicator of the typical performance of an organization (Lenox *et al.*, 2005;

MSQ
20,5

462

Peteraff and Reed, 2007). Overall, we can argue that using the industry level data can be a good proxy for the performance of a typical airline.

3.1 Variables and measures
Several measures for productivity, quality, and profitability have been used in this study. A list of variables along with their definition within the airline industry has been provided as follows:

- *Labor productivity (LPR):* labor productivity is defined as output per unit of labor and is calculated by dividing output by a measure of the labor input (typically labor hours). For air transportation, output is measured in terms of passenger-miles and ton-miles. Labor productivity has been used as a measure of productivity.
- *On-time performance (OT):* the percentage of flights that were departed on-time (less than 15 minutes late). On-time performance has been used as a measure of quality (conformance quality).
- *Gas price (GAS):* the average gas price per year. GAS is a measure of operational cost.
- *Employee salary (SAL):* average employee salary per year. SAL is a measure of operational cost.
- *Maintenance cost per flight hours (MC):* the average cost of maintaining the aircraft divided by the total number of flight hours per year. MC is a measure of operational cost.
- *Passenger load factor (PLF):* the number of passenger-kilometers traveled as a percentage of the total seat-kilometers available. PLF is a measure of profitability.

Utilization of resources is directly related to profitability (D'Aveni, 1989; Hammesfahr *et al.*, 1993). Passenger load factor is a measure of utilization of resources and has been recommended as a measure of profitability in the airline industry (De Vany, 1975; Spiller, 1983; Baltagi *et al.*, 1998). Previous studies indicate that a difference of one percentage in load factor could result in profitability difference as high as five percent (Wyckoff and Maister, 1977). It has been argued that differences in accounting policies may provide misleading information when using financial data from secondary sources (Venkatraman and Ramanujam, 1986). Using passenger load factor as the measure of profitability provides consistent measure for profitability. In terms of quality, previous studies have used on-time performance as the measure of service quality (Mazzeo, 2003). Therefore, these operational variables can be acceptable measures of productivity, quality and profitability in the airline industry.

4. Methodology
The data for this study have been obtained from the Bureau of Transportation Statistics of the US Department of Transportation (DOT). Our analysis is based on the operational performance of all domestic airlines (network and low-cost carriers) from 1989 to 2008. We focused on the operational performance of the entire industry for the following reasons: First, tracking individual airlines within the scope of 20 years is very difficult and in some cases impossible since some of the airlines ceased operations

(due to the bankruptcy, merging, etc). Second, some of the performance measures have been reported at the industry level (e.g. labor productivity). We used annual measures of performance since they provide a more accurate assessment (by removing the seasonal effect of the data).

An advantage of this dataset is its richness in terms of providing a variety of operational measures. In addition, objective measures of performance are free from bias. Using objective measures of performance for a single industry is appropriate because it allows for precise determination of the sources of performance (Venkatraman and Ramanujam, 1986; Garvin, 1988; Tsikriktsis, 2007). Therefore, the data used in this study is appropriate to address the research questions being investigated.

5. Data analysis
The mean and standard deviation along with measures of skewness and kurtosis for each variable have been calculated and the results have been presented in Table I. At the level of significance of 0.01 ($\alpha = 0.01$), the critical value of skewness is ± 1.174. For kurtosis, a value in the range of -1.21 and 2.86 satisfies the requirement of normality ($\alpha = 0.02$). With the exception of gas price (GAS), which exceeds skewness threshold and salary (SAL), which exceeds the kurtosis threshold, other variables are within the threshold of skewness and kurtosis.

To further investigate the normality of the data, we conducted the Kolmogorov-Smirnov (KS) test of normality. The result showed that all variables are coming from a normal distribution.

5.1 Correlation between variables
Correlation between variables is presented in Table II. The findings from Table II shows that passenger load factor (PLF) is significantly correlated with labor productivity (LPR). Therefore, $H1$ is supported ($r = 0.946$, $p - \text{value} = 0.0001$).

On-time performance is significantly correlated with passenger load factor (PLF). However, the correlation is negative indicating that improvement in on-time performance may negatively affect profitability ($r = -0.72$, $p - \text{value} = 0.001$). This is counterintuitive since it was expected that quality and profitability are significantly and positively related. This could be an indication of spurious correlation where the relationship between OT and PLF is influenced by another variable (e.g. labor productivity).

5.2 Stepwise regression on profitability
To further investigate the effect of operational variables on profitability, a stepwise regression analysis was conducted. Productivity (LPR), quality (OT), maintenance cost

Variables	Minimum	Maximum	Mean	Std deviation	Skewness	Kurtosis
OT (%)	76.74	87.88	82.32	3.53	0.107	-1.143
LPR (%)	78	145	101.45	20.76	1.016	0.082
GAS ($)	1.35	2.80	1.87	0.44	1.273	0.41
MC ($)	1.26	3.54	2.06	0.65	1.168	0.431
SAL ($)	32,000	65,000	46,245	2,574	0.295	-1.652
PLF (%)	60	79.88	69.34	6.46	0.198	-0.97

Table I.
Descriptive statistics

MSQ
20,5

464

	OT	LPR	GAS	MC	SAL	PLF
OT	1	-0.699^{**}	-0.522^{*}	0.307	-0.563^{**}	-0.720^{**}
Sig.		0.0001	0.018	0.188	0.01	0.0001
LPR	-0.699^{**}	1	0.859^{*}	-0.185	0.810^{**}	0.946^{**}
Sig.	0.0001		0.0001	0.435	0.0001	0.0001
GAS	-0.522^{*}	0.859^{**}	1	-0.373	0.709^{**}	0.733^{**}
Sig.	0.018	0.0001		0.105	0.0001	0.0001
MC	0.307	-0.185	-0.373	1	-0.508^{*}	-0.319
Sig.	0.188	0.435	0.105		0.022	0.171
SAL	-0.563^{**}	0.810^{**}	0.709^{**}	-0.508^{*}	1	0.908^{**}
Sig.	0.01	0.0001	0.0001	0.022		0.0001
PLF	-0.720^{**}	0.946^{**}	0.733^{**}	-0.319	0.908^{*}	1
Sig.	0.0001	0.0001	0.0001	0.171	0.0001	

Table II.
Correlation between
variables

Notes: *Correlation is significant at the 0.05 level (two-tailed); **Correlation is significant at the 0.01 level (two-tailed)

per flight hours per year (MC), and employee salary (SAL) were regressed on profitability (PLF). The result is shown in Table III.

Stepwise regression was used to determine the significance of each variable. This procedure has been used in previous studies (Hatten *et al.*, 1978; Eisenhardt and Schoonhoven, 1990; Ramaswamy *et al.*, 1994). Since productivity (LPR) and on-time performance (OT) were both significantly correlated with profitability (PLF), stepwise regression was used to determine the significant variable(s) in the presence of other variables. Because of the potential problem of autocorrelation with time series data, a Durbin-Watson (DW) test statistic was calculated for the regression equation (Neter and Wasserman, 1974; Gujarati, 1995). If the DW statistics is substantially less than two, there is evidence of positive serial correlation. Alternatively, a DT statistic close to four is an indication of negative autocorrelation. The DW test statistic is 1.803, which is close to two. Therefore, it was concluded that autocorrelation does not influence the results.

The model is significant which explain 99 percent of variability of profitability. On-time performance is not a significant variable (Table IV). According to the regression model (Table IV), the effect of labor productivity (LPR) and salary (SAL) on profitability is positive while there is negative impact regarding the effect of gas price (GAS) and maintenance cost per miles flown (MC) on profitability. To check for the existence of multicollinearity, variance inflation factors (VIF) have been calculated. A value inflation factor greater than 10 is an indication of the existence of multicolinearity (Kutner *et al.*, 2004; Hair *et al.*, 2009). From Table IV it is found that all VIFs are less than 10 therefore multicollinearity does not influence the results. Therefore, it was concluded that the model is a good predicator of profitability.

From Table IV, it is found that GAS has a negative standardized coefficient in both Model 3 (-0.327) and Model 4 (-0.432) while the zero-order correlation between GAS and PLF is positive (0.733). This suggests the existence of suppression. We tested this using the partial correlation procedure by using LPR as the control variable when correlating GAS with PLF. The partial correlation between GAS and PLF while controlling for LPR is -0.479 (p-value $= 0.038$). This indicates that LPR positively affects the dependent variable (PLF) through one path and negatively affects through

Model	R	R square	Adjusted R square	Std error of the estimate	R square change	Change statistics				Durbin-Watson
						F change	df1	df2	Sig. F change	
1	0.946[a]	0.894	0.888	2.15806	0.894	152.370	1	18	0.000	
2	0.976[b]	0.953	0.948	1.47488	0.059	21.538	1	17	0.000	
3	0.991[c]	0.981	0.978	0.96474	0.028	23.732	1	16	0.000	
4	0.995[d]	0.990	0.987	0.73971	0.008	12.216	1	15	0.003	1.803

Notes: [a] Predictors: (Constant), LPR; [b] Predictors: (Constant), LPR, SAL; [c] Predictors: (Constant), LPR, SAL, GAS; [d] Predictors: (Constant), LPR, SAL, GAS, MC

Table III.
Model summary

Table IV.
Coefficient

Model		Unstandardized coefficients B	Std. error	Standardized coefficients Beta	t	Sig.	Correlations Zero-order	Partial	Part	Collinearity statistics Tolerance	VIF
1	(Constant)	39.476	2.467		15.999	0.0001					
	LPR	0.294	0.024	0.946	12.344	0.0001	0.946	0.946	0.946	1.000	1.000
2	(Constant)	39.315	1.687		23.311	0.0001					
	LPR	0.190	0.028	0.611	6.845	0.0001	0.946	0.857	0.358	0.345	2.902
	SAL	0.0001	0.0001	0.414	4.641	0.0001	0.908	0.748	0.243	0.345	2.902
3	(Constant)	39.324	1.103		35.645	0.0001					
	LPR	0.274	0.025	0.881	10.940	0.0001	0.946	0.939	0.375	0.181	5.527
	SAL	0.0001	0.0001	0.427	7.305	0.0001	0.908	0.877	0.250	0.344	2.908
	GAS	-4.745	0.974	-0.327	-4.872	0.0001	0.733	-0.773	-0.167	0.261	3.830
4	(Constant)	43.048	1.360		31.647	0.0001					
	LPR	0.330	0.025	1.059	13.225	0.0001	0.946	0.960	0.347	0.108	9.301
	SAL	0.0001	0.0001	0.287	4.789	0.0001	0.908	0.778	0.126	0.192	5.216
	GAS	-6.284	0.867	-0.432	-7.248	0.0001	0.733	-0.882	-0.190	0.194	5.161
	MC	-1.384	0.396	-0.138	-3.495	0.003	-0.319	-0.670	-0.092	0.441	2.268

another path (GAS). In other words, LPR suppresses the correlation of GAS with PLF. The negative partial correlation between GAS and PLF means that for airlines with the same LPR the correlation of GAS with PLF is actually negative.

A similar phenomenon is observed in the relationship between LPR and PLF in Model 4. The zero-order correlation is 0.946 while the partial correlation is higher (0.960) which is an indication of suppression. To examine the existence of this observation, we examined the partial correlation between LPR and PLF controlling for GAS and MC. The partial correlation was 0.980, which was higher than the first-order correlation (0.946). This suggests that the correlation between LPR and PLF for the same level of GAS and MC is higher. Since GAS and MC are relatively standard cost items (i.e. airlines cannot control these items too much) it highlights the effectiveness of labor productivity in the airline industry.

6. Discussion
In this study, two research questions in the context of the US airline industry were investigated. First, the relationship between productivity and quality with profitability was examined. The correlation analysis indicated that labor productivity and profitability are positively related. However, the relationship between on-time performance and profitability was found to be negative. While this finding appears to be counterintuitive, there are several explanations for this. First, from Table II it is found that the first-order correlation between OT (on-time performance) and profitability (PLF) is negative and significant. The partial correlation between OT and PLF controlling for LPR (labor productivity) is non-significant ($r = -0.254$; p-value $= 0.296$). This can be interpreted as spurious relationship indicating that such a relationship between on-time performance and profitability does not exist (Hair et al., 2009). This has been confirmed from the multiple regression analysis as well where on-time performance is not a significant variable. Second, this finding can be attributed to the role of airline safety and security. It has been argued that on-time performance may jeopardize safety (Siegmund, 1990). From this perspective, if safety and profitability are related, the negative correlation between on-time performance and profitability can be attributed to the moderating role of safety in the relationship between on-time performance and profitability. While we did not address airline safety in this study, it is recommended that future studies consider the link between safety, productivity, and quality on profitability.

The findings of this study can be interpreted from the perspective of the sand cone model (Ferdows and De Meyer, 1990). According to the sand cone model there is a sequence in which operations objectives should be achieved. This starts with quality, followed by flexibility and delivery and ends with cost. Empirical studies support the validity of the sand cone model in the US airline industry where tradeoff among different operational objectives is inevitable (Schmenner and Swink, 1998; Lapré and Scudder, 2004). Our findings suggest that operational performance (measured by labor productivity) is the most important operational objective for the airlines. Emphasis on operational excellence has deteriorated on-time performance due to the trade-off between operational excellence and on-time performance.

Alternatively, the negative link between on-time performance and profitability can be explained though mutual forbearance theory, which asserts that firms which compete in multiple markets compete less aggressively because of the risk of response by the rivals in all markets. Within the US airline industry, it has been found that an increase in multimarket contacts deteriorates service quality (Prince and Simon, 2009). From this perspective, the findings of this study may suggest that due to the intensity of rivalry among air carriers, airlines do not have the incentive to improve on-time performance since it may increase the likelihood of severe responses by rivals in all markets.

Furthermore, the results showed that labor productivity is the major determinant of profitability in the US airline industry (it has the largest coefficient and emerged as the most significant variable in the stepwise regression). The importance of human resource productivity and improvement in workforce on airline performance has been addressed in the literature. According to Gittell *et al.* (2005) resolving financial problems and crisis in the airline industry cannot be resolved through reduction in wages and salaries. While these efforts may provide short-term solution to the problem, sustainable performance is achieved through focusing on relational factors such as employee relationships, shared governance, and wages (Gittell *et al.*, 2005). In line with previous studies, our result confirms the significance of human resource practices on profitability in the US airline industry.

The emergence of employee salary as a significant variable in the regression analysis may be counterintuitive. While employee salary may be viewed as a cost item, we expect to see a negative coefficient for this variable (SAL) in the regression model. Surprisingly, the coefficient is positive (B = 0.278). There is one possible explanation for that. In the service industry, there is a positive link between employee satisfaction and customer satisfaction (Hennig-Thurau, 2004; Kattara *et al.* 2008). Assuming that higher wages and salaries may be an indication of higher employee satisfaction, addressing employee satisfaction (in this case through higher salary) will result in higher customer satisfaction. From quality management perspective, customer satisfaction is one of the key determinants of business performance and profitability. Therefore, if customer satisfaction is important to the airline industry, managers should look for effective strategies to enhance employee satisfaction.

An important finding of this study is the effect of on-time performance on profitability. While on-time performance was initially correlated with profitability, it did not emerge as a significant variable in the regression analysis. This suggests that conformance quality (measured by on-time performance) is not a significant predictor of profitability. Future studies can consider other measures for quality (e.g. baggage handling, in-flight service, etc). For example, empirical studies suggest that passengers do equate size of the aircraft with quality of service (e.g. Truitt and Haynes, 1994). Therefore, we recommend that future studies treat quality as a multidimensional construct (Kaynak, 2003). Research in quality management indicates that quality is a multi-dimensional construct. From this perspective, different variables need to be considered to collectively measure airline quality. We suggest that future studies develop multidimensional scales for quality as well as productivity.

6.1 Managerial implications
The findings of this study can provide insight for management and operations of airlines. In terms of the effect of productivity and quality on profitability our findings suggest that labor productivity is the most significant contributor to productivity. According to the regression model (Table IV), one unit improvement in labor productivity results in 1.059 increase in profitability. Therefore, we recommend airlines to develop strategies to improve their labor productivity.

Regarding quality, we did not find a significant relationship between on-time performance and profitability. This means that on-time performance does not have a significant effect on profitability. While on-time performance has been used a measure of service quality, it appears that it does not have a significant effect on profitability, taking into account other factors such a labor productivity or salary. We do not recommend that airlines should abandon their on-time performance initiatives. Rather, we argue that on-time performance is not as important as other factors.

In terms of employee salary, we recommend that airlines develop sound and productive human resource management practices to have healthy and productive employees. The link between employee satisfaction and customer satisfaction leads to higher profitability. We suggest investment in human resource management practices such as training, employee involvement in decision making and empowerment to improve their job satisfaction.

As it could be expected gas price and maintenance costs negatively affect profitability. Fuel cost is more significant than maintenance cost; therefore if airlines have a choice between these two cost items we recommend airlines to seek strategies to minimize their fuel cost. We do not recommend that airlines should abandon their maintenance policy (e.g. outsourcing maintenance) since that is an integral part of the airline safety practice. Rather, we do recommend emphasizing reduction in fuel cost more aggressively than investment in maintenance contracts and outscoring in terms of their effect on profitability.

6.2 Limitations and future research

There are a few limitations in this study. Above all, the small sample size of the study should be addressed. It is recommended that future research be conducted with a larger sample size.

Hair et al. (2009) recommend a ratio of 5:1 for the sample size and the number of independent variables (five observations for each independent variable) when there is no measurement error. While our sample size satisfies this requirement (objective measures used in this study are unbiased and do not exhibit measurement error) we recommend replicating this study using a larger sample. Furthermore, we used annual performance measurements for the airline industry. While we could use semi-annual or monthly data to increase the sample size, we decided not to do so for a couple of reasons. Using annual performance data provides a better assessment of operational and performance outcomes. Quarterly data may be highly correlated due to the seasonality effect.

In this study we focused on the performance of the entire airline industry. This approach enabled us to determine how productivity and quality affect profitability. Some studies have looked at the performance of individual airlines and have assessed performance of different air carriers based on their business model (e.g. Tsikriktsis, 2007). We were unable to conduct such an analysis since there have been considerable changes in the US airline industry (due to the bankruptcies, mergers and acquisitions). In that regards, future studies should replicate this study utilizing some kind of control variables (e.g. aircraft size, number of employees, full service vs. focused, etc) to better determine the effect of productivity and quality on profitability based on these control variables.

One important aspect of the airline industry is safety regulations. The effect of safety on profitability is a debatable issue. While some studies indicate there is no relationship between safety and profitability (e.g. Golbe, 1986) others argue that there

MSQ
20,5

is a positive link between safety and profitability (e.g. Sinha, 2007). In that regards, further analysis is needed to determine the effect of safety on profitability along with quality and productivity.

While there are contextual and industry specific factors that may influence the effect of operational variables on profitability, we believe the findings of this study can be generalized to similar industries, especially in industries that are efficiency driven, capital-intensive, and exhibit some level of regulation. The findings of this study can be generalized to other sectors of the transportation industry such as trucking, cargo and cruise. In addition, the findings of this study can be extended to industries that have some level of federal regulation (e.g. safety) or are capital-intensive such as the petroleum industry and the electric power industry, to name a few.

470

Finally, our conceptualization of airline quality was assessed through on-time performance. While several studies have used on-time performance as a measure for service quality, there are other attributes for service quality in the airline industry such as baggage handling and flight service. Therefore, future studies can develop a multi-dimensional definition of airline service quality.

7. Conclusion
In this paper the effect of productivity and quality on profitability in the US airline industry was addressed. We established a positive link between productivity and profitability. We did not find a link between conformance quality and profitability. The regression analysis revealed key operational measures that affect profitability. Our findings suggest that labor productivity, employee salary, gas price and maintenance cost significantly affect profitability. Among them, labor productivity appears to be the most significant variable that contributes to profitability.

The significance of labor productivity as the most important variable in explaining variability in profitability asserts the long existing belief in focusing on efficiency-driven practices in the airline industry. While in this study we just focused on labor productivity, we believe that improvement in other types of productivity (e.g. multifactor, equipment, etc) will have significant impact on profitability. Improve productivity requires changes in organizational operations, processes, and routines. In that regards, we recommend airlines to initiate, develop and maintain programs such as lean system and Six Sigma. There is evidence in the airline industry that such programs will result in improvement in operations and higher level of performance (e.g. Southwest Airlines).

The usefulness of on-time performance as a measure of quality can be questioned. Quality is a multidimensional construct and using on-time performance may not fully address airline service quality. Further investigation is needed to address the relationship between safety, productivity, and quality as well as their effect on profitability in the airline industry.

Notes
1. Asset frontier is formed by structural choices made by a company regarding investment in plant and equipment (Schmenner and Swink, 1998).

2. Focused airlines serve specific geographical areas, and use one type of aircraft (e.g. Southwest). Full service airlines use a mix of aircrafts, and serve both domestic and international markets (e.g. Delta, American, and United Airlines).

3. An example for this could be the baggage fee which was first implemented by United Airlines in 2008. Later, other airlines initiated similar policies for baggage fees.

References

Adrangi, B., Chow, G. and Raffiee, K. (1997), "Airline deregulation, safety, and profitability in the USA", *Transportation Journal*, Vol. 36 No. 4, pp. 44-52.

Anderson, E.W., Fornell, C. and Lehman, D.R. (1994), "Customer satisfaction, market share and profitability: findings from Sweden", *Journal of Marketing*, Vol. 58 No. 3, pp. 53-66.

Anderson, E.W., Fornell, C. and Rust, R.T. (1997), "Customer satisfaction, productivity and profitability: differences between goods and services", *Marketing Science*, Vol. 16 No. 2, pp. 129-45.

Bailey, E. and Williams, J.R. (1988), "Sources of economic rent in the deregulated airline industry", *Journal of Law and Economics*, Vol. 31 No. 1, pp. 173-202.

Baltagi, B.H., Griffin, J.M., Vadali, S.R. and Sharada, R. (1998), "Excess capacity: a permanent characteristic of US airlines?", *Journal of Applied Econometrics*, Vol. 13 No. 6, pp. 645-57.

Barney, J. (1991), "Firm resources and sustained competitive advantage", *Journal of Management*, Vol. 17 No. 1, pp. 99-120.

Barney, J. (1995), "Looking inside for competitive advantage", *Academy of Management Executive*, Vol. 9 No. 4, pp. 49-61.

Buzzell, R. and Gale, B. (1987), *The PIMS Principle: Linking Strategy to Performance*, Free Press, New York, NY.

D'Aveni, R.A. (1989), "The aftermath of organizational decline: a longitudinal study of the strategic and managerial characteristics of declining firms", *Academy of Management Journal*, Vol. 32 No. 3, pp. 577-605.

De Vany, A.S. (1975), "The effect of price and entry regulation on airline output, capacity and efficiency", *The Bell Journal of Economics*, Vol. 6 No. 1, pp. 327-45.

Deephouse, D.L. (1996), "Does isomorphism legitimate?", *Academy of Management Journal*, Vol. 39 No. 4, pp. 1024-39.

Douglas, T.J. and Judge, W.Q. Jr (2001), "Total quality management implementation and competitive advantage: the role of structural control and exploration", *Academy of Management Journal*, Vol. 44 No. 1, pp. 158-69.

Eisenhardt, K. and Schoonhoven, C.B. (1990), "Organizational growth: linking founding team strategy, environment and growth among US semiconductor ventures", *Administrative Science Quarterly*, Vol. 35 No. 3, pp. 504-29.

Ferdows, K. and De Meyer, A. (1990), "Lasting improvements in manufacturing performance: in search of a new theory", *Journal of Operations Management*, Vol. 9 No. 2, pp. 168-84.

Garvin, D. (1988), *Managing Quality: The Strategic and Competitive Edge*, Free Press, New York, NY.

Gittell, J.H., Von Nordenflycht, A. and Kochan, T.A. (2005), "Mutual gains or zero sum? Labor relations and firm performance in the airline industry", *Industrial and Labor Relations Review*, Vol. 57 No. 2, pp. 163-80.

Golbe, D.L. (1986), "Safety and profits in the airline industry", *Journal of Industrial Economics*, Vol. 34 No. 3, pp. 305-18.

Gujarati, D.N. (1995), *Basic Econometrics*, 3rd ed., McGraw-Hill, New York, NY.

Hair, J.F., Black, W.C. and Babin, B.J. (2009), *Multivariate Data Analysis*, 7th ed., Pearson Education, Harlow.

MSQ
20,5

472

Hammesfahr, J.R.D., Pope, J.A. and Ardalan, A. (1993), "Strategic planning for production capacity", *International Journal of Operations & Production Management*, Vol. 13 No. 5, pp. 41-53.

Hatten, K.J., Schendel, D.E. and Cooper, A.C. (1978), "A strategic model of the United States brewing industry: 1952-1971", *Academy of Management Journal*, Vol. 21 No. 4, pp. 592-610.

Hennig-Thurau, T. (2004), "Customer orientation of service employees: its impact on customer satisfaction, commitment, and retention", *International Journal of Service Industry Management*, Vol. 15 No. 5, pp. 460-78.

Heskett, J.L., Sasser, W.E. Jr and Schlesinger, L.A. (1997), *The Service Profit Chain*, Free Press, New York, NY.

Kattara, H.S., Weheba, D. and El-Siad, O.A. (2008), "The impact of employee behavior on customers' service quality perceptions and overall satisfaction", *Tourism & Hospitality Research*, Vol. 8 No. 4, pp. 309-23.

Kaynak, H. (2003), "The relationship between total quality management practices and their effects on firm performance", *Journal of Operations Management*, Vol. 21 No. 4, pp. 405-35.

Kutner, M., Nachtsheim, C. and Neter, J. (2004), *Applied Linear Regression Models*, 4th ed., McGraw-Hill Irwin, New York, NY.

Lapré, M.A. and Scudder, G.D. (2004), "Performance improvement paths in the US airline industry: linking trade-offs to asset frontiers", *Production and Operations Management*, Vol. 13 No. 2, pp. 123-34.

Lenox, M., Rockart, S. and Lewin, A. (2005), "Firm and industry profits when complementarities drive resource and capability heterogeneity", working paper, Duke University, Durham, NC.

Listes, O. and Dekker, R. (2005), "Scenario aggregation-based approach for determining a robust airline fleet composition for dynamic capacity allocation", *Transportation Science*, Vol. 39 No. 3, pp. 367-82.

Loveman, G. (1998), "Employee satisfaction, customer loyalty, and financial performance", *Journal of Service Research*, Vol. 1 No. 1, pp. 18-31.

Mazzeo, M.J. (2003), "Competition and service quality in the US airline industry", *Review of Industrial Organization*, Vol. 22 No. 4, pp. 275-96.

Moore, T.G. (1986), "US airline deregulation: its effects on passengers, capital, and labor", *Journal of Law and Economics*, Vol. 29 No. 1, pp. 1-28.

Murphy, N.B. (1969), "Sources of productivity increases in the US passenger airline industry", *Transportation Science*, Vol. 3 No. 3, pp. 233-8.

Nelson, E., Rust, R.T., Zahorik, A., Rose, R.L., Batalden, P.A. and Siemanski, B.A. (1992), "Do patient perceptions of quality relate to hospital financial performance?", *Journal of Health Care Marketing*, Vol. 12 No. 4, pp. 6-13.

Neter, J. and Wasserman, W. (1974), *Applied Linear Statistical Models*, Richard D. Irwin & Co., Homewood, IL.

Peteraff, M. and Reed, R. (2007), "Managerial discretion and internal alignment under regulatory constraints and change", *Strategic Management Journal*, Vol. 28 No. 11, pp. 1089-112.

Prince, J.T. and Simon, D.H. (2009), "Multimarket contact and service quality: evidence from on-time performance in the US airline industry", *Academy of Management Journal*, Vol. 52 No. 2, pp. 336-54.

Raghavan, S. and Rhoades, D.L. (2008), "Core competencies, competitive advantage, and outsourcing in the US airline industry", *International Journal of Strategic Management*, Vol. 8 No. 2, pp. 125-35.

Ramaswamy, K., Thomas, A.S. and Litschert, R.J. (1994), "Organizational performance in a regulated environment: the role of strategic orientation", *Strategic Management Journal*, Vol. 15 No. 1, pp. 63-74.

Roth, A.V. and Jackson, W.E. III (1995), "Strategic determinants of service quality and performance: evidence from the banking industry", *Management Science*, Vol. 41 No. 11, pp. 1720-33.

Rust, R.T., Zahorik, A.J. and Keiningham, T.L. (1995), "Return on quality (ROQ): making service quality financially accountable", *Journal of Marketing*, Vol. 59 No. 2, pp. 58-70.

Schefczyk, M. (1993), "Operational performance of airlines: an extension of traditional measurement paradigms", *Strategic Management Journal*, Vol. 14 No. 4, pp. 301-17.

Schmenner, R.W. and Swink, M.L. (1998), "On theory in operations management", *Journal of Operations Management*, Vol. 17 No. 1, pp. 97-113.

Siegmund, F. (1990), "Competition and performance in the airline industry", *Policy Studies Review*, Vol. 9 No. 4, pp. 649-63.

Sinha, D. (2007), "Safety, profitability and the load factor for airlines in the USA", *Economics Bulletin*, Vol. 12 No. 6, pp. 1-7.

Smith, T.M. and Reece, J.S. (1999), "The relationship of strategy, fit, productivity and business performance in a services setting", *Journal of Operations Management*, Vol. 17 No. 2, pp. 145-61.

Spiller, P.T. (1983), "The differential impact of airline regulation on individual firms and markets: an empirical analysis", *Journal of Law and Economics*, Vol. 26 No. 3, pp. 655-89.

Suzuki, Y. (2000), "The relationship between on-time performance and airline market share: a new approach", *Transportation Research Part E*, Vol. 36 No. 2, pp. 139-54.

Taneja, N.K. (1988), *The International Airline Industry*, Lexington Press, Lexington, KY.

Taneja, N.K. (2003), *Airline Survival Kit: Breaking out of the Zero Profit Game*, Ashgate Publishing, Aldershot.

Trapani, J.M. and Olson, C.V. (1982), "An analysis of the impact of open economy on price and the quality of service in the airline industry", *Review of Economics and Statistics*, Vol. 64 No. 1, pp. 67-76.

Treacy, M. and Wiersema, F. (1995), *The Discipline of Market Leaders*, Perseus Books, New York, NY.

Truitt, L.J. and Haynes, R. (1994), "Evaluating service quality and productivity in the regional airline industry", *Transportation Journal*, Vol. 33 No. 2, pp. 21-32.

Tsikriktsis, N. (2007), "The effect of operational performance and focus on profitability: a longitudinal study of the US airline industry", *Manufacturing and Service Operations Management*, Vol. 9 No. 4, pp. 506-17.

Venkatraman, N. and Ramanujam, V. (1986), "Measurement of business performance in strategy research: a comparison of approaches", *Academy of Management Review*, Vol. 11 No. 4, pp. 801-14.

Voss, C., Tsikriktsis, N., Funk, B., Yarrow, D. and Owen, J. (2005), "Managerial choice and performance in service management: a comparison of private sector organizations with further education colleges", *Journal of Operations Management*, Vol. 23 No. 2, pp. 179-95.

Williams, G. (2002), *Airline Competition: Deregulation's Mixed Legacy*, Ashgate Publishing, Aldershot.

Profitability in
US airline
industry

473

MSQ
20,5

474

Wright, P.M., McMahan, G. and McWilliams, A. (1994), "Human resources and sustained competitive advantage: a resource-based perspective", *International Journal of Human Resource Management*, Vol. 5 No. 2, pp. 301-26.

Wyckoff, D.D. and Maister, D.H. (1977), *The Domestic Airline Industry*, Lexington Books, Lexington, MA.

Yeung, A.C.L., Cheng, T.C. and Lai, K. (2006), "An operational and institutional perspective on total quality management", *Production and Operations Management*, Vol. 15 No. 1, pp. 156-70.

Zeithaml, V.A., Berry, L.L. and Parasuraman, A. (1996), "The behavioral consequences of service quality", *Journal of Marketing*, Vol. 60 No. 2, pp. 31-46.

Zhao, X., Yeung, A.C.L. and Lee, T.S. (2004), "Quality management and organizational context in selected service industries of China", *Journal of Operations Management*, Vol. 22 No. 6, pp. 575-87.

Further reading

Skinner, W. (1974), "The focused factory", *Harvard Business Review*, Vol. 52 No. 3, pp. 113-21.

Smith, K.G., Grimm, C.M., Gannon, M.J. and Chen, M. (1991), "Organizational information processing, competitive responses, and performance in the US domestic airline industry", *Academy of Management Journal*, Vol. 34 No. 1, pp. 60-85.

Snipes, R.L., Oswald, S.L., LaTour, M. and Armenakis, A.A. (2005), "The effects of specific job satisfaction facets on customer perceptions of service quality: an employee-level analysis", *Journal of Business Research*, Vol. 58 No. 10, pp. 1330-9.

Part III:

Service delivery and service quality

18

International service variants: airline passenger expectations and perceptions of service quality

Fareena Sultan

Merlin C. Simpson, Jr

Keywords *Consumer behaviour, Service quality, Service levels, Customer satisfaction, Airlines*

Abstract *The primary objectives of this study are to determine if consumer expectations and perceptions of airline service quality vary by nationality. The study also examines whether the relative importance attributed to service quality dimensions in domestic settings can be replicated internationally. An empirical examination of airline passengers is conducted for airlines competing on the transatlantic corridor using a survey instrument in three languages. The study is the first application of an existing model, SERVQUAL, to examine consumer expectations and perceptions in an international environment. It differs from earlier published SERVQUAL research in two significant respects; first, it applies the model internationally in a general classification of business, i.e. international airline service, rather than to individual domestic business enterprises. Second, it applies a portion of the SERVQUAL model to assess service quality by comparing the expectations and perceptions that European and US airline passengers have of both European and US airline groups.*

Introduction

As corporations increasingly are attracted to international markets to overcome stagnant domestic market growth and stimulate revenues in various industries, enlightened appreciation of the needs and wants of consumers of other countries are increasingly important for those companies espousing the marketing concept. Major airline industry competitors, seeking to gain or expand market share globally or regionally, provide an opportunity to explore the service expectations and perceptions of customers of different nationalities.

Domestic market

Beginning in the early 1990s, US airlines sought to overcome then stagnant domestic markets and the limitations of existing nation-to-nation agreements governing international service routes by establishing code-sharing alliances with foreign airlines. "Code-sharing" is based on airline designators used in airline industry computer systems; although code-sharing agreements most commonly are recognized in airline alliances as marketing strategies, they vary in nature based on the interests of the cooperating airlines. By virtue of a marketing arrangement with a foreign airline, e.g. as proposed between American Airlines and British Airways, an American Airlines ticket could be issued to a passenger to Munich, Germany, although American Airlines does not fly between the USA and that city. The passenger travels to Munich on American Airlines and British Airways aircraft, without separate ticketing as earlier had been the case. Such arrangements essentially allow airlines to operate almost as one entity, such as the "STAR" alliance (involving Air Canada, Varig, SAS, Lufthansa, Thai Airlines and United Airlines) while retaining their separate national identities, thus enabling the airlines to achieve a market position other than that achievable as their national identity suggests, and to overcome in degree the restrictions of the Chicago Conference on International Aviation in 1944, which continues to define freedoms allowed to airlines serving international markets.

Market share

As they strive to improve market share and further enhance financial performance through international markets, US airlines need a better understanding of the variables likely to determine the success of new ventures, e.g. expectations and perceptions of airline passengers from other countries, most immediately those of the nations represented by their new code-sharing partners. If significant variances were to be found in the perceptions of airline passengers (by nationality) for the service quality of the different airline groups, improvements would be needed to improve the marketing mix to overcome noted deficiencies.

It has been widely accepted that overseas airlines *are* better; "No US airline has service 'as good as most foreign airlines'" (McClenahan, 1991). Airline service quality among US carriers has been considered an oxymoron by many travelers, while major foreign carriers, Lufthansa German Airlines, Swissair, British Airways and Singapore Airlines, are recognized service quality leaders (Oneal, 1991; McClenahan, 1991), receiving enthusiastic reviews from airline passengers for exceptional customer service. In the absence of a service-quality focus among competing US airlines, devising and implementing such a customer-focused marketing strategy is nonetheless seen increasingly important to those US airlines seeking to compete in international markets, where they confront foreign carriers recognized for excellent customer service.

Overcome limitations

Alliances with highly recognized airlines from other countries, may afford the opportunity to overcome limitations of bilateral international agreements and to improve service offerings. Dynamics associated with the international operating environment increasingly requires companies to collaborate with foreign partners for market efficiency, and responsiveness (Bartlett and Ghoshal, 1987). Alliances are increasingly advocated as a means to overcome obstacles and market complexities preventing companies from achieving strategic aims, particularly in globalizing markets (Ohmae, 1989). However, alliances are not to be seen as conveniences to be implemented without commitment to long-run purpose; to do so is to compromise the inherent advantages of such strategic arrangements, however, this is often found to be the case with US-based corporations, which often abandon alliances before achieving their original purposes (Ohmae, 1989). It may be that contemporary alliances undertaken by otherwise competing airlines conflict with requirements for global competition: top management may not intend to change the fundamental way it thinks about and operates its business (Hout *et al.*, 1982).

Successful service quality strategies are generally characterized by customer segmentation, customized service, guarantees, continuous customer feedback, and comprehensive measurement of company performance. The experience in many industries and companies demonstrates that this process, although generally acknowledged, is not universally implemented. Market segmentation by customer expectations, to create separate levels of service that exceed those levels of expectations, has also been found essential to attract customers and create customer loyalty (Porter, 1980, 1985). Knowing accurately what customers prefer, successful service companies are able to give customers exactly what they want by customizing the product or service, to surprise and "delight" them (Porter, 1980; Albrecht, 1992).

Optimum levels

Determining optimum levels of customer service is understood to depend on accurately assessing customer expectations, so that companies are able to meet highly-valued customer expectations and avoid employing those services that customers do not value; regular customer feedback has been determined essential to such successful customer satisfaction strategies (Evelyn and DeCarlo, 1992; Miller, 1992; Peters and Waterman, 1982; Peters and Austin, 1985; Sonnenberg, 1991). Successful customer service focused companies measure their service to ascertain how well they are satisfying their customers (Peters and Waterman, 1982; Evelyn and DeCarlo, 1992; Albrecht, 1992), and superior companies have been shown to be consistently excellent listeners to their customers (Albrecht, 1992).

The purpose of this study is to determine (i) whether service quality expectations and perceptions vary by nationality, (ii) the relative importance attributed to five service quality dimensions according to passenger nationality groups, and (iii) if a portion of the SERVQUAL model (Zeithaml *et al.*, 1990) dealing with consumer expectations and perceptions could be replicated internationally.

Accepting the general validity of the SERVQUAL model (Zeithaml *et al.*, 1990), which assesses gaps between customer expectations of service quality and their perceptions of its actual delivery by the provider, this study explores the adaptability of the SERVQUAL model to international markets, from earlier domestic applications for aggregate assessments of customer service quality (Boulding *et al.*, 1993; Carman, 1990; McDougall and Snetsinger, 1990; Parasuraman *et al.*, 1994; Brown and Swartz, 1989; Webster, 1989, 1991; Lambert and Harrington, 1989).

Five "gaps"

The SERVQUAL model concentrates on five "gaps" (Figure 1) impairing the delivery of excellent service quality; this study focuses on Gap 5: the difference between airline passenger expectations and perceptions of service. Before concerted efforts can be successfully undertaken to redress service management problems that impede the delivery of truly excellent service quality, it is essential to know to what degree customer perceptions of existing service fail to meet expectations; this study focuses on that primary issue. Thereafter it becomes important to know whether differences exist in management perceptions of customer expectations (Gap 1), a discrepancy in managment perceptions and the service specifications that are enacted (Gap 2), etc. Thus we study Gap 5 which focuses on the differences between consumer expectations and perceptions. This is also the only gap that can be examined solely on the data from the consumer; study of other gaps, while important, would require data collection from companies themselves.

This study differs from earlier research in two significant respects. First, this study applies the SERVQUAL model to compare the performance of groups of major competitors in international airline service, incorporating multiple passenger and airline nationalities, using a survey instrument in three languages. Published accounts of the SERVQUAL model have been generally applied to individual business enterprises in a country-by-country, or "domestic" context, evaluating the degree to which they fulfill the expectations of their customers, identifying factors essential to improve delivered service quality in those cases studied. Although individual companies are thought to have used the model for this purpose, the results also have been largely treated as proprietary. Moreover, no literature could be

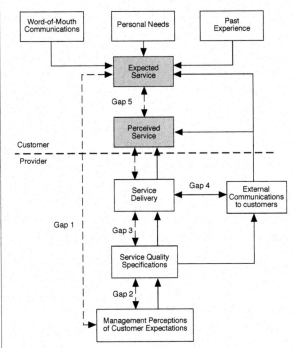

Source: Valarie A. Zeithaml, A. Parasuraman, Leonard L. Berry. Delivering Quality Service: Balancing Customer Perceptions and Expectations. New York: The Free Press, 1990

Figure 1. Conceptual model of service quality

found on the use of the SERVQUAL model to compare major groups of major competitors in international airline service. Second, this study applies a portion of the model to an international rather than a domestic setting, comparing the expectations and perceptions of airline passengers from various countries to airlines from Europe and the USA. It contributes to the service quality literature by applying Gap 5 (the difference between customer perceptions and expectations) of the SERVQUAL model to an international environment. It provides empirical evidence of the usefulness of service models to assess companies competing in global markets, and describes the role of nationality in forming service quality expectations and perceptions.

Additionally, this research seeks to assess US airlines' potential to implement a service quality-based marketing strategy, and to determine if major US airlines are positioned to attract greater numbers of European passengers, thereby improving market share on the transatlantic corridor, and to suggest the potential for realizing similar opportunities in other global markets, e.g. Asia.

Literature
Customer perceptions and expectations of service quality are increasingly used to forecast company profitability and prospects for improved market

share. Although many other "quality-focused" initiatives have often failed to enhance company performance, customer-perceived service improvements have been shown empirically to improve profitability (Buzzell and Gale, 1987). The shift from an industrial to a customer-value paradigm (Albrecht, 1992) places service at the center of company efforts to improve profitability. As virtually all organizations compete to some degree on a basis of service (Zeithaml *et al.*, 1990), and as the US economy has become a predominantly "service economy" (Albrecht and Zemke, 1985), service quality then becomes significantly important to achieve a genuine and sustainable competitive advantage. Service-based companies are compelled by their nature to provide excellent service in order to prosper in increasingly competitive domestic and global marketplaces, i.e. there is no "tangible" product to equate otherwise to quality.

Satisfying customer preferences

Customer-driven strategies require satisfying customer preferences; it is first necessary to identify the customer (Sonnenberg, 1991), which is also found to be prerequisite to successful global competition (Butterworth, 1990) and service competition generally (Whiteley, 1991; Parasuraman *et al.*, 1988). Many companies intending to employ a customer service-based strategy find the process of identifying and measuring customer preferences very difficult, often owing to mistaken business perceptions of customer wants (Drucker, 1964; Miller, 1992; Andrews *et al.*, 1987; Fornell, 1992). Nonetheless, providing superior service quality requires creating a distinct relationship between what the customer wants and that which the company provides, or a relationship between customer requirements and essential business elements (Evelyn and DeCarlo, 1992; Schneider and Bowen, 1995).

Service quality literature recognizes expectations as an instrumental influence in consumer evaluations of service quality (Grönroos, 1982; Parasuraman *et al.*, 1985; Brown and Swartz, 1989). Expectations are understood as the desires or wants of customers, i.e. what the service provider should offer (Parasuraman *et al.*, 1988), and studying companies understood to be leaders in various industries (and not limited to direct competitors), i.e. "benchmarking" or "studying the winners", has become a vital source in identifying gaps that exist between customer expectations and company performance (Park and Smith, 1990; Drege, 1991; Whiteley, 1991; Albrecht, 1992) as perceived by its customers (Miller, 1992).

Difficult challenges

Meeting rising customer expectations has proved to be one of the most difficult challenges to service businesses (Sonnenberg, 1991; Drege, 1991). Quality is found to be measured most accurately through the eyes of the customer (Miller, 1992), and it is not found to improve unless it is regularly measured (Reichheld and Sasser, 1990). Customers are therefore never mistaken when they say that (service) quality is bad, because if they perceive it so, it necessarily *is* so (Schneider and Bowen, 1995). Companies that actively search for and incorporate the best service methods and processes to improve the performance, regardless of sources, and ultimately the perceptions of their customers, are found to excel in relation to their competitors (Sellers, 1991). In practice, companies that exceed customer expectations without impairing profit margins have frequently been found to develop a solid foundation of customer loyalty, based on segmented service (Drucker, 1964; Porter, 1980, 1985; Farber and Wycoff, 1991).

Recognizing the importance of measuring service quality perceptions and expectations to improve performance, and the importance of international markets to the success of companies in numerous service industries, it is significant that no studies have been performed to investigate the differences that might exist based on nationality and culture (Winsted, 1997).

Importance of quality

The general importance of quality to the airline industry is recognized in the annual *Airline Quality Report* (Bowen and Headley, 1995) for domestic airlines, which incorporates an internally-focused model based on financial data, fares, passenger load factors, service related issues, etc. As service quality strategies fundamentally focus *externally* on the customer and satisfaction (a market orientation), rather than internally on company profits and costs (a production orientation), a distinctive and unequivocal management approach as well as organization commitment is required (Peters and Waterman, 1982; Whiteley, 1991; Carlzon, 1989).

In order to formulate successful service strategies internationally, this study proposes that there is a need to examine consumer expectations and perceptions in an international setting. As an example we focus on the airline service industry.

Research methodology

Series of propositions

We focus on Gap 5 of the SERVQUAL model (Expectation-Perception Gap, Figure 1). The conceptual framework for this aggregate study is illustrated by Figure 2, by which we examine the expectations-perceptions gap along the various links illustrated. We wish to examine how US and European passengers evaluate groups of US and European airlines, examining each of the links indicated. We propose a series of propositions to test the expectations and perceptions along the links depicted in Figure 2. After analyzing possible differences in the service quality expectations of European and US passengers (Figure 2, link 5), this study assesses differences in European and US passenger perceptions of service quality of individual US and European airline groups (Figure 2, links 1/4 and 2/3) and passenger group perceptions of a single airline group (Figure 2, links 1/3 and 2/4).

SERVQUAL model application.
This empirical research study applies the gap-theory methodology of the SERVQUAL model (Zeithaml *et al.*, 1990) to the links in Figure 2. It measures service quality of US and European airline groups, and seeks to ascertain:

(1) if national origin of passengers influences expectations and perceptions of domestic and foreign airline service quality, and

(2) if Gap 5 of the SERVQUAL model and the associated dimensions tested by earlier studies can be extended to an international application.

The SERVQUAL model is formulated using statements grouped to constitute five dimensions representing the core criteria by which customers have been determined to evaluate service quality (Zeithaml *et al.*, 1990). The five dimensions of service identified in this "expectations-perceptions" gap model (Tangibles, Reliability, Assurance, Responsiveness, and Empathy) are used to assess overall service quality of companies, as well as performance in any of five dimensions. This analysis does not address individual SERVQUAL dimensions, rather focuses on aggregate assessment of service quality of airline groups as perceived by two passenger groups.

The primary dependent variable in this research is overall airline service quality, measurement of which can be accomplished in three ways: individually for 22 service quality statements [defined in Appendix A

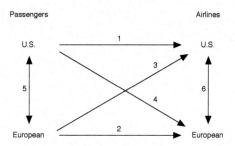

Figure 2. Airline service quality research framework

(Zeithaml *et al.*, 1990)], for five dimensions, or as an aggregate service quality value. Airline passenger responses to individual statements, providing unique insights to consumer perceptions and expectations of the service rendered, also provide the foundation for aggregate dimension scores, which are further combined to provide an overall service quality score for each airline group.

Propositions
Earlier SERVQUAL research had identified Reliability as the most important and Tangibles as the least important of the five dimensions influencing overall service quality ratings of service companies (Zeithaml *et al.*, 1990). Determining the relative importance of the same dimensions in international airline service is an integral part of this study, and based on the previous research, we propose that relative importance should remain the same. In addition, we propose that nationality of passenger groups influences perceptions and expectations of airline service quality; and therefore it is expected that there will be differences in the expectations and perceptions by nationality. The eight propositions to be tested are described below:

P1. The relative importance attributed to dimensions influencing customer service quality expectations and perceptions does not vary by nationality of airline passengers.

P2. Service quality expectations of airline service quality vary by nationality.

P3. Service quality perceptions of airline groups vary by nationality.

P4. Overall assessments of airline service quality vary by nationality.

P5. European passengers perceive delivered service quality of US and European airline groups to vary (Figure 2, links 2 and 3).

P6. US passengers perceive delivered service quality of US and European airline groups to vary (Figure 2, links 1 and 4).

P7. European and US passengers perceive the US airline group to vary in service quality (Figure 2, links 1 and 3).

P8. European and US passengers perceive the European airline group to vary in service quality (Figure 2, links 2 and 4).

The methodology used to explore these propositions is examined based on overall service quality. Unweighted SERVQUAL values are calculated, i.e.

expressing the degree to which a service quality provider *absolutely* exceeds or fails to meet customer (passenger) expectations. Additional proposition testing can be accomplished using weighted data (by incorporating respondent values for individual service quality dimensions) to indicate *relative* levels of service quality provided, e.g. by airlines, or by dimension which would indicate the service quality dimension(s) requiring the most attention to overcome customer dissatisfaction with service quality. For the sake of brevity, this study focuses on unweighted data; weighted data results are available from the authors.

SERVQUAL models

Individual airline service quality feature scores

Individual service quality

An individual service quality (SERVQUAL) feature score for airline passenger respondents is determined by calculating the difference between passenger-assigned scores to expectation and perception statements (Gap 5) distinguishing the five dimensions:

$$x_{ijk} = p_{ijk} - e_{ijk} \tag{1}$$

where x is the respondent difference score between perception (p) and expectation (e), of respondents (i) for any of the 22 statements (Appendix A) representing an expression of service quality ($i = 1, \ldots N$, where N = number of respondents); while j represents the SERVQUAL dimensions (1 through 5) and k represents the number of statements (four or five) in a SERVQUAL dimension.

Airline SERVQUAL dimension scores

An airline's quality of service in any SERVQUAL dimension [Reliability, Responsiveness, Assurance, Empathy, and Tangibles] is determined by the aggregate scores of airline passenger respondents for statements associated with individual SERVQUAL dimensions, dividing the product of respondent difference scores (x_{ijk}) by the number of statements comprising the dimension (k_j), summing the average passenger scores and dividing by the number of respondents (N):

$$ASQ_j = \sum_{i=1}^{N} \left[\frac{\sum_{k=1}^{K_j} \frac{x_{ijk}}{K_j}}{N} \right] \tag{2}$$

where ASQ_j represents the aggregate service quality score for each of five dimensions ($j = 1, 2, 3, 4, 5$), k represents individual statements in the respective dimension (four or five statements comprising a dimension, as described in Appendix B), j represents the SERVQUAL dimensions (1 through 5), k_j represents the number of statements in the jth dimension, and N equals the number of respondents.

Overall airline SERVQUAL score

Aggregate airline service quality (ASQ) scores for the five dimensions are averaged to provide an overall unweighted measure of service quality, by dividing the cumulative dimension scores by five:

$$ASQ_u = \frac{\sum_{j=1}^{5} ASQ_j}{5} \tag{3}$$

where ASQ_u represents an overall (unweighted, absolute) measurement of service quality of a provider, e.g. airline, calculated by dividing the sum of aggregate SERVQUAL dimension scores by the number of SERVQUAL dimensions (5).

Operationalization of variables

Resulting scores in equations (1), (2), or (3) indicate the absolute difference by which passenger expectations and perceptions of airline service quality vary; negative airline SERVQUAL scores in the three categories (features, dimensions, or overall) indicate the degree to which passenger perceptions of airline service quality fail to meet expectations of service quality, a lower negative score approaching $p - e = 0$, reflecting a higher service quality level. Individual statement differentials pinpoint features within respective dimensions to address service quality priorities of customers, i.e. which service characteristics or features are most (or least) important to respondents and to address service quality deficiencies. The independent variables (expectations and perceptions) used to assess airline passenger service quality are operationalized using an airline passenger survey in three languages, adapting the five SERVQUAL dimensions. The operationalization of the expectation statements related to the five SERVQUAL dimensions is shown in Appendix C. The operationalization of perception statements related to these dimensions is shown in Appendix D. A Likert seven-point scale in which (1) means "strongly disagree" and (7) means "strongly agree" is used to measure consumer expectations and perceptions for each of these statements.

Empirical examination

Transatlantic corridor

This study focuses on groups of US and European airlines (Figure 2) competing on the transatlantic corridor between Europe and USA[1]. As bilateral international agreements fundamentally dictate which airlines are allowed to compete on individual international routes (and for which reason code-sharing initiatives have been otherwise adopted by many airlines), the airlines and cities included in this research reflected the agreements existing between individual governments for the airlines providing service on the transatlantic corridor between the respective countries.

Major competing airlines were invited to participate in the research by distributing a survey instrument to their passengers during flights between the USA and Europe. Five airlines initially agreed to participate: American Airlines, British Airways, Delta Air Lines, Lufthansa German Airlines, and United Air Lines. British Airways and Delta Airlines later withdrew and were replaced by Air Canada and Scandinavian Airlines System (SAS). As a result of these changes the number of airports and countries through which surveys were collected, and the nationalities represented in the research were greatly increased. The study results are limited to US and European passengers, Air Canada flights providing additional data from European passengers traveling on the transatlantic corridor.

Survey instrument

A common passenger survey instrument was provided for each airline's use to collect data from international travelers on the North Atlantic corridor. The survey was translated into French for use on Air Canada flights from Montreal and Toronto to Frankfurt and Paris, and German for use on Lufthansa flights from Frankfurt to New York.

Airline passengers were asked to identify the European and/or US airline on which they most frequently traveled between the United States and Europe; which resulted in the creation of two airline groups, creating the basis for the study analysis by passenger groups[2]. For example a European passenger flying on Air Canada could provide survey data on either or both of a US and European airline. The survey instrument consisted of four parts: airline service quality expectations and perceptions of airline service quality, flying habits and preferences, and demographic data. Airline Service Quality Expectations were captured by two sets of constructs: the importance of service quality (SERVQUAL) dimensions (ratio scale) (Appendix B); and expectations of airline service quality, using the 22 SERVQUAL dimension statements adapted for airline industry context (Appendices C and D), using a Likert strongly disagree (1)-strongly agree (7) seven-point scale.

Quality perception

Since respondents identified the airline(s) most-frequently flown in one or both of two airline groups between the USA and Europe, service quality perception statements (Appendix D) were applied to these designated airline(s), providing the basis for two airline groups to be compared. It did not matter on which airline a passenger was flying, rather the airline designated as being the primary carrier for such travel, together with the nationality of the passenger.

Flying habits and preferences of passengers were assessed to provide additional information concerning: overall frequency of air travel and international air travel between Europe and the USA, the primary purpose (business or vacation) for international travel, classes of service flown on international travel, and airlines most likely to be chosen for business and vacation travel.

A total of 7,511 surveys were distributed to passengers by the five participating airlines; 5,555 surveys returned by airlines could not be included in the research database, e.g. blank surveys resulting from not being distributed as scheduled by respective airline flight personnel or not completed by passengers; surveys returned without nationality being disclosed, lacking airline designation, containing an excessive number of unanswered expectation or perception statements, or a single value being circled for all perception statements, evidencing "frivolous" response.

Five airlines

Of those originally distributed, 1,956 completed passenger surveys were collected from the five participating airlines in the second half of 1994, a response rate of 26.04 percent, with 716 responses obtained from US citizens and 1,078 from Europeans representing 12 countries,[3] from August through October 1994, addressing 12 airlines (in two groups of five US and seven European airlines). The US airlines included American Airlines, Continental Airlines, Delta Air Lines, TWA, and United Airlines; European airlines included Air France, British Airways, Iberia, KLM Royal Dutch Airlines, Lufthansa German National Airlines, Scandinavian Airline System (SAS), and Virgin Atlantic Airways.

Data analysis

Overall means analysis of service quality expectation and perceptions dimensions were used to:

(1) determine and compare the absolute importance attributed to five service quality dimensions by passenger (nationality) groups;

(2) directly compare aggregate European to US passenger group data; and

(3) measure passenger group assessments of airline groups service quality overall[4].

T-tests of passenger expectations, perceptions and assessments of airline service quality were used to test respective propositions, i.e. t-tests were used to compare European and US passenger group expectations and perceptions, and to analyze data associated with importance of individual SERVQUAL dimensions.

Test of propositions
Importance of dimensions by passenger nationality
P1. The relative importance of dimensions influencing customer service quality expectations and perceptions does not vary by the nationality of airline passengers.

Passenger responses

The relative importance of each of five service quality dimensions was determined by passenger responses using a ratio scale of zero through 100 points, as implemented in the original SERVQUAL research (Appendix B); means analysis of data was calculated by individual nationalities, aggregated to reference groups (USA and Europe). The importance of SERVQUAL dimensions in terms of mean percentage points is shown in Table I, by nationality groups. For example 716 US respondents attributed 31.7 percentage points of importance to Reliability.

The rank order importance of dimensions for both of the passenger groups of US and European passengers coincides with earlier research findings. Airline passenger data parallels original SERVQUAL research results: Reliability is the most important dimension in measuring international airline service, followed by Responsiveness, Assurance, Empathy, and Tangibles.

This is supported by independent responses to statements ranking the importance of service quality dimensions (Appendix B); 60 percent of responding passengers (1,122) indicated Reliability to be the most important service quality feature, 43 percent (803) indicated Responsiveness as the second most important, and 47.4 percent (804) indicated Tangibles as the least important.

We additionally did a difference in means test between the two passenger groups. Reliability and Tangibles have statistically significant differences; Responsiveness Assurance and Empathy do not. Nevertheless, since the rank order of importance of service quality dimensions is found to match original SERVQUAL research findings for both US and European passenger groups, P1 is accepted. On the basis of this analysis, we conclude that there is no difference in the order of importance of service quality dimensions by nationality; Reliability is most important among the service quality dimensions and Tangibles least.

Passenger expectations by nationality
P2. Service quality expectations vary by nationality.

Difference score

Service quality assessment in this research is based on the calculation of a difference score between passenger expectations and perceptions. The passenger groups consisted of 1,078 European and 716 US passengers who provided expectations data (Appendix C). This is the basis for assessing airline service quality when compared to "paired"[5] perception statements (Appendix D).

US and European passenger group expectation mean values, understood as an expression of customer wants (Parasuraman *et al.*, 1988) are shown in Table II. In this table ETAN1 refers to the expectations of the tangible TAN 1, as described in Appendix C (Excellent airlines will have modern-looking aircraft). Similar interpretation holds for all of the variables in Table II.

	Dimension	US passenger [n = 716]	European passenger [n = 1,078]	Difference in means	t-value*	Prob> |T|
Most	Reliability	0.3170	0.2987	0.0183	−2.4144*	0.0149
important	Responsiveness	0.2042	0.2041	0.0001	−0.2720	0.9783
	Assurance	0.1708	0.1770	−0.0062	1.5395	0.1238
Least	Empathy	0.1641	0.1636	0.0005	−0.1083	0.9138
important	Tangibles	0.1436	0.1558	−0.0122	2.6288*	0.0086

Notes: * α: $p < 0.05$; critical t-value > 1.96*

Table I. Importance of SERVQUAL dimensions, by passenger groups (mean percentage)

Expectations of both passenger groups were highest for Reliability and Assurance dimensions (values exceeding six, using Likert seven-point scale, with the single exception of European passenger group results for EASR4, "Employees in excellent airlines will have the knowledge to answer customers' questions"), and the lowest for Tangibles (values for multiple

	Passenger groups (mean value)				
SERVQUAL factor	US [n = 716]	Europe [n = 1,078]	Difference	t-value*	Prob > |T|
Tangibles					
1. ETAN1	5.5251	5.5288	0.0037	0.0537	0.9571
2. ETAN2	5.6997	5.5343	0.1654	−2.7823*	0.0055
3. ETAN3	6.2318	5.8608	0.3710	−7.2708*	0.0000
4. ETAN4	5.5307	5.3553	0.1754	−2.8849*	0.0040
Reliability					
5. EREL1	6.5056	6.5260	0.0204	0.4883	0.6254
6. EREL2	6.6927	6.6735	0.0192	−0.5304	0.5959
7. EREL3	6.3729	6.1660	0.2069	−4.2660*	0.0000
8. EREL4	6.5042	6.4527	0.0515	−1.2164	0.2240
9. EREL5	6.1983	6.0222	0.1761	−3.2324*	0.0012
Responsiveness					
10. ERSP1	6.0768	5.9100	0.1668	−3.0309*	0.0030
11. ERSP2	6.5056	6.3052	0.2004	−5.0167*	0.0000
12. ERSP3	6.6522	6.5686	0.0836	−2.3062*	0.0212
13. ERSP4	6.1969	6.0334	0.1635	−3.2008*	0.0016
Assurance					
14. EASR1	6.5223	6.3256	0.1967	−4.8363*	0.0000
15. EASR2	6.5307	6.3961	0.1346	−3.3170*	0.0012
16. EASR3	6.6173	6.3042	0.3131	−8.0079*	0.0000
17. EASR4	6.2556	5.9490	0.3066	−6.2854*	0.0000
Empathy					
18. EEMP1	6.1494	5.8377	0.3117	-6.0839*	0.0000
19. EEMP2	6.0992	5.8377	0.2615	−4.8260*	0.0000
20. EEMP3	6.1858	5.9174	0.2684	−5.3651*	0.0000
21. EEMP4	6.4525	6.3265	0.1260	−2.8011*	0.0058
22. EEMP5	6.1606	6.0538	0.1068	−2.1463*	0.0320

Notes:
α: $p < 0.05$; critical t-value > 1.96*
** t-values being determined using Likert seven-point scale, one being "strongly disagree" and seven "strongly agree". [Appendix D]; t-values are calculated using Europe-US mean values

Table II. US and European passenger mean** service quality expectations

	t-values	
	US airline group (1)**	European airline group (2)**
Tangibles		
1. PTAN1	−6.0647*	−1.5655
2. PTAN2	−6.0973*	−2.0609*
3. PTAN3	−8.6707*	−7.5007*
4. PTAN4	−7.3249*	−3.7587*
Reliability		
5. PREL1	−3.0812*	−6.5228*
6. PREL2	−3.4030*	−3.3167*
7. PREL3	−5.1796*	−5.9431*
8. PREL4	−4.7867*	−5.4919*
9. PREL5	−5.6285*	−4.1028*
Responsiveness		
10. PRSP1	−3.2394*	−3.5418*
11. PRSP2	−3.5587*	−3.5155*
12. PRSP3	−1.2915	−2.2390*
13. PRSP4	−1.7250	−3.1881*
Assurance		
14. PASR1	−4.0949*	−3.7960*
15. PASR2	−5.0222*	−1.8967
16. PASR3	−2.5114*	−5.0572*
17. PASR4	−5.5201*	−5.0151*
Empathy		
18. PEMP1	−4.5372*	−5.5256*
19. PEMP2	−5.8280*	−5.7490*
20. PEMP3	−5.3686*	−5.4187*
21. PEMP4	−2.9205*	−3.5307*
22. PEMP5	−3.8095*	−4.0826*

Notes:
α: $p < 0.05$; critical t-value > 1.96*
(1) Individual SERVQUAL feature t-value for mean differences for the US airline group by US and European passengers. The passenger groups compared consisted of 760 European and 660 US passengers who had designated a US airline on the transatlantic corridor.
(2) Individual SERVQUAL feature t-value for mean differences for the European airline group by US and European passengers. The groups compared consisted of 849 European and 361 US passengers who had designated a European airline on the transatlantic corridor. ** For each airline group mean differences are calculated as European-US

Table III. Passenger perception differences of airline groups, by SERVQUAL feature[9]

items in the dimension being less than six on Likert seven-point scale). Both passenger group expectation values for Tangible features (the appearance of physical facilities, equipment, personnel and communications materials) were lowest among the 22 service quality features, except for airline employee appearance (ETAN3).

The differences between US and European passenger group expectations were found to be statistically significant in 18 of 22 service quality feature statements. On this basis, *P2* is accepted. We conclude that service quality expectations do vary by nationality.

Passenger perceptions by nationality
P3. Service quality perceptions vary by nationality.

Airline origin***	Passenger origin***		t-value
	Europe	USA	
Europe	5.4205	5.8023	−5.1461*
USA	5.4779	5.6927	−3.2940*
t-value	−1.0410	1.5350	

Notes:
α: $p < 0.05$; critical t-value > 1.96*
** "The service quality of this airline is excellent"; values being determined using Likert seven-point scale, 1 = "strongly disagree" and 7 = "strongly agree".
*** In both row and column comparisons, mean differences are calculated as European-US

*Table IV. Airline group mean excellence rating ** by passenger group*

Differences in perceptions of European and US airline groups were determined using SERVQUAL statements (Appendix D) from European and US passengers. When addressing the US airline group, the two passenger groups are found to have statistically different mean values for 20 of 22 service quality features (US Airline Group Column, Table III). The two features for which a statistically significant difference was not evidenced were in the Responsiveness dimension: "Employees of this airline are always willing to help customers" (PRSP3) and "Employees of this airline are never too busy to respond to customer requests" (PRSP4).

Significant difference

When the two passenger group perception scores for the European airline group were examined, a statistically significant difference in mean values was also determined for 20 of 22 statements (European airline column, Table III). However, in this instance, the two features that did not have significant differences were in the Tangibles dimension, "This airline has modern-looking aircraft" (PTAN1) and the Assurance dimension, "Customers of this airline will feel safe in their transactions" (PASR2).

As the differences between US and European passenger group perceptions of the two airline groups were each found to be statistically significant in 20 of 22 service quality feature statements, *P3* is accepted. We conclude that service quality perceptions do vary by nationality.

Overall assessments of service quality by nationality independent of the SERVQUAL model
P4. Overall service quality assessments vary by passenger nationality.

This proposition was tested by an analysis separate from the SERVQUAL model. For the designated airline, passengers responded to an independent survey statement, "The service quality of this airline is excellent", on a

Airline group	Passenger group		t-value
	Europe	USA	
Europe	−0.7505	−0.6258	−2.2472*
USA	−0.8029	−0.6596	−2.7721*
t-value	1.4010	0.5798	

Notes:
α: p < 0.05; critical t-value > 1.96*
** In both row and column comparisons, mean differences are calculated as European-US

*Table V. Overall SERQUAL rating of US and European airline groups, by passenger group ***

seven point disagree-agree Likert scale. The results shown in Table IV indicate that US passengers rated *both* European and US airlines significantly higher than did European passengers.

Higher level of service

US passengers considered European airlines (as a group) to provide a higher level of service quality (5.8023) than did European passengers (5.4205); US passengers also considered US airlines to provide a higher level of service quality (5.6927) than did European passengers (5.4779), again using a Likert seven-point scale. The differences in mean results between US and European passenger groups were statistically significant. On this basis, *P4* is accepted and we conclude that overall service quality assessments vary by nationality.

Proposition testing: P5 *through* P8
European and US passenger assessments of US and European airline group service quality were sequentially examined based on overall airline group service quality using overall SERVQUAL ratings calculated by equation (3).

European passenger ratings of overall service quality by airline group
P5. European passengers perceive delivered service quality of US and European airline groups to vary (Figure 2, links 2 and 3).

Perceptions

This propositions examines perceptions of European passengers; 849 European passengers provided perceptions of European airlines and 760 of US airlines. The difference in the number of passengers reporting expectations and perceptions of airline groups is owing to differing numbers of passengers addressing both a US *and* a European airline if they had travel experience with both, or a single response if international experience was limited to a single airline group, US *or* European.

Both airline groups failed to meet European passengers' service quality expectations (a lower negative score, approaching $p - e = 0$, reflecting a higher service quality level). Table V (Europe column) indicates that the European passenger group found the US airline group to provide lower overall unweighted service quality (–0.8029) than the European airline group (–0.7505); however, the difference was not statistically significant ($t = 1.4010$)[6].

From this data it can be concluded that although European passengers considered European airlines to perform (overall) more closely to expectations than US airlines, when the five SERVQUAL dimensions were

Proposition	Testing result
P1: The relative importance of dimensions influencing customer service quality expectations and perceptions does not vary by the nationality of airline passengers	Accepted
P2: Service quality expectations vary by nationality	Accepted
P3: Service quality perceptions vary by nationality	Accepted
P4: Overall service quality assessments vary by passenger nationality	Accepted
P5: European passengers perceive delivered service quality of US and European airline groups to vary (Figure 2, links 2 and 3)	Rejected
P6: The US passenger group perceives delivered service quality of US and European airline groups to vary (Figure 2, links 1 and 4)	Rejected
P7: European and US passengers perceive the US airline group to vary in service quality (Figure 2, links 1 and 3)	Accepted
P8: European and US passengers perceive the European airline group to vary in service quality (Figure 2, links 2 and 4)	Accepted

Table VI. Summary of proposition testing

combined to provide the overall service quality rating, the difference is not statistically significant. Therefore *P5* is not accepted and we cannot conclude that European passengers' perceptions of US and European airlines vary.

US passenger ratings of overall service quality by airline group
P6. The US passenger group perceives delivered service quality of US and European airline groups to vary (Figure 2, links 1 and 4).

This proposition examines perceptions of US passengers; 660 US passengers provided perceptions of US airlines and 361 of European airlines. Table V indicates (US column) that although also failing to meet expectations (negative *p-e* scores), the US passenger group found US airlines to provide lower overall service quality (−0.6596) than European airlines (−0.6258); however, the difference was not statistically significant ($t = 0.5798$). On this basis *P6* is not accepted. We cannot conclude that US passenger perceptions of US and European airlines vary.

US airline group service quality by passenger group
P7. European and US passengers perceive the US airline group to vary in service quality (Figure 2, links 1 and 3).

This proposition examines perceptions of US airlines. Analysis was performed to compare passenger group assessments of the US airline group. 760 European and 660 US passengers evaluated the service quality of the US airline group.

Table V (US row) indicates that the US passenger group considered the US airline group to more closely meet overall service quality expectations (−0.6596) than did the European passenger group (−0.8029), a statistical difference being evidenced ($t = -2.7721$). Therefore, European and US passenger groups perceive US airline group service quality to be different, and on this basis *P7* is accepted.

European airline group service quality by passenger group
P8. European and US passengers perceive the European airline group to vary in service quality (Figure 2, links 2 and 4).

Variation in quality

This proposition examines perceptions of European airlines. 849 European and 361 US passengers evaluated European airline group service quality. Table V indicates (Europe row) that the US passenger group considered European airline service quality to more closely meet expectations (−0.6258) than did the European passenger group (−0.7505), as indicated by a service quality value (*p-e*) closer to zero, and for which a statistical difference was also evidenced ($t = -2.2472$). On this basis it can be concluded that European and US passengers do view European airline service to vary in quality; *P8* is accepted by this method.

Thus proposition testing results indicate that six of the eight propositions are accepted. Table VI summarizes the tests of the propositions.

Research findings and implications
SERVQUAL model
This empirical study further validates the SERVQUAL model and demonstrates its potential value in an international setting using a common survey instrument in multiple languages. The study results suggest that service quality models may be applied reliably in other international scenarios.

The two passenger groups agreed that Reliability is the most important among the five SERVQUAL dimensions, followed in sequence by Responsiveness, Assurance, Empathy and Tangibles (Table I). The study found Reliability to be the dominant dimension in the service quality paradigm as applied to international airline travel, consistent with the findings of the earlier SERVQUAL exploratory and quantitative research (Zeithaml *et al.*, 1990).

Model research

Earlier SERVQUAL model research indicates that businesses find it easier to meet customer expectations in the dimension found least important by customers generally (Tangibles), while finding it most difficult to meet expectations in the dimension most valued by customers (Reliability) (Zeithaml *et al.*, 1990). These assessments would suggest that the airlines intent on improving customer service quality should spend more management attention and resources on improving the Reliability dimension and less on Tangibles.

Differences in expectations by nationalities
In this study we find that expectations of service quality vary by nationality groups. Statistically significant differences are found in 18 of 22 expectation statements (Table II). US passenger group expectations for service quality are also found significantly higher than the European passenger group in 17 of these service quality features.

Expectations: the primacy of Reliability
Reliability is deemed the most important service quality dimension by both passenger groups; the highest mean value for expectation is attributed by both passenger groups to a Reliability feature: "When a customer has a problem, an excellent airline shows a sincere interest in solving it" (EREL2, Table II). Comparably high expectation scores were attributed by both passenger groups to two other Reliability features, "When excellent airlines promise to do something by a certain time, they will do so" (EREL1) and "Excellent airlines will provide their services at the time they promise to do so" (EREL4).

Not statistically significant

Although the differences between passenger groups for each of these service quality features are not statistically significant, the expectation values (greater than 6.3 using a seven-point Likert scale) strongly indicate the primacy both passenger groups attribute to Reliability features overall.

Additional passenger comments suggest why airlines fail to meet passenger expectations for Reliability: "Late every time I have used this airline", "Food was terrible, ran out of food that was printed on the menu", "I do not expect to stand in line for over one hour to check in first thing in the morning ... bad start to our holiday", and "... to be kept in line for 90 minutes and then not given actual seat assignments is not acceptable!".

Expectations of Responsiveness
Passengers appear to expect airline personnel to be responsive and prepared to meet their requests, further suggesting that although passengers may acknowledge that errors and that problems may occasionally occur, airline employees are expected to respond to customer needs in a constructive and considerate manner. Airlines concerned about building long-term passenger loyalty, and sustained profits earned thereby (Reichheld and Sasser, 1990), will not be distracted from their attention to the passenger even when economic prosperity may obscure the need for doing so.

Several additional passenger comments on individual surveys exemplify why both airline groups fail to meet expectations in the Responsiveness dimension: "Many flight attendants appear exceptionally bothered by working" and "Aircraft personnel were 'reasonable' when seen, but service was spasmodic and of variable quality".

Expectations of Assurance

High values

Both passenger groups attribute relatively high values (greater than 6 on 7-point Likert scale, Table II) to their expectations for Assurance features, except for the European score for "Employees in excellent airlines will have the knowledge to answer customers' questions" (5.9, EASR4). The emphasis that passengers ascribe to employee behavior instilling confidence in customers (EASR1), feeling safe in their transactions (with the airline) (EASR2), employees being consistently courteous with customers (EASR3), and employees having the knowledge to answer customers' questions (EASR4), may relate to the general insecurity that many airline passengers have for flying. Everything associated with the flight, e.g. the check-in process, how schedule changes are handled, the conduct of airline employees, becomes critical to passengers (Schneider and Bowen, 1995). The significance of Assurance features is reflected in the extemporaneous survey comments of some passengers, e.g. "Frankfurt (staff) was not nearly as courteous or helpful", "... European airline staff seem to be more naturally caring", and "Polite, attentive staff".

Expectations of Empathy

The Empathy features for which expectations are greatest include: "Excellent airlines will have the best interests of the passenger at heart" (EEMP4, Table II), and "The employees of excellent airlines will understand the specific needs of their customers" (EEMP5, Table II), the scores for both passenger groups exceeding 6. US passenger mean expectations were statistically greater for all Empathy features than the European group.

Companies are often shown to violate the customer's best interests or specific needs, by rationalizing the causes of complaints made by customers, e.g. the reason for a lost reservation is explained by an employee in terms of what the customer did wrong (Schneider and Bowen, 1995), rather than the provider – e.g. the airline. Thus airlines must also continue to address the fundamental importance of Empathy-related issues in the overall delivery of service to ensure that passenger interests and needs are served.

Expectations of Tangibles

Both passenger groups impute the lowest expectations for Tangibles among service quality features (Table II); mean expectation values for all Tangibles features are less than 5.7 (using the Likert seven-point disagree-agree scale) except the US passenger group expectation for the appearance of aircraft personnel (ETAN3, Table II).

Lowest expectations

Both groups have lowest expectations among *all* features for ETAN1 "Excellent airlines will have modern-looking aircraft" (Table II). The US passenger group attributes a statistically higher expectation for the appearance of airline office, terminal, and gate facilities (ETAN2), than the European passenger group. The US passenger group also are found to have statistically greater expectations than the European passenger group for airline personnel appearance (ETAN3).

The differences in the importance accorded to the appearance of airline facilities and staff by US passengers may be related to higher "security needs" among these passengers, as some people consider airline travel threatening (Bitner, 1990; Schneider and Bowen, 1995). To these people, boarding an airplane is a life-and-death issue, so that even Tangible aspects associated with the flight, e.g. the cleanliness of the airport and the appearance of airline employees, become critical to them (Schneider and Bowen, 1995). In a disorganized environment, including airline facilities or employees whose appearance is unkempt, the physical clues may also suggest incompetence and inefficiency (Bitner, 1990), thereby heightening passenger anxieties about airline travel.

Tangibles

For example, in terms of Tangibles, the prominent attention given to new paint schemes for aircraft, and the adoption of high-technology inflight entertainment capabilities indicate that airline management focus may be somewhat misdirected. Comments from one passenger survey illustrate the issue clearly: "Your new paint scheme stinks. It has to be a balance (price and service quality). Low service low price succeeds because expectations are met. This (named) airline provides 'fake' value in its services".

Although passengers consider Tangible aspects of international airline travel to be relatively less important than Reliability and Responsiveness, airlines can ill-afford to ignore the absolute importance of those Tangibles-related aspects which influence passenger travel anxiety and their assessments of service quality.

Differences in perceptions by nationality
This study finds that differences exist in the service quality perceptions of the two passenger groups. As compared to European passengers, the US passenger group perceive the European and US airline service quality to be significantly higher in 20 of 22 individual service quality statements (Table III). With US passengers giving higher perception scores to both airline groups, and European passengers giving lower scores to both airline groups, the findings suggest that airlines need to energetically address their weaknesses as perceived by customers of various nationalities. If they intend to successfully employ service quality strategies to increase their international market presence, marketing communications must acknowledge differences in perceptions by nationality.

Negative scores

Differences in overall SERVQUAL ratings by nationality
Both European and US airlines are perceived by both passenger groups to *not* meet expectations, as indicated by negative scores for overall service quality (Table V). A significant difference in overall service quality ratings is determined when data for an individual airline group is compared by passenger groups, i.e. direct comparison of US and European airline group service quality by a particular passenger group (Table V). However, a statistically significant difference is not indicated when the US and European passenger groups compared the service quality of *each* airline group (Table V). These results are corroborated by the mean service excellence ratings independent of the SERVQUAL model shown in Table IV.

The service quality ratings of European passengers are significantly lower than those of the US passenger group (Table IV), indicating that the European group is generally more critical of service quality. Similar results are found by using SERVQUAL ratings (Table V) viz. that European passengers consider both groups to provide lower service quality scores than do US passengers, indicating that European passengers are more critical of service quality overall.

Managerial implications

It has been observed that the lure of a universal product may be false (Ohmae, 1989), as may be the goal in alliances among international airlines. This research suggests that there are significant service quality perception differences among passenger groups that they would seek to attract. Since European passengers found the service quality of US airlines to be less than that of their own international carriers, substantial efforts may be required to improve the service offering (changes in the marketing mix as well) in order to attract those passengers. It is also unclear that US carriers are in fact committed to improving their service quality through such alliances as have been recently been created, or merely seeking to circumvent the provisions of international laws governing their ability to reach what appear as attractive markets. They might be inclined to abandon such alliances when management problems and disagreements occur with their new partners (Ohmae, 1989).

Research differences

The research findings also suggest that those businesses intending to expand their activities to international markets should carefully consider the different levels of nationality-based expectations that may exist, carefully research those differences to determine how marketing strategies should be altered for the greatest effect, e.g. to structure marketing communications to various passenger groups based on nationality, and to invest in improved training and development of service provider staff to more effectively respond to the expectations of customers. As Bitner *et al.* (1990) suggest, companies seeking to deliver excellent service quality as a business strategy, need to inspire their employees to meet customer needs: proper responses can lead to increased customer satisfaction. As this research indicates, it should not be assumed that the service delivered or delivery in one country will meet the expectations of customers from another country.

Gain market-share

On the basis of this research, customers from some countries, e.g. European passengers as illustrated by this research, may be seen as more discerning and critical of service than their counterparts in other countries, having higher expectations and/or lower perceptions of service quality provided. This research calls into question whether US airlines are positioned to improve market share on the transatlantic corridor by employing a service quality-based strategy because of the observed lower perception of the service delivered by European respondents. More generally it questions whether various service businesses can successfully enter international markets without first refining both their service offering and delivery. Without significant commitment to service excellence initiatives, businesses may experience more difficulty in attracting foreign customers and improving market share as intended. In this research, US airlines may be seen to have greater difficulty in attracting significantly greater numbers of European passengers on the most heavily-traveled airline route in commercial aviation, other than through code-sharing arrangements. However, there is a corresponding potential for European airlines to attract greater numbers of US passengers and gain market share at the expense of US competitors if "open-skies"[7] treaties are implemented between the US and European nations (and Asian as well), because of the perception of their service offering by US passengers. In the absence of such agreements to overcome restrictions imposed by international agreements, international alliances become a more attractive, but not problem-free alternative to entering global markets.

Global markets

The research questions whether alliances, while popular means of entering foreign markets for less-restricted businesses (Ohmae, 1989), are suitable to various service providers to enter international markets. If partners are perceived not to offer the same level of service (in terms of product or delivery), the long-term success of such alliance may be impaired, as well as the reputation, brand equity and profitability of individual partners. This suggests that service providers seeking to enter global markets by means of alliances will have to carefully scrutinize the service practices and capabilities of their intended partners to avoid the adverse consequences that may otherwise occur, to the frustration of their established market goals. Some partners with apparent market size and capability may in fact not strategically fit the needs of a business on this basis. Thereby alliances may alone not be a viable solution; as one respondent in this research commented about a KLM code-sharing flight using Northwest Airlines, "I don't like surprises".

These research findings mean that, concurrent with efforts to improve perceptions and overall ratings of service quality, businesses should also seek to alter customer expectations of service quality, e.g. in their choices and applications of company communications. In this research, airline advertising which creates images of experiences that are subsequently not met during the travel experience can only serve to widen the gap between passenger expectations and perceptions of service. The consequences of expectations unrealistically set is that service quality will rarely (and most likely only inconsistently) meet the expectations of customers.

This research indicates that the marketing strategies and solutions that airlines (and other service businesses generally) implement to expand internationally must take into account and be *consistent* with different expectations and perceptions that exist based on nationality. Otherwise there is little likelihood that appreciable change will be recognized in future studies of this kind, and more importantly that these businesses will succeed in their international efforts.

Contributions, limitations and future research

The major contributions of this study are: (i) the *first* examination of consumer expectations and perceptions of service quality in an international setting, (ii) the application of the service quality model, viz. the SERVQUAL model, in an international setting, and (iii) empirical evidence that service quality expectations and perceptions vary based on nationality.

Justifications

The study provides justification to the belief that differences may exist in consumer perceptions and expectations based on nationality. Although it is understood that practitioners had used the SERVQUAL model in various countries, it represents the first use of the model across borders and nationalities. The study provides empirical evidence for the expectations and perceptions differences that may be expected in service quality and may significantly impact companies that depend increasingly on international markets and customers. Airline passengers have different expectations for airline service quality based on nationality, as well as perceiving the service quality of airlines to vary in terms of SERVQUAL model features and overall service quality.

It is also suggested that similar studies be conducted to identify specific quality issues affecting other service sectors, as this study concentrated on international airline service only. This study was also limited to airlines service in a specific international market, i.e. US and European airlines competing on the transatlantic corridor between the USA and Europe. The nature of this research precluded airlines renowned for service quality internationally which do not compete on the designated routes, e.g. Singapore Airlines, Cathay Pacific, and Japan Airlines. As future growth for airlines competing internationally is forecast to be increasingly in Asia and Eastern Europe, studies of service quality issues and the influence of regional cultures would appear appropriate. Future international airline service quality study should include Pacific routes, and involve those Asian airlines highly reputed for service quality. However, in examining service quality in an international setting such as Asia, one also needs to take into account whether understanding of underlying dimensions of service quality, e.g. semantic differences, remain the same (Winsted, 1997).

Higher scores

The appearance of a pattern of higher scores by US passengers[8] in this study also suggests the opportunity for studying how culturally-based ratings affect the ability of airlines to accurately monitor customer expectations and perceptions of performance, e.g. by inflight surveys of "today's flight".

Another avenue to extend this research would be to perform longitudinal studies using the transatlantic corridor to enhance the usefulness of data collected during this research. Studies of the remaining gaps identified in the SERVQUAL model would be instructive and potentially beneficial to the participating airlines to isolate issues affecting perception-expectation differences; however, such a research project would require the direct cooperation and involvement of the airlines.

Notes

1. Chosen owing to it being the most heavily competed and traveled route in international airline service.
2. Each passenger could evaluate a European airline that they most frequently used for transatlantic travel, as well as a US airline flown most frequently on the transatlantic corridor. If they had not flown one of the two airline categories, instructions were provided to leave the associated portions of the survey blank.
3. The remaining 162 surveys were completed by passengers of other nationalities not included in the scope of this study.
4. Tables of data supporting the individual hypotheses are available from the authors.
5. "Paired" refers to the match between related expectation and perception statements, e.g. "Excellent airlines have modern-looking aircraft" (expectation), and "This airline has modern-looking aircraft" (perception).
6. This result is corroborated by the independent calculation of the quality of repective airline groups (Table IV); the difference in European group ratings of overall service quality of European and US airlines is not statistically significant ($t = -1.0410$).
7. Bilateral "open-skies" treaties allow airlines of the respective nations to implement airlines service between the countries in addition to those airlines already approved under provisions of the Bermuda I and II agreements.
8. US passenger group perceptions of service quality, irrespective of airline group, are greater than that of European passengers in all cases. Mean values of passenger group percpetions by SERVQUAL features can be obtained from the authors.

References

Albrecht, K. (1992), *The Only Thing That Matters*, Harper Collins, New York, NY.

Albrecht, K. and Zemke, R. (1985), *Service America!*, Warner Books, New York, NY.

Andrews, J.F., Drew, J.H., English, M.J. and Rys, M. (1987), "Service quality surveys in a telecommunications environment: an integrating force", in Czepiel, J.A., Congram, C.A. and Shanahan, J. (Eds), *The Services Challenge: Integrating for Competitive Advantage*, American Marketing Association Proceedings Series, Chicago, IL, pp. 27-31 .

Bartlett, C.A. and Ghoshal, S. (1987), "Managing across borders: new strategic requirements", *Sloan Management Review*, Summer, pp. 7-17.

Bitner, M.J. (1990), "Evaluating service encounters: the effects of physical surrounding and employee responses", *Journal of Marketing*, Vol. 54 No. 2, April, pp. 69-82.

Bitner, M.J., Booms, B.M. and Tetreault, M. (1990), "The service encounter: diagnosing favorable and unfavorable incidents", *Journal of Marketing*, Vol. 54 No. 1, pp. 71-84.

Boulding, W., Kalra, A., Staelin, R. and Zeithaml, V.A. (1993), "A dynamic process model of service quality: from expectations to behavioral intentions", *Journal of Marketing Research*, Vol. 30, pp. 7-27.

Bowen, B.D. and Headley, D.E. (1995), *The Airline Quality Report 1995* (NIAR Report 95-11), National Institute for Aviation Research, Wichita State University, Wichita, KA.

Brown, S. and Swartz, T.A. (1989), "A gap analysis of professional service quality", *Journal of Marketing*, Vol. 53, April, pp. 92-8.

Butterworth, K. (1990), "To compete globally, American firms must know their customers", in *American Manufacturing in a Global Market*, Kluwer Academic Publishers, Boston, MA.

Buzzell, R.D. and Gale, B.T. (1987), *The PIMS Principles*, Free Press, New York, NY.

Carlzon, J. (1989), *Moments of Truth*, Harper and Row, New York, NY.

Carman, J.M. (1990), "Consumer perceptions of service quality: an assessment of the SERVQUAL dimensions", *Journal of Retailing*, Vol. 66 No. 1, pp. 33-55.

Drege, S. (1991), "Customer retention strategies", *Business Mexico*, December, pp. 52-3.

Drucker, P.F. (1964), "The customer is the business", in *Managing for Results*, Harper and Row, New York, NY.

Evelyn, J.J. and DeCarlo, N.J. (1992), "Customer focus helps utility see the light", *The Journal of Business Strategy*, January/February, pp. 8-12.

Farber, B. and Wycoff, J. (1991), "Customer service: evolution and revolution", *Sales and Marketing Management*, May, pp. 44-9.

Fornell, C. (1992), "A national customer satisfaction barometer: the Swedish experience", *Journal of Marketing*, Vol. 56, January, pp. 6-21.

Grönroos, C. (1984), "A service quality model and the marketing implications", *European Journal of Marketing*, Vol. 18 No. 4, pp. 36-44.

Hout, T., Porter, M.E. and Rudden, E. (1982), "How global companies win out", *Harvard Business Review*, No. 5, September-October, pp. 98-108.

Lambert, D.M. and Harrington, T.C. (1989), "Establishing customer service strategies within the marketing mix: more empirical evidence", *Journal of Business Logistics*, Vol. 10 No. 2, pp. 44-60.

McClenahen, J.S. (1991), "Welcome to the unfriendly skies: why business people hate to fly", *Industry Week*, 3 June, pp. 14-16.

McDougall, G.H.G. and Snetsinger, D. (1990), "The intangibility of services: measurement and competitive perspectives", *Journal of Services Marketing*, Vol. 4 No. 4, pp. 27-40.

Miller, T.O. (1992), "A customer's definition of quality", *The Journal of Business Strategy*, January-February, pp. 4-7.

Ohmae, K. (1989), "The global logic of strategic alliances", *Harvard Business Review*, Vol. 67 No. 2, pp. 143-54.

Oneal, M.D. (1991), "Straighten up and fly right", *Business Week/Quality*, pp. 116-17.

Parasuraman, A., Zeithaml, V.A. and Berry, L.L. (1994), "Reassessment of expectations as a comparison standard in measuring service quality: implications for further research", *Journal of Marketing*, January, pp. 111-24.

Parasuraman, A., Zeithaml, V.A. and Berry, L.L. (1988), "SERVQUAL: a multiple-item scale for measuring consumer perceptions of service quality", *Journal of Retailing*, Vol. 64, Spring, pp. 12-40.

Parasuraman, A. (1985), "A conceptual model of service quality and its implications for future research", *Journal of Marketing*, Vol. 49, Fall, pp. 41-50.

Park, C.W. and Smith, D.C. (1990), "Product class competitors as sources of innovative marketing strategies", *Journal of Consumer Marketing*, Vol. 7 No. 2, pp. 27-38.

Peters, T.J. and Austin, N. (1985), *A Passion for Excellence*, Random House, New York, NY.

Peters, T.J. and Waterman Jr, R.H. (1982), *In Search of Excellence*, Harper and Row, New York, NY.

Porter, M.E. (1980), *Competitive Strategy: Techniques for Analyzing Industries and Competitors*, Free Press, New York, NY.

Porter, M.E. (1985), "Generic competitive strategies", in *Competitive Advantage: Creating and Sustaining Superior Performance*, Free Press, New York, NY.

Reichheld, F.F., and Sasser Jr, W.E. (1990), "Zero defections: quality comes to services", *Harvard Business Review*, September-October, pp. 105-11.

Schneider, B. and Bowen, D.E. (1995), *Winning the Service Game*, Harvard Business School Press, Boston, MA.

Sellers, P. (1991), "Pepsi keeps going after No. 1", *Fortune*, 11 March, pp. 62-70.

Sonnenberg, F.K. (1991), *Marketing To Win*, Harper and Row, New York, NY.

Webster, C. (1989), "Can consumers be segmented on the basis of their service quality expectations?", *Journal of Services Marketing*, Vol. 3 No. 2, pp. 35-53.

Webster, C. (1991), "Influences upon consumer expectations of services", *Journal of Services Marketing*, Vol. 5 No. 1, pp. 5-17.

Whiteley, R.C. (1991), *The Customer Driven Company*, Addison-Wesley Publishing, Reading, MA.

Winsted, K.F. (1997), "The service experience in two cultures: a behavioral perspective", *Journal of Retailing*, Vol. 73 No. 3, pp. 337-60.

Zeithaml, V.A., Parasuraman, A. and Berry, L.L. (1990), *Delivering Quality Service*, The Free Press, New York, NY.

(The appendices follow overleaf.)

Appendix A. SERVQUAL model statements [by dimension]

Service quality dimension	Statement number/code	Text
Tangibles	(1) TAN1	Excellent – companies will have modern-looking equipment
	(2) TAN2	The physical facilities at excellent _____ companies will be visually appealing
	(3) TAN3	Employees at excellent _____ will be neat appearing
	(4) TAN4	Materials associated with the service (such as pamphlets or statements), will be visually appealing in an excellent _____ company
Reliability	(5) REL1	When excellent _____ companies promise to do something by a certain time, they will do so
	(6) REL2	When a customer has a problem, excellent_____ companies show a sincere interest in solving it
	(7) REL3	Excellent _____ companies will perform the service right the first time
	(8) REL4	Excellent _____ companies will provide their services at the time they promise to do so
	(9) REL5	Excellent _____ companies will insist on error-free records
Responsiveness	(10) RSP1	Employees in excellent ____ companies will tell customers exactly when services will be performed
	(11) RSP2	Employees in excellent _____ companies will give prompt service to customers
	(12) RSP3	Employees in excellent _____ companies will always be willing to help customers
	(13) RSP4	Employees in excellent airlines will never be too busy to respond to customer requests
Assurance	(14) ASR1	The behavior of employees in excellent _____ companies will instill confidence in customers
	(15) ASR2	Customers of excellent _____ companies will feel safe in their transactions
	(16) ASR3	Employees in excellent _____ companies will be consistently courteous with customers
	(17) ASR4	Employees in excellent _____ companies will have the knowledge to answer customers' questions
Empathy	(18) EMP1	Excellent _____ companies will give customers individual attention
	(19) EMP2	Excellent _____ companies have operating hours convenient to all their customers
	(20) EMP3	Excellent _____ companies will have employees who give customers personal attention
	(21) EMP4	Excellent _____ companies will have the customer's best interests at heart
	(22) EMP5	The employees of excellent _____ companies will understand the specific needs of their customers

Source: Zeithaml *et al.* (1990).

Table AI.

Appendix B. Importance of service quality dimensions

1. The appearance of the airline's ground facilities, aircraft, personnel and communications materials.	_____ points
2. The airline's ability to perform the promised service dependably and accurately.	_____ points
3. The airline's willingness to help customers and provide prompt service.	_____ points
4. The knowledge and courtesy of airline's employees and their ability to convey trust and confidence.	_____ points
5. The caring, individualized attention the airline provides its customers.	_____ points

TOTAL points allocated: 100 points

Table AII.

Appendix C. Operationalized SERVQUAL expectation statements

Service quality dimension	Statement number/code	Text
Tangibles	(1) TAN1	Excellent airlines will have modern-looking aircraft.
	(2) TAN2	The office, terminal and gate facilities of excellent airlines will be visually appealing
	(3) TAN3	An excellent airline's employees will be neat appearing
	(4) TAN4	An excellent airline's materials associated with its service, e.g. pamphlets or statements, will be visually appealing
Reliability	(5) REL1	When excellent airlines promise to do something by a certain time, they will do so
	(6) REL2	When a customer has a problem, an excellent airline shows a sincere interest in solving it
	(7) REL3	Excellent airlines will perform the service right the first time
	(8) REL4	Excellent airlines will provide their services at the time they promise to do so
	(9) REL5	Excellent airlines will insist on error-free records
Responsiveness	(10) RSP1	Employees of excellent airlines will tell customers exactly when services will be performed
	(11) RSP2	Employees in excellent airlines will give prompt service to customers
	(12) RSP3	Employees of excellent airlines will always be willing to help customers
	(13) RSP4	Employees in excellent airlines will never be too busy to respond to customer requests
Assurance	(14) ASR1	The behavior of employees in excellent airlines will instill confidence in customers
	(15) ASR2	Customers of excellent airlines will feel safe in their transactions
	(16) ASR3	Employees in excellent airlines will be consistently courteous with customers
	(17) ASR4	Employees in excellent airlines will have the knowledge to answer customers' questions
Empathy	(18) EMP1	Excellent airlines will give customers individual attention
	(19) EMP2	Excellent airlines have operating hours convenient to all their customers
	(20) EMP3	Excellent airlines will have employees who give customers personal attention
	(21) EMP4	Excellent airlines will have the customer's best interests at heart
	(22) EMP5	The employees of excellent airlines will understand the specific needs of their customers

Table AIII.

Appendix D. Operationalized SERVQUAL perception statements

Service quality dimension	Statement number/code	Text
Tangibles	(1) TAN1	Excellent airlines will have modern-looking aircraft
	(2) TAN2	The office, terminal and gate facilities of excellent airlines will be visually appealing
	(3) TAN3	An excellent airline's employees will be neat appearing
	(4) TAN4	An excellent airline's materials associated with its service, e.g. pamphlets or statements, will be visually appealing
Reliability	(5) REL1	When excellent airlines promise to do something by a certain time, they will do so
	(6) REL2	When a customer has a problem, an excellent airline shows a sincere interest in solving it
	(7) REL3	This airline performs the service right the first time
	(8) REL4	This airline provide its services at the time it promises
	(9) REL5	This airline insists on error-free records
Responsiveness	(10) RSP1	Employees of this airline tells its customers exactly when services will be performed
	(11) RSP2	Employees in this airline give prompt service to customers
	(12) RSP3	Employees of this airline are always willing to help customers
	(13) RSP4	Employees of this airline are never too busy to respond to customer requests
Assurance	(14) ASR1	The behavior of employees in this airline instill confidence in customers
	(15) ASR2	Customers of this airline will feel safe in their transactions
	(16) ASR3	Employees in this airline are consistently courteous with customers
	(17) ASR4	Employees in this airline have the knowledge to answer customers' questions
Empathy	(18) EMP1	This airline gives customers individual attention
	(19) EMP2	This airline has operating hours convenient to all their customers
	(20) EMP3	This airline has employees who give customers personal attention
	(21) EMP4	This airline has the customer's best interests at heart
	(22) EMP5	Employees of this airline understand the specific needs of their customers

Table AIV.

■

This summary has been provided to allow managers and executives a rapid appreciation of the content of this article. Those with a particular interest in the topic covered may then read the article in toto to take advantage of the more comprehensive description of the research undertaken and its results to get the full benefit of the material present

Executive summary and implications for managers and executives

International service variants: airline passenger expectations and perceptions of service quality

It is widely accepted in the USA that foreign airlines tend to offer a better quality of service than US carriers. Sultan and Simpson examine whether customer expectations and perceptions of airline service quality really do vary by nationality. The authors focus in particular on the difference between passengers' expectations and perceptions of service.

The study examines US and European airlines competing on trans-Atlantic routes. Questionnaires were distributed to passengers travelling on American Airlines, Lufthansa, United, Air Canada and SAS, although their responses covered around a dozen airlines in total.

Reliability is the most important factor

The results reveal that Americans and Europeans believe that reliability is the most important aspect of airline-service quality and "tangibles" (which includes factors such as the appearance of the aircraft and of its employees) is least important. Ironically, airlines find it easier to meet customer expectations in the area customers rate as least important (tangibles), while finding it most difficult to meet expectations of reliability – the factor most valued by customers. These assessments suggest that airlines keen to improve customer-service quality should devote more time and money to improving reliability, and less to factors such as aircraft livery and staff uniforms.

Where US and European passengers concur and differ

US and European passengers appear to expect airline employees to be responsive and prepared to meet their requests. Passengers acknowledge that errors and problems may occasionally occur, but airline employees are always expected to respond to customer needs in a constructive and considerate manner.

US and European passengers believe it is important for airline employees to instil a sense of confidence. This may be because of the unease that many passengers feel while flying.

US passengers have higher expectations than Europeans of "empathy" aspect of airline service. Companies were too often shown to violate customers' best interests or specific needs by, for example, explaining the reason for a lost reservation in terms of what the customer rather than the airline did wrong.

US passengers also tend to have higher expectations than Europeans about tangible factors such as the appearance of the terminal, aircraft and employees.

Both expectations and perceptions of service quality vary by nationality, as do overall service-quality assessments. US passengers rated both European and US airlines significantly higher than did European passengers. Neither US nor European airlines met the service-quality expectations of European passengers. While the European passengers considered the European airlines' overall performance to come closer to expectations than that of US airlines, the difference between the two was not statistically significant. US passengers found that US airlines provided lower overall service quality *than European airlines, but again the difference was not statistically significant.*

Airline alliances and service quality

Since European passengers found the service quality of US airlines to be less than that of their own international carriers, substantial efforts may be needed by US carriers to improve the service they offer in order to attract Europeans. This has obvious implications for airline alliances, such as the Star alliance between Air Canada, Varig, SAS, Lufthansa, Thai Airlines and United Airlines. It remains unclear, however, whether US carriers see these alliances as a way of improving their service quality, or whether they are merely seeking to circumvent international laws governing their ability to reach what appear to be attractive markets. In the long term, the success of an alliance may be jeopardised if partners are perceived not to offer the same level of service.

"Open skies" may benefit European airlines

The research appears to reveal the potential for European airlines to attract more US customers if "open skies" treaties are implemented between the US and European nations, because US passengers perceive European airlines to offer better service quality than their American counterparts.

Moreover, the research suggests that marketing communications should differ for different passenger groups, based on nationality.

(A precis of the article "International service variants: airline passenger expectations and perceptions of service quality". Supplied by Marketing Consultants for MCB University Press.)

19

The evaluation of airline service quality by fuzzy MCDM

Sheng-Hshiung Tsaur, Te-Yi Chang, Chang-Hua Yen

Abstract

This study applies the fuzzy set theory to evaluate the service quality of airline. Service quality is a composite of various attributes, among them many intangible attributes are difficult to measure. This characteristic introduces the obstacles for respondent in replying to the survey. In order to overcome the issue, we invite fuzzy set theory into the measurement of performance. By applying AHP in obtaining criteria weight and TOPSIS in ranking, we found the most concerned aspects of service quality are tangible and the least is empathy. The most concerned attribute is courtesy, safety and comfort. © 2002 Elsevier Science Ltd. All rights reserved.

Keywords: AHP; Fuzzy MCDM; TOPSIS; Airline; Service quality

1. Introduction

In Taiwan, the air travel market, both domestic and international, have been experiencing great competition in recent years due to both the deregulation and the increasing of customers awareness of service quality. Under the circumstance, airlines not only attempt to establish more convenient routes, but also introduce more promotional incentives, including mileage rewards, frequent flyer membership program, sweepstakes, and so on. Airlines hope to consolidate the market share and enhance profitability. However, the marginal benefits of marketing strategies gradually reduce because most of the airlines act similarly. Recognizing this limitation of the marketing strategies, some of air carriers now tend to focus on the commitment of improving customer service quality.

The air carriers provide a range of services to customers including ticket reservation, purchase, airport ground service, on-board service and the service at the destination. Airline service also consists of the assistance associated with disruptions such as lost-baggage handling and service for delayed passengers.

Service quality can be regarded as a composite of various attributes. It not only consists of tangible attributes, but also intangible/subjective attributes such as safety, comfort, which are difficult to measure accurately. Different individual usually has wide range of perceptions toward quality service, depending on their preference structures and roles in process (service providers/receivers). To measure service quality, conventional measurement tools are devised on cardinal or ordinal scales. Most of the criticism about scale based on measurement is that scores do not necessarily represent user preference. This is because respondents have to internally convert preference to scores and the conversion may introduce distortion of the preference being captured.

Since service industry contains intangibility, perishability, inseparability and heterogeneity, it makes peoples more difficult to measure service quality. To explore the past related research document, most of the methods for evaluating airline service quality employs statistics method. 5-point of Likert Scales is the major way to evaluate service quality in the past. Nowadays, the fuzzy set theory has been applied to the field of management science, like decision making (Hutchinson, 1998; Viswanathan, 1999; Xia et al., 2000), however, it is scarcely used in the field of service quality.

Lingual expressions, for example, satisfied, fair, dissatisfied, are regarded as the natural representation of the preference or judgement. These characteristics indicate the applicability of fuzzy set theory in capturing the decision makers' preference structure fuzzy set theory aids in measuring the ambiguity of concepts that are associated with human being's subjective judgment. Since the evaluation is resulted from the different evaluator's view of linguistic variables, its evaluation must therefore be conducted in an uncertain, fuzzy environment. During the process of evaluators are imprecise with too large an allowance for error. Therefore, this study includes Fuzzy Multiple Criteria Decision-Making (MCDM) theory to strengthen the comprehensiveness and reasonableness of the decision-making process.

The rest of this study is structured as follows: The first part describes important aspects for the assessment of service quality of airline and presents the evaluation framework and methodology. Next part discusses the procedure and results of empirical study. The final results of the empirical study are presented and discussed in the final section.

2. Evaluation framework and methods of airline service quality

The evaluation procedure of this study consists of several steps as shown in Fig. 1. First, we identify the service quality aspects and attributes that customers consider the most important. After constructing the evaluation criteria hierarchy, we calculate the criteria weights by applying Analytic Hierarchy Process (AHP) method. The measurement of performance corresponding to each criterion is conducted under the setting of fuzzy set theory. Finally, we conduct Technique for Order Preference by Similarity to Ideal Solution (TOPSIS) to achieve the final ranking results. The detailed descriptions of each step are elaborated in each of the following sub-section.

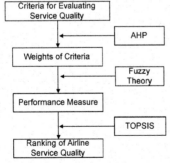

Fig. 1. Evaluation framework of airline service quality.

2.1. Evaluation aspects and criteria

The typical multiple criteria evaluation problem focuses on a set of feasible alternatives and considers more than one criterion to determine a priority ranking for alternative implementation. Keeney and Raiffa (1976) suggest that five principles to be considered when criteria are being formulated: completeness, operational, decomposable, non-redundancy, and minimum size.

There are many empirical studies concerned about service quality. Parasuraman, Zeithaml, and Berry (1985a, b) proposed ten aspects of evaluation criteria in assessing service quality. Many scholars measured the discrepancy in the perception of service quality between airline managers and passengers. Gourdin (1988) have categorized airline service quality into three items: price, safety and timelines. Elliott and Roach (1993) pointed out that timelines, the luggage transportation, the quality of F&B, the comfort of seat, the check in process and inboard service are the six guidelines for evaluating airline service quality. In Ostrowski, O'Brien, and Gordon's (1993) empirical study of service quality and customer royalty, they took timeliness, F&B quality, comfort of seat as the factors of surveying service quality. Truitt and Haynes (1994) uses the check-in process, the convenience of transit, the process of luggage, the timeliness, the clearness of seat, the F&B quality and the customer complaints handing as the standards for measuring service quality.

This study incorporates the revised five-aspect representation of service quality proposed by Parasuraman, Zeithaml, and Berry (1985a, b). The five aspects include tangibility, reliability, responsiveness, assurance and empathy. Tangibility means the physical service presentation such as on-board equipment, quality of the food and so on; reliability stands for the how credible the airline is in terms of safety and pilot navigating skills; responsiveness aspect describes how ground or on-board crew interact with customers; assurance aspect represents the certainty that airline provides for customers and the empathy aspect represents how airline deal with the customer complaints and provide thoughtful services.

Taking the structure of the five aspects as the skeleton and synthesize the other literatures as well as the practical consideration, we established these evaluation criteria include five aspects and 15 service quality evaluation criteria, the details of which can be found in Table 1.

2.2. Analytic hierarchy process (AHP)

The AHP was first proposed by Thomas L. Saaty in 1980 (Saaty, 1980). For years it has been used in tourism planning, (Ryan, 1991; Moutinho & Curry, 1994) and in several areas of social management sciences. It

S.-H. Tsaur et al. / Tourism Management 23 (2002) 107–115

109

Table 1
The evaluation criteria for airline service quality

Objective	Attribute
Tangibility	Comfort and cleanness of seat
	Food
	On-board entertainment
	Appearance of crew
Reliability	Professional skill of crew
	Timeliness
	Safety
Responsiveness	Courtesy of crew
	Responsiveness of crew
Assurance	Actively providing service
	Convenient departure and arrival time
	Language skill crew
Empathy	Convenient ticketing process
	Customer complaints handing
	Extended travel service

integrates opinion and evaluation of experts and devises the complex decision making system into a simple element hierarchy system. Then, evaluation method in terms of ratio scale is employed to proceed with relative importance of pairwise comparison among every criterion. This method decomposes complicated problems from higher hierarchies to lower ones. Furthermore, it also systematizes the problem by employing the subsystem perspective endowed in the system. Based on the hierarchical for the airline service quality in this way.

The AHP weighting is mainly determined by the decision-makers who conduct the pairwise comparisons, so as to reveal the comparative importance between two criteria. If there are n evaluation criteria, then while deciding the decision-making the decision-makers have to condusect $C(n, 2) = n(n - 1)/2$ pairwise comparisons. Furthermore, the comparative importance derived from the pairwise comparisons allows a certain degree of inconsistency within a domain. Saaty used the principal eigenvector of the pairwise comparison matrix contrived by scaling ratio to find the comparative weight among the criteria.

For example, the evaluation hierarchy structure of airline service quality in Table 1, there were three evaluation criteria in the objective level of "Reliability", including "Professional Skill", "Timeliness" and "Safety". Then the evaluation measurement of ratio scale is employed to conduct pairwise comparison to clarity the relative importance of each attributes among above attributes. Therefore, the comparison has to make for three times. To have a further explanation of the compassion, the evaluators would make the comparison between that of the importance of "Professional Skill" and "Timeliness". Besides, the evaluators also would make the comparison between "Professional Skill" and

"Safety". At last, the evaluators would make the comparison between "Timeliness" and "Safety". By means of the comparative importance derived from the pairwise comparisons allows a certain degree of inconsistency within a domain. We should be used the principal eigenvector of the pairwise comparison matrix to find the comparative weight among the criteria. The AHP method should be an exact measure of the difference of attribute preference for consumers and results of this approach are better than the others. For the reasons, this study utilizes AHP method to evaluate the preference weights of airline service attributes for customers.

2.3. Fuzzy set theory

"Not very clear", "probably so", "very likely", these terms of expression can be heard very often in daily life, and their commonality is that they are more or less tainted with uncertainty. With different daily decision-making problems of diverse intensity, the results can be misleading if the fuzziness of human decision-making is not taken into account. However, since Zadeh (1965) was first proposed fuzzy set theory, and Bellman and Zadeh (1970) described the decision-making method in fuzzy environments, an increasing number of studies have dealt with uncertain fuzzy problems by applying fuzzy set theory. With such an idea in mind, this study includes fuzzy decision-making theory, considering the possible fuzzy subjective judgment of the evaluators during airline service quality evaluation. This method for establishing airline service quality can be made more objective. The applications of fuzzy theory in this study are elaborated as follows:

2.3.1. Fuzzy number

Fuzzy numbers are a fuzzy subset of real numbers, and they represent the expansion of the idea of confidence interval. According to the definition made by Dubois and Prade (1978), Those numbers that can satisfy these three requirements will then be called fuzzy numbers, and the following is the explanation for the features and calculation of the triangular fuzzy number.

For example, the expression "airline service quality" represents a linguistic variable in the context of this study. It may take on values such as "fair", the membership functions of expression values can be indicated by triangular fuzzy numbers (TFN) $\mu_A \times (X) = (L, M, U)$ within the scale range of 0–100, the evaluators can subjectively assume their personal range of the linguistic variable μ_A (fair) $= (20, 50, 80)$, which are as shown in Fig. 2. Comparing with the traditional investigative research, the importance degree for the serving attribute used 5-points of Likert Scale, applying TFN that the utilization of linguistic variables is rather widespread at the present time, and the linguistic values

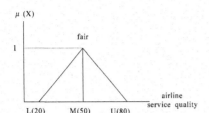

Fig. 2. Triangular membership function of fuzzy number.

found in this study are primarily used to assess the linguistic ratings given by the evaluators.

According to the nature of TFN and the extension principle put forward by Zadeh (1965), the algebraic calculation of the triangular fuzzy number.

Addition of triangular fuzzy number $\oplus$;

$$(L_1, M_1, U_1) \oplus (L_2, M_2, U_2)$$
$$= (L_1 + L_2, M_1 + M_2, U_1 + U_2). \qquad (1)$$

Multiplication of a triangular fuzzy number $\odot$;

A. $(L_1, M_1, U_1) \odot (L_2, M_2, U_2)$
$$= P(L_1/L_2, M_1M_2, U_1U_2) \quad L_1 \geqslant 0, L_2 \geqslant 0. \quad (2)$$

B. Any real number k,

$$K \odot \mu_A(X) = (K, K, K) \odot (L, M, U)$$
$$= (KL, KM, KU). \qquad (3)$$

Subtraction of a triangular fuzzy number $\ominus$;

$$(L_1, M_1, U_1)(L_2, M_2, U_2)$$
$$= (L_1 - L_2, M_1 - M_2, U_1 - U_2). \qquad (4)$$

2.3.2. Linguistic variable

According to Zadeh (1975), it is very difficult for conventional quantification to express reasonably those situations that are overtly complex or hard to define; thus, notion of a linguistic variable is necessary in such situations. A linguistic variable is a variable with lingual expression as its values. One example for the linguistic variable is "airline service quality". It means the service quality that passenger experiences during the flight carried by the airline. The possible values for this variable could be: 'very dissatisfied", "not satisfied", "fair", "satisfied", and "very satisfied". The evaluators were asked to conduct their judgments, and each linguistic variable can be indicated by a triangular fuzzy number within the scale range of 0–100. Also the evaluators can subjectively assume their personal range of the linguistic variable.

2.3.3. The overall valuation of the fuzzy judgement

The overall valuation of the fuzzy judgement copes with the fact that every respondent perceives differently

toward every criterion. The subsequent valuation of the linguistic variable certainly varies among individuals. We integrate the overall fuzzy judgement by Eq. (5).

$$E_{ij} = (1/m) \odot (E_{ij}^1 \oplus E_{ij}^2, \cdots, \oplus E_{ij}^m), \qquad (5)$$

where $\odot$ is the muplication of fuzzy numbers, $\oplus$ the add operation of fuzzy numbers, E_{ij} the overall average performance valuation of airline i under criterion j over m assessors.

E_{ij} as a fuzzy number can be represented by triangular membership function as Eq. (6) shows

$$E_{ij} = (LE_{ij}, ME_{ij}, UE_{ij}), \qquad (6)$$

Buckley (1985) stated that the three end points can be calculated by the method proposed as:

$$LE_{ij} = \left(\sum_{k=1}^{m} LE_{ij}^k \right) \Big/ m, \qquad (7)$$

$$ME_{ij} = \left(\sum_{k=1}^{m} ME_{ij}^k \right) \Big/ m, \qquad (8)$$

$$UE_{ij} = \left(\sum_{k=1}^{m} UE_{ij}^k \right) \Big/ m. \qquad (9)$$

2.3.4. Defuzzification

The result of fuzzy synthetic decision of each alternative is a fuzzy number. Therefore, it is necessary that the nonfuzzy ranking method for fuzzy numbers be employed during service quality comparison for each alternative. In other words, Defuzzification is a technique to convert the fuzzy number into crisp real numbers, the procedure of defuzzification is to locate the Best Nonfuzzy Performance (BNP) value. There are several available methods serve this purpose. Mean-of-Maximum, Center-of-Area, and α-cut Method (Zhao & Govind, 1991) are the most common approaches. This study utilizes the Center-of-Area method due to its simplicity and does not require analyst's personal judgement.

The defuzzified value of fuzzy number can be obtained from Eq. (10).

$$BNP_{ij} = [(UE_{ij} - LE_{ij}) + (ME_{ij} - LE_{ij})]/3 + LE_{ij} \quad \forall i, j. \qquad (10)$$

When we use the fuzzy approach on vague objects such as the satisfaction of airline service quality. Because the evaluation is resulted from the different evaluators view of linguistic variables, it will have the difference and ambiguity. In addition, the traditional evaluation method required the evaluators to make the choice among 'very dissatisfied", "not satisfied", "fair", "satisfied", and "very satisfied". That would force the evaluator's to do an over-high or over-low appraisal, Consequently, it would influence the accuracy of the

S.-H. Tsaur et al. / Tourism Management 23 (2002) 107–115   111

evaluation. In this study, using the membership function to measure the linguistic variables to achieve the better result, which can fairly and exactly reflects the different service quality of each airline. Therefore, the fuzzy logic, thinking and results of the fuzzy approach are better than the traditional statistic approach.

2.4. TOPSIS

The TOPSIS was first proposed by Hwang and Yoon (1981). The underlying logic of TOPSIS is to define the ideal solution and the negative ideal solution. The ideal solution is the solution that maximizes the benefit criteria and minimizes the cost criteria; whereas the negative ideal solution maximizes the cost criteria and minimizes the benefit criteria. The optimal alternative is the one, which is closest to the ideal solution and farthest to the negative ideal solution. The ranking of alternatives in TOPSIS is based on 'the relative similarity to the ideal solution', which avoids from the situation of having same similarity to both ideal and negative ideal solutions.

To sum up, ideal solution is composed of all best values attainable of criteria, whereas negative ideal solution is made up of all worst values attainable of criteria. During the processes of alternative selection, the best alternative would be the one that is nearest to the ideal solution and farthest from the negative ideal solution. Take the objective space of the two criteria as example which is indicated in Fig. 3. A^+ and A^- are, respectively, the ideal solution and negative ideal solution, and alternation A_1 is shorter in distance in regard to the ideal solution (A^+) and negative ideal solution (A^-) than alternatives A_2. As a matter of fact, the ups and downs of these two alternatives are beyond comparison, only TOPSIS has defined such "relative closeness" so as to consider and correlate, as a whole,

the distance to the ideal solution and the negative ideal solution. The calculation processes of the method are as following:

2.4.1. Establish the normalized performance matrix

The purpose of normalizing the performance matrix is to unify the unit of matrix entries. Assume the original performance matrix is

$$\mathbf{X} = (X_{ij}) \quad \forall i,j, \tag{11}$$

where X_{ij} is the performance of alternative i to criterion j.

2.4.2. Create the weighted normalized performance matrix

TOPSIS defines the weighted normalized performance matrix as:

$$\mathbf{V} = (V_{ij}) \quad \forall i,j, \tag{12}$$

$$V_{ij} = w_j \times r_{ij} \quad \forall i,j,$$

where w_j is the weight of criterion j.

2.4.3. Determine the ideal solution and negative ideal solution

The ideal solution is computed based on the following equations:

$$A^* = \{(\max V_{ij}|j \in J), (\min V_{ij}|j \in J'), i = 1, 2, \ldots, m\}, \tag{13}$$

$$A^- = \{(\min V_{ij}|j \in J), (\min V_{ij}|j \in J'), i = 1, 2, \ldots, m\}, \tag{14}$$

where

$$j = \{j = 1, 2, \ldots, n | j \text{ belongs to benefit criteria}\},$$

$$j' = \{j = 1, 2, \ldots, n | j \text{ belongs to cost criteria}\}.$$

2.4.4. Calculate the distance between idea solution and negative ideal solution for each alternative

$$S_i^* = \sqrt{\sum_{j=1}^{n} (V_{ij} - V_j^*)^2} \quad i = 1, 2, \ldots, m, \tag{15}$$

$$S_i^- = \sqrt{\sum_{j=1}^{n} (V_{ij} - V_j^-)^2} \quad i = 1, 2, \ldots, m. \tag{16}$$

2.4.5. Calculate the relative closeness to the ideal solution of each alternative

$$C_i^* = \frac{S_i^-}{S_i^* + S_i^-} \quad i = 1, 2, \ldots, m, \tag{17}$$

where $0 \leqslant C_i^* \leqslant 1$ that is, an alternative i is closer to A^* as C_i^* approaches to 1.

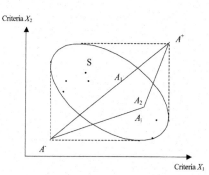

Criteria X_2

Criteria X_1

Fig. 3. The objective space of the two criteria—the distance between idea solution and negative ideal solution for each alternative.

112   S.-H. Tsaur et al. / Tourism Management 23 (2002) 107–115

2.4.6. Rank the preference order

A set of alternatives can be preference ranked according to the descending order of C_i^*.

3. Empirical study of airline service quality

3.1. Survey

In an effort of conducting the survey, 450 questionnaires are sent out to licensed tour guides in 29 general travel agencies. The reason of restricting the qualification of respondents was that we wished respondents had the experience of traveling with all airlines to be evaluated. The licensed tour guides were the most natural choices due to their frequent travels. Among the 450 surveys, 211 were returned for a return rate of 47%. The other demographic statistics were: 21% were at their age of 21–41; 99.05% received at least high school education; average working experience in tourism industry was 5.9 years.

The questionnaire of service quality evaluation mainly was composed of two parts: questions for evaluating the relative importance of criteria and airline's performance corresponding to each criterion. AHP method was used in obtaining the relative weight of criteria. As for the performance corresponding to criteria of every airline, we used linguistic expression to measure the expressed performance. In order to establish the membership function associated with each linguistic expression term, we asked respondents to specify the range from 1 to 100 corresponding to linguistic term 'very dissatisfied', 'dissatisfied', 'fair', 'satisfied' and 'very satisfied'. These score were later pooled to calibrate the membership functions.

We picked three major air carriers as the objects of this empirical study. Airline A, the oldest airline in Taiwan, with more than 30 years history, gains the highest market share by nearly 30%. The market share of airline B, although is only 20% currently, is rapidly growing because of the positive image and reputation. Airline C is a rather young jetliner with less than 10 years of operation history. The market share of airline C is the least out of the three airlines at about 13%.

3.2. The weights of evaluation criteria

Fig. 4 shows the relative weights of the five aspects of service quality, which are obtained by applying AHP. The weights for each of the aspect are: tangibility (0.245), reliability (0.231), responsiveness (0.189), assurance (0.170) and empathy (0.165). The weights describe in general that customer more concern the physical feature than the psychological or empathetical aspects.

Ranked by the weights, the top six evaluation criteria are: courtesy of attendants (0.105), comfort and cleanness of seat (0.09), safety (0.09), responsiveness of the attendants (0.084), on-board entertainment (0.045), extended travel service (0.044). Apparently, customers concern how well they are treated and served during the airborne time. Courteous ground or flight crew soothes the unease of air travel and makes the trip pleasant. The ranks also reflect why the new design of cabin or seat and on-board features are always welcomed by customers. Particularly for the international flight, which usually incur long airborne time, the physical comfort is

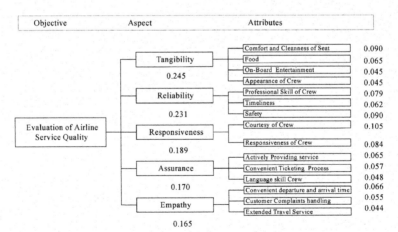

Fig. 4. Weights of the fifteen criteria.

S.-H. Tsaur et al. / Tourism Management 23 (2002) 107–115

113

Table 2
Fuzzy performance measures of airlines[a]

Service quality evaluation criteria	Airline A	Airline B	Airline C
Courtesy of attendants	(52.01, 61.91, 70.80)	(52.61, 62.19, 71.04)	(55.35, 65.05, 73.67)
Safety	(39.25, 48.40, 58.36)	(55.10, 67.66, 73.73)	(53.19, 63.04, 71.68)
Comfort and cleanness of seat	(51.60, 61.46, 70.23)	(53.65, 63.19, 71.74)	(56.21, 66.19, 74.85)
Responsiveness of attendants	(53.25, 62.86, 71.79)	(54.31, 63.71, 72.50)	(45.54, 54.88, 64.33)
Professional skills	(54.14, 67.94, 72.76)	(56.27, 66.04, 74.54)	(47.33, 56.75, 66.03)
Convenient departure time	(54.27, 64.05, 72.73)	(54.88, 64.10, 72.81)	(53.00, 62.64, 71.31)
Food	(52.71, 62.67, 71.21)	(51.19, 60.77, 68.96)	(51.66, 61.32, 70.09)
Actively providing service	(52.55, 58.81, 67.60)	(47.47, 59.01, 65.55)	(49.09, 58.55, 67.28)
Timeliness	(45.15, 54.93, 64.10)	(53.02, 61.91, 71.05)	(51.48, 61.09, 69.81)
Convenient ticketing process	(54.18, 63.82, 72.68)	(54.61, 64.15, 72.72)	(53.09, 62.81, 71.71)
Customer complaints handling	(44.15, 53.58, 62.95)	(46.01, 55.57, 65.02)	(45.46, 55.15, 64.56)
Language skill of airline attendant	(58.53, 68.36, 80.33)	(60.96, 68.04, 76.73)	(49.43, 58.70, 67.73)
On-board entertainment	(59.86, 69.84, 77.90)	(57.98, 70.35, 76.48)	(56.51, 66.48, 74.70)
Appearance of crew	(51.60, 61.33, 70.05)	(48.35, 57.54, 67.09)	(49.93, 59.61, 68.59)
Extended travel service	(49.58, 59.19, 67.91)	(51.45, 61.20, 69.98)	(49.32, 59.08, 68.00)

[a] Is the best performance out of the three airlines.

Table 3
Overall performance measures of airlines

Service Quality Evaluation Criteria	Airline A	Airline B	Airline C
Courtesy of attendants	61.57	61.95	64.69[a]
Safety	48.67	65.50[a]	62.64
Comfort and cleanness of seat	61.10	62.86	65.75[a]
Responsiveness of attendants	62.63	63.51[a]	54.91
Professional skills	64.95	65.61[a]	56.70
Convenient departure time	63.69	63.93[a]	62.31
Food	62.20[a]	60.30	61.02
Actively providing service	59.65[a]	57.34	58.30
Timeliness	54.73	62.00[a]	60.79
Convenient ticketing process	63.56	63.82[a]	62.54
Customer complaints handling	53.56	55.54	55.06[a]
Language skill of airline attendant	69.07[a]	68.58	58.62
On-board entertainment	69.20[a]	68.27	65.90
Appearance of crew	60.99[a]	57.66	59.38
Extended travel service	58.89	60.88[a]	58.50

[a] The final ranking results show that airline B is the best of the three airlines in terms of service quality, followed by airline C and A.

Table 4
Final ranking of airlines

Rank	Airline	Similarity to ideal solution
1	B	0.8155
2	C	0.5534
3	A	0.3857

respondents are then calculated by Eqs. (5)–(9) to obtain the overall performance measure for each airline. Table 2 lists the fuzzy performance measure for the three airlines.

After obtaining the performance measure in terms of fuzzy number, we defuzzify the fuzzy numbers into crisp numbers so as to conduct TOPSIS ranking procedure. We used Center-of-Area method (as Eq. (10)) to defuzzify the fuzzy numbers, which are as shown in Table 3.

In general overview, airline A performs better in physical attributes, while airline B outperforms in professional aspect and airline C has better interaction with customers.

the substantial need for the customers. Safety of air travel nowadays becomes a public distress due to several serious jetliner crashes in recent years. Customers are more aware that safety is the essential requirement of any trip.

3.4. Final ranking

In this paper, we use AHP method in obtaining criteria weight, and apply TFN to assess the linguistic ratings given by the evaluators. By using TOPSIS, we aggregate the weight of evaluate criteria and the matrix of performance to evaluate the three airline service quality, the service quality evaluation results can be seen in Table 4.

3.3. Performance measure of service quality

From the criteria weights obtained from AHP (Fig. 4), the performance of alternatives corresponding to each evaluation criterion evaluated by respondents is measured as fuzzy number with triangular membership function. The performance measure of each

4. Conclusions and implications

The concept of quality service goes beyond the technical aspects of providing the service—it includes customers' perception of what the services should be and how the services is to be conveyed.

In investigating both concerns, we establish the procedures for identifying the most important attributes of service quality for customers and capture customers' assessment of three airlines based on these attributes. The evaluation procedures consists of the following steps: (1) identify the evaluation criteria for airline service quality; (2) assess the average importance of each criterion by Analytic Hierarchical Process over all the respondents. (3) represent the performance assessment of air carriers for each criterion by fuzzy numbers, which explicitly attempts to accurately capture the real preference of assessors. Individual assessment then is aggregated as an overall assessment for each airline under each criterion. (4) Use TOPSIS as the main device in ranking the service quality of the three air carriers.

The significant findings of this study cover several perspectives. Customers are mainly concerned about the physical aspect of the service and less concerned about the empathy aspect. The finding suggests that airlines should maintain their physical features about a certain level and keep renovation necessary.

Among the fifteen service criteria, the most important attributes are 'courtesy of attendants', 'safety', 'comfort and cleanness of seat' and 'responsiveness of attendants'. These results suggest the direction for service improvement. Airline manager also should be more committed to management improvement and be alert the implication of poor management to service quality.

The final ranking results show that airline B is the best of the three airlines in terms of service quality, followed by airline C and A. It is interesting to note that assessment of the service quality is not strongly reflected in the market share. (airline A rank as the third in service quality whereas it has the largest market share). This suggests that even though customer service has an vital impact on air travel business, other factors such as fare promotion program also play the important role. Further more, customer perception of service quality is also dynamic and sensitive to some major incidents such as accidents or events, which are not necessarily promptly reflected in the market share.

In traditional investigative research, the importance degree for the serving attribute used the 5-points of Likert Scale. In this paper, we used the AHP rule and the concept of hierarchical structure to make the pairwise comparison among elements. In cases where there are many attributes, the investigation time is increased and the interviewee may feel impatient.

Interactive design using the computer aid system can be used, and the above disadvantage may be improved. On other hand, we use the fuzzy approach on vague objects such as the satisfaction of airline service quality. In this study, using the membership function to measure the linguistic variables to achieve the better result, which can fairly and exactly reflects the different service quality of each airline. Therefore, the fuzzy logic, thinking and results of the fuzzy approach are better than the traditional statistic approach.

This study possess a few limitations. Firstly, our survey respondents were chosen from tour guides due to sample size limitation and response quality considerations. This may raise questions regarding representativeness of preference of a general travelers. However it may be argued that tour guides are professionals in tourism and are more sensitive to service quality because they judge on behalf of their clients. Their opinions may be treated as those of 'experts' in this field.

References

Bellman, R. E., & Zadeh, L. A. (1970). Decision making in a fuzzy environment. *Management Science, 17*(4), 141–164.

Buckley, J. J. (1985). Ranking alternatives. Using fuzzy numbers. *Fuzzy Sets and System, 15*, 21–31.

Dubois, D., & Prade, H. (1978). Operations on fuzzy number. *International Journal of System Science, 9*(6), 613–626.

Elliott, K., & Roach, D. W. (1993). Service quality in the airline industry: are carriers getting an unbiased evaluation from consumers? *Journal of Professional Service Marketing, 9*(2), 71–82.

Gourdin, K. (1988). Bringing quality back to commercial travel. *Transportation Journal, 27*(3), 23–29.

Hutchinson, M. O. (1998). The use of fuzzy logic in business decision-making. *Derivatives Quarely, 4*(4), 53–67.

Hwang, C., & Yoon, K. (1981). *Multiple attribute decision making: Methods and application*. New York: Springer.

Keeney, R., & Raiffa, H. (1976). *Decision with multiple objective: Preference and value tradeoffs*. New York: Wiley.

Moutinho, L., & Curry, B. (1994). Modelling site location decisions in tourism. *Journal of Travel & Tourism Marketing, 3*(2), 35–56.

Ostrowski, P. L., O'Brien, T. V., & Gordon, G. L. (1993). Service quality and customer loyalty in the commercial airline industry. *Journal of Travel Research, 32*(2), 16–24.

Parasuraman, A., Zeithaml, V. A., & Berry, L. L. (1985a). A conceptual model of service quality and its implications for future research. *Journal of Marketing, 49*(Fall), 41–50.

Parasuraman, A., Zeithaml, V. A., & Berry, L. L. (1985b). SERVQUAL: a multiple-item scale for measuring consumer perceptions of service quality. *Journal of Retailing, 64*(1), 38–39.

Ryan, C. (1991). *Recreational tourism—a social science perspective*. London: Routledge.

Saaty, T. L. (1980). *The analytic hierarchy process: planning, priority setting*. New York: McGraw Hill International Book Co..

Truitt, L. J., & Haynes, R. (1994). Evaluating service quality and productivity in the regional airline industry. *Transportation Journal, 33*(2), 21–32.

Viswanathan, M. (1999). Understanding how product attributes influence product categorization: development and validation of fuzzy set-based measures of gradedness in product categories. *Journal of Marketing Research, 36*(1), 75–95.

Xia, X., Wang, Z., & Gao, Y. (2000). Estimation of non-statistical uncertainty using fuzzy-set theory. *Measurement Science & Technology, 11*(4), 430–435.

Zadeh, L. A. (1965). Fuzzy Sets. *Information and Control, 8,* 338–353.

Zadeh, L. A. (1975). The concept of a linguistic variable and its application to approximate reasoning. *Information sciences,* Part 1: *8,* 199–249; Part 2: *8,* 301–357; Part 3: *9,* 43–80.

Zhao, R., & Govind, R. (1991). Algebraic characteristics of extended fuzzy number. *Information Science, 54,* 103–130.

20

Competition and Service Quality in the U.S. Airline Industry

MICHAEL J. MAZZEO*

Abstract. The U.S. government, media, and flying public have expressed great concern in recent years over both airline market concentration and flight delays. This study explores potential connections between the two by examining whether the lack of competition on a particular route results in worse on-time performance. Analysis of data from the U.S. Bureau of Transportation Statistics in 2000 indicates that both the prevalence and duration of flight delays are significantly greater on routes where only one airline provides direct service. Additional competition is correlated with better on-time performance. Weather, congestion, and scheduling decisions also contribute significantly to explaining flight delays.

Key words: Airlines, competition, flight delays, quality.

JEL Classifications: L13, L43, L93

I. Introduction

Deregulation of commercial airline transportation in the United States has contributed to a striking overhaul in an industry that is crucially important to the American economy. Economists predicted that unregulated competition among airlines would result in lower costs and reduced fares for consumers. It was also hoped that consumers would benefit as competing airlines offered improved levels of service to attract demand. While the skies have been somewhat bumpy for carriers – particularly those unable to successfully cut costs – the most efficient airlines have been able to thrive in the two decades since deregulation.

One concern that accompanied deregulation was that scale economies inherent in air transport might hold down entry and leave the number of airlines operating in a competitive system relatively small. If particular markets were concentrated as a result, consumers would be vulnerable to higher prices. Indeed, studies of airline pricing have demonstrated that while deregulation has reduced most fares, prices are lower when the number of airlines flying between a given pair of cities

---
* Thanks to Meghan Busse, Cory Capps, participants at the IDEI/CSIO workshop in Toulouse, two anonymous referees, and the editor John Kwoka for very useful insights. Special thanks to Scott Schaefer for his assistance and suggestions.

is larger. The interplay between cost savings from scale and the potential threat of high fares due to the exercise of market power has informed the debate over airline competition policy since deregulation.[1]

A separate set of recent government overtures toward re-regulation has focused on the underprovision of service by the airline industry. Both the executive and legislative branches have applied pressure on the industry by threatening to impose strict requirements on the quality of service airlines provide. To avert passage of a "Passengers' Bill of Rights" in 2000, the industry made promises to improve service quality, temporarily mollifying supporters of re-regulation. However, the industry's failure to improve service – in particular, their worsening record of delayed and cancelled flights – has prompted many prominent legislators continue to push for government intervention into the competitive landscape.

It is interesting to note that policy makers are continuing to closely monitor concentration within the airline industry, though not necessarily making the connection between concentration and service quality. The U.S. Department of Justice recently pursued a case against American Airlines, asserting that they engaged in illegal practices to maintain monopoly status on specific routes to and from the Dallas-Fort Worth Airport. The proposed merger between United Airlines and USAir – which many analysts believe would have precipitated further industry consolidation – was scrapped after intense scrutiny by antitrust authorities. That the primary focus of such inquiries is the effect of concentration on price is not surprising. However, one might expect more attention to be focused on the potential effects on service quality, particularly given the simultaneous call for action regarding flight delays.

This paper systematically examines the connection between high market concentration and poor airline service. The analysis focuses on on-time performance – the most common category of customer complaints – on a flight-by-flight basis using data from the Airline Information database maintained by the U.S. Bureau of Transportation Statistics. Airlines have argued that weather conditions beyond their control are the cause of most delays; I will incorporate data from the National Weather Service to control for such problems. Critics, however, argue that airlines have considerable flexibility regarding schedule changes. Delays will hurt airlines' profitability less if they are imposed on consumers who have fewer alternatives. I address this particular assertion by comparing on-time performance with measures of competitiveness across the various routes. The findings indicate that flight delays are more common and longer in duration on routes where only one airline provides direct service and through airports where the carrier represents a larger share of total flights. This suggests that airlines may lack sufficient incentive to provide service quality in markets where they do not face competition.

---

[1] Borenstein's (1992) survey provides a summary of the important results.

II. Quality, Competition and Airlines

Over the past several years, considerable attention has been devoted to service levels in the U.S. airline industry – with the predominant view that quality is poor and rapidly deteriorating. While the industry has been deregulated for 15 years, substantial monitoring of firm conduct continues. In part, this results from the high concentration that (associated with airlines' hub-and-spoke route system) persists in many travel markets.[2] The industry also seems to be a popular target for crusading politicians. Since early 1999, the U.S. Congress has held numerous hearings on service problems, pressured the airlines to agree to a new "Airline Customer Service Commitment," and subsequently held additional hearings after service levels failed to improve. I focus here on on-time performance as a proxy for service quality, as many industry observers do.[3]

Weather, congestion and other exogenous factors undoubtedly contribute to air delays. Nevertheless, airlines could take actions or make investments that would improve their on-time performance. For example, a delay caused by a failed pre-flight maintenance inspection could be mitigated if an extra, unscheduled aircraft was on hand or if large, expert repair crews were employed. Stand-by crewmembers stationed at airports might prevent delays caused by unanticipated employee absences. Adopting such measures would add substantial costs; airlines' willingness to incur these costs to improve quality ought to differ based on the extent to which delayed flights cost the airlines in the long run. In fact, current on-time performance by airlines may well be at the profit-maximizing level.

An airline's costs associated with delayed flights will likely depend on its market structure. If the voices clamoring for reduced delays are correct, expected on-time performance is a key non-pecuniary component of an air traveler's utility function. Such a consumer would compare prices and expected on-time performance of the competing carriers on the route for which he or she was buying a ticket. To the extent that consumers' expectation of future delays are based on a carrier's past on-time performance on that route, one potential cost of flight delays for airlines is reduction in future demand. However, since the demand for air travel is quite inelastic for many consumers, the reduction in utility would represent higher costs for the airline when consumers have other carriers as a potential alternative on the route they are planning to fly. If an airline is the only carrier serving a particular route, the future revenue implication of delayed flights would be less severe. Having additional competition should provide incentives for the profit-

---

[2] As detailed in the next section, more that half the routes in the dataset examined here are served directly by only one firm.

[3] For example, in their widely cited "Airline Quality Rating" series, Bowen and Headley (2001) devise an overall quality metric composed mostly of flight delay rates and factors that are exacerbated by delayed flights (e.g., customer complaints, lost baggage). Dresner and Xu (1995) also find a strong connection between delayed flights and customers filing complaints on those flights.

maximizing airline to invest in delay prevention, since the cost of delays are greater when consumers have additional options.[4]

A recent paper by Suzuki (2000) suggests how an airline's on-time performance could affect future market share in competitive markets. In the same spirit as I describe above, consumers in Suzuki's model incorporate past flight delays in their choice of carrier. As a result, passengers' propensity to switch airlines increases if they have experienced prior flight delays. He calibrates the model using data from the Atlanta-O'Hare city pair market and finds that fluctuations in market share between American, Delta and United from 1990 to 1997 can be explained by passengers' experiences with past on-time performance. This sort of evidence supports the conjecture that the consequences of poor on-time performance can be substantial in competitive markets.[5]

The data presented in the following section demonstrates considerable variety in the competitiveness of the individual routes that each airline serves. By the argument sketched above, airlines incur a greater cost associated with delayed flights on routes where other firms also offer service, all else equal. In order to maximize firm-wide profits, therefore, airlines may allocate resources so that better on-time performance is generated on their more competitive routes. In many cases, the production inputs are sufficiently fungible to accommodate quick reactions to schedule disruptions. For example, American Airlines flies the same type of aircraft on its routes from Dallas to Nashville and Dallas to Indianapolis. If the Dallas pre-flight maintenance check on the plane planned for Nashville (where Delta also flies from Dallas) indicates a problem that will take an hour to fix, the plane planned for Indianapolis (no competitors) could be substituted. Likewise, a flight attendant could be pulled from the plane bound for Indianapolis if a crewmember on the Nashville flight called in sick. With advanced planning additional resource deployments are possible – aircraft closer to their next scheduled maintenance could be disproportionately assigned to noncompetitive routes, for example. Advances in technology

---

[4] A considerable theoretical literature analyses the connection between market structure and product quality more formally. Swan (1970) argued that quality (durability) choice was independent of market structure; however, subsequent authors reversed this result by relaxing some restrictive assumptions. For example, Spence (1975) finds that a price regulated monopolist would underprovide quality. Costs matter as well – if the cost of providing additional quality increases slower than demand increases with higher quality, a profit-maximizing monopolist would provide the highest possible quality level. Schmalensee's (1979) review of this literature highlights the situations in which market concentration would lower product quality, but also concludes that "there is an obvious need for empirical work to confront the implications of the theoretical literature with data."

[5] Since flight-level price data are not available, there is no effort made in this paper to estimate consumers' willingness-to-pay for on-time performance in a serious way. Instead, by comparing quality outcomes across markets, I hope to generate some evidence to suggest that competitive forces provide an incentive for firms to provide additional quality to consumers.

used by airlines to support operations have made this sort of profitability-enhancing input manipulation much easier in recent years.[6]

In the empirical work, I will examine whether there are within-airline differences in on-time performance that are correlated with the competitiveness of individual routes. While not as widespread as the literature on competition and prices, several empirical papers examine the connection between quality provision and market concentration.[7] For example, Hoxby (2000) finds that metropolitan areas with more school districts have higher quality in terms of greater student achievement levels. Dranove and White (1994) summarize the evidence of the connection between quality provision and market competition in hospital markets and Domberger and Sherr (1989) look at markets for legal services. In the airline industry, an early study by Douglas and Miller (1974) investigates flight frequency as the measure of quality across city pair markets. Borenstein and Netz (1999) examine the connection between market competition and the times when flights are scheduled. Mayer and Sinai (2002) perform an extensive empirical evaluation of on-time performance, focusing on the effects of congestion on flight delays and the externalities imposed by certain patterns of flight scheduling. Finally, Foreman and Shea (1999) find evidence that average delays decreased after the airlines were required to publish on-time performance rates. They also find a positive correlation between on-time performance and competition, but their competition measure is very crude.[8]

III. Data

The data for this analysis were put together from a variety of sources. Partially in response to the growing concern over air traffic delays, the U.S. government has been compiling and publishing more detailed information about the on-time performance of airlines. Several airline and travel websites will present the average "on-time" performance – percentage of flights less than 15 minutes late, rounded to the nearest 10 percent – for each flight number to consumers along with details

---

[6] McCartney (2000) reports on systems used by Continental Airlines to allocate staff at hubs, organize crew schedules and overnight maintenance, and even adjust meal quality based on passenger load.

[7] Sutton (1991) discusses how firms' exogenous investments to promote consumer willingness-to-pay can ultimately lead to market concentration. As of now, there is no evidence that relatively poor on-time performance has driven any firm out of a particular city-pair market. The maintained assumption here is that airlines take route structure as exogenous and fixed when deciding on their investments to provide quality service.

[8] The empirical work analyzes the effects of actual competitors only. Theoretically, airline markets could be contestable if sunk costs are low enough – thus, potential entrants would discipline monopolists to provide better on-time service. Though contestability was an early motivation for deregulating the airline industry, subsequent analyses (e.g., Morrison and Winston, 1987; Peteraf, 1994) have found empirical evidence incompatible with contestability in terms of fares. To the extent that the results for quality are similar, this paper may provide further evidence that the airline industry is not contestable.

about price, schedule and equipment. On a monthly basis, the Department of Transportation publishes the "Air Traffic Consumer Report," which includes summary
statistics on flight delays, as well as mishandled baggage, oversales and customer
complaints. The Bureau of Transportation Statistics (BTS) maintains the extensive
compendium of information on which these averages are based. The BTS's Office
of Airline Information tracks the entire domestic system of the (then) ten major
U.S. airlines (Alaska, America West, American, Continental, Delta, Northwest,
Southwest, TWA, United and USAir).[9] The airlines submit their entire flight schedules and subsequently provide the actual gate departure and arrival times for each
flight.

The data are available to download from the BTS website – the dataset used for
this analysis contains all the flights scheduled between 50 major airports in January,
April, and July of 2000. The airports were selected to include all of the major airline
hubs and a sample of facilities in smaller cities. The list of airports, and the number
of flights in the dataset taking off and landing from each, is presented in Table I.
Over 800,000 individual flight observations are included in the dataset.[10]

As discussed above, the summary data typically report a flight as "late" if
it arrives at the gate more than 15 minutes past its scheduled arrival time. The
flight level data from the BTS report adherence to schedule rounded to the nearest
minute, which permits a more accurate analysis. The average flight in the dataset
was 10.7 minutes late. Figure 1 displays the frequency of observations in 15-minute
intervals around their scheduled arrival time. It is interesting to note that a substantial portion of the flights recorded were "early" – 9.7 percent of flights reached their
gate prior to the scheduled arrival time. This does suggest that a certain amount of
slack may be built into the airlines' schedules; I will consider whether this may
be done strategically below. On the other hand, an almost identical 9.8 percent of
flights in the dataset were 45 minutes or more late. To the extent that passengers'
frustration with poor service grows by the minute, it will be useful to investigate the
continuous measure of on-time performance in addition to the industry's definition
of "late."

To isolate the effect of market structure on on-time performance, it is necessary
to control for factors that affect the ability to adhere to schedule, but which carriers
have less ability to manage. Weather is the primary example, as particular weather
conditions may require additional preparations for takeoff or landing or may limit
the use of the full complement of an airport's runways. The National Weather Service (NWS) maintains an archive of daily atmospheric conditions at various sites

---

[9] The data collected for this paper are from a period prior to the bankruptcy of TWA and its
subsequent takeover by American. Therefore, TWA remains in the analysis here.

[10] The data are maintained in a searchable database at http://199.79.179.77/ntda/oai/ DetailedS-
tatistics. Note that the BTS maintains a separate file for flights that are cancelled. Cancelled flights
clearly make consumers worse off; however, it is difficult to integrate them into the analysis without
making *ad hoc* assumptions regarding their comparability. Therefore, only completed flights are
included in this analysis.

Table I. Summary of airports, flights and carriers in the dataset

Airport	Outbound flights	Inbound flights	Share of total flights by carrier									
			Alaska	Am. West	American	Continental	Delta	Northwest	Southwest	TWA	United	US Air
Albuquerque (ABQ)	6603	6118	0.0%	8.1%	7.4%	6.9%	11.0%	2.8%	46.8%	0.0%	10.4%	0.0%
Atlanta (ATL)	44469	33523	0.0%	1.0%	3.5%	4.0%	77.6%	3.5%	0.0%	1.4%	4.2%	4.8%
Birmingham (BHM)	3659	3952	0.0%	0.0%	5.0%	4.5%	22.1%	11.0%	42.0%	0.0%	3.3%	12.1%
Boise (BOI)	2504	2506	0.0%	7.2%	0.0%	0.0%	13.3%	8.6%	39.5%	0.0%	31.4%	0.0%
Boston (BOS)	24222	25336	0.0%	2.9%	12.6%	8.9%	21.8%	6.8%	0.0%	2.6%	15.9%	28.5%
Buffalo (BUF)	4240	4489	0.0%	0.0%	7.8%	9.9%	8.5%	13.6%	0.0%	0.0%	10.5%	49.7%
Charlotte (CLT)	20382	20813	0.0%	0.0%	1.9%	1.6%	2.6%	3.1%	0.0%	1.8%	1.9%	87.0%
Chicago O'Hare (ORD)	55231	50100	0.0%	1.2%	34.1%	3.1%	3.5%	4.3%	0.0%	1.7%	48.6%	3.5%
Cleveland (CLE)	10878	11175	0.0%	0.9%	3.3%	56.4%	6.6%	8.3%	6.4%	3.7%	6.8%	7.6%
Cincinnati (CVG)	14238	14565	0.0%	0.0%	1.3%	0.2%	91.8%	0.7%	0.0%	2.4%	3.7%	0.0%
Columbus (CMH)	8036	8337	0.0%	16.6%	3.0%	6.3%	16.2%	10.4%	8.6%	6.6%	8.8%	23.4%
Dallas (DFW)	42026	34080	0.0%	1.4%	66.7%	4.1%	15.5%	3.2%	0.0%	2.1%	4.7%	2.3%
Denver (DEN)	26392	27859	0.0%	2.4%	4.8%	4.2%	6.1%	3.7%	0.0%	2.1%	73.9%	2.8%
Des Moines (DSM)	1557	1619	0.0%	0.0%	9.8%	0.0%	0.0%	5.7%	0.0%	33.1%	51.3%	0.0%
Detroit (DTW)	26070	26776	0.0%	1.7%	3.5%	3.7%	2.9%	74.9%	3.0%	2.1%	4.0%	4.4%
Hartford (BDL)	7060	7519	0.0%	1.7%	9.8%	5.1%	17.7%	10.2%	3.7%	5.2%	14.9%	31.7%
Honolulu (HNL)	2789	2917	0.0%	0.0%	16.7%	9.7%	18.6%	19.9%	0.0%	3.3%	31.9%	0.0%
Houston (IAH)	23617	24791	0.0%	2.3%	5.1%	73.5%	2.9%	4.5%	0.0%	1.5%	5.9%	4.2%
Indianapolis (IND)	7782	8132	0.0%	3.6%	3.2%	7.2%	10.8%	20.1%	11.1%	7.0%	13.4%	23.7%
Jacksonville (JAX)	4537	4927	0.0%	0.0%	4.0%	10.9%	23.3%	10.1%	16.0%	6.0%	4.1%	25.6%
Las Vegas (LAS)	24276	25204	3.6%	24.2%	5.5%	6.1%	9.4%	4.2%	28.2%	2.1%	14.5%	2.2%
Lexington (LEX)	778	904	0.0%	0.0%	0.0%	0.0%	65.8%	0.0%	0.0%	0.0%	0.0%	34.2%
Los Angeles (LAX)	39546	41530	5.6%	6.1%	16.0%	4.7%	9.7%	4.5%	12.3%	2.2%	35.9%	3.1%
Louisville (SDF)	4386	4704	0.0%	0.0%	4.2%	3.9%	26.8%	11.2%	19.9%	9.5%	2.8%	21.7%
Memphis (MEM)	10228	10695	0.0%	0.0%	2.9%	0.0%	9.6%	79.2%	0.0%	0.0%	3.8%	4.4%
Miami (MIA)	14683	15714	0.0%	1.3%	53.9%	7.7%	6.5%	6.1%	0.0%	4.5%	10.8%	9.2%
Minneapolis (MSP)	25069	25831	0.0%	1.7%	4.1%	2.7%	3.6%	74.4%	0.0%	3.3%	7.4%	2.9%

Table I. Continued

Airport	Outbound flights	Inbound flights	Share of total flights by carrier									
			Alaska	Am. West	American	Continental	Delta	Northwest	Southwest	TWA	United	US Air
Nashville (BNA)	10316	10969	0.0%	0.0%	12.7%	4.1%	13.2%	11.3%	37.3%	5.0%	4.4%	12.1%
New Orleans (MSY)	9356	9872	0.0%	0.3%	8.2%	16.6%	15.7%	8.5%	24.8%	5.5%	9.7%	10.7%
New York Kennedy (JFK)	9320	9488	0.0%	7.5%	23.3%	0.0%	29.3%	4.1%	0.0%	18.6%	17.3%	0.0%
New York LaGuardia (LGA)	20570	22396	0.0%	0.0%	16.1%	6.3%	25.4%	8.4%	0.0%	2.9%	12.7%	28.2%
Newark (EWR)	24907	26063	0.0%	3.3%	7.5%	55.3%	9.2%	6.8%	0.0%	2.2%	10.8%	5.0%
Oklahoma City (OKC)	3103	3367	0.0%	0.0%	15.4%	11.2%	15.6%	9.6%	16.9%	17.0%	14.4%	0.0%
Omaha (OMA)	3588	3816	0.0%	11.3%	6.8%	2.5%	4.8%	17.5%	16.6%	14.7%	25.9%	0.0%
Orlando (MCO)	19865	20723	0.0%	1.0%	7.4%	8.7%	34.2%	7.4%	8.3%	4.9%	10.2%	17.8%
Philadelphia (PHL)	22440	23549	0.0%	2.0%	5.8%	3.2%	7.0%	6.4%	0.0%	2.3%	10.2%	63.1%
Phoenix (PHX)	30783	33458	3.1%	39.3%	3.8%	3.4%	5.9%	3.6%	26.5%	1.9%	9.9%	2.7%
Pittsburgh (PIT)	17369	17394	0.0%	0.0%	1.1%	1.7%	3.6%	2.8%	0.0%	2.9%	3.1%	84.9%
Portland (PDX)	10140	10403	22.4%	5.7%	3.6%	2.9%	17.1%	5.3%	11.5%	3.0%	28.5%	0.0%
Raleigh (RDU)	7763	8446	0.0%	0.0%	12.5%	8.4%	15.2%	10.4%	9.3%	4.5%	5.0%	34.8%
Richmond (RIC)	3796	4215	0.0%	0.0%	3.2%	6.8%	18.0%	8.7%	0.0%	4.3%	11.2%	47.8%
Sacramento (SMF)	7171	7338	6.3%	8.4%	3.4%	0.9%	6.4%	3.1%	46.3%	3.0%	22.4%	0.0%
St. Louis (STL)	28150	29185	0.0%	0.7%	2.8%	1.3%	2.1%	3.5%	12.4%	71.7%	2.7%	3.0%
Salt Lake City (SLC)	14591	15251	0.0%	2.9%	2.5%	2.0%	62.6%	2.2%	16.7%	1.9%	9.2%	0.0%
San Diego (SAN)	14187	15032	7.5%	6.4%	8.4%	5.4%	9.2%	4.4%	29.3%	3.0%	22.6%	3.9%
San Francisco (SFO)	27925	28726	5.0%	3.6%	10.3%	4.8%	7.4%	4.9%	4.6%	2.2%	53.8%	3.6%
Seattle (SEA)	16944	17500	29.1%	3.8%	6.1%	4.5%	9.0%	9.4%	8.0%	3.2%	23.4%	3.6%
Tampa (TPA)	12432	13236	0.0%	1.5%	8.1%	10.4%	20.1%	8.5%	15.4%	4.5%	8.3%	23.3%
Washington Dulles (IAD)	15545	16036	0.0%	0.1%	5.6%	1.3%	7.6%	5.0%	0.0%	2.3%	54.7%	23.6%
Washington National (DCA)	17581	18639	0.0%	0.9%	12.3%	10.4%	20.5%	9.5%	0.0%	3.4%	8.2%	34.6%

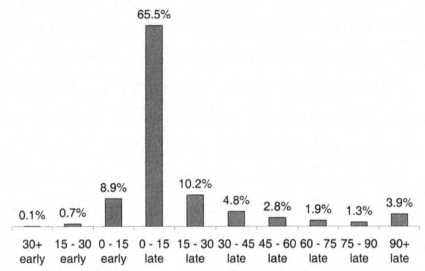

Figure 1. Histogram of "minutes late" in the dataset.

throughout the country that is also accessible through the Internet.[11] Conveniently, the reporting site for a particular city is typically its airport – all 50 airports selected have archived data on the NWS website. For each of the 92 days represented in the flight data, I have collected the average, minimum and maximum temperature for each airport. The NWS also maintains records on "significant" weather; I know if rain, snow, fog, haze, or thunderstorms were reported at each airport on each day. Table II provides definitions and summary statistics for all the variables used in the empirical analysis.

Airport congestion is also cited as an explanation for poor on-time performance. To be sure, airlines do have at least some control over airport congestion levels – airports become more congested as individual airlines schedule additional flights. However, the airlines do not control the schedules of their competitors and most airports do vary in their congestion levels at different times of the day.[12] Furthermore, airlines' schedules are set well in advance of other decisions (crew deployment, aircraft utilization) carriers make that potentially affect on-time performance. I have constructed the variable CONGEST to equal the number of flights (from all U.S. airports) scheduled to land at the same airport during the same hour as each flight in the dataset. I also include airport fixed effects in the regressions to control for capacity and other airport-specific factors that I cannot measure directly.

---

[11] The NWS archived data are located at http://nndc.noaa.gov/?http://ols.ncdc.noaa.gov/cgi-bin/nndc/buyOL-002.cgi.

[12] Mayer and Sinai (2002) attribute the differential performance of hub airlines and other operating at hubs to scheduling differences – to achieve network benefits, hub airline flights are necessarily scheduled at congested times. By counting the actual number of flights scheduled to land each hour, I can control for this more directly.

Table II. Variable definitions and summary statistics

Variable	Definition	Mean	Std. dev.
Weather conditions			
COLD	Dummy Variable = 1 if origin or destination airport reported temp. below 30 on day of flight	0.408	0.49
THUNDER	Dummy Variable = 1 if origin or destination airport reported thunderstorms on day of flight	0.172	0.38
RAIN	Dummy Variable = 1 if origin or destination airport reported rain on day of flight	0.192	0.39
SNOW	Dummy Variable = 1 if origin or destination airport reported snow on day of flight	0.105	0.31
FOG	Dummy Variable = 1 if origin or destination airport reported fog on day of flight	0.657	0.48
HAZE	Dummy Variable = 1 if origin or destination airport reported haze on day of flight	0.462	0.50
Flight, airport & airplane characteristics			
ARR_TIME	Scheduled arrival time of flight (0 = 12:01 am; 1 = midnight)	0.637	0.21
MILES	Length of flight in miles	872.7	609.2
TOEAST	Compass direction of flight, 1 = E; −1 = W	−9.11e-6	0.73
INTOHUB	Dummy Variable = 1 if destination is a hub for that carrier (list of hub/airline combination in footnote 18)	0.415	0.49
OUTOFHUB	Dummy Variable = 1 if origin is a hub for that carrier (list of hub/airline combination in footnote 18)	0.433	0.50
CONGEST	Number of flights scheduled to land in the same hour at the destination airport of the flight	22.75	15.08
AGE	Age of aircraft used for flight	14.13	10.14
NO_SEATS	Number of seats on aircraft used for flight	151.90	70.31
AIRBUS	Dummy Variable = 1 if aircraft used on flight was manufactured by Airbus	0.83	0.28
BOEING	Dummy Variable = 1 if aircraft used on flight was manufactured by Boeing	0.481	0.50
Concentration measures			
SOLO	Dummy Variable = 1 if only 1 airline serves the city-pair market Non-stop	0.377	0.49
HHI	Hershman–Herfindahl Index for all carriers offering service between origin and destination airports (revenue-weighted market shares, non-stop and multi-segment)	0.505	0.18
APT_SHARE	Airline's share of total flights at origin airport + airline's share of total flights at destination airport	0.753	0.27
SUBAVAIL	SOLO*OUTOFHUB	0.180	0.38

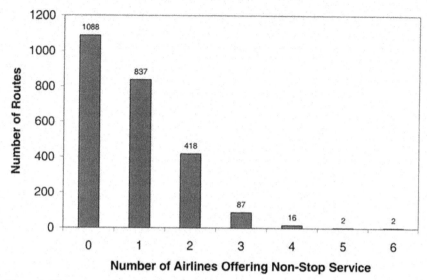

Figure 2. Direct competition in airport-pair routes.

The flight level on-time data kept by the BTS also includes the "tail number" of the aircraft that flew on each completed flight. The tail number is a unique aircraft identifier that was matched to the U.S. Civil Aviation Registry maintained by the Federal Aviation Administration (FAA).[13] For each aircraft, the FAA data contains ownership information, manufacturer and model of the aircraft and its engines, the year the plane was manufactured, and the maximum number of seats possible on the plane. Matching these data with the flight level dataset permits investigation of whether aircraft characteristics (e.g., age) are correlated with on-time performance. It would also be possible to determine whether aircraft are deployed strategically – older planes on less competitive routes, for example.

To evaluate the main hypothesis that carriers keep to their schedules less closely in more concentrated markets, I created several alternate measures of competition. For each of the 2,450 origin/destination pairs, I have counted up how many of the ten airlines provide nonstop service between the two airports. There is considerable variety in the degree of direct competition across the markets, as displayed in Figure 2. For about 44 percent of the airport pairs, no airline provides nonstop service. For some close airport pairs service is impractical (e.g., no airline flies from Kennedy to LaGuardia or from Dulles to National). For many others, no airline flies nonstop, but several airlines offer connecting service (e.g., between San Diego, CA and Richmond, VA). Among the airport pairs where non-stop service is offered, there is only one option just over 60 percent of the time. On the remaining routes, consumers have the ability to select from two or more carriers.

---

[13] The FAA database is located at www.landings.com/_landings/pages/search/search_nnr.html.

Analysts have also found that indirect service can be a relevant substitute for nonstop service between cities. For example, Reiss and Spiller (1989) find that airlines providing indirect service do have a competitive effect on firms offering non-stop service between two cities. To incorporate this substitute into a measure of concentration, I computed a Hirschman–Herfindahl Index for all service between each pair of airports in the dataset. The U.S. Department of Transportation maintains data on carrier revenue by airport pair that includes multiple segment itineraries as well as non-stop flights.[14] The variable HHI represents the concentration index using airport-pair carrier revenues for 2000. Using revenue-weighted market shares is particularly useful in this context, since the extent to which connecting service constitutes competition to an airline that provides non-stop service will vary across markets depending on the distance between airports and the schedules available to make the necessary connections.

Finally, I constructed measures of the share of total traffic accounted for by each airline at each airport. Passengers dissatisfied with poor on-time performance likely travel to several cities from their home airport, so it will by crucial to incorporate the consumers' ability to choose an alternative carrier on other routes as well. This is particularly true in markets where there is relatively little direct service. Returning to Table I, we see that airport concentration varies substantially. At one extreme is Oklahoma City, a small airport where seven of the ten airlines are represented and each has between 10 and 17 percent of the total flights. On the other hand, several of the hub airports are dominated by a single airline – USAir represents 87 percent of the flights in and out of Charlotte, while over 91 percent of Cincinnati's flights are on Delta.

IV. Empirical Analysis

This section contains empirical analyses of service quality using the data described above. The empirical model evaluates various measures of on-time performance as a function of (1) weather conditions; (2) flight, airport and airplane characteristics; and (3) concentration. Table III displays the OLS regressions in which "Minutes Late" is the dependent variable. Table IV examines alternative dependent variables, including probits predicting whether a flight is 15 and 45 or more minutes late and RELLATE, which is defined as the minutes late for the flight divided by the average minutes late for all flights into that airport during the same time period.[15] For each estimation, the unit of observation is an individual flight. It is important to note that these estimations include airport and carrier fixed effects; the estimated parameters indicate a particular variable's effect on flight delays after

---

[14] The data are on the website of the DOT's Office of the Assistant Secretary for Aviation & International Affairs, and can be found at http://ostpxweb.dot.gov/aviation/aptcomp/aptcomp2000.htm.

[15] I divided each day into four six-hour blocks to calculate the average minutes late for comparison purposes. This dependent variable gives an alternate method for controlling for effects other than concentration. I thank one of the referees for suggesting this specification.

controlling for unobserved factors at each airport and for each airline's average on-time performance.[16]

As expected, the weather variables are very significant predictors of on-time performance. In particular, if thunder, snow, rain or fog is reported at either the origin or destination airport, the flight has a statistically significant chance of arriving later than its scheduled time. The delay is particularly long – more than 12 minutes on average – on a day with thunderstorm activity. Cold weather appears to reduce delays; however, this result may show up because days with a very low minimum temperature also have several hours where temperatures are warm enough not to affect flight preparations.

The remaining flight-specific variables reflect additional characteristics that may affect on-time performance. The variable ARR_TIME indicates the scheduled arrival time of each flight, with the 24-hour day converted to a scale from zero to one. The estimated effect of arrival time is very large: the average flight arriving at 8 pm is about 9 minutes more behind schedule than flights arriving at 8 am. The variable MILES represents the flight's distance and TOEAST its direction ("to east" equals 1 if the flight travels from west to east, -1 from east to west, and the fraction in between for intermediate compass points). The parameter estimates on both of these variables are negative and significant, suggesting that it may be possible to "make time up in the air" on longer flights or when wind conditions are favorable. The coefficient on CONGEST is positive and significant, indicating that flight delays are greater when the number of flights scheduled to land in a given hour is higher. Controlling for these factors, an airline's performance at its own hub is better than average. In particular, the INTOHUB variable is negative and significant.[17] Hub carriers have a greater incentive to keep connecting passengers from missing flights, as the costs to rebook passengers onto new connections and to monitor interrupted baggage are substantial. In addition, a passenger's delay – and frustration – may be compounded if delays cause a connecting flight to be missed. Interestingly, the OUTOFHUB dummy has a much smaller effect, particularly for determining whether a flight is more than 15 or 45 minutes late.

---

[16] The estimated airline fixed effects roughly correlate with average on-time performance for the airlines as reported by Bowen and Headley (2001), and the estimated airport fixed effects are also as expected. Dummy variables were also included for each month's data – delays were much greater in July than in January or April. This may indicate that delays are getting worse over time, but with only one year's data some other seasonal variation cannot be ruled out. Day of the week controls indicated that flights were more likely to be on-time on light travel days (Tuesday and Saturday), while Friday flights had significantly longer delays. These results are not reported in Tables II and III, but are available from the author on request.

[17] INTOHUB is a dummy variable whose value is one if the flight's destination is one of the airline's major hubs *and* if the carrier on the flight is the airline whose hub is in that city. Therefore, INTOHUB equals one for the following carrier/destination pairs: America West/Las Vegas, Phoenix; American/O'Hare, Dallas; Continental/Cleveland, Houston, Newark; Delta/Atlanta, Cincinnati, Salt Lake City; Northwest/Detroit, Memphis, Minneapolis; TWA/St. Louis; United/O'Hare, Denver, Los Angeles, Dulles, San Francisco; US Air/Charlotte, Philadelphia, Pittsburgh. The OUTOFHUB dummy is one for flights originating in hubs – with the same list of carrier/origin pairs.

Table III. OLS Regressions of airline delay length (flight-level regressions – number of observations = 769,782; dependent variable: minutes late (time between scheduled and actual gate arrival) mean = 10.7 minutes)

	Panel 1 – base regression			Panel 2 – alternate concentration variable			Panel 3 – base regression including SUBAVAIL		
	Coeff.	Std. err.	t-stat.	Coeff.	Std. err.	t-stat.	Coeff.	Std. err.	t-stat.
CONSTANT	-9.478	0.516	-18.36	-11.037	0.545	-20.203	-9.324	0.517	-18.03
COLD	-3.778	0.133	-28.34	-3.773	0.133	-28.23	-3.781	0.133	-28.35
THUNDER	12.631	0.128	98.95	12.639	0.128	98.77	12.631	0.128	98.95
RAIN	6.309	0.121	52.07	6.319	0.121	52.04	6.309	0.121	52.08
SNOW	8.636	0.158	54.76	8.627	0.158	54.57	8.638	0.158	54.77
FOG	2.319	0.113	20.50	2.349	0.113	20.71	2.318	0.113	20.49
HAZE	-0.192	0.098	-1.95	-0.189	0.099	-1.92	-0.191	0.098	-1.94
ARR_TIME	18.590	0.196	94.96	18.607	0.196	94.82	18.556	0.196	94.72
MILES (00s)	-0.077	0.008	-9.21	-2.9e-4	8.8e-5	-3.30	-0.076	0.008	-9.14
TOEAST	-1.213	0.057	-21.32	-1.216	0.057	-21.32	-1.222	0.057	-21.46
INTOHUB	-3.746	0.211	-17.74	-3.745	0.212	-17.69	-3.681	0.212	-17.39
OUTOFHUB	-1.150	0.210	-5.48	-1.130	0.210	-5.38	-1.401	0.217	-6.47
CONGEST	0.029	0.004	8.27	0.030	0.004	8.48	0.030	0.004	8.53
APT. SHARE	4.387	0.355	12.36	3.974	0.368	10.79	4.257	0.356	11.96
SOLO	1.353	0.131	10.35	–	–	–	0.977	0.153	6.37
HHI	–	–	–	3.96	0.398	9.95	–	–	–
SUBAVAIL	–	–	–	–	–	–	0.830	0.177	4.68
Adjusted R^2			0.073			0.074			0.074

Fixed-effect dummy variables for each month, day of the week, airport and carrier were also included in these regressions.

Table IV. Airline delay analyses – alternate dependent variables (flight-level regressions – number of observations = 769,782)

	Panel 1 – probit Dep. var. = I(min. late > 15)			Panel 2 – probit Dep. var. = I(min. late > 45)			Panel 3 – OLS regression Dep. var. = RELLATE		
	Coeff.	Std. err.	z	Coeff.	Std. err.	z	Coeff.	Std. err.	t-stat.
CONSTANT	−1.569	0.020	−78.48	−2.373	0.027	−89.16	−8.375	0.515	−16.25
COLD	−0.120	0.005	−22.75	−0.175	0.007	−25.20	−3.763	0.133	−28.27
THUNDER	0.371	0.005	76.92	0.449	0.006	75.85	12.649	0.127	99.24
RAIN	0.249	0.005	53.89	0.269	0.006	46.08	6.290	0.121	52.04
SNOW	0.319	0.006	53.14	0.341	0.008	44.46	8.731	0.157	55.45
FOG	0.098	0.004	21.87	0.103	0.006	17.57	2.306	0.113	20.41
HAZE	−0.021	0.004	−5.41	−0.004	0.005	−0.91	−0.170	0.098	7.73
ARR_TIME	0.764	0.008	99.12	0.929	0.010	92.16	1.543	0.195	7.90
MILES (00s)	0.005	0.000	17.34	−0.002	0.000	−4.84	0.001	8.30e-5	−13.02
TOEAST	−0.061	0.002	−27.87	−0.037	0.003	−13.12	−1.156	0.568	−20.25
INTOHUB	−0.154	0.008	−19.19	−0.131	0.010	−12.99	−2.831	0.211	−13.43
OUTOFHUB	0.016	0.008	2.04	−0.001	0.010	−0.05	−1.042	0.209	−4.97
CONGEST	0.002	0.001	11.70	0.001	0.000	5.44	0.005	0.004	1.48
APT. SHARE	0.159	0.014	11.58	0.046	0.017	2.61	3.048	0.354	8.60
SOLO	0.061	0.005	11.94	0.061	0.007	9.43	1.442	0.131	11.05
Pseudo-R^2/R^2	0.065			0.085			0.049		

Fixed-effect dummy variables for each month, day of the week, airport and carrier were also included in these probits.

The remaining rows of Tables III and IV contain the key variables of interest in evaluating the hypothesis that airlines have worse on-time performance on their least competitive routes. The estimates here provide empirical support for this hypothesis, as the SOLO dummy (equals one if there is only one carrier flying direct on the route), the HHI measure (including both nonstop and connecting service), and the APT_SHARE variable (percent of flights from the origin and destination airports the carrier represents) are positive and significant in the minutes late regression and the late flight probits. Note that these effects may come from somewhat different sources. SOLO and HHI capture direct effects that may influence fliers who commonly take a particular route. APT_SHARE reflects airports where frequent fliers have less choice among all the places they intend to fly.[18] In the third panel of Table III, I split up the SOLO variable by including an interaction between the SOLO and OUTOFHUB dummy variables. This new variable, SUBAVAIL, represents flights whose equipment or crew could easily be borrowed by a flight on competitive route at the same hub, if needed. The effect is incremental, and the coefficient estimate is positive and significant. While delays are significantly greater on the less competitive routes, the effect appears to be more acute at airports where competitive routes also originate. This suggests that airlines may be organizing their production inputs with the competitiveness of their routes in mind.

Table V reproduces the base "minutes late" regression with the airplane characteristic variables collected from the FAA added. Here, I have included the age of the aircraft on each flight, the maximum number of seats that can be configured in the aircraft, and dummy variables for aircraft manufactured by BOEING and AIRBUS.[19] Not surprisingly, the older planes arrive at their destination later than planned more often. In addition, AIRBUS planes are about 1.6 minutes later than planes manufactured by other firms, on average. The NO_SEATS coefficient is positive and significant, even though more passengers are potentially inconvenienced if a larger plane is delayed. Of course, NO_SEATS does not reflect the actual number of passengers on each flight. The airlines know precise loads on individual flights and may well take actions to maintain better service when a larger number of customers are involved. Finally, no evidence was found to suggest that aircraft with characteristics that predicted flight delays were disproportionately deployed on non-competitive routes.

Table VI presents a regression whose dependent variable is the scheduled elapsed time for each flight in the dataset. Airlines have been criticized for "pad-

---

[18] The magnitude of the effects can also be determined from these results. A flight on a monopoly route is on average 1.35 minutes later than a similar flight on a competitive route, and if the carrier has 22% greater origin or destination market share the average delay on the flight increases by one minute. Computing derivatives using the estimates from Table IV indicates that a particular flight is between 1 and 2 percent more likely to be late if it is operated by the only carrier that flies between the two cities.

[19] The excluded category includes equipment manufactured by firms such as Fokker and McDonell-Douglas.

Table V. Minutes late regression including aircraft characteristics flight-level regressions – number of observations = 769,782; dependent variable: minutes late (time between scheduled and actual gate arrival) mean = 11.4 minutes

	Coeff.	Std. err.	t-stat.	p-value
CONSTANT	−12.359	0.597	−20.71	0.000
COLD	−4.092	0.150	−27.24	0.000
THUNDER	13.768	0.143	96.11	0.000
RAIN	6.969	0.135	51.51	0.000
SNOW	10.068	0.176	57.17	0.000
FOG	2.104	0.127	16.55	0.000
HAZE	−0.246	0.110	−2.23	0.026
ARR_TIME	19.058	0.218	87.28	0.000
MILES (00s)	−0.085	0.010	−8.70	0.000
TOEAST	−1.375	0.064	−21.54	0.000
INTOHUB	−3.913	0.252	−15.50	0.000
OUTOFHUB	−1.164	0.252	−4.63	0.000
CONGEST	0.026	0.004	6.66	0.000
APT. SHARE	5.010	0.441	11.36	0.000
SOLO	1.458	0.147	9.89	0.000
AGE	0.180	0.008	22.62	0.000
NO_SEATS	0.007	0.001	6.00	0.000
AIRBUS	1.647	0.229	7.19	0.000
BOEING	0.272	0.128	2.12	0.034

Fixed-effect dummy variables for each month, day of the week, airport and carrier were also included in these regressions.

ding" their schedules to avoid missing their scheduled arrival times; this could potentially bias the results from Tables III and IV. Of course, scheduled time is prescribed mostly by the flight's distance and direction. The schedules also appear to reflect realities regarding congestion and time of day effects. It is interesting to note that flights out of the hub have a longer than scheduled flight time on average, while flights into the hub do not. This may partially reflect the logistical difficulties associated with turning around large banks of flights at busy hub airports.

There are mixed results for the concentration variables in the scheduling regression. SOLO flight schedules appear to be padded; as a result, the SOLO coefficient may be biased downward in the on-time estimations. This may also reflect consumers' preference for reaching their destination more quickly – airlines respond with a more accurate schedule on routes where consumers have more than one option. The airport share variable, however, is negative and significant. While airport and airline dummies are included, there may be interactions correlated with airport share that affect scheduling. For example, a dominant carrier may have access to

Table VI. OLS regression of airline flight scheduling (flight-level regressions – number of observations = 769,782; dependent variable: scheduled duration of each flight; mean = 144.4 minutes)

	Coeff.	Std. err.	t-stat.	p-value
Constant	31.819	0.114	278.18	0.000
APRIL	−0.774	0.024	−32.28	0.000
JULY	−1.973	0.024	−83.22	0.000
MONDAY	−0.106	0.034	−3.13	0.002
TUESDAY	−0.084	0.035	−2.38	0.017
WEDNESDAY	−0.120	0.035	−3.43	0.001
THURSDAY	−0.127	0.035	−3.61	0.000
FRIDAY	−0.134	0.035	−3.82	0.000
SATURDAY	0.292	0.034	8.52	0.000
Miles	0.118	0.000	6170.61	0.000
"To East"	−10.271	0.013	−782.66	0.000
ARR_TIME	5.223	0.045	115.73	0.000
INTOHUB	−0.342	0.049	−7.02	0.000
OUTOFHUB	1.239	0.048	25.63	0.000
CONGEST	0.116	0.001	142.54	0.000
APT. SHARE	−0.862	0.081	−10.54	0.000
SOLO	0.195	0.030	6.47	0.000
Adjusted R^2		0.9874		

Fixed-effect dummy variables for each airport and carrier were also included in this regression.

more convenient airport gates. The data for scheduled time on the runway are not available, but I do know the actual "taxi in" times for the flights in the dataset. There is a significant negative correlation between taxi in time and airport share; this may be reflected in scheduling.

Figure 3 displays the estimated carrier fixed effects from the on-time and scheduling regressions along side the raw average minutes late for each carrier in the dataset. The fixed-effect estimates from the minutes late regressions follow the raw averages reasonably closely. It does appear, however, that some airlines benefit from selection effects in keeping to their schedules. For example, the average flight on American is nearly four minutes later than the average flight on Northwest, but their estimated carrier fixed effects are almost identical. Although a substantial portion of United's poor performance in 2000 was carrier-specific, it appears that their flights were particularly susceptible to weather, congestion, and airport-related delays.[20] The carrier fixed effects from the scheduled elapsed time

---

[20] United's average minutes late is 5.7 minutes greater than the next worst performer (America West) and 14.0 minutes more than the best (Northwest) carrier's average delay. However, United's

COMPETITION AND SERVICE QUALITY IN THE U.S. AIRLINE INDUSTRY   293

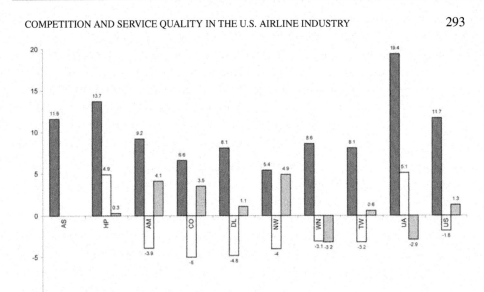

Figure 3. Carrier fixed effects on delays and schedules

regression suggest that some airlines' relatively good on-time performance may result from allowing more time on similar flights rather than from getting passengers to their destination more quickly. Among the five airlines with the lowest fixed effects estimates in the minutes late regression, three (American, Continental and Northwest) have the largest estimated fixed effects in the scheduled elapsed time regressions. This at least partially offsets the quality of these airlines' service, although consumers likely receive utility from being on-time as well as from getting to their destination quickly. Southwest is notable for having estimated carrier fixed effects that are negative and significant in both regressions. It also appears that United has set itself up to be delayed more often by scheduling a shorter amount of time for its flights.

The results in this section reveal factors that explain the on-time performance of flights. Weather, congestion and carrier/airport fixed effects are significant predictors of whether a flight arrives at its destination on time and how long delays last. Controlling for these factors helps to isolate the effects of market concentration – flights on routes with no direct competition have significantly longer schedule times and significantly longer delays. When comparing on-time performance of airlines in the aggregate, it is crucial to account for route selection effects, as the difference between the minutes late averages and the carrier fixed effects estimates suggests.

estimated carrier fixed effect was only 0.2 minutes greater than the next worst (America West) and only 10.1 higher than the lowest carrier fixed effect (Continental). Note that Alaska is the excluded carrier in both the on-time and the scheduled time regressions.

It is important to reiterate two caveats to the results presented above. First, without incorporating data on demand it is difficult to make a reliable welfare statement about the relationship between quality and market structure. The analysis here cannot rule out the possibility that worse on-time performance in monopoly markets disproportionately affect consumers who value time less and are willing to trade delays for lower prices. I collected data on the per capita income of the MSAs associated with each airport – variation in the origin/destination income had no explanatory power in the minutes-late regression. Unfortunately, price data were not available to match with this flight-level on-time dataset; however, none of the many other studies of market concentration and airline fares suggest a negative correlation between monopoly routes and fares.[21]

Finally, recall that the results presented on the connection between market structure and on-time performance are conditional on the schedules the airlines have established. To the extent that there is some unobserved factor explaining delays on particular routes that is correlated with the propensity for airlines to offer service on that route, the effects of market structure on performance may be biased. While some delay-prone routes may be monopolies rather than duopolies, others might not attract any direct service, making it difficult to sign the potential bias. A model that predicts the market structure of city-pair routes, as well as on-time performance, may be a valuable extension to further examine these striking correlations.

V. Conclusion

With several mergers being proposed or considered and increasing calls for government intervention to address on-time performance, competition policy analysis is at the forefront in the U.S. airline industry. Unlike previous studies that focus on prices, this paper examines the hypothesis that the market power which dominant carriers enjoy allows them to provide a lower quality of service – through increased flight delays – to their customers on less competitive routes. Margins may be higher on monopoly routes because airlines that do not face competitive pressure can save the costs that would be needed to provide higher quality, on-time service. The results in this paper indicate that, in fact, flights are less frequently on time on routes that are served by only one airline and in cases where the carriers market share at the airports served are higher. Accounting for scheduling suggests that the actual quality provided is even worse; the airlines schedule longer flight times on their monopoly routes, all else equal.

More broadly, this study is among the first to quantify the link between competition and product quality, which will inform policy makers when assessing the competitiveness of markets, evaluating potential mergers, and imposing industry

---

[21] See, for example, Borenstein (1989), Hurdle et al. (1989), Morrison and Winston (1990), etc. Even studies like Evans and Kossides (1994) that fail to find a significant positive correlation between concentration and fares do not suggest that the correlation is negative.

standards. Welfare analysis ought to address how firms' incentives to provide quality vary with different levels of market concentration and how consumers value higher or lower quality services. For airlines, an extension that estimates demand for air travel as a function of prices and on-time performance would be a useful exercise. This may provide a better understanding of the economic forces airlines face when making and adhering to their schedules and the potential connection between market structure regulation and the provision of quality service for the public.

References

Borenstein, Severin (1992) 'The Evolution of Airline Competition', *Journal of Economic Perspectives*, **6**(2), 45–73.

Borenstein, Severin (1989) 'Hubs and High Fares: Dominance and Power in the U.S. Airline Industry', *Rand Journal of Economics*, **20**(3), 344–365.

Borenstein, Severin, and Janet Netz (1999) 'Why do All the Flights Leave at 8 am?: Competition and Departure-Time Differentiation in Airline Markets', *International Journal of Industrial Organization*, **20**(3), 344–365.

Bowen, Brent, and Dean Headley (2001) 'The Airline Quality Rating 2001', mimeo

Dranove, David, and William D. White (1994) 'Recent Theory and Evidence on Competition in Hospital Markets', *Journal of Economics and Management Strategy*, **3**(1), 169–209.

Domberger, Simon, and Avrom Sherr (1989) 'The Impact of Competition on Pricing and Quality of Legal Services', *International Review of Law and Economics*, **9**, 41–56.

Douglas, George W., and James C. Miller III (1974) 'Quality Competition, Industry Equilibrium, and Efficiency in the Price-Constrained Airline Market', *American Economic Review*, **64**(4), 657–669.

Dresner, Martin, and Kefeng Xu (1995) 'Customer Service, Customer Satisfaction, and Corporate Performance in the Service Sector', *Journal of Business Logistics*, **16**(1), 23–40.

Evans, William N., and Ioannis N. Kessides (1993) 'Localized Market Power in the U.S. Airline Industry', *The Review of Economics and Statistics*, **75**(1), 66–75.

Foreman, Stephen Earl, and Dennis G. Shea (1999) 'Publication of Information and Market Response: The Case of Airline on Time Performance Reports', *Review of Industrial Organization*, **14**, 147–162.

Hoxby, Caroline (2000) 'Does Competition Among Public School Benefit Students and Taxpayers?', *American Economic Review*, **90**(5), 1209–1238.

Hurdle, Gloria J., Richard L. Johnson, Andrew S. Joskow, Gregory J. Werden, and Michael A. Williams (1989) 'Concentration, Potential Entry, and Performance in the Airline Industry', *Journal of Industrial Economics*, **38**(2), 119–139.

Mayer, Christopher, and Todd Sinai (2002) 'Network Effects, Congestion Externalities and Air Traffic Delays: Or Why Not All Delays are Evil', *American Economic Review*, forthcoming.

McCartney, Scott (2000) 'Computer Class: Airlines Find a Bag of High-Tech Tricks to Keep Income Aloft', *The Wall Street Journal*, January 20, A1.

Morrison, Steven A., and Clifford Winston (1990) 'The Dynamics of Airline Pricing and Competition', *American Economic Review*, **80**(2), 389–393.

Morrison, Steven A., and Clifford Winston (1987) 'Empirical Implications and Tests of the Contestability Hypothesis', *Journal of Law and Economics*, **30**(1): 53–66.

Peteraf, Margaret and Randal Reed (1994) 'Pricing and Performance in Monopoly Airline Markets', *Journal of Law and Economics*, **37**(1), 193–213.

Reiss, Peter C. and Pablo T. Spiller (1989) 'Competition and Entry in Small Airline Markets', *Journal of Law and Economics*, **32**, S179–S202.

Schmalensee, Richard (1979) 'Market Structure, Durability, and Quality: A Selective Survey', *Economic Inquiry*, **17**(2), 177–196.

Spence, A. Michael (1975) 'Monopoly, Quality and Regulation', *Bell Journal of Economics*, **6**(2), 407–414.

Sutton, John (1991) *Sunk Costs and Market Structure*, Cambridge, MA: MIT Press.

Suzuki, Yoshinori (2000) 'The Relationship between On-Time Performance and Airline Market Share: A New Approach', *Transportation Research Part E*, **36**, 139–154.

Swan, P. L. (1970) 'Durability of Consumer Goods, *American Economic Review*, **60**(5), 884–894.

21

Overall level of service measures for airport passenger terminals

Anderson R. Correia, S.C. Wirasinghe, Alexandre G. de Barros

Abstract

Overall level of service (LOS) measures for airport passenger terminals are presented in this paper. These measures are useful to evaluate the overall LOS in a single scale, according to user perceptions. The procedure consists of observing passengers and collecting several socio-economic and physical variables that might influence the user evaluation of the airport as a whole. A psychometric scaling technique is used to obtain quantitative LOS ratings from survey data. Regression analysis is used to obtain mathematical relationships between the quantitative LOS ratings and global indices (total service time, total walking distance and two orientation indices). The methodology is illustrated with its application at São Paulo/Guarulhos International Airport in Brazil.
© 2007 Elsevier Ltd. All rights reserved.

Keywords: Airport; Passenger terminal; Level of service; Overall analysis; Global index; Passenger perception

1. Introduction

The development of level of service (LOS) measures for airport passenger terminals has been one of the major issues for airport operators in the last decades. This has motivated a number of LOS studies by many air transportation agencies, including the Federal Aviation Administration – FAA (Transportation Research Board, 1987), Airports Council International – ACI (2000) and Transport Canada (1979). Despite the effort of these agencies, the LOS standards and methods provided by them have been the subject of criticism by airport professionals. One of the main concerns is the lack of passenger input. In those studies, the LOS standards have been developed arbitrarily. Several studies have also been undertaken to develop methods for LOS evaluation taking into account the user's perceptions. Most of them have provided results based on a poor database, and were not able to provide a high level of significance for testing the hypothesis considered.

AVIATION PERFORMANCE AND PRODUCTIVITY

A.R. Correia et al. / Transportation Research Part A 42 (2008) 330–346   331

Additionally, most studies have focused on individual components of the airport passenger terminal (check-in counter, departure lounge, etc.), neglecting the overall evaluation.

A wide measure reflecting the LOS of the terminal as a whole would be very useful at the planning, design and management level. The main challenge to develop an overall measure is the data collection. It is relatively simple to collect characteristics of individual facilities (e.g. individual waiting time at the check-in counter) as opposed to obtaining overall measures (e.g. total walking distance by an individual). Several issues have to be addressed before a research effort is developed to collect overall measures. It is the purpose of this paper to provide a methodology for such an effort, illustrating it with the case study of São Paulo/Guarulhos International Airport.

A thorough review of the past research on LOS was presented in Correia and Wirasinghe (2004). Mumayiz and Ashford (1986) provided a method called perception–response concept, using graphical displays constructed from passenger responses concerning the LOS provided at airports in England. Omer and Khan (1988) employed the concept of utility theory to develop a relationship between characteristics of facilities (e.g. waiting time, space available) and user responses (0–1) about the LOS offered. Müller and Gosling (1991) applied a psychometric scaling technique to obtain a quantitative measure of LOS that might be used in a relationship similar to the one developed by Omer and Khan (1988). Seneviratne and Martel (1991) developed LOS standards for several components of the airport passenger terminal. The selection of the most important components and measures was based on a survey of Canadian airports (Martel and Seneviratne, 1990). Ndoh and Ashford (1993) employed theories of perception and scaling to evaluate LOS on airport access, using 12 attributes (e.g. mode economy, mode comfort, access information, etc.). Park (1994) used fuzzy logic to derive LOS measures for specific components of the airport passenger terminal. The methodology was applied in a case study of the Seoul Kimpo Airport. Yen (1995) conducted a survey at Austin Municipal Airport in Texas, USA. He applied binary logit models to estimate a "long" model and a "short" model to predict the probabilities that a passenger will rate a service on the basis of perceived time measures. Yen et al. (2001) presents a quantitative model to define the level of service at airport passenger terminals. The model uses the fuzzy concept to relate subjective service ratings to time measurements of associated waiting or service processes. Fernandes and Pacheco (2002) utilize data envelopment analysis to evaluate the capacity of 35 Brazilian airports, based on several operational parameters (e.g. number of check-in counters, average space available per passenger, etc.). Studies similar to Fernandes and Pacheco (2002) have been developed to analyze the efficiency of airlines, however employing variables that are more related to the airlines' perspective; see Inglada et al. (2006), for instance. Magri and Alves (2003) evaluate the LOS offered by six Brazilian airports as a function of 36 subjective parameters suggested by the Airports Council International (2000). De Barros et al. (2007) use regression analysis to evaluate the relative importance of transfer passenger ratings of individual facilities and services at Bandaranaike International Airport in Sri Lanka.

All the above studies concentrate on the LOS evaluation of individual components. No study has developed an objective overall LOS measure, reflecting the LOS provided by the airport passenger terminal represented by a single scale. This lack motivated the development of overall level of service measures, which is the object of this paper.

2. Facility characteristics

One of the first steps prior to developing an appropriate survey is the identification of the most important facility characteristics that have an influence on the user perception of the overall LOS. The Airports Council International (Airports Council International, 2000) sent a questionnaire to its 512 airport members, with questions concerning the quality evaluation process. Tables 1 and 2 provide the results of the survey concerning the objective and subjective criteria, respectively, employed to evaluate the overall quality of the airport.

It is possible to measure some of these criteria (e.g. waiting time, walking distance, punctuality). However, the measurement of very subjective criteria (e.g. overall attitude of staff, airport security, etc.) is very complex. On the other hand, the application of a multi-attribute model to evaluate the overall LOS demands the selection of the most important attributes. It is not feasible to employ too many variables – the data needs would be extremely high to validate such a model with a high level of significance. In this case, it is necessary to pick the attributes that have the greatest impact on the user perception of the overall LOS.

332   *A.R. Correia et al. / Transportation Research Part A 42 (2008) 330–346*

Table 1
Objective criteria employed by ACI airports

Objective criteria	# of airports
Response to/analysis of complaints/mail/comments	13
Response to phone calls	8
Flight information display system (FIDS)	4
Monitoring of information to passengers	3
Availability of automated services	2
Ticketing waiting time	2
Availability of telecommunications	1
Availability of lifts/escalators/moving walkways/conveyors/stairs	12
Repair/maintenance monitoring	3
Availability of trolleys	20
Cleanliness	12
Availability of assistance for disabled	4
Seat congestion	2

Table 2
Subjective criteria employed by ACI airports

Subjective criteria	# of airports
Overall customer satisfaction at the airport/overall attractiveness/convenience of airport/overall quality of service	24
Signage/access and user-friendliness of terminal/finding your way/signs for pedestrian	36
Disabled accessibility/assistance	6
Quality of public announcements	10
Walking distance/walking time	9
Terminal atmosphere/comfort	13
Terminal temperature/air conditioning	13
Terminal decor/aesthetics/style	7
Usefulness of electronic ticketing systems	1
Modernity of facilities	2
Overall cleanliness/cleanliness of terminal	37
Toilets/restrooms-overall standard	10
Cleanliness of restrooms	18
Availability/number of restrooms	6
Ease of finding restrooms	2
Noise	1
Waiting times in general	2
Escalators/elevators/moving walkways	3
Seating areas	13
Number of telephone booths/telecommunication facilities	18
Entertainment in terminals/children's play areas	5
Nurseries	2
Art and exhibitions	1
Advertisement of the airport	1
Smoking lounge/areas	3
Airport development	1
Airlines/tour operators/choice and frequency of destination	5
Prices and rates in general	1
Punctuality	4
Service in case of flight delay	1
Security/airport safety	12
Overall attitude of staff	8
Staff appearance	2
Ease of locating staff	1
Competence/responsiveness of staff	5
Courtesy and friendliness/empathy of staff	6
Availability/reliability of staff	1
Availability of airport security staff	1

A.R. Correia et al. / Transportation Research Part A 42 (2008) 330–346   333

Seneviratne and Martel (1991) provided a list of the most important performance variables according to user perceptions, based on a survey of Canadian airports (Figs. 1–3). The variables are grouped into three categories as a function of the element types (circulation, waiting areas and processing elements).

The analysis of the surveys developed by Airports Council International (2000) and by Seneviratne and Martel (1991) suggested the application of the following variables at the overall level:

1. Waiting time.
2. Processing time.
3. Walking time.
4. Walking distance.
5. Level changes.
6. Orientation/information.
7. Space availability for passengers.

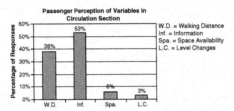

Fig. 1. Passenger Perception of Variables in Circulation Section (Martel and Seneviratne, 1990).

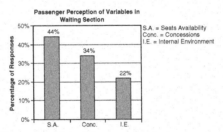

Fig. 2. Passenger Perception of Variables in Waiting Section (Martel and Seneviratne, 1990).

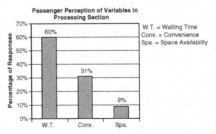

Fig. 3. Passenger Perception of Variables in Circulation Section (Martel and Seneviratne, 1990).

8. Space availability for cars at the curbside.
9. Number of seats.

In addition to reflecting the user perceptions of LOS, these variables indicate the state of the art of airport passenger terminal planning, design and management. For instance, walking distance has been used as an important parameter to evaluate airport passenger terminal configurations (De Neufville et al. (2002); Correia (2000); Bandara and Wirasinghe (1992)); processing time, waiting time and space available have been suggested as some of the most important performance variables of an airport passenger terminal (Horonjeff and McKelvey, 1994); several research reports have been written to deal with the subject orientation/information at airport passenger terminals (Dada (1997); Dada and Wirasinghe (1999); Caves and Pickard (2001)); the number of seats is recognized as one of the most important parameters to consider on the design level of a departure lounge (Omer and Khan (1988); Seneviratine and Martel (1994); Wirasinghe and Shehata (1988)).

In addition to the objective variables previously mentioned, one could consider including factors that account for the quality of the passenger experience in the terminal on a subjective level. These factors include security environment, variety of retailing facilities, baggage handling, punctuality of flights, etc. Another aspect that could be handled in a LOS study is the value of time of a passenger, associated with the time spent either waiting or walking (Fosgerau, 2007). Nevertheless, the focus of this research is the provision of LOS standards for the planning and design stages of an airport; in this case, objective variables are more appropriate.

Following the identification of the representative variables, the challenge is to measure these variables in an objective and precise way. The following sections will deal with this subject.

3. Survey methodology

One drawback of the simple survey method is that much of the information obtained is based on passenger statements describing what they have done or expect to do in the future. With respect to past actions, the interviewed passengers can make mistakes in trying to recall what has happened, particularly when some time has elapsed since the event. The same kind of problem also applies to their intended actions, since these may also differ markedly from what actually happens. On the other hand, observation involves the personal or mechanical monitoring of selected activities and records actions as they occur. Proctor (2000) affirms that three conditions usually exist if the observation method is to be effectively carried out:

1. The event must be observable.
2. The event must occur frequently or be predictable.
3. The event must be completed over a short period of time.

The modeling of level of service in this paper assumes that there is a causal relationship between passenger perceptions (ratings obtained from questionnaire application) and actual physical measures experienced by the passenger. For this reason, several variables will be measured from the curbside to the departure lounge for departing passengers, before the interview process. Simultaneously, the surveyor observes several airport service performance measures for a passenger, for instance, waiting time, service processing time and availability of space. In this case, a passenger is acting as a 'client' in timing his or her own sequential movements and the surveyor is acting as 'monitor'. At the departure lounge, surveyors complete a questionnaire, via a question and answer session, about the passenger's subjective perception of the provision of service level through each facility. The respondent and monitored passenger at each service facility is the same person.

The advantages of the method are: (1) detailed information can be obtained by the tracing and monitoring of the passenger movements at each service activity facility, (2) the respondent for the evaluation questionnaire and monitored passenger are one, so the reliability of data can be maximized and (3) it is possible to compare the passenger perception of the provided service with actual measures of service performance.

AVIATION PERFORMANCE AND PRODUCTIVITY

A.R. Correia et al. / Transportation Research Part A 42 (2008) 330–346

3.1. Questionnaires

A sequence of logical steps that must be followed to develop a good questionnaire as suggested by Aaker et al. (1998) were applied to develop the questionnaire. It was applied to a preliminary survey at three Brazilian airports during the summer of 2003. Some corrections were made and it was finally applied at the São Paulo/Guarulhos International airport during the summer of 2004. The basic changes were the inclusion of some variables that needed to be present in the LOS evaluation. These variables were suggestions made by aiport users to the interviewers: orientation, walking distance and security environment. Some changes were also made based on the preliminary statistical analysis. Some variables presented a high degree of correlation and were removed from the analysis. That was the case for the curbside evaluation. The three variables – space available for cars, walking distance and waiting time – were highly correlated. For this reason it was decided to evaluate the curbside by the space available for cars only.

The questionnaires were developed with the purpose of getting the following specific information:

- Type of flight: international or domestic.
- Trip purpose: business or non-business. Passengers' expectations are very different depending on the trip purpose.
- Movement type: arriving or departing.
- Gender: Male or Female.
- Airline.
- User opinions about LOS: Five categories are proposed for passengers' ratings: excellent, good, fair, poor and unacceptable.
- Facility characteristics.

4. Theoretical framework

The theoretical framework adopted for LOS evaluation is based on the psychometric scaling technique developed by Bock and Jones (1968) and further applied by Müller (1987) and Ndoh and Ashford (1993).

Psychometrics and psychological scaling theory have given extensive consideration to the behavior of subjects, sampled from a specific population, in choosing among alternatives (Bock and Jones, 1968). These ideas can be applied to passenger level of service evaluation of an airport terminal by considering passengers as subject to the experience of being processed at the terminal during the transition between their access and egress mode (whether by ground or air), and then being asked to choose a rating for the quality of that experience (Müller and Gosling, 1991). Most of the studies on this subject have been developed from the work of Thurstone (1959). He introduced the fundamental concept of a sensory continuum, which remains an essential part of current psychological theory.

There are many methods available based on psychometric scaling theory. We could divide them into two categories. There are the methods where judges assess a stimulus directly in terms of other objects, in which categories are included the constant, paired comparisons and rank order methods. The other category, successive-categories judgments, however, depends upon passenger evaluations of the stimulus as a function of rating categories. For the purpose of measuring terminal LOS, it is supposed that the passenger will experience a stimulus only once during his/her trip experience, which is being measured; in this case constant, paired comparisons and rank order methods are not useful for measuring performance variables, i.e. LOS of different terminal components. Considering this, the successive categories method will be employed, since it is the most suitable for measuring airport passenger terminal LOS. The method has been mathematically developed by Bock and Jones (1968), as presented below.

The psychometrical scaling technique allows the scaling of user perceptions of LOS attributes from categorical data. Categorical data are collected by most airports from passenger surveys in which passengers are asked to rate service attributes of preference, importance or satisfaction. In applying the psychometric technique it is assumed that:

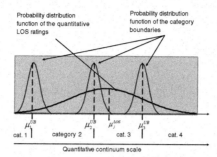

Fig. 4. Illustration of the Successive Categories Method for all Passengers.

- A scale continuum, partitioned into several category boundaries is defined. Any given LOS attribute j (e.g. walking distance), has a unique perception scale value μ_j^{LOS} that can be placed between two category boundaries. This scale value is unique irrespective of the person providing the scale measure.
- A category k in which the mean scale value μ_j^{LOS} is placed has a lower and an upper boundary μ_k^{UB} on the scale continuum. The lower boundary of the first category is minus infinity, and the upper boundary of the last category is plus infinity.
- Any passenger i providing a perception scale for an attribute j will ascribe a scale value v_{ji}^{LOS}, which is related to the mean scale value μ_j^{LOS} of j, the category boundaries, and a variance value specific to the passenger. The location of the category boundaries are defined as composed of fixed components on the continuum and a random component that allows for variations in the interpretation of the category boundary k by different passengers. Fig. 4 shows the spatial descriptions of the scale values and category boundaries.
- Over the whole population or a homogeneous sample, the sample mean scale value for any LOS attribute can be determined. The deduced scale is a discriminant process based on a specified probability distribution function. The normal distribution is assumed as this distribution for both the scale value and the category boundaries.

The details of the theoretical framework have been provided by Correia (2005). Application of the method provides a quantitative measure μ_j^{LOS} representing the level of service evaluation of a given attribute j (e.g. walking distance); this numerical measure can be applied by regression analysis to be correlated to actual performance measures (e.g. walking distance in meters) obtained through surveys and observation of several airport users.

5. Case study of São Paulo/Guarulhos International Airport

Construction of São Paulo/Guarulhos International Airport started in 1980, with operations starting in 1985. It has an area of 14 km^2 with two terminals, which were initially designed to operate only domestic flights; at that time, the majority of international flights to Brazil were handled by Rio de Janeiro International Airport. During the last two decades, many airlines transferred their operations to São Paulo, which in 2000 handled 13 million passengers, making it the busiest airport in South America. Not only is the passenger traffic large, but also there is a daily circulation of 100,000 people in this airport, including passengers, employees and visitors. There are 370 companies operating and 41 airlines. The schematic view of the airport is presented in Fig. 5.

On the main floor the deplaning operations are processed, while the enplaning operations are processed on the upper floor. The terminals are designed as pier-fingers. On the mezzanine floor are some minor commercial stores and services like post office, pharmacy and banks.

Terminal 2   **Terminal 1**

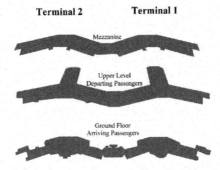

Fig. 5. Layout of São Paulo/Guarulhos International Airport. Adapted from INFRAERO (2005).

6. Summary of responses

Hundred and nineteen passengers have been interviewed in two surveys done at São Paulo/Guarulhos International Airport. The pilot survey was done during June, 16–22, 2003, where 40 passengers were observed and interviewed. The final survey was done during May, 10–16, 2004 where 79 passengers were observed and interviewed. From the 119 passengers, 47.1% were on a domestic trip, while 52.9% were on an international trip. 44.5% were on a non-business flight, while 55.5% were on a business/combined flight. Finally, 72.3% were male and 27.7% were female.

Several measures were collected for each passenger at individual components during both surveys (119 passengers):

Curbside: curbside utilization, walking distance, waiting time.

Check-in counter: waiting time, processing time, and space available per passenger, party size, number of baggage carts.

Security screening: waiting time, processing time and space available per passenger.

Departure lounge: number of seats per passenger, waiting time and space available per passenger.

All these variables can be combined to obtain an overall LOS measure (Correia, 2005). In addition to the characteristics of facilities at the components level, four overall measures were collected for each observed passenger in the second survey in 2004 (79 passengers):

1. Walking distance.
2. Total service time (waiting time + processing time).
3. Actual walking distance/minimum walking distance (measure of orientation).
4. Tardity-differential (measure of orientation).

It is assumed that a bad orientation system at the terminal result in additional walking distance, especially for users who are not familiar with the airport. If the terminal planning provides a good orientation system, the users will be able to get to their desired destinations by walking the minimum distance necessary; otherwise, they might walk considerably more than the minimum. This idea suggested the creation of the following orientation index:

$$O_I = \frac{\text{Real Operational Walking Distance}}{\text{Minimum Walking Distance}}.$$

A perfect orientation system would have O_I equaling 1.0. Increasing values of O_I would be associated with an increasingly bad orientation system. This orientation index will be correlated to the user opinions on the orientation level of service.

Another measure of orientation considered was the tardity-differential. One of the effects of a bad orientation program is that visitors and passengers will remain in the terminal longer than would be necessary, thus

338   *A.R. Correia et al. / Transportation Research Part A 42 (2008) 330–346*

causing accumulations that might require additional building space. This additional time was researched by Dada (1997), who developed an orientation index called *tardity differential* – defined as walking time difference between experts and novices (T), divided by the route length (D). Higher values of tardity-differential may signify some difficulty in wayfinding. In this research, an attempt was made to correlate this tardity-differential to the user opinions about orientation level of service. The expert walking time was defined as the minimum walking time (walking time of the surveyor). The novices walking time was the user walking time collected by the surveyor. This index will be called O_{II} hereafter.

The user responses on the level of service of these three overall measures (walking distance, orientation and total service time) were collected during the second survey at São Paulo/Guarulhos International Airport. Table 3 and Fig. 6 present the distribution of responses.

The responses were provided on a 1–5 scale (1, unacceptable; 2, poor; 3, fair; 4, good; 5, excellent). According to Table 3 and Fig. 6, the majority of the passengers interviewed are pleased (good/excellent) with the overall services provided at São Paulo/Guarulhos International Airport. However, a considerable number of respondents rated the service as poor/fair. No passenger rated the walking distance or service time as unacceptable and only two passengers rated the orientation as unacceptable.

The values of characteristics of facilities were grouped by similar values to facilitate their presentation in this paper. They are presented in Tables 4–7, where the last column (*Obs*) represents the number of passengers observed in each group of similar values.

The actual walking distance for each passenger interviewed was measured from the curbside to the boarding gate, excluding the distance walked to/between non-operational components (concessions, toilets, etc.). This distance will be called operational walking distance in this paper. The minimum walking distance was defined as the minimum feasible distance from the curbside to the boarding gate.

Table 4 indicates that most passengers are processed with a service time shorter than 100 min. However, 10 passengers had to stay longer than this time in holding/processing components. It is important to mention that this time does not include time spent in concession/service components outside the departure lounge.

The operational walking distance was shorter than 500 m for the majority of passengers, as Table 5 indicates. Only six passengers had to walk longer than this distance. Perhaps this value would have been

Table 3
Rating of overall measures

Rating category	Responses					
	Walking distance		Orientation		Total service time	
1	0	0.0%	2	2.6%	0	0.0%
2	9	11.7%	9	11.7%	4	5.1%
3	21	27.3%	14	18.2%	18	23.1%
4	38	49.4%	41	53.2%	43	55.1%
5	9	11.7%	11	14.3%	13	16.7%
Total	77	100.0%	77	100.0%	78	100.0%

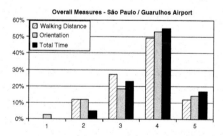

Fig. 6. Overall Measures – Distribution of Responses.

Table 4
Total service time data

Group	Service time range (min)	Average service time (min)	Obs
1	0–9	6.4	5
2	10–29	21.4	16
3	30–49	35.7	16
4	50–59	54.4	7
5	60–69	64.4	12
6	70–99	83.7	12
7	100–129	109.3	7
8	>130	237.7	3

Table 5
Actual operational walking distance data

Group	Walking distance range (m)	Average walking distance (m)	Obs
1	<100	44.33	9
2	100–199	165.23	13
3	200–249	224.08	13
4	250–349	288.91	23
5	350–399	363.70	8
6	400–499	420.00	5
7	>500	538.50	6

Table 6
Orientation I data

Group	O_I range	Average O_I	Obs
1	1.0	1.00	30
2	1.1	1.10	10
3	1.2	1.20	12
4	1.3–1.4	1.40	10
5	1.5–1.6	1.60	4
6	1.7–1.9	1.80	4
7	>2.0	3.40	7

Table 7
Orientation II data

Group (j)	O_{II} range (s/m)	Average O_{II} (s/m)	Obs
1	<0.00	−0.04	11
2	0.01–0.10	0.06	11
3	0.11–0.20	0.15	8
4	0.21–0.30	0.26	9
5	0.31–0.60	0.46	12
6	0.61–0.90	0.72	12
7	0.91–1.50	1.13	8
8	>1.50	1.50	7

considerably higher if connecting passengers had been interviewed. This study included only departing passengers using the curbside.

An analysis of Table 6 reveals that 30 passengers were able to walk from the curbside to the departure lounge in the shortest path (minimum walking distance). The remaining passengers walked more than the necessary distance, indicating that they may have had some orientation/information problems. Most probably, these users are not very familiar with the airport. Table 7 presents information similar to Table 6, but walking times are analyzed, as opposed to walking distance.

7. Data analysis

The user responses have been analyzed through application of the methodology provided, using the successive categories method to obtain the quantitative level of service ratings (μ_j^{LOS}).

7.1. Total service time

Table 8 presents the μ_j^{LOS} values for total service time in the last column. For instance, $\mu_2^{LOS} = 1.17$. This value indicates that the mean quantitative rating of the overall service time for the interviewed passengers whose service time averaged 21.4 min is 1.17. It can be seen that the mean quantitative ratings decrease as the total service time increases, with the exception of group 4. For the worst case (average time = 237.7 min), $\mu_8^{LOS} = -0.89$. This proportionality indicates that a model could be developed to obtain a correlation function between LOS quantitative ratings and time values. Using linear regression, the model is given by

$$\mu_{\text{SaoPaulo}}^{LOS} = 4.542 - 0.911 \ln(T_{WT+PT}),$$
$$(t = 7.655)(t = -6.198)$$

(1)

with $R^2 = 0.86$, $F = 38.420$, $\chi^2 = 6.465$, $\chi_{\text{critic}}^2 = 23.685$ (5% signif. – 14 d.f.). Several types of functions have been suggested (e.g. exponential, linear, log, ln), but the ln function provided the best fit to the existing data (Fig. 7).

Table 9 provides the suggested LOS standards, obtained by substitution of the LOS category boundaries (μ_k^{UB}) in Eq. (1). According to the suggested LOS standards, passengers evaluate the LOS of the terminal as good (LOS B) if the total service time is shorter than 88 min. When the service time is longer than 242 min, the level of service will be evaluated as poor (LOS D). No passenger evaluated the service time as unacceptable (LOS E). In this case, it was impossible to generate the LOS E standard.

These LOS standards might not be applicable to airports that have characteristics that are different from São Paulo/Guarulhos International Airport. The high values of service times corresponding to LOS C and LOS D are due to the following reasons:

Table 8
Total service time data

Group (j)	Total service time (min)	μ_j^{LOS}
1	6.4	2.99
2	21.4	1.17
3	35.7	1.42
4	54.4	0.57
5	64.4	1.15
6	83.7	0.84
7	109.3	0.63
8	237.7	-0.89

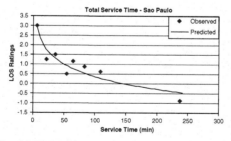

Fig. 7. Plot of the Data and the Regression Line - Total Service Time - São Paulo.

A.R. Correia et al. / Transportation Research Part A 42 (2008) 330–346   341

Table 9
Suggested level of service standards – total service time

LOS	Total service time (min)
A	0–14
B	14 88
C	88–242
D	>242

- The airport has a great share of inter-continental flights. For these flights, around 300 passengers/flight are processed with only three check-in counters serving economy class. Besides, passengers are asked to arrive at the departure lounge 90 min before departure and to arrive at the airport 3–4 h before departure. For some Europeans flights, boarding takes more than 30 min.
- The ride to the airport from downtown can take 30–60 min. Some passengers do not want to take the risk of missing the flight and arrive very early at the airport. In this case, they have more time to stand in long queues.

7.2. Walking distance

The LOS analysis of walking distances has been done analogously to the total service time analysis previously developed. Table 10 presents the μ_j^{LOS} values corresponding to the user responses of passengers in groups 1–7.

Using the values of columns (2 and 3) of Table 10, a linear regression model was developed to obtain a correlation between LOS quantitative ratings and walking distances:

$$\mu_{SaoPaulo}^{LOS} = 1.117 - 0.002(Wd_{op})$$
$$(t = 6.170)(t = -3.045)$$

(2)

with $R^2 = 0.65$, $F = 9.27$, $\chi^2 = 8.352$, $\chi^2_{critic} = 21.026$ (5% signif. – 14 d.f.).

Fig. 8 provides the plot of the data and the regression line. Table 11 provides the LOS standards.

Table 10
Real operational walking distance

Group	Wd_{op} value (m)	μ_j^{LOS}
1	44.33	1.06
2	165.23	0.76
3	224.08	0.61
4	288.91	0.57
5	363.70	0.93
6	420.00	0.45
7	538.50	0.01

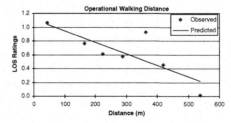

Fig. 8. Plot of the Data and the Regression Line – Oper. Walking Distance - São Paulo.

Table 11
Suggested LOS standards – operational walking distance

LOS	$Wd_{op}(m)$
A/B	0–415
C	415–922
D	>922

In addition to overall LOS measures of total service time and walking distance, this work intended to provide overall LOS measures based on orientation indices. The following two sections will deal with two orientation indices. "Orientation I" will explore the relation between actual walking distances and minimum walking distances. "Orientation II" will explore use of the tardity-differential ratio (O_{II}), which has been previously explained.

7.3. Orientation I

Table 12 presents the ratio (O_I) between actual walking distances and minimum walking distances. When this index is 1.00, it indicates that passengers in this group have walked the minimum distance required. Increasing values of this ratio indicate that passengers have walked an additional unnecessary distance. For instance, passengers in Group 2, have walked 10% more than the minimum walking distance ($O_I = 1.10$).

As was the case for overall service time and walking distance, a linear regression model (Eq. (3)) is built to correlate quantitative LOS ratings of orientation to the O_I index:

$$\mu_j^{LOS} = 1.280 - 1.443 LN(O_I)$$
$$(t = 7.756)(t = -4.925) \tag{3}$$

with $R^2 = 0.83$, $F = 24.254$, $\chi^2 = 11.950$, $\chi^2_{critic} = 21.026$ (5% signif. – 12 d.f.).

Fig. 9 presents the plot of the data and the regression line and Table 13 proposes the suggested LOS standards.

These suggested LOS standards (Table 13) indicate that an excellent level of service (LOS A) will exist when passengers walk just the minimum walking distance. A good level of service (LOS B) will be achieved when

Table 12
Orientation data

Group (j)	O_I	μ_j^{LOS}
1	1.00	1.14
2	1.10	1.41
3	1.20	1.21
4	1.40	0.92
5	1.60	0.38
6	1.80	-0.01
7	3.40	-0.27

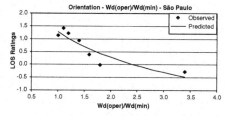

Fig. 9. Plot of the Data and the Regression Line - Orientation - São Paulo.

A.R. Correia et al. / Transportation Research Part A 42 (2008) 330–346   343

Table 13
Suggested LOS standards – orientation

LOS	$O_I = Wd_{op}/Wd_{min}$
A	1.0
B	1.0–2.1
C	2.1–3.4
D	3.4–4.5
E	>4.5

people walk up to two times the minimum walking distance. The minimum walking distances for São Paulo/ Guarulhos International Airport range from 150 to 350 m (from curbside to gate). Other large international airports around the world may have minimum walking distances much longer than these ones (e.g. Dallas Fort Worth, Frankfurt, Toronto Pearson). In these airports, the acceptable O_I indices might be different, because people would not be happy to walk very long distances.

7.4. Orientation II

Table 14 shows the splitting of passengers into eight groups of similar O_{II} values. The relationship between O_{II} and LOS responses of orientation is

$$\mu_j^{LOS} = 1.820 - 1.294(T/D)$$
$$(t = 7.07)(t = -3.71)$$

(4)

with $R^2 = 0.70$, $F = 13.733$, $\chi^2 = 8.191$, $\chi^2_{critic} = 23.685$ (5% signif. – 14 d.f.).

Fig. 10 shows the plot of the data and the regression line. Table 15 presents the suggested LOS standards.

The advantage of using this index is that it may be correlated to physical measures of the building and then be used for planning purposes. Dada (1997) developed an association between the tardity-differential (O_{II}) and the number of decision points and number of level changes. A decision point is usually an intersection of

Table 14
Tardity differential (O_{II}) data

Group (j)	O_{II} average value (s/m)	μ_j^{LOS}
1	−0.04	1.29
2	0.06	2.62
3	0.15	1.60
4	0.26	1.56
5	0.46	0.96
6	0.72	0.50
7	1.13	0.79
8	1.50	−0.24

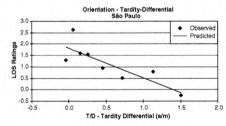

Fig. 10. Plot of the Data and the Regression Line - Tardity Differential - São Paulo.

Table 15
Suggested LOS standards – tardity-differential

LOS	T/D (s/m)
A	<-0.35
B	-0.35–1.08
C	1.08–1.73
D	1.73–2.42
E	>2.42

Table 16
Factors influencing user orientation (Dada, 1997)

Route number	Number of decision points	Distance (m)	Time difference (s)	Number of level changes
1	4	66	16.05	2
2	5	75	10.08	1
3	6	162	31.40	1
4	6	155	48.09	2
5	13	265	27.89	0

corridors, where a user has to choose between two or more routes, or where there is a need for further information on which to base a direction finding decision.

The research for the development of this correlation was done at a building complex at the University of Calgary. Two groups of subjects (31 each) were recruited for this investigation. One group was composed of users familiar with the building. The other group was composed of novices. Five routes were selected for these two groups. The results of this investigation are presented in Table 16.

Using that data, a regression analysis was performed between the tardity-differential (O_{II}), number of decision points (N) and number of level changes (L_c):

$$O_{II} = (8.681N + 107.236L_c)10^{-3}. \tag{5}$$

Eq. (5) has the power to identify how the physical measures of the building have an impact on the ease of wayfinding. In this case, the two-step process to evaluate the level of service of a planned building would be to define the number of decision points and level changes of a given route. These two measures would provide the tardity-differential through Eq. (5). Finally, Table 16 would indicate the LOS associated with this tardity-differential. The only drawback of this process is that Eq. (5) was obtained from an investigation undertaken in Calgary – Canada, but the LOS standards of Table 16 were developed with data from São Paulo/Guarulhos International Airport. To solve this deficiency, an investigation should be undertaken to obtain a relationship similar to Eq. (5), but applied to São Paulo/Guarulhos International Airport.

8. Conclusions

This unique research has provided a method to collect passenger responses about the overall LOS provided at the airport passenger terminal along with the most important overall measures for each interviewed passenger. Although this is a complex research, it was capable of obtaining overall measures that have been used to derive quantitative relationships between physical measures and passenger responses.

The overall measures represent an important step for the overall level of service evaluation for airport passenger terminals. Although the process of obtaining data are complex, a reasonable sample of 100 passengers can be obtained with the participation of four trained surveyors collecting data during a week (8 h shift).

The importance of these new LOS standards is stressed, given the lack of research on this subject. Not only are the standards useful for application at São Paulo/Guarulhos International Airport, but this paper has indicated how this methodology can be further applied. It would be useful to apply this methodology in other airports located in Brazil and even internationally. This effort would provide a more comprehensive understanding of the relationship between overall terminal measures and the level of service associated with them.

Acknowledgements

This research was supported in part by a Brazilian Government Scholarship (CAPES), by the Natural Sciences and Engineering Research Council of Canada, and the University of Calgary.

References

Aaker, D., Kumar, V., Day, G., 1998. Marketing Research, sixth ed. Wiley, New York.

Airports Council International, 2000. Quality of service at airports: standards & measurements. ACI World Headquarters, Geneva, Switzerland.

Bandara, S., Wirasinghe, S.C., 1992. Walking distance minimization for airport terminal configurations. Transportation Research A 22 (1), 59–74.

Bock, R.D., Jones, L.V., 1968. The measurement and prediction of judgment and choice. San Francisco, Holden-Day.

Caves, R.E., Pickard, C.D., 2001. The satisfaction of human needs in airport passenger terminals. Proceedings of the Institution of Civil Engineers, Transport 147 (February Issue I), 9–15.

Correia, A.R., 2000. Quantitative evaluation of airport passenger terminal configurations.M.Sc. Dissertation, Aeronautical Institute of Technology, Brazil.

Correia, A.R., 2005. Evaluation of level of service at airport passenger terminals: individual components and overall perspectives. Ph.D. Thesis, University of Calgary, Canada.

Correia, A.R., Wirasinghe, S.C., 2004. Evaluation of level of service at airport passenger terminals: a review of research approaches. Transportation Research Record 1888, TRB, National Research Council, Washington, DC, pp. 1–6.

Dada, E.S., 1997. Quantitative measures of orientation in airport terminals. Ph.D. Thesis, University of Calgary, Canada.

Dada, E.S., Wirasinghe, S.C., 1999. Development of a new orientation index for airport terminals. Transportation Research Record 1662, TRB, National Research Council, Washington, DC, pp. 41–47.

De Barros, A.G., Somasundaraswaran, A.K., Wirasinghe, S.C., 2007. Evaluation of level of service for transfer passengers at airports. Journal of Air Transport Management 13 (5), 293–298.

De Neufville, R., de Barros, A.G., Belin, S.C., 2002. Optimal configuration of airport passenger buildings for travelers. Journal of Transportation Engineering of ASCE 128 (3), 211–217.

Fernandes, E., Pacheco, R.R., 2002. Efficient use of airport capacity. Transportation Research A 36 (3), 225–238.

Fosgerau, M., 2007. Using nonparametrics to specify a model to measure the value of travel time. Transportation Research A 41 (9), 842–856.

Horonjeff, R., McKelvey, F.X., 1994. Planning and Design of Airports, fourth ed. McGraw-Hill, New York.

Inglada, V., Rey, B., Rodríguez-Alvarez, A., Coto-Milan, P., 2006. Liberalisation and efficiency in international air transport. Transportation Research A 40 (2), 95–204.

Magri, A.A., Alves, C.J.P., 2003. Convenient airports: point of view of the passengers, Proceedings of the 7th Air Transport Research Society World Conference, Toulouse, France.

Martel, N., Seneviratne, P.N., 1990. Analysis of factors influencing quality of service in passenger terminal buildings. Transportation Research Record 1273, TRB, National Research Council, Washington, DC.

Müller, C., 1987. A framework for quality of service evaluation at airport terminals. Ph.D. Thesis, University of California at Berkeley, USA.

Müller, C., Gosling, G.D., 1991. A framework for evaluating level of service for airport terminals. Transportation Planning and Technology 16, 45–61.

Mumayiz, S.A., Ashford, N.J., 1986. Methodology for planning and operations management of airport terminal facilities. Transportation Research Record 1094, TRB, National Research Council, Washington, DC, pp. 24–35.

Ndoh, N.N., Ashford, N.J., 1993. Evaluation of airport access level of service. Transportation Research Record 1423, TRB, National Research Council, Washington, DC, pp. 34–39.

Omer, K.F., Khan, A.M., 1988. Airport landside level of service estimation: utility theoretic approach. Transportation Research Record 1199, TRB, National Research Council, Washington, DC, pp. 33–40.

Park, Y.H., 1994. An evaluation methodology for the level of service at the airport landside system. Ph.D. Thesis, Loughborough University of Technology, UK.

Proctor, T., 2000. Essentials of Marketing Research. Financial Times, second ed. Prentice-Hall, Englewood Cliffs, NJ.

Seneviratne, P.N., Martel, N., 1991. Variables Influencing Performance of Air Terminal Buildings. Transportation Planning and Technology 16 (1), 1177–1179.

Seneviratine, P.N., Martel, N., 1994. Criteria for Evaluating Quality of Service in Air Terminals. Transportation Research Record 1461, TRB, National Research Council, Washington, DC, pp. 24–30.

Thurstone, L.L., 1959. The Measurement of Values. University of Chicago Press, Chicago.

Transport Canada, 1979. A discussion paper on level of service definition and methodology for calculating airport capacity. Report TP 2027.

Transportation Research Board, 1987. Special Report 215: Measuring airport landside capacity. TRB, National Research Council, Washington, DC.

Wirasinghe, S.C., Shehata, M., 1988. Departure lounge sizing and optimal seating capacity for a given aircraft/flight mix – (i) single gate; (ii) several gates. Transportation Planning and Technology 13, 57–71.

Yen, J.-R., 1995. A new approach to measure the level of service of procedures in the airport landside. Transportation Planning Journal 24 (3), 323–336.

Yen, J.-R., Teng, C.-R., Chen, P.S., 2001. Measuring the level of service at airport passenger terminals: comparison of perceived and observed time. Transportation Research Record 1744, TRB, National Research Council, Washington, DC, pp. 17–23.

22

Measuring airport quality from the airlines' viewpoint: an application of data envelopment analysis

Nicole Adler, Joseph Berechman

Abstract

The main objective of this paper is to develop a model to determine the relative efficiency and quality of airports. This factor seems to have a strong effect on the airlines' choice of hubs. Previous studies of airport quality have used subjective passenger data whereas in this study airport quality is defined from the airlines' viewpoint. Accordingly, we have solicited airlines' evaluations of a number of European and non-European airports by means of a detailed questionnaire. Statistical analysis of the median score has shown that these evaluations vary considerably relative to quality factors and airports. The key methodology used in this study to determine the relative quality level of the airports is Data Envelopment Analysis (DEA), which has been adapted through the use of principle component analysis. Of the set of West-European airports analyzed, Geneva, Milan and Munich received uniformly high, relative efficiency scores. In contrast, Charles de Gaulle, Athens and Manchester consistently appear low in the rankings. © 2001 Elsevier Science Ltd. All rights reserved.

Keywords: DEA; Principal component analysis; Airport quality; Policy analysis

1. Introduction

This paper is based on a large-scale study on airport quality measurement see Berechman and Adler (1999). The main objective of this paper is to examine the quality of various airports, mostly West European, from the perspective of the airlines. The importance of the subject stems from the fact that airport quality studies undertaken to date, by and large, were carried out from the point-of-view of passengers. Thus, the quality measures used in these studies relate mainly to airport amenities for passengers such as the number of restaurants, ease of access by surface transport or passengers' processing time etc. (see for example Adler and Golany, 2001). Notwithstanding the importance of this information, it has lesser relevance to airlines deciding from which airports to operate.

Specifically, an airline when choosing a hub must consider, in addition to demand and network factors, airport quality factors that will have a direct bearing on their costs of operation. These include factors such as delay data, runway capacity, local labor force costs and the reliability of airport traffic control. In this study we analyze the results of a questionnaire sent to various airlines, in order to ascertain their perception of the quality of airport services. Using this information, we employ a methodology capable of ranking airports relative to their quality level. The methodology chosen was Data Envelopment Analysis (DEA), which can analyze airports with multiple inputs and outputs simultaneously.

Two papers have been published in the field of airport analyses and DEA. Gillen and Lall (1997) develop two DEA models based on terminal and airside operations. They use number of runways, gates, employees, baggage collection belts, public parking spots and terminal area to explain number of passengers and pounds of cargo. The second model uses airport area, number of runways, employees and runway area to explain air carrier and commuter movements. The data was collated over a five year period and the results define the changes within and across airports over time. The second paper by Parker (1999) analyzed the performance of BAA before and after privatization. Using employment, capital stock, non-labor and capital costs as inputs and number of passengers and cargo and mail handled as outputs, he discovered that privatization had no noticeable impact on technical efficiency. In addition, the research reveals that economies of scale at airports exist, thus encouraging the use of the variable-returns-to-scale DEA model. This research is different from the two papers mentioned because it attempts to measure the quality of airports from an airline's viewpoint. The analysis uses objective input data to explain ordinal, subjective rankings of airports based on airline evaluations. The analysis can in turn be used by airports to understand which improvements are important to their airline clients.

The main source of data for this study was a questionnaire whose objective was to evaluate the quality level of a set of 26 airports in Western Europe, North America and the Far East, from the point-of-view of the airlines. The specific questions are detailed in Appendix A. Section 2 provides an initial, exploratory data analysis of the results of the questionnaire according to questions and airports. Section 3 uses canonical correlation analysis to evaluate the linear connection between two sets of data, namely the results of the questionnaire vs. a set of collectible data on the resources available and managerial strategies at the relevant airports. Section 4 presents the Data Envelopment Analysis (DEA) methodology, including DEA models utilized to rank the airports in the study, according to their perceived quality. Section 5 discusses some policy implications of the results and Section 6 summarizes the results of the model and draws major conclusions.

Appendix B specifies the results of the Canonical Correlation Analysis used to show the linear correlation between the two sets of data. Appendix C specifies the airport codes used throughout this paper.

2. The database and exploratory data analysis

In this study we have distinguished between two types of data: 'subjective' data and 'objective' data. The main source of subjective data for this study was a questionnaire, which was sent to 61 different airlines, of which 19 replied. The objective input data were collated from many sources.

The questionnaire's subjective answers (i.e. the responses of the airlines in the sample) are scored from 1 (poor performance of an airport) to 5 (excellent performance). The subjective data was then evaluated using the median of the distribution of the responses to each question. Generally when analyzing ordinal data of the sort described, a median statistic is used. However we also evaluated alternative statistics, such as the standardized mean. Certain standard deviations were close to or equal to zero, which resulted in implausible results. After corrections, the results proved very similar to those of the median, consequently we have chosen to analyze the median results alone.

The 'objective' input data was collected in order to explain the airlines' differing levels of satisfaction from each airport as indicated by their response to the questionnaire. The objective data was collated to account for the various services that the airports provide the airlines. The dataset includes peak, short and medium haul charges, international (int'l) –domestic (dom), int'l–int'l and dom–dom minimum connecting times, average delay times, number of terminals, number of runways and distance to the nearest major city-center, which is a surrogate, surface-transportation, non-discretionary

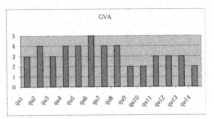

Fig. 1. Geneva.

variable. The specific variables were chosen so as to include both long-term managerial variables i.e. number of terminals and runways and shorter term, more accessible variables i.e. minimum connecting times and charges. Sensitivity analyses were run as was an additional, partial analysis including delay data, which was available for the majority of the West European airports in the sample.

It should first be noted that whilst most airlines chose scores above the middle value of 3, they generally considered the costs of using these airports, in both labor and other terms, as heavy. In the final questions, regarding the potential congruity of airports to airlines' wave system and potential demand (questions 13, 14), the average score value lay at around two. The key factor to observe from these distributions is that there is no recognizable pattern common to them all. Thus, qualitatively we can say that the airlines' evaluations of the airports varied considerably relative to quality factors (score distribution within answers) and airports (scores between airports). We reach this conclusion because the airlines' answers to the questions did not cluster around any particular score and showed a variety of different distributions.

To further illustrate, we consider here two West European airports, Geneva which attained amongst the highest median score and Athens which attained amongst the lowest (Figs. 1 and 2).

Geneva received consistently high scores, particularly in turn-around times (question 6). Within Europe, it is clear that whilst some airports received consistently low scores such as Athens (see Fig. 2), others show a clear trade-off

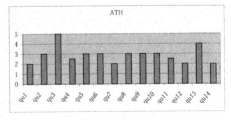

Fig. 2. Athens airport.

N. Adler, J. Berechman / Transport Policy 8 (2001) 171–181

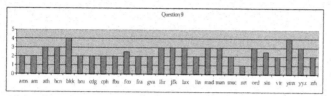

Fig. 3. Question 9 results.

between the quality levels and associated costs, such as Zurich and Vienna.

When evaluating the scores of airports across questions, one can see that certain questions resulted in varied answers whereas others showed more uniform results across airports. For illustrative purposes, consider question 9 on labor costs, which are a prime factor affecting airport quality from the airlines' viewpoint. Question 9 (what is your assessment of the costs of employing local labor force at each of these airports?) reflects a variation in results, as shown in Fig. 3.

The respondents gave considerably lower scores to all airports in response to this question, suggesting that all airlines would like to reduce their labor costs. However, except for Tokyo, labor costs in the Far East are substantially lower than other regions, which clearly explain the relatively high scores received by BKK and SIN. Tokyo is extremely expensive, explaining why NRT received the worst score amongst all sample airports. Amongst North American airports, YMX received the top score, although JFK, LAX, ORD and YYZ were not far behind. The most expensive region, Western Europe, indeed received amongst the lowest scores, as expected.

Table 1 shows the complete ranking according to the median, overall, questionnaire scores.

3. Canonical correlation analysis

A Canonical Correlation Analysis (CCA) was undertaken to evaluate the degree to which the scores from the questionnaire could be explained by the managerial and objective data. If the CCA shows a high correlation between two sets of data, we can ascertain that the input variables explain the subjective, questionnaire scores. CCA is similar to regression analysis, where a single variable is explained by a set of variables in a linear fashion so as to minimize the summed square of errors. In CCA, the difference is that we have two sets of variables from which we want to establish a relationship, assuming that one set is a linear function of the other set.

To carry out this analysis it was necessary first to categorize the results of the questionnaire into five grouped responses, namely Variable Groups A to E, in order to reduce the number of criteria. The median responses were summed to attain the grouped data (and normalized in the subsequent principal component analysis). The questionnaire contained questions of five types (see also Appendix A):

- Group A: the suitability of a given airport to an airline, underlying the aviation rationale of servicing an airport by an airline (Q1–Q3).
- Group B: the operational reliability and convenience of an airport (Q4–Q7).
- Group C: the costs of using an airport (Q8–Q10).
- Group D: the overall satisfaction and quality of an airport (Q11–Q12).
- Group E: factual questions with respect to the wave system and demand (Q13–Q14).

Specifically, CCA calculates common weights, a_i and b_j, for all the airports by maximizing the correlation between linear combinations of two sets of data (see Tatsuoka and

Table 1
Sample airports ranked according to median questionnaire scores

Rank	Airport code	Median overall questionnaire score
1	ORD	3.821
1	SIN	3.821
3	YMX	3.464
4	LAX	3.429
5	BKK	3.357
6	CPH	3.286
6	GVA	3.286
8	AMS	3.250
8	MUC	3.250
10	ARN	3.214
10	FCO	3.214
10	LHR	3.214
10	MAN	3.214
14	VIE	3.179
15	BCN	3.107
15	ZRH	3.107
17	FRA	3.071
18	MAD	3.000
19	BRU	2.964
19	CDG	2.964
19	YYZ	2.964
22	JFK	2.929
22	NRT	2.929
24	ATH	2.857
25	FBU	2.821
26	LIN	2.786

174   *N. Adler, J. Berechman / Transport Policy 8 (2001) 171–181*

Lohnes, 1988 for a more detailed discussion). The composite input of airport a is

$$\chi_a = \sum_{i=1}^{R} a_i x_{ij}$$

where x_{ij} represents the input data and the composite output of airport a is

$$\eta_a = \sum_{j=1}^{S} b_j y_{ij},$$

where y_{ij} represents the questionnaire data. The weights, a_i and b_j, represent decision variables within the model.

As can be seen in Appendix B (in the column marked $\chi'\eta$)), the results of the CCA show a correlation of 0.99 between the two sets of data. This suggests a strong linear association between the two groups, implying that the selected objective data are good indicators and clearly explain the variability of the subjective data. As a result, it would seem reasonable to use a linear model to rank the airports in terms of the objective and subjective data chosen.

4. Data envelopment analysis

We now present the major methodology used to determine the degree of efficiency (or quality) of various airports in our sample. The data for this analysis includes both the subjective and objective data described in Section 2. Airports can be regarded as organizations that make decisions about how to use their inputs (e.g. number of runways) to produce specific outputs (e.g. service satisfaction). Since it is reasonable to assume that all airports use similar inputs to produce the same outputs, we regard them as homogeneous Decision-Making Units (DMUs). Our objective is to determine the efficiency of various airports in carrying out these tasks. Since airports produce multiple outputs utilizing multiple inputs without an obvious production function connecting them, we chose a non-parametric methodology that enables us to derive a single measure of efficiency that encompasses all inputs and outputs. Data Envelopment Analysis (DEA) was the methodology chosen to develop the measure of efficiency and was first developed by Charnes et al. (1978).

Clearly, not all the airports are homogeneous in size. Five large hub operators exist within Europe, including AMS, BRU, CDG, FRA and LHR (see Appendix C with regard to the symbols). The size of their operations is substantially larger than other European airports such as Barcelona or Vienna. Consequently, we have chosen a DEA model that does not assume constant-returns-to-scale, which would be disadvantageous to the smaller airports (and is also in line with the findings of Parker (1999)). Thus, a variable-returns-to-scale, input minimization approach was deemed the most appropriate (see Banker et al. (BCC), 1984). The BCC model compares N units (airports) with S outputs denoted

by y_j, $j = 1,...,S$ and R inputs denoted by x_i, $i = 1,...,R$. The efficiency score for DMU a can be evaluated as shown in model (1).

$$\underset{w_j, v_i}{\text{Min}} \; e_a = \frac{\sum_{i=1}^{R} v_i x_{ia}}{\sum_{j=1}^{S} w_j y_{ja}} - c_a$$

$$\text{subject to}: \frac{\sum_{i=1}^{R} v_i x_{im}}{\sum_{j=1}^{S} w_j y_{jm}} + c_a \leq 1 \text{ for } m = 1,...,N$$

$$w_j \geq 0 \text{ for } j = 1,...,S$$

$$v_i \geq 0 \text{ for } i = 1,...,R \tag{1}$$

The constraints ensure that the weights chosen by the mathematical model, w_j and v_i, when applied to all airports, do not allow another airport to achieve efficiency greater than one. Thus the efficiency ratio ranges from zero to one, with the decision-making unit a being considered relatively efficient if it receives a score of one. Each DMU will choose weights so as to maximize its own efficiency, given the constraints. This ratio problem can be transformed into a linear program relatively easily. The results of the DEA analysis are dichotomous; an efficient set of airports, all receiving a relative efficiency score of one and an inefficient set of airports.

We are attempting to explain the airlines' level of satisfaction mainly with respect to the various West-European airports and also some Far Eastern and North American airports. The outputs, which represent levels of satisfaction from use of each airport, have been categorized to produce five summed variables based on grouped questions (see Section 3).

Inputs to the DEA model are the "objective data" which are to be minimized because they are affected by airport policy directly. In this manner, we can evaluate which inputs should be improved in order to achieve the same or higher levels of satisfaction efficiently.[1] One input variable, namely distance in kilometers to the nearest city center, is an airport variable whose value cannot be changed as a result of managerial decision-making i.e. it has been included in the analysis as a non-discretionary variable (see Banker and Morey (1986)). Hence, the key variables used (for 1996), are airport charges, minimum connecting times,[2] number of passenger terminals, number of runways

---

[1] Since we would prefer to maximize some of the input variables e.g. number of passenger terminals and runways, the inverse values have been used in these instances.

[2] Minimum Connecting Times data was available for all airports in the sample for 1998, thus this data has been used.

N. Adler, J. Berechman / Transport Policy 8 (2001) 171–181

175

and distance to nearest city center. The data is presented in Appendix B.

One of the frequent problems of DEA is a lack of differentiation between the DMUs, which can be caused by an excessive number of criteria with respect to the total number of DMUs in the respective analysis. One way of dealing with this problem is to reduce the total number of criteria through an extensive search and detailed discussion with the decision-makers as to the most appropriate inputs and outputs. Another method that can aid in the ranking of DMUs involves the addition of a virtual or target airport into the sample. In this manner, the airports are compared to the pre-specified target, as was undertaken in Berechman and Adler (1999). However, one still needs to consult with experts in the field in order to attain appropriate preference information. Another methodology developed in Adler and Golany (2001) is the combination of Principal Component Analysis (PCA), which describes a matrix of data through a reduced number of variables or principal components, and DEA. The advantage of this technique is that it does not require additional, expert opinion.

PCA explains the variance structure of a matrix of data through linear combinations of variables, consequently reducing the data to a few principal components, which generally describe 80–90% of the variance in the data. If most of the population variance can be attributed to the first few components, then they can replace the original variables without much loss of information. As stated in Johnson and Wichern (1982), let the random vector $X = [X_1, X_2,..., X_p]$ have the covariance matrix V with eigenvalues $\lambda_1 \geq \lambda_2 \geq ... \geq \lambda_p \geq 0$ and normalized eigenvectors $l_1, l_2,...,l_p$. Consider the linear combinations, where the superscript t represents the transpose operator:

$$X_{PC_i} = l_i^t X = l_{1i}X_1 + l_{2i}X_2 + \cdots + l_{pi}X_p$$

$$\text{Var}(X_{PC_i}) = l_i^t V l_i, \quad i = 1, 2, ..., p$$

$$\text{Cov}(X_{PC_i}, X_{PC_k}) = l_i^t V l_k, \quad i = 1, 2, ..., p, k = 1, 2, ..., p$$

The principal components are the uncorrelated linear combinations $X_{PC_1}, X_{PC_2}, ..., X_{PC_p}$ ranked by their variances in descending order.

Generally inputs and outputs of a data envelopment analysis need to be strictly positive (some papers have dealt with the issue of zero data, see for example Thompson et al., 1993). However, the results of a PCA can have negative values. An affine transformation of data can be utilized with no change in the results when using the additive model (see Charnes et al., 1985) or without a change in the definition of efficient DMUs when using the BCC model (see Ali and Seiford, 1990). Indeed, Pastor (1996) proves that the BCC output-oriented model is input translation invariant and vice versa. Consequently all PC output data used subsequently in the input-oriented DEA have been increased by the most negative

Table 2
Eigenanalysis of the correlation matrix

Eigenvalue	1.7567	1.3994	0.9538	0.5273	0.3628
Proportion	0.351	0.280	0.191	0.105	0.073
Cumulative	0.351	0.631	0.822	0.927	1.000

Variable	PC1	PC2	PC3	PC4	PC5
A	−0.657	0.168	−0.047	0.167	0.714
B	−0.005	0.736	−0.002	−0.676	−0.020
C	−0.640	0.150	−0.254	0.188	−0.685
D	0.294	0.632	0.210	0.686	−0.026
E	0.270	0.091	−0.943	0.096	0.143

value in the vector plus one when necessary, thus ensuring strictly positive data.

$$\tilde{X}_{PC_i} = X_{PC} + b \quad \text{where } b = \text{Min}\{X_{PC_i}\} + 1$$

This technique was used to reduce the five output variables drawn from the questionnaire data to three principal components, which explain 82.2% of the variance in the original data as can be seen from the results in Table 2.

The first PC explains 35% of the variance of the original data matrix and represents a combined weighted average of Grouped Data A and C vs. D and E. The second PC explains an additional 28% of the variance and consists of a weighted average of all the data with greater emphasis on grouped questions B and D.

For a detailed description of the modified DEA model utilizing PCA refer to Adler (1999); Adler and Golany (2001). It should be noted that the PCA-DEA modified model is equivalent mathematically to the original formulation if all PCs are included and the objective function is modified to account for the PC weights (the results of both analyses in this case are identical). However, since we do not include all the PCs, a minimal amount of information is lost, as is some of the translucence in reading the results. Therefore, when applying the modified model it is important to replace only the input (output) data that does not appear in the objective function. This model is based on input minimization and the PCA was applied to outputs only.

Since we are looking not only to differentiate between DMUs but also fully rank the airports in the sample, we used an additional technique alongside the PCA-DEA model. The super-efficient DEA model was chosen, in which Andersen and Petersen (1993) achieve a full ranking by undertaking a DEA without assessing the DMU itself and then evaluating the extent to which the envelope frontier is extended when including the efficient DMU under assessment. This is achieved by evaluating the constraints only for $m \neq a$ (see model (1)), thus unit a can receive a score greater than one. The advantage of this technique is the lack of preference information required in order to rank the set of efficient DMUs. The results of the super-efficient PCA-DEA model are presented in Section 4.1.

176   N. Adler, J. Berechman / Transport Policy 8 (2001) 171–181

Table 3
Results from the PCA-DEA base run model

DMU	Base run score
NRT	48.45%
BKK	60.89%
YMX	64.04%
CDG	87.15%
YYZ	89.98%
ATH	95.35%
MAN	97.44%
FRA	100.78%
ZRH	110.68%
BRU	111.26%
LHR	116.17%
BCN	119.77%
FCO	120.60%
MAD	121.12%
ARN	121.17%
VIE	131.67%
AMS	152.93%
JFK	180.00%
CPH	216.93%
FBU	225.00%
ORD	227.68%
LAX	249.85%
MUC	257.16%
GVA	greater than 400%
LIN	greater than 400%
SIN	greater than 400%

Table 4
Results from the PCA-DEA model including delay data

DMU	Delay score
CDG	104.27%
ZRH	111.96%
FRA	112.09%
BRU	115.38%
FCO	130.64%
VIE	133.21%
ARN	136.91%
LHR	145.85%
AMS	166.67%
MAD	169.18%
ATH	218.49%
CPH	221.17%
GVA	greater than 400%
LIN	greater than 400%
MUC	greater than 400%

4.1. Results of data envelopment analysis model[3]

The input-minimization, variable-returns-to-scale, super-efficient, PCA-modified model was then applied to the data gathered (i.e. the results of the questionnaire and the objective data). Any airport receiving a score lower than 100 could improve its position relative to the efficient DMUs (those that received a score of 100 or more) by minimizing one or more of its inputs to achieve the same level of airline satisfaction. Table 3 presents the results from this run, which we have labeled the Base Run (see Appendix C for airport codes).

The most efficient, quality-driven airports, according to this DEA analysis, include Geneva, Milan and Singapore. The worst, or least efficient airports would appear to be Narita, Bangkok and Montreal, whilst the least quality driven European airports include Charles de Gaulle, Athens and Manchester. Finally, it should be noted that the super-efficiency model could produce unbounded results when comparing extreme efficient DMUs. When this occurs, the efficiency score is simply reported as large (see Seiford and Zhu, 1999 for a discussion and explanation).

4.2. Limited data envelopment analysis model including delay data

In this sensitivity analysis we included delay data as an

additional input variable, however we were able to gather data on only 15 out of the 26 airports in the sample. The delay data represents the average delay per Aircraft Movement (ACM) in minutes.[4] Table 4 presents the results of the model including delay data.

Once again, Geneva, Milan and Munich have excelled relatively. However, both Athens and LHR have improved their relative ranking as a result of the inclusion of the delay data. Indeed, Athens position improved quite dramatically. Athens' average delay per movement is less than half that of Munich, which may explain the surprising improvement.

5. Policy analysis tests

To ascertain the stability of the base run, and examine certain policies aimed at affecting the quality factors of airports, we have undertaken several analyses. The first analysis examines the effect of changing landing charges on the airport quality ranking. The second test investigates the effect of changing the minimum connecting time variable on the overall ranking. The third test takes account of both the number of passenger terminals and freight terminals.

The first analysis evaluated the effect of changing the short-haul, peak-landing charge at each airport (in $ per Maximum Take Off Weight) with the long-haul peak-charge. On average, the increase in charges is around 200%, though it should be noted that some airports have a single charge system, whilst others charge 400% higher long-haul charges. The results are as indicated in Table 5.

Whilst there are some differences in the DEA ranking, as can be seen in Table 5, the change in landing charges had little effect on the most efficient, quality driven airports. However, LHR and Madrid became inefficient and Munich reduced its' ranking, whilst Toronto went from inefficient to

---

[3] We have used the EMS DEA Software Package. See references (EMS DEA program) for the http address.

[4] As evaluated by the ATFM.

N. Adler, J. Berechman / Transport Policy 8 (2001) 171–181 177

Table 5
PCA-DEA ranking with short-haul vs. long-haul charges

DMU	Score	DMU	Score
	Short Haul Charges		Long Haul Charges
NRT	48.45%	NRT	48.62%
BKK	60.89%	YMX	74.97%
YMX	64.04%	CDG	79.06%
CDG	87.15%	BKK	82.17%
YYZ	89.98%	LHR	93.87%
ATH	95.35%	ATH	95.35%
MAN	97.44%	MAN	97.44%
FRA	100.78%	FRA	98.63%
ZRH	110.68%	MAD	99.61%
BRU	111.26%	YYZ	101.90%
LHR	116.17%	BRU	104.51%
BCN	119.77%	ZRH	109.43%
FCO	120.60%	ARN	112.17%
MAD	121.12%	BCN	114.60%
ARN	121.17%	FCO	125.57%
VIE	131.67%	VIE	131.67%
AMS	152.93%	AMS	133.78%
JFK	180.00%	MUC	171.43%
CPH	216.93%	JFK	180.00%
FBU	225.00%	CPH	216.93%
ORD	227.68%	FBU	225.00%
LAX	249.85%	ORD	227.68%
MUC	257.16%	LAX	249.85%
GVA	greater than 400%	GVA	greater than 400%
LIN	greater than 400%	LIN	greater than 400%
SIN	greater than 400%	SIN	greater than 400%

efficient. These results may well reflect the managerial choices made by airport management when considering which airlines and routes to attract.

In the second policy analyses, which focus on the impact of connection times, three different minimum connecting times are applied individually in three models, ceteris paribus. International to international (Int'l–Int'l) routes, international to domestic (Int'l–Dom) routes and domestic to domestic (Dom–Dom) routes are each applied separately. The Int'l–Dom route variable has been used in the base run and Table 6 displays the results of the base-run and the results when the Int'l–Dom minimum connecting time was replaced by one of the other two measures. The Int'l–Dom connecting time is similar to the Int'l–Int'l times, approximately 60 min, but substantially higher than the Dom–Dom connecting times, which average out over the sample to 40 min.

As evident from the results in Table 6, some airports have changed their rankings, however the changes are small and the leading airports remain in the same ranked positions. In the Int'l–Int'l minimum connecting times model, both Manchester and Vienna have reduced their rankings, though the latter remained relatively efficient. However, in the dom–dom minimum connecting times model, Vienna becomes inefficient suggesting that greater relative attention is paid to Int'l–dom routes at this airport. Stockholm, on the other hand, improves its relative position in the dom–dom model.

In the third test, we introduced an additional variable to the basic run, namely the inverse number of freight terminals (see footnote 1 for an explanation). The results are given in Table 7.

Whilst yet again the main three airports remain stable at the top of the ranking, three airports have changed their positions dramatically. Both JFK and FRA improve their rankings somewhat, but CDG becomes efficient, which is a major change. This may suggest that airports heavy in freight ought to be analyzed separately from passenger-oriented airports when analyzing efficiency and quality.

6. Summary and conclusions

The main objective of this study was to determine the relative efficiency or quality ranking of various West-European and other airports. Previous studies of airport quality generally have used subjective passenger data to determine the degree to which users regard an airport to be of high, medium or low quality, using airport passenger amenities as the key quality attributes. In contrast, we have defined airport quality from the perspective of the airlines. Accordingly, we have solicited airlines' evaluations of a large number of European and non-European airports by means of a detailed questionnaire, which asked for their assessment of various airport operational, cost and demand attributes, for example, airport turn-around times, local labor costs and potential demand.

The main results of this analysis showed that that the airlines' evaluations of the airports vary considerably relative to quality factors and airports. This is an important statistical result since, were all answers to cluster around a particular score with little variation among airports, not much could have been inferred from the data. Amongst the Western European airports, Geneva and Copenhagen, followed by Munich and Amsterdam, achieved the highest scores, though non-European airports were regarded by the airlines as offering the highest quality, the highest being Chicago and Singapore. One important result from this analysis is that in evaluating the overall quality of an airport, airlines clearly recognize the trade-off between the quality attributes of an airport. In other words, while an airport may achieve a high score for some quality attributes, e.g. perceived quality of local traffic control, it may score low on other attributes, e.g. the perceived costs of doing business.

This research compiled a database that was divided into two groups: 'objective' and 'subjective' data. The former include factual variables such as peak short and medium haul charges and minimum connecting times on international and inter-European routes. The subjective variables include the responses of the airlines in the sample (i.e. the questionnaire). The database contains the responses of 19 airlines (out of 61) that completely filled the questionnaire, and 26 airports (of which 16 are West European). Thus, in

Table 6
DEA ranking using different minimum connecting times

DMU	Score Int'l–Dom	DMU	Score Int'l–Int'l	DMU	Score Dom–Dom
NRT	48.45%	NRT	44.64%	NRT	53.92%
BKK	60.89%	BKK	69.76%	YMX	66.20%
YMX	64.04%	YMX	69.89%	VIE	80.02%
CDG	87.15%	MAN	83.97%	BKK	87.11%
YYZ	89.98%	CDG	87.15%	CDG	87.15%
ATH	95.35%	YYZ	89.98%	YYZ	90.73%
MAN	97.44%	ATH	95.35%	MAN	90.90%
FRA	100.78%	FRA	100.78%	ATH	95.35%
ZRH	110.68%	VIE	105.28%	FRA	100.78%
BRU	111.26%	ZRH	106.60%	ZRH	106.56%
LHR	116.17%	BRU	111.26%	BRU	111.26%
BCN	119.77%	LHR	116.17%	LHR	116.17%
FCO	120.60%	BCN	117.42%	FCO	120.60%
MAD	121.12%	FCO	120.60%	MAD	121.12%
ARN	121.17%	MAD	121.12%	BCN	124.37%
VIE	131.67%	ARN	128.92%	AMS	153.43%
AMS	152.93%	AMS	152.93%	JFK	180.00%
JFK	180.00%	JFK	180.00%	ARN	195.24%
CPH	216.93%	CPH	216.93%	CPH	216.93%
FBU	225.00%	FBU	225.00%	FBU	225.00%
ORD	227.68%	ORD	227.68%	ORD	227.68%
LAX	249.85%	LAX	249.85%	LAX	249.85%
MUC	257.16%	MUC	257.16%	MUC	257.16%
GVA	greater than 400%	GVA	greater than 400%	GVA	greater than 400%
LIN	greater than 400%	LIN	greater than 400%	LIN	greater than 400%
SIN	greater than 400%	SIN	greater than 400%	SIN	greater than 400%

Table 7
DEA ranking with passenger vs. freight terminals

DMU	Score (only passengers)	DMU	Score (freight and passengers)
NRT	48.45%	BKK	60.89%
BKK	60.89%	NRT	64.02%
YMX	64.04%	YMX	67.33%
CDG	87.15%	YYZ	91.59%
YYZ	89.98%	ATH	95.35%
ATH	95.35%	MAN	97.72%
MAN	97.44%	ZRH	110.68%
FRA	100.78%	BRU	111.26%
ZRH	110.68%	LHR	116.17%
BRU	111.26%	BCN	119.77%
LHR	116.17%	MAD	121.12%
BCN	119.77%	FCO	124.50%
FCO	120.60%	VIE	131.67%
MAD	121.12%	ARN	157.70%
ARN	121.17%	AMS	163.25%
VIE	131.67%	CPH	216.93%
AMS	152.93%	ORD	227.68%
JFK	180.00%	CDG	237.83%
CPH	216.93%	FBU	245.27%
FBU	225.00%	MUC	257.16%
ORD	227.68%	LAX	275.57%
LAX	249.85%	FRA	276.09%
MUC	257.16%	JFK	333.83%
GVA	greater than 400%	GVA	greater than 400%
LIN	greater than 400%	LIN	greater than 400%
SIN	greater than 400%	SIN	greater than 400%

this analysis we attempted to ascertain whether the objective, input data explains the airlines' differing levels of satisfaction from each airport, as indicated by their response to the questionnaire. Using canonical correlation analysis, it was shown that the objective data linearly explains the variability of the subjective data, thus implying that the particular characteristics of each airport are important factors in determining quality.

The main methodology used in this study to determine the relative quality level of the airports in our sample was data envelopment analysis (DEA). This model computes the position of each airport relative to an efficient frontier, delineated by airports in the sample. A variable-returns-to-scale, input-minimization, DEA model was used, after the output data was reduced using Principal Component Analysis. In order to attain a complete ranking of all airports, the super-efficient technique was applied. The results from several PCA-DEA runs, including a base-run and those of the limited sample delay-data run and sensitivity/policy analyses, were quite similar. This suggests that the results from the PCA-DEA model are relatively stable. Key results from the analysis show that of the set of West-European airports evaluated in this analysis, Geneva and Milan appear to consistently lead the efficiency scales. Since Milan appeared lowest in the ranking of the questionnaire results alone, this would suggest that the airport utilizes minimal

Table 8

	Peak Short and Medium Haul Charges ($)	Inverse Passenger Terminals	Inverse Runways	Distance to City Center (km)	Minimum Connecting Times Int'l–Int'l (minutes per movement)	a	χ	Median Group A	Median Group B	Median Group C	Median Group D	Median Group E	b	η	
AMS	1940	1.00	0.20	14	50	0.0000	0.1779	9.5	16	7	7.5	5.5	0.0090	0.1816	$\chi'\chi$ 1
ARN	1433	0.25	0.50	42	30	0.0397	0.1883	10	16	8	6	5	−0.0015	0.1845	$\eta'\eta$ 1
ATH	2045	0.50	0.50	8	60	0.1014	0.1992	10	10.5	9	4.5	6	0.0064	0.2082	
BCN	987	0.33	0.50	10	45	0.0018	0.1724	11	14	8.5	6	4	0.0015	0.1882	$\chi*\eta$
BKK	6764	0.50	0.50	22	75	0.0022	0.2144	12	14.5	10.5	4	6	0.0115	0.2292	0.9937
BRU	1834	1.00	0.33	16	50		0.1959	10	14	7	5	5.5		0.1853	
CDG	1712	0.50	0.50	27	60		0.2357	9.5	13.5	6	6.5	6		0.1831	
CPH	1464	0.50	0.33	8	45		0.1543	12	16	8	5	5		0.2010	
FBU	1772	0.33	0.50	8	30		0.1285	8	14.5	7.5	5	4.5		0.1582	
FCO	1054	0.50	0.33	35	45		0.2056	11	13	8.5	7	5.5		0.2084	
FRA	2223	0.50	0.33	12	45		0.1545	8	15	7	7	6		0.1746	
GVA	1649	1.00	1.00	4.5	40		0.2228	10	17	8	6	5		0.1831	
LHR	2720	0.25	0.33	24	60		0.1945	7.5	14	8.5	7	8		0.2041	
JFK	14296	0.11	0.20	25	120		0.2054	10	12	7.5	4.5	7		0.2079	
LAX	8614	0.13	0.20	20	120		0.2486	12	15	9	5.5	6.5		0.2269	
LIN	1056	1.00	0.50	7	40		0.1818	9	12	6.5	5.5	6		0.1825	
MAD	987	0.33	0.50	10	45		0.1724	11.5	12	9	6	3.5		0.1931	
MAN	2582	0.50	1.00	14	40		0.2113	10.5	16	9.5	5	4		0.1857	
MUC	14684	0.50	1.00	57.5	35		0.1673	10	16	7.5	7	5		0.1829	
NRT	13742	0.20	0.14	16	110		0.1701	6	15.5	6	5.5	8		0.1701	
ORD	5696	0.50	0.50	20	90		0.2538	13	17.5	10	7	8		0.2352	
SIN	2215	0.33	0.50	28.5	60		0.2272	12.5	17	9.5	6.5	6		0.2504	
VIE	2838	1.00	0.50	18	30		0.1629	9.5	16	7	6.5	8		0.1801	
YMX	7820	1.00	0.50	53	60		0.2461	10	15	11	6	5.5		0.2225	
YYZ	7647	0.33	0.33	27	75		0.1917	10.5	13.5	9	5.5	6.5		0.1754	
ZRH	1674	0.50	0.33	11	40		0.1466	8	16	8	7	4.5		0.1623	

180 *N. Adler, J. Berechman / Transport Policy 8 (2001) 171–181*

inputs to achieve its subjective grade. In contrast, Charles de Gaulle, Athens and Manchester consistently appear low in the rankings.

Further research in this field should include a connection between the airport quality issue and the airlines' choice of hub networks. Some work in this field has been undertaken, however no study has gone far enough. Since the airport charges represent approximately 5–7% of the airlines' total operating costs, clearly airport quality levels should also be a part of the hub location choice problem. The question then becomes how to combine financial, location, demand and quality issues in one model. This will become more important as global alliances require newly formed affiliations to choose hubs on multiple continents.

Acknowledgements

The authors wish to acknowledge financial and data collection support from the Directorate General of Civil Aviation at the Dutch Ministry of Transport. We wish to thank Prof. Jaap de Wit and his assistants for their kind support and encouragement.

Nicole Adler would also like to thank the Recanati Foundation for partial funding.

Appendix A. The questionnaire

Question 1: How well does each of these airports contribute to your airline's results?

Question 2: What is your assessment of the level of slot availability, at times you mostly need it, at each of these airports?

Question 3: What is your assessment of the level of difficulty your airline faces in using each of these airports due to environmental and night operations restrictions?

Question 4: How reliable (in terms of time precision) is the local air traffic control at each of these airports?

Question 5: How reliable (predictable) is passenger-processing time at each of these airports?

Question 6: How reliable is this airport with respect to overall turn-around time?

Question 7: How satisfied is your airline with the overall design and layout of each of these airports?

Question 8: What is your assessment of the quality (*performance not the costs*) of the local labor force at each of these airports?

Question 9: What is your assessment of the costs of employing local labor force at each of these airports?

Question 10: What is your assessment of the costs of procuring local services (such as office space, food, fuel and communication) at each of these airports?

Question 11: If there were no institutional, operational or significant costs constraints, mark the airports on this list in terms of your airline's preference to switch to or add to your network?

Question 12: What is your overall assessment of the quality of each of these airports from your airline's perspective?

Question 13: How well does each of these airports fit with your wave system (if you have any)?

Question 14: From your airline's perspective how large is the actual demand accommodated through this airport? (1 = very small (less than 50,000 pass. per year); 2 = small (50,000–150,000); 3 = medium (150,000–250,000); 4 = large (250,000–500,000); 5 = very large (above 500,000); n.a = not applicable)

Appendix B. Raw data and canonical correlation analysis

(Table 8)

Appendix C. Airports in sample

The following airports and their codes are utilized in the sample analysis provided in this report: (Table 9)

Table 9

Airport	Code
Amsterdam	AMS
Stockholm	ARN
Athens	ATH
Barcelona	BCN
Brussels	BRU
Paris	CDG
Copenhagen	CPH
Oslo	FBU
Rome	FCO
Frankfurt	FRA
Geneva	GVA
London	LHR
Milan	LIN
Madrid	MAD
Manchester	MAN
Munich	MUC
Vienna	VIE
Zurich	ZRH
Bangkok	BKK
New York	JFK
Los Angeles	LAX
Tokyo	NRT
Chicago	ORD
Singapore	SIN
Montreal	YMX
Toronto	YYZ

References

Adler, N., 1999. The Choice of Optimal Multi-Hub Networks in a Liberalized Aviation Market, PhD, Faculty of Management, Tel Aviv University, Israel.

Adler, N., Golany, B., 2001. Evaluation of deregulated airline networks using data envelopment analysis combined with principal component

N. Adler, J. Berechman / Transport Policy 8 (2001) 171–181   181

analysis with an application to Western Europe. European Journal of Operational Research 132 (2), 18–31.

Ali, A.I., Seiford, L.M., 1990. Translation invariance in data envelopment analysis. Operations Research Letters 9, 403–405.

Andersen, P., Petersen, N.C., 1993. A procedure for ranking efficient units in data envelopment analysis. Management Science 39 (10), 1261–1294.

Banker, R.D., Morey, R.C., 1986. The use of categorical variables in data envelopment analysis. Management Science 32 (12), 1613–1627.

Banker, R.D., Charnes, A., Cooper, W.W., 1984. Some models for estimating technical and scale inefficiencies in data envelopment analysis. Management Science 30 (9), 1078–1092.

Berechman, J., Adler, N., 1999. 'Methodology and Measurement of Airport Quality from the Airlines Viewpoint and its Effect on an Airline's Choice of a West-European Hub Airport', Final Report (two volumes). The Netherlands Ministry of Transportation, Directorate General of Aviation.

Charnes, A., Cooper, W.W., Rhodes, E., 1978. Measuring the efficiency of decision making units. European Journal of Operational Research 2, 429–444.

Charnes, A., Cooper, W.W., Golany, B., Seiford, L., Stutz, J., 1985. Foundations of data envelopment analysis for Pareto-Koopmans efficient empirical production functions. Journal of Econometrics 30, 91–107.

EMS DEA program: http://www.wiso.uni-dortmund.de/lsfg/or/scheel/ems.

Gillen, D., Lall, A., 1997. Developing measures of airport productivity and performance: an application of data envelopment analysis. Transportation Research E 33 (4), 261–273.

Johnson, R.A., Wichern, D.W., 1982. Applied Multivariate Statistical Analysis. Prentice-Hall Inc.

Parker, D., 1999. The performance of BAA before and after privatization. Journal of Transport Economics and Policy 33, 133–145.

Pastor, J., 1996. Translation invariance in data envelopment analysis: a generalization. Annals of Operations Research 66, 93–102.

Seiford, L.M., Zhu, J., 1999. Infeasibility of super-efficiency data envelopment analysis models. INFOR 37 (2), 174–187.

Tatsuoka, M.M., Lohnes, P.R., 1988. Multivariable Analysis: Techniques for Educational and Psychological Research. Macmillan Publishing, New York.

Thompson, R.G., Dharmapala, P.S., Thrall, R.M., 1993. Importance for DEA of zeros in data, multipliers and solutions. The Journal of Productivity Analysis 4, 379–390.

Part IV:

Human Resources and Industrial Relations

23

Airline labour cost reduction: post-liberalisation experience in the USA and Europe

Fariba E. Alamdari and Peter Morrell

US and European carriers have been developing strategies to reduce costs in response to the growing competition in their markets following airline deregulation in the USA since 1978, and liberalisation in Europe since 1988. The most obvious area of costs for airlines to tackle has been labour. This paper analyses trends in labour unit costs (labour expenses per available tonne kilometre) of major US and European carriers from 1978 and 1985 respectively. The results indicate that both US and European airlines have been successful in reducing labour unit costs. This was achieved in the US by some reduction in real wages (labour costs per employee) and periods of increased productivity (ATKs per employee). European airlines reduced unit labour costs by productivity increases, offset by increases in real wage levels. In Europe, some reduction in real wage levels might be expected, following the US experience and in order that they might achieve globally competitive unit labour costs. These might be accompanied by the more widespread use of profit sharing and stock options. © 1997 Elsevier Science Ltd.

Introduction

The air transport industry both in the USA and in Europe has recently gone through a period of tremendous change. Domestic airline deregulation in the US in 1978 and the liberalisation of air transport in Europe, started on a Community-wide basis in 1988 with the passage of the first package of measures, brought competition to an industry which had been enjoying a high degree of government support and involvement for so long. Such changes in the airline regulatory environment affected many aspects of the aviation industry. The economic impact of these changes has been widely discussed in previous studies, both for the US (see, for example, Meyer *et al.*, 1981 and Meyer and Oster, 1984), and in Europe (CAA, 1993; CAA, 1995; Comité des Sages, 1994; Cranfield, 1997 etc).

More intensive competition amongst established carriers and relative ease of entry by lower cost carriers have made the ability to control costs crucial for major airlines' existence. For example, 15% of the US domestic air travel market is now served by lower cost carriers who offer very low fares (US Department of Transportation, 1996). In Europe, a similar trend can be observed with the entry of such carriers such as EasyJet, Ryanair, and EBA (now Virgin Express), all offering very low fares, although not as yet on a very large number of city pairs.

One of the major areas of operating costs affected by cost cutting activities is labour expenses. This is because labour costs normally account for between one quarter and one third of airline operating costs, and are an area over which managers can exert influence. The array of measures to reduce costs that have been used includes: voluntary or compulsory staff redundancy, reductions in wages, introduction of two-tier wage rates, contracting out of labour, the use of overseas-based employees, the use of cheaper overseas labour, and franchising. Employees in some airlines in the US have traded concessions for profit sharing and increased participation in management through stock ownership and board representation. The former measure has also been adopted in Europe.

The above trends raise a number of questions:

- Have American and European majors been successful in reducing their labour costs, and has this been encouraged by trends towards increased competition?
- Which categories of staff are most affected by the cost cutting measures?
- Are there large variations amongst airlines in reducing their staff costs?
- Does the longer US experience since deregulation provide any pointers for the future direction of labour costs in Europe?

To address the above questions this paper focuses on two regions of airline operations which have experienced liberalisation, the US and Europe. An earlier study identified some parallels between US developments in the 1980s and recent policy changes in Europe, but concluded that a transformation of European labour costs had not yet occurred (Robinson, 1994). More recent evidence is examined here, together with an analysis of trends in US and European airlines as a whole since the removal of regulatory constraints in both regions (over the period of 1978–1994, and 1985–1994 respectively). In addition, a more detailed look will be taken at labour cost trends for individual US and European carriers.

Main factors driving airline operating costs

Unit airline operating costs are affected by *input prices* (eg costs of fuel, airport charges or labour), *operational characteristics* (eg scheduled/charter or short/long haul) and *productivity*, which is a measure of the relationship between an airline's inputs to its output (eg available tonne-kms per employee).

Input prices such as those of fuel and airport charges are beyond airline management's control and significant cost reduction through productivity or efficiency improvements may take many years to achieve (eg fleet replacement) or could be ineffective (eg airport charges). However labour costs, which account for between 25–35% of total operating costs, are more amenable to control by airline management.

There are many *operational characteristics* of airlines which can influence performance measures, especially unit costs and labour productivity. However, sector distance, passenger length of haul, aircraft size and the degree of involvement in freight operation have been found to have the most significant impact on airline unit costs (Alamdari *et al.*, 1995). The longer the average sector distance or passenger haul the lower will be the unit cost of operations, all other things being equal. Similarly, the larger the aircraft size the lower are likely to be the unit costs. The higher the percentage of freight carried, the lower the unit costs, particularly when an airline operates all-cargo aircraft. The cost of flying a tonne of freight is considerably less than the cost of flying an equivalent volume of passengers, who demand numerous additional services both on the ground and in the air.

Increases in *productivity* and efficiency are the key to cost reduction, particularly for large and well established carriers. Several studies in the past have tried to construct a single composite productivity measure to compare airlines' efficiency (see, for example, ATA, 1974 and Morrell and Taneja, 1979). However, due to the diversity found in the nature of carriers' operations it is very difficult to arrive at such a measure which is both meaningful and of use to airline managers. A common index used to measure productivity is Total Factor Productivity (TFP). This index has gone through various stages of growth and application through the efforts of many researchers (Dogramaci, 1981). TFP is the ratio of the quantity of output produced to a weighted combination of quantities of different input factors used. The application of TFP in air transport industry can be found in many studies including those of Caves *et al.* (1981, 1983, 1987) and Windle (1991), and the

Oum and Yu (1995) study which compared the productivity and cost of US and non-US airlines.

Partial productivity measures relate airline output to labour or other inputs. A large number of measures could be used in this respect. For example, Pollack (1979) suggested 69 measures to monitor the activity and efficiency of scheduled airlines, many of them involving labour. Similarly, a British Airways study in 1982 adopted 40 measures for labour productivity alone (British Airways, 1982), and other studies have examined 12 or so measures of productivity and efficiency (Doganis, 1986 and Doganis *et al.*, 1994). Given the availability of data and the aggregate nature of the analysis, the focus here will be on output expressed in available tonne-kms and input in terms of both staff numbers and costs.

Airline labour costs

Unit labour costs are generally defined in relation to total production (available tonne-kms), and the relationship between these two determinants of unit costs is given by the following identities:

Unit Labour Costs = Labour costs ÷ Available Tonne-kms

> or   Labour Cost per Employee ÷ Employee Productivity

> or   Average Wages/Salaries per Employee ÷ Average ATKs per Employee

Trends in these two determinants of unit costs will be examined over time, on an annual basis. The major problem in relating labour costs to an airline's production is the change over time in the share of that production performed *by other firms* (contracting out), and conversely the change in work performed by the airline's employees *for other firms* (contracting in). Maintenance, ground handling and catering staff categories are likely to most subject to these distortions.

More recently some airlines have considered contracting out all of their information technology and computing requirements. Furthermore, capacity pools and block space agreements are effectively contracting out flight operations to other carriers, and would thus distort flying crew and maintenance staff numbers.

In the past, many of these agreements might have been reciprocal, with one carrier performing ground handling at its home base for other carriers and vice versa. This might also be the case with more recent alliances, where each airline's sales staff work for both alliance partners in their respective home countries. On the other hand, work is also increasingly contracted out to wholly or partly owned subsidiary companies, such as Lufthansa's shift of aircraft maintenance to Shannon Aerospace, as well as other independent firms, often in countries with lower wages or social costs.

The growing use of temporary staff to meet seasonal peaks might also pose problems in interpreting trends, although these can be minimised by conversion of such staff to annual equivalents.

Airline labour cost reduction: F Alamdari and P Morrell

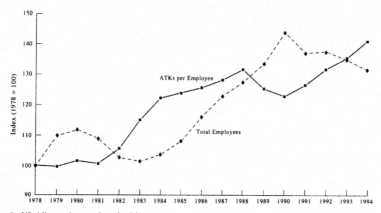

Figure 1 US airline employment & productivity.
Source: Compiled from Air Transport Association of America (ATA) data.

Post-deregulation US airlines

Established US airlines faced significant competition from new entrants, particularly in the initial period following deregulation in 1978. These new airlines were generally not unionised, and operated with labour costs which were well below those of the large incumbents. They also achieved higher productivity and more flexible work practices. How the larger airlines reacted to this new competition, as well as two economic recessions has important implications for an evaluation of the effects of deregulation, and possibly for airline labour cost developments in Europe, which are discussed the next section. First, developments over the period 1978 to 1994 will be analysed for US airlines.

Employment levels and productivity

Overall, the number employed by the major and national airlines[1] in the US has increased over the period 1978 to 1994, and was 36% higher in 1990 compared to 1978 (see *Figure 1*). However, between 1990 and the third quarter of 1995 the numbers employed had fallen by 12%, following lay-offs induced by the recession and resultant large financial losses.

Surprisingly, the period immediately following deregulation (1978–1981) produced no overall gains in productivity measured in ATK per employee, even though in the first three years output was increasing. A possible reason for this was the introduction of services to new cities requiring proportionately more staff, and more intensive service competition, resulting in the need for more customer contact staff per unit of output. From 1981 to 1984,

however, labour productivity increased by about 6% a year, before levelling out from 1984 to 1990. Since 1990, growth resumed at 3.5% a year.

Spencer and Cassell (1987a) identified the following measures taken by US airlines to increase employee productivity:

- Crew size reductions (2 vs 3 man cockpit crews, reduced cabin crew numbers per flight)
- Cross-utilisation of staff and multi-tasking
- Greater use of part time staff
- Reduced numbers of reserve crews
- Revised crew scheduling rules

The first area is dependent on replacing aircraft such as the three crew B727 with the two crew B737. Even so there was strong union resistance to dispensing with the flight engineer on the newer B737s, especially at United. The second area was largely confined to non-unionised, smaller or start-up airlines such as People Express, and was unlikely to have had a very significant effect on the national and major airlines included in *Figure 1*. It is difficult to quantify the effect of the remaining areas listed above, but they were probably less important.

Labour costs per employee

The average cost per employee increased at a steady rate in current terms since deregulation, except during the period 1983 to 1987 when no increases were obtained against a background of a surplus of available skilled labour. In the period immediately following deregulation, wages were bid up by new entrant airlines. Average employee productivity moved broadly in line with average wage/salary costs in the years 1982 to 1988, but in the early period (1978 to 1982) and since 1988 wage costs have

---

[1]Majors are US airlines with annual revenues of over US$ 1 billion, and nationals of between $100 million and $ 1 billion

Airline labour cost reduction: F Alamdari and P Morrell

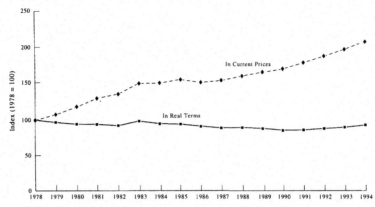

Figure 2 US airline labour costs per employee.
Source: Compiled from ATA data.

tended to increase faster than productivity gains (see *Figures 1* and *2*).

In constant prices, the average labour cost per employee has declined slowly (apart from a small increase in 1983) over the period 1978 to 1994, particularly over the first three years following deregulation (*Figure 2*). As discussed above, staff productivity had only increased marginally in the first three years following deregulation.

The share of pensions, related benefits and payroll taxes increased somewhat from 18% of labour costs in 1978 to 20% in 1994. The share of employee compensation costs declined from 41.4% of total operating costs in 1978 to 33.7% in 1994, almost all of the drop occurring in the initial part of the period to 1982, after which time this percentage was largely unchanged. The initial fall was principally due to the significant increase in the share of fuel costs in the total, but an increase in labour's share might have been expected in the period after 1982 with the subsequent fall in fuel costs.

US airline success in controlling labour costs per employee was due initially to competition from low cost, non-unionised, new entrant airlines (eg Southwest and People Express), and was combined with the early 1990s oil crisis and recession which led to a temporary over-supply of airline personnel. A more detailed analysis of airline responses to this new situation is well documented by Spencer and Cassell (1987a,b, 1989), and can be summarised under:

- Wage and compensation adjustments
- Benefit adjustments
- Work force allocation and utilisation

Under the first heading, airline unions were forced in the early part of the 1980s to concede wage cuts and freezes, or deferral of wage increases (eg Eastern, Pan Am). Two-

tier (a and b) wage scales were introduced by some airlines (notably by American), while flexible wage plans were traded for Employee Stock Ownership and Purchase plans, as well as profit sharing (Eastern and later Northwest and United). Under benefit changes, early retirement incentives were offered, and reductions in holiday, sick leave and other entitlements. In 1995, American Airlines incurred $332 million in costs associated with the early retirement of 350 flight attendants and over 2000 dispatchers and mechanics.

The third category includes a number of changes designed to increase productivity and make work practices more flexible, some of which were touched on in the previous section.

Unit labour costs

The ultimate success of US airline management in controlling labour costs can be judged by examining labour costs per ATK. This combines trends in employment levels, productivity and wage levels, which were described above. Experience since deregulation can be split into the first three years before the economic recession, the recession period, the cyclical upswing and the second recession. *Figure 3* shows how US airline labour costs per ATK declined between 1983 and 1987 in current prices, following increases over the years immediately following deregulation when a large number of new entrant airlines bid up the cost of hiring skilled personnel. Between 1987 and 1991, the pressure on labour costs increased again with staff shortages occurring and some return of union power, levelling off in the early 1990s because of the economic recession, major airline collapses and some downsizing.

Whereas between 1978 and 1994, unit labour costs, in current prices, rose by 47%, the US consumer price index increased by 127%, resulting in an overall fall in these

Airline labour cost reduction: F Alamdari and P Morrell

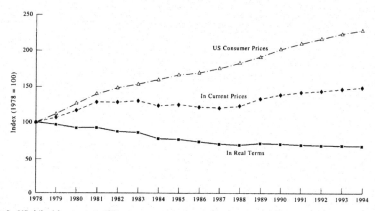

Figure 3 US airline labour cost per ATK
Source: Compiled from ATA data.

costs in real terms of 35%, or by just under 2% a year. The most significant period of unit labour cost reduction was 1983 to 1987, when costs declined by 5.4% a year. This was the period of introduction of b-scales and significant industry consolidation.

Previous research compared pre- and post-deregulation trends: over the six years prior to 1978, labour costs for the major US carriers increased at an average annual rate of 3.8% above the consumer price index, falling to 1% below the rate of inflation from 1979 to 1982 (Transportation Research Board, 1991).

Analysis by employee category

Around 60% of employees of the major US airlines are unionised, with few regional airlines or new entrants having union representation. Delta Air Lines is exceptional in having only cockpit crew unionisation. The three staff categories with the most powerful and often militant unions were the pilots (100% unionisation), the cabin crew and the maintenance engineers (both having around 80% unionisation). All three groups often require substantial training and are harder to replace than other staff categories.

The three most heavily unionised staff categories, namely cockpit and cabin crew and maintenance engineers, accounted for 54.7% of total wage/salary cost in 1993 (markedly higher than the 47% in 1978), so agreement on both productivity and wage levels in these areas was and still remains crucial to the control of unit costs (see *Table 1*)[2]. Amongst these three groups, cockpit crew increased in importance throughout the period, and flight attendants up to 1985. The small decline in the importance of

---

[2]Air Transport Association of America (ATA) data has been used rather than ICAO, since the latter did not appear reliable for the distribution of labour costs by staff category.

Table 1 US airline staff costs by staff category (%)

	1978	1985	1993
Flying operations	25.4	26.2	29.2
Flight attendants	10.4	13.4	13.5
Direct aircraft maintenance	11.2	10.5	12.0
Aircraft/traffic personnel	34.8	33.7	31.1
General management	1.1	1.3	0.6
Other	17.1	14.9	13.6
Total	100.0	100.0	100.0

Source: Air Transport Association of America data for major and national airlines.

maintenance staff between 1985 and 1993 can be attributed to increased productivity and some outsourcing. ATA reported that, by the end of 1995, 24.6% of direct maintenance was performed for majors and nationals by outside firms, compared to 19.9% in early 1988 (Feldman, 1996).

Table 2 shows that all the staff categories except maintenance just kept pace with inflation in their average remuneration between 1978 and 1985. Over the more recent period of 1985 to 1993, however, all categories' average pay declined in real terms, especially cabin crew and other staff. Over the period as a whole, all staff categories suffered a fall in real pay, with ticketing, sales and promotion least affected and other categories most affected. Maintenance staff and cockpit crew unions had more success in maintaining their members' pay in real terms since 1985. It is interesting to note that the ratio of cockpit crew pay to the average pay for all categories increased from 2.25 in 1978 to 2.32 in 1985, and again to 2.53 in 1993. On the other hand, pilot productivity measured in flying hours per cockpit crew member increased only marginally between 1983 and 1988, and actually fell between 1988 and 1993 (Alamdari *et al.*, 1995).

57

Airline labour cost reduction: F Alamdari and P Morrell

Table 2   US airline staff costs per employee by staff category

	US$ (000) expressed at 1993 prices				
	1978	1985	Average annual change 1978–85	1993	Average annual change 1985–93
Cockpit crew	111.4	114.8	+0.4%	107.4	−0.9%
Cabin crew	35.1	37.5	+0.9%	29.5	−3.4%
Maintenance	45.3	43.8	−0.5%	41.6	−0.7%
Ticketing, sales and promotion	35.1	35.9	+0.3%	34.0	−0.8%
Other	45.1	46.5	+0.4%	34.6	−4.1%
Average	49.5	49.4	+0.0%	42.4	−2.2%

Source: ICAO Personnel Statistics by airline for AA, CO, UA, TW, DL, NW and US.

Analysis by individual airline

To obtain a better understanding of post-deregulation trends, a more detailed examination was made of individual US airlines, in particular the three largest which have operated continuously since 1978, and today account for around 57% of total domestic RPKs, namely United, American, and Delta.

Over the period 1978 to 1993, labour productivity for Delta and United increased by a greater percentage than for American (*Figure 4*). Whereas by 1989 they had all achieved average gains of around 4% a year, since then the former two airlines had advanced more strongly. United's trends are distorted by a strike in 1985, and the subsequent acquisition of Pan Am's Pacific operations. The airline suffered from low productivity on short haul routes in the earlier years due to their inability to persuade unions to operate the B737-100s with two rather than three cockpit crew (these aircraft were retired by 1984).

Automation and outsourcing were two important factors causing increased labour productivity. Revenue accounting is one task that has been largely automated over the past five years: American Airlines both automated revenue accounting, and moved it to a wholly owned subsidiary in Barbados which also performs similar operations for other industries. This and other measures to increase productivity appeared to be more successful for American in the early part of the 1980s. Delta, on the other hand, experienced slower productivity growth in the earlier period.

For the period as a whole, American Airlines achieved the greatest fall in real wage/salary cost per employee. The airline was especially concerned at the threat from New York Air, which started operating in 1980. Labour costs for this airline and People Express were low, both because they were based on lower post-deregulation market prices, and because they were start-up airlines having average wage rates close to entry levels. American's response was to try to start up a new airline within the airline, based on b-scale wage rates. This would mean that, for example, newly hired cabin attendants would

Figure 4   US airline ATKs per employee.
Source: Compiled from ATA data.

Airline labour cost reduction: F Alamdari and P Morrell

be paid an annual wage of $15 000 compared to the average of $30 000 paid to existing cabin crew.

The main problem with this approach was that the b-scale employees began to feel that they were underpaid for doing similar work to many of their colleagues, although American's management campaigned to persuade them that the more senior staff were overpaid on regulated industry rates. The plan also required a rapid growth in operations to be effective, since natural retirement of older staff would not, by itself, make much difference to the average. While American did grow rapidly during the 1980s, the growing b-scale workforce became more highly unionised towards the end of the decade: as a result, the two-tier system became less effective. However, American's approach was very successful over the period 1982 to 1987, particularly over the latter part of this period (*Figure 5*).

United Airlines initially had little success in reducing real labour costs per employee, but substantial subsequent success over the period 1983 to 1985 took its toll on staff morale, and the damaging strike in 1985 significantly reversed the reductions that had been achieved. Attempts to introduce b-scales in 1985 were effectively killed by a month long shut down of all United's operations. It was at this time that plans for an employee buy-out of the airline were first formulated, driven largely by their pilots' union. Such plans nearly came off in 1989, when British Airways were willing to invest $750 million in the airline in return for a grand alliance, but the plan collapsed because of the high level of foreign participation in the airline, which was not acceptable to the US government. Success was finally achieved in mid-1994, when 55% of the airline was transferred to the unions in return for wage concessions, and *de facto* b-scales of pay for the low cost subsidiary, Shuttle by United.

Delta Air Lines' average wage rates increased steadily in real terms between 1980 and 1993, apart from 1987

when they absorbed the lower wage carrier Western Airlines. Western employees' wage rates, however, were brought up to Delta levels over the subsequent two to three years. They did, however, achieve a substantial fall in average rates in the first two years following deregulation.

The combined effect of productivity and wage rates resulted in the three major airlines' unit labour costs falling in real terms by broadly the same amount over the period (*Figure 6*). Delta did particularly well in the period since 1989, and United since 1991. American, on the other hand, had achieved most of their gains by 1988.

In summary, a significant increase in US airline competition following deregulation has resulted in a steady decline in average pay in real terms, accompanied by productivity gains (more in the early 1980s) despite an increase in numbers employed (especially over the period of economic growth between 1983 and 1990). This has combined to give good gains in unit labour costs, particularly from 1978 to 1988, when they levelled out or fell more slowly.

Unions faced a weakening position in the first half of the 1980s, but have since rallied. Overall they have become more flexible in terms of acceptance of both lower pay, at least in real terms, and also productivity increases in order to maintain employment levels over the longer term. Their position has depended on the supply/demand balance in the labour markets and in some cases the threat of bankruptcies, which was not a major factor before 1978. The latter also led them to become more involved in discussions on airline strategic planning, achieved in some cases by board representation and shareholding.

Post-liberalisation Europe

European liberalisation formally started from 1988 with the passage of the first liberalisation package (see Crans,

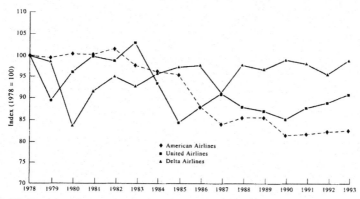

Figure 5 US airline average labour cost per employee in real terms.
Source: Compiled from ATA data.

Airline labour cost reduction: F Alamdari and P Morrell

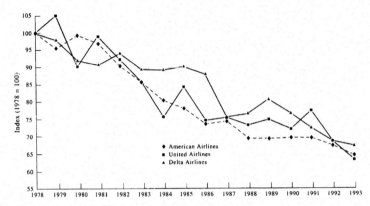

Figure 6 US airline labour cost per ATK.
Source: Compiled from IATA data.

1992 and AEA Yearbook, 1993 for detailed information on EU air liberalisation packages). However, since 1984, countries such as UK and Netherlands began the move towards a more liberal regime by signing more liberalised air services agreements. The airlines' main response to the growing competition in Europe has been to reduce labour costs as part of a range of cost cutting activities. The intensified level of international competition from major carriers outside Europe, mainly US airlines, and the need to recover from economic recession which resulted in financial deficits, have also increased the need for the European carriers to reduce labour costs.

Efforts to reduce costs and bring about improved working practices have met strong resistance in many European countries. Since 1993, work stoppages, most of short duration, have affected SAS (ground staff), Austrian Airlines (flying crew), TAP Air Portugal (all staff), Air France (all staff) and Alitalia (pilots). British Airways' pilots' union recently settled a dispute after a threatened strike. The climate is gradually changing, however, and unions are beginning to take seriously the actual or threatened withdrawal of government support. There is also evidence of unions making some of the demands for a greater say in management, profit sharing and share ownership that their US counterparts made in the 1980s.

Employment levels and productivity

Amongst the many policies adopted by European carriers to reduce labour costs, one has been a reduction in the number of staff. Some carriers have been more successful in reducing staff numbers than others, partly due to factors beyond management control such as cultural and social influences, the strength of labour unions and government attitudes to redundancies. For example it

has been more difficult for carriers such as Iberia to shed jobs, operating from a country with over 20% unemployment. Iberia's restructuring proposal in December 1994 which included 2,120 layoffs was met with two one-day strikes costing the carrier $16 million in loss of revenue.

Figure 7 illustrates the development in the level of employment for a sample of major EU scheduled airlines[3], from 1985 to 1994. The year 1985 is used as the base, since the movement towards liberalisation began in 1985 through more liberal air services agreements between EU member countries. It has been said that the 1990s were going to be characterised by staff reductions, and the trend in the *Figure 7* supports such a view.

It ought to be mentioned that the reduction in the number of employees has not always meant a worsening level of job losses to the industry as a whole. In some cases labour moves from one organisation to another. This happens when airlines outsource some of their activities such as maintenance and catering. For example, Shannon Aerospace in Ireland carry out aircraft maintenance on behalf of a number of European carriers including its shareholders, Swissair and Lufthansa. Lufthansa has recently announced that it will transfer more maintenance work to this company, which is effectively transferring jobs to a lower wage rate country within the EU. However in other cases airlines have moved an entire function or part of it to lower cost countries outside the EU, resulting in net job losses. For example, Swissair transferred revenue accounting tasks to India in 1992, employing over 100 staff at a facility near Bombay (Donoghue, 1993).

---

[3]Air France, Alitalia, British Airways, Iberia, KLM, Lufthansa, SAS, Sabena and TAP Air Portugal

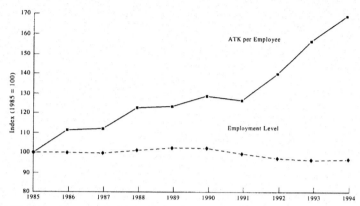

Figure 7   EU airline employment & productivity.
Source: Compiled from ATA data.

While it is difficult to quantify the impact of EU liberalisation measures on the reduction in the airlines' staff levels, it is clear that the measures have encouraged such a trend. It is wrong to assume that the development in EU airlines' staff levels is entirely due to increased competition in the EU countries. However a survey of 18 EU airlines revealed that almost two thirds of surveyed carriers believe that EU liberalisation measures affected their policy in relation to staffing (Cranfield, 1997).

Although the level of employment by EU carriers has declined in recent years, staff productivity measured by ATKs (Available Tonne Kms) per employee has increased. *Figure 7* above, illustrates employee productivity (ATKs per employee) trends for a number of EU airlines from 1985 to 1994. The increase in the labour productivity is more noticeable since 1991, three years after the passage of the first liberalisation package in 1988. The decline in employee numbers was accompanied by higher labour productivity, which in theory should put the airlines in a more competitive position, assuming that it is not accompanied by higher wages.

The survey of EU airlines (Cranfield, 1997) can shed some light on the extent to which the increase in airline labour productivity has been due to EU liberalisation. Almost all the airlines surveyed (94%) believed that competition from EU airlines, which has been intensified by the adoption of EU measures, has affected airlines' improvement in efficiency. However it ought to be mentioned that the economic recession of 1990–1993 must have played its role in increasing the pressure for higher productivity.

Labour costs per employee

Clearly reductions in the number of staff or increases in labour productivity do not necessarily translate into lower labour cost. It is possible to lower the number of employees and at the same time ask for increased productivity from the remaining staff in return for higher wages. Therefore it is important to analyse the average wage and salary levels of the EU carriers.

To remove the impact of exchange rates, each carriers' expenses per employee are expressed in their local currency, and indexed on 1985 as the base year. Then, to arrive at a composite unit representing EU airlines' average labour cost, the airlines' labour expenses (in an index form) are weighted by their staff numbers and aggregated. To establish the changes in employee expenses in real terms all the figures are adjusted by local Consumer Price Indices (CPI) and are expressed in 1994 prices.

It can be seen from *Figure 8* that carriers overall have experienced a rise in their labour costs in current prices. However, even in real terms, the average expenses per employee has risen by almost 10% over the whole period. Therefore it could be concluded that airlines' employees have increased their productivity, in return for which they have received on average a slightly higher salary in real terms.

Unit labour cost

Reducing labour unit cost, without adversely affecting service levels, ought to be the prime aim of the airlines in Europe, especially in the more recent years when European aviation markets has become increasingly liberalised, and therefore competition amongst EU carriers has gathered pace.

The overall trend in EU airlines' unit labour cost as illustrated in *Figure 9* indicates that EU airlines have been successful in controlling and reducing their unit labour cost in real terms, especially since 1991. This is because since then the rate of increase in staff productivity has

Airline labour cost reduction: F Alamdari and P Morrell

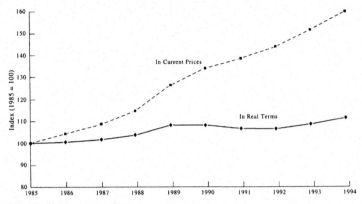

Figure 8   EU airline labour costs per employee.
Source: ICAO statistics and airline annual reports.

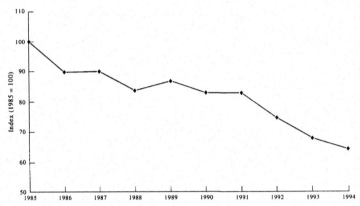

Figure 9   EU airline labour cost per ATK in real terms.
Source: ICAO statistics and airline annual reports.

been greater than the increase in average wage levels (as illustrated in *Figures 7* and *8*). Such trends have also been affected by outsourcing of certain activities.

Labour costs analysis by employee category

As *Table 3* indicates, cockpit crew salaries constituted a higher proportion of total labour costs in 1993 than 1985. The same applies to cabin crew. Other categories, which include airport, handling, catering and staff involved with head office planning and operations, have declined in importance. The increasing share of cockpit crew costs occurred because the relatively higher salaries (*Table 4*)

more than outweighed the relatively higher productivity increases over this period (Alamdari *et al.,* 1995). For cabin crew, their relatively higher salaries compared to other staff categories were accompanied by a much poorer productivity performance.

The analysis of EU airline labour costs by staff category from 1985 to 1993 shows that all categories of airline staff salaries in the EU, unlike their counter-parts in the US, have increased in real terms, such that the gap between the two has widened. (*Tables 4* and *2*). However, cockpit crew have received the largest increase in their salary (an average of 7.4%) while the ticketing, sales and promotion

Airline labour cost reduction: F Alamdari and P Morrell

Table 3 EU airline staff costs by staff category (%)

	1985	1993
Cockpit crew	15%	18%
Cabin crew	12%	15%
Maintenance	20%	19%
TSP	10%	9%
Other	42%	39%
Total	100%	100%

Source: ICAO Personnel Statistics by airline for BA, IB, LH, SK, TP.

Table 4 EU airline staff costs per employee by category

US$	US$ (000) expressed at 1993 prices		
	1985	1993	Av. annual change 1985–93
Cockpit crew	72 309	128 022	7.4%
Cabin Crew	26 934	42 198	5.8%
Maintenance	25 899	43 180	6.6%
TSP	28 350	39 971	4.4%
Other	26 029	45 254	7.1%
Average	29 105	49 436	6.8%

Source: ICAO Personnel Statistics by airline for BA, IB, LH, SK, TP.

(TSP) staff received the lowest increase (an average of 4.3%). With the exception of cockpit crew, all the airline employees received on average an annual salary of around $49 000 in 1993. Cockpit crew salaries in the same year was nearly 3 times higher than the rest of staff. This ratio was somewhat higher than that recorded by US airlines.

Analysis by individual airline

The above analysis focused on EU labour costs on average, whereas in order to establish the success of individual EU carriers in reducing their labour costs, a number of European carriers'[4] productivity, expenses per employee and unit labour cost are analysed next. This analysis is carried out for the period 1985 to 1994.

Labour productivity. *Figure 10* illustrates trends in employee productivity (ATK per employee) for a number of EU airlines (the airlines are ranked according to their 1994 performance with the highest on the left). It can be seen that the majority of airlines have continued to increase their labour productivity over the years, with KLM,

---

[4]Air France, British Airways, Iberia, KLM, Lufthansa, SAS, Sabena, TAP Air Portugal.

Lufthansa and British Airways at a higher rate than other carriers. The only carrier that has not achieved growth in employee productivity in recent years is Sabena, largely because of a radical reduction in capacity since 1991 (although this was largely confined to intercontinental routes). However, despite the decrease in Sabena's general employee productivity, previous research shows that the airline's cockpit crew achieved the highest growth in productivity compared with the other EU airlines during the period from 1983 to 1993 (Alamdari *et al.*, 1995).

Labour cost per employee. The analyses of labour costs per employee for the three years, 1985, 1989 and 1994, allows a comparison between the labour costs of different carriers, and establishes the changes in actual labour expenses.

The average cost per employee for the study carriers, in 1994 US dollars, is illustrated in *Figure 11* (the airlines are ranked according to their 1994 performance). To take into account the differences in the cost of living of different

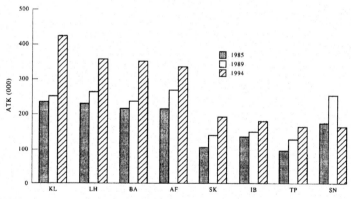

Figure 10 EU airline ATKs per employee.
Source: ICAO statistics and airline annual reports.

Airline labour cost reduction: F Alamdari and P Morrell

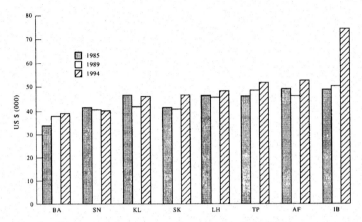

Figure 11   EU airline labour cost per employee (1994 prices). Using purchasing power parity exchange rates.
Source: ICAO statistics and airline annual reports.

countries the Purchasing Power Parity (PPP)[5] exchange rates were used to convert labour costs in national currencies to US dollars. Using this rather than market exchange rates removes the cost of living variations from the comparison.

It can be seen that in most cases the airlines' average labour cost has increased, in real terms, especially in Iberia's case between 1989 and 1993. Sabena was the only airline in the sample which experienced declining average labour costs.

Air France has continuously reduced average labour cost until the merger with UTA in 1992 after which average labour costs rose. For example, cost-saving measures introduced by Air France in September 1993 met with considerable hostility from its work force. The resulting industrial action led to the government intervening to force the company to withdraw its proposed cuts. In exchange for reductions in salaries, the airline changed the holding company structure to allow up to 20% of the shares to be owned by staff (Air France, 1995). Other airlines operating from countries experiencing high levels of unemployment also have found it difficult to lay off workers.

Lufthansa, in response to its increasing labour costs started from April 1996 employing regional flight attendants based in Delhi, Bangkok and Singapore. Sabena has also been successful in reducing labour costs in recent

[5]PPP exchange rates convert currencies on the basis of what money will buy, rather than on the basis of a market evaluation. Therefore they are the rates of currency conversion that equalise the purchasing power of different currencies. This means that a given sum of money, when converted into different currencies at the PPP rate, will buy the same basket of goods and services in all countries. Thus PPPs are the rate of currency conversion which eliminate differences in price levels between countries.

years. KLM has generally managed to maintain its labour costs below that of the 1985 level throughout the past decade, despite an increase in more recent years. British Airways, SAS, and TAP have experienced some increase in their average labour costs. As British Airways has the lowest unit labour cost, such an increase has a less detrimental effect on the company compared to TAP which has the third highest unit labour costs. Despite that, British Airways has recently announced that 5000 of its employees would be offered voluntary redundancy. Iberia is the only carrier which has been faced with a continuous increase in its labour costs through the period 1985–1994.

Unit labour cost. Airlines unit labour costs which take into account not only labour wage rates but also labour productivity, provide a different picture compared to the trend in labour cost per employee. It can be seen from *Figure 12* that with the exception of Iberia and Sabena, the airlines' labour cost per ATK has declined.

It is apparent that the majority of EU carriers reduced unit labour costs mainly through increase in productivity, while carriers such as KLM and to some extent Lufthansa reduced labour unit cost through both an increase in productivity and a reduction in wage rates. Sabena's case is different, as despite success in lowering labour wage rate its labour unit costs have increased slightly through lower productivity. It is interesting to note that the two southern European carriers, TAP and Iberia, pay their employees much more than other airlines for producing one ATK, while KLM and British Airways pay the lowest for the same level of output.

In conclusion, EU airlines have certainly reduced staff numbers and increased labour productivity both in terms

Airline labour cost reduction: F Alamdari and P Morrell

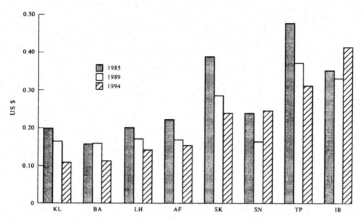

Figure 12 EU airline labour cost per ATK (1994 prices). Using purchasing power parity exchange rates. *Source*: ICAO statistics and airline annual reports.

of increases in ATK per employee and reductions in labour costs per ATK. However, they have not been successful in reducing employee's wages, even in real terms. Therefore it appears that the airlines are paying their staff on average slightly more in return for proportionately greater productivity increases. This is possibly because the increase in outsourcing, while reducing the number of lower paid employees (eg cleaning and catering) and boosting productivity, has a tendency to increase average unit labour costs.

Such trends are clearly affected by EU measures, international competition from carriers outside Europe, and by the world and European economic climate. However from the Cranfield survey of 18 EU carriers it has become clear that EU liberalisation measures have certainly played an important role in accelerating the reduction in staff numbers and increased labour productivity and in controlling labour costs.

Conclusions

Success in labour cost reduction should ultimately be judged in terms of trends in labour cost per unit of output (ATK), relative to trends in prices in general. This reflected both productivity gains and the degree to which labour was compensated in higher wages.

The US had an initial period after deregulation without a recession, which made it harder for management to achieve reduced real labour costs per employee. Europe, on the other hand, had the benefit of an common external threat of economic downturn to provide the catalyst for management action and union acceptance for change. But the threats of increased competition were more gradual and arguably less severe in Europe.

In the four years following deregulation, US airlines achieved reductions in unit labour costs of around 10% in real terms; this was caused by real reductions in wage and salary levels, with productivity broadly unchanged. Only once the economic recession took effect over the next four years did US airlines experience significant advances in productivity, accompanied, however, by broadly unchanged real wages. This gave a 17% fall in unit labour costs in real terms. Since 1988, unit labour costs in real terms have levelled out, initially with a decline in real wage offset by a fall in productivity, and more recently with higher productivity accompanied by higher real wages.

European experience was somewhat similar to post-deregulation experience in the US, *once the recession set in*. The key differences were that European airlines were not successful in moderating real wages, but at the same time they achieved higher productivity gains. Thus in the period 1991 to 1994, unit labour costs fell by around 23%, as a result of fast growth in productivity, offset by some increases in real wages. In the earlier period, before liberalisation had gathered pace, EU airlines achieved more modest productivity gains, and experienced small real wage increases and modest reductions in real unit costs.

In the eight years following deregulation, the salaries of US airline pilots and cabin crew grew slightly faster than inflation, while maintenance staff were the only category that experience a real reduction in pay. Over the past eight years, cabin crew and other categories suffered the worst erosion in their real pay, with pilots, maintenance and ticketing/sales/promotion staff the least affected. All European airline staff categories increased their real pay substantially over the past eight years, pilots by the largest percentage and ticketing/sales/promotion staff by the lowest.

Airline labour cost reduction: F Alamdari and P Morrell

Based on the US experience, pilots and cockpit crew might be expected to suffer least in a fall in real incomes in the future, but it should be noted that European cabin crew appear proportionately more expensive in 1993 *vis-à-vis* US carriers compared with other staff categories. While the larger US airlines experienced broadly similar trends in labour productivity, costs per employee and per ATK following deregulation, European airlines showed large variations. This might be expected from the uniform US domestic market and economy, as opposed to the diversity that still exists in Europe. Since 1989, British Airways, KLM and Lufthansa achieved significant reductions in labour costs per ATK in constant prices, Air France obtained modest reductions, while Iberia and Sabena were faced with increases.

Finally, it can be concluded from what happened in the US under deregulation after the first recession, that European airlines will achieve further reductions in real unit labour costs, driven by productivity gains, and more importantly reduced real wages. Such reductions might be traded for profit sharing or stock option schemes.

References

Air France (1995) *Group Annual Report, 1994–1995.*
Alamdari, F., Doganis, R. and Lobbenberg, A. (1995) *Efficiency of the World's Major Airlines.* Cranfield Research Report, No. 4, March.
AEA (1993) *Yearbook 1993.* Association of European Airlines, April.
ATA (1974) *US Airline Industry Costs and Productivity, 1967–1973.* Air Transport Association of America, May 17.
British Airways (1982) *Compass 82,* Volumes 1 and 2.
Caves, D. W., Christensen, L. R. and Tretheway, M. W. (1981) US trunk carriers, 1972–1977: A multilateral comparison of total factor productivity. *Productivity Measurement in Regulated Industries,* eds. T. G. Gowing and R. E. Stevenson. Academic Press.
Caves, D. W., Christensen, L. R. and Tretheway, M. W. (1983) Productivity performance of US trunk and local service airlines in the era of deregulation, *Economic Inquiry,* **XXI** (July), 312–324
Caves, D. W., Christensen, L. R. and Windle, R. J. (1987) An assessment of the efficiency effect of US airline deregulation via an international comparison. *Public Regulation: New Perspectives on Institutions and policies,* ed. E. E. Bailey. MIT Press. Cambridge, Mass.

Civil Aviation Authority, UK (1993) *Airline Competition in the Single European Market.* November, CAP 623.
Civil Aviation Authority, UK (1995) *The Single European Aviation Market—Progress So Far.* September, CAP 654.
Crans, B. (1992) *EC Aviation Scene, Air and Space Law,* **XVII** (4/5)
Cranfield (1997) *Single Market Review 1996· Impact on Services—Air Transport,* Kogan Page for the European Commission March 1997.
Comité des Sages (1994) *Expanding Horizons.* A report for the European Commission, January.
Doganis, R. (1986) Measure for Measure. *Airline Business,* May.
Doganis, R., Alamdari, F. and Lobbenberg, A. (1994) Who is lean and mean? *Airline Business,* November.
Dogramaci, A. (1981) *Productivity Analysis, A Range of Perspectives.* Martinus Nijhoff Publishing.
Donoghue (1993) Back offices, far afield and frugal. *Air Transport World.* December.
Feldman, J. (1996) Was this trip necessary. *Air Transport World,* September.
Meyer, J. R., Oster, C. V., Morgan, I. P., Berman, B. and Strassmann, D. (1981) *Airline Deregulation: The Early Experience.* Auburn House.
Meyer, J. and Oster, C. (1984) *Deregulation and the New Airline Entrepreneurs,* MIT Press.
Morrell, P. S. and Taneja, N. K. (1979) Airline productivity re-defined: an analysis of US and European carriers. *Transportation,* 8/1979, Elsevier, Amsterdam.
Oum, Tae Hoon and Yu, Chunyan (1995) A productivity comparison of the world's major airlines. *Journal of Air Transport Management,* **2** (3/5)
Pollack, M. (1979) Measures of airline activity and efficiency: A descriptive survey. *Transportation Research,* **13A,** 345–349
Robinson, O. (1994) Employment policy and deregulation in European air transport. *The Service Industries Journal,* **14** (1)
Spencer, F. and Cassell, F. (1987a) *Eight Years of US Airline Deregulation: Management and Labor Adaptions; Re-emergence of Oligopoly.* The Transportation Center, Northwestern University.
Spencer, F. and Cassell, F. (1987b) *US Airline Labour Relations under Deregulation.*
Spencer, F. and Cassell, F. (1989) Labour strategies. *Airline Business,* August.
Transportation Research Board (1991) *Winds of Change: Domestic Air Transport Since Deregulation,* Special Report 230, National Research Council, Washington DC.
US Department of Transportation (1996) *The Low Cost Airline Service Revolution,* April.
Windle, R. J. (1991) The world's airlines, a cost and productivity comparison. *Journal of Transport Economics and Policy, January,* **XXV** (1), 31–49

24

Low Cost Airlines: Business Model and Employment Relations

LAURIE HUNTER

The passenger air travel industry is experiencing increasing competition between low cost/no frills carriers (LCC) and the more traditional full service carriers. This paper explores the comparative business models with a view to identifying areas where these might be expected to generate different HR and employment relations practices, and checking the findings against available evidence. While some of the expectations are confirmed, unionisation is higher than anticipated in the LCC sector and a relatively high percentage of staff were on regular rather than contingent contracts. Differences in approach are observed among LCC airlines, and the evidence indicates some convergence between the two sectors as competition heightens.

Keywords: Airlines, Competition, Employment relations, Low cost carriers, Business models

Introduction

The passenger air travel industry is characterised by the emergence of a low-cost/no frills sector alongside and partly in competition with the incumbent full service carriers. [1] These two sectors offer strong contrasts in their business and competitive strategy, effectively providing competing models of operation. Although it is now widely accepted that there is no necessary and unique connection between an organisation's business model and its HR and employment relations strategy, there is still some expectation that the latter will be influenced by, and have some interaction with, the business strategy. The aim of this short paper is to explore the comparative business models (Section 2), to identify areas where these

might be expected to generate different HR and employment relations practices (Section 3), and check these expectations against the available evidence. This may in turn raise questions regarding tendencies to divergence or convergence between the two sectors, and about their respective HR responses to major market shocks.

Competing Business Models

We will refer to the two models as the full service carrier (FSC) and low cost carrier (LCC) models. The FSC model is essentially one based on a differentiation strategy, in contrast to the LCC approach based on cost leadership or cost minimisation (Alamdari and Fagan (2005)): within each model companies will seek competitive advantage through some variation in their operational vision, business routines, architecture and practice. [2] Thus we should expect to see some heterogeneity within sectors as well as between sectors. However, it is possible to present a 'typical' profile of an FSC and LCC model organisation as follows (Table 1):

It is clear from this comparison that the FSC bears much heavier overheads necessitated by the hub and spoke *modus operandi*, which is based on the premise of the need to build up capacity utilisation by links to feeder routes at the hubs; and generally higher operating costs on account of the extra services provided, for which a premium price is charged. Airline alliances in recent years can be seen as a device to share the overheads and use aircraft capacity more effectively. Even so, the level of capacity utilisation on many routes will be moderate, though off peak and other promotional fares have been introduced to increase capacity. (Scheduled

LOW COST AIRLINES: BUSINESS MODEL AND EMPLOYMENT RELATIONS

Table 1 Operational Characteristics of FSC and LCC Airline

Characteristic feature	FSC	LCC
Generic strategy	Differentiation	Cost minimisation/cost leadership, entrepreneurial in character
Scale	Typically large	Generally smaller, but some major players (e.g. Ryanair, EasyJet)
Operational model	Hub and spoke/Multiple hub and spoke, linking with feeder routes	Point to point, no interlining, short sector length (400–600 nautical miles)
	Mix of short/medium/ and long-haul routes	Mainly short haul
	Various aircraft type and engines	Uniform aircraft type
	Moderate capacity utilisation (c. 60%)	High capacity utilisation, (c. 70–80%) rapid turnround between sectors, low margins
Market	Normally in competition with other FSCs, leading to differentiation by class (quality) of service, with high service image, including:	Cheap travel sector of the market, segmentation by time of booking and choice of flight
		Quality of service basic, e.g.:
		Little flexibility of flight changes (use or lose!)
	Frequent scheduling & flight flexibility	No catering, or meals charged for
	Extensive in-flight services	Ground services typically outsourced (but can be
	Comprehensive ground services	problematic, e.g. easyJet)
	Use of principal airports	Typically use secondary airports
Inventory Management	Pre arranged tickets and seats: reservation system complex, due to feeder routes: use of travel agents	Inventory management simplified: direct or online bookings, ticketless, no use of travel agents

Source: This table draws on: ITF (2002): and Alderighi *et al.* (2004).

flights, once committed to, are a sunk cost which can with benefit be spread by marginal cost pricing of spare capacity.) Travellers such as business passengers with a need for frequent scheduling, inter-flight flexibility and ground service linkages are the backbone of the FSC market, for which a premium fare is paid, with differentiation being offered through personal space and comfort on-board, inflight entertainment and free food and alcoholic drinks, frequent flier programmes, free airport lounges and use of major city airports (typically with higher landing charges). All these features raise seat costs.

By contrast, the LCC has cut costs significantly by reducing overheads, providing a no frills service and often using secondary airports with cheaper landing charges. Inventory management is simplified by the absence of feeder routes, direct or online booking and ticketless operation. By significantly reducing costs and fares, the LCCs have opened up a much wider range of point to point journeys, many not served by the FSCs,[3] and in so doing have attracted at least some price-conscious passengers from the high-fare FSCs. On routes between UK and Ireland, Aer Lingus business passengers mainly work for companies employing over 100, while Ryanair business passengers are usually self employed or work for smaller companies (Binggeli and Pompeo (2005)).

Faced with this competition, FSCs have attempted to fight back by adopting some of the LCCs' characteristics – with increasing online sales, more rapid turnround times and reduced use of travel agents or lower commission rates. Some have gone as far as to set up their own 'budget airline' within the main

organisation (examples include BA and GO (later sold off): British Midland and bmibaby: KLM and Transavia). But in general they still have a long way to go and these airlines will pursue differentiated strategies (c.f. British Airways' current (2005) plans to expand the share of capacity allocated to high fare/high yield business class passengers by upgrading seating quality).[4]

Comparative HR and Employment Relations Strategies

Discussion of business strategies and their relation to HR and employment relations strategies strictly requires a detailed analysis of the meaning of business strategy, HR strategy and practice, and the interplay between them.[5] This is not feasible in the context of this short paper. Instead, we follow the general thrust adopted by Boxall (1999),[6] who found the contingency hypothesis linking business strategy and HR policy overly simplistic in terms of both strategy and HR/employment relations. Business strategy is not a given, but is seen as critically interactive with HRM. Purcell and Alhstrand (1994) note that large scale multi-divisional enterprises are able to have different strategies for different segments or levels of the business, and likewise may deploy a segmented labour force with differentiated contracts of employment to reflect the different market circumstances. This permits a pluralist view of the firm, rather than the often implied assumption that strategy will be accepted by a homogeneous workforce adopting a unitary frame of reference. It allows for

LOW COST AIRLINES: BUSINESS MODEL AND EMPLOYMENT RELATIONS

the possibility of response to competitive pressures by selective contingent contractual arrangements (de-layering, right-sizing, outsourcing or contingent labour). Thus a high commitment strategy for HR need not be applied to the whole labour force, but only to the strategic core. A resource based view of strategy (Barney, 1991) permits variation in the business models used by competing firms, rather than the notion that there is a unique best practice model to which those who wish to survive in the longer term will have to conform. Instead, firms able to identify, develop and deploy distinctive and difficult to replicate competitive advantages or core competencies can enjoy flexibility and highly effective performance, and dynamic capabilities (Teece and David (2000): 'the ability to sense and then seize new opportunities, and reconfigure and protect knowledge assets, competences and complementary assets and technologies to achieve sustainable competitive advantage' (p 26). Businesses will, however, be path dependent – not all choices will be available to the firm at a point of time, and strategic choice will be influenced by its historic path and the way in which its strategy and strategic resources have been built up. Boxall also draws a distinction in employment strategy between <u>human capital advantage</u> (recruiting and retaining outstanding human talent, able to be used to exploit opportunities) and <u>human process advantage</u> (fostering learning, cooperation and innovation). In the last resort a firm's labour advantage may be seen as a product of these two forms of advantage, but individual firms may tend to concentrate on one rather than the other at any phase of its development.

With such a framework in mind, how can we use this to tease out some of the likely differences between the FSC and LCC sectors of the air travel market? As a first step it may be helpful to identify a list of alternative HR/employment relations practices or strategies, as in Table 2:

We can take as our starting point the main strategic distinction between FSC and LCC types – the former pursuing differentiation, the latter cost leadership. That would immediately suggest that *rewards* would be lower in the LCC, reflected in some combination of lower basic pay, more extended working hours, and lower vacation and leave arrangements. This might also suggest a lower *trade union presence*, assuming unions are able to negotiate a share of corporate rent in the form of a union differential: the FSCs on the other hand, as major employers, many with national carrier responsibilities, would be more likely to recognise and bargain terms and conditions with appropriate unions.[7] More problematic is the use of *contingent labour*. On the one hand, the opportunity to reduce costs by employment of flexible labour might seem to be more attractive to the low cost operations, but this may also be appropriate to the FSCs with more extensive ground services. The alternative, of course, is to *outsource* non-core activi-

Table 2 Alternative HR/employment Relations Strategy Elements

Type of element	Policy/practice alternatives
Culture/philosophy	Unitarist/Pluralist
Work organisation	High commitment/control or compliance
	High trust/low trust
	Human process advantage/human capital advantage
	High/low use of outsourcing
	High division of labour/job or task flexibility
Employment contract	High/low weekly hours
	Regular or contingent contract
Effort/Rewards	High/low basic pay
	Hours of work high/low
	Paid leave or holiday entitlement high/low
	Contingent pay or not (e.g. profit sharing, performance related pay, etc.)
Union stance	Union recognition/non-union
	Formal collective bargaining or not
	Alternative forms of employee voice (consultation, works committees, etc.)

ties, and as already noted, the LCCs outsource many of their ground services (see Table 3).

The issue is further complicated by the respective approaches to *work organisation*. There may be some presumption that the FSCs will tend to adopt a developed form of division of labour and task specialisation, given the generally larger scale, longer history and a more extensive range of activities managed in-house. LCCs might therefore be expected to demand more functional flexibility and multi-tasking from their employees – which might be eased if indeed there is a lower level of union organisation. The expectation is that unions would support job specialisation and resist multi-skilling and tasking, to safeguard jobs and maintain pay for specialist job functions.

If these arguments are along the right lines, we would predict that the LCCs will be a more informal, less highly structured and more flexible form of organisation, perhaps therefore more inclined to operate on a *unitarist* philosophy, with a strong 'family' atmosphere among employees and between employees and managers. FSCs will tend to be more bureaucratised and mechanistic, reflecting larger scale, greater organisational complexity (from market segregation, route structure and more complex coordination requirements), pointing to a *compliance* model of employment relations rather than a *high commitment* model. This is not to say, of course, that the FSCs will be blind to the attractions promised through a high commitment, high trust route to high performance. Teamworking, quality management, workgroup autonomy and bottom up involvement in decision taking, key distinctive elements in the

LOW COST AIRLINES: BUSINESS MODEL AND EMPLOYMENT RELATIONS

Table 3 Hypothetical HR Policies Compared: LCC and FSC Models

Policy/practice alternatives	LCC Model	FSC Model	Comment
Unitarist/Pluralist	Unitarist	Pluralist	Some ambiguity here?
High commitment/control or compliance	Commitment	Compliance	
High trust/low trust	High trust	Desirable but hard to achieve	
Human process advantage/human capital advantage	Human process	Human capital	Elements of both likely to be found but variation in emphasis.
High/low use of outsourcing	High use	Moderate use	
High division of labour/job or task flexibility	High flexibility	Specialisation	
High/low weekly hours	Higher hours	Lower hours	
Regular or contingent contract	More contingent	Some contingent but lower	Employment security was badly affected by the post 9/11 downturn in air travel and substantial layoffs: 4/6 US mainline carriers are in bankruptcy protection and layoffs continue.
High/low basic pay	Lower pay	Higher pay	
Hours of work high/low	Higher	Lower	
Paid leave or holiday entitlement high/low	Lower	Higher	
Contingent pay or not (e.g. profit sharing, performance related pay, etc.)	Profit sharing (e.g. original Southwest Airlines model)	??	A priori arguments for and against this ambiguous
Union recognition/non-union	Less unionised	More unionised	
Collective bargaining	Less likely	More likely	But note that SWA adopted union recognition and collective bargaining in the seminal LCC model
Alternative forms of employee voice (consultation, upward communication)	More likely	Some, probably formalised through unions (e.g. works councils)	

high performance workplace paradigm, may be desirable but more difficult to achieve in a hierarchical context with a complex workforce with different goals and interests in the employment relationship: in effect a more *pluralist* form of organisation. We would probably expect, nonetheless, that the FSCs would make some efforts in these directions, but with their history of stability might possibly find it hard to achieve adaptation to change and to build and sustain the requisite levels of trust. (Hill and Rothaermel, 2003).

Finally, with respect to the choice between human capital and human process advantage, our expectation would be that the FSCs would be more inclined to emphasise human capital advantage, and the LCCs more the labour process advantage (though the outcome will depend on their cumulative effect and neither can be ignored). As we have argued, the LCCs will be more dependent on informal and flexible working arrangements, which will require more fluid communications across job and functional boundaries, a cooperative spirit and (probably implied) a higher degree of trust in employee relations. In contrast, the needs of the more specialised labour force, more mechanistic structures and rou-

tines, and divergent occupational interests seem more likely to edge in the direction of depending on acquiring and developing high skilled, high quality labour capable of delivering the quality of service expected by the main customer base.

Comment

This preliminary view is speculative and in some cases the categorisation is ambiguous and in need of further examination, preferably with the help of additional data. However, there is some suggestion of a differentiated profile on the basis of *a priori* reasoning. It is also clear, however, that in addition to some ambiguity in matching the airline types with policy alternatives, there is likely to be some variation within each of the airline types: competitive differentiation in the two models is almost certain to produce different philosophy and practices, and country institutions and regulations may themselves shape some aspects of policy. This suggests the possibility of a 'some frills' model[8] which could be used either by the LCCs or the FSCs: a middle ground with frill features selected in such a way as to offer prospects of market extension and profit growth. Indeed it is to be expected that such a development will occur as the newer LCCs achieve maturity and look to grow further in an increasingly saturated market segment, while the FSCs seek to take a share of the low cost operators' market. However, it should be noted that Alamdari and Fagan (2005) present evidence suggesting that the adoption of a 'some frills' strategy does not necessarily achieve higher profit margins than their rivals, and that adherence to the original low-cost paradigm may well be the most profitable option.

Preliminary Evidence

It is expected that empirical information on the variables discussed in the two previous sections will become available in more detail from the second phase of the MIT Global Airlines Industry study. Differences between airlines and between global regions or countries will almost certainly be discovered. However, it is possible to report some preliminary empirical evidence relating to the hypotheses of Section 3. Much of this is based on the ITF survey (2002), reported by researchers working on behalf of the International Transport Workers Federation (ITF), which at least reduces the possibility of employer bias. The survey covered 21 countries and 30 airlines. For brevity the findings are reported in bullet points:

❖ A large majority of LCCs offer poorer pay and working conditions compared with FSCs (estimated at between 5% and 40%). The few cases that match FSCs seem likely to be where a new carrier is created within an existing mainline company (the carrier–within–carrier model).

❖ Monthly block hours for aircrew and for ground staff are respectively 10–35% and 10–20% higher than in FSCs: Days off and vacation entitlement are reduced by 5–20% relative to the FSC.

❖ ITF affiliated unions have gained or retained recognition in 70% of the low cost airlines studied, using legal rights of organisation and traditional methods. In some cases, however, recognition is limited (some countries or some categories of employees). Some airlines, like Ryanair, have adopted a deliberate non-union stance though this has come under pressure recently (c.f. Wallace et al., 2006). It is not known if airport employees and subcontract handling and maintenance agents are unionised.

❖ A majority of recruits to the LCCs come from jobs in the aviation industry, many of them already members of relevant unions.

❖ A majority of LCCs employ a mix of approximately equal numbers of workers on unlimited contracts and on fixed term contracts.

❖ Management in LCCs seems to have created a special 'company atmosphere' by emphasising the 'us against the others' mentality, so that loyalty is built to the employer. Paternalistic methods are employed to support loyalty and to

some extent 'underdog' community spirit. More detailed case study evidence exists on this for airlines such as Southwest, JetBlue, easyJet, etc.

More generally, a number of FSCs have reacted to the presence of a successful LCC either by developing a lower cost model while still retaining the essential features of the full service airline or setting up a separate low cost airline. Aer Lingus provide an example of the former, while Qantas's creation of Jetstar as a competitor to the low cost Virgin Blue in Australia comes into the latter category. As Wallace et al. (2006) observe, Aer Lingus appears to have made a good recovery from the 9/11 events, through cost reductions, the addition of new point to point routes to increase passenger numbers and associated redundancies and re-structuring, but still faces major challenges in terms of its future ownership and industrial relations. Qantas on the other hand established Jetstar as a direct competitor to Virgin Blue (Bamber et al., 2006). Both the LCCs have been based on strong brands and perhaps because of this have moved into the 'some frills' market, targeting part of the corporate market, and interestingly, both have opted for a high customer service high workforce commitment model to support this. However, while Virgin Blue have committed to union recognition, Jetstar appear to be following a union avoidance strategy. The evidence from these cases and elsewhere strongly suggests the tendency to convergence into the 'some frills' arena, with the choice being governed by a mix or market structure, the degree of independence from the parent company and decisions about the labour model they want to pursue.

Conclusions

In general, our expectations are reasonably well supported by the evidence so far. However, although pay and working conditions generally follow prediction, unionisation is higher than expected in LCCs (possibly explained by the start-up LCCs recruiting staff from the FSCs, where they were already unionised); and half the workforce enjoys regular (unlimited) rather than contingent contracts. The overall picture, however would seem to support the general proposition that the LCCs would be more flexible and entrepreneurial, and therefore better equipped to respond to opportunities – and to change and/or market shocks (such as 9/11—though in fairness it should be pointed out that the national 'flag' airlines were more likely to be terrorist targets).

On the down side, the lower pay and conditions offered by the LCCs might be suggestive of an exploitative employment contract (though we have no comparison of the respective human capital profiles on which to judge). This might be reflected in higher turnover rates in the LCCs[9] and lower job satisfaction or low morale. But against this, we have the evidence of a paternalistic approach on the part of at least some LCCs and (following the pioneering Southwest model based on careful recruitment of staff with the right attitudes for *this* airline) a strong loyalty and high commitment (as for example in Virgin Blue). In other words, there may be a fairly complex set of influences at work here within the psychological contract, where somewhat lower pay and conditions are balanced by other positive factors in the implicit contract: this might include the (unexpected) high level of unionisation, providing an outlet for employee voice) or a high level of employee loyalty. That would tend to support the unitarist thesis, in contrast to the FSCs, where recent evidence from airlines such as British Airways and Aer Lingus [10] suggests greater conflict in the employment relation (disputes, strikes and other industrial action affecting different groups of staff).

We have noted earlier the response of some of the FSCs to the LCC challenge, by either setting up their own low cost alternative (carrier within carrier) or adapting their own model to borrow some of the key characteristics of the LCCs. The evidence on this indicates (a) that the carrier within carrier model is rarely successful since the operational structure and high service culture do not sit easily in the no-frills paradigm: (b) the cost discrepancy cannot be made up by marginal adjustment to the basic FSC model, so that although costs have been cut the cost advantage is still sizeable. Real cost savings are more likely to be made by major staff cuts and economies in sub-contract arrangements – but these will tend to reinforce the compliance tendency of the FSCs, increase concerns about employment security, reduce trust and generate grievances and a confrontational rather than cooperative employment relationship. As yet, however, the development of the 'some frills' market is in its infancy and there is little doubt that further innovation and experimentation will take place in the near future.

Notes

1. A third sector – the chartered airlines – is also present, but is not considered for the present purpose.
2. For further helpful discussion of alternative models, see Doganis (2001).
3. FSCs face direct competition from LCCs on only 4% of their routes (6% of capacity): Binggeli and Pompeo, 2005.
4. For some evidence on customer preferences, see O'Connell and Williams (2005).
5. The companion papers in this journal issue provide some of this analysis from differing perspectives.

6. This summary needs some revision and refinement but ay serve as a platform for the initial exploration.
7. We should note however that Southwest Airlines, the pioneering LCC, opted for straightforward union recognition and in that sense unionisation could be seen as a core element in pure LCCs.
8. This variant is described as the 'New World Carrier' model, Bamber *et al.* (2006).
9. Evidence on this should emerge from the MIT global airlines industry study.
10. See for example: the BA case study in Blyton and Turnbull (2004), Wallace *et al.* (2006) on Aer Lingus.

References

Alamdari, F. and Fagan, S. (2005) Impact of the adherence to the original low-cost model on the profitability of low-cost airlines. *Transport Reviews* **25**(3), 377–392.

Alderighi, M., Cento, A., Nijkamp, P. and Rietveld, P. (2004) The entry of low cost airlines, tinbergen institute discussion paper 074/3.

Bamber, G., Lansbury, R.D., Rainthorpe, K. and Yazbeck, (2006) Low-cost airlines' product and labour-market strategic choices: Towards' new world carriers' in Australia (paper presented at Labor and Employment Relations Association 58th annual meeting, Boston).

Barney, J. (1991) Firm resources and sustained competitive advantage. *Journal of Management* **17**(1), 99–120.

Binggeli, U. and Pompeo, L. (2005) The battle for Europe's low-fare flyers, McKinsey Quarterly (web exclusive, August).

Blyton, P. and Turnbull, P. (2004) The Dynamics of Employee Relations. 3rd edition. Houndmills, Macmillan–Palgrave.

Boxall, P. (1999) The Strategic HRM debate and the resource-based view of the firm (reprinted as Chapter 4). In *Strategic Human Resource Management*, (eds) R.S. Schuler and S.E. Jackson, pp. 73–89. Blackwell, Oxford.

Doganis, R. (2001) *The Airline Business in the 21st Century*. Routledge, London.

Hill, C.W.L. and Rothaermel, F.T. (2003) The Performance of incumbent firms in the face of radical technological innovation. *Academy of Management Review* **28**(2), 257–274.

ITF (2002) ITF Survey: The Industrial Landscape of Low Cost Carriers, London.

O'Connell, J.F. and Williams, G. (2005) Passengers' perceptions of low cost airlines and full service carriers: a case study involving Ryanair, Aer Lingus, Air Malaysia and Malaysian Airlines. *Journal of Air Transport Management* **11**(4), 259–272.

Purcell, J. and Alhstrand, B. (1994) *Human Resource Management in the Multi-divisional Company*. Oxford University Press, Oxford.

Teece and David, J. (2000) Managing Intellectual Capital: Oxford University Press, Oxford.

Wallace, J., Tiernan, S. and White, L. (2006) Industrial relations conflict and collaboration: Adapting to a low fares business model in Aer Lingus (companion paper in this issue).

25

Employment Relations, Management Style and Flight Crew Attitudes at Low Cost Airline Subsidiaries:
The Cases of British Airways/Go and bmi/bmibaby

GERAINT HARVEY
PETER TURNBULL

In response to the challenge of low costs airlines, several full service carriers (FSCs) around the world have created their own low cost subsidiary. In the UK, two successful examples of this strategy are bmibaby (bmi) and Go (British Airways). To compete with their low cost rivals, these subsidiaries need to create a similar low cost employment system and human resource management policies to support this system, which will be very different from that of the parent company. More importantly, in a 'customer facing' industry such as civil aviation, how staff respond to these management practices will have a crucial bearing on the success (or otherwise) of the airline. In this paper we assess the degree of decentralization of employment relations to subsidiary management at both airlines; we discern the man- agement style towards flight crew at the low cost subsidiaries; and finally, we analyse the response of flight crew to the management style adopted. © 2006 Elsevier Ltd. All rights reserved.

Keywords: Industrial relations, Employment rela- tions, Management style, Airlines, Civil aviation, Low cost, Subsidiary, Decentralisation, Pilots, Employee attitudes

Introduction

Progressive liberalization of the civil aviation indus- try in the UK and Europe, throughout the 1980s and

European Management Journal Vol. 24, No. 5, pp. 330–337, October 2006

1990s, encouraged a host of new entrant airlines to compete with full service carriers (FSCs) (Vlaar *et al.*, 2005). Airlines were no longer required to demonstrate financial fitness in order to operate, nor did they need to gain permission to reduce fares. Lower fares, pioneered by the new entrant airlines such as Ryanair and easyJet, placed considerable pressure on other airlines to reduce costs. Given that the new entrant low cost airlines operate, on average, at just 43% of FSCs' operating costs, it is hardly surprising that they have flourished while established airlines struggle. For example, in the immediate aftermath of September 11th, Ryanair had a stock market valuation of £1.8 billion (in 2002), some £30 million more than British Airways (BA). While FSCs such as BA reported significant financial losses post-2001, Ryanair and easyJet reported healthy profits. In Europe, the anticipated growth rate for FSCs is now dwarfed by the expected growth of the low cost carriers (ECA, 2002, 12).

In response to the low cost phenomenon, several FSCs created their own low cost subsidiary, including British Airway's Go and bmi's bmibaby. While this strategy enabled FSCs to compete head on with low cost new entrants, it is not without inherent difficulties. For example, how will the new subsidiary affect the 'brand' of the FSC? How, and to what extent, can management 'ring fence' the pay and conditions of low cost subsidiary employees – after all, if FSC wage rates and other conditions of employment were adopted there would be little or no cost advantage – and will the subsidiary airline be able to develop a distinctive 'management style' to support the low cost strategy? Crucially, how will this (new) style of management be perceived by airline staff, and how will it affect their commitment to the organization and the airline's ability to deliver an appropriate 'flight experience' for passengers?

We address these questions, first, by reviewing the constraints and (strategic) choices that management face when determining an appropriate 'style' for employee relations and human resource management within subsidiary operations. In particular, will a centralised strategy prevail under centripetal pressures or will subsidiary management be able to harness centrifugal forces to differentiate their chosen style from that of the FSC? We then examine two low cost subsidiaries established by FSCs, namely bmibaby and Go, utilising data from the first major study of British flight crew since Blain's (1972) study more than 30 years ago (Harvey, 2004). As pilots are a pivotal employee group for any airline, but a rather esoteric profession, we offer a brief review of their work and conditions of employment before exploring their attitudes to work and management at the new low cost subsidiaries. In both these cases, in addition to the comparatively high cost of employment at the parent (legacy) company, there is a 'legacy' of adversarial industrial relations that might permeate the management style of the new low cost

subsidiary. Under these circumstances, there is a premium on centrifugal forces and the development of a distinctive management style. Where management was able to harness these forces, as in the case of Go, pilots displayed a more positive attitude to their work and the management of the airline.

Subsidiary Employment Relations and Management Style

The extent to which authority is devolved to units within the divisional firm and the extent of subsidiary autonomy is an important determinant of employee relations and organizational performance (Ferner *et al.*, 2004). The nature and extent of any devolution will be influenced by a range of structural factors, such as the size of the subsidiary relative to that of the parent company, the import of the subsidiary to the performance of the parent, the age of the subsidiary, and whether it is a green-field or brown-field site (e.g. Edwards *et al.*, 1993) as well as a variety of strategic factors that have been classified as either centripetal or centrifugal pressures on employee relations (Kinnie, 1987). The centripetal pressures include the desire to exclude trade unions from business strategy decisions (i.e. limiting any union influence to the local level, thereby allowing head office greater autonomy); the need to centrally control certain employee-related costs, such as pensions, which have implications throughout the organization; and the need to ensure some kind of consistency of practice to avoid anomalies within different divisions or subsidiaries that might lead to comparability or other claims (ibid, 473-4). For FSCs establishing a low cost subsidiary, there will clearly be a desire to 'localise' any trade union influence, but this will be part of a strategy to 'isolate' rather than 'integrate' the subsidiary. In particular, the imperative of securing significantly lower labour costs puts a premium on centrifugal rather than centripetal forces.

The centrifugal forces that encourage the devolution of employment relations to local management are twofold (Kinnie, 1987, 475). First, it may be more advantageous to allow local management to decide on those policies that affect the local level and of which they have greater awareness than central management. Secondly, so as to ensure institutional separation, local managers should be seen to act autonomously. This will reinforce the perception that local management have discretion in other strategic decision-making areas. In particular, the degree of decentralization of employment relations authority has implications for the 'management style' at the subsidiary. In general, 'while management style is most likely to be set at corporate level it could in some firms be determined at intermediate and local levels' (Purcell, 1987, 544). For the low cost subsidiaries of FSCs, this autonomy to determine management style is crucial.

Purcell's (1987) concept of management style refers to the choices made and the underlying rationale for the way in which management treats its employees. It infers a 'distinctive set of guiding principles, written or otherwise, which set parameters to and signposts for management action in the way employees are treated and particular events handled' (ibid, 535). Management style may be assessed in terms of individualism and collectivism. Purcell describes individualism as 'the extent to which the firm gives credence to the feelings and sentiments of each employee and seeks to develop and encourage each employee's capacity and role at work' (ibid, 536). This notion of individualism reflects key facets of HR practice, such as 'internal labour markets with careful selection at restricted points of entry, internal training schemes, promotion ladders and extensive welfare provisions' (ibid).

Collectivism in management style is defined as 'the extent to which the organisation recognises the rights of employees to have a say in those aspects of management decision making which concerns them' (ibid, 538). Thus, collectivism reflects the extent to which management recognise the collective interests of employees, their collective involvement in the decision making processes and the legitimacy accorded the collective by management. Although typically associated with trade union representation, Purcell notes that high levels of collectivism in management style can be also be manifest in non-union firms (e.g. in the legitimacy afforded by management to such representative mechanisms as works councils) (ibid, 539). Consequently, the essence of collectivism is the 'approach of management in operating these joint structures. Do they seek to minimise or oppose them or actively co-operate with them?' (ibid, 538). This is crucial because the simple act of trade union recognition or the existence of a works council may offer a false indication of the collectivism in management style. Indeed, as Purcell observes,

In many cases unions have fought to be recognised against management's wishes and labour law is important in some countries in imposing requirements on firms to deal with work councils or recognise trade unions. Given the existence of collective employee organisations, management can however choose the extent to which they legitimise, *de facto*, the collective and joint structures of negotiation and consultation (ibid, 539).

On this basis, Purcell (1987, 541) plots the degree of collectivism in management style along a continuum from unitarism, through adversarialism, towards co-operation.

Within the subsidiaries of multi-divisional firms, distinctive management styles often prevail (ibid, 544). Divergence from the corporate approach appears to depend largely on 'the type of product and product markets' (ibid, 545). Technology and the skill level of the dominant group(s) of staff are also important

variables (ibid). This is nowhere better illustrated than in relation to the management of flight crew at the low cost subsidiaries of FSCs. Before exploring our two case studies in more detail, the impact of pilots' skills and the nature of the low cost product market are briefly reviewed.

The Airline Pilot

The airline pilot is an atypical employee who poses a particular challenge to management as a result of two features of the pilot's work: their substantial bargaining power and the disincentive for a pilot to leave an airline. As Johnson (2002, 22) points out, pilots possess 'strategic skills' as – technically and legally – no airline can fly aircraft without a pilot. The low substitutability of airline pilots is the result of both general and specific skills: the former derive from the extensive experience (700 hours flying) that all pilots must have before qualifying for a commercial pilots licence, having also passed the Air Law examination and an Instrument Rating Flight Test (Eaton, 2001, 100), while the latter derive from the standard operating procedures of the specific airline (which differ from one carrier to the next). As a result, the replacement of pilots during a strike is virtually impossible (Johnson, 2002, 22), and any disruption will of course have an immediate impact on the airline (as the product cannot be 'stockpiled'). As Chris Darke, the former General Secretary of the British Air Line Pilots' Association (BALPA) was keen to point out, pilots enjoy 'unrivalled' bargaining power:

I'm not saying that other groups of people can't effect, by strike, influence over their employer, but there aren't many that can have that immediate, absolute effect. Pilots can (interview notes, August 2001).

The second peculiarity of the work of flight crew arises from the disincentive for pilots to leave their employer. As Cappelli (1985, 332) notes of pilots in the USA, the skills learned and utilised by airline pilots have little or no transferability in alternative employment, outside of flying aircraft, but more important is the binding effect of seniority rules. This limits movement between airlines as well as occupations, as any transfer to another carrier would result in the loss of seniority rights, with consequent loss of roster privileges and a sharp pay cut. The advantage to management, of course, is that they can invest in pilot training without the fear of losing human capital to a rival carrier. This is not to suggest that pilots are modern-day vassals – flight crew turnover at easyJet, for example, was recently estimated to be around 10% (BALPA February 2004) – rather to highlight the fact that when employees are reluctant to exit they are more likely to exercise voice (Hirschman, 1970; Freeman and Medoff, 1984). Pilots have a deserved reputation for being highly vociferous.

As already noted in this issue (Hunter, 2006), it is anticipated that pay, benefits and other conditions of employment will be inferior at low cost airlines. For pilots, this is indeed the case. For example, low cost airline pilots fly on average 210 days per annum, whereas FSC pilots fly on average only 184 days per annum (ECA, 2002, 7). Superior utilization is one reason why salary costs as a proportion of total operating costs are much lower at low cost airlines, but basic salaries are also much lower. On average, low cost airline pilot salaries are 27% less than their FSC counterparts (ibid, 5). In addition, there is a significantly larger variable component of the low cost airline pilot's remuneration, which is usually contingent on the number of flights (or sectors) the pilot flies. The average variable component for First Officers flying with FSCs is around 5% compared to 18% for First Officers flying with low cost airlines. The respective figures for Captains are 8% and 20% (ibid).

The 'low cost service' of low cost airlines is 'matched by', or more accurately is 'constructed upon', low cost employment policies. But this need not consign the low cost airline to a 'traditional' or 'adversarial' management style. In fact, as both bmibaby and Go sought to bring a higher quality service to the low cost market, both airlines were conscious of the need to develop 'high quality relationships'[1] with key employee groups, most notably pilots. However, where centripetal forces prevailed, as at bmibaby, this proved far more problematic than where centrifugal forces held sway, as at Go. Whereas bmibaby was saddled with the legacy of adversarial industrial relations and a confrontational management style, Go was able to develop a more cooperative management style.

Bmibaby – Centred on Adversarialism

bmi commenced passenger services as Derby Aviation in 1949. In 1964 the airline moved its base to the East Midlands Airport and changed its name to British Midland Airways. In 1978, a team of directors, led by Michael Bishop, purchased a principal shareholding in the airline. British Midland (as it was then known after a name change in 1986) was the first airline in the UK to offer a booking service with payment over the internet. The airline joined the Star Alliance of international carriers in July 2000 and Lufthansa acquired a 30% stake in the airline. In February 2001, the airline was re-branded as British Midland International (bmi) in preparation for its alliance with United Airlines and the commencement of its transatlantic service (operating scheduled flights to Washington DC and Chicago). Just one year later a low cost subsidiary, bmibaby, was announced (January 2002). Thus, the BMI Group represents a multi-specialist carrier (Binggeli and Pompeo, 2002) in that it operates several specialized airlines under the bmi brand: bmi mainline, bmi regional and bmibaby.

Advertised as the UK's second largest full service airline, bmi currently holds 12% of take-off and landing slots at London Heathrow; operates 1,700 flights per week with a fleet of 41 jet aircraft; and flies to 25 destinations in ten countries. The airline has traditionally competed on service quality, receiving over 50 industry awards since 1990 (www.bmi.com). It has received twelve consecutive awards for best UK domestic service, and in May 2002 the airline received a maximum rating from *Business Traveller* magazine for its London to Washington service. Indeed, the airline markets itself as an innovator and a quality service provider and is actively involved in the implementation of industry standards for passenger care, called Airline Passenger Service Commitments (APSC).

The competitive strategy of bmibaby reflects that of the mainline carrier, emphasising quality of service where other low costs airlines such as easyJet and Ryanair have simply stripped it out. The airline's website allows passengers to change their booking and reserve seats on-line. In 3 years of operations, the low cost brand increased its passenger numbers to over 3 million and has won the *Daily Telegraph* award for best low cost airline each year. In 2004, a joint marketing deal was agreed with Germanwings, a low cost airline in which Lufthansa has a major stake, further strengthening the relationship between the German flag carrier and bmi.

Although senior managers within the BMI Group have commented that authority for the subsidiary was devolved entirely to the local management level (interview notes, November 2005) employee relations at all three airlines within the BMI Group are still determined centrally, with a single HR function responsible for all bmi employees. Under centralised direction, bmi mainline pilots were offered 'inferior contracts' (specifically longer hours of work) with bmibaby at a time when the Group had just announced 600 redundancies. As a spokesperson for the company commented at the time, recruitment difficulties were 'not anticipated' at the new subsidiary.

Under the direction of the corporate HR department, management claim to have implemented a 'full complement' of so-called best practice HRM (e.g. extensive consultation and flexible work practices), but a survey of pilots undertaken in 2002 revealed only 'sparse' recognition of these policies amongst flight crew at bmi.[2] More telling, the survey revealed considerable dissatisfaction with the relationship between management and flight crew throughout the BMI Group.[3] Dissatisfaction with other aspects of employment was also evident, as reported in Table 1.

In less guarded moments, bmi managers acknowledge that senior management have, at times, displayed a 'horrendous attitude towards pilots'

Table 1 Flight Crew Satisfaction at bmi

Aspect of Work	% Dissatisfied	% Satisfied
Salary	22	78
Pension	10	90
Leave entitlement	6	94
Sickness benefits	4	96
Access to flight manager	32	68
Disciplinary procedures	32	62
Status	42	58
Job security	73	27
Relationship (flight crew and management)	88	12
Management of human relations problems	71	27
Management of industrial relations problems	94	5
Flight rosters	84	16

$n = 95$.

(quoted by Harvey, 2004). Some of the additional comments made by respondents to the 2002 survey of flight crew illustrate a level of enmity between management and flight crew:

I work for a very good airline in many ways (safety, training, customer satisfaction). But the way employees are treated is terrible. Industrial relations are at an all time low. There is no trust between pilots and management. We are blamed for much of the company's inept management. 9/11 has been used as an excuse, and the way HR issues have been handled during redundancy/restructuring has been without compassion. (First Officer QRN 145)[4]

...the customer perceives pilots as highly trained and respected professionals, whereas the management view pilots as whinging encumbrances, who are overpaid and a drain on the company. (First Officer, QRN 212)

What is the point of having a working partnership with management when any agreements that they sign (in writing from ops director) are NOT honoured? Where are we going as an industry when flight crew don't have any trust in management agreements? (Captain, QRN 662)

Trade union officials corroborated pilots' claim that bmi management still follow an adversarial management style across all three component airlines within the group. In fact, bmi members of the British Air Line Pilots' Association (BALPA) were balloted for industrial action in 2004 and in 2005 rejected a pay deal offered by the company. Managements' response was to unilaterally impose the new pay structure for pilots (interview notes, October 2005). Frustration with this management policy was again illustrated when BALPA threatened strike action on behalf of its unionised members at bmibaby in 2006. In response to a more recent survey conducted by BALPA in early 2004, 65% of respondents at bmi indicated that they did not believe that they would be working for the airline in the foreseeable future.

Go – Devolving Co-operation

Go commenced operations on 22nd May 1998 and became a highly profitable airline within barely 4 years. Passenger numbers increased by 41% over this period and pre-tax profits rose by 51% to £16.9 million in the 6 months leading up to 30th September 2001. Go was sold soon after Rod Eddington took the helm of BA in 2000. Believing that Go represented an image that the British flag carrier would rather eschew, and in recognition that that its low cost subsidiary was competing with BA's own short haul service, Go was bought out by its senior management team, backed by venture capital group 3i, in June 2001 for £110 million. One year later (August 2002) the airline was acquired by easyJet for £374 million.

Former chief executive, Barbara Cassani, defined the Go brand as 'energetic, passionate and tenacious' (quoted in *Marketing*, August 31st 2000), attributing the success of the firm to a combination of low prices and being able to 'surprise customers with the service and the way the whole experience feels' (*ibid*). Cassani described this approach as the '3X + Y formula', whereby '3X means all the basics done cheaply and simply' and the 'Y' is for the quality surprises to which the customer would be treated (Cassani and Kemp, 2003, 94). For example, cafetiere coffee was served on flights; more 'flexible' tickets were made available to passengers with assigned seating to eradicate the 'free-for-all' onboard other low cost airlines; and free city guide brochures of the destination were offered to customers. The quality of service marked Go's strategy of differentiation. The airline competed not merely on tariff, but also by offering the customer a comfortable experience. In doing so, the airline was more appealing to the business traveller. Go was voted the best low cost airline by *Business Traveller* in October 2001.

Thus, wherever and whenever feasible, the airline supplemented its low cost strategy with service quality, a strategy which set it apart from its low cost competitors in the UK. Whereas Ryanair and easyJet were committed to an austere 'no frills' approach, Go emphasised quality as well as cost – hence it is *low* frills as opposed to *no* frills. As Korczynski (2002, 15) amongst others notes, where there is intense competition there is increased necessity for firms to compete simultaneously on lower costs *and* service quality, as 'customers can increasingly now aim to settle for correct and efficient service outcomes, with a favourable service process as well' (see also Blyton and Turnbull, 1995). In the intense competitive market for air transport, Go's strategy offered higher 'customer value' (Heskett et al., 1997).

Whereas management at other low cost airlines such as easyJet likened their pilots to bus drivers (Rigby, 1997, 52), to the detriment of flight crew commitment

EMPLOYMENT RELATIONS, MANAGEMENT STYLE AND FLIGHT CREW ATTITUDES AT LOW COST AIRLINE

(Harvey, 2004),[5] Cassani avoided a similar *faux pas* when BA's low cost subsidiary was being named. A London design agency charged with developing the brand of the new airline offered the names 'Go' and 'The Bus'. Cassani refused the latter because it conveyed the wrong image for the company (Cassani and Kemp, 2003, 90). Although her decision about the name of the airline had little to do with possible ramifications for relationship between management and staff, Cassani was well aware of the detrimental effect that a poor relationship with employees generally, and flight crew specifically, would have. An early addition to the airline's senior management team was Ed Winter, a former Chief Pilot with British Airways and veteran of 'tough industrial relations' bargaining with flight crew (Cassani and Kemp, 2003, 51). Consequently, there was a concerted effort to develop a (collectivist) management style based on mutuality and co-operation rather than adversarialism, contrary to the prevailing pattern of industrial relations at BA (Blyton and Turnbull, 2004, 91-9 and Colling, 1995). From its inception, the airline recognized several unions for the purpose of collective bargaining including BALPA.

In the preliminary development of Go, senior management generated a 'what-not-to-do' list, elaborated by Cassani in her retrospective on the company. Flight crew featured heavily in these 'guidelines':

Develop an antagonistic relationship with unions and allow poor employee morale to eat away at your organisation. *No thanks, I'd seen enough of that in the US airline industry* (Cassani and Kemp, 2003, 43).

Run the airline in compartments so one part has no idea what's going on anywhere else. Make sure your pilots never meet or talk to commercial people. And vice versa. *My personal bete noire (ibid, 44).*

Hire pilots and not pay attention to their personalities – pilots just fly planes and cabin crew should be hired for good looks, shouldn't they? *Sorry but no; this one really winds me up (ibid).*

When recruiting flight crew at the airline, management focused on evaluating pilots on the merits of their skills outside of technical competency. Pilots were assessed on whether they would be comfortable with the Go philosophy and management style, a process that was far from easy (*ibid*, 123). As Cassani later reflected,

In our interviews we wanted to find out what kind of people they were. Many pilots are not accustomed to being interviewed at trendy ad agencies. These interviews were a signal that we wanted flexible people, as much as skilled pilots. Ed [Winter] and I agreed we wanted pilots to become involved and learn about the whole business, and not to work in cliques. Even during the times when qualified 737 trained pilots were at their most scarce, we turned away people who wouldn't fit in. In some airlines, pilots become too domineering, creating tension with other colleagues and management … I rejected the first captain

we interviewed because she was too concerned about the perks and benefits she was hoping to get. It was a shame because it would have been a nice touch to hire a woman, but she could have poisoned the place with comments about how much better everything was in traditional airlines (*ibid*).

Although centripetal forces were not entirely absent – Cassani points out that 'Initially we recognised unions at Bob Ayling's request to avoid industrial strife at British Airways [but] later we embraced the approach because we thought it right to give people the choice of being represented by a union' (Cassani and Kemp, 2003, 132) – centrifugal forces clearly held sway. This allowed Go to develop a management style that is perhaps best described as 'consultative' (as defined by Purcell, 1987), with a commitment to both individual employee needs and collective representation. Evidence of this approach at the airline is the Consultative Group which involved management, employee representatives and trade union representatives,

Through the Consultative Group, we included employees in important decisions and we shared how the business was doing – warts and all … We worked well together on the committee not because we had to but because we wanted Go to be successful and a good place to work. It just seemed like the right way to run a company' (Cassani and Kemp, 2003, 133).

Human resource management policies at Go were certainly well received by flight crew. In response to the survey of unionised UK pilots conducted in 2002 (Harvey, 2004), flight crew employed by Go reported widespread satisfaction with various aspects of their work. In fact, they were among the most satisfied pilots in the UK. Indicative data are reported in Table 2.

Table 2 Flight Crew Satisfaction at Go

Aspect of Work	% Dissatisfied	% Satisfied
Salary	4	96
Pension	56	33
Leave entitlement	26	74
Sickness benefits	22	74
Access to flight manager	0	100
Disciplinary procedures	4	92
Status	7	93
Job security	22	78
Relationship (flight crew and management)	19	81
Management of human relations problems	7	89
Management of industrial relations problems	11	85
Flight rosters	11	85

n = 27.

Several respondents at Go were moved to comment on the positive relationship between flight crew and management. For example:

I doubt many airlines have been set up, and run like "Go", but then no other airline had Barbara Cassani as a boss! Ask me the same questions in 12 months time under easy-Jet management, I do hope I will feel the same. (First Officer, QRN 415)

I was flying for Go when it was taken over by easyJet thus I am a reluctant easyJet pilot. Go was an excellent company under the leadership of Barbara Cassani (CEO Go). My answers to the above questions would have been very different had that still been the case. There is no doubt that the CEO of a company has a major impact on industrial and human relations. (Captain, QRN 1009)

Go sadly has now been bought by easyJet. While Cassani was in charge morale, enthusiasm, and loyalty were all at a high level. With the advent of the take-over people generally are much less enthusiastic about the future. (QRN 1142)

It has been the best work decision of my life to join Go ... There is a good flow of information between the management and the air crew – there is a real 'open door' policy and communication is easy with all the senior managers – leading to no 'us and them' atmosphere. Secondly, the rostering is absolutely fantastic – it is stable and the rosterers are human beings who will help to arrange duties around pilot lifestyles ... I just hope that this will remain when the company is integrated with easyJet. (First Officer, QRN 426)

At Go's parent (legacy) airline, the legacy of adversarial industrial relations lives on, despite a formal 'partnership agreement' between BA and BALPA (Blyton and Turnbull, 2004, 91-9 and Turnbull et al., 2004). With a flight crew community more than ten times the size of that of Go, managers at BA are more 'constrained' in their ability to deal with individuals

directly, although other large employers (Purcell, 1987) including several airlines (Gittell et al., 2004; Kochan et al., 2003) have been able to develop a distinctive form of individualism alongside high quality relationships with trade unions. At BA, however, in stark contrast to Go, there were much higher levels of dissatisfaction, as illustrated in Table 3.

Conclusion

Although a low cost product market strategy need not consign airlines to low cost (or 'low road') employment relations, for the subsidiary operations of FSCs it seems that high quality relationships (or 'high road' employment relations) are more likely where centrifugal rather than centripetal forces hold sway. In the former case, management at the low cost subsidiary has greater scope to forge a new and distinctive management style, and more importantly in the case of Go a style that was divorced from the adversarial relationships that have characterised management-labour relations at British Airways. Where centripetal forces prevail, as at bmibaby, the legacy of adversarialism lives on.

In both these cases, management sought to combine a low cost operating system with higher quality service (certainly in comparison to that offered by rival low cost airlines such as easyJet and Ryanair). Both carriers succeeded, but at bmibaby this was at the expense of flight crew commitment and job satisfaction. At Go, the new management team were arguably too successful for the parent company, competing for passengers on short haul routes with the BA brand behind them, but at much lower fares, with 'service surprises', and staff who were prepared to 'go the extra mile' for the customer. Go's acquisition by easyJet will imply further changes for the management of employee relations, and as with so many other UK companies that have grown through a process of merger and acquisition this may well spell the end of its distinctive and successful management style.

Notes

1. This phrase is widely used to describe the employment relations and HR policies of Southwest Airlines (e.g. Gittell et al., 2004; Kochan et al., 2003) one of the pioneers of the low cost model.
2. The questionnaire was mailed to 4,765 members of BALPA. A total of 1,451 pilots responded, from 24 different airlines (Harvey, 2004).
3. Only one-in-ten respondents employed by the three BMI Group airline operations were satisfied with the relationship between flight crew and management. As only a small number of bmibaby pilots responded to the survey, the data reported here refer to all flight crew employed by the BMI Group. However, there were no significant differences between bmibaby and bmi mainline pilots in terms of satisfaction with management-employee relations and other aspects of work and employment.

Table 3 Flight Crew Satisfaction at British Airways

Aspect of Work	% Dissatisfied	% Satisfied
Salary	66	34
Pension	28	72
Leave entitlement	9	91
Sickness benefits	18	81
Access to flight manager	23	76
Disciplinary procedures	61	35
Status	72	28
Job security	33	66
Relationship (flight crew and management)	74	26
Management of human relations problems	51	47
Management of industrial relations problems	85	15
Flight rosters	27	73

n = 395.

4. 'QRN' is simply the Questionnaire Respondent Number (based on the chronological order in which the questionnaire was returned).
5. easyJet pilots reported the lowest levels of job satisfaction and commitment of all BALPA members who responded to the survey.

References

Binggeli, U. and Pompeo, L. (2002) Hyped hopes for Europe's low cost airlines. *McKinsey Quarterly* **4**, 87–97.

Blain, A.N.J. (1972) *Pilots and Management*. George Allen & Unwin, London.

Blyton, P. and Turnbull, P. (1995) Growing turbulence in the European airline industry. *European Industrial Relations Review* 255(April), 14–16.

Blyton, P. and Turnbull, P. (2004) *The Dynamics of Employee Relations*. (3rd edition). Macmillan-Palgrave, Houndmills.

Cappelli, P. (1985) Competitive pressures and labor relations in the airline industry. *Industrial Relations* 25(4), 316–338.

Cassani, B. and Kemp, K. (2003) Go: *An Airline Adventure*. Time Warner Books, London.

Colling, T. (1995) Experiencing turbulence: competition, strategic choice and the management of human resources in british airways. *Human Resource Management Journal* 5(5), 18–32.

Eaton, J. (2001) *Globalisation and Human Resource Management in the Airline Industry*. Ashgate, Aldershot.

Edwards, P., Ferner, A. and Sisson, K. (1993). *People and the Process of management in the multinational company: A review with some illustrations. Warwick Papers in industrial Relations* 43. Industrial Relations Research Unit, Coventry.

European Cockpit Association Report, (2002) *Low Cost Carriers in the European Aviation Single Market*. Brussels.

Ferner, A., Almond, P., Clark, I., Colling, T., Holden, L., Edwards, T. and Muller-Camen, M. (2004) The dynamics of central control and subsidiary autonomy in the management of human resources: Case-study evidence from US MNCs in the UK. *Organization Studies* 25(3), 363–391.

Freeman, R.B. and Medoff, J.L. (1984) *What Do Unions Do?* Basic Books, New York.

Gittell, J.H., Von Nordenflycht, A. and Kochan, T. (2004) Mutual gains or zero sum? Labour relations and firm performance in the airline industry. *Industrial and Labour Relations Review* 57(2), 163–180.

Harvey, G. (2004) *The Management of Pilots*. PhD thesis, Cardiff University.

Heskett, J., Sasser, W. and Schlesinger, L. (1997) *The Profit Service Chain*. The Free Press, New York.

Hirschman, A.O. (1970) *Exit, Voice and Loyalty: Responses to Decline in Firms, Organizations and States*. Harvard University Press, Cambridge MA.

Hunter, L.C. (2006) Low cost airlines: Business model and employment relations. *European Management Journal* **24**, in press.

Johnson, N.B. (2002) Airlines: Can collective bargaining weather the storm? In *Collective Bargaining in the Private Sector*, (eds) P.F. Clark, J.T. Delaney and A.C. Frost, pp. 15–53. Industrial Relations Research Association Series, Illinois.

Kinnie, N. (1987) Bargaining within the Enterprise: Centralized or Decentralized? *Journal of Management Studies* 24(5), 463–477.

Kochan, T., von Nordenflycht, A., McKersie, R. and Gittell, J.H., (2003) Out of the ashes: Options for rebuilding airline labour relations. Institute for Work and Employment Research (IWER) Working Paper 04-2004.

Korczynski, M. (2002) *Human Resource Management in Service Work*. Palgrave, London.

Purcell, J. (1987) Mapping management styles in employment relations. *Journal of Management Studies* **24**(5), 533–548.

Rigby, R. (1997) Cheap and cheerful. *Management Today* **(August)**, 52–54.

Turnbull, P., Blyton, P. and Harvey, G. (2004) Cleared for take-off? Management-labour partnership in the european civil aviation industry. *European Journal of Industrial Relations* 10(3), 281–301.

Vlaar, P., de Vries, P. and Willenborg, M. (2005) Why incumbents struggle to extract value from new strategic options: Case of the European airline industry. *European Management Journal* 23(2), 54–169.

26

EMOTIONAL LABOUR AND SEXUAL DIFFERENCE IN THE AIRLINE INDUSTRY

Steve Taylor and Melissa Tyler

Introduction

This paper examines service work within the contemporary airline industry. On the basis of original empirical research, it is argued that gendered emotional labour and the production of sexual difference are prominent aspects of employment within this economic sector. 'Emotional labour' refers to 'feeling' management, during social interaction within the labour process, as shaped by the requirements of capital accumulation (Hochschild 1983). 'Sexual differentiation' is the process through which social significance is attached to anatomical differences which serve to assign particular social beings to distinct social collectivities: wherein 'sexual difference' is constructed and appropriated (Guillauman 1995).

Hochschild (1983: 33) suggests two main ways in which employees may engage in emotional labour: 'surface acting' and 'deep acting'. The former involves pretending 'to feel what we do not . . . we deceive others about what we really feel, but we do not deceive ourselves'. 'Deep acting' means 'deceiving oneself as much as deceiving others . . . we make feigning easy by making it unnecessary'. Hochschild advances two major forms of deep acting: the direct exhortation of feeling and the use of a trained imagination. We will be examining the gendered deployment of surface acting and deep acting in the service of valorisation within parts of the airline industry, as implicated in the production of sexual difference. Emotional labour cannot be regarded as a 'gender-neutral' phenomenon, with empirical research demonstrating that forms of employment which demand significant amounts of emotional labour are dominated by women (Hochschild 1983; Smith 1992; James 1992). Attention must centre upon the relationship between emotional labour and sexual differentiation.

The airline industry has been shaped by recent managerial programmes aiming to maximise 'service quality' and 'customer satisfaction'. Previous papers in this journal (Rosenthal *et al.* 1997; Jones *et al.* 1997; Knights and McCabe 1998) have offered empirically informed assessments of such initiatives within other areas of the service sector, focusing particularly upon managerial attempts to mobilise the subjective commitment of employees to the delivery of quality customer service. As the performance of emotional labour can draw upon and shape the subjectivity of employees, we present a contribution to an expanding debate. While recognising that gendered emotional labour and the production of sexual difference have, at least since the 1950s, been central elements of airline service work (Mills 1998), three specific arguments will be drawn from our empirical research:

1. Recent competitive pressures and accompanying managerial initiatives are intensifying demands upon female employees for the production of emotional labour, subjective commitment to organisational aims and sexual difference within parts of the airline industry.

2. Despite the enormous power of these managerial demands, the 'spaces' for female employees to 'comply, consent and resist' (Pollert 1996) remain 'open' within the aspects of the industry studied. This is consistent with the findings of Rosenthal *et al.* (1997), Jones *et al.* (1997) and Knights and McCabe (1998).

3. In order to explain and analyse the complex processes involved in the above, recourse to the notion of 'patriarchal structures' (Walby 1990) is inadequate (Bradley 1989; Pollert 1996). Rather, the power of the gendered managerial prescription investigated here is related to the way it is embedded within the structural and inequitable capital-labour relation. Discourses stressing the importance of gendered employee/customer interactions and the emotional labour this involves, for capital accumulation within an intensely competitive airline industry, are embedded within

managerial selection, training, supervision and evaluation of employees. The resources of the female service workers under consideration, to respond to the attempted emotional and cultural control of their working lives which these managerial demands represent, are limited when compared to the managerial resources mobilised in an attempt to operationalise the aforementioned discourses. This managerial mobilisation is driven, at least partly, by the 'structural constraints' (Pollert 1996: 643) imposed by the social reproduction of the capitalist mode of production, of which the social relations of airline service production are a part. We differ here from Rosenthal et al. (1997) and Knights and McCabe (1998). These studies fail to sufficiently address the way in which structural power can shape subjective employment experience. Our approach is informed by those who place the process of gendering inside class relations, and stress the need to empirically interrogate the historically-specific 'lived experience' of gendered power relations in order to adequately analyse and explain such phenomena (Cockburn 1983; Pollert 1996; Acker 1998). We will be suggesting that sexual difference, and the consolidation of gendered power relations, are produced through historically-situated capitalist and gendered labour processes (Bradley 1989). Once we investigate the lived experience of employment, we reveal that 'gender relations are everywhere' (Pollert 1996: 645). They shape and are shaped by the capital-labour relation.

The Research Sites

We conducted ethnographic research into two aspects of the airline industry: the telephone sales of airline services by telephone sales agents (TSAs) representing a major British airline ('Flightpath'); and airline service delivery by flight attendants within the same airline and one other, both of which are 'key players' in an intensely competitive market. The research was conducted between 1994 and 1996, during which time both airlines implemented a quality management programme.

TSA employment involves receiving, and dealing with, calls from people who are interested in purchasing or reserving Flightpath services. Agents work within a large open-plan office (a 'community'). They are equipped with a headset, a telephone system and a computer system. 'Dealing with' calls usually involves placing the caller on hold and accessing information from the computer system. Full-time TSAs work an eight-hour shift constituted by constant call taking and are divided into teams of nine. TSAs are managed by one Sales Team Supervisor (STS). A team of eight supervisors is responsible to one Sales Team Leader (STL). There were five STLs at the completion of the research. These are, as a team, responsible to the Unit Manager of the telephone sales centre studied. S/he is then accountable to the head of Telephone Sales, UK. Everyone within the centre is on performance-related pay.

The research at Flightpath consisted of non-participant observation and interviewing at all levels of the above structure, focusing upon TSA recruitment and training, the nature of the labour process and the way in which the introduction of a quality management programme had affected the work situation. Particular attention was paid to the operationalisation of managerial prescription, supervision and evaluation of the TSA labour process. Much of the two weeks of observation was spent sitting with TSAs and 'listening in' to their telephone interaction with customers. The researcher also observed sales team meetings, the final training session and award ceremony for successful trainees, the Flightpath Telephone Sales Annual Conference and general TSA-management interaction.

Interviews were semi-structured and audio-taped. The one (male) unit manager was interviewed three times while four (three male and one female) of the five (one female) STLs were interviewed once. These interviews were similar in length, lasting approximately 45 minutes. Thirteen (eight female, five male) of the forty (52 per cent female) STSs were interviewed. These varied greatly in length—between a minimum of 15 minutes and a maximum of 90 minutes. Of the 360 TSAs (81 per cent female), 23 were interviewed (six male, seventeen female). Each interview lasted an average of forty minutes. The latter included interviews with representatives of the Transport and General Workers Union and were also supplemented by four 'focus group' discussions with groups of six TSAs. Additionally, representatives from the Training Section within the site were interviewed. The opportunity also arose to interview the head of Flightpath Telephone Sales UK. This lasted approximately thirty minutes.

The empirical research into the work of flight attendants was split into three main phases, all focusing upon recruitment, training and supervision of flight attendants. The first stage involved an analysis of company documentation at both airlines, followed by observational flights in various classes of travel with both organisations (ten in total). During these flights, particular attention was paid to interaction between flight attendants and between flight attendants and passengers. The research focused upon what flight attendants actually do, how and why they do it, with what implications and how all this had been affected by recent managerial quality initiatives.

The second phase of the fieldwork involved semi-structured, audio-taped interviews with a representative sample of airline personnel and passengers: with applicants to airlines (12 in total, 9 women and 3 men); with trainee and experienced flight attendants, including those who were involved in the recruitment, triaining and supervision of other flight attendants (25 in total, 19 women and 6 men); and with passengers (48 in total, 33 men and 15 women). For comparative purposes, the following headings were used: what is a flight attendant; what makes a good flight attendant; what makes a bad flight attendant; what kind of services are flight attendants expected to provide; why are women attracted to the job of flight attendant; why are men attracted to the job of flight attendant; reflections upon respondents own experiences of flying.

The third stage of the research entailed a content analysis of airline documentation, ranging from company mission statements, recruitment and training literature to advertising and marketing materials depicting female flight attendants obtained from some 48 airlines (out of 64 which were contacted).

All the labour processes studied are nominally and substantively forms of gendered employment in that the majority of those employed are women and, as will be illustrated below, all involve skills and abilities which women are deemed to possess by virtue of being female. We shall now go on to report our research findings, firstly into the telephone sales labour process, and secondly into the work of flight attendants. In the former, we will largely concentrate upon deep acting as emotional labour; in the latter, surface acting. We will be assessing the extent to which managerially-imposed constraints to engage in both forms of emotional labour produce gendered subjective experiences and serve to reify sexual difference.

'Quality Service' and Emotional Labour Within the Airline Industry

Managerial programmes which aim to shape the feeling management of service employees during their interaction with customers often emphasise the importance of 'quality service' and 'customer satisfaction' within an increasingly competitive business environment (Rosenthal et al. 1997; Jones et al. 1997; Taylor 1997). Within parts of the service sector, quality of customer service is perceived as one, if not *the*, key differentiation strategy by management (Fuller and Smith 1991; Leidner 1993; Hughes and Tadic 1998). Such strategies have been identified within the airline industry (Colling 1995; Boyd and Bain 1998), as competition for passengers increases in the context of European de-regulation of airline services, globalisation of the airline business and the perceived ever-heightening individualised expectations of airline passengers. Managerial discourses, emphasising the centrality of service quality, were evident within all of our research sites.

An essential characteristic of a managerial focus upon customer satisfaction is the perception of senior management that there is a requirement to actively manage the delivery of quality service (Fuller and Smith 1991; Jones et al. 1997). Active management of service delivery which involves employee/customer interaction clearly has implications for the feeling management of employees. However, within both of the cases under consideration here, and this is also noted elsewhere (Jones et al. 1997;

Rosenthal *et al.* 1997), the delivery of service quality, and the feeling management this can involve, should (according to management) simultaneously be achieved through the 'empowerment' and autonomy of workers rather than through managerial prescription. Flightpath as a whole, and the telephone sales centre studied in particular, achieved huge commercial success within the research period. Telephone sales management attributed this to a 'culture change' sweeping through the organisation, 'empowering' TSAs, and enabling them to deliver quality customer service 'spontaneously' and 'naturally'. The mobilisation of employee commitment to an organisational aim of service quality is a crucial element in the quality management programme at Flightpath.

The nature of interaction between flight attendant and customer has always been seen, by airline management, as central to customer perceptions of quality service (Hochschild 1983; Mills 1998). However, both airlines where the work of flight attendants was researched were further affected by recent managerial programmes emphasising the importance of 'quality service' and 'customer satisfaction' (Tyler 1997). One of the most significant developments in this respect was that one airline established Standards Development Officers (SDOs) as part of the cabin crew on all flights. SDOs were also experienced flight attendants. This represents an attempt to reduce managerial hierarchy, blur previously rigid distinctions between management and non-managerial employees and secure cabin crew commitment to the service quality ethos. Furthermore, within both airlines studied, clear attempts were made by management to stress the importance of flight attendant autonomy, spontaneity and 'natural personality', for the attainment of 'customer satisfaction' during interaction with customers (Tyler 1997).

Thus, competitive pressures within the airline industry have facilitated managerial initiatives which attempt to 'manage' the 'natural' delivery of quality customer service during employee-customer interactions. We wish to argue that this development has particularly gendered consequences.

The Telephone Sales Labour Process

Despite managerial claims of 'empowered' employees at Flightpath, the work of individual TSAs was supervised and measured in a most thoroughgoing manner. The major form of work measurement at the telephone sales centre studied consists of monthly targets which individual TSAs must surpass. These targets were divided into 'hard' and 'soft' dimensions.

'Hard' targets refer to quantitative measurement. Each individual TSA has a revenue target, relating to the value of airline services which are sold to customers, and they are expected to surpass this each month. STSs in turn have a team target which has to be attained on a monthly basis. STLs are targeted in terms of the monthly monetary performance of (eight) STSs within their community. The Unit Manager is ultimately responsible for ensuring that STLs deliver monthly returns to target. The unit as a whole is targeted within the telephone sales division according to these calculations. There are other hard targets, described by management as 'productivity' evaluation. This involves measurement of the number of calls answered per agent per week, the amount of time spent in conversation with passengers per week and the amount of time spent in 'wrap up'—the time between the termination of one call and the opening of a new one. Each individual has a particular productivity target.

The evaluation of the TSA labour process by 'soft' standards is more ambiguous. They were described by management as referring to 'teamwork, commitment and also their actual call structure, their job skills if you like' (STS). Management stressed that overall evaluation of agents was a 50/50 split between hard and soft standards. This measurement directly shaped performance-related pay.

The supervision and evaluation of TSA/customer interactions according to soft standards largely takes place through 'remote' and 'known' monitoring. The telephone system within the unit enables STSs, STLs and training staff to 'listen in' to the content of any call between agent and customer at any time during the working day. This can be done with or without the knowledge of the agent in question. STSs claimed that they randomly engaged in remote monitoring, and sometimes taping, as a form of 'quality assurance'. Furthermore, STSs routinely observe and tape the telephone interaction of each team member with their full knowledge. This is then used in review and appraisal weekly meetings between agent and supervisor. TSA performance-related pay is shaped by an STS monthly report, resulting from the weekly review and appraisal meeting. This is based upon evaluation according to both hard and soft standards. Management stressed that the targeting system is flexible. Individual TSAs targets, which arise from the weekly meetings and monthly reviews and appraisals between STSs and their team members, can vary from month to month depending upon the perceived strengths and weaknesses of particular employees.

The individualised managerial surveillance system at Flightpath has gendered assumptions about the 'natural' skills and capacities of women and men embedded within it. Firstly, this can be observed within managerial selection of TSAs. Selection panels argued that they attempted to select 'personalities' who will 'naturally' deliver quality service. The personalities selected were overwhelmingly female. When questioned, selectors (overwhelmingly male) openly articulated their gendered assumptions:

> The vast, vast majority of the agents we select are women . . . it's not as if we don't get men applying for the job . . . they just seem to fit it better, they're

better at it . . . we are looking for people who can chat to people, interact, build
rapport. What we find is that women can do this more, they're definitely more
natural when they do it anyway. It doesn't sound as forced, perhaps they're
used to doing it all the time anyway . . . women are naturally good at that sort
of thing. I think they have a higher tolerance level than men . . . I suppose we
do, yes, if we're honest about it, select women sometimes because they are
women rather than anything they've particularly shown in the interview (STL).

Once selected, agents are expected to deploy their 'natural' personality
within employee/customer interactions, regardless of the emotional stance
which customers may adopt towards agents. These gendered beliefs, and
the way in which they are also inscribed within the training, supervision
and evaluation of TSAs represent demands for gendered emotional labour
and the production of sexual difference during employee/customer
interaction.

TSAs are, to some extent, trained in the techniques of emotional
labour. They are instructed to respond to the perceived feelings and
expressions of customers in a manner which upholds the commercial
interests of Flightpath. These managerial demands do not only encompass
surface acting. Examples were observed, during the training process, of
TSAs being taught how to 'deal with' customers that appeared 'insulting'
through actively 'working on', shaping and changing feeling. Gendered
assumptions inhered within such managerial prescription of TSA deep
acting. Thus, female TSAs were expected to respond in a 'polite' manner
to male customers who interacted in an insulting, often sexualised,
manner. One comment from a trainer, which illustrates this prescription,
describes TSA training in a technique of deep acting which Hochschild
(1979) labels 'bodily emotion work':

> If a man's having a go at you . . . he might even be embarrassing you . . . don't
> get ruffled, you've got to keep your cool. Remember that you are trying to offer
> him something and get him to pay for the privilege. He can really talk to you
> how he wants. Your job is to deal with it . . . *just take a few deep breaths and let
> the irritation cool down* . . . think to yourself he's not worth it (our emphasis)

Despite the above examples of managerial prescription, TSAs, telephone sales management and members of the training section stressed
that the training programme was only a framework for the delivery of
quality service, within which employees were expected to use discretion.
The nature of every possible worker/customer interaction cannot be
prescribed through the training programme. TSAs argued that they
frequently, with the encouragement of management, interact with
customers in their own personal or 'natural' manner. This is known as
'building rapport'. However, the individualised surveillance and remuneration system outlined above encourages 'positive divergences' while
aiming to eliminate 'negative divergences' from managerial prescription
within agent/customer interaction (Taylor 1998). Unless TSAs 'spon-

taneous' feelings or 'emotion work' (Hochschild 1979) can be utilised as 'positive discretion' (i.e. to deliver quality service as defined by management), many employees are coerced into deploying emotional labour, given the knowledge that they can be supervised at any time—through the targeting system, direct observation, known and remote monitoring. It is important to remember that the results of this supervision will shape both the material and symbolic remuneration which TSAs receive from their employment. With management also explicitly stating that consistent TSA failure to meet monthly targets would result in dismissal, we are witnessing here the mobilisation of powerful managerial resources in demand of emotional labour. This mobilisation has been driven by the structural constraints imposed by the capitalist mode of production and exhibits the inequitable nature of the capitalist employment relationship. There is clear evidence from our research of coerced surface and deep acting. In relation to the latter, a female TSA commented;

> You can't let yourself be impolite towards a customer or feel angry with them . . . As we are always told, they pay our wages . . . I suppose it's something that I learnt to do since I came here . . . you're taught to think about the customers, to think about what they're like and to try and get on with them whatever they're like.

Crucially, gendered managerial expectations about who can and cannot perform emotional labour are inscribed within supervision and evaluation at Flighpath. Many female TSAs expressed similar sentiments to the following:

> They expect us to put up with a lot more from customers than the blokes . . . if someone is having a go . . . and we get some real dirty bastards . . . especially on American calls when it's the middle of the night over there . . . you're just expected to put up with it . . . because 'you never know, you might get a sale'. It's seen as normal behaviour, men just having a laugh . . . one supervisor said to me . . . 'just because it's not your sense of humour, it doesn't mean you have to get offended by someone else's' . . . they tell us 'you've got to have a thick skin, you can't let it affect you, get rid of the feeling'. . . . I suppose it's bound to affect how you respond in your social life, your tolerance levels (TSA).

Gendered assumptions about the 'natural' abilities and 'personalities' of women and men, including the capacity of female employees to engage in and 'put up with' sexualised encounters (Filby 1992; Hughes and Tadic 1998), are inscribed within managerial attempts to prescribe TSA emotional labour and facilitate deep acting and 'natural' social interaction at Flightpath.

The majority of female and male TSAs interviewed also agreed that the few male TSAs within the telephone sales centre studied were actually supervised and evaluated according to different criteria. Females tended to be judged according to both 'hard' *and* 'soft' standards—the latter referring to the nature of their interaction with customers which, as we have seen, can involve significant amounts of emotional labour. For male TSAs, the nature of this interaction could be overlooked if one was considered a 'good seller' (i.e. consistently surpassed revenue and productivity ('hard') targets). Consequently, we are suggesting that the demands for TSAs to deep act are not only structurally induced by the dictates of capital accumulation, they are also distinctly gendered—aimed particularly at female TSAs.

Flight Attendants

From our research into the work of flight attendants, it became clear that the role is defined (by airline management, cabin crew themselves and passengers) as 'women's work'; it is deemed to involve skills which women are seen to possess simply by virtue of being women. A regular (male) business traveller outlined these skills:

> A good flight attendant, or hostess ... should be organised and attentive, she should ideally be helpful and knowledgeable, she should be well-prepared and trained, and should be sincere. ... She should be perceptive and be able to work alongside her colleagues to ensure that all passengers' needs are taken care of. ... She should be able to anticipate the needs of her passengers and go beyond their expectations. ... He or she should be firm and self-confident, and be able ... to think for themselves and so plan ahead (note that the female pronoun is used until this respondent refers to being 'firm and self-confident').

Such assumptions shaped the selection of flight attendants. A male recruiter told us that 'women are best suited to this role because they are much more patient and caring than men ... of other people's needs ... they are much more thoughtful by nature'. The work is deemed to involve 'caring', physically and emotionally, for others and women are seen as capable of carrying out this work, by virtue of their sexual difference from men. The skills involved in airline service provision are not recognised as skills by many of those who provide and consume the service, but are seen as 'common-sense' ways of being a woman; that is, of anticipating the needs and (exceeding the) expectations of others. In the case of the flight attendant, women were not only deemed capable of (naturally) caring for others, but also themselves. Female flight attendants were seen as inherently capable of presenting themselves as 'feminine', as aesthetically pleasing, not only by their employers, but also by customers and many flight attendants.

Our research actually suggested that the level of 'quality service' delivered by flight attendants—or 'personal servicing' (which can include both surface and deep acting) which is involved in flight attendant/ passenger interaction—increases relative to the cost of the service itself. At one of the airlines studied, a training course was held for junior flight attendants who had been promoted to a flight attendant in first class travel. Throughout this training, emphasis was placed upon using passenger names, as well as memorising their drink and meal require-ments, to provide a more 'personal' service. Trainees were told by their (female) instructor: 'Go around and introduce yourself by name to all of the passengers . . . it's much more personal and that's what they expect from us in First Class, after all, that's what they're paying us for'. The trainees were also instructed to use their 'body language'. 'Above all, use your hips, hands, arms and your voice' (Instructor).

Three particular uses of body language—which can be seen as an element of either surface or deep acting—were considered fundamental to the establishment of a 'rapport' with passengers, and to the production of customer satisfaction. A training instructor told trainee flight attendants to:

> always walk softly through the cabin, always make eye contact with each and every passenger, and always smile at them. This makes for a much more personal service, and is what first class travel and (we) as a company are all about.

In a similar vein to the TSAs, in addition to the above types of prescription, it was suggested by management that flight attendants should exercise their own discretion when interacting with customers. Management expect females to be particularly adept at 'naturally' exer-cising this work autonomy. Thus, in terms of developing a rapport with passengers, confronting emergency situations, dealing with sick or nervous passengers, applying 'TLC' and deploying appropriate 'body language', trainees were often told that 'basically, you just have to use your common-sense' (Instructor).

The presentation and performance of a female body as feminine was particularly deemed (by management, employees and passengers) a skill which female flight attendants were expected to be capable of deploying, yet they are given little training in this respect. The femininity of women workers is largely perceived in terms of aesthetics; to be a woman is to look feminine according to dominant occupational and organisational discourses. Key words which have emerged from the analysis of interview transcripts include being 'polished', 'well groomed' and 'flawless'. Expectations of the type of bodily presentation, on behalf of management, cabin crew and passengers, were also found to contain explicitly sexualised elements (Tyler 1997).

However, despite managerial claims that flight attendants are expected to regulate their own appearance maintenance and emotion work, it can be argued that the work of the flight attendants studied has recently been subjected to increased managerial surveillance. One example of such supervision in relation to surface acting is the enforcement of Uniform and Grooming Regulations at both airlines. Flight attendants were under the line management of a Standards Development Officer (SDO) who was responsible for checking and monitoring the appearance of flight attendants through spot checks and pre-flight 'grooming checks'. These 'managers' were also senior flight attendants and part of the cabin crew. They were supervised and appraised by senior management who were not part of the cabin crew. This further supervision often took the form of 'mystery shopping' upon randomly selected flights. SDOs are responsible for the enforcement of the company's uniform regulations which for women involve wearing the company's uniform, regulation make-up and hairdressing and also behaving in a particular way whilst in uniform. SDOs held appraisals with flight attendants on a three monthly basis, monitoring and recommending improvements to appearance, particularly conformance to a weight-height ratio. These recent uniform regulations are reinforced by a more informal network of peer pressure and self-appraisal. In many ways, a strong 'culture of femininity' was observed among female flight attendants. Such cultural participation may offer valuable resources in terms of 'coping' with and 'managing' the daily work of a flight attendant (emotional labour is only one part of a complex and health-threatening job—see Boyd and Bain 1998), while simultneously aiding the production and reproduction of sexual difference (Westwood 1984). The system through which flight attendants at both airlines are evaluated also focused upon deep acting. SDO's appraised flight attendants of their 'care' and 'commitment' towards passengers, often suggesting areas in which this could be improved.

'Compliance', 'Consent', 'Resistance'

Some suggest that managerial initiatives such as those described above facilitate 'total' managerial control of the emotional labour process (Hochschild 1983; Sewell and Wilkinson 1992). This view concurs with managerial perceptions within our research sites of wholesale 'culture changes' sweeping through the respective organisations. Of course, the major difference between these perspectives is the meaning attached to the representation, with the former lamenting and the latter celebrating. However, our research findings suggest that gendered managerial control of the emotional labour process is not 'total', an argument which concurs with the findings of Rosenthal et al. (1997), Jones et al. (1997) and Knights and McCabe (1998). Despite managerial attempts at detailed prescription and surveillance of the labour process, the female emotional labourers under consideration here were still able to 'negotiate' the production of their sexual difference from men. We wish to highlight the significance of this 'action in process . . . whether compliance, consent or resistance' (Pollert 1996: 648).

In the case of TSAs, it was argued above that managerial methods to control employee/customer interaction include employee selection procedures which contain within them assumptions about the 'natural' capacities of women and men—their sexual difference. However, having selected employees according to their 'natural' abilties and 'personality', it is then very difficult for management to control that personality further:

> I've had loads of battles with my supervisor 'cos she'll say 'change the way you say this' and I'll say 'but that's the way I do it, that's me, that's my personality. I can't change myself'. She says 'well you'll have to', but I don't. They (management) either want us to be natural when interacting with customers or they don't, they can't have it both ways (female TSA).

It was suggested above that 'remote monitoring' is another method whereby telephone sales management attempt to ensure deep acting during TSA/customer interaction. However, many female TSAs claimed that, with experience, they learnt to ascertain when their conversations were being supervised. Situated within an open-plan office, this was recognised by the actions of the supervisor and regular gazes in their direction. When convinced they are not under supervision, many reported that they deviated from managerial prescription, particularly when dealing with 'rude' or 'insulting' customers. Clearly, remote and known monitoring can shape TSAs emotional *displays* during some employee/customer interactions. Managerial control mechanisms can also shape the feeling behind the display, as some of the earlier examples of deep acting indicated. However, there were numerous examples of TSAs expressing 'deviant' feelings, and operating according to the rules of 'equal emotional exchange' (Hochschild 1983), when given the opportunity to do so. Some agents were observed disconnecting calls from rude or ignorant customers. This was an especially common practice amongst female TSAs as a response to 'slimy', 'insulting' or 'patronising' male callers. All these practices occurred when TSAs were sure they were not being observed, physically or electronically.

A common female TSA practice, revealing emotional discretion and resistance to deep acting within the labour process, involves limiting the information given to a rude or offensive caller. Many revealed that they deliberately withold relevant service information from customers who provoke anger or irritation within them. A related practice is talking to such passengers in a 'distant', 'disinterested' manner:

> If I don't like someone . . . it's difficult to explain but I will be efficient with them, giving them what they want and no more, but I will not be really friendly. . . . I sometimes have a really monotone voice, sounding a bit cold. . . . I will not laugh at their jokes for example (TSA)

The surveillance through which management in the cases studied attempted to shape the emotional labour of flight attendants also allowed 'space' for employee negotiation. Some of the examples below may not be seen as resistance to the sexual differentiation process itself, but could be construed as 'coping strategies' which make the flight attendant's role more tolerable.

One example was that of several lesbian flight attendants' performance of their organisational roles. These women are strongly heterosexualised by the various organisational discourses (which are embedded in managerial prescription, supervision and evaluation of the labour process) on feminine sexuality. However, there was evidence that these women played with sexuality and gender, almost as a subversive strategy of resisting organisational identification and the production of sexual difference. The element of performance in the role of flight attendant potentially allows for this as a valuable and pleasurable strategy of resistance to organisational identification and heterosexualisation (as the regulative norm of organisational, sexual subjectivity). We also observed several male flight attendants playing with the stereotype of the 'cabin crew queer'. Some gay employees were able to 'cope' with the job by literally parodying their roles and the rules which govern them. One female flight attendant in particular suggested that she was able to use her lesbian identity as a strategy for resisiting organisational identification and the wholesale manipulation of her feelings and identity; as a means of distinguishing between her own (private) sexuality and her (public) heterosexualised organisational role: 'It's good to be able to put on an act all of the time. I do it to protect myself from it. Keep myself immune to it'.

Thus, just as the management and manipulation of employee feelings and identity is an element in the management of the labour process through which sexual difference is produced, so it can be a significant element within coping strategies or even strategies of (albeit individualised) resistance to such management. The above research findings suggest that the organisational body of the flight attendant is a 'contested surface' upon which an organisational identity is inscribed. Management selection, training, supervision and evaluation in relation to the work of flight attendants appears to shape the surface acting of employees. Surveillance is an ever-present threat and so flight attendants may *behave* in accordance with prescription. They may develop a 'look' so they appear compliant. However, our research suggests that for some, behind the look, there may be a 'distance' from the role.

Reflecting upon interactions with customers, some female flight attendants spoke of 'faking': 'Of course I still smile, I just don't go out of my way to . . . hide the fact that it's a pretend smile'. Others apparently decided that the best coping strategy was to emphasise their safety, first aid and rescue skills, and to underplay the service element of their work. This is perhaps the more difficult of the two strategies to maintain in a working environment which constantly stresses professionalism based on appearance, service and presentation.

Conclusion

Our research demonstrates that the delivery of 'quality service' through employee–customer interaction, which inevitably draws upon employee capacities for feeling management, is currently considered important to capital accumulation by management within companies that are world leaders in the airline industry. We are not suggesting that this is the only differentiation strategy being pursued within an increasingly competitive industry. However, we have shown how management within our research sites have embedded discourses of 'quality service' within their selection, training, supervisory and evaluative processes.

Inherent to the quality management programmes established within both aspects of the airline industry studied is an expectation that service employees will work beyond managerial prescription when interacting with customers and delivering service quality. Our central argument throughout this paper has been that management, within all of our research sites, assume that women workers in particular can accomplish this 'discretionary' aspect of the job, utilising skills which they supposedly possess by virtue of their sexual difference from men: capacities which are deemed to derive from women's 'Otherness'. However, quality management programmes which aim to emphasise the significance, and tap the presumed potential, of this (gendered) discretion simultaneously involve heightened surveillance and control of the labour process in an attempt to eradicate 'negative divergencies' from managerial prescription. This erodes rather than expands employee autonomy, intensifying demands for the production of gendered emotional labour and sexual difference from employees.

Emotional labour is seen as 'women's work' in that the majority of those employed to undertake it are women, and it is deemed to draw on abilities which women are supposed to possess by virtue of their sexual difference from some norm of masculinity. As new managerial initiatives within the airline industry stress the increasing importance of emotional labour, the assumption that women are more capable of 'naturally' performing it remains. Our empirical evidence has shown a managerial emphasis upon the selection and training of specifically female employees for the very purposes of emotional labour, and the development of mechanisms enabling detailed, thoroughgoing supervision and evaluation of a gendered emotional labour process. Our research also indicates a concomitant managerial demand for (particularly) female employees to develop subjective commitment to organisational aims of service quality and customer satisfaction. This is perfectly illustrated by the suggestion above that female TSAs are expected to deep act in order to deliver quality and sell services, and this directly effects their evaluation and remuneration. In contrast, it seems that the few male TSAs in the telephone sales centre studied are expected to sell by whatever means. 'You have to have a few hard sellers as well. . . . I suppose we would say that many of the blokes do this' (STS). Men are employed in the cases reported, and they do perform emotional labour. However, they cannot be produced as sexually different from a normative masculinity in the same way as women. These boundaries become blurred in all of our cases, from a managerial point of view, when male employees were perceived by management to be gay.

One major difference between the two aspects of the airline industry studied is the employee remuneration systems. Individualised performance-related pay at Flightpath Telephone Sales affords greater power to management in the demand for gendered emotional labour, female subjective commitment and the production of sexual difference, when compared to managerial supervison of flight attendant-customer inter-action which is not directly tied to the individual pay of cabin crew members. We have argued throughout that the power of the gendered managerial demands being investigated here must be related to their inscription within the structurally induced and vastly inequitable capital-labour relation. The greater the resources of management (in this case individualised surveillance and reward systems at Flightpath), the more inequitable the relation and the more intense the managerial demands (for gendered emotional labour). We have advocated the mutual constitution of gender and class relations, while simultaneously recognising that these phenomena are of a different analytic order. 'While class relations can be conceived abstractly in a mode of production, gender relations have to be analysed in lived experience . . . (but we are demonstrating) one system, not two' (Pollert 1996: 646–7).

Our findings differ from two previous *WES* contributions, which attempt to assess the impact of quality management within the service sector upon the subjectivity of employees, in some important respects. Our evaluation of quality management, focusing upon the erosion of (particularly) female employee autonomy and the emotional exploitation which can accompany managerial demands for employee emotional labour, is clearly contrary to the argument of Rosenthal *et al.* (1997: 481) who claim their 'empirical findings lend more to the optimistic view that modern . . . quality . . . management can benefit employees'. From research at 'Shopco', they go on to state (491–2) that 'employees appeared strongly to endorse the idea and aims of the (quality) programme' and that 'front-line staff . . . reported high levels of the kind of customer-oriented behaviour sought by management'. Furthermore, staff 'discretion and responsibility have increased noticeably . . . (and) this new discretion was not accompanied by any increase in human or technological surveillance'.

The above contentions are based upon a survey of managerial and employee perceptions of a quality management initiative. How these perceptions related to the actual operation of the labour process was not studied. We would agree with Knights and McCabe (1998: 435–6) 'that only if observational research complements . . . other (research) methods is it likely that research can penetrate beneath the surface of specific accounts and rationalisations (of quality management)', especially when one is considering the depth of employee emotional commitment to managerial objectives, as Rosenthal *et al.* claim to do. In fact, our own findings demonstrate how a *surface* commitment or act can conceal 'deep' or 'genuine' resentment and cynicism of quality improvement programmes in the service sector. Moreover, although Rosenthal *et al.* (1997: 493–4) concede that 'organisational rules' at 'Shopco' limit the freedom and discretion of employees, particularly during their interaction with customers, no empirical detail is given as to *how* 'they are still governed'. As we have seen, the nature of managerial supervision, evaluation and remuneration of service employees can be crucial in disabling work autonomy which appears to be promoted through quality management.

Arguably, both Rosenthal *et al.* (1997) and Knights and McCabe (1998) underplay the extent to which the structural and vastly superior power of capital, in relation to labour, can shape service employee subjectivity. These studies examine the power (or partial failure) of quality management, and employee responses to it, almost entirely at a *discursive* level. We have argued throughout that the power effects of the 'discourse of quality', and the capacity of employees to respond to this, within the airline industry, must be related to the extent of its 'embeddedness' within the inequitable and structurally produced capital-labour relation. We are not denying the discursive effects of quality management, nor the discursive nature of employee 'consent, compliance and resistance', we are merely arguing that structural and material power must also be taken into account. Pursuing this argument in relation to the gendered nature of quality management also leads us to oppose those (Swan 1994) who contend that sexual difference and gendered power relations are primarily produced through the identity effects of dominant discourses of masculinity and femininity. Knights and McCabe (1998:435) actually talk generally of workplaces as situations where 'power, hierarchy and inequality are . . . so stacked against a majority of employees'. However, this general view is not fully integrated within their specific study of TQM at 'Qualbank'. Ironically, their empirical findings suggest that the partial 'failure' of TQM, in this particular case, could be traced to the structural capital-labour relation, and the contradictions inhering within it.

Despite the power of the gendered managerial demands identified by this paper, it is vital to remember we have also argued, in line with Rosenthal *et al.* and Knights and McCabe, that managerial control of female emotional labour, the production of sexual difference and female employee subjective commitment to the ethos of service quality, within the aspects of the airline industry studied, is not 'total'. Rather, precisely because women are deemed to possess a 'natural' capacity for emotional labour, prescription can be limited. The prevalence, nature and extent of surface and deep acting can be open to contestation and negotiation from female employees. In fact, there is some evidence that the more management attempt to prescribe the performance of emotional labour, the stronger resistance and contestation from female employees. This is why managerial attempts to control gendered emotional labour must still be seen as a 'double-edged sword' (Filby 1992).

References

Acker, J. (1998) 'The Future of "Gender and Organizations": Connections and boundaries', *Gender, Work and Organization*, 5, 4, 195–206.

Boyd, C. and Bain, P. (1998) '"Once I Get You Up There, Where the Air is Rarified": Health, safety and the working conditions of cabin crews', *New Technology, Work and Employment*, 13, 1, 16–28.

Bradley, H. (1989) *Men's Work, Women's Work*, Cambridge: Polity Press.

Cockburn, C. (1983) *Brothers*, London: Pluto Press.

Colling, T. (1995) 'Experiencing Turbulence: British Airways' management of human resources', *Human Resource Management Journal*, 5, 5, 18–32.

Filby, M. (1992) '"The Figures, The Personalities and The Bums": Service work and sexuality', *Work, Employment and Society*, 6, 1, 23–42.

Fuller, L. and Smith, V. (1991) '"Consumers" Reports: Management by customers in a changing economy', *Work, Employment and Society*, 5, 1, 1–16.

Guillaumin, C. (1995) *Racism, Sexism, Power and Ideology*, London: Routledge.

Hochschild, A. R. (1979) 'Emotion Work, Feeling Rules and Social Structure', *American Journal of Sociology*, 85, 551–75.

Hochschild, A. R. (1983) *The Managed Heart: The commercialization of human feeling*, Berkeley: University of California Press.

Hughes, K. D. and Tadic, V. (1998) '"Something to Deal With": Customer sexual harrassment and women's retail service work in Canada', *Gender, Work and Organization*, 5, 4, 207–19.

James, N. (1992) 'Care=Organisation+Physical Labour+Emotional Labour', *Sociology of Health and Illness*, 14, 4, 488–509.

Jones, C., Taylor, G. and Nickson, D. (1997) 'Whatever it Takes? Managing "Empowered" Employees and the Service Encounter in an International Hotel Chain', *Work, Employment and Society*, 11, 1, 541–54.

Knights, D. and McCabe, D. (1998) 'Dreams and Designs on Strategy: A critical analysis of TQM and management control', *Work, Employment and Society*, 12, 3, 433–56.

Leidner, R. (1993) *Fast Food, Fast Talk: Service work and the routinization of everyday life*, Berkeley: University of California Press.

Mills, A. (1998) 'Cockpits, Hangars, Boys and Galleys: Corporate masculinities and the development of British Airways', *Gender, Work and Organization*, 5, 3, 172–88.

Pollert, A. (1996) 'Gender and Class Revisited; Or, "The Poverty of Patriarchy"', *Sociology*, 30, 4, 639–59.

Rosenthal, P., Hill, S. and Peccei, R. (1997) 'Checking Out Service: Evaluating excellence, HRM and TQM in retailing', *Work, Employment and Society*, 11, 3, 481–503.

Sewell, G. and Wilkinson, B. (1992) ' "Someone to Watch Over Me": Surveillance, discipline and the just-in-time labour process', *Sociology*, 26, 2, 271–90.

Smith, P. (1992) *The Emotional Division of Labour in Nursing*, Basingstoke: Macmillan Educational Books.

Swan, E. (1994) 'Managing Emotion', in Morgan, T. (ed.), *Women in Management: A developing presence*, London: Routledge.

Taylor, S. (1997) ' "Empowerment" or "Degradation"? Total Quality Management and the Service Sector', in R. K. Brown, (ed.), *The Changing Shape of Work*, London: Macmillan.

Taylor, S. (1998) 'Emotional Labour and the New Workplace', in P. Thompson and C. Warhurst (eds.), *Workplaces of the Future*, London: Macmillan.

Tyler, M. (1997) *Women's Work as the Labour of Sexual Difference: female employment in the airline industry*, unpublished Ph.D thesis, University of Derby.

Walby, S. (1990) *Theorizing Patriarchy*, Oxford: Blackwell.

Westwood, S. (1984) *All Day, Every Day: Factory and family in the making of women's lives*, London: Pluto Press.

Index